— Pyramids at the Louvre —

Pyramids at the
— Louvre —

*Music, Culture, and Collage
from Stravinsky to the
Postmodernists*

Glenn Watkins

The Belknap Press of
Harvard University Press

Cambridge, Massachusetts
London, England
1994

This book is printed on acid-free paper, and its binding materials
have been chosen for strength and durability.

The epigraph on p. xi is from *A Net of Fireflies: Japanese Haiku and Haiku Paintings,* trans.
Harold Stewart, copyright 1960 in Japan by Charles E. Tuttle Co., Inc.; all rights reserved.

Library of Congress Cataloging-in-Publication Data

Watkins, Glenn, 1927–
Pyramids at the Louvre: music, culture, and collage from
Stravinsky to the postmodernists / Glenn Watkins.
p.   cm.
Includes bibliographical references and index.
ISBN 0-674-74083-1 (acid-free paper)
1. Music—20th century—History and criticism.   2. Music—
Philosophy and aesthetics.   I. Title.
ML197.W437   1994
780'.9'04—dc20   93-31703
CIP
MN

For
Oso, Iso, and Ichiban

— Contents —

Masquerades

Cut and Paste

—— Acknowledgments ——

In the course of writing a book that wisely or not sought to incorporate perspectives from several disciplines I benefited from the repeated counsel of numerous colleagues in the performance and creative arts, in musicology and art history, and in various branches of sociology, cultural history, and literary criticism. A sabbatical leave followed by a year as Senior Fellow at the Institute for the Humanities at the University of Michigan provided the opportunity to test some of these perspectives as well as organizational stratagems critical to the completion of the project, and for such a luxurious span of time and its associations it is impossible to express my gratitude adequately.

I am especially indebted to the School of Music and the Office of the Vice President for Research of the University of Michigan for subventions which provided crucial support, as well as to the staff of the University's Music Library, and particularly to John Powell, who courteously responded to endless requests for assistance.

To Marvin Eisenberg, who read an early version of the book, made substantive comments and suggestions, and meticulously scrutinized page proofs; to Richard Crawford, who read and commented on the chapters on Primitivism; to John Wiley, who brought to my attention several Russian sources that I would otherwise never have encountered; and to Robert Craft, Karlheinz Stockhausen, Alfred Schnittke, Luciano Berio, William Albright, Christopher Rouse, Michael Daugherty, David Gompper, H. Robert Reynolds, and Jeffrey Lyman, all of whom provided timely answers to specific questions, I offer special thanks.

Finally, for the wisdom and care in the final pruning and shaping of the typescript I owe an enormous debt to Margaretta Fulton, General Editor for the Humanities at Harvard University Press, and to Nancy Clemente, Senior Editor, whose talents clearly belong to a vanishing breed.

Lighting one candle with
another's flame
At dusk in spring—the same
yet not the same.

Buson

Preludes and Postulates

Myths are the agents of stability, fictions the agents of change.

Frank Kermode

If, as suggested in some quarters today, we are not only in a period of Postmodernism but in one of Post-History, a certain urgency surrounds our need to understand the forces that contributed to the Modernist movement of the twentieth century as well as its announced successors. Asserting an essentially ahistorical posture, most Postmodern critics have maintained that in the arts the doctrines of influence and intentionality ought to be debated, disentangled or jettisoned, and if retained allowed to remarry as the facts allow or as the fancy prefers. The truth is to be measured only in the power of the idea thus formed, and as such subject to continuing modification.

Yet in the absence of history, nostalgia for signs of continuity persists: *imitation* and *emulation,* recognized more or less continually from the time of the ancients, have been reviewed and retagged *misreading,* and juxtaposition and contrast have resurfaced with new and powerful claims to contemporaneity under the rubric of collage. Collage: cut-and-paste, assemblage, re-contexting of images collected from both quotidian experience and our knowledge of the past. In the foreword to a recent study Kim Levin has spoken of collage as "the all-purpose twentieth-century device." Noting the capacity of the technique to support a variety of artistic movements from the first decade to the present, Levin traces its vitality to a dexterity in accommodating a series of emerging avant-gardes while simultaneously aiding in the definition of what was new in each of them.[1] Indeed, from the early decades of the twentieth-century the very idea of Modernism has been likened to a curio cabinet, where unrelated objects are placed together and achieve cohesion through arrangement and proximity. But from the enigmatic federation of such a highly diverse complex of attitudes some have concluded that all hopes for communicating with a large public audience

1

were abandoned, that the autonomy of the arts was proclaimed, and that obscurity of intention was elevated to the status of a credo.

Despite the appeal of such sweeping judgments on an age, the reduction of so varied a round of evidence to so limited and potentially demeaning a verdict does very little honor either to the practice of history or to the richness of an era. Thus in trying to grasp the voices of Modernism, alternately judged as now past or currently thriving, as well as of Postmodernism, its paradoxical companion and non-successor, the practice of collage in music virtually refuses discussion in isolation, for many of its techniques as well as its philosophical underpinnings are observable in both literature and the fine arts. Eschewing loose analogy wherever possible, I have tried to conjure up the methods, the effects, and the contexts of artistic theory, social inference, and technological progress as they relate to the issue at hand; to demonstrate that rather than promoting a disoriented, incoherent jumble of contradictions, collage has exhibited a vigorous capacity to enlighten through juxtaposition, to forgo resolution, to sponsor pluralistic conclusions, and to promote understanding of an order that eludes all edicts.

From Cubism, Futurism, Dada, and Surrealism to the numerous aesthetic turnovers of the 1960s, 1970s, 1980s and 1990s, collage has sustained its vitality. Although the layman may readily recall the pasted snippets of newspaper or music in the art of Picasso and Braque, and be vaguely aware of the power of citation and allusion in the works of Joyce and Eliot, the central role of collage's guiding hand in music has been considered only incidentally and unsystematically. Yet in music's reshuffling of bits and scraps of memory, in the unsuspected confrontation and unusual alliance of materials, and in the manipulation of both time and space through a new set of coordinates, a sense of discovery was already being heralded from the first dozen years of the century in the music of such notables as Debussy, Ravel, and Stravinsky. The temptation to relate such developments to the emergence of Cubism in Paris between 1906 and 1914 is encouraged by the fact that its most famous practitioners were well known to the musicians.

Pierre Boulez has correctly pointed to Stravinsky's love for manipulating musical objects, a delight in taking things apart and putting them together again in a different fashion, thereby giving them "significance."[2] For Stravinsky the invocation of a known and one's expectations regarding it became the starting point of the creative process. In this gloss of pre-existent material, however, Stravinsky was obliged to define his own voice with increasing precision. A personal style was thus coined not so much through the appropriation of ingredients from a particular historical or cultural model as through their fracture and purposeful reassemblage: criticism of received materials becomes the modus operandi for the creative act. "Why was it that the world of quotation and reference . . . exercised such a fascination on the most brilliant spirits of the day, and why does that same fascination persist today though the borrowed clothes are new and the masking ideology has lowered its claims?"[3] By asking this question in such a perplexed tone at the time of Stravinsky's death in 1971, Boulez highlighted the persistence of one of the most important issues of contemporary musical thought: the seductiveness of cultural outreach and the power of appropriation as a creative stimulus. In an age when the activities of the most distant provinces as well as the customs and habits of our neighbors are brought both sonically and visually into our living room daily, it need come as no surprise that many composers of our time have been moved to register a similar fascination both with the elusiveness of global fraternity and with the diversity and richness of local traditions. Once again the agency of collage seems to have been ready-made for such an inquiry.

It should be understood from the outset, however, that the term *collage* is used here as a metaphor; that citation typically refers less to thematic recall of familiar tunes than to the assemblage and rearrangement of a rich parade of cultural loans involving textures, timbres, temperaments, and generative procedures ranging from the banal to the esoteric; that juxtaposition characteristically italicizes complementary qualities in the seemingly contradictory; and as a consequence surfacing questions more often evoke polychromatic illumination rather than single-hued answers.

But beyond the identification and definition of collage as a technique, we will need to question at every turn the reasons for its rising tide of glamor. The opening chapters on Orientalism and Primitivism consider presumably discrete topics in the early definition of Modernism. Yet while Primitivism may appear to relate to the issue of the authority of the past (backward in time) and Orientalism to authorities of the present (geographically outward), both involve recognition of forces at some remove from the here-and-now implied in the modish stem of Modernism's name. The Western idea of the Orient in the early twentieth century was not only of a physically displaced Other embued with qualities of the exotic but of one that quickly came to be fused with a search for the primitive, for an elusive "first times" containing the roots of expression. The ultimate paradox was finally proposed by the Surrealists in their attempt to distance the everyday. During the first two decades of the twentieth century, then, not only was there an attempt to congest ethnic diversity into a primal, global vision, but the authority of first times was collapsed to include the present.

Other fictive constructions that aided in this interpretive realignment centered on the temptation, voiced from the time of its premiere, to view *Le Sacre du printemps* as a kind of *musique nègre,* paralleling the taste for *art nègre* in the visual and literary domains. The perception of Africa as the quintessential locus for Primitivism in turn gave rise to further attempts at promoting fusions between European folk primitive and American popular expressions. For with Europe's increasing awareness of Afro-American musical developments in ragtime and jazz, a richly prepared cultural theory of transference was forwarded in numerous quarters.

Just as the increasingly variegated rush of daily urban experience— coupled to neonationalist sentiments suddenly tempered by the suspicion that the Age of Colonialism was on the eve of extinction— accounted in part for the Cubist vogue for collage in the period 1909–1914, so the ultimate rage for ragtime and jazz can be ascribed to multiple causes. For the feverish embrace of this Afro-American musical expression was surely due not only to the visceral attraction of its rhythms and timbres but also to the weight of social inference which it carried both at home and abroad. Reflective of an energetic and rising young nation and its ethnic diversity, it was ultimately graced with an elevated cachet in America following Europe's capitulation to its charm. Yet, prolonged confusion and debate over source repertoires and sponsorship, in jazz as well as in other forms, has frequently obscured the observation that it was the liaison of diverse circumstances and materials, typically fractured and juxtaposed in an unfamiliar mosaic, that constituted not so much the seeds of a predicament as the basis of a new power.

Simultaneously and paradoxically, whether in *Le Jazz* or *Le Sacre,* the search for Urtexts capable of transcending contemporary local traditions, of speaking of the very source of culture, gradually and collectively came to preoccupy most artists of the twentieth century who were interested in resuscitating their art in a radical new way. Indeed, a search for the elusive and necessarily mythical roots of inspiration soon identified the center of a new quest. Whether in allusions to African sculpture, even if ascertainably of recent vintage, that prized conceptual rudimentariness over perceptual beauty; whether in the formal appropriation of a trenchant haiku or of a Chinese ideogram—both of which, more than mere geographical displacements, appeared to Westerners ignorant of Oriental languages as standing altogether outside of history; whether in the arrangement of folk tunes or other derivative materials shorn from anthologies as though they were prized discoveries from a field dig; or in the deconstructed guitars and clarinets, beverage and tobacco labels, as well as in the cropping of newsprint into chunks that resonated like recently discovered relics from a previous age; the ideal model for a new foundation was hypothesized. Following an avalanche of such reassemblages, the critic's interpretive game—the search for a contemporary meaning in the sum of these fragments—began.

The thought gradually surfaced that with the journey to the primordium might come visions of an artistic millennium, and there can be little doubt that this perception helps to account for the current interest in reviewing an earlier attraction to Primitivism by an age with its own millennial preoccupations. The notion of Primitivism as encompassing more than a concern for preindustrial or tribal societies, however, allows us to recognize that a significant part of the twentieth-century cultural explosion, which would ultimately require reconstitution through collage, involved an obsession not so much with primitive societies of a distant past as with the search for an energizing authority in two equally elusive models—one involving outreach to geographically distant shores densely impacted with legend, and another which sought to forward the mechanisms of modern society and everyday life as contemporary counterparts to ancient ritual.

Such polyfocal perspectives prospered under freshly colored banners of relativity in both science and art, where a new sense of time fostered illuminations available only through simultaneous projection. In this endeavor, the painters and the dramatists literally set the stage. The masks of the Greeks and of Japanese No drama were retrieved, and wedded to the traditions of the Italian *commedia dell'arte,* Russian *lubok,* French *image d'Épinal,* and other folk traditions, they aided in the 1920s not only in the fabrication of Neoclassicism, Constructivism, and a Theater of the Absurd but in the definition of a new mechanico-urban age and, somewhat later, a review of their collective force for a second postwar era.

Then, in the 1930s, a new impetus to cultural collage came with the wholesale exodus of artists, intellectuals, and scientists from Europe to the United States and the simultaneous dispersal of newly formed civilian armies under varied auspices and from numerous countries to every corner of the globe, forcing in the process not only a review of attitudes held in the first half of the century but the contemplation of alternative courses of action for the future. After World War II, advance in the formats as well as the speed of communication soon made available such a smorgasbord of materials that it was natural, if not inevitable, that the sheer quantity of options seemed to dictate the final abandonment of any desirability, let alone possibility, of separation: high and low, black and white, homegrown and exotic flourished under the patronage of new dimensions of time and social structure, intimated in the early part of the century but now projected with exhilarating intensity and an accompanying philosophy. Loudly debated, the widespread celebration of cultural diversity and the construction and consideration of seemingly endless lists of binaries led at century's close not only to a reconsideration of the Western canon but to the denial of any appeal to historical resonance in the consideration of materials from such a swollen base. The new perspectives gradually and resolutely began to deny former restricted aesthetic approaches that tended to promote a sense of enduring formal values and at the same time often yielded to the temptation to turn every work of art into a sociopolitical document.[4]

In appraising the long arch of these developments, the historian characteristically recognizes the advantages of viewing various aesthetic movements according to a combination of formal and social dicta. Schoenberg is frequently described as a Viennese Jew, an intellectual, and an Expressionist; Stravinsky as an Italo-Russian Slav, intuitive in approach, and a Primitivist. Yet in the period 1909–1914, the essential qualities typically attributed to these two men can readily be reversed. Schoenberg's compositional process was much less structured, more involuntary, and more conditioned by Expressionist tenets of "inner necessity" than Stravinsky's, which, for all its Primitivist reliance upon a folk melos and rhythm, had already by 1912–1914 demonstrated an understanding of the mathematical formalizations of the Cubists and their usefulness for establishing control over a potential runaway organism. Even more interesting is the argument that there was something of the Russian in the German point of view and vice versa, that the intellectual carried a substantial intuitive component, that the Expressionists shared many of the basic concerns of the so-called Primitivists, and that newly constituted formalisms could serve as agents for a range of metaphysical perceptions.

Recognizing that the pressure placed upon any artist to stand for an age is defensible only to the extent that individuals are understood to belong to larger circles, the historian rightly takes pause when faced with the daunting task of controlling multiple histories. At the same time, in broadcasting our arrival at a new, Postmodern era, he has also laid claim not only to a chronological distance sufficient to permit a measured perspective concerning the issues attendant to the birth of Modernism but to a contemporary vision capable of tracing lines of continuity from the inception to the end of an age now closed.

This concept of Postmodernism, however, has clouded our sense of a contemporary identity at least as much as it has clarified it. If the concept of an avant-garde has been interred and the idea of the masterpiece is suspect, it is not the first time in this century. Furthermore, current notions of multiculturalism increasingly demand recognition of a lineage that is traceable to the last fin de siècle; an early period's devotion to the simultaneous projection of competing authorities continues to thrive under the new banner of stylistic pluralism; and, as in the past, music continues the struggle to comprehend the range of its societal functions. Thus, the story that surfaces here announces neither the demise of Modernism nor its retrospective failure. Rather it tries to clarify the ways in which Modernism served as a natural conduit to and claimed continued residency in a Postmodern age. Indeed, the penultimate chapter, "Pyramids at the Louvre," stands as an interdisciplinary test case of this very proposition and, prior to an *envoi*, retrospectively seeks to justify the metaphor which serves as a title for the collection as a whole.

Neither an attempt to discredit Postmodernism as a term nor an assault upon its tumescent literature, the present volume merely joins the battle for its clarification. Though for a book with such high aims a round of disclaimers might well be expected, the first is nonetheless registered as an appeasement: namely, that I felt no obligation to recount the Postmodern debate *ab ovo* through a heady litany of its most prominent interlocutors, since to address their texts directly would force review of a terrain that has been excessively debated and broadly interpreted. Though their importance is openly acknowledged in the many references to sources that take note of their arguments, the fleeting allusions to such important figures as Jean-François Lyotard, Jürgen Habermas, and Frederic Jameson stand as a coded confession of my interest in but general sense of dismay at much of the circularity surrounding the concept of Postmodernism and the feeling that a detailed reconsideration of this vast literature ought not enter the body of the present discussion. By the same token, I willingly admit that before undertaking the present project I was more inclined to take issue with the deconstructionists' repudiation of the autonomy of the musical text. In the act of parsing the issue of collage for the twentieth century, however, I have at least begun to appreciate the reasoning behind their claim "that critics are no more parasites than the texts they interpret."[5] At the same time, if the Postmodern fraternity has appropriately been charged with the abandonment of metanarratives, the present volume eludes membership through the dispatch of a series of *petits récits* that pretend to enchain in the formation of a larger organism.

My indebtedness to other disciplines, however, is immense, and on occasion I have approached the primary sources outside of music history directly, as with Albert Gleizes and Cubist theory. But for the rest I have called upon important intepretations that surfaced in the studies and debates attendant to several pertinent and lively art exhibitions: the "Primitivism" and the "High/Low" shows at the Museum of Modern Art, for example, or the Los Angeles County Museum Diaghilev and Constructivist exhibitions.[6] Thus, while frequent reliance upon interpretations in art history and theater fostered a deductive approach, my concern for dealing directly with the central musical sources promoted a more inductive methodology. For the present at least, I have viewed this as the only prudent course in an interdisciplinary study where I stray so frequently from my central field of expertise.

Finally, I would like to add that the perceptions recorded here were intended less as a lively, frontal assault on a recent species of musicological reductionism given to pruning away contextual detail than as an affectionate attempt to return to the musicological discourse many of the approaches that have been somewhat aggressively strained out in recent years. Theories of criticism, however, tend to spawn a never-ending chain of more theory that frequently fails to test the basic assertions through concrete example. For all of the appeal of Jacques Derrida's denial that criticism can ever achieve scientific status and

Nietzsche's view that the historian's objectivity is essentially that of the artist, not the scientist—that history itself is "pure story, fabulation, myth conceived as the verbal equivalent of the spirit of music," such a belief only facilitates what Hayden White has termed the "dissolution of the dream of a method by which history-in-general can be endowed with any sense at all."[7] Consequently, a continuing search for the ingenious melodies of narrative history as cohorts to scientific accountability persists as the perpetually elusive goal.

Regardless of what objectives may be defined as proper to a responsible history of the future, the music historian has always been, and continues to be, seduced by his role as a story teller and at the same time tamed by a sense of obligation to the musical object which ought not become buried in a sea of theory—critical, aesthetic, or formalistic. As a purely practical and defensive act, then, the music historian is obliged to sidestep the invitation to confect a unified world theory, to color his story with only a touch of philosophy, and, like the artists about whom he writes, to construct a narrative that is seasoned as much by intuition and affection as by methodology. Contrarily, he knows that free-wheeling criticism quickly tends to polemic and the odor of a hothouse exercise. Some years ago, before the current brand of criticism had surfaced as a fashionable enterprise, before "discourse" and "text" had need of quotation marks, Virgil Thomson pronounced the following sobering judgment: "Musicology is all right, when useful. Analysis and professional judgments are cardinal to the act. But polemical esthetics, commonly referred to as 'criticism,' are for any purpose but salesmanship, so far as I am concerned, pure lotus-eating."[8]

However we choose to write our story, the impossibility of structuring a definitive history or of arguing the truth beyond narrow parameters forces us to accept the fact that the ideological proportions of history and criticism are fated to twist and turn in a perpetual state of flux and to be endlessly reconstituted for every age. Thus, while claims to comprehensiveness invariably elude all cultural histories, I hope that readers who note grand omissions and shocking gaps in the present study will be moved to enlarge and complement from personal experience the observations recorded here, and to view this collection of essays as a coherent exercise in collage itself—one that only hints at a set of possibilities and settles for the fabrication and elaboration of a consistent fiction.

Finally, with a sensitivity to current definitions of fashion and propriety, it is fair to warn that this book provides no comprehensive account of popular or folk music cultures, modern dance and theater, or the integration of musical and social agendas. Yet it is perhaps no paradox that all of these issues surface repeatedly and in no way superficially. Indeed, it is precisely their relevance to some of the icons of musical Modernism as well as Postmodernism that constitutes the present story. As a consequence, concern will be noted for the current fin de siècle's claim to the discovery of multiculturalism. Such a perspective, which in any case cannot be forestalled, need not, in my mind, be rejected out of hand but may be regarded rather as the familiar and perennial wedding of radical contemporary theory with the best of a grand tradition—a tradition briefly jettisoned but now returned with a new pigment and a revitalized sense of utility. Thus, the aim here is not so much to discredit a contemporary report as to implore recognition of a rich chain of events from the turn of the last century. No doubt the introduction of such an appeal is in part reflective of the fact that slightly before the midpoint of the present centennial curve the author, owing to the caprices of war, learned an Oriental language before he studied a modern European one and lived in Tokyo before he ever traveled to Paris.

Marcel Proust purportedly once asked his housekeeper, "Do you ever read novels, Celeste?" "Occasionally, monsieur," she replied. "Why?" he continued. "They take me out of myself," she responded; to which Proust retorted, "They should take you into yourself."[9] The same may reasonably be claimed for the writing as well as the reading of history.

— THE ORIENT —

— 1 —

"And the Moon Descends over the Temple That Was"

I would like to see Persia and India and then China, the mandarins paunchy beneath their umbrellas, and the princesses with slender hands, and the learned ones who argue about poetry and about beauty . . . I would like to see assassins smiling as the executioner strikes an innocent neck with his great, curved oriental sabre . . . I would like to see paupers and queens . . . I would like to see those who die for love as well as those who die for hatred. And then I would return later to speak of my adventure to those curious about dreams, raising, like Sinbad, my old Arabian cup from time to time to my lips to interrupt the story artfully.

Tristan Klingsor

How will you talk about Spain once you have been there?

Heinrich Heine

From earliest times a tradition persistent in the West that ceremonies performed at dawn toward the rising sun carried a special power resulted in the orientation of temples and sacred buildings toward the east. As a consequence, from Mesopotamia and Egypt to Mayan Central America and Stonehenge in England, entrances were pointed eastward, and the custom endured in the positioning of Christian sanctuaries of both Europe and the Americas from the Middle Ages to the present day. Every child is familiar with Kipling's judgment that

> Oh, East is East, and West is West,
>   and never the twain shall meet,

13

> Till Earth and Sky stand presently at
> God's great Judgment Seat.

Yet the seeming truism of the opening line ignores not only the root of the word *orientation,* but Kipling's own conclusion:

> But there is neither East nor West,
> border, nor breed, nor birth,
> When two strong men stand face to face,
> though they come from the ends of the earth!

Indeed, East and West have met and through successive encounters have renewed each other's culture and thought in a fashion inconceivable without such a confrontation. In the West the luxuriant atmosphere of Tristan Klingsor's apostrophe, which Ravel so seductively summoned in his *Shéhérazade* of 1903, had already been richly appropriated throughout the nineteenth century in the work of numerous writers, painters, and musicians in a manner that did not always transcend colonialist attitudes. For at a fundamental level, the emphasis which the West placed upon the individual in its own society contrasted notably with the collective mystery and ineffable intangibility which it attributed to the Orient.

Orientalism has been the object of wide-ranging critical scrutiny, and in the post–World War II period has been subject to revision and reinterpretation. The idea of the Orient—meaning east, or, more specifically, east of Europe—was with good reason increasingly held to betray the speaker's Eurocentrism. It should be added that for Europeans, especially the English and French, the term "Orient" has traditionally implied the Near East, the Bible lands, and North Africa, while for Americans it has tended to connote the Far East—especially China and Japan. Depending upon the vantage point, it could also include India and Malaysia, particularly for the British, and Indonesia, for the Dutch. Finally, Russia has continued to loom as an equivocal and marginal entity—a chameleon whose capacity to assume Eastern or Western colors changed according to context.

In this light, it is understandable that Orientalism provided a ready-made forum for numerous political and colonialist arguments which began to be forwarded in the late 1970s.[1] But just as Eric R. Wolf warned against the perpetuation of East and West as monolithic categories and encouraged the search for dynamic types of interconnectedness and mutual dependency beyond the static models of nation and colony,[2] so one of the principal lures of the Orient for literature, art, and music has resided in its capacity first to be imagined (reverie in life or art), experienced (the voyage), and finally recalled (reconstituted through travel diaries, pictures, novels, musical portraits, and other creative reminiscences) in a fashion closely tied to purely aesthetic needs. Clearly, the ease with which Western Europe has adopted Oriental motifs suggests the embrace of issues well beyond any momentary vogue and reflects the value of viewing the self obliquely—not in search of a faithful photographic image nor in order to establish cultural hegemony, but rather to encounter attributes not readily discernible in daily life. Thus the major challenge of the Orient for writers, painters, and musicians alike has been to search, appropriate, reveal, and transform, rather than to render the exotic impotent. And in retrospect it is clear that the idea of multiculturalism, both as a sociological notion and as a vibrant aesthetic touchstone, was as powerful for the nineteenth-century fin de siècle as for the millennial turnover one hundred years later.

The West is aware that it has historically drawn sustenance from the East in a variety of ways and in so doing has found a radical cultural contestant and rich source of inspiration. The arts of the seventeenth through the nineteenth centuries clearly reflected many of these regional preoccupations. Yet the superior tone of the West in observing the Orient has been repeatedly noted by political and social historians, and the notion that the Orient has at times served as a plaything of the Western mind did not escape criticism well before the 1980s and 1990s. That artists have not always avoided value judgements and have exhibited an occasional tendency to devalue as they plundered, cannot be denied. The view of the East as opulent, colorful, and intriguing but also by turns sinister, menacing, and erotic has clearly fueled Western appetites both political and artistic. On all fronts, however, investigation generally has led not so much to a discovery of passions felt in the East that were absent in the West as to the capacity to paint them in more vivid tones for having been observed at some remove from mundane experience.

It is not surprising that this view from a distance has promoted the natural tendency to blur distinctions between the peoples and cultures of non-Western civilizations, and writers and artists have frequently been charged with seeing all non-Europeans as an undifferentiated if motley society.[3] It follows as a corollary that the Westerner has also periodically proclaimed a predestined role as interpreter for the essentially inarticulate Orient. This Occidental perception of the essential muteness of the East is a reflection not only of the stoic silence of its great Sphinxes and Buddhas but of the Westerner's prevailing ignorance of its languages, both literary and musical.

Beneath this reasonably guileless facade, Western interest gradually developed not just in the literature of the Orient, access to which continued to be hampered by the need for translation, but especially in its art, which could more readily counter claims of voicelessness. Throughout the nineteenth century musicians, too, increasingly sought out the structural and timbral bases of non-Western musics, both of which ultimately served as important sources in the definition of Modernism. As a companion to Primitivism, Orientalism in the early twentieth century soon began to place less emphasis upon the exotic as a source of local color and to attach an enhanced significance to those qualities which could transcend national boundaries and historical chronologies.

As a symptomatic if somewhat recondite example, Josef Hauer (1883–1959), a Viennese theoretician-composer who momentarily posed a philosophical challenge to Arnold Schoenberg in the 1920s, expressed a pronounced antipathy to the Greek philosophers and claimed descendancy for his most revolutionary ideas from ancient Chinese thought. He even suggested that the Chinese knew a kind of twelve-tone music. Finally, his division of the twelve pitches of the chromatic scale into two hexachordal tropes he attributed to a study of the *I Ching* (*pace* John Cage) and recognition of its hexagrams and adjacent trigrams.[4] The illustration, while not especially important in and of itself, is reflective of the almost compulsive appropriation of the Orient in the twentieth century, not just as a non-Western source but as a culture with roots perceived to be even more ancient than those of the Greco-Roman tradition. Thus, in the world of music, the Western intellectualisms of the trope and the series as well as the capriciousness of chance and the "happening" have all been laid at the doorstep of the Far East.

In the act of filtering the Orient through their Western eyes and ears, Goethe, Delacroix, Baudelaire, and Berlioz; Hesse, Hauer, Cowell, and Cage; Messiaen, McPhee, Stockhausen, and Boulez have all promoted the notion that the consideration of an alien culture could provide new sources of authority and aid in the expansion of resources, sonorities, and themes in the search for global values. Although the Modern view

of the Orient has differed from the Romantic one, its continuing appropriation should not surprise us, for each age has a way of returning to
the same sources, the same myths, to the same elementary ideas in the
act of translating them into a contemporary account of a perennial philosophy.[5]

Despite the rash of ethnographic criticism that has scrutinized the
Western artist's adoption of Eastern culture and charged exploitation
if not piracy, it may be well to assert the simple and perhaps somewhat
obvious fact that a great deal of the fascination with the Orient, both
in the nineteenth century and in the early twentieth, resided in the
sheer story-telling allure of *The Thousand and One Nights* and other related fairy tales from Charles Perrault to Hans Christian Andersen. It
is clear that the quality of the universal which attends such literature is
heightened and clarified both by the remoteness of the setting and by
the readily translatable social stereotypes attendant to all myths. Any
child can follow the clearly etched personae of contrasting station and
ethical values: the emperors and queens both good and bad, princes
and paupers, sorcerers, warriors, ambassadors, evil spirits and magical
birds. The nineteenth-century Symbolists did not invent them, but they
noted and appreciated their potency as well as their availability.[6]

Though the category of the "Other," capitalized or in quotes or
both, had yet to be defined by the Symbolists, the very name of their
movement advertised its devotion to a related sensibility: namely, that
the human condition can best, perhaps only, be observed through some
distancing technique. Despite periodic colonialist attitudes in the invocation of such contrasts, a sense of the collective mystery of the Orient
increasingly permitted the Western artist to recall Eastern locales for
aesthetic purposes devoid of all political or moral judgments based upon
ethnic stereotypes. On the level of visual color alone, the Orient was
alive with possibilities that seemed to be missing from the Western palette. Chinese red, for example, implied not just an orangy cast but a
sheen attributable to the qualities of a lacquered surface, familiar in the
West in any number of *objets d'art* of Sino-Japanese origin. Gold drawn
from the same lexicon conjured up not a blinding brilliance but one
shadowed with the misty gray undertones that float beneath the gilt
surface of a painted Oriental screen, giving the impression of a considerable antiquity. And embrace of the Orient in the world of sound
through the invocation of a pentatonic scale was seductive precisely

because the tuning of its five notes could be only approximated in the equal temperament of Western music and because its use left audible gaps in the familiar diatonic octave. Timbral or sonic color codes, as we shall see, were also developed as cohorts in conjuring up the Orient. Ultimately, as Edward Said himself eventually asserted, it was this very dialectic of the shaping forces of colonialism and the surfacing aesthetic options that encouraged, even demanded, a contrapuntal reading of the canon of Western literature.[7]

The Russian musician's fascination with the Far East, the Near East, and Southeast Asia was pronounced throughout the nineteenth century. From Glinka's Oriental dances in *Ruslan and Lyudmila* (1837–1842) and Balakirev's Oriental fantasy *Islamey* (1869) to Glazunov's *Oriental Rhapsody* (1889) and Tchaikovsky's *Nutcracker Suite* (1892), the vogue for the Chinese, Japanese, Hindu, Persian, and Turkish march and dance flourished. Authenticity was seldom a burning issue, although distinctions between ethnic groups were in general more successfully portrayed than in the age of Rameau's *Les Indes galantes* (1735), when a procession of only vaguely differentiated dances from exotic locales became not only à la mode but de rigueur in the ongoing conflation of the genres of opera and ballet.[8] Even Jean Jacques Rousseau included examples of Chinese and North American Indian music in his music dictionary of 1768, and Carl Maria von Weber used one of them, which in turn served Paul Hindemith for the "Turandot" movement of his *Symphonic Metamorphosis on Themes of Carl Maria von Weber* of 1943.[9] Theoretical interest in analyzing scalar formations of diverse cultures also became a preoccupation of the Romantic Age, and by the early twentieth century claims to authenticity were still occasionally invoked by composers through the quotation of melodies drawn from Eastern lands—as in Ravel's use of Persian melodies in his orchestral overture *Shéhérazade,* Holst's citation of Japanese melodies in his *Japanese Suite,* or Puccini's use of Japanese source materials in *Madama Butterfly,*[10] native Indian melodies in *Girl of the Golden West,* and ancient Chinese song in *Turandot.* But cachet was also frequently achieved through the invention of reductive symbols only obliquely related to the cultures in question. Even when composers were searching out the roots of their native culture, the move away from citation and toward synthesis, as with Stravinsky and Bartók, often proved to be the most compelling course, while the extended use of genuine tunes was increasingly reserved for sets of folk melodies with "modern" accompaniments.

Paris and the Far East at the Turn of the Century

The Paris International Exposition of 1889, celebrating the hundredth anniversary of the French Revolution, was far more symbolic than the similar fairs of 1878 and 1900 and in many ways eclipsed both of them in importance. Following their defeat in the Franco-Prussian War of 1870, the French were intent on demonstrating not only their cultural richness but their rightful claims to technological parity, if not superiority, within the European community. The construction of the Galérie des Machines may have been an impressive advocate of French progress,[11] but it was the Exposition's Eiffel Tower that stood as the most potent emblem of this assertion. It is worthy of note that even earlier plans for demonstrating technological prowess through a symbolic tower by both British and American engineers were drawn in consort with obelisks, domes, and pyramids—all emblems of architectural achievement in ancient and distant cultures (Figure 1.1).[12] On the other side of the cultural ledger, France could point not only to its own distinguished roster of painters, writers, and composers from the Romantic Age, but could, in harmony with the theme of an international exposition, demonstrate its awareness and appreciation of societies from around the globe. In addition to dissipating the more repellent aspects of economic colonialism, such a posture clearly reflected the Symbolist attraction to and vivifying respect for distant lands that had long since transcended a rudimentary infatuation.

Although throughout the nineteenth century French interest in the Far East was less well developed than in the Near East and North Africa, the International Expositions of 1889 and 1900 in Paris brought the world of Southeast Asia, China, and Japan to the attention of artists and musicians alike. Yet though such international expositions were replete with artifacts and entertainment, one of their primary purposes was to promote commerce. The Dutch, for example, having deprived the Javanese of their political rights at home, nonetheless allowed them to retain and practice their native arts, typically performed at court and hence an emblem of power. As purveyors of an export commodity at an international exhibition, the Dutch could express pride in their sponsorship of these Javanese ensembles and dancers. The presentation of such dances, which were normally outside the experience even of the Javanese except in courtly circles, indicates a surprising cultural openness. A witness of these performances spoke of a quartet of lady dancers from the twenty-eight who constituted the *troupe de ballet* of the prince Mangok-Negoro, sovereign of Java residing at Solo (Surakarta): "All four belonged to the highest class of their profession, the Sarimpi, of a privileged cast, whose members were born, lived and died in the company of the prince. From their youth they were trained in the dance which they were to perform, they remained virgins and enjoyed great esteem, in contrast to the public dancers."[13] As a special dispensation, the Prince of Solo authorized the dancers to bring their richly ornamented ceremonial and courtly costumes with them to Paris.

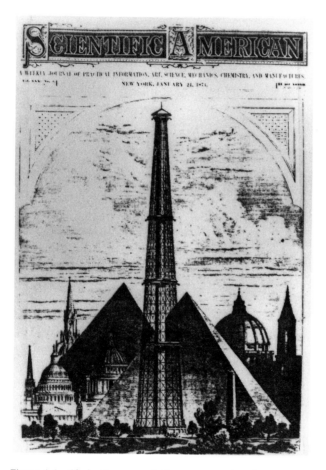

Figure 1.1. Clark, Reeves and Company, project for a Philadelphia Centennial Tower, 1874.

Scientific American, January 1874.

Ultimately, it was an arrangement of some apparent satisfaction to colonialist and native alike, with Dutch concessions to art being incorporated as part of an economic showcase that carried potential connotations of taste and cultural richness.

Not surprisingly these visiting troupes proved to be stimulating for
both musicians and visual artists, and the vividness of the impression
can be seen in Rodin's 1908 watercolors of Cambodian dancing girls
as well as in the scores of numerous Parisian composers. At the 1878
Exposition interest had centered especially on the music of the Hungarian gypsies and the Tunisian and Algerian cafés-concerts, but in 1889
the attention of the visitors turned principally to the *théâtre annamite*
and the Javanese dances. Critical descriptions of the latter varied from
"a strange music, sometimes bizarre" to "very beautiful sounds, very
plain, in no way disagreeable" to "howlingly ferocious and made up
of metallic sonorities which pierce the ears."

The music of Annam, then a French protectorate and now a part of
Vietnam, was described by Saint-Saëns as "only bad Chinese music in
decline; true Chinese music is atrocious to our ears, but when one takes
the pains to study it, it offers considerable interest, which is missing
here." Reports of the musical offerings were chiefly made by journalists,
however, and only Julien Tiersot brought a musicological expertise to
his accounts. Having heard the Javanese musicians on innumerable afternoons, Tiersot attempted his own transcriptions, only to concede
that a phonograph would be necessary to make a proper record of the
music.[14]

Throughout the nineteenth century the West had been attracted to
portraying the seductive and even the violent aura of the Orient, and
artists from Delacroix to Gautier and Flaubert have been repeatedly
blamed for assisting in the establishment of stereotypes and even a sense
of Western moral superiority. By 1889 there can be no arguing that
the Exposition hoped to rely upon a flourishing sensitivity to anthropology and history to assist in portraying a sense of progress through the
ages. The Eurocentric bias is evident in the official report, which announced the organizational plan of the Exposition according to the relative primitiveness of various civilizations. The five continents were recognized as representing distinct degrees along an imaginary civilizational
curve: Oceania, the most primitive; Africa, showing the effects of the
first contacts with civilization; Asia, odalisque quietly sleeping in a sensual pose; America, in search of fortune and commercial supremacy; and

Europe, magnifying its own speculative nature, thoughts, and position through the emblem of the word and the book.[15]

The assumption that there was an automatic and corresponding transferral of such perspectives to value judgments in music and the other arts must be resisted, however. For just as an open letter of 1887 by a group of writers, painters, sculptors, and architects protested the emphasis upon technological progress implied in the erecting of the Eiffel Tower, so numerous artists viewed the imported civilizational component of the Exposition from anything but an official angle. Judith Gautier, the daughter of the poet Théophile, for example, was an avid Orientalist throughout her life, and although she never visited China or Japan, she studied their languages and regarded them with a profound affection throughout her life. She also prompted her devoted and life-long assistant, Louis Benedictus, to make transcriptions of the music heard at the expositions of both 1889 and 1900 to accompany her own published translations of their poetry.[16] Questions regarding the accuracy of their transcriptions and translations aside, the sincerity of their combined commitment to the arts of the Far East can scarcely be questioned. A similar respect and affection is apparent in the remarks of Debussy, who summed up the potency of the draught in terms that, somewhat dramatically, imply a naiveté on the part of Western music, rather than the possibly more predictable charge of an undeveloped harmonic system in the Orient. The following familiar words are from a letter to the poet Pierre Louÿs of January 22, 1895: "Do you not remember the Javanese music able to express every nuance of meaning, even unmentionable shades, and which make our tonic and dominant seem like empty phantoms for the use of unwise infants. Try no more to place before us poor old 'mi, la, re, do' of an ancient and doubtful nobility."[17]

Musicians will note the emphasis that Debussy placed upon pitch in this letter, an emphasis that unwittingly diminishes the obvious impact of other parameters, such as rhythm, heterophony, and especially timbre, as italicizers of modality and tuning in Javanese music. The exclusive attention which Debussy drew to a brief melodic event of pentatonic implications, recalled from a live performance at the Exposition, may explain his self-acknowledged failure to capture the aura of the Javanese ensemble in his *Fantaisie* for piano and orchestra of 1890.[18] It was a judgment shared by several writers, including Robert Godet as late as 1926, who seemed eager to excuse Debussy's early interpretation of the Javanese ensemble: "Not for a minute has Debussy thought of reproducing with Western instrumental resources the effect of polyphony and, especially, of percussive poly-rhythms." He concluded that the ultimate importance of Debussy's exposure to this source came later, through "the grouping of scattered materials . . . in his memory and his imagination."[19] The Romantic notion of an Orient imagined, and if visited only later remembered, is forwarded as a creative norm.

Indeed, in spite of Debussy's possible familiarity with a Javanese gamelan sent to the Paris Conservatoire by the Dutch government in 1887[20] and his observance of numerous performances at the International Exposition of 1889, it was only in a series of later pieces that Debussy's memory synthesized the potential of the encounter. In addition to the obvious appropriation of pentatonic patterns already well known from contexts totally divorced from any experience with live Oriental ensembles, composers of the early twentieth century continued to develop the Romantic arsenal of timbral effects capable of conjuring up the Orient. Debussy in particular repeatedly hinted at his view of the East through his choice of register and timbre.

This is especially evident in the 1900 version of "Pour la danseuse aux crotales" and "Pour l'égyptienne" from Louÿs's *Chansons de Bilitis* for reciter and chamber ensemble of two flutes, two harps, and celesta. But even when Debussy composed for a single monochromatic instrument such as the piano, his explorations of timbre and register were far from routine. In "Et la lune descend sur le temple qui fut" from the second book of *Images* of 1907, Debussy successfully hypothesized a not totally imaginary Oriental ensemble on the modern piano by several means. These include descending arpeggiated fifths in the bass register to approximate the resonating sheen of the gong (Example 1.1, mm. 6, 7, 9). The impression of this sonority for those who attended the 1889 Exposition is made explicit by Tiersot, who referred to "the sounds of the enormous gongs, full and sonorous as a bell of a cathedral" and to "gongs of diverse kinds and of all dimensions including the largest, all projecting a perceptible note, although sometimes very low, tuned in the manner of tympanies."[21] Many years later Debussy also recalled the music's sonority: "Amongst the Annamites, one witnesses a kind of embryonic lyric drama influenced by the Chinese . . . An angry little clarinet guides the emotions; a tam-tam organizes the terror . . . and that is all."[22]

Even more alluring qualities surround the appearance of the grace

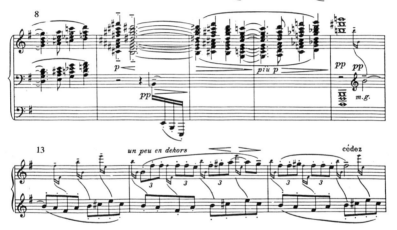

Example 1.1. Claude Debussy, *Images,* Book II, "Et la lune descend sur le temple qui fut," mm. 1–15.

notes articulated in multiple octave registers. In "Et la lune descend" (Example 1.1, mm. 12–15) these figures not only accentuate the overtone structure of an inversionally symmetrical pentatonic fragment characteristic of Javanese music (F♯, A, B, C♯, E) but correspond closely to the function of the *saron peking* or *saron panerus* in a Javanese gamelan.[23] The highest pitched of the metallophones, these instruments typically articulate the quickly decaying upper octave anticipations of principal melodic notes, and Debussy's vivid portrayal is undoubtedly instrument specific.

Finally, the prevailing initial harmonic unit of fourth and fifth above a root (or fourth with added second) presented as an opening and closing frame for the piece can be plausibly argued as a reflection of harmonies common to Cambodian and Javanese instrumental ensembles which Louis Laloy had recently strained to describe at the 1906 Congress of the International Musical Society in Brussels:

> It is also necessary to remark that a sense of harmony begins to force its way through: besides octaves, very frequently on the two *Roneat,* one often hears genuine chords struck which do not justify any melodic movement: there are seconds, fourths, seconds and fourths, or seconds and thirds, quite beautiful in sound, which give a sense of consonance more than of dissonance . . . It is probable that if the music of the Far East continues to develop, it will construct a good and proper system of harmony; its evolution will be quite parallel to that of our music, though divergent.[24]

Laloy's observations about Cambodian harmony, which attempt to amend the notion of Southeast Asian music as being guided by strictly polyphonic activity, are reflected in Debussy's harmonic choices at the very beginning of the piece both in the characteristic fourth plus second (Example 1.1, m. 1: E, A, B), quickly subjected to parallel motion, and in the occasional contractions to a third plus second (m. 3: F♯, A, B). They also reflect, pitch specifically, the harmonic evidence of a transcription made in 1900 by Louis Benedictus entitled "Danse javanaise" (Example 1.2). All of these vertical "simultaneities" are, indeed, familiar sounds coincidental to a gamelan polyphony restricted to the five–note *slendro.*[25]

It is of no small interest that "Et la lune descend sur le temple qui fut" is dedicated to Louis Laloy himself, and apparently the title was actually confected by him following the completion of the work.[26] The author of tracts on Greek music, Rameau, and Ronsard as well as the first study in French on Debussy (1909), Laloy also wrote a monograph entitled *La Musique chinoise* in 1912.[27] That Laloy was familiar with the latest developments of the time is confirmed by the fact that prior to

Example 1.2. "Danse javanaise" (Benedictus, 1900).

its premiere Debussy and Stravinsky read *Le sacre du printemps* at Laloy's residence in Bellevue, Debussy playing the bass. Laloy reported: "We were speechless, as though knocked to the ground by a hurricane which came from the depth of the ages."[28] The appearance of Laloy's article on Cambodian music in the year just prior to Debussy's "Et la lune," as well as the eventual dedication of the work to him, carries the resonance of cause and effect, or at the very least the force of a memory jogged. Although in his 1909 study of the composer Laloy failed to speak directly of the technical means employed by Debussy, he was generous in his evocation of the atmosphere of the piece and explicit in proclaiming the Far East as the locus of its sound world:

> The second piece [of *Images,* series II] transports us to another country, without posting letters and beyond a measurable distance, a country of dreams where we would gladly go together: *Et la lune descend sur le temple qui fut.* More remote than *Pagodes,* in a Far East less torrid and more serious, thoughts are collected and music is condensed, free of any egoist mixture, a gem translucid and compressed, born of space and of silence.[29]

On the day following Debussy's death Robert Godet wrote a lengthy homage in which he specifically alluded to the composer's Oriental strain. Although the details could be argued, the account is worth recalling:

> I pass on to an Orient now extinct, which the French genius of Debussy, along with Flaubert, restored and naturalized: *Canope, Danseuses de Delphes, La Terrasse des audiences du clair de lune* . . . I pass on finally to the Far East, fictitious but nourished by tested realities: *Pagodes* (Cambodia and Java, filtered through the imaginary flight provided by admirable exhibitions), *Et la lune descend sur le temple qui fut* . . . (an India reflecting the world of Kipling, but sifted and refined through distant archipelagos).[30]

Regardless of the setting one may wish to claim for Debussy's temple, his memory of the Javanese gamelan is both more precise and more evocative than in his early *Fantaisie* for piano and orchestra. And both Godet and Georges Jean-Aubry were quick to note the connection.[31] More recently Pierre Boulez has fastened on the remarkableness of this very work: "The composer who received this [Eastern] influence at the deepest level and transcended it in the most marvellous way was Debussy. I am thinking not of *Pagodes* but of 'La lune descend sur le temple qui fut.' Here the concepts of time and sonority are clearly determined."[32]

Debussy was not alone in his evocation of the Orient through timbral as well as scalar symbols. For though Mahler drew upon an obligatory and pervasive pentatonicism in the setting of Chinese texts in *Das Lied von der Erde*,[33] his employment of tam-tam (the temple gong both as Oriental reference and as symbol of Death) and oboe (to the Western ear, the Oriental color par excellence) in the opening frame of its final movement endorsed an accepted timbral code that promoted the adoption of pedal points, ostinati, harp, mandolin, and flute as members of an imitation Oriental ensemble. Varieties of gongs (Chinese tam-tam, Javanese kempul, kenong) and flutes (Japanese shakuhachi, Javanese suling) as well as oboes (including the four- and five-reed instruments of various Southeast Asian gamelans and the *hichiriki* of the Japanese Gagaku ensemble) are common throughout the East, but Mahler's timbral choices as well as his pentatonicism were as approximate as Hans Bethge's translations of Li-Tai Po and other Chinese poets. The authorization, even the need and purpose, for such interpretive license, however, was taken for granted by audiences well beyond Paris, Vienna, or Munich, where the work was premiered in November of 1911.

In *Das Lied von der Erde* Mahler painted pictures suitable for a screen or a porcelain cup—blossoms in the spring, pagodas and arched bridges, fluttering kimonos. But he also used his Oriental backcloth in the first movement to speak of the crouched and ghostly figure of an ape whose "howling pierces life's sweet fragrance," and in the last movement to suggest a "coolness in the shade of my pine-trees" at the impending heartbreak of farewell. Nature and the Orient are fused.[34] Similarly, while Debussy's "Poissons d'or" may be dismissed as an attractive allusion to goldfish as ornament, the aesthetic values which drew the composer to the subject can best be sensed through a lacquer screen that portrays both the stillness and motion of a magical carp gliding beneath bending willows—a screen owned by Debussy and contemplated during the composition of the music (Figure 1.2). The peripatetic mood of the music responds to the alternating stasis and mercurial darting of the goldfish, a mesmerizing *tableau vivant* seemingly without issue but carrying a seductive invitation to contemplation of motifs beneath the surface. As in "Pagodes" from his *Estampes* of 1903, so in "Et la lune descend sur le temple qui fut" Debussy clearly sought not to preach but rather to fashion an atmosphere of serenity and mystery denied to

Figure 1.2. "Poissons d'or." Lacquer panel owned by Claude Debussy.

dwellers in Paris and other modern urban environments. It was not that Notre-Dame or Sacré Coeur lacked mystery because they were too near at hand; Debussy's mythical temple simply no longer existed, indeed, never had: ". . . and the moon descends on the temple that was." Time and place are not merely elusive, they are forever out of reach.

Ravel's explorations of Asia were similar in numerous technical details, including the pentatonicism, quartal grace notes, secundal clashes, and timbral evocations through register such as appear in "Laideronette, Empress of the Pagodas." But his locus is at a still further remove. Whether in "Asie" by Tristan Klingsor, which opens his *Shéhérazade* of 1903 (see the epigraph at the beginning of this chapter), the porcelain figures of Perrault's fairy tales *(Mother Goose),* or the Chinese cup of *L'Enfant et les sortilèges* (1920–1925), Ravel's Orient is both more fanciful, more imaginary, and more private. Thus in the second movement of his Piano Trio (1914), rhythmic nuances and formal solutions clearly reflect his exposure to the heterophony of Malayan ensembles at the Paris International Expositions. Labeled a Pantoum, a Malayan verse form characterized by four-line stanzas whose second and fourth lines are repeated as the first and third of the following stanza, the movement explores a structure adopted by several French poets in the fin de siècle, including Théodore de Banville, who described it in detail in his *Petit traité de poésie française* in 1871. Ravel's solution is anything but obvious, however, and one of the most telling examples of formal transference comes in the recall of the first two themes in 3/4 meter against the 4/2 meter of the third—the whole adapted to the classical musical form of a traditional scherzo and trio.[35] But this is Southeast Asian Orientalism at a considerable remove, involving connoisseurship and interdisciplinary enlightenment more than a practiced ear on the part of the listener.

Like Debussy, Ravel drew inspiration from another Orient—though it lay to the west of France—one more extrovert than the Far East but also more personal: Spain, a land closer to home but equally mysterious and whose culture and Oriental connections Ravel knew well. An attempt to secure this link is made by Ravel in the first movement of the same Piano Trio whose second movement is a Pantoum, wherein he adopts the Basque rhythms of the *zortziko* (8/8 divided into 3 + 2 + 3/8). For all of its base in additive ethnic folk metrics, its affable movement and graceful lilt register as distant relatives to Bartók's Bulgarian dance rhythms (Example 1.3). Elsewhere the Spanish note was sounded independently throughout the composer's career, beginning with the *Habanera* of 1895–1897, and continuing with the rhythms, repeated notes, and glissandi of "Alborada del gracioso" (*Miroirs,* 1905),

Example 1.3. Maurice Ravel, Piano Trio, mvt. 1, mm. 1–4.

the multiple evocations of *Rapsodie espagnole* (1907–8), the hypnotizing *Boléro* of 1928, and the successive explorations in *Don Quichotte à Dulcinée* (1932–33) of the alternating 6/8–3/4 rhythms of the Spanish *quajira* in the first song, the quintuple metrics of the *zortziko* in the second, and the rhythm and triple metrics of the *jota* in the concluding drinking song. Ravel's interest in a Spain characterized by more than the superficialities of local color was shared by Debussy, who also explored its distinctive rhythms in "Soirée dans Grenade" (*Estampes,* 1903), "Ibéria" (*Images,* 1906–1912) and "La Puerta del vino" (*Préludes,* Book II, 1910–1913). And in light of Russian interest in the Iberian peninsula from the time of Glinka, it is not surprising that as late as 1921 Stravinsky took note of the prevailing notion of Spain as a kind of Orient and hence of Russia's innate predilection for its music:

> It is very natural that we want to be inspired by, and, if I may say so, to take with us a bit of Spain. The question is, what can be transported? Certain wines must be consumed where they are made. Others, those which can stand the trip, we bring with us.
>
> Affinities and resemblances can be remarked between Spanish music, especially that of Andalusia, and the music of Russia, no doubt through their common Oriental origins. Certain Andalusian songs remind me of Russian ones, and I enjoy these atavistic memories. Musically speaking, the Andalusians are not at all Latin, their rhythms being of Oriental inheritance.[36]

Ravel ultimately demonstrated that allusion to the East could be useful even when he had no need of invoking the Orient precisely, however. His opera *L'Enfant et les sortilèges,* for example, is set in a child's world of make-believe, and the central events take place largely in the child's imagination. It is noteworthy that as the opera opens, Ravel creates the fairy-tale—not the Oriental—atmosphere of the work through the use of a set of patently Oriental symbols: the color of the oboe, pentatonic pitch material, and open fifths and fourths laid over a changing metric grid (Example 1.4). The distancing capacity of an Eastern musical code is metamorphosed into an invitation to a contemporary child's world of dreams. But we realize the reference is to the universal fantasy world of the child wherever he may be, in Peking or in Paris.[37]

In the process of surveying their several Orients and filtering their

Example 1.4. Maurice Ravel, *L'Enfant et les sortilèges* (1920–1925), Act I, mm. 12–19.

discoveries through private, subjective experience, the aspirations of all three composers to musical authenticity were diluted and converted by a personal program. Though it can be argued that in the process colonialist agendas were notably submerged, it is possible to claim that their approach was totally in keeping with what has been called "France's venerable tradition of aestheticizing colonial expansion."[38] Nonetheless, Debussy and Ravel clearly shared a concept of *musique du monde* akin to Goethe's concept of *Weltliteratur,* advanced in his *Chinesische Jahres- und Tageszeiten* of 1830, which aimed through translation and criticism to advance civilization through understanding and respect.[39] The possibility of reading such courteous inferences into the Westerner's view of the Orient in an Age of Colonialism is a point of view that is seldom advanced. In fact recent investigations of Orientalism tied to questions of Western cultural leverage and political power brokerage have almost universally ignored the potential role of the artist as a sympathetic commentator.[40] Yet not only is the East–West relationship more complex than social and political historians might have us believe, but it ought to be characterized in substantial measure by qualities which reflect a profound Western appreciation of the artistic and aesthetic legacy of the East.[41]

Diaghilev and the Orient

Russia had historically been perceived as a kind of Orient, perpetually teetering between Eastern and Western values. In the nineteenth century Vladimir Stasov (1824–1906), art historian, critic, and music lover, had attributed the Oriental element in Russian music to a logical perpetuation of its medieval heritage. "Nowhere in Europe does it play such a predominant role as it does with our musicians," he observed.[42]

Sergei Diaghilev's introduction of the music of the Russian Five in his second Parisian season of 1907 not only showcased the Russian mode but confirmed a taste for the Orient that had been shared by Russia and France throughout the nineteenth century. Then, in 1908 he achieved total Parisian capitulation with the Imperial Theater's production of Musorgsky's *Boris Godunov,* with Chaliapin in the title role and Alexandre Benois and Alexandre Golovin as designers of the decor and costumes. Expansion of the original plan was virtually inevitable, and in 1909 Léon Bakst virtually swept Paris off its feet with his fantasy decor for *Orientales* and *Shéhérazade,* as did Nikolas Roerich with his sets for Borodin's *Prince Igor.*

Music had now been joined by a visual Oriental component characterized by a prevailing brilliance of Fauvist color and a sense of motion that was delightful to the eye and escapist for the mind. Thematically, however, the repertory of ballets which appeared up to 1912 was submerged in a sea of Orientalia marked by a collection of familiar loci and fabled personalities, all typically projected for their surface exoticism as well as for their occasional prurient Decadence. A combination of pantomime and classical dance joined to the coloration of national and folk dances[43] typical of the age of Marius Petipa also continued to prosper, but this, too, was destined to change.

Diaghilev's ballet *Le Dieu bleu* of 1909 illustrated the continuing power of resurrected themes such as the pseudo-Hindu world of Léon Minkus' *La Bayadère,* one of Petipa's notable successes in St. Petersburg in 1877. Yet, while stage decor and costume brought the brilliance and fresh perspectives of the Fauvists' colors to the stage in a manner that mesmerized audiences, *Le Dieu bleu* only reviewed and corroborated

the fact that a great deal of the nineteenth-century's classical ballet production was unveiled in the presence of routine music by the likes of
Minkus and Cesare Pugni. André Levinson, one of the most important
St. Petersburg dance critics from 1909 until he moved permanently to
Paris in 1921 following the Revolution, openly charged that, with the
exception of a few notable scores by Tchaikovsky, music, for all its
"aptness for balletic forms," had been the weakest link in the classical
ballet.[44] It was an issue that Diaghilev was finally forced to confront in
large measure due to his experience with *Le Dieu bleu*.

Diaghilev chose Jean Cocteau to devise a scenario, Reynaldo Hahn
to write the score, and Léon Bakst to execute the costumes (Figure 1.3)
and scenic designs, which he bathed in orange, blue, and green. Among
the coterie of artists whose services Diaghilev enlisted, Bakst had provided a singularly powerful thrust to the *World of Art* program, which
sought to invigorate the Russian avant-garde both through a renewed
interested in its national heritage and a revitalized contact with the
mainstream of Western European culture. In his costumes Bakst relied
increasingly on tunics, boleros, harem pants, split skirts, and nude male
torsos. In this he claimed to be prompted not only by a desire to under-
line the erotic component purportedly justified by an Eastern setting,
but also by an interest in ethnic and historical accuracy.[45] In this regard
Bakst's influence extended to matters of choreography. Bronislava Nijinska has related how, working with Michel Fokine, Bakst would illus-
trate "the proper position of a hand or the movement of an arm, sometimes even demonstrating an oriental pose for us and explaining the
way we should move our bodies during the dance."[46]

In the four ballets with Far Eastern locales (*Cléopâtre, Shéhérazade,
Thamar,* and *Le Dieu bleu*) which Bakst mounted for Diaghilev, the
designer addressed a taste simultaneously prevalent in London, Paris,
Moscow, and St. Petersburg. It was further fueled by an important literary tradition of the Russian romantic poets. For example, *Egyptian
Nights,* first produced by Fokine at the Maryinsky Theater in St. Petersburg in 1908 and later renamed *Cléopâtre* by Diaghilev, was based upon
a story by Pushkin, who together with Lermontov paved the way for
the Russian Symbolist's dedication to themes of love and death in exotic
settings.[47] Yet France's contribution to the movement was perhaps the
richest of all, for in the nineteenth century painters (Eugène Delacroix,
Gustave Moreau, and Jean-Léon Gérôme) and writers (Gustave Flaubert, Théophile Gautier) alike had capitulated to its allure. And in the

Figure 1.3. Léon Bakst, costume for a Negro dancer in *Le Dieu bleu,* 1912.
Private collection.

world of music the Orient of the Bible lands and North Africa had been tapped by composers from Félicien David and Berlioz to Bizet, Massenet, Delibes, and Saint-Saëns. Thus Diaghilev's Ballets Russes built upon a literary, visual, and musical foundation that had developed over a considerable period of time both at home and abroad.

Just as Rodin's watercolors of 1908 were inspired by the sight of Cambodian dancing girls at the International Exposition of 1900 and on later visits, so Fokine and Bakst fell under the spell of performances of the Ballet Troupe of the royal Siamese Court in the Imperial Theaters of St. Petersburg as early as October 28–29, 1900. The impact of these performances is clear in Bakst's painting *A Siamese Sacred Dance,* from 1902, the background of which forecasts numerous details of his back-drop for *Le Dieu bleu* in its reliance upon diagonal composition, figures of Hindu deities, and cavernous temples.[48] If the European taste for the opulent and decadent was soon to recede, it cannot be denied that Bakst provided new and authentic visual sources based upon first-hand, though imported, experience. His subsequent exportations of this mate-rial at least hinted at an expression that transcended hackneyed exotic entertainment.

On the musical front, however, the inherent problems of a banal Orientalism remained largely unaddressed. Reynaldo Hahn, who pro-vided the score for the ballet, is little remembered today as a personality, except as a friend of Marcel Proust and Sarah Bernhardt. Similarly, he is forgotten as a composer but for a few *mélodies,* which Hahn sang at the time to his own accompaniment in the salons of Paris. Though it was the first ballet to be commissioned by Diaghilev from a non-Russian, Hahn's single contribution to Diaghilev's world, *Le Dieu bleu* (1909), is today only a title, long eclipsed by its more illustrious com-panions. A glance at the score reveals the reasons for its disappearance and the symptoms that would oblige Diaghilev to reconsider the role of the Orient in his future productions. A slender bit of exotica, the work contains monophonic solos, both chromatic and whole-tone, as well as various ostinati and open-fifth accompaniments by way of an exercise in Orientalia. Hahn's statement that his ballet was "to be of the Impressionist school" is confirmed in the music that accompanies the appearance of a Hindu goddess from the lotus pool—an overt and symbolic stylization of the undulating rhythmic quirk that characterizes the right hand of Ravel's "Ondine," the water sprite, at the opening of *Gaspard de la nuit,* published the year before.[49] But this is a rarefied symbolism for connoisseurs and insufficient to salvage the work as a whole.

Edward Gordon Craig, one of the visionaries of the contemporary theater and a critic of the power which Diaghilev had acceded to Bakst in his use of Fauvist color, wrote a devastating review of *Le Dieu bleu* in his periodical *The Mask* under the nom de plume J. Van Holt. Declaring that the desire of Hahn and Diaghilev to do away with "the senseless traditions of the ballet skirt with its antiquated poses and gesture" had come too late in light of the recent accomplishments of his friend Isadora Duncan, he poked fun at the Oriental trappings and concluded: "These certainly are very extraordinary experiments, but why not make them and keep them in the bathroom? Or if Madame Rubinstein, in gilt and diamonds, went out to tea to the Countess of Winkleboro and M. Nijinsky, dyed blue, could be persuaded to take black coffee at the Reform Club, might not nearly as great a sensation be produced? Why drag in the Theatre?"[50]

It is understandable that Cocteau, who also made his debut with Diaghilev as coauthor of the scenario, failed to find his expected success in it, and that, following the premiere of *Le Sacre,* he would be obliged to go in search of a liaison with Stravinsky in hopes of "astonishing" the director of the Ballets Russes elsewhere.

Astonishment, as it was to turn out, would require more than a locale, and would involve a complex of ingredients that had been forming under Diaghilev's sponsorship. Primary among them had been the concept of an integration of the arts, which to that point had more often than not amounted merely to interface. Though it was possible to rely upon the brilliance of costume and set invited by an Oriental subject, increasing parity was sought between the several components, and both music and the visual arts were soon to be challenged to a role beyond mere accompaniment to the dance. Diaghilev's desire to treat the so-called decorative and fine arts as equal was not just a footnote to Art Nouveau taste but entailed a vision of a new aesthetic—the hope that radical dimensions discovered in one art might be covertly resident in another. The feeling prevailed that one could not be sure which art, at any given time, might show the way. Not only decorative art but utilitarian and folk crafts and music were now deemed capable of a powerful and propelling expression.[51] Diaghilev also believed that Russian artists enriched their palette through a thorough assimilation of Western art and encouraged fusion between Eastern and Western values as a source of aesthetic vitality. He even believed that Russian artists had demonstrated that they did their best work only after such a confrontation.[52]

But Hahn, born in Venezuela, was not a Russian, and his music flourished in the most banal exotic waters of contemporary Paris. In an earlier age of Russian ballet, Hahn's slight music would have been sufficient to the purposes at hand. In the developing climate around 1910, Hahn's product was emblematic of the dissolution of an age. Stravinsky explained Hahn's relationship to the Ballets Russes clearly: "I saw him quite often at one time, but always in company with Marcel Proust. Diaghilev needed him and therefore staged his *Dieu Bleu:* he was the salon idol of Paris, and salon support was very useful to Diaghilev at that time. After the war, however, Diaghilev dropped him for the very reason that he had once found him important—his salon reputation."[53]

The implications are clear and by extension are capable of being interpreted as an assessment of the decline of interest in things Oriental. Such a conclusion would fall short of the true state of affairs, however. Mahler, Debussy, and Ravel had recently provided models for transcending the commonplace and the cliché in the appropriation of the Orient. Now Stravinsky, in a pair of encounters with the Orient immediately following Hahn's farewell to Diaghilev's company, was to press the argument even further that confrontation with the East could promote the discovery of a radical new musical language. In the act of constructing this language in tandem with the requirements of a ballet company, the age of Petipa and Minkus would be left behind.

— 2 —

Of Nightingales and Ukiyo-e

I would even say, without any sense of paradox, that the more the windows to the outside are small the more my imagination is strengthened. Too great a knowledge of things inspires respect in us and prohibits spontaneous usage. On the contrary, a scattered knowledge fires the imagination; it is from such a small nucleus, much as the grain of sand in the oyster nurtures the pearl, that our ideas take shape, without being preoccupied with a profound preliminary study of civilizations.

Pierre Boulez

Le Rossignol

The first step in forging a more intimate relationship between the composer and the other contributors to the Ballets Russes came through Stravinsky's reconstitution of the power of folk music. Initially preserving the chromatic/diatonic (magic/mundane) distinctions of Rimsky-Korsakov's nationalist operas in his *Firebird,* he quickly transformed the nucleus of this inheritance in his next two ballets, *Petrushka* and *Le Sacre du printemps,* developing a new language whose architectonic qualities were increasingly dominant.

Following the spectacular reception of *Petrushka* and *Le Sacre* in 1911 and 1913, Stravinsky could have been expected to adjust quickly and decisively to this changing fashion. Paradoxically, however, there were two significant pieces of Orientalia which were being written by him at this time, the *Three Japanese Lyrics* (1912–13) and the opera *Le Rossignol,* begun as early as 1908 but not completed until 1914. Rimsky-Korsakov had seen sketches for the first act of *Le Rossignol,* but it had languished when Diaghilev called on Stravinsky to write *Firebird.* Stravinsky might never have finished it but for a commission from the newly formed

Free Theater of Moscow to complete the opera. In the event the company folded, and Diaghilev picked up the opera and presented it on May 26, 1914. Having returned to his opera immediately following the composition in quick succession of his three early ballets, Stravinsky was obviously faced with a stylistic dilemma. It was resolved by allowing the quiet, essentially static first act to serve as a kind of prologue. As Stravinsky put it in his *Chronicle*,

> . . . the forest with its nightingale, the pure soul of the child who falls in love with its song—all this gentle poetry of Hans Andersen's could not be expressed in the same way as the baroque luxury of the Chinese court, with its bizarre etiquette, its fêtes, its thousands of little bells and lanterns, and the grotesque humming of the mechanical Japanese nightingale . . . In short, all this exotic fantasy, obviously demanded a different musical idiom.[1]

The musical contrast is, indeed, audible even to first-time listeners, and the near plagiarism of Debussy's *Nuages* in the opening of Act I seldom goes unremarked.[2] But beyond the charges of youthful imitation which are traditionally forwarded with respect to this passage, Stravinsky's initial audiences would have recognized a clear and appropriate symbolism: Debussy's nebulous world of "clouds" purloined and intoned before Alexandre Benois's misty seascape, "a transparent parchment drop" in front of the main setting (Figure 2.1). The play has not yet begun, and the music prepares the first words of the Fisherman, whose text ("The heavenly spirit casts its net") is sung by a tenor out of view in the orchestra pit. The composer invites the audience to enter the world of fairy tales by a pair of non-Oriental distancing techniques, a scrim and a musical allusion to clouds. Writing Benois from Ustilug on August 12, 1913, Stravinsky noted that by that time he had begun work on the second act, whose beginning he insisted "must take place behind a lowered transparent tulle curtain, and with Chinese shadows." He also announced that he considered his discovery of a "fausse-chinoise" scale a "happy find."[3] Benois, too, related how sets and costumes reflected his growing attachment to Chinese folk-style colored prints. The result, he admitted, was eclectic and "far from pedantic accuracy" but was somehow congruent with Stravinsky's music, which he felt oscillated between a "style of authenticity" (the Chinese march, the arias of the Nightingale and Death) and everything else that "sounded rather 'European.'"

In light of Stravinsky's galloping stylistic advances by the time he got

Figure 2.1. Alexandre Benois, "The Sea Shore." Sketch of the backdrop for the "Song of the Fisherman" at the opening of Stravinsky's *Le Rossignol*.

Private collection. © 1994 ARS, New York / SPADEM, Paris

around to writing Acts II and III, it might be assumed that there would be an absence of formulae, and precious little concession to pervading musical Oriental codes. The number of conventions at the ready to portray the Chinese, however, virtually guaranteed the adoption of both familiar orchestral maneuvers and scalar constructions. A note of newness is apparent, however, in the discordant edge which he applies against the black-note pentatonic collection through a parallel formation of alternating harmonic major and minor sevenths.[4] Indeed, brushes with polytonality enliven "The Chinese Emperor's March" at the beginning of the second act and seem to advertise a Modernist commentary upon the received traditions of *musique chinoise*. Elsewhere in the second act Stravinsky openly acknowledged Russian traditions in approaching the Chinese, and his teacher Rimsky-Korsakov specifically, through the adaptation of the principal melody from *Le Coq d'or* (Example 2.1) for the real nightingale's opening vocalise before the Emperor (Example 2.2). But Rimsky's cockerel was a magical bird, and in the wholesale transference of its chromatic idiom to Andersen's real nightingale and the use of a diatonic melody for the mechanical bird presented by the Japanese ambassador, Stravinsky seemingly reverses the types.[5]

Yet while the racket of the accompaniment to the mechanical nightingale's song may have prompted Stravinsky to speak of its "grotesque humming," the pervading contrast is between the gentle and ethereal aura of the real bird and the pro forma use of the Oriental pentatonic for the Japanese ambassador's contraption. Any momentary confusion of conventions may also be seen as an attempt to play upon the deceptiveness of appearances. For though the mechanical nightingale momentarily wins the affections of the Emperor, it is the real bird which ultimately steals his heart and saves him from Death's icy grip. Later adumbrations of this material, limited to the head motif and shorn of its continuing chromatic cascades, appear in the final act over arpeggiated accompaniments which promote a restless, somewhat obscured tonality.[6] Such vacillations, however, are totally in keeping with Stravinsky's flirtation with dual perceptions at the very root of the opera. Nothing could better clarify the truth of this observation than the composer's own remarks: "the intentional meaning of the opera, the triumph of Life over Death, is reversed at times in the depths of the music; in the brave little parade of Music through the gates of Death, for example, the flute charms the Keeper into a stay of execution, but the piece is a funeral march, nonetheless."[7]

Other dichotomies are also preserved, and the tonally distended instrumental introduction to the vocal coloratura of Example 2.2 confirms

Example 2.1. Nikolai Rimsky-Korsakov, *Le Coq d'or*, Act I.

Robert Craft's observation that the retrospective vocal style of *Le Rossignol* is distinctly at odds with its more progressive instrumental language.[8] Selectively, and under special circumstances in this opera, formulaic imitation gives way to subtler varieties of transformative
emulation, and in the end new vocabularies are identified and secured
for potential entry into a Modernist musical lexicon. Not only the musical idioms had been subjected to change, however; implications regarding the Orient as cohort to other developments had been opened up
for discussion as well. Let us see how this is so.

It had been determined well before the premiere of *Le Rossignol,*
which took place on May 26, 1914, that the soprano assigned to the
role of the Nightingale should not be seen. As a consequence both
the Nightingale and the Fisherman—the latter mimed onstage—were
placed out of view in the pit. It was a solution, interestingly enough,
that echoed Diaghilev's staging of Rimsky-Korsakov's *Le Coq d'or* only
two nights earlier on May 24, in a production italicized by the radiant
costumes and sets of Natalia Goncharova, an extraordinarily brilliant
painter whose reputation as a Cubo-Futurist-Primitivist had preceded
her arrival in Paris from St. Petersburg.

In *Le Coq d'or* Goncharova made her debut with Diaghilev employing a lapidary use of color, a distorted perspective, and motivic
stylization redolent of Byzantine icons and the rudimentariness of peasant crafts (Figures 2.2 and 2.3). All this contrasted dramatically with
Bakst's rich Art Nouveau elegance which, despite a common ground
in Fauvist color, portrayed an Orientalism that was pronouncedly more
luxuriant. Furthermore, Goncharova's interpretation of the folk now
carried with it a "primitivizing directness . . . pulsating with raw, vulgar

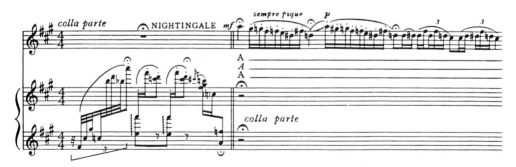

Example 2.2. Igor Stravinsky, *Le Rossignol,* Act II.
Reprinted with permission of Boosey & Hawkes, Inc.

Figure 2.2. The embroidered end of a towel from the North Dvinsk province of Russia. The motif is known as "Cavaliers and Ladies." Such folk art directly influenced the work of Natalia Goncharova and Kasimir Malevich in the period 1909–1912 (see Figure 2.3).

energy."[9] She had demonstrated to an approving public that the essential Otherness of the Orient no longer resided in the refinements of *chinoiserie* and, moreover, that the Oriental was capable of being translated and merchandised as Primitivism *à la russe* and, in an extraordinary act of clairvoyance, even as Constructivism—thus anticipating a new Soviet age not yet proclaimed.

If the Modernist aesthetic was out of sight in Rimsky-Korsakov's score, though unflinchingly present in the mise-en-scène where it was equated visually with neoprimitive color and figure (Figure 2.4), one detail in the production of *Le Coq d'or* was clearly provocative. For, at the suggestion of Benois, the opera was performed as a ballet with the principal roles mimed by dancers. As a consequence Goncharova placed the singers on steep ramps projected on either side of the stage, turning the stage "into a three-dimensional *lubok*."[10] Of the force of the *lubok*, an illustrated popular woodcut or broadside of ancient origins typically projected in primitive, colorful style and frequently incorporating language, Michel Larionov had spoken in the preface to an exhibition of 1913. Describing the variable traditions of these lithographs hand-painted on copper and wood with the aid of a stencil, he noted that

Figure 2.3. Natalia Goncharova, sketch of a woman's costume for *Le Coq d'or,* 1914.
Victoria and Albert Museum, London. © 1994 ARS / ADAGP, Paris.

they were either colored within the limits of a contour or allowed to overflow. Larionov observed that a primitive vision of an object, while remaining completely intact, was reassessed from different positions, and concluded that "the *lubok* exposes some of the most complicated constructions such as we find in the visions of Picasso and Braque. The fact that this conception is forwarded simultaneously by the *luboks* and by our present-day painters is the best demonstration of the negation of time, because, in the same moment, one discovers that which can

Figure 2.4. Natalia Goncharova. Set for Act I of *Le Coq d'or*.
Robert L. B. Tobin Collection, San Antonio. © 1994 ARS / ADAGP, Paris.

only be perceived by going around the object, and this demands a certain duration."[11]

Goncharova also spoke directly to the importance of the *lubok* in a preface to the same exhibition, emphasizing the importance of the Oriental component for contemporary Occidental perception, claiming a grander civilization for the former, but a great culture, profundity of spirit, and sense of nature in the latter. She recalled that the Orient, which includes the Slavs, possessed traditions that went farther back than those of ancient Europe, had a greater love of synthesis in attempting to comprehend the surrounding world, and was attracted to a decorative style in the reproduction of it: *The Thousand and One Nights,* Hindu and Persian miniatures, Chinese, Hindu, Russian and Persian *lubki,* Russian *babas* (stone sculpture), and Japanese prints did not copy nature or embellish it, she said, but re-created it.[12]

Serge Grigoriev, régisseur général of the company, recalled the production of Rimsky-Korsakov's opera vividly, noting that Diaghilev had decided that the soloists and chorus were to sing only, the scenic action being confined to their "doubles" in the ballet.

> It was for this reason that Diaghilev decided to place the principals in the orchestra pit, but at rehearsals, it proved to be impractical. It thus became necessary to find a solution which would not compromise the essential plan. Different propositions were made, but Diaghilev rejected them all. Finally Goncharova suggested constructing on both sides of the front stage some ladders in the form of pyramids, incorporated into the decor, placing the soloists and chorus there— all dressed as "boyards" or noblemen. This proposal pleased Diaghilev and the question was settled.[13]

Although Benois has been credited with the original suggestion to separate singing and movement, he disliked the protrusion of Goncharova's scenery, "which seemed to impede the action"—an effect which cannot be judged from the surviving sketches.[14] Benois's verdict notwithstanding, Grigoriev reported that the opera was enthusiasically received by the public, and Serge Volkonsky, noting that Goncharova had transformed the stage into a huge children's book, declared that "if the walls of the French Grand Opera had vocal organs, they would have gasped with surprise at the sight of what was shown there on May 21, 1914."[15] A comparative review of *Le Rossignol* and *Le Coq d'or* on June 6 did complain of the unsupportable cacophony of the music for *Le Rossignol,* yet praised the freshness and clarity of Mme. Dobrowolska, who sang the role of the Nightingale from the orchestra pit. The reviewer also asserted not only that Goncharova's solution in *Le Coq d'or* was well received, but that he could hardly imagine a return to the original production.[16]

A potential model for the separation of text and action has been proposed in the innovations of the Roman Livius Andronicus, who charged the singer to remain immobile while a mimer presented the action.[17] Yet a more recent prototype—almost surely known to Benois and Diaghilev—had appeared under the pressure of practical circumstances encountered by Jean-Georges Noverre (1727–1810), reigning ballet master at the court of Vienna and the Paris Opéra only a century before. In his *Lettres sur la danse* of 1760 Noverre related that Gluck, unable to find singers for his chorus except from the local cathedral in

Vienna, was informed that they were not permitted to appear on stage in a secular theater. The ballet master hit upon the idea of having the singers remain in the wings with the action portrayed by the dancers on stage.[18] It is of no small interest that George Balanchine appropriated the same solution many years later in a 1930s production of Gluck's *Orfeo.*

Even though the Fisherman's singing at the beginning of *Le Rossignol* could be held analogous to that of the Virtues which typically introduce Baroque opera, his performance from the pit introduced a new dimension. And while a recent prototype for the Nightingale could possibly have been recalled from the forest bird of Wagner's *Siegfried,* Stravinsky's offstage projection could be said not only to have emphasized the mythical qualities attendant to all fairy tales and legends but also to have highlighted the enchantment and mystery of its Oriental setting. Nonetheless the chronological proximity of *Le Rossignol's* premiere to Goncharova's more radical treatment in *Le Coq d'or* forced a reconsideration of *Le Rossignol's* message and an awareness of other dramaturgical experiments being undertaken in the early decades of the twentieth century.

Goncharova's visual conflation of the neoprimitive and the Oriental in *Le Coq d'or* forwarded the discovery of a new and powerful Other, audaciously synthetic and energetically projected. But the spatial component, immediately picked up in the production of *Le Rossignol,* was, for all of its tentativeness, an equally daring, if complementary, move. In both productions, the extraction and separation of the text from corporeal action appealed to perceptions clearly allied to potent Eastern theatrical and metaphysical attitudes. The resourcefulness of the diagnosis and the pointedness of the prescription were extraordinary. The production also placed in bold relief a set of similar proposals—known only to Stravinsky at the time—that Cocteau had proposed the previous February in his plan for the ill-fated project *David.*[19] Cocteau was to scrutinize the idea further, however, in the production of *Parade* and finally with consequential effect in *Les Mariés de la Tour Eiffel,* and Stravinsky would overtly and repeatedly explore its potential over the next decade.

If the principals involved in the staging of *Le Coq d'or* were unaware of the range of Far Eastern theatrical traditions, their solution was decidedly not independent of it. Similar conventions are operative in Japanese Bunraku, or puppet theater, where the central problem concerning the rapport between actor, manipulator, marionette, and mask is that of the voice, where the narrator is separated from the manipulator and the voice is not related to the marionette in any way.[20] Stravinsky's close friend Maurice Delage had returned from Japan in 1912, and it is entirely possible that he experienced Bunraku and No theater there, later conveying his impressions to members of the Diaghilev circle. Earlier evidence of Parisian infatuation for the appropriated components can be located as early as 1888, when Judith Gautier, inveterate Orientalist, had written a Chinese marionette play, later given a Japanese locus and entitled *La Marchande de sourires,* with music by Louis Benedictus. By 1894 she had established a marionette theater, the Petit Théâtre, in her Japanese-style apartment in the rue Washington. In light of recurring comparisons between the Mahabharata epic—familiar from performances by the Javanese shadow puppet theater—and Wagner's Ring cycle based on a shared mythic grandeur, it may come as no surprise that on one occasion Gautier, a friend of Wagner, mounted *Die Walküre* as marionette theater with live singers. Gautier, who was a sculptor as well as poet, modeled the marionettes herself, and since the attitudes of the figures were unchanging, she was obliged to create several versions for each character. Pierre Louÿs attended and recorded the indelible impression that Gautier's performance made upon the guests.[21]

When Diaghilev and Stravinsky discussed the possibility of extracting a ballet from the last two acts of *Le Rossignol* as early as September 1916, practical considerations obviously worked in tandem with a collection of theatrical experiences, including the 1914 productions of *Le Coq d'or* and *Le Rossignol.* First heard in a concert setting in December 1919, *Le Chant du rossignol* was mounted as a ballet in February 1920 with decor by Matisse and choreography by Leonide Massine. Louis Laloy reflected not only his own cultural inclinations but a rich Parisian tradition in an appreciative review of the transformation from opera to ballet: "The two nightingales are no longer singers but dancers, and the episodes follow one another without transition or explanation. The music has achieved the solidity of a symphony."[22]

Years later Virgil Thomson, without any reference to, but clearly not oblivious of, its early production history made the following characterization of *Le Rossignol* and *Le Chant du rossignol:* "The opera version is almost a ballet. And the ballet is almost an opera, though in the ballet both the real nightingale, originally a soprano, and the toy nightingale are evoked by orchestral means. The ballet version, nevertheless, still yearns to sing, just as the opera version strained toward the dance."[23]

Other manifestations of this new perspective appeared in the works of Stravinsky in quick succession with *Renard, L'Histoire du soldat, Pulcinella,* and *Les Noces.* In the last production Goncharova's guiding hand was once again in evidence. Together with Nijinska's choreography, the so-called Russian period was not so much brought to an end as summarized with respect to the various developments in the period 1912–1922, indicating in the process the possibility of their future impact upon the international stage. In the 1914 productions of *Le Coq d'or* and *Le Rossignol* both artist and musician serendipitously chanced upon new conduits for the articulation of Modernist values through an Oriental legacy and were quick to note their force. These fresh perspectives constituted far more than a passing directorial decree on the one hand or respect for a set of traditions on the other, and were destined to resonate in numerous disguises.

Critical reaction by other composers to Stravinsky's music for *Le Rossignol* is of no small interest. Rather than dismissing the score as the unfortunate completion of an early indiscretion, numerous composers sensed that Stravinsky had struck a new note. Though Reynaldo Hahn might not have been the ideal observer, he rhapsodized that "the music . . . suggests the barbaric and sensual China of legend, with an intensity bordering on the neuropathological." Even more significantly both Ravel and Bartók praised the score's audacities and proclaimed that the music betrayed an indebtedness to Schoenberg![24]

The Stravinsky-Schoenberg connection was subject to a considerable amount of exaggeration at precisely this time, reflecting the need of the critics to identify and suggest parity among contenders to leadership in the avant-garde. Yet while it would be imprudent to weigh here the numerous claims of affinity with Schoenberg—as well as those made later by both Bartók and Ravel with respect to their own music— the ease and frequency with which such judgments of modernity were made within the purview of an Oriental backdrop is worth noting. Equally provocative is the observation that in Germany a conflation of Oriental and *commedia dell'arte* theater thrived openly from the time of Schoenberg's *Pierrot lunaire* to the Bauhaus productions of the twenties.[25]

Three Japanese Lyrics

Begun in October 1912—a month before Stravinsky concluded the composition of *Le Sacre*—and completed in January 1913 well before the ballet's premiere, *Three Japanese Lyrics* was forced to find an appropriately discrete language in direct competition with a visceral and spellbinding score. Here, however, the composer's Japanese orientation is not to ambassadors and mechanical nightingales as in *Le Rossignol,* but to haiku poetry, whose brevity and trenchant focus encourages the composer to suggest more than to insist, and in the process to abstract more than to paint. Such traits propose a set of contrasting corollaries to the traditional view of a lurid and flamboyant Orient, and simultaneously point to the recognition of a rich complement of interdisciplinary and intercultural values in the genesis of these songs. For example, in an article of 1906 regarding emerging values in the *mélodie moderne française,* Camille Mauclair suggested that "Japan's wonderful haïku resemble Verlaine's *ariettes,*" and claimed affinity between the highest forms of poetry in all nations.[26] Stravinsky, who made his own settings of Verlaine in a group of orchestral songs of 1910, might have agreed.

An equally important background to the *Three Japanese Lyrics* lies not only in the extent to which Japanese fashion had been ascendant in Western Europe, and especially in France, at the turn of the century, but also in the virility of cultural crisscrossing in the visual arts generally. In spite of the antiquity of the Japanese print tradition, for example, Dutch graphic art had influenced Japanese painting as early as the seventeenth century, leading in the eighteenth to the discovery of a new type of art in the form of woodblock prints known as Ukiyo-e ("painting from the floating world"). In turn, their subjective treatment of everyday life strongly influenced artists such as Van Gogh, Gauguin, Toulouse-Lautrec, Edouard Manet, and Claude Monet. The continuing allure of Japan was undoubtedly due in part to late nineteenth-century interest in things Japanese following Admiral Perry's visit in 1853–54—an event which ended centuries of social and economic isolation. By the time of the Paris Exposition of 1878 French infatuation with the Japanese had reached such a point under the patronage of Edmond de Goncourt that *La République des lettres* could proclaim, "The Japanese is triumphant."[27]

Though the reaction of the musicians to the Javanese at the International Exposition of 1889 has been repeatedly assessed, there were other musical delights as well. Louis Benedictus published his attempts at transcriptions of the sounds he heard in the exhibition villages of Algeria, Persia, Romania, Annam, and Japan in a collection entitled *Les Musiques bizarres* together with French translations of the poetry by his friend

Judith Gautier.[28] Similarly in 1900 Benedictus fashioned a second collection in six pamphlets devoted to the music of Japan, China, Indo-China, Java, Egypt, and Madagascar which he had heard at the Exposition.[29] Gautier was ecstatic and proclaimed that Benedictus had "accomplished a tour de force, and caught in flight the indiscernible music which is never written down. He has fixed it and wonderfully caught its enveloping charm."[30]

Access to the visual world of the Orient, as Gautier's comments suggest, had always been easier than to its music, and Takashi Funayama has offered the following important distinction: "Whereas Japonaiserie in its manifold forms was introduced into Europe on occasions like the three great international exhibitions, Japanese traditional music was almost never performed in Europe. French musicians who attended the 1900 exhibition, such as Debussy, Satie, Ravel, and Chabrier, were deeply moved upon hearing Indonesian gamelan music, but they had no knowledge whatsoever of Japanese music."[31] Though Japanese music may have been anything but commonplace, it is not quite accurate to claim that opportunities for exposure to this music were totally absent. At the same time, even if a few Japanese melodies had been published in Benedictus' two collections of *Musiques bizarres,* their limited number and distribution would have been insufficient to give Western composers more than a superficial bearing on the music. Furthermore, reports of performances of this music at the 1900 Exposition emphasize the surrounding noise and general hubbub, which precluded the possibility of coming to significant terms with the music.

For the second of the *Japanese Lyrics* Stravinsky composed an elaborate and virtuoso introduction that momentarily seems to prefigure the style of the second and third acts of *Le Rossignol* through the quasi-heterophonic admixture of diatonic, chromatic, and tonally undirected lines. The reversal of diatonic and chromatic function in the role of the two nightingales has been taken a step further to a simultaneous union. And the brief pentatonic patterns in both the second song and the third are so fused with the artifical techniques of Stravinsky's extended tonality that their exotic origins are almost totally obliterated.[32]

In the third of the *Japanese Lyrics* Schoenberg's shadow has been claimed to have fallen once again, and initial encouragement for such a thesis stems not only from the instrumental ensemble which mirrors Schoenberg's *Pierrot lunaire* but from its less secure tonal orientation promoted by melodic sevenths and other unstable intervals. With no intention of promoting an unwarranted fiction, it is interesting to note in this regard, however, that "Harou-samé," one of three Japanese melodies cited by Benedictus in his *Les Musiques bizarres* of 1889 and subtitled "Chant japonais antique," is characterized by numerous cadential melodic sevenths. Yet Benedictus' transcription, rather than capturing a bizarre intervallic conceit, undoubtedly reflects the need of the samisen, having exhausted its lower range, to break back up to the higher octave (Example 2.3, mm. 4, 10.).[33] Schoenberg and Benedictus aside, it is obligatory to recall that such intervals are not infrequently found in Russian folk melodies, and that they appear in abundance in *Le Sacre du printemps,* a score in progress at the time. The coda to the third song sums up the alliance of these various materials and discloses the ways in which Stravinsky endorsed new techniques along with faded reminiscences of a former musical *japonisme:* leanness of texture, pentatonic allusion (upper voices, second and third measures from the end), contrapuntal manipulation involving figural diminution in the drive to the cadence (final two measures), and closure through parallel perfect fifths in the upper voices (Example 2.4).

Example 2.3. "Harou-samé: Chant japonais antique," transcribed by Louis Benedictus in *Les Musique bizarres à l'Exposition* (1889).

Example 2.4. Igor Stravinsky, *Three Japanese Lyrics,* "Taraiuki," coda.
Reprinted with permission of Boosey & Hawkes, Inc.

In the prevailing absence of musical models either from source books or from experience, many Parisians, including Debussy, André Messager, and D. E. Inghelbrecht, translated their fascination for Japan into music based upon their impressions of nonmusical sources and the reallocation of traits visible in prints as well as in features discussed in *Paris illustré,* edited by Tadamasa Hayashi. As noted earlier, Delage was exceptional among Parisians in that he had visited Japan in person in 1912 on the same business trip with his father that had taken him to India, and he was to resurrect his memory of it in later years in his *Sept haikai* (1925) for soprano and instrumental ensemble and "In morte di un samurai" for voice and piano (1951). In the second of these, penned many years later following the end of World War II, Delage portrayed the death of a samurai and the tolling of Japanese temple bells through a specific and compelling evocation of Ravel's bells sounded in his "Vallée des cloches" *(Miroirs)*—a work, it should be noted, that Ravel had dedicated to Delage. It is evident that the routes to an interpreted *japonisme* were characteristically circuitous. Thus in recalling the open quartal harmonies of Ravel, Delage made reference not only to his teacher but to a structural feature securely rooted in a French musical tradition independent of Oriental associations.

Delage had only recently returned from his trip to Japan, however, when Stravinsky dedicated the first of his *Japanese Lyrics* to him. The dedication thus discloses both the intimacy of friendship and the probability of further, if second-hand, cultural exposure. Despite the apparent absence of any direct familiarity with Japanese music, Stravinsky's awareness of Japan's art and poetry is readily confirmable. It was to be expected in light of recent advances in his personal language that Stravinsky's intentions in the composition of these pieces would be radically different from those of composers in preceding decades when faced with Oriental subjects, and would soon play a part in the completion of a languishing *Rossignol,* resurrected the next year.

On the surface the economical style of the *Three Japanese Lyrics* appears to be a self-conscious antidote to the explosive language which the composer was developing concurrently in *Le Sacre,* yet technically it is a mirror of many of the practices emerging in that very score. Nonetheless, Stravinsky later specified an underlying aesthetic program for these songs that sought an equivocal fusion between Japanese visual and Russian prosodic concerns. Having read a small anthology of Japanese poems in Russian translation during the summer of 1912, he was impressed with their similarity to Japanese paintings and engravings, openly declaring that "the graphic solution of problems of perspective and space shown by their art incited me to find something analogous in music. Nothing could have lent itself better to this than the Russian version of the Japanese poems, owing to the well-known fact that Russian verse allows the tonic accent only. I gave myself up to this task, and succeeded by a metrical and rhythmic process too complex to be explained here."[34]

Asked about his *Japanese Lyrics* on his first visit to Japan in April 1959, Stravinsky confided to an interviewer: "I was interested at the time in Japanese woodblock prints. What attracted me was that this was a two-dimensional art without any sense of solidity. I discovered this sense of the two-dimensional in some Russian translations of poetry, and attempted to express this sense in my music. However, the Russian critics of the time attacked me severely for creating two-dimensional music."[35]

How did Stravinsky create this two-dimensional quality? It obviously had little to do with the citation of authentic melodies such as Holst was to summon in his *Japanese Suite* of 1916, or with the invocation of a filtered pentatonicism (see Example 2.4), a grace-note style equally commensurate with his current Russian manner (Example 2.5), or with timbral allusion to gongs through open fifths or fourths in low registers

Example 2.5. Igor Stravinsky, *Three Japanese Lyrics,* "Akahito," mm. 1–4.
Reprinted with permission of Boosey & Hawkes, Inc.

in the first song—except as each of these details was capable of identifying the distinctive planar attributes that Stravinsky required. The reduction of instrumental forces, however, not only complemented the terse terrain of a haiku setting but also permitted the firm projection of a linear independence between voice and accompaniment that was further emphasized by skewed prosodic solutions. These features in turn were capable of being claimed as analogous to the two-dimensional space of Japanese paintings and prints. The disconcerting result in the first song, which can only be appreciated by those familiar with the Russian language, was clearly described in a letter to Prokofiev from Nikolai Miaskovsky, written in June 1913, in which he noted that the correct declamation could be achieved by moving the music one eighth note to the left. The manuscript sketches from October 1912 show that this was indeed Stravinsky's initial solution. In the final solution the grace notes of the accompaniment aid in marking the placement of Stravinsky's altered prosody (see Example 2.5).

But there is a third side to the coin. For at the very time he was working out analogies with Japanese visual perspective, Stravinsky simultaneously experienced a "rejoicing discovery" in noting a similar accentual alteration in the singing of his native Russian *pribaoutki*.[36] Equally intriguing is the prospect that had Stravinsky known at the time of the non-accentual qualities of the Japanese language, he might have been tempted to set the texts in their original language. But in this bringing together of Japanese pictoral aesthetics, haiku text, Russian translation, peasant prosodic practice, and the timbre of a contemporary Viennese ensemble, Stravinsky achieved one of his first massive acts of agglutination. As was characteristic of a later habit, however, in so doing Stravinsky in no wise confused authenticity with authority.

Part of the appeal in Stravinsky's rethinking of the Oriental quotient can be compared with the role accorded Asia in the regeneration of Europe by the Romantics. But if the Romantic Age conferred the status of a spiritual hero on anyone who mastered an Oriental language, the same could not be claimed with respect to music. For at the turn of the century knowledge of Indian, Chinese, and Javanese musics was extremely meager, and of Japanese music virtually nonexistent. Musical explorers, in the sense of the modern ethnomusicologist, were few and far between, and the discipline as such was only dimly perceived. The option of working by symbol and by analogy, however, beckoned as an attractive possibility for the early twentieth-century composer who was intent not on learning an exotic language but on rethinking his native tongue anew. In such a frame of mind, reduced evidence and analogical scrutiny offered an ideal starting point for the reconstitution of a language.

In this quest the *idea* of the Orient as well as the Primitive proved catalytic.[37] The push for the neoprimitive through Goncharova's sets in *Le Coq d'or* and soon thereafter through a rethinking of Russian prosody as evidenced in peasant *pribaoutki* in Stravinsky's *Three Japanese Lyrics* both suppressed uses of a clichéd Oriental code that could have been predicted from text and title alone. Stravinsky's work with Nicolas Roerich in confecting a scenario for *Le Sacre du printemps* as well as the memory of Rimsky-Korsakov's devotion to pagan rituals in his other operas were near at hand and served the transformation process well. Thus, Stravinsky's two Oriental pieces of 1913–14, while seemingly reflective of two discrete adaptations of the East, were both as much temporal reconstructions as geographical reinterpretations. *Le Rossignol,* later described by the composer as an attempt to recapture an element of his childhood via the land of fairy tales, embraced the Orient as a mythic land of dreams wherein the child is allowed to sense those universals more common to the world of the adult: beauty, ritual, death, and fate, as well as the magical force of music and its capacity to seduce or even deceive. As the result of a delayed production, musical values discovered elsewhere were appliquéd by Stravinsky onto an aging musical torso with a sense of *amplification* but without any intent of *betrayal* of the original literary text.

Despite Judith Gautier's expressed view that the Japanese were aggressive and exploitive while the Chinese were peace-loving and artistic, Stravinsky's reference to "the grotesque humming of the mechanical Japanese nightingale" is scarcely sufficient to promote the thesis that the opera contains more than an oblique reference to the Russo-Japanese War of 1904. And the *Japanese Lyrics,* by the composer's admission, had addressed from the beginning a specific set of *aesthetic* issues inherent in Japanese painting and Russian peasant prosodic practices in an attempt to explore the possibility of a musical analogue.[38] Although developments in art do not proceed in a vacuum, their genesis may spring from reasonably circumscribed events. The denial of the force of aesthetic choice and the insistence upon art as a totally socially determined by-product can narrow the perspective and skew the message. Though social and aesthetic forces are characteristically intertwined, either is capable of momentarily claiming a virtually preemptive ascendancy. The naturalness of approaching the Chinese and the Japanese as a source in Russian art was a given for Stravinsky, supported not only by Russia's own claims to Orientalness but by a venerable tradition of appropriating the foreign in the service of defining the familiar.

Like the Greeks, who also promoted self-discovery through confrontation with the Orient, the early twentieth century's appropriation was neither a coloring, a suffusion, nor mere self-congratulatory xenophobia.[39] But the Orient's mythic and colorful past had now been recalled and sublimated by a new age for a fresh purpose. Stravinsky's pan-ethnic solutions knowingly transcended the boundaries of the original text, casting a glance at the past while providing a glimpse of the future. His commandeering of the Orient in both *Le Rossignol* and *Three Japanese Lyrics* reflected not so much opportunism, misrepresentation, or expediency, as affection and an abiding interest in the gentler as well as the more radical consequences of transformative emulation as a creative gambit. Both the taste and the range were to persist into old age. In 1939 the composer lucidly stated his basic philosophy of the matter with the judgment that "the danger lies not in the borrowing of clichés. The danger lies in fabricating them."[40]

The mysterious Orient, which to a certain extent had always connoted a land residing in a kind of time warp or at least one that was hardly contemporaneous with Western Europe, was now relocated through reference to Primitivist and peasant practice in a still more indeterminate, though perceivably earlier, "first times." The maneuvers, for all their audacity and arguable appropriateness, were less arbitrary than reflective of an almost compulsive tendency of the age to relocate the beginnings of all things; of an attempt not so much to revitalize a musical language as to invent a new one constituted from the most basic conceivable elements; and, above all, of a search for a contemporary identity. The quest, inevitably, led to the formation of new myths. Like all myths, however, they were empowered and rendered palpable through that sense of discovery attendant to personal crusades. It must have been clear to the participants that only in the search to define others was one likely to stumble across the shadow of the self; that one of their richest resources lay in a consideration of the tension between the "past" and the "elsewhere" and the meaning both could have for the "here and now."

By the second decade of the century, the invocation of the Chinese in Ezra Pound's poetry carried the power of both the Orient and the Primitive through his collage accession of ideographs that vibrated with the energy of prehistoric neumes. But by the mid-1920s Janet Flanner, who observed the Parisian scene as acutely as anyone, felt free to voice disdain for such an attitude: "I like neither Pound's arbitrary historicity, nor his condensed violence, nor his floating Chinese quotations such as marked the poetry he wrote for the *Little Review,* nor all his weighty, ancient, mixed linguistics, like stony chips whacked off with *hauteur* from the old statuary of the scholarly mind."[41] Clearly intimated was the opinion that the Oriental-Primitivist collusion was démodé, that it could no longer pretend to leadership in the avant-garde, that it reflected anything but an intuitive allocation, and that it potentially mocked the force and vitality of its origins in an intellectualization that now appeared strained. Such a view also effectively announced the passing of Cubism and the banality of theoretical disquisitions on *simultan-isme* as well.[42] Flanner undoubtedly felt secure in her judgment. For she realized that the dominance of Eastern exoticism as a salon commodity was clearly faltering, and that Stravinsky's insistence that his *Three Pieces for String Quartet* had been expressly written for performance in the Chinese room of Misia Sert's Paris apartment was insufficient to capture the patroness's affection for a work totally beyond her comprehension and, at least on the surface, devoid of all Oriental implications.[43] Where residues were still visible or audible they were clearly evaporating rapidly or accommodating drastically under the pressure of competing forces: the Chinese Magician in Erik Satie's *Parade* (1917) was a conjurer from a sideshow, and Bartók's *Miraculous Mandarin* (1918–1923) sounded the last echo of a moribund Decadent aesthetic in consort with forces recently excavated in *Le Sacre*. Flanner also understood that Neoclassicism had swung into full view as a potent option, and about that she too sounded a warning.

But fashion had taken only a slight turn to the right, and the masking ideology had, if anything, heightened its claims. Indeed, "time traveling," as Constance Lambert later dubbed it, as well as simultaneity, collage, and a persisting fascination for distant times and cultures were to continue to prosper, albeit outfitted with a new wardrobe. Many years later, Boulez, speaking of the exotic instrumental references in his *Le Marteau sans maître* (1953–1955)—specifically those to the African balafron through the use of the xylophone, to the Balinese gender in the employment of the vibraphone, and to the Japanese koto in his choice of the guitar—identified the continuing viability of the impulse and its capacity for metamorphosis:

> My aim was rather to enrich the European sound vocabulary by means of non-European listening habits, some of our traditional classical sound combinations having become so charged with "history" that we must open our windows wide in order to avoid being asphyxiated. This reaction of mine has nothing whatever to do with the clumsy appropriation of a "colonial" musical vocabulary as seen in the innumerable short-lived *rhapsodies malgaches* and *rhapsodies cambodgiennes* that appeared during the early years of the present century.[44]

Boulez's remarks could be taken to refer specifically to a *Rapsodie cambodgienne* written in 1882 by Louis Bourgault-Ducoudray (1840–1910), a composer and professor of music history at the Paris Conser-

vatoire from 1878 on, where he gave courses on Renaissance polyphony, the folk music of France, chant, and Oriental and Russian music.
His lectures on Rousseau's theories of recitative, on Rimsky-Korsakov
and Musorgsky as early as 1880 and a special course on Russian music
in 1903, are all believed to have exerted an influence upon Debussy,
who was his pupil. Though Bourgault-Ducoudray's orchestral *rapsodie,*
like Debussy's only slightly later *fantaisie,* may have failed to capture the
full force of the supporting aesthetic, he had paradoxically articulated
Boulez's *ideal* some eighty-five years earlier in a lecture prepared especially for the Paris Universal Exposition of 1878.

> No element of expression existing in a tune of any kind, however
> ancient, however remote in origin, must be banished from our musical
> idiom. All modes, old or new, European or exotic, insofar as they are
> capable of serving an expressive purpose, must be admitted by us and
> used by composers. I believe that the polyphonic principle may be
> applied to all kinds of scales. Our two modes, the major and the minor,
> have been so thoroughly exploited that we should welcome all ele-
> ments of expression by which the musical idiom may be rejuvenated.[45]

Numerous composers of the early twentieth century shared this view.
For even as they were aware of the shallowness of some of their confected Oriental codes, they also acknowledged their usefulness—not
just in portraying the chasm that separated East from West but in illuminating unsuspected affinities or the complementarity of inescapable
contrasts. While in later years Stravinsky insisted that intimate access to
the time world of the Orient remained out of reach, he also posited
the argument—repeatedly advanced throughout his life—that an angle
can sometimes provide an empowering advantage.[46]

— THE PRIMITIVE —

— 3 —

Out of Africa and the Steppes

The beginning as primordial asceticism has an obsessive persistence in the mind . . . Formally, the mind wants to conceive a point in either time or space that marks the beginning of all things.

Edward Said

This Primitivism advocated by Gauguin became perhaps an even more lasting influence on modern art than either Van Gogh's Expressionism or Cézanne's way to Cubism.

E. H. Gombrich

Music historians are perhaps even more suspicious of "isms" than art historians. Both have exhibited appropriate caution, not to say anxiety, in arguing the usefulness of such canopies to designate large style periods (Classicism, Romanticism) as well as more narrowly focused aesthetic phenomena (Mannerism, Neoclassicism). At the same time, in the constant alternation between broadened perspectives and refined details, historians have had periodic recourse to the enlightenment which each could provide. None of these terms has been the subject of greater debate than Primitivism, however; certainly few have been so exhaustively and variably appropriated over a greater chronological, sociological, and aesthetic range.

As one of Modernism's subtexts "Primitivism" is frequently encountered in the discussion and criticism of twentieth-century art and music, where it tends to imply a return to first principles through the discovery of some elemental and vitalizing energy observable in preindustrial societies, and particularly in peasant, tribal, and folk repertoires. Such repertoires, it should be understood, are typically the properties of musically nonliterate peoples and as such are unwritten and preserved only in oral form. Characteristically, Primitivism tends to connote those tribal or folk expressions which carry the suggestion of the unaffected and the unstudied, the powerful and the essential, and which hint at a communion with the primordium typically observable in art developed outside the system of patronage in Western culture. The naturalness with which a Primitive so defined fuses with the Exotic is apparent. It is well to note, however, that these oral traditions may carry only the *appearance* of antiquity, of some mythical Ur-melody or rhythm, and that written repertoires may frequently antedate them.

In an attempt to assess the role of Primitivism in the birth of Modernism, the history of art has provided several fundamental studies.[1] In light of the fact that one of the most recent of these, which accompanied an important exhibition in 1984 at the Museum of Modern Art in New York, could claim the help of at least two prior efforts of considerable erudition over the past fifty years, it is somewhat surprising to discover that Primitivism—a word not unfamiliar to twentieth-century concert-goers—is missing as an entry in any of the standard music dictionaries and encyclopedias currently in use.[2] Although the Museum of Modern Art exhibition demonstrated that the implications of the term for our time are still in the process of being sorted out and some of the basic questions may not even have been asked, let alone answered, the art historians have sketched a foundation unusually rich and potentially useful for any attempt at interdisciplinary collusion. Criticism of the Museum of Modern Art show centered on the need to extend our view beyond the recognition of formal analogies to a consideration of cultural contexts and especially to the social and political issues of the time potentially reflected in the works themselves. Without the work of the MOMA show, however, it would have been more difficult to advance this line of inquiry. Yet with it in hand, we should proceed with caution. To turn every work of art into an intensely social or political document already suggests an agenda on the part of the critic that may lead to a procrustean exercise. To ignore such matters altogether, however, can imply an isolationist role for the arts in society.

If the anthropologists' and ethnomusicologists' investigations into the concept of Primitivism have seldom shown an interest in Modernist problems, it can be countered that art historians and historical musicologists have seldom advanced more than a superficial recognition of the role of the tribal, the folk, or the primitive in the assessment of vocabularies potentially seminal to the development of contemporary artistic and musical thought. Direct interdisciplinary transferral, however, is rarely possible, and a quest for the clarification of the generative forces of musical Primitivism in the twentieth century is aided in only the most oblique way by a review of events which promoted accession of the term in the plastic arts. This is largely due to the fact that many, if not most, of the propelling artifacts central to the formation of visual Primitivism in the early part of the century came from areas (Africa and Oceania) whose musical materials were little known to Western musicians or, if available, already radically transformed.

Among those rare publications which dealt with the music, Henri-Alexandre Junod's study *Les Chants et les contes des Ba-Ronga* (Lausanne, 1897) was one of the earliest to include the notation of African melodies. Not only did the art dealer Paul Guillaume express his gratitude for its disclosure of "the unusual subtlety of African musical rhythms,"[3] but the composer Samuel Coleridge-Taylor openly acknowledged his debt to the music included in Junod's "excellent and sympathetic little book" in his own collection of variations on *Negro Melodies* of 1904. In his preface Coleridge-Taylor attempted to make a distinction between African Negro and American Negro melodies, judging that the former were more martial and free in character, the latter more personal and tender. Both, he felt, displayed a perceptible affinity to the music of the Caucasian race, unlike the music of India, China, and Japan, which he claimed contemporary cultivated ears found most unsatisfactory. The music of Africa he felt provided a noteworthy exception among non-Western cultures: "Primitive as it is, it nevertheless has all the elements of the European folk-song and it is remarkable that no alterations have had to be made before treating the Melodies."[4]

Coleridge-Taylor's emphasis upon melody, his perception of similitude to European folk repertoires, and his seeming innocence of the role of dance and polyrhythm virtually dictates the reasons that his example was ignored as a source by most European composers. At the same time, the dyadic basis of much West African harmony, which relied prominently upon parallel singing in thirds, undoubtedly helps to explain both Coleridge-Taylor's perceptions and the ease with which the transition from an African to a European standard of harmony took place in the American South.[5] Indeed, it is not surprising that as a composer Coleridge-Taylor is remembered not for his variations on Negro melodies, but for his oratorio, *Hiawatha,* a work which focused upon Native-American culture and which in the early twentieth century rivaled Handel's *Messiah* in popularity with English choral societies. Since Coleridge-Taylor was an English composer of African descent whose father had left him and his mother in order to return to his native land, his exemplification of African music could have claimed a degree of authenticity had the time and place been right, but in the event his impact on the issue at hand was negligible. The same might be said of Richard Wallaschek's somewhat earlier but more than slightly prejudicial *Primitive Music* of 1893; Junod's more admirable, appreciated, but limited study of 1897; and Henry Edward Krehbiel's later and somewhat more analytical *Afro-American Folksong: A Study in Racial and National Music* of 1914.[6] Some would say that the slightness of their collective influence was fortunate given their restricted knowledge of the range and subtlety of African music.

If accretions to knowledge of black music of any provenance predictably came slowly, in bits and pieces, and with considerable geographical confusion, Europe's delayed but gradually accelerating response to *musique nègre* during the first two decades of the twentieth century in the guise of various African-American hybrids can be attributed to the eventual introduction and recognition of many of the factors missing from Coleridge-Taylor's formula. Initially, the general lack of information about African music and a limited acquaintance with African-American music through exposure to cakewalk and ragtime meant that the impulse to claim developments similar to those surrounding *art nègre* were reasonably circumscribed in the world of sound. But the extent to which the search for parallels in the absence of models was not totally suppressed can be sensed in a remark attributed to Debussy, who had written his own "Golliwog's Cakewalk" and "Le petit nègre" for piano by 1906. As Stravinsky later recalled: "Hahn was an enthusiast of *Le Sacre du Printemps,* as indeed almost everyone in Paris had become—except for Debussy, who persisted in calling it '*une musique nègre,*' and the few conservatives, who were calling it '*Massacre du Printemps.*'"[7]

A review of the factors that fed into musical developments at the time is therefore necessary if we are to intuit the extent to which the idea of Primitivism was of moment for musicians and composers alike. Like the Museum of Modern Art exhibition, the present search aims less to consider the original function of the catalytic source materials, except as it may have been acknowledged by or demonstrably known to the composers who appropriated them, than to assess the impetus and the auspices under which such materials were put to use.[8]

Despite such a recital of caveats, it is clear that the basic impulse behind the attraction to the Primitivist ideal can frequently be shown to have been the same in music as in the visual arts and in literature. More to the point, many of the artists, composers, and littérateurs knew one another personally, even worked in close proximity, and reacted within a close chronological frame. Music's ultimate response to fashion and patronage, like that of the other arts, forces a consideration of Cocteau's observation in 1920 that *art nègre,* rather than a fundamental new impulse, was simply an assimilation to a slightly earlier and contemporary taste for *japonisme.*[9] Indeed, in light of the fact that African or Oceanian musical models were sparse, Western Europe's willingness to press analogies with *art nègre* in improbable places is not surprising, as Proust's remarkable testimony in *À la recherche du temps perdu* (1913) suggests. Noting the effect of the mise en scène upon those who were given to making hollow distinctions among the Russian ballets, Proust provided testimony of the natural tendency to fusion between Orientalism and Primitivism by observing that some were tempted to claim *Shéhérazade* as a kind of *art nègre.*[10] Noting the proclivity of ballet's exotic male hero to follow his instincts and to realize his true nature by living outside the rules of society, Lynn Garafola has remarked that Nijinsky's realization of the Golden Slave in *Shéhérazade* "was exemplary in this regard: a primitive who from the moment he bolted onstage until the final spasm of his death exalted the fully liberated self and its inevitable clash with society."[11] Bakst's brilliant costumes of silver and gold against darkskinned eunuchs and slaves readily endorsed such a perception (Figure 3.1).

But like *japonisme,* Primitivism in music ultimately related not only to a desire for enlarged perspectives similar to those in the visual arts, but led to technical solutions which may be described as analogous to the achievements in the world of painting and literature. Indeed, the association of Primitivism with Cubism, Expressionism, and Dada is, not unexpectedly, demonstrable in the world of music.

From Orientalism to Primitivism

European "high" culture's fascination with black Africa can be traced to the fourteenth and fifteenth centuries, but the emblems of black cul-

Figure 3.1. Léon Bakst, costume of the "silver" Negro in *Shéhérazade,* 1910.
Museum of Fine Arts, Strasbourg.

ture were typically placed in special curio cabinets and seldom influenced literary or visual art except as a surface feature. The theme of
the American Indian is also recurrent throughout this same period following the first expeditions of Columbus, who returned not only with
artifacts but with a small coterie of natives. Bead and feather work occasionally appeared in paintings of the fifteenth through the seventeenth
centuries, but it was not until the eighteenth century that the figure of
the Indian began to captivate English literature. Following the French
Revolution and the rise of nationalist impulses and attendant colonial-

ism, further extensions of the Exotic Dream continued to prosper in the nineteenth century and encompassed, in addition to an interest in Asia, America, Africa, Oceania, and the Caribbean, a fascination for the local roots of Western European and Near Eastern cultures.

It is tempting to claim that, rather than extending from the preceding age's infatuation with the Orient and the Exotic, the appropriation of *art nègre* as a vital model at the birth of Modernism in the visual and literary arts stemmed more from a desire to return to the historically earliest times in search of fundamental perspectives regarding a new world view. Yet even though we search for distinctions as we move from one aesthetic order to another, underlying continuities persistently surface. Thus it is with the relationship between Orientalism and Primitivism. An accentuated belief in the antiquity of the Orient had already been expressed by Goethe in his poem "Hegire," wherein he proclaimed a persistent urgency to return to the Orient, which for him encompassed "the profound origins of the human race."[12] But while this challenge to the prevailing Renaissance veneration of the Greco-Roman foundations of Western European civilization may sound extraordinary to a modern reader, it was not the first. For just as Marc Lescarbot had likened the Indians of Central and South America to the Spartans of the Golden Age in his popular *Histoire de la Nouvelle France* of 1609, so others had identified the Indians with the most exalted species of ancient barbarians. Consequently, by the time of John Dryden's invocation of the phrase "noble savage" in *The Conquest of Granada* in 1670, the way had been well prepared for the coinage of such an expression. The Age of the Renaissance was over, and the exclusivity of a Greco-Roman orientation had become a thing of the past.

As Hayden White has stated, the theme of the Noble Savage—having been subject to careful scrutiny by the historians, its functions and origins identified, and its pedigree precisely established—"may be one of the few historical topics about which there is nothing more to say."[13] And yet we continue to analyze not only the persistence of the idea but the proliferation of contexts which have invited its appropriation. And in the recognition of such variable contexts we are obliged to note the seemingly contradictory meanings which attached to the notion of the Primitive.[14]

For the pervasive inclination of Western societies to recurring bouts of self-doubt repeatedly prompted praise of the barbarian's innocence as well as his natural goodness. As John Ellis has noted, this notion has been a recurring Western fantasy from Tacitus to Rousseau to Herder and Margaret Mead.[15] Yet, if history has been unkind to their various illusions regarding a social order, it has also gained nourishment from them. We need only recall the extent to which the compulsion to locate and recall this state of original innocence, to get back to "first times," to the "fons et origo" of human civilization, was clearly manifest in colonial America, where the Puritans repeatedly forwarded the view of a new land based upon an evocation of the primordium and the "first church."[16] Similarly, for the creative artist, the primordium offers a fatal attraction: by claiming access to it, all intermediate influences can be refuted and their attendant anxieties short-circuited.

Already from the early years of the century infatuation with Primitivist, frequently African, sources on the part of artists from Picasso, Braque, Vlaminck, and Picabia to Jarry, Apollinaire, and Cendrars had helped clarify a series of goals well beyond neonationalism, including the search for universals on the one hand and for a personal identity on the other. Though Creation and the Garden of Eden continued to be appropriated as themes, they were quickly wedded not so much to notions of purity and an eventual loss of innocence as to the idea of a primal energy. Toward this end the visual artists gradually appropriated primitive artifacts less as commemorative aesthetic objects than as sources of a ritualistic, even potentially magical power; and rarely, except for cartoonists, did these artists use them as anticolonialist indictments.[17]

But in painting and literature as well as in music, interest in cultural Primitivism clearly had ramifications beyond the recognition of art from the "Dark Continent" and Oceania. The search for the roots of human expression ranged from the wholesale investigation of folk art and music in Western Europe to the study of Scythian civilization and peasant design in Russia, both securely rooted in nineteenth-century studies. The mixture of these differing views of "primitive" culture are readily observable in the Expressionist almanac *Der Blaue Reiter* of 1912, wherein the folk, the Oriental, and the tribal are assembled in a common celebration. The Fauvists, who were also represented in the almanac, were attracted to African sculpture in large part by its strangeness more than its formal qualities, the discovery of which would be left to the Cubists. Yet appreciation of more recent types of African sculpture, even though technically less advanced than ancient Benin examples, was understandable. Paul Guillaume, whose exhibitions of *art nègre* took

Paris by storm in 1917, illuminated the distinction a decade later in his book on primitive Negro sculpture:

> No civilized influence ever contributed materially to the art of the fetish-maker . . . In only one case, the fifteenth and sixteenth century Portuguese colony of Benin, did the union of black and white cultures bear creditable fruit. Here, in southern Nigeria, the natives learned the process of casting bronze with moulds of wax and clay, and with it turned out figures of themselves and their conquerors. It is a hybrid art, weak, but yet a distinctive form, combining both African and European elements. Elsewhere the coming of the white man has meant the passing of the negro artist . . . The art-producing negro, then, was the negro untouched by foreign influences.[18]

Thus, in spite of their closer chronological proximity, more recent traditional African crafts were prized precisely because of their failure to approximate Western standards of art, for those untutored qualities which were held to be quintessentially primitive and reflective of their function in ritual, and increasingly for their emphasis on the abstractness of geometrical forms rather than naturalistic representation.[19] In turn these more current examples served the sensibility of contemporary artists in the confection of a new and vigorous art. In such a predilection we see at once the distinction between the archaic and the primitive—the former implying idealization of a remote ancestry, the latter reflective of the expressive state of mind of any group not yet totally conditioned by the standards of civilizational discipline.[20] Such a distinction helps to explain the preference of early twentieth-century Russian artists for local folk cultures of more recent vintage over that of the advanced and more ancient art of Scythian civilization, even though the latter possessed a highly developed technique and employed precious materials. In spite of their lesser antiquity, the absence of those "finished" qualities common to "high" art and the presence of characteristics perceived as "elemental" permitted folk and peasant art to be readily comprehended as ideally primitive.

In music, however, there was no counterpart to Benin sculpture or Scythian artifacts. A record of the earliest musics from both cultures had long since dissolved in the mists of time. A notation was missing, indeed had never existed, and whatever remained through oral tradition over the centuries could lay only the most tenuous claim to authenticity in reflecting an ancient culture. Yet, as we can imagine in light of the response of the other arts, this situation offered few problems for composers in search of a cultural utopia to serve as the springboard for a contemporary art. They realized that repertoires, however recent, which carried the suggestion of the untutored and spontaneous could serve as a valid touchstone in the search to revivify fundamental values. In Manuel de Falla's quest for a native Iberian melos, for example, he organized, together with Federico García Lorca, a festival of the *cante jondo* in 1922, which he labeled a *canto primitivo andaluz*.[21] His interest in locating a repertoire for which he could assert not only a considerable antiquity but even the attributes of an Ur-song is apparent from his remark that "we must state that this Andalusian song is perhaps the only European song which preserves in all its purity—both in structure and style—the highest qualities inherent in the primitive songs of the Orient."

Alas, Falla's own description already carries the seeds of destruction for any concept of purity in its acknowledgment of cross-cultural fusion, and recalls Gertrude Stein's evaluations of Picasso's creative source book—one which promoted a recognition of the Spanish, the Moorish, and the Russian.[22] But if Picasso and many of his contemporaries became admiring conserver-collectors of Iberian as well as African masks and sculpture, Falla's campaign to preserve the *canto primitivo andaluz* was based upon the more urgent belief that its beauty was "not only threatened with ruin, but on the point of disappearing forever."[23] The notion of the vanishing rarity, which carries connotations of value and which had repeatedly been introduced by anthropologists, collectors, and littérateurs, had been appropriated by the world of music to good effect. Judith Gautier's earlier warning following the excavations that uncovered Gezer, one of the oldest cities of Palestine, now echoed with a new force: "We must make haste, for civilization is penetrating everywhere."[24] Imperialism and colonialism, rather than serving as springboards for the appropriation and transformation of Primitivist values, are held to be the potential source for their ruination or disappearance altogether, and the artist now spearheads the formation of a crusade to check the negative consequences.

Yet, despite Falla's seeming interest in locating the earliest musical expression of his native country, it is no less than paradoxical that he had earlier discovered the possibility of finding "truth without authenticity" in a seven-year sojourn in Paris, where he found himself totally captivated by Debussy's intuitive understanding of the Spanish manner.[25] Falla's claims to primitive status for the *cante jondo* notwithstanding, both Iberian and other concerted efforts to uncover demonstrably authentic sources lacked a carbon test or other consequential means of determining their vintage. Whether in the folk collections of the late nineteenth-century Russians, in Bartók's transcriptions of Hungarian, Bulgarian, Romanian, and Arabic tunes in the early twentieth, or in the new hybrid fantasy of Afro-American jazz, a melos of untestable origins, rooted in the *Volk,* carried connotations of first times, encouraged composers to perceive such repertoires as the earliest recoverable musical materials, and served the composer's need for an idealized model. Obviously, the primary allure of such folk models resided in the potential for claiming access to ancient times in one's own culture and for speculating on the meaning of shared features in diverse cultural repertoires. Even if the idea of the Primitive promoted the notion of a psychological as much as a temporal or geographical Other, the capacity to locate it close to home served to refocus questions of cultural identity as much as or more than those of nationality. France's dexterity in identifying with Spain, for example—on grounds of geographical and cultural proximity on the one hand and because of distancing Oriental-Moorish associations on the other—provided totally different perspectives for Bizet, Chabrier, Debussy, and Ravel in their interpretation of Spanish culture from those entertained by Glinka (*Souvenir of a Summer Night in Madrid,* 1848–1851) and Rimsky-Korsakov (*Spanish Caprice,* 1887) or Liszt (*Spanish Rhapsody,* 1864), Schumann (*Spanisches Liederspiel,* 1849), and Hugo Wolf (*Spanisches Liederbuch,* 1889–90).

Something of this revisionist call upon native locales is visible in Picasso's early attention to Iberian sculpture as well as in the emphasis which Vlaminck and Derain placed upon provincial and popular arts such as the *images d'Epinal* previously used by Gauguin. Such adjustments in perspective of the near-at-hand were in part prompted by the dissipating energy of overworked repertoires. Just as the painters had begun to sense that the Egyptian and the Asiatic were no longer "bizarre enough for inclusion in this modern curio collection,"[26] so the persistent reworking of Oriental motifs in music of the late nineteenth and early twentieth centuries had now begun to rob them of their colorful essence and threatened to disenfranchise them for the task at hand. The difference between the subjects chosen for Diaghilev's Ballets Russes before and after 1912 is clear evidence not only of a change in fashion but of the need for an equally vivid but underexposed model.

German Primitivism: *Der Blaue Reiter*

In one sense the twentieth century's attention to the power of folk music and peasant arts can be seen as a continuing reflection of the burgeoning forces of nationalism in the nineteenth century and the tendency of developing nations to search for the roots of their culture in quest of a collective identity. A fruitful search for temporally distant origins carried the potential of bolstering the legitimacy of contemporary claims to cultural richness. It is a point of view which Brahms, as well as Mahler and later Hindemith, understood well, and the invocation of a *Volkslied* by Herder as an epigraph to Brahms's op. 117, no. 1, for example, is open advertisement of it. Johann Gottfried von Herder, openly reacting to French cultural domination in the Age of Enlightenment, sought to elevate the German position through a call to poetry, which he claimed existed in its greatest purity and power in the uncivilized periods of every nation (*Über den Ursprung der Sprache,* 1772). This concern led him to promote a concerted effort to retrieve German folksongs, Norse poetry, and mythology as well as the repertoires of the Minnesänger and Martin Luther in collections which he published in 1774 and 1778. Herder's genetic view of history led him to an assessment of the past as an aid for comprehending the present and laying the course for the future. But his invention of a multicultural theory and his call for cultural relativism promoting the equality of all cultures was soon abandoned. For Herder ultimately denounced high culture as artificial and venerated the *Volk* as the only genuine repository. Parallels have been noted with modern multiculturalists who begin by requesting a celebration of difference and conclude with the denouncement of Western culture as elitist.[27]

A similar belief in the power of these repertoires promoted the *Wunderhorn* collections of Arnim and Brentano, which not incidentally were published between 1805 and 1808, in the wake of Napoleon's invasion of Germany, the *Kinder-und Hausmärchen* of the Brothers Grimm in 1812, the Afzelius–Geijer collection of Swedish folksongs prompted by Sweden's loss of Finland to Russia in 1809, and Alexander Afanasiev's *Narodny russkii skazki* (1855 on). And Sir Walter Scott believed as strongly as any other poet of his time in the value and antiquity of the border ballads, agonizing that both the repertoires and the minstrel balladeers were part of a vanishing breed.[28] Thus Germany's protracted attempts to clarify the important role of folk music was matched by many other Western European nations as well.

In the collective and consuming urge to search out the roots of society and culture, two German-based groups who labeled themselves Die Brücke and Der Blaue Reiter were among the earliest to spell out the categorical range of their alliance. The mixture of visual, literary, and musical materials in the almanac *Der Blaue Reiter* of 1912, which was edited by Wassily Kandinsky and Franz Marc, is astonishing, and many a first reader has wondered what to make of such a potpourri. For alongside paintings by Kandinsky, Marc, Picasso, Matisse, Cézanne, and Gauguin, musical compositions of Schoenberg, Berg, and Webern, and articles on Skriabin and the relationship of text and music appear a series of reproductions from the New Hebrides, stone sculpture from Mexico, a Brazilian mask, a statue carved from wood, an Egyptian doll, a Japanese woodblock print, painting on Bavarian glass from the fifteenth and sixteenth centuries, and a mosaic from San Marco as well as drawings and watercolors of children.

Africa and the South Pacific are also represented by wooden sculpture from the Cameroons and Easter Island, a Benin plaque, and a Gabon mask (see Figure 3.2). They share a common factor: art which in the first decade of the twentieth century had yet to be received into the aesthetic canon. Kandinsky's emigration from Moscow to Munich in 1897 placed him in touch with the rise of *Jugendstil* values that embraced non-European art as a source of inspiration in the period of German colonial expansion after 1896. In the process the German Primitivist movement had, like the Russian one, increasingly placed a premium upon the function of the decorative arts in aspiring to a vital union of art and life. The final stance reflected a conflagration of internal and external aesthetic and political aspirations that was noteworthy for the pluralism of its sponsorship.

What may have appeared as a confusion between the art of children, Western folk art, and the art of black cultures was in effect the result of an attempt to provide a new orientation and promote fresh perspectives among the seemingly dissimilar.[29] A potentially binding force behind such variety was a concern for the Spiritual which encompassed the legacy of the Rosicrucians and the Theosophists in Russia, Germany, and France. The attendant mystical speculation of these separate but complementary spiritualist movements transcended national-colonialist aspirations or histories and somehow sought a fusion of the primitive, the peasant, and the child in search of a metaphysical world of color and form.

It can be argued, for example, that the elemental pitch and color properties which Schoenberg probed in his first ventures into atonality constituted an approach to the primordial condition. The scrambling of pitches without strongly defined tonal goals and the periodic substitution of a dialectic of color for thematics, as in his invention of *Klangfarbenmelodie,* sounded the death knell of powerful traditions in effect from the earliest recorded music and promoted in a special harmonic way from the time of the Renaissance. But emotionally the move toward atonality carried with it a sense of urgency that seemed to stem from a consideration of the raw materials of art. To many listeners dis-

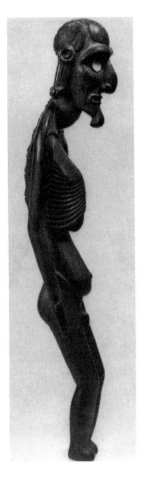

Figure 3.2. Two illustrations from *Der Blaue Reiter* (1912): (left) Easter Island sculpture; (right) Benin bronze.

turbed by initial encounters with *Erwartung* or the *Five Pieces for Orchestra,* both written in 1909, such an interpretation may sound like a titillating rationale for a disturbing music. Yet Schoenberg would have been in accord with the essence of this judgment, as the text to *Erwartung* confirms, though its Freudian cast clearly confronts the primal seepage of the mind rather than a geological primordium. The occasional, seemingly fortuitous formation of patterns in Schoenberg's score through localized repetition (as opposed to a dialectic based upon the logical development of tonal ideas) promoted a link with the accidental repetitions of nature as well as the random structure of dreams. The need to order this chaos, while preserving its freshest qualities, ultimately forced the reactionary discovery of serialism in the 1920s. But this was clearly a later attempt to tidy up a terrain which, at its birth, was prized precisely because of its search for the foundations of expression, and whose frenetic tonal behavior linked effortlessly with the concept of the subconscious as a dominant ingredient in early twentieth-century concepts of the Primitive.

To connect Schoenberg with the Blaue Reiter movement is no fanciful bit of story telling. Included in the almanac were two paintings by him, *Vision* and *Self Portrait,* as well as an article, "The Relationship to the Text," and a musical composition reproduced in facsimile, *Herzgewächse.* This last work, first introduced in the pages of *Der Blaue Reiter,* may appear to carry a discernible Christian iconography in its textual reference to a lily and the gradual ascension of a very high soprano accompanied by an ensemble of harp, harmonium, and celesta. In fact, however, it is nonsectarian and non-Christian, endorsing transcendental and theosophical spiritual notions in harmony with Skriabin's primordial-millennial excursions in *Prometheus* and *Mysterium.*[30] And *Erwartung,* written only slightly earlier in 1909, though it seems far removed from any notion of the primitive as it was being defined by the Russian neonationalists, was clearly in tune with Freudian explorations of the primal scream and the interpretation of dreams.

Unlike their French and English counterparts, German painters made infrequent journeys outside of Europe before 1913 and relied heavily upon the treasures of the ethnological museums in the formation of their views and myths about non-Europeans. In March 1910, for example, the Dresden Ethnographic Museum displayed the famous Benin bronzes as well as artifacts of the Mexican Pueblos. And during the summer months between 1905 and 1910 the same city's zoo also set up Samoan, Sudanese, and Indian villages as part of a typical summer's entertainment. In contrast to contemporaneous practices at the Bronx Zoo, the villagers were not displayed as captives in cages but were presented as commercial *Völkerschauen* in the zoological gardens.[31] They were viewed as complements to the museum presentations on the one hand and on the other as counterparts both to the European universal exposition villages and to the highly successful Wild West shows that had been touring Europe since the 1880s and had visited Dresden as recently as 1906–7. Clearly, such a varied assortment of non-threatening exposures played heavily in the formation of benign or sanitized Primitivist values by the Brücke artists, a Dresden-based Expressionist group that flourished between 1905 and 1913 and provided the basis for a Modernist transformation of values.[32]

For although, among the visual artists, Max Pechstein and Emil Nolde ultimately made their way to the South Seas beginning in 1914, Primitivism's initial voice in Germany during the previous decade had been largely formed by conjuring up the spiritual and the subconscious in an attempt to forge a natural link with the anxieties of urban life. Among the Germans, it was especially evident in the urban scenes of Karl Schmidt-Rottluff and particularly Ernst Ludwig Kirchner. The latter's paintings in particular are remarkable for the litany of strolling women, alone or in pairs, who amble through the city streets like mannequins whose visage reflects not only their indebtedness to tribal masks but an artificiality stemming from the numbing pressures of contemporary existence. Such ideas received further confirmation in the work not only of Schoenberg but of Freud, who made open connections between the neuroses of modern man and his primitive roots; and selectively in the manifestos of Futurists such as Marinetti, who dismissing non-European style as superficial and archaic, nonetheless viewed modernity as ahistorical and essentially Primitivist.[33] A perfect illustration of this attitude is the Futurists' indifference to African tribal music on the one hand and their reverence for the dynamism of urban life and the polyphony of noises inspired by the machine age on the other, which resulted in the mythic invention around 1914 of a consort of modern-Primitivist noisemakers called *intonarumori*.

Beyond such attempts to spell the relevance of the Primitivist angle for city dwellers, both the diversity and the pervasive glamour of non-urban cultures were also underscored in the inclusion of seven nineteenth-century Russian peasant woodcuts in the Blaue Reiter

Munich exhibition of 1911. The impression was enlarged by the projection of countless "primitive artifacts," listed earlier, alongside Russian folkprints in the *Der Blaue Reiter* journal of 1912. The message was compounded and sealed with the reproduction of Matisse's *The Dance* and articles entitled "Masks" by August Macke, "The 'Savages' of Germany" by Franz Marc, and "The 'Savages' of Russia" by David Burliuk in the same volume—all of which clearly echoed earlier Fauve inclinations. One must resist a rush to judgment in the use of the term "savages," however, for the authors applied the word in anything but a pejorative sense both to themselves and to other artists of the avant-garde who shared their common goals. It was a point of view that Kandinsky pursued in his treatise *The Art of Spiritual Harmony* of 1914, wherein he praised the Primitives' renunciation of external form in their desire to express only internal truth,[34] and one that clearly runs contrary to all notions of subjugation and senseless cultural rape attendant to "the scramble for Africa" and other colonialist accessions in the Age of Imperialism.[35]

If one of imperialism's basic goals was "to set out quite consciously to modernize, develop, instruct, and civilize the natives," it must also be countered that one of the Western artists' primary concerns centered on an equally idealized desire to sensitize their own society to values inherent in the Primitive.[36] Isolated from the rest of the world, Africa continued to be viewed, as Hegel had romantically described it, as "lying beyond the day of self-conscious history," preserving its detachment in a land enveloped by the innocence of childhood.[37] The force of this ambivalence that attended the Primitivist-Modernist coalition is frequently ignored by critics who exclusively promote either personal social agendas or exhilarating aesthetic appeals.

Although the Expressionists' concern with Primitivism led to interpretations somewhat different from those of the Parisian Fauves and Cubists, fascination with the subconscious and the search for the foundations of expression was not propelled by a veneration of distortion in and of itself. Rather, interest centered on the exploration of the chaos that preceded creation and ultimately on those formations, either in nature or society, that could be identified as Ur-texts and therefore loaded with a generative potential. Edvard Munch's *The Scream,* Kandinsky's early canvases titled *Composition,* or Schoenberg's several *Visions* are seminal examples in the visual arts. And the lacerating cry for help ("Hilfe") by the Woman in Schoenberg's *Erwartung* (1909) as well as the only slightly later invention of *Sprechstimme* in his *Pierrot lunaire* (1912), though traceable to Wagner's Kundry and nineteenth-century *melodrama* respectively, undoubtedly reflect a radical inquiry into the foundations, not of language, but of vocal expression.[38] The consequences of a continuing obsession with this issue were to resonate throughout the remainder of the twentieth century.[39]

Other expressions of the musical avant-garde that connected centrally or marginally with spiritual concerns tuned to the primordium-millennium paradox include an article by Leonid Sabaneyev on Skriabin's *Prometheus*, N. Kulbin's "Die Freie Musik" and Thomas Hartmann's "Über die Anarchie in der Musik," and Kandinsky's Light-Sound-Color play *The Yellow Sound*. Yet while the fascination of the visual artists among the Blaue Reiter group for Africa and Oceania finds no direct musical counterpart, a *musique nègre* was soon to be sought out, repertoires were to be appropriated, and myths soberly developed.

Russian Primitivism

The late nineteenth-century Russian neonationalist movement had sought to identify repositories of the native spirit in its folklore and peasant crafts, and it is in this search that the modern Russian movement in art is typically said to have begun. From the 1870s Savva Mamontov and Princess Maria Tenisheva were the primary catalytic forces in the identification and promotion of traditional peasant styles with respect to both the simplicity of motifs and the structural use of form and space.[40] At Mamontov's estate at Abramtsevo near Moscow, a colony of painters, composers, singers, actors, architects, art historians, and archaeologists, who dubbed themselves "The Wanderers," threw the first challenge to the official Petersburg Academy of Art, which had dominated taste since the time of Catherine the Great in the mid-eighteenth century. In an attempt to define an art that was useful to the people, they rejected, not unlike Herder in Germany, the Western aesthetic of "art for art's sake" and sought to formulate an art based on their Russian national heritage.

The archaeological and historical constituency among the colony's membership led a systematic search for native Russian materials, placing a focus on Scythian civilization, medieval icons, and national peasant art and costume. The taste was already visible in both the stage settings and costume designs by Victor Vasnetzov of Mamontov's group for the

1885 production of Rimsky-Korsakov's *The Snow Maiden*. Although Glinka, the father of Russian nationalist music, had early shown the way with respect to the incorporation of folk melodies, Rimsky-Korsakov's two compilations of Russian folksongs, published in 1877 and 1882, provided further evidence of the increasing involvement with folk materials and themes. And in his opera *May Night* (1878–79), based on peasant life in the Ukraine, the composer waxed enthusiastic on this new alliance: "I managed to connect, with a subject I adored, that ceremonial side of folk-life which gives expression to the survivals from ancient paganism."[41] In his next opera, *Snow Maiden,* Rimsky-Korsakov demonstrated an ever-widening interest in the earliest roots of Russian culture, and later he disclosed that his previously mild interest in Russian customs and heathen pantheism "flamed up. There seemed no better subject than this . . . no better religion and philosophy of life than the worship of the Sun God, Yarilo."[42] Finally, in the preface to his opera *Christmas Eve* (1895), the composer spoke of his juxtaposition of a series of pagan ritual figures with a tale of Gogol as part of a series in which he explored seasonal associations and the solar cycle. The latent power of collage techniques as well as the vitalizing themes of Primitivism had been clearly anticipated.

In France a dawning fascination with Russian music became evident when Rimsky-Korsakov and Alexander Glazunov introduced works such as Musorgsky's *A Night on Bald Mountain* and Borodin's *On the Steppes of Central Asia* in concerts given at the Exposition of 1889. Such works were received primarily as a kind of traditional Russian Orientalism, however, and Rimsky-Korsakov's Primitivism, which was not accompanied by radical musical discoveries, relied to a pronounced extent upon a set of visual and literary symbols. But both in his use of modal folk materials and the confection of a diatonic/chromatic dichotomy as a musical code for the mundane and the magical, he not only provided the necessary musical link with the discoveries of the Mamontov group and a rational connection with the folk motifs of Viktor Vasnetzov's decor for *The Snow Maiden,* but encouraged an alliance with emerging anticlassical choreographies. He also supplied the basis for our current understanding of the ease with which Stravinsky reacted to the topics of his first three ballets: *Firebird, Petrushka,* and *The Rite of Spring.* By the same token, Rimsky-Korsakov and others of his generation and circle were as much interested in subject matter as style, and already by 1880 Rimsky-Korsakov's reaction against Yulii Melgunov, an early ethnographer who undertook to transcribe "Russian Songs Directly from the Voices of the People," was unequivocal.[43]

Such lack of interest among composerly circles did not stall the ethnographic movement, however, and in 1897 Evgeniia Linyova, aided by a phonograph, began the patient work of recording the heterophonic practices that had eluded the transcribers. Between 1904 and 1909 she published a total of sixty-five numbers in three sets of polyphonic song transcriptions, and it is well documented that Stravinsky knew her work and expressed continuing interest in such investigations.[44] Much as Picasso's early primitivism flourished under the sponsorship of a fin de siècle interest in the archaic and the exotic as exhibited by Gauguin and later by the art collectors,[45] Stravinsky took his cultural bearings from a similar set of engagements on the part of his Russian elders and transcended them.

The neonationalist energies of the Mamontov group were also imitated by others, and the establishment of an artist's colony in 1895 by Princess Maria Tenisheva (1867–1928) at Talaskino was openly modeled after and intended to surpass that at Abramtsevo. Ultimately the two groups linked together, and promoted by the energies of Benois, Bakst, and Roerich the foundation was laid for the formation of the World of Art movement by Diaghilev in the late 1890s as a rallying point for the Russian artistic avant-garde. Diaghilev's *World of Art (Mir Iskusstva)* magazine was inaugurated in 1898, and its elevated, even Messianic tone, forwarded the notion of art as a mystical experience, a tone readily relatable to Kandinsky's later Blaue Reiter group. It endorsed, toward this end, not only the contemporary Western movements of the French Impressionists and the Viennese Secessionists, but French interests in primitive and folk art as well. The pages of this journal typically displayed a mixture of the cultivated and the primitive not unlike the later *Blaue Reiter:* reproductions of works by Puvis de Chavannes and Gustave Moreau appeared alongside photographs of peasant dress, furniture, and embroidery. Gradually the idea emerged that from such a confrontation could spring a new art, honoring not so much the subject matter as the inherent beauty of Russia's heritage.

Diaghilev's decision in 1906 to promote a Russian section at the annual Salon d'Automne in Paris followed exhibitions in St. Peterburg and the folding of the *World of Art* magazine in 1903. Through this move Diaghilev set out to introduce Russian art to the West through a massive exhibition of icon paintings and examples of Russian art from the eighteenth and nineteenth centuries. The exhibition concluded with the work of a group of the youngest Muscovites, Larionov and Goncharova, who by 1909 were to launch a Russian style openly labeled Primitivism.

As early as 1897 Diaghilev's urge to promote this new Russian view abroad was fueled not only by his entrepreneurial sensibilities but by a genuine belief in the interface of Eastern and Western cultures. Russia, observed by the West as a hybrid from the East, was now prepared to offer and promote an enriched self-portrait that traded upon an identifiable Russianness drawn from its deepest societal roots. John Bowlt has alerted us to the fact that "well before the first Paris productions of the Ballets Russes in 1909, European audiences had already been primed for the 'exotic barbarism' of Russia" by Mamontov and by Tenisheva, who had earlier been responsible for the presentation of Russian arts and crafts at the Paris Universal Exposition of 1900.[46] Furthermore, artists from Mamontov's private opera such as Konstantin Korovin, later employed by Diaghilev, proved to be the force behind a revolution in stage design, initiated by Vasnetzov, that removed it from its former role as a simple backdrop.

Roerich and Stravinsky together made a personal visit to Princess Tenisheva's collections in order to avail themselves of source materials in preparation for *Le Sacre du printemps*. And previously, in 1907, she had organized an exhibition, "Objets d'art russes anciens faisant partie des collections de la princesse Marie Ténichév" at the Musée des Arts Décoratifs in Paris in an open effort to outstrip Diaghilev's plans to export Russian culture to the West. Gradually, then, a plan developed that sponsored not only internal neonationalist aspirations but also a program for external distribution whose objective was clearly the assertion of Russian leadership, even preeminence. In light of Russia's historic connection with France as well as the latter's current claims to leadership in the international avant-garde movement, Paris was the ideal venue for launching a dynamic cultural campaign with anything but parochial aims.

— 4 —

"Massacre" and Other Neologisms

> The *Rite of Spring* serves as a point of reference to all who seek
> to establish the birth certificate of what is still called "contempo-
> rary" music. A kind of manifesto work, somewhat in the same
> way and probably for the same reasons as Picasso's *Demoiselles
> d'Avignon,* it has not ceased to engender, first, polemics, then,
> praise, and, finally, the necessary clarification.
>
> *Pierre Boulez*

Le Sacre: Music, Dance, and the Critics

The ballet is a discipline unto itself, and yet its story is in great measure
a story of music as well. It is virtually impossible to appreciate the initial
reaction to a work like Stravinsky's *Le Sacre* without some awareness
of the developing conventions of ballet. Although to sketch even the
barest outlines of its history is impractical, recognition of certain national roles is essential. It is possible to trace with reasonable clarity, for
example, the emphasis upon discipline and technique that Italy brought
to the dance from the fifteenth century on, to note its transference to
France during the Renaissance, and through that country's agency its
transportation throughout Europe in the eighteenth and nineteenth
centuries. Subject to various stages of transformation and reform under
the guidance of masters such as Jean-George Noverre (1727–1810),
Jean Dauberval (1742–1806), and Charles Didelot (1767–1837), its
classical form was ultimately defined by a Franco-Russian *danse de
l'école.*[1]

Rise of the *ballet en action* in the early nineteenth century brought
an emphasis upon expressive mime-dance and dramatic integration of
the corps de ballet. Yet, however summary the judgment may be, the

pursuit of formalism in France was eventually held responsible for the loss of expressiveness in the Romantic ballet, and it was the Russians, under the guidance of Marius Petipa (1818–1910), who led the way to its revivification in the second half of the nineteenth century with works such as *Konyok gorbunyok* ("The little hump-backed horse," 1864), *La Bayadère* (1877), *Sleeping Beauty* (1890), and *Raymonda* (1899). Demonstrating a kinship with the French form in its emphasis upon the ballerina, Petipa also showcased the male dancer, made use of the quite different talents of Pugni, Minkus, Tchaikovsky, and Glazunov respectively in the above four works, instructed them on the requirements of music in company with dance, and breathed a new life into the genre before—once again succumbing to the pressures of a new age—he was forced into retirement in 1903.

It was in such an atmosphere that Diaghilev sensed a ripe opportunity. Having presented *Boris Godunov* in Paris during the 1908 season, he extended his musical presentations in 1909 to include ballet. Fokine was responsible for the choreography of all the initial productions, and he enlisted a distinguished roster of talents including the dancers Pavlova, Karsavina, and Nijinsky and the designers Benois, Bakst, and Roerich. But though Fokine clearly built upon his knowledge of and experience with the Petipa repertory, he had also been impressed by the innovations in modern dance that Isadora Duncan had brought to Russia in 1905 and 1908, and her approach to *danse libre,* which many charged as simply untutored, had left a decided impact upon him.

The musical component of Fokine's ballets originally included the anthology type with music by several composers (*Cléopâtre,* 1909, music by Arensky, Glazunov, Glinka, Musorgsky, Rimsky-Korsakov, Taneyev, and Tcherepnine) as well as by a single composer (*Chopiniana,* 1908, renamed *Les Sylphides* for Paris, 1909), in addition to the more popular spectacles with an integrated narrative and music originally intended for each other. Yet even though the latter condition had prevailed earlier in the case of Pugni and Minkus, their music, which was tailor-made to the demands of Petipa, frequently fulfilled the requirements of the dance without achieving the independent interest that was the mark of Tchaikovsky's scores. With Fokine at his side from the beginning of his Paris venture, Diaghilev virtually eliminated the anthology ballets after 1910, began to showcase the variety and talent of his troupe, and gradually pressed the possibility of a partnership with the visual and musical avant-gardes. The revival in 1912 of Debussy's

Afternoon of a Faun (1894) to a choreography devised by Nijinsky and the sumptuous Art Nouveau sets of Bakst signaled that some of the ingredients of a new alliance had been identified. But those who witnessed the introduction of an unknown and untested musical force with Stravinsky's *Firebird* in 1910 could hardly have foreseen that *Petrushka* (1911) and *Le Sacre du printemps* (1913) were just around the corner.

The collaborative efforts of the new Ballets Russes have been frequently detailed, but it is well to remember that the preparation for such an interdisciplinary collusion had been undertaken over a number of years and on a variety of fronts. Bakst, for example, had been familiar with the anitiquities of the Hermitage in St. Petersburg even before he was introduced to the marvels of the Louvre as a student in Paris in the 1890s. Then, following his journey to Greece in the summer of 1907, he returned eager to put his burgeoning knowledge of ancient art and culture to theatrical account. As with the staging of Diaghilev's Oriental productions, Bakst not only contributed in matters of design and the introduction of motifs drawn from Attic black-figure ware but also guided Fokine in the choreographic details of *Daphnis et Chloë,* produced in 1912. In the same season Bakst similarly instructed Nijinsky in the creation of a choreography that created a frieze-like effect in the production of Debussy's *L'Après-midi d'un faune.* Emphasizing a two-dimensional quality through the dancer's movement in profile across the stage, Nijinsky approximated the poses of Greek vase painting by having the dancers pause after each change of position. Although a composite of influences, including Isadora Duncan on Fokine and Vsevolod Meyerhold's stylized *drame statique* on Nijinsky, was operative in both ballets, Stravinsky later spoke of *L'Après-midi d'un faune* as an "animated bas-relief" and claimed that "Bakst dominated this production . . . and inspired the slightest gesture and choreographic movement."[2]

Attention to the Greco-Roman foundations of Western culture was in some ways as much a natural anticipation of the fascination with musical Primitivism in the early teens as it was a preparation for the Neoclassicism of the twenties. Obviously the idea of Primitivism sought to tap the even more distant origins of expression prior to the beginning of recorded Western culture, and in music this implied the need to study and resurrect the oral traditions of folk music and dance for traces of a rudimentary and ancient diction. This was obviously the angle which had interested the Russians from the late nineteenth century, long before it entered the mainstream of high culture in the West and prior to its introduction in the music of a new avant-garde as defined by Stravinsky, Bartók, and Prokofiev. For Western Europeans, however, *art nègre* held a romantic advantage as the Primitivist source par excellence because, unlike folk cultures or localized Moorish cross-fertilizations, it had an essentially sub-Saharan and Oceanic base that laid no claim to either a European or an Oriental lineage.

In the critical response to Stravinsky's *Le Sacre du printemps* the Primitive stamp was explicitly and repeatedly noted from the beginning. Adolphe Boschot, in a review of the dress rehearsal that was reasonably uncomprehending though accurate in several details, identified the Primitivist qualities with respect to both dance and music:

> They wish to demonstrate for us the dances of prehistoric Russia: therefore they offer us, in order to "go primitive," some dances of savages, of the Caribs and Kanakas . . . All well and good, but it is impossible to keep a straight face . . . they repeat the same gesture a hundred times over: they paw the ground, they stamp, they stamp, they stamp, they stamp and they stamp . . . Evidently all of this is defensible; it is prehistoric dance. The more ugly and deformed it is, the more prehistoric. Well, that's one conception of it . . . I would prefer another that leads to beauty and not to ugliness. And perhaps it would contain as much truth. One of the contortions which seems to please Nijinsky is a twisting of his dancers into figures of the most ancient bas-reliefs. But the deficiencies in design of primitive artists do not prove that the men themselves were deformed, any more than the pictures of the *cubists* prove that our amiable contemporaries are only an agglomeration of tetrahedrons.

The reference to physical contortions akin to "the most ancient bas-reliefs" suggests that memory of Nijinsky's solutions for the *Faun* was still fresh; and in the allusion to the Cubists we note the critic's interest in forwarding connections with current developments in the painterly arts.[3] Yet the repetitive stamping apparently failed to recall gestures that surviving choreographic notation hints had already been entrusted to twelfth-century Polovtsians by Lev Ivanov in the Act II *danse générale* of Borodin's *Prince Igor* in its original production of 1890.[4] Roerich's evocative scenery for a production of this excerpt in 1909 later contributed to the general Primitivist effect of the work and prompted Benois to exclaim: "Roerich's 'panoramic' background, devoid of lateral wings, represented the sky, golden and blood-red, over the infinite expanse of the steppe, with columns of smoke rising from the motley, squat yurts of the nomads—it was perfect!"[5] Yet if there was a lineage traceable to Ivanov's original choreography for *Prince Igor*—a work performed alongside *Le Sacre* at its premiere but with a new choreography by Fokine, critics failed to note a developing anticlassical choreographic tradition in the Russian theater, one that had been previously favored by Rimsky-Korsakov and a few others who shared his archaeological bent.[6] Boschot concluded instead that in an attempt to "go primitive" the choreographer had been obliged to dredge up some dances of the Caribs, warlike cannibal tribes from the Lesser Antilles, and the Kanakas from the South Seas.

If the choreography presented a problem for Boschot, the music was no less troubling. Stating that the music was both disconcerting and disagreeable in its attempt to mirror the barbaric choreography, he claimed that Stravinsky had endeavored "to formulate a music of noise," a judgment that clearly sought to place the Russian composer in the camp of the Italian Futurists. Bochot encouraged the reader to discover Stravinsky's means for the destruction of tonality with the following experiment:

> You can get an idea of it that corresponds to my impression: play on two pianos, or with four hands, transposing it by a tone in one part but not the other: thus, for example, when you hear *do mi sol* on one side, you will hear *ré fa la* on the other, *and at the same time*. Or, if you prefer to play out of tune by a semitone, go right ahead. It is only a matter of almost never allowing one of those ignoble harmonies which formerly passed as being consonant. And this savage music, which lasts half an hour, accompanies some dances of the Caribs.[7]

Jean Chantavoine, also writing of the premiere performance, was quick to connect the spastic choreography—the "stampings, the nodding of heads, and mechanical shakes"—to both "the archaism of the *Faune* (once again!) and the clownish puppetries of *Petrushka*."[8] And Gustave de Pawlowski was the first to introduce the expression "Massacre du Printemps," largely with respect to audience behavior.[9]

Émile Vuillermoz, in an article that undertook to review both *Le Sacre* and Debussy's *Jeux* premiered a week before, echoed Chantavoine in emphasizing the Dalcrozian, what he called marionette, style—a new aesthetic of "divine puppets" that he felt perpetuated the automism and unfeeling character of *Petrushka*.[10] Nijinsky had been the choreographer in all three ballets. The charge of a Dalcrozian bias for the choreography is not idle speculation, for Émile Jaques-Dalcroze had undertaken a tour of Russia in January 1912,[11] where he had been observed by both Diaghilev and Nijinsky. As a result of this encounter as well as two later trips to the Dalcroze Institute at Hellerau, beginning in November 1912, Marie Rambert, one of Dalcroze's brightest pupils, was invited to join the Ballets Russes, and she directly assisted Nijinsky in the choreography of both *Jeux* and *Le Sacre du printemps*.[12] But Vuillermoz's reference to "marionette" style and "divine puppets" also clearly betrays an awareness of the writings of Edward Gordon Craig, which had begun to appear in his journal *The Mask* in 1908. No one could have suspected at this time, however, the future impact of the underlying aesthetic both upon the theater and upon the works of Stravinsky in particular.[13]

In light of his Oriental proclivities, it was understandable that Louis Laloy, who had heard *Le Sacre* played by Debussy and Stravinsky on the piano the year before, would review the final production in terms of the instrumental riches of the Chinese, Cambodians, Siamese, and Javanese in their combinations of strings, pipes, plates, bells, and stones. Laloy praised the capacity of Eastern cultures to conceive of sound as something that transcends the note on the printed page and intimated that the modern age in the West was perhaps just now beginning to sense the potential of such a perspective. Judging that Stravinsky had taken noise as a point of departure rather than as an object for direct imitation as in Mahler's wind machines or the *intonarumori* of the Italian Futurists, Laloy praised the score's masterful orchestration using only traditional instruments.[14]

But Laloy was also one of the few to note a Primitivist affinity between the composer and the painters. In so doing he not only joined Boschot in dilating the geographical purview but underscored Nijinsky's announced infatuation with Gauguin at this very time with the claim that Stravinsky, too, "profited from the lessons of primitive majesty that Gauguin and his emulators sought among savage peoples."[15] Speaking of a "simian-like tremolando of little old wobblers who look like a handful of puppets shaken in little jerks by an unseen operator," the critic Maurice Touchard seemed to reinforce Vuillermoz's theme. But with his question "why were these prehistoric men dressed as Indians?"[16] he not only echoed Boschot's impression that he had witnessed dances of the Caribs but introduced an observation compatible with the choreographic and costume reconstructions of Millicent Hodson's 1987 production of *Le Sacre*.[17] Indeed, for numerous modern-day viewers, as for Touchard, the use of headbanded, bent, and stamping figures performing line and circle dances was clearly redolent of early cowboy and Indian movies.[18] Long before American Indians appeared in the movies, however, they had been studied and romanticized by the French, the Germans, the English, and the Russians in their literature and in their museums.

Amerindians and Euro-Primitivism

The Amerindian question raised by Touchard's and Boschot's reviews deserves momentary consideration in light of the variety and depth of its appeal for Europeans throughout the nineteenth and early twentieth centuries. James Fenimore Cooper's *The Last of the Mohicans,* for example, was published in French translation in 1826 only a few months after it first appeared in America. Franz Schubert knew it as well as other novels of Cooper in their German versions, and one of his last requests, made in a letter written only a week before his death in November 1828, was for additional writings by the American author. In the same year visiting members of the Osage tribe were introduced to Italian royalty, and in 1845 George Catlin had American Indians perform tribal dances at the opening of an exhibition of his Indian paintings at the Salle Valentino in Paris. Both Eugène Delacroix and George Sand were there, and Delacroix captured one of the scalping scenes in a pen and india ink drawing,[19] while Sand caught both the sight and the sound in a remarkably vivid essay "Les Sauvages de Paris," which appeared in 1846.[20]

In 1876 the Dresdener Karl May began his career of fantasizing the Native American in a series of novels that achieved widespread popularity in the 1890s, and by 1886 a group of Sioux Indians traveling under the sponsorship of a Berlin agent had made their way to Budapest, where they set up their tents on the grounds of the Zoological Garden. The presentation of their dances in a special performance for the press on May 29, 1886, occasioned numerous lively descriptions: "the dance was accompanied by loud howling, similar to the howl of a dog or jackal, a dance in which the feet were lifted in a way similar to the Hungarian czardas with rapid foot movement. They bend forward repeatedly as though seeking an invisible enemy, attentively anchor their faces towards the earth and wave their horrible weapons to the left and right." At other times it was noted that the Indians seemed to be just "waddling to a monotonous drumming" in which they appeared to "simper about in one place, at most shaking their elbows a bit to the music."[21] Parts of the description could virtually be passed off as a later review of *Le Sacre*. At the same time recognition of the compatibility of foreign tribal practices with national folk traditions clearly augmented the potential impact of such dances.

In the following year Buffalo Bill's Wild West Show, which depended prominently upon Native Americans, gave two command performances for Queen Victoria in honor of her Golden Jubilee during its tour of the United Kingdom, and on his next trip to Europe William Cody's show traveled to Paris for the 1889 Exposition, where the Indians were taken up the Eiffel Tower in full regalia. Opening on May 19, 1889, they stayed for seven months. Trips to Spain, Italy, Austria, Germany, Belgium, Scotland, and Ireland followed. In Milan, where they performed for eleven days, the young Giacomo Puccini recorded how deeply he had been moved by the show in a period well before the writing of *The Girl of the Golden West* (1910),[22] and the American sculptor Frederic Remington, in England at the time of the group's return there in 1892, noted that among tourists the Tower, Parliament, Westminster, and London Bridge all took a back seat to the Wild West Shows when they were in town.[23] Returning to America in 1893, Cody's group came once more to Europe for a protracted stay during 1902–1906. In all instances the European press reported them as a vanishing race, destined according to laws of social Darwinism to disappear under the domination of white civilization.[24] Despite persistent notice of the Indian's alternatingly docile and wild behavior, in this new view the Noble Savage of the Enlightenment was accorded the additional Romantic quality of the *pathétique*.

Specific Russian interest in and knowledge of the American Indian is verifiable from numerous pieces of evidence, including the fact that Catherine the Great at the end of the eighteenth century wrote George Washington and Benjamin Franklin asking for a list of Indian words to be included in a comparative dictionary. Russian curiosity about the Pacific northwest coast of North America can be traced to the voyages of Vitus Bering and Alexei Chirikov in 1741 and the contacts of Adam von Krusenstern with Aleuts in 1805, which led to the establishment in St. Petersburg of Indian artifact collections. In time, growing interest in the American Indian, whose ancestors had migrated from Asia across the Bering Strait twenty thousand to thirty-five thousand years before, meshed not only with the Russian folk tales *(skaskas)* of the Cossacks and the North Sea fisherman *(pomors)* but with the literary interests of Pushkin and Lermontov, both of whom knew and admired James Fenimore Cooper's *Last of the Mohicans*.[25] Similarly, Longfellow's poem "The Song of Hiawatha" received numerous Russian translations including one by Konstantin Balmont, and Anton Chekhov's "Malchiki," a short story that tells of a schoolboy running away from home to join the wild Indians, speaks to the fascination of several generations of Russian youth.[26]

Although Buffalo Bill had yet to play in Russia, in 1892 he sent his agent C. M. Ercole there in order to make arrangements for a group of Cossacks to join his show for performances in London that year. The printed "Programme" for 1893, which saw Cody's group performing at the Chicago World Colombian Exposition from spring until October, states that among the nineteen scheduled numbers—including the Capture of the Deadwood Mail Coach by the Indians and sharpshooting demonstrations by the renowned Annie Oakley—three incorporated Russian soldiers among the armies of various countries, and number seven was devoted solely to the "Cossacks, of the Caucasus of Russia, in Feats of Horsemanship, Native Dances, etc."[27]

Cody may have brought a bit of Russia to his show as early as 1892, but William F. Carver had already done him one better by taking his entire company to Moscow and St. Petersburg two years before.[28] A celebrated marksman who had given command performances for the Prince of Wales and Kaiser Wilhelm in 1879–80, Carver had been a cofounder of the Wild West Show with Buffalo Bill in 1883. Following a falling out and ultimate court action, Carver went his own way while maintaining a bitter enmity toward Cody to the end of his life. Beginning in 1889 Carver took his own competing Cowboy and Indian troupe to Hamburg, Berlin, and Vienna, where he played before royalty, and in 1890 he moved on to Budapest, Warsaw, Moscow, and finally St. Petersburg, where the show played before the Czar, various grand dukes and duchesses, and the Queen of Greece.[29]

Describing the impression created by Carver's "Wild West" or "Wild America" shows in St. Petersburg at performances on Tsaritsyn Lug (the Czar's meadow)—site of the *balagany* entertainments of Butterweek Fair following the Admiralty Square fire at Shrovetide

1872[30]—a report in an illustrated weekly for June 23, 1890, made special note of the bravery and daring of the Sioux, Cheyenne, and Ogala Indians. It also asserted that it was possible for the spectators to completely familiarize themselves with Indian culture. Citing such practical activities as the painting of tents and clothes design, the report contained numerous illustrations and further observed that the Indians "demonstrate their art and agility in their people's war and wedding dances" as well as their marksmanship with bow and arrow. The cowboys were described as "more civilized" though still manifesting a "half-wild" image owing to their "life amidst primitive nature" and their constant exposure to the danger of the Indians.[31]

These multiple and sustained visits of groups of American Indians throughout Western Europe and Russia in the period 1886–1893 and again between 1902 and 1906 resulted in a broad exposure. They never lived in hotels but pitched their tents near the Exposition grounds in Paris and in the Colosseum in Rome, performed in the Arena at Verona, and did their war dances in the shadow of Vesuvius in Naples.[32] They were given an audience with Pope Leo XIII on the occasion of his eleventh anniversary as pontiff in 1889, played to the Czar of Russia in 1890, thrilled Queen Victoria along with the crown heads of Belgium, Denmark, Greece, and Saxony in 1887 and Edward VII as well as the future Kings Edward VIII and George VI in 1903. Thus, knowledge of their ritual body movements was obviously much more available to a broad public than anything comparable drawn from ancient Russian civilization, which had to be largely concocted and idealized.[33]

German sensibility to themes of the American Indian was especially keen not only in the nineteenth century but well into the twentieth under a variety of sponsorships. In his earliest sketchbooks from 1905, for example, the artist George Grosz recalled the fantasy games of his childhood, also reported in his autobiography: "we would play Cowboys and Indians on the meadow . . . and fire off hand-made catapults like so many characters out of Karl May's novels."[34] And throughout the teens and twenties Grosz, Otto Dix, and Rudolph Schlichter promoted Indian themes variously: initially as general expressions of admiration for American culture, then as antiwar propoganda, and finally in the postwar period as an emblem of America's aggressive meddling in European domestic and economic policies.[35] Another German, August Macke, had painted canvases with American Indian themes as early as 1910, and in his essay "Masks," which appeared in the *Blaue*

Reiter almanac, he underscored the compatibility of the American Indian with contemporary constructions of Primitivism through specific references to war paint and Indian dress, the latter enriched by an example from the Museum für Völkerkunde in Munich.

Among European composers, the first to respond to such themes were two Italians: Giacomo Puccini incorporated Native-American melodies in his *Girl of the Golden West,* which premiered at the Metropolitan Opera in 1910 under the baton of Arturo Toscanini with Enrico Caruso, Emmy Destinn, and Pasquale Amato in the principal roles; and Ferruccio Busoni wrote his *Indian Fantasy* of 1913 and the three-part *Indianisches Tagebuch* of 1917 after having been introduced to Indian melodies through his student Natalie Curtis. In both instances, however, the appropriation of authentic source materials was more symptomatic of the fascination of a period than they were emblematic of a compelling confrontation.

Thus, Russian claims to spiritual kinship with the American Indian were not unique, and similar statements of affinity made in virtually all countries of Europe gradually confirmed a growing Romantic preoccupation. Yet, both the virtuosity of the Cossacks as riders and the origins of the Maryinsky Theater as a horse theater, which after 1860 was taken over by the state and made available to a larger public, undoubtedly provided a congenial linkage to imported Wild West shows. In turn, a sense of the natural rapport between such entertainments and the advancing neonationalist sponsorship of Primitivism could have fostered a deliberate or subliminal accession of Amerindian elements to the purposes of *Le Sacre.*

Touchard's question "why were these prehistoric men dressed as Indians?" clearly indicates that, while he may have been innocent of the Russian pedigree in many of the details of the costume designs, for many Parisian observers the introduction of headbands, bearskins, and embroidery analogous to beadwork coincided naturally with their recent exposure to North American Indian exhibitions (Figure 4.1). Although increased attention to integrity of design, a general rejection of ethnographic eclecticism, and a persistent concern for accurate national and historical backgrounds increasingly became a mark of the designers of Russia's Silver Age such as Bakst, Benois, Roerich, Goncharova, and Larionov,[36] from the beginning, and of necessity, historical credibility had always been allied to a lively interpretive imagination.

André Levinson's charge that contemporary choreography had failed

Figure 4.1. Costume and gesture for *Le Sacre du printemps*. Marie Rambert is second from the left.

primarily owing to a lack "of immersion, no real knowledge, no reverence for the treasures taken over from antiquity"[37] was also in large
measure an attack on the undermining effects of eurhythmics. For the
Dalcrozian approach was not a dance method but a program for the
study of rhythm through bodily motion, and at its base lay a perspective
that emphasized a fundamental, some would say excessive, tendency to
assign a single movement for every note. Yet, its usefulness in fashioning
an anti-balletic, earthbound choreography suggestive of a broad ethnic
spectrum but devoid of specific alliances was obvious.

Furthermore, while animal impersonations, headbands, line and circle formations, stamping, jumping, percussion and a pervasive pulse are
common to numerous folk and tribal dance traditions, through a range
of confrontations, including press illustrations, Marie Rambert could
hardly have remained untouched by a broad range of stimuli well beyond her first-hand encounters with the Grecian poses of Isadora Duncan and the Hindu traceries of Ruth St. Denis. Her report of Nijinsky's
setting of the steps may confirm the reports of the ballet critics, but it
is also compatible with descriptions of a variety of ethnic dances and

says nothing that would limit the initial inspiration of *Le Sacre*'s chore-ography to Russian sources: "feet very turned in, knees slightly bent, arms held in reverse of the classical position, a primitive, prehistoric posture. The steps were very simple: walking smoothly or stamping, jumps mostly off both feet, landing heavily."[38]

Perhaps the most vivid image of the Native American was promoted by the advent of photography and ultimately the cinema. Already in the 1890s Thomas Edison had made numerous film vignettes for the penny arcade peep shows with titles such as *Sioux Ghost Dance,* from 1894, and *Black Dance, Eagle Dance,* and *Parade of Buffalo Bill's Wild West,* all from 1898. Of the several hundred movies made by D. W. Griffith, thirty were about Indians. And prior to the premiere of *Le Sacre,* well over 400 movies had been made dealing with Indian themes, including Pathé's *Justice of a Redskin* (1908) and Gaumont's *Red Man's Revenge* (1908), both filmed in France. Indeed, the period 1909–1914 was a period in which the fast-growing film industry was virtually del-uged with Indian movies: 50 in 1909; 100 in 1910; 150 in 1912. Close to 200 Indian pictures were released in 1911, a year in which it was claimed that six million people went to the pictures every day of the year in the United States alone.[39] Though distortions in both conduct and costume have been attributed to many of these movies, hundreds of Native Americans were recorded on film leaving behind at least a trace of authenticity with respect to dress and dance.

Further confirmation of the contemporary Parisian fascination with American Indians came with an announcement by the Nouveau Cirque in June 1900 of a special attraction, a musical play about American cow-boys and Indians, entitled *Les Indiens Sioux.* The extent of the appeal for composers and performers alike was soon made evident in the for-mation in 1902 of a group who began to gather on Saturday evenings following concerts and who emphasized their rebellious nature by call-ing themselves Apaches. Among the group were Ravel, Delage, Tristan Klingsor, Calvocoressi, the pianist Ricardo Viñes, and the conductor Désiré Inghelbrecht. Florent Schmitt early became a member of their group, which by 1909 also included Stravinsky. And Diaghilev's notice of the Apaches had come as early as 1907, when the group met with him in order to persuade him to perform *Boris Godunov* in lieu of a projected Tchaikovsky opera the next year.[40]

But Jacques Rivière identified the overriding Primitivist credential of *Le Sacre du printemps* most in tune with exposure to such a variety of events when he called it a sociological ballet that moved beyond reconstructions from scientific documents and relied instead upon the imagination, emphasizing in the process an age in which individuality takes a back seat to the mass, the group, the colony. Indeed, the personal and narcissistic element of Nijinsky's first ballets had been jettisoned, and in its place a new social component was thrust to the fore.[41]

The preceding detour into Western European and Russian fascination with Amerindian culture should be viewed neither as an attempt to justify Touchard's and Boschot's remarks in their reviews of the premiere of *Le Sacre* nor as a revisionist ploy aimed at discrediting Roerich's and Stravinsky's initial search for the basis of a genuinely Russian expression. Rather it should help us to understand the force and breadth of the sources of Primitivism for Russian artists and French critics around 1910–1912 and to explain the pervasive and supranational appeal of a cultural aesthetic for an age. Ivan Bilibin, illustrator of a series on the legend of the *Firebird,* had virtually sealed the connection in an article that he wrote for *Mir Iskusstva* in 1904 on the folk art of the Russian north, in which he explicitly summoned the image of America in the formation of neonationalist aspirations: "Only very recently, like an America, we discovered the ancient Rus' of art." Such a perspective was anchored to the European view of the Amerindian as the ultimate Other primarily because, unlike the Asian and the African, he "had been ignored by both the ancient Greco-Roman world and by the Bible."[42]

Ethnomusical Postmortems

As early as 1918 the dance critic André Levinson noted the fragmentary nature of *Le Sacre*. Hypothesizing that the many two- and four-note motifs were built partly on folksong, he emphasized the role of repetition and lack of development. It was a surprising forecast of the description of the score made by Bartók two years later. Noting that Stravinsky never mentioned the sources of his themes, Bartók confessed:

> Lacking any data, I am unable to tell which themes of Stravinsky's from his so-called "Russian period" are his own inventions and which are borrowed from folk music. This much is certain, that if among the thematic material of Stravinsky's there are some of his own invention (and who can doubt that there are), these are the most faithful and clever imitations of folk songs. It is also notable that during his Russian period, from *Le Sacre du Printemps* onward, he seldom uses

melodies of a closed form consisting of three or four lines, but short motives of two or three bars and repeats them "à la ostinato." These recurring primitive motifs are very characteristic of Russian music of a certain category. This type of construction occurs in some of our old music for wind instruments and also in Arab peasant dances.[43]

Many years later, patient research in the folktune collections and a study of the sketchbook of *Le Sacre* confirmed Levinson's and Bartók's suspicions concerning the fragmentation and folk origins of the score in almost every detail.[44]

Stravinsky never verbalized the difference between the nuclear use of folktune fragments as the basis of composition and the extensive quotation of tunes. It was a distinction that he made, however, in his own music, as the progress from *Firebird* to *Petrushka, The Rite,* the *Three Pieces for String Quartet,* and *Les Noces* clearly illustrates. As his dependence upon folktune repertories receded, Stravinsky began not only to deny their presence in his music but to decry their use in the work of others, including Bartók. Although in his late years he "bowed deeply" to Bartók's religiosity, his musicianship, and the acuity of his ear, and also called it a social tragedy that an artist of such stature should have finished his career "in circumstances of actual need," he concluded: "However, I never could share his lifelong gusto for his native folklore. This devotion was certainly real and touching, but I couldn't help regretting it in the great musician."[45] Even more pertinent is the fact that his continuing denial of the folktune content of *The Rite* now began to appear in tandem with claims that promoted the genesis of the work as a personal revelation. "Very little tradition lies behind *Le Sacre du printemps,*" he wrote in 1960. "I had only my ear to help me. I heard and I wrote what I heard. I am the vessel through which *Le Sacre* passed."[46] While such a retrospective assessment may seem extraordinary, it only confirms that by his seventy-fifth year Stravinsky openly viewed the long arch of his career as responding to multiple authorities and regarded the Russian factor, however fundamental, as a generative stimulus more than an aesthetic goal.

Thus, beyond the definition of national values, the investigation of folk repertoires placed the creative artist in contact with sources that ultimately proved to be powerful as much for their structural as for their referential potential. Stravinsky's attraction embraced both factors, and his immediate model for the employment of Russian folktunes in *Fire-*

bird and *Petrushka* was undoubtedly Rimsky-Korsakov in a fashion not dissimilar to the role played by Mahler for Berg or Liszt for Bartók. Both of these early ballets built upon late nineteenth-century interests in the folk, and it was through this conduit that the stage was set for the composition of *Le Sacre du printemps*. Abandoning quotation as a constructive principle, Stravinsky now distilled a hypothetical folk melos into mosaic-like components and redeployed them in an imaginary ritual drawn from "first times." The means by which the cellular building-blocks create the feverish excitement to which Bartók alluded has been the object of repeated examination,[47] and Olivier Messiaen undertook fundamental investigations that disclosed what he labeled *personnages rythmiques* as early as 1939. Many years later, one of his pupils, Pierre Boulez, elaborating on Messiaen's observations, demonstrated the audible contraction, expansion, and stasis of the three compact cells that articulate the opening of the "Danse sacrale."[48]

In tandem with Cubist fracture and heterophonic folk performance practice, ritual structure had displaced narrative (the composer stated, "The piece has no plot."), and pantomime had been abandoned. Though Diaghilev had merchandised the erotic potion of the Symbolist Decadents successfully in a number of his early ballets, in "The Sacrificial Dance," the closing scene of *Le Sacre du printemps,* Stravinsky plumbed the notion of eros to its roots and served it up as something neither primitive nor pagan but primal, a view of man's passion as the fundamental and generating life force. *Le Sacre* also played upon the Symbolists' and the Decadents' infatuation with horror and especially human sacrifice, and, while transporting the issue well beyond the world of Strauss's *Salome* of 1905, provided an uncanny prophecy of the barbarisms and emblematic slaughter of innocents in a modern world. Beginnings are counterbalanced by endings, and the celebration of earth at its dawn brings with it the ritualistic extinction of life.

Despite the powerful symbolism, it is something of a paradox that, with the exception of a few effective stagings, including a notable recent one directed at a recovery of the original production, *The Rite* has endured and made its reputation more as a concert piece than as a ballet. In retrospect we are obliged to review the entire Primitivist sponsorship for what it was: a catalyst for the disclosure of new and potent forces which could serve as the basis for an avant-garde. Noting that the composition does not depend on the argument of a ballet, Boulez adroitly summed up the meaning of *Le Sacre*. "This ritual of 'Pagan Russia' attains a dimension quite beyond its point of departure; it has become the ritual—and the myth—of modern music."[49]

Musique nègre: Cakewalk and Ragtime

It was not until the end of World War I that the cult of *art nègre* moved into full swing. In literature Apollinaire had signaled its virtues and potency as early as 1912, but in the visual arts, following the lead of Fauvist and Cubist painters, Paul Guillaume's African and Oceanic exhibit at the Devambez Gallery in 1919 and the journal *Action,* in particular, were among the earliest important stimuli for a growing craze. Clouzot and Level's preface to the catalogue of Guillaume's "Art nègre et art océanien" exhibition wavered between formal and spiritual criteria as a basis for judgment, yet boldly ranked the arts of Oceania and Africa "in terms of their plastic values—the more geometric pieces being the more esteemed—and the supposed state of savagery of the groups that produced them."[50]

It was precisely at this time that the movement found a tardy but powerful ally in a music that was perceived to stem directly from black America. Gradually, Europe's fin-de-siècle interest in trans-Atlantic culture via Native Americans not surprisingly began to shift to a transplanted African culture in the domain of music in the face of new and attractive repertoires with a broad base of appeal.[51] The arrival of "Le jazz" served the long-felt need for an *art nègre* in music with a viable model, and Stravinsky was one of the first to promote this liaison at precisely the time he was making his first forays into Neoclassicism. The possibility of a fusion between Russian and Afro-American "primitivist" sources was first explored in *L'Histoire du soldat* (1918), in *Ragtime* (1919), and later in many other works besides the *Ebony Concerto* of 1945.

It would be false to suggest, however, that models of African-American musical expression had not been made available to Europe before this time. Gabriel Astruc (1860–1938), who was later to become Diaghilev's French producer, had been exposed to the cakewalk when he attended the Columbian World's Fair in Chicago in 1893 as secretary to the Principal Commissioner for Fine Arts in France. Upon his return he not only described the encounter in an article in *Figaro* but claimed a role in its early popularization in Paris:

The *Cake-Walk* obtained consecration and the publicity of reviews by the end of the year. A competition was organized at the Nouveau-Cirque which excited the world of entertainment and the theater. Even official artists did not escape the contagion. One day, at the home of James-H. Hyde, the grand American who is more jovial than his austere bearing would seem to indicate, a tournament was improvised in the presence of M. d'Estournelles de Constant, representative of Fine Arts, and the cake-walk prize was carried off by Mlle. Carlotta Zambelli, star *danseuse* of the Opera, whose partner I was.[52]

Shortly thereafter, in 1898, Will Marion Cook's popular and historically important show *Clorindy, or the Origin of the Cakewalk*—"the first time an all-black effort played at a major house . . . patronized exclusively by whites"[53]—appeared at the Casino Theater in New York; as early as 1900 John Philip Sousa's success in playing ragtime selections on his European tours led a San Francisco newspaper to print the headline "Paris Has Gone Ragtime Wild";[54] and in 1904 Cocteau reported the continuing presence of Negro dancers at the Nouveau Cirque in Paris, where the strutting elegance of the cakewalk made "everything else turn pale and flee." Just as the clown Chocolat had inspired Toulouse-Lautrec and later, in a duo act with Footit, captivated the young Pablo Picasso, the dancing team M. et Mme. Elks left Cocteau spellbound.

> They danced: skinny, crooked, beribboned, glittering with sequins, spangled with gaudy lights, hats raked over their eyes, their ears, knees higher than their thrust-out chins, hands twirling flexible canes, wrenching their gestures from themselves and hammering the artificial floor with taps on their patent leather shoes. They danced, they glided, they reared, they kicked, they broke themselves in two, three, four, then they stood up again, they bowed . . . And behind them the whole city, the whole of Europe, began dancing.[55]

Not only the whole of Western Europe, it might be added, but Russia as well, if we can believe the report that at a gathering of Rimsky-Korsakov's pupils on February 17, 1904, Nicolas Richter scandalized the composer's wife by playing a cakewalk whose steps were demonstrated by Stepan Mitusov, future co-librettist of *Le Rossignol,* and the twenty-one year old Stravinsky.[56] Two years later Debussy acknowledged the prevailing force of these early Afro-American popular styles in "Golliwog's Cakewalk" (1906–1908) and "Le petit nègre" (1906), and in America the four-year-old Edna St. Vincent Millay was already dancing the cakewalk to her mother's accompaniment on the piano.[57]

By the teens a coalition of Primitivist values and the jazz mode encouraged Cocteau to announce the triumph of the Art of the Everyday in its broadest terms, and to forward the proposal that the sounds of the cabaret, the music hall, the cinema, and the circus awaited the composer as a vital new resource.[58] Once the sounds of jazz, increasingly made popular to Europeans through exposure to American bands and ensembles from 1917 on, were wedded to Stravinsky's rhythmic manner previously announced under the Russian Primitivist banner, there was an increasing desire to interpret the results as a kind of *art nègre*. Stravinsky's knowledge of jazz may have been limited, but an awareness of its timbral qualities and its virile endorsement of syncopation and pulse made it a ready and natural ally in the genesis of works like *Histoire du soldat*. By Stravinsky's own later admission the Russian folk-primitive had teamed up with the Harlem equivalent of the *bals-musette*, and his music had taken a new turn.

> My choice of instruments was influenced by a very important event in my life at that time, the discovery of American jazz . . . The *Histoire* ensemble resembles the jazz band in that each instrumental category—strings, woodwinds, brass, percussion—is represented by both treble and bass components. The instruments themselves are jazz legitimates, too, except the bassoon, which is my substitution for the saxophone . . . The percussion part must also be considered as a manifestation of my enthusiasm for jazz . . . Jazz meant, in any case, a wholly new sound in my music, and *Histoire* marks my final break with the Russian orchestral school in which I had been fostered.[59]

In retrospect it is easy to see how the repetitive patterns, syncopations, and small but characteristic instrumental groupings of jazz were so readily reconcilable with the ostinati, shifting accentuation, and chamber ensembles of Stravinsky's post-*Sacre* production. The introduction of jazz and other vernacular styles into the world of "high art" in the late teens and throughout the 1920s was not merely an accommodation to popular taste, however, but rather a reflection of a developing awareness of the multiple functions and meanings of "high" and "low" as musical categories. Their potential juxtaposition, in variable levels of integration, became a central topic of the time, and was discretely addressed in works for instrumental ensemble, ballet, and opera. The composite output of Satie, Stravinsky, Poulenc, and Milhaud in the period 1917–1924 demands recognition of this prospering attitude, and Poulenc's *Rapsodie nègre* (1917), Stravinsky's *Ragtime* (1918), Milhaud's *La Création du monde* (1924) as well as a host of less familiar works are scarcely comprehensible without attention to the collision of multiple Primitivist-Modernist values observable in text, scenario, and musical language alike.

Sponsorship of such a fusion appeared in numerous quarters. By the time of the Société Lyre et Palette's first séance of music and painting, organized by Blaise Cendrars and Moïse Kisling from November 19 to December 5, 1916, the appeal of *art nègre* to high society was under way. At the vernissage which took place at the Salle Huyghens on the afternoon of 19 November, music of Satie was played alongside works by Picasso, Matisse, and examples of *sculptures nègres,* and the attendant sense of chic was captured by Albert Guillaume in his *La Maladie noire* (Figure 4.2).[60] Satie occasionally came here to try out new ideas or to

Figure 4.2. Albert Guillaume, *La Maladie noire* (n.d.), reproduced on a postcard.

play rags of Ferd "Jelly-Roll" Morton, whose recordings Satie, like Stravinsky, had been introduced to by Ansermet.[61] In December 1916 Satie was busy composing *Parade,* which though not premiered until May of the next year, was to include a ragtime piece for the little American girl.

But though Satie's rags were no more authentic African music than Stravinsky's similar adventures of 1918 and 1919, the invitation to try one's hand at concocting a work that could lay claim to the current fashion must have been irresistible. The young Poulenc's opus 1, a *Rapsodie nègre* dedicated to Satie and premiered at one of Jane Bathori's Vieux-Colombier Concerts on December 11, 1917, is clearly such a specimen. Shortly thereafter, in August 1918, Count Étienne de Beaumont gathered the *beau monde* for a *fête nègre* as part of a series of *bals masqués* for which he appropriated Poulenc's work.[62] The third movement, an *intermède vocal* entitled "Honoloulou," utilized a three-stanza nonsense text of pseudo-African doggerel. Purportedly taken from a collection of verse entitled *Les Poésies de Makoko Kangourou,* the textual model was to be found in the Dada poetry of Tristan Tzara, who had introduced the mock-African textual element in his 1916 play *La Première Aventure céleste de M. Antipyrine.*[63]

Speaking of early performances at the Vieux-Colombier by the group of young composers who came to be known as Les Six, Poulenc later recalled the first performance of *Rapsodie nègre* thus:

> I vividly remember the moment when young Arthur Honegger, dressed as a troubadour, played the drum for the play of *Robin et Marion.* As far as my *Rapsodie nègre* is concerned, the performance didn't pass without incident. This work, a reflection of the taste for negro art which had flourished since 1912 under the impetus of Apollinaire, included four instrumental movements and a vocal interlude. The latter was a setting of an imitation negro poem by a friend who signed himself "Makoko Kangourou." You can just imagine the effect *that* had! At the last minute the singer threw in the sponge, saying it was too silly and that he didn't want to look a fool. Quite unexpectedly, masked by a big music stand, I had to sing that interlude myself. Since I was already in uniform, you can just imagine the unusual effect produced by a soldier bawling out songs in pseudo-Malagasy![64]

Poulenc's report actually conflates two performances, Honegger having appeared nine days earlier at a Vieux-Colombier concert on December 2, 1917. But Poulenc's vocal achievement in *Rapsodie nègre* need be neither doubted nor overestimated. The piano accompaniment, *lent et monotone,* drones along in alterations of two repeated eighth-note chords while the voice sings only four pitches in a descending scalar pattern (Example 4.1) to the following syllabically set text:

Honoloulou pota la ma,
Honoloulou, Honoloulou,
Kata mako mosi bolou,
Rata Kousira po lama.

Wata Kovsi mo ta ma sou
Etcha pango, Etche panga
tota nou nou, nou nou ranga
lo lo lulu ma ta ma sou.

Pata ta bo banana lou
mandes Golas Glebes ikrous
Banana lou ito kous kous
pota la ma Honoloulou

Example 4.1. Francis Poulenc, *Rapsodie nègre,* mvt. 3, "Honoloulou" *(intermède vocal),* mm. 1–9.

The extent to which the spoof was perpetuated, or perhaps misunderstood, is left open to speculation by the remark of Jane Bathori, one of the most knowledgable singers of contemporary repertoires of her day, that the limited melodic range of the third movement "gives an extraordinary color and Negro atmosphere."[65] The other four movements, entitled "Prélude," "Ronde," "Pastorale," and "Final," are each characterized by ostinato figures typically announced at the beginning of each movement and then subjected to adjacent or simultaneous juxtaposition without any evidence of development. But the heavy reliance on ostinati, the open parallel intervals which in the first movement carry a vaguely exotic-primitive note (Example 4.2), the double key signature of the piano part in the second movement (seven flats in the left hand, none in the right), the Dada textual element, and the simultaneous white-key/black-key glissandi which collapse on a tone cluster at the close of the piece collectively announce Poulenc's desire to align himself with the *esprit moderne*.

In the same year at the Cabaret Voltaire in Zurich Richard Huelsenbeck confirmed the Dadaists' involvement with the *art nègre* movement

Example 4.2. Francis Poulenc, *Rapsodie nègre*, mvt. 1, "Prélude," mm. 1–3.

by chanting "authentic" Negro poems ending in shouts of "Umba, umba" to tom-tom accompaniments. He observed:

> There was a witches' sabbath such as you cannot imagine, a hurrying and scurrying from morning till evening, an intoxication of drums and tom-toms, an ecstasy of tap and Cubist dances . . . The Cabaret Voltaire was our experimental stage, where we gropingly tried to understand what we had in common. Together we created a wonderful Negro singsong with clappers, wooden mallets, and many primitive instruments . . . our Cubist dances with masks by Janco and home-made costumes of colored cardboard and tinsel.[66]

And in June 1917 Apollinaire's *Les Mamelles de Tirésias,* which was later to be turned into an opera by Poulenc, had premiered with a black mute character outfitted with noisemakers cast as "the people of Zanzibar." The force and directness of the alliance was sealed in 1919 with Guillaume's exhibition of African and Oceanic art at the Galerie Devambez. This was followed by a *Fête nègre* presented at the Théâtre des Champs-Élysées at a time when the theater was officially closed following bankruptcy.[67] In his introduction to the *Fête nègre* Guillaume is less than specific, but his opening remarks verify the collaborative nature of the event: "The artists, musicians, painters, dancers, and poets of France have contributed an important work in order to present to you this evening a unique spectacle destined to be remembered in the history of dramatic pageantry of this century."[68] A later comment suggests that poetry from the region of the Wele, a river in the northeast of the Belgian Congo (now Zaire), was chanted in a manner that recalled Homer, but no mention is made of the performers or the sources utilized.[69]

A few brief critical reviews included in *Les Arts à Paris* are as enticing as they are inexplicit. *L'Europe nouvelle* reported that "the fête nègre organized by Paul Guillaume at the Théâtre des Champs-Élysées was an astonishing thing,"[70] and André Billy communicated the following intriguing remarks in *L'Opinion:* "Of the *Légende de la Création* I will say only this: its inspiration is moving, and religious literature has produced nothing greatly superior to it with respect to the sentiments of awe and humility in the eyes of the Creator. But why did the public never stop laughing? Is it necessary to remark that it was not a *jazz band* performance?"[71]

In the absence of specifics the reference to music is provocative. We know that Blaise Cendrars wrote an "interprétation scénique" subtitled "un poème dansé" for Guillaume's production whose textual component was undoubtedly drawn from material which he had started to assemble as early as 1919 for his *Anthologie nègre*.[72] Whether it was actually danced on this occasion is not known, but it clearly could not have had anything to do with Milhaud's score, which was not envisioned before 1922. Since the presence of a jazz band appears to be ruled out by the report, it is possible that Poulenc's *Rapsodie nègre*, already performed in 1917, was enlisted in this entertainment. Jean Börlin presumably could not have appeared either, in light of the fact that his Paris debut, which included his *Sculpture nègre* to music of Poulenc, occurred a few months later, on March 25, 1920.[73] Though a poster of the event hangs on the wall in a 1930 photograph of Guillaume, the program is undecipherable.[74] Whatever spiritual ancestry the *Légende de la Création* may share with Milhaud-Léger's *La Création du monde,* which appeared a few years later, in his *Fête nègre* Guillaume had proved that music, dance, costume, and recitation all held a power that was potentially as strong as sculpture and painting in fostering an alliance with *art nègre.* In like fashion, following the example of the German Expressionist cabarets frequented by Arp and Ernst, Tristan Tzara published translations of Maori songs in 1917 which he declaimed at Dada soirées in Zurich. It was a tradition that André Breton continued at the Grand Palais, where he danced a New Caledonian Pilou-Pilou some four years before his Surrealist Manifesto of 1924.[75]

Thus, Poulenc's choice of ingredients, typically spoken of as a spoof, was knowingly made, not so much in the hope of provoking a scandal as of appealing, in a somewhat wry manner, to the taste for Negro art which was currently laying claims to high fashion. The petition to *art nègre* was made almost exclusively through the text, however, for the instrumental ensemble had been directly lifted from Schoenberg's *Pierrot lunaire,* and the music itself, despite Bathori's claims for a "Negro atmosphere," transmitted only the faintest African or Afro-American overtones.

Thus, spectacles such as Beaumont and Guillaume introduced in Paris in 1918 and 1919 were entertainment but at the same time a reflection of the Parisian craze for *art nègre* and its pluralistic sponsorship. For despite exposure to the cakewalk by Gabriel Astruc in the 1890s and by Cocteau and others at the Nouveau Cirque in 1904 as well as to ragtime by John Philip Sousa's band as early as 1900 and to its rhythms in works by Debussy, Satie, and Stravinsky before the end of World War I, it was not until the end of hostilities that the full force of American popular dance music was felt in Europe. Building on an earlier exposure provided by American soldiers and a few phonograph recordings of New Orleans jazz, the arrival of Sidney Bechet in Louis Mitchell's band in 1917 constituted an important turn, and by 1918 black American jazz ensembles were playing at the Casino de Paris. Finally, at Beaumont's private soirée American Negro soldiers provided entertainment alongside the music of Poulenc, and the juxtaposition, if not fusion, of "high" and "low" art heralded the sense of radical chic to which *art nègre* now aspired.

But Poulenc, Apollinaire, Cocteau, Guillaume, Picasso, Bechet, and Beaumont were only the tip of the iceberg. As early as 1913 Francis Picabia had painted *Negro Song I* and *II,* while the undisputed theorist of the Cubists, Albert Gleizes, had painted his *Jazz* in New York by 1915. In the following years Blaise Cendrars persuaded Picasso to execute the cover drawing for Stravinsky's *Ragtime* (1919) (Figure 4.3), which he published under the imprint of his and Cocteau's Editions de La Sirène. And shortly thereafter he published his own *Anthologie nègre* in 1921 and somewhat later his *African Saga* (1927) and *Little Black Stories for Little White Children* (1929). Nancy Cunard also brought out her anthology entitled *Negro* in 1931–1933. All of these publications were clearly an extension of the same infatuation with an idealized black culture.

The list could be amplified in the world of music by many peripheral pieces such as Milhaud's *Caramel mou,* which he wrote for an avant-garde show staged by Pierre Bertin in May 1921. Using a text by Cocteau, Milhaud concocted a shimmy for clarinet, saxophone, trumpet, trombone, and percussion that served as an accompaniment to a black dancer named Graton. And Jean Wiéner's *Trois blues chantés* of 1924 for voice and piano included the indication that the textless vocal part was to be performed "à la saxophoniste nègre." Wiéner's jazz performances with the black American saxophonist Vance Lowry had repeatedly drawn Cocteau and members of Les Six to the Bar Gaya from February 1921 on. Both there and later at Le Boeuf sur le Toit, Cocteau, Picabia, and Milhaud were reported to have taken turns as jazz drummers themselves. Wiéner's interests were not restricted to jazz, however, and he specifically endorsed the presentation of "high" and

Figure 4.3. Pablo Picasso's front cover for the first edition (1919) of Stravinsky's piano arrangement of *Ragtime*. The two musicians are drawn in a single line.

"low" music together. His career still remains to be detailed, but it is easy to understand how the mechanical piano performance of Stravinsky's *Le Sacre du printemps* during a concert that featured Billy Arnold's jazz band, and the playing of Satie's *Socrate* and *Blues* ("Danse américaine") alongside Schoenberg's *Pierrot lunaire* and Stravinsky's *Ragtime,* must have drawn the curious and provided sufficient variety to give everyone something to talk about. Ultimately, the composite of these forces and figures was to congeal in a new alliance with heightened aspirations. Milhaud, Léger, and Cendrars were to be the central figures, but they were to be supported in their dreams by a new Swedish ballet company whose French name, Ballets Suédois, reflected not only its Parisian locus of operations but its aesthetic target.

— 5 —

The Creation of the World

Underneath, in the waters of the vast primeval swamp, the reflected images of the moon . . . And the principal character is
Man, over whom the primitive forces have resumed their sway
. . . all the beasts, all the sounds of the everlasting forest come
to gaze at him, filling his ears with their music.

Paul Claudel

The desire to promote alternatives to the Russian formula as well as
sheer audacity lay behind the formation of Rolf de Maré's Ballets
Suédois in October 1920. The idea for a company of Swedish dancers,
drawn primarily from the Stockholm Opera, to take up residency in
Paris in direct competition with the Ballets Russes had been jointly
conceived by de Maré and Fokine. In preparation for the venture Jean
Börlin undertook an apprenticeship with Fokine, and in France de
Maré quickly struck an alliance with Cocteau and Les Six—initially
with a production of Darius Milhaud's *L'Homme et son désir* premiered
on June 6, 1921, and shortly thereafter with *Les Mariés de la Tour Eiffel,*
premiered on June 21 with music by five of the six composers.

The impetus for the first of these productions, *L'Homme et son désir,*
may be said to have sprung from a visit of the Russian Ballet to Rio
de Janeiro in September 1913. For it was at that time that the young and
as yet unknown Heitor Villa-Lobos (1887–1959) received his initial
exposure to ballet as a member of the theater orchestra. Having already
undertaken numerous treks into the Brazilian interior, he now ventured
on his first foray into musical Primitivism in a set of piano pieces, *Danças
características africanas,* soon transcribed for orchestra in 1914–15. Following an entire concert devoted to his own compositions in 1915,

Villa-Lobos then decided to try his hand at ballet, and in 1917 completed two orchestral scores whose orientation emphasized the aboriginal base of his native Brazil: *Amazon,* quite unknown even today, and the more familiar *Uirapuru.* Milhaud had arrived in Rio as secretary to Paul Claudel at the French Legation in 1916, and Villa-Lobos had quickly taken the young Frenchman under his arm, "introducing him to the *choroes* and carnival music, and explaining to him the *macumba* fetishist rites."[1]

While Milhaud's *Saudades do Brasil, Scaramouche,* and even *Le Boeuf sur le toit* are frequently cited as reflections of his Brazilian experience, Villa-Lobos' *Amazon* and *Uirapuru*[2] have been ignored as potential stimulants for Milhaud's *L'Homme et son désir.* Yet it is perhaps no coincidence that Milhaud's 1918 ballet—graced by Claudel's scenario, excerpted in the epigraph above—centered on the freeing of Man by a phantom Woman, and like Villa-Lobos's *Amazon* was set in a Brazilian rain forest and featured an expanded use of percussion.

In addition to fifteen percussionists Milhaud also used four quartets: vocal; string; oboe, trumpet, harp, doublebass; piccolo, flute, clarinet, bass clarinet—the last of which could be viewed as *Pierrot*-inspired.[3] Milhaud's textless vocal quartet, whatever its Primitivist or Expressionist legacy, was in effect not far removed from Debussy's chorus in *Sirènes,* and the persistent patchwork of diatonic dance tunes clearly adumbrates the Brazilian maxixes in *Le Boeuf sur le toit.*[4] With his percussionists, however, Milhaud evokes a genuine sense of mystery, delicate and atmospheric, whose originality could only have intrigued Edgard Varèse. The circle was later completed when Varèse befriended Villa-Lobos upon his arrival in Paris in 1923. In sum, *L'Homme et son désir* clearly signaled a call to the primitive through South American venues and vernaculars and without recourse to Slavic, African, or Afro-American musical prototypes. Yet Milhaud's specification that the stage be divided into four levels and Fernand Léger's use of large cutout figures directly forecast several features of their next cooperative venture, *La Création du monde* (see Figure 11.10). And Börlin's nude choreography, which incorporated a more plastic version of his *Sculpture nègre,* appears in retrospect, as Marvin Eisenberg put it, "like a Brancusi come to life" (Figure 5.1).

The gradual transition from the musical language of *L'Homme et son désir,* completed in 1918, to the sound world of *La Création,* written in 1923, was to be directly biased by Milhaud's exposure to the world

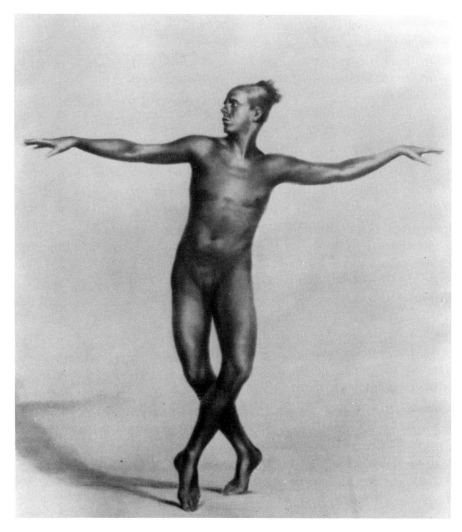

Figure 5.1. Jean Börlin, smeared in shiny yellowish makeup for *L'Homme et son désir* (1921).

Photo, Dansmuseet, Stockholm.

of jazz, however, both in its export variety, such as he had witnessed in London in 1920, and through a direct encounter in Harlem itself. When Milhaud first heard Billy Arnold's band in London in 1920, he was mesmerized:

> The new music was extremely subtle in its use of timbre; the saxophone breaking in, squeezing out the juice of dreams, or the trumpet, dramatic or languorous by turns, the clarinet, frequently played in its upper register, the lyrical use of the trombone, glancing with its slide over quarter-tones in crescendos of volume and pitch . . . The constant use of syncopation in the melody was of such contrapuntal freedom that it gave the impression of unregulated improvisation, whereas in actual fact it was elaborately rehearsed daily, down to the last detail. I had the idea of using these timbres and rhythms in a chamber music, but first I had to penetrate more deeply into the arcana of this new musical form, whose technique still baffled me.[5]

Upon his arrival in New York in 1922, Milhaud commented to the press that European music was to a considerable degree influenced by American music, by which he did not mean Edward Macdowell or John Alden Carpenter but "jazz." The headlines read "Milhaud Admires Jazz" and "Jazz Dictates the Future of European Music," and Milhaud was suddenly flanked by admirers, including the chairman of the Negro musicians' union and Harry T. Burleigh, a well-known arranger of Negro spirituals. His eventual introduction to New Orleans jazz was through the chanteuse Yvonne George, who took him to Harlem, which according to Milhaud was as yet undiscovered by

> snobs and aesthetes: we were the only white folk there. The music I heard was absolutely different from anything I had ever heard before and was a revelation to me. Against the beat of the drums the melodic lines crisscrossed in a breathless pattern of broken and twisted rhythms. A Negress whose grating voice seemed to come from the depths of the centuries sang in front of the various tables. With despairing pathos and dramatic feeling she sang over and over again, to the point of exhaustion, the same refrain, to which the constantly changing melodic pattern of the orchestra wove a kaleidoscopic background. This authentic music had its roots in the darkest corners of the Negro soul, the vestigial traces of Africa, no doubt. Its effect on me was so overwhelming that I could not tear myself away.[6]

Incantation, African roots, first times: the familiar slogans of *art nègre*. Primitivism had now been clearly identified by the younger generation of French composers, whose mission centered not on the prolongation of an aesthetic but on the opportunity which they sensed awaited them to vivify, to modify, and to update. Milhaud had been exposed first-hand to a music that would allow him to provide the note of authenticity missing from Poulenc's *Rapsodie nègre,* and Parisian soil had been further enriched by the arrival of an impertinent new ballet company.

The first fruit of the conjunction of these multiple aesthetic and institutional forces was *La Création du monde,* and it epitomized more clearly than any other work to that date the potential of a high/low, jazz/classical, primitive/contemporary conspiracy. De Maré's model for the Ballets Suédois was clearly the Ballets Russes with respect to its collaborative objectives, and for this project, which premiered at the Théâtre des Champs-Élysées on October 25, 1923, he enlisted the services of Blaise Cendrars to join Milhaud, Léger, and Börlin.

Milhaud had registered his musical impressions of Brazil not only in *L'Homme et son désir* but in a more popular vein in *Le Boeuf sur le toit* and *Saudades do Brasil,* both of which stemmed from his exposure to tangos and maxixes. Now to memories of his South American adventure Milhaud wedded his exposure to Parisian locales in response to Cocteau's injunction to tap the popular strain of the music hall and circus as a source of creative stimulus. Milhaud's testimony to the influence of these variable forces on all three principals is exceptionally clear. In his *Autobiography* he verified that Cendrars and Léger were frequenters of *bals-musette* and that they took him with them. They quickly became familiar with the strains of the accordion, sometimes accompanied by the clarinet, the cornet, the trombone, or the violin, issuing from cafes at every turn. Milhaud confessed that they were also intrigued with the sight of West Indian womenfolk dancing the beguine, "whose irregular rhythm conjured up the palm trees and savannas of their islands. During our rounds Léger, Cendrars, and I were working out the details of our ballet."[7]

If, as the above remarks suggest, the fusion of Caribbean, South American, and Parisian popular musics provided indispensable ingredients for *La Création du monde* of 1923, it was Milhaud's exposure to Afro-American jazz that rounded out the equation, completing and clinching his call to the Primitive. For it was immediately following his visit to New York in 1922 that Milhaud contacted Léger and Cendrars with a proposal to create a jazz ballet, noting later that "I adopted the same orchestra as used in Harlem, seventeen solo instruments [two flutes, oboe, two clarinets, bassoon, horn, two trumpets, trombone, piano, percussion, two violins, saxophone, cello, double bass], and I made wholesale use of the jazz style to convey a purely classical style."[8] The use of seventeen solo instruments coincided with many European composers' fascination with ad hoc ensembles (as in *Pierrot lunaire* and *L'Histoire du soldat*), which ultimately fused with Les Six's interest in the instrumentation of the *bals-musette* café orchestra. Poulenc had already introduced a prototype ensemble in his *Cocards* (1919) before Milhaud's *La Création du monde*.

The initial touchstone which helped Milhaud to define his style in the ballet was timbral. His use of saxophones, trumpets, and trombones in the opening scene successfully conjures up the pastoral mood prior to the opening of the curtain. One automatically recalls Stravinsky's claims regarding the force of timbre in procuring the Primitivist note in *Le Sacre*. But there were other ingredients in Milhaud's arsenal of effects, including blue notes and syncopations prominently displayed in the second section of the ballet, that blatantly announced his Afro-American alliance. Many of the same melodic blue-note figurations appeared in "St. Louis Blues" and Gershwin's *Rhapsody in Blue* (1924), and successor-predecessor relationships were repeatedly cited between these two works and Milhaud's *Creation of the World* (1923).[9] Milhaud similarly appropriated secondary ragtime rhythms that pitted eighth-note patterns in groups of three against a pattern of three quarter notes barred in four as an advertisement of his orientation. Constant Lambert later claimed that Milhaud had represented the primeval incantations of a trio of gods "by a three-part jazz fugato over a percussion accompaniment . . . Crudely and naively analyzed, the percussion background provides the necessary barbaric atmosphere, the jazz inflections of the tune suggest a stylized negro speech, the counterpoint provides the element of mingled and growing effort."[10] But programmatic issues aside, if from a technical point of view the use of counterpoint was calculated to support Milhaud's announced intention "to convey a purely classical style," the question arises, "Why a classical style?" Beyond its potential function of signaling order in the act of creation following primal chaos, it was also in tune with the fusion of jazz and a virulent Neoclassicism that was currently in vogue in the works of Stravinsky. To this was also added an element of cyclic repetition throughout the five scenes of the ballet, and its integrative potential served the requirements of both abstract musical developments and the narrative progress of the ballet. But perhaps the best way of sensing the compatibility of jazz and the classical component is to try to understand the degree to which jazz was held to possess its own classical nature. Milhaud summed it up in the following telling reminiscence:

> Jean Wiéner played syncopated music with aerial grace and sensitivity, with an especially light rhythm. We loved to listen to his playing, and to that of his partner, Vance, the Negro, who was an admirable saxophonist and banjo-player. Without any transition these two would pass from fashionable ragtime and fox trots to the most celebrated works of Bach. Besides, syncopated music calls for a rhythm as inexorably regular as that of Bach himself, which has the same basis.[11]

There was a final symbol which was readily available to Milhaud for the fourth section of the ballet, the dance of desire and mating. Indeed, given the current popularity of the tango as the ultimate dance of seduction, its inclusion was virtually demanded—or, should we say, its absence would have been noted. Yet Milhaud's suggestion of one of its principal rhythms (a syncopated figure followed by two notes of equal value) is so fractured that the ultimate effect is more that of a spasm than a reflection of the tango teas which had been the rage of Paris and London from the early teens. Milhaud's rhythms are distant as well from those works that had immediately followed his Brazilian adventure— *Le Boeuf sur le toit* (1919) and *Saudades do Brasil* (1920–21). Even so, Milhaud delivers a score that is perhaps more scrupulous about its musical manners than about a commitment to Cendrars's scenario; the concluding section's recall of the first and second movements, for example, seems calculated as much to a sense of reprise as to any association with lovers in the springtime.[12]

Léger, who created the decor and costumes, had behind him the experience of Cubism as well as exposure to the mechanics of Mondrian. Both were importuned in the service of conjuring up a spectacle of modern vitality, urban dynamics, and the elements of surprise and motion dear to Cocteau and his circle, who took as their highest mission the recognition of an Art of the Everyday. The idea that everything had to be in constant motion suggests not only a certain nervosity, but the hustle and bustle, the "on-the-go" mentality of urban life.[13]

Léger's formula for incorporating this point of view in a Theater of Spectacle involved the continuous movement of both figure and scenery in a rapid series of compressed events that resulted in a perpetual collision of visual images. The concept of the "star" performer was to be absorbed into a two-dimensional scenic landscape, achieving unity with it through a mechanical choreography.[14] The scenery included clouds and geometric shapes as well as three African deities, Nzamé, Mébère, and N'kava, each some twenty-six feet in height. The totemic quality of these figures was obviously calculated to conjure up global counterparts varying in both time and place, from the Kamakura Daibutsu to the Eiffel Tower and New York skyscrapers. The iconic analogy was pressed home in another work premiered that evening on the same program: Cole Porter's *Within the Quota,* to scenario and sets by Gerald Murphy, pumped "authentic" American syncopations orchestrated by Charles Koechlin against a backdrop consisting of an immense blown-up newspaper page sporting an American skyscraper and an ocean liner turned on end next to a headline reading: "Unknown Banker Buys Atlantic."[15]

At a more specific level, however, Léger modeled the faces and figures for drop curtain, decor, and costumes directly after drawings, some of which are virtually tracings, made from Carl Einstein's *Negerplastik* (1915) and Marius de Zayas' *African Negro Art: Its Influence on Modern Art* (1916), much as Milhaud patterned his instrumentation after Harlem jazz ensembles (Figures 5.2 and 5.3).[16] Mobile, flat, cut-out figures, they were at once mythical and larger than life, presiding as they were over the first signs of animal and plant activity on the day of creation. The lower orders placed in front of them included the demigods and, finally, the plants, animals, and dancers. The costumes for the animals and insects disclose an affinity for solutions previously made by both Larionov and Goncharova,[17] but concerning the use of masks generally Léger offered the following appraisal: "The mask dominated the ancient stage and the most primitive peoples use it in creating a spectacle. In spite of the feeble means at their disposal, they realized that the human likeness on the stage hindered the development of a lyrical state, of a state of astonishment . . . the individual must be made to disappear in order to utilize the human material properly."[18]

Léger had originally hoped to use skins, which were to be inflated with gas at the moment of creation and sent aloft. Potential interference with the music from the noise of the pumps led him to the use of masks for both face and body, achieving in the process the illusion of African sculpture for the principal actors. Mask and sculpture, fundamental touchstones of *art nègre,* promoted a sense of spectacle commensurate with the surrounding scenery. The mask was to assume an extraordinary role in the theater of numerous countries during the 1920s and, beyond the African connection, was legitimized through its recall of the traditions of Greek theater, No drama, and the early plays of the Expressionists. Meyerhold, Craig, Appia, Lermontov, Kaiser, O'Neill, Eliot, Cocteau, and a host of dramatists, who sensed the power of the mask's attendant anonymity and universality, participated in its revival.[19] With them, Léger acknowledged the potential of the mask to transcend the individual and to suggest human universals. Masks were also capable of striking a sense of terror and awe which Léger deemed essential to the purpose at hand. Among the basic affirmations regarding the nature of Cubism as it was defined by artists in the circle around Apollinaire and Jean Metzinger in the period up to 1912 was the notion that "the Truth

Figure 5.2. Fernand Léger, set and costumes of figures and insects for *La Création du monde*.

Photo, Dansmuseet, Stockholm. © 1994 ARS, New York / SPADEM, Paris.

Figure 5.3. Helmet mask from the Ivory Coast. Published in Carl Einstein, *Negerplastik,* 1915.

the Cubist seeks is opposed to the semblance of truth that is offered by the 'exterior appearance of objects.' "[20] The ritual message of the African mask served this purpose admirably, and its value and force were manifestly still operative in the 1920s when Léger joined with Milhaud in a telling of the creation story.

Creation myths are the most sacred myths of all cultures, containing as they do both societal structure and value. Though their number is astronomical, similarity among them is extraordinary.[21] All seek to fix the origins of life from which all meaning proceeds. The version of this story forwarded by Cendrars in his scenario is clearly traceable to his own *L'Anthologie nègre,* which had appeared only two years before in 1921. A curious collection of accounts by missionaries and explorers of African lore, animal fables, and mythical tales, the anthology contained as its second tale a piece entitled "The Story of the Beginning of Things." In confecting his scenario, however, Cendrars set aside individual relationships and transformed the narrative tale of his anthology into an anonymous telling of the creation story in five parts: during the chaos before creation three gigantic deities consult together; from the mass at the center, animal and vegetable life sprouts; man and woman appear; a dance of desire and mating follows; the conclusion brings calm, the kiss, spring, the spreading of life.[22] Cendrars was a restless voyager, and made journeys, either real or imagined, to Siberia, Panama, New York, and Alaska. All such trips carried a drastically compressed or expanded perspective of duration in comparison to real time, and in *La Création du monde* he postulated the most distant, elusive and yet fascinating of all temporal encounters.

Léger's solutions, too, were a direct reflection of attitudes which he and others had been addressing for some years. In painting *The Card Game* of 1919, for example, he had made a specific attempt to humanize his earlier abstractions through a directly perceivable subject and to comment upon it through the introduction of simple pictorial elements, namely "metallic cylinders clashing against flat angular shapes." Just as he rendered the soldiers in this painting "mechanically anonymous and given the potential for irresistible action,"[23] Léger infused his deities with the same properties in *La Création du monde*. Persisting in his predilection for monumentality and brilliant flat colors in the mechanization of the human form, he adapted his interest in Byzantine mosaics and stained-glass windows to the theatrical stage. In addition, he reflected various approaches to *simultaneity,* visible in the earlier work of Robert and Sonia Delaunay as well as Blaise Cendrars and Guillaume Apollinaire, in the planar overlap and intercut of the sets and figures, suggesting the force of a new synthesis. Building upon his experience with *L'Homme et son désir,* which had incorporated a four-tiered structure, Léger now had his totemic deities loom as ancient versions of urban skyscrapers, and their planar physical projection, viewed against the sounds of Milhaud's music, invited contemplation of the ancient-modern relationship.

Jean Börlin, who choreographed the Ballets Suédois production, had seen Isadora Duncan as early as 1906 and Émile Jaques-Dalcroze by 1911, both of whom were to be as strong an influence on him as they were on Fokine. The first evidence of his interest in the theme which was to dominate *La Création du monde* appeared in a solo dance, entitled *Sculpture nègre,* which he performed at his Paris debut on March 25, 1920, a good seven months before the premiere of the company. The program was comprised of seven compositions without decor and supported by an orchestra of forty-five players. Photographs of *Sculpture nègre* (Figure 5.4) clearly reflect a degree of ethnographic research, and the critic Pierre Scize has left us with a clear idea of the overall impression. Noting that Börlin was dressed in a costume imitating a wooden African statuette that would find later echoes in *La Création du monde,* he detailed the deliberately ponderous effect of the whole: "The body's flexible points all bend as if under the weight of an abominable compulsion . . . It rose up, slowly and as if ossified by years of contemplative immobility. And what this god unveiled before our eyes was the primitive eurhythmics of the first beings: an extraordinary vision in three-dimensional form."[24]

The description is sufficiently precise to permit a comparison with an important aspect of Nijinsky's choreographic solution for *Le Sacre.* As described by Rambert, Levinson, and others, prominence was given there to bending and straightening the knees and to the raising and lowering of the heels, which they attributed to the pedagogical method of Jaques-Dalcroze. To the extent that Börlin had prepared his choreography as much through thoughtful research of African dance movement as through a study of Dalcrozian gymnastics, the expression "primitive eurhythmics" by the critic above and the remarks of independent observers of African dance take on a special relevance in promoting an understanding of Börlin's approach. John Miller Chernoff has observed that in contrast to Western dance, which aspires to the conveying of a feeling or idea through movement, posture, and pantomime, the African dancer "through the certainty of feet placed squarely on the ground, knees slightly bent, weight moving downward, is communicating a sense of rootedness and solidity in the world, the security of an unambiguous tribal life."[25] Clearly the airy grace of the classical ballet, which takes pains to promote the illusion that the dancer has escaped the force of gravity, had been abandoned by Börlin for a type of dance that is its diametrical opposite.

Prior to *La Création du monde* the Ballets Suédois under the direction of Börlin had enlisted a variety of national approaches including Siamese, Spanish, and Swedish folk dance and, in addition to *Sculpture nègre* and *L'Homme et son désir* (June 6, 1921), a third Primitivist exercise, *Offerlunden.* Based upon a Viking sacrifical theme, it opened on May 25, 1923. Levinson, charging cheap imitation, dubbed it "un *Sacre* scandinave," and the production was soon discontinued.

Börlin's next production was *La Création du monde,* and in preparing

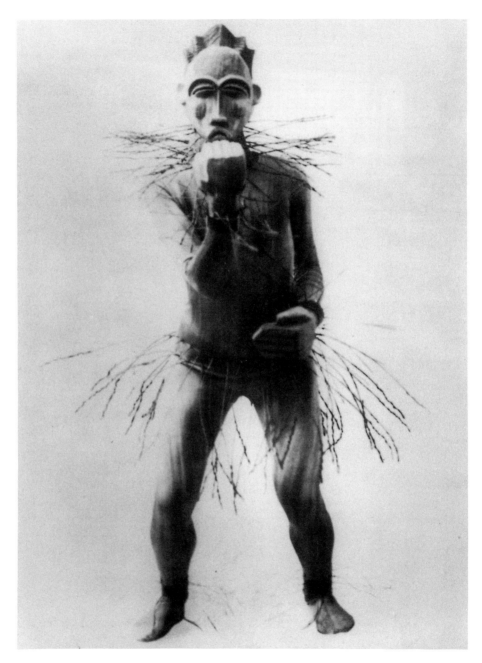

Figure 5.4. Jean Börlin's costume by Paul Colin for *Sculpture nègre*, 1920.

Photo, Dansmuseet, Stockholm.

the choreography he pursued his search for a valid ethnic base. Investigations into the dances of black Africa were based principally upon the research of Rolf de Maré, who, fearful that non-European dance traditions were fated to oblivion, had traveled first to Indonesia, where he shot twenty documentary films, and then to Africa, Asia, and South America.[26] Börlin's concerns, previously expressed in the costumes and choreography for *Sculpture nègre,* were now extended to "the first European ballet in which the choreography was essentially derived from African dance."[27] In spite of such claims, however, his efforts continued to puzzle the critics. Some deemed the choreography too classically inclined for the subject, while the dancers took exception to having their role reduced to the pushing of scenery and painted figures about the stage. Such encumbrances to classical dancing had already been prefigured by the heavy enclosures of the dancers in Cocteau's *Les Mariés de la Tour Eiffel,* whose costumes "were created over a wire frame to carry the thick padding, while a mask concealed the dancer's face."

Some have argued that Jean Börlin "was not a great dancer"[28] and that his choreographic ideas invariably developed in the shadow of strong personalities such as Fokine, de Maré, Cocteau, and Léger. Yet, whatever the truth of the judgment that the dancing of *La Création du monde* lacked "any great choreographic merit,"[29] it is important to note the change that had taken place in the world of the ballet. From a time in the nineteenth century when dance was preeminent and the music and scenery were frequently of routine interest, we have passed through the early Ballets Russes seasons when costume and sets competed successfully with the dance, then to a period from 1911 when music and choreography increasingly reigned, to a time when music and scenery could triumph over the choreography—one might even say to a point where the movement of the scenery and cardboard figures *was* the choreography. But the rootedness of the choreography could also legitimately pretend to a degree of ethnic authenticity, and the legacy of mask and marionette, of Edward Gordon Craig as well as *Petrushka,* had surfaced once again and had projected the possibility of a new affiliation between scenery, costume, action, and dance. The importance and the relationship of ballet's constituent parts changed from work to work throughout the 1920s—not just in the brief tenure of the Ballets Suédois but in the final decade of the Ballets Russes as well, when any pair of the triumvirate were capable of assuming a dominating role.

Thus the path had been cleared earlier for the contributions of all three collaborators to *La Création du monde*. Léger's orientation was obviously toward an African Primitivism already familiar to audiences from the work of the Cubists and the exhibits at the Trocadéro's Musée de l'Homme. But, as Levinson noted, the idea behind the costumes could be variously traced to Goncharova's designs for *Le Coq d'or* and to the managers' costumes by Picasso for *Parade*. Milhaud's music, too, had its familiar reference points and could readily be associated with the sounds of an Afro-American jazz which were increasingly popular in Parisian theatres, concerts, and dance halls. Also clearly within memory was his fascination for "beginnings" as it had surfaced in his *L'Homme et son désir* in the company of a wordless vocal quartet and an expanded use of percussion. And Börlin's choreography, beyond its direct reliance upon ethnic models, was undoubtedly seen as representative of a new, free-spirited kind of dance promoted by Ruth St. Denis, Isadora Duncan, Bronislava Nijinska, and Vaslav Nijinsky during the preceding two decades and previously projected by Börlin in three projects with Primitivist themes.

Just how modern was the ballet viewed to be at the time? Vuillermoz's report, which appeared in the *Revue musicale* only two months after the premiere, openly deflates the announced objectives of its creators:

> The scenario by Blaise Cendrars and the decor and costumes by Fernand Léger seemed intent on making of this evening an audacious manifestation of the avant-garde. This did not happen, however. Milhaud's technique, which has never been really revolutionary, becomes meeker with each passing day, and Léger's cubism, which seemed so aggressive in his *Skating Rink,* could not shock anyone when applied to the theme of original chaos.[30]

Xavier de Courville, writing in the *Revue musicale* as late as February 1925, cut through all the aesthetic claims with respect to the visual component, proclaiming a lack of genuine modernity, reliance on overly familiar stylisations, and a cubist decor which he felt was conventional.[31]

Finally André Levinson, whose perspectives on *The Rite* have been noted above and who was already living in Paris by the time of the premiere of *The Creation of the World,* called the bodily contortions of the dancers in imitation of the exotic sculptures an aberration. He also charged that the excessive glamor attached to Negro sculpture was due to the exaltations of the great modern artists and the snobs who followed them.[32]

The multiple impulses of Primitivism behind *La Création du monde* may provide a more interesting story in the long run than the work itself. For the allegory had its roots in various tendencies articulated from the turn of the century. More specifically, the Ur-text–Primitive collaborative had already been clearly established in *Le Sacre du printemps,* and the Milhaud-Léger-Cendrars-Börlin consortium was clearly an attempt to update its social message for the 1920s.

The reaction of the critics above nonetheless camouflages the persisting factors which provided a sense of urgency for the ballet at its conception. The condition to which *La Création* responded was more fundamental than the desire for another *succès d'estime.* T. S. Eliot posed the question in a review of 1924, "Is it possible or justifiable for art, the creation of beautiful objects and of literature, to persist indefinitely without its primitive purposes: is it possible for the aesthetic object to be a direct object of attention?" Eliot believed that the very viability of art depended upon its capacity to retain its primitive aura: "the stage—not only in its remotest origins but always—is a ritual, and the failure of the contemporary stage to satisfy the craving for ritual is one of the reasons why it is not a living art."[33] And Ezra Pound had proclaimed that "a return to origins invigorates because it is a return to nature and reason."[34]

Not only would Léger and Milhaud have understood both Eliot and Pound, but the subject which *La Création du monde* addressed was one familar to and perhaps directly prompted by another prominent artist then living in Paris. Constantin Brancusi (1876–1957), of Romanian birth but resident in Paris from 1904, had already achieved recognition as a sculptor by the end of the century's first decade. The initial version of the *Kiss* appeared by 1908, and the *Pasarea maiastra (Magic Bird)* by 1910–1912. The shape of the latter has been persuasively linked to one of the headresses designed by Alexandre Golovin for the premiere of Stravinsky's *Firebird* on June 25, 1910, and both the ballet's theme of the magic bird and the egg as an emblem of the soul have been convincingly related to the Romanian folk story that Brancusi forwarded in connection with *Maiastra.*[35] (See Figures 5.5–5.7.) Beyond these specifics of shared design and ethnic base, the sculpture proved to be important as the launching station for a sequence of magical birds that was to culminate in 1922 in the first of a group entitled *Bird in Space,* and

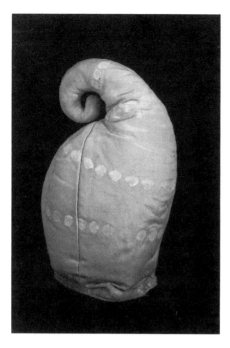

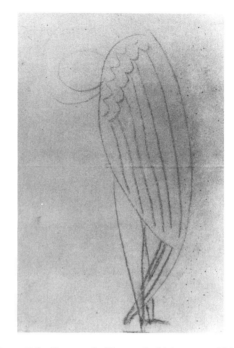

Figure 5.5. Alexandre Golovin, Headdress for an attendant to King Kastchei in Stravinsky's *The Firebird,* Paris, 1910 (facsimile of original design, made 1936–37).

Whitworth Art Gallery, University of Manchester, Manchester, England.

Figure 5.6. Constantin Brancusi, *Maiastra,* ca. 1910. Private collection. © 1994 ARS, New York / ADAGP, Paris.

equally important as the progenitor for a renowned series of egglike forms whose relevance to the contemporary musical scene will be hypothesized below.

From the beginning the reductive form of many of Brancusi's early pieces suggested the idea of a primal expression to various observers. Even a specific association with African Primitivism was claimed for numerous works from *The First Step* (1913) through *Caryatid* (1915), *Adam and Eve* (1916–1921), *Chimera* (1918), and *The White Negress* (1923). Though the idealization of many of his ovoidal figures, from the time of *Prometheus* (1911) through increasingly simplified versions entitled *The Newborn* (1915) and *The First Cry* (1917), suggests an independence from African sculpture, it clearly underscores Brancusi's infatuation with beginnings. The first work to eliminate all markings and

Figure 5.7. Constantin Brancusi, *Pasarea Maiastra,* 1912.
Tate Gallery, London. © 1994 ARS, New York / ADAGP, Paris.

to reduce form to a perfect ovoid was entitled *Sculpture for the Blind*
(1916). A few years later Brancusi announced an even more universal
implication by calling his next, nearly identical, example *Beginning of
the World* (1920) (Figure 5.8).[36] As Eric Shanes has put it, "Because the
beginning of the world for most species involves the fertilization of an
egg, it is surely permissible to see Brancusi's ovoid as an egg . . . It is
perhaps the most essential of all the essential statements in Brancusi's
art."[37]

The willingness on the part of the sculptor Barbara Hepworth to
sense connections between such developments and the world of music
is remarkable, but her seemingly automatic introduction of Stravinsky
in assessing Brancusi was clearly reflective not only of the power of *Le
Sacre* or the persistence of its developing mythology but of the continuing need to identify a musical repertoire that could lay claim to contemporary social relevance: "I think Brancusi's understanding of these time-
less elements of sculpture is very close to Stravinsky's understanding

Figure 5.8. Constantin Brancusi, *Beginning of the World,* ca. 1920.

Dallas Museum of Art; Foundation for the Arts Collection; Gift of Mr. and Mrs. James H. Clark. © 1994 ARS, New York / ADAGP, Paris.

of rhythm—they are elements which belong to the primaeval forces activating man's sensibilities; but they are, at the same time, sophisticated in the sense that they apprehend contemporary needs and passions and reaffirm the continuity of life."[38]

Could Milhaud have known of Brancusi's *Beginning of the World* when he suggested the project of *The Creation of the World* to Léger on his return to Paris from New York in 1922? The composer's autobiography reveals that he had apparently been introduced to more than Harlem and jazz on his visit to America and virtually eliminates speculation on the question:

> The wife of the publisher of the *Washington Post,* Mrs. Eugene Meyer, a great friend of Bibi Picabia and Germaine Survage, asked me to play some contemporary music at her home. She owned some very lovely modern paintings, as well as sculptures by Brancusi, whom she had induced to come to the United States for an exhibition of his works, and they had remained on excellent terms. A year or two later I met her again in Paris at a dinner in Brancusi's house, to which Satie and I had also been invited. We ate a delicious dinner cooked in the sculptor's great furnace.[39]

Brancusi's black marble portrait of Mrs. Meyer, made in 1930, ultimately offered vivid testimony of their association. Brancusi and Milhaud, as members of the Satie circle, both tended the composer in his final illness in 1925, and the sculptor incised Satie's name on the stone cross placed at his grave.

Ultimately, there is no need to insist upon aesthetic parallels or transferrals between Milhaud's musical language and the art of Brancusi—as some have done with the sculptor and Satie[40]—in order to substantiate Milhaud's undisputable awareness of Brancusi and particularly his themes in the early 1920s. The period of *La Création du monde* has traditionally been characterized as one concerned with a return to the universals of mankind following a war commonly labeled the "war to end all wars," and Léger's and Milhaud's ritualistic and mythic presentation has been held to reflect these concerns. But as Bengt Häger has reminded us, beyond such issues *La Création du monde* was retrospectively seen to have been an important touchstone for numerous later aesthetic developments as well: Léger's mobile forms, which introduced the idea of art in movement, preceded his meeting with Calder by seven years; abstract choreography freed of the limitations of the human form was also later exemplified in the work of Alwin Nikolais and others; and especially the notion that music and choreography could exist side by side, in a symbiotic yet quite independent relationship, was to be taken to further extremes in the work of John Cage and Merce Cunningham.[41]

Initial critical reaction to Milhaud's ballet may have been mixed, but despite the view of some that his music was "frivolous and more suitable for a restaurant or a dance hall," Milhaud noted and obviously took satisfaction in the fact that only ten years later "the self-same critics were discussing the philosophy of jazz and learnedly demonstrating that *La Création du monde* was the best of my works."[42] By 1933 the seminal role of *La Création du monde* was increasingly, if quietly, acknowledged, as New York critics, citing its affinity with Gershwin's *Rhapsody in Blue,* noted that Milhaud's ballet had premiered the year before. By then the question regarding the authentic relationship between American jazz and African tribal music or the relationship of either to Milhaud's score was no longer an issue.[43]

Milhaud had acknowledged his source in the timbral code of a Harlem ensemble and had left other detectable signs of an alliance in both melody and rhythm through the use of blue notes, syncopations, and ostinati. However, Léger's prediction that *La Création du monde* would be "the only possible ballet nègre in the entire world" and that it would "remain as a model of the genre"[44] in large part went untested. Just as Roerich's scenery and costumes and Nijinsky's choreography for *Le Sacre* quickly evaporated from the public conscience while Stravinsky's music continued to hold the boards, so Milhaud's music had to withstand the test of time for the ballet as a whole. Though it is hardly a damning judgment to suggest that Milhaud's score failed to secure and sustain the same independent interest as Stravinsky's, it is intriguing to consider why the music for *La Création* now sounds like a 1920s period piece. It is hardly sufficient to point to the fact that in Stravinsky's score the folk model is submerged, while in Milhaud's work the jazz component sits boldly on the surface in the manner of the models for the New Classicism. *Petrushka,* as well as *Pulcinella,* could be discounted for the same reason.

Ultimately, neither the symbolism, the easy recognition of source materials, nor the degree of their integration appears to prove fundamental to an enduring acceptance. Nor, as Theodor Adorno might suggest, is it in the absence of complexity that we should look for a rationale.[45] Boulez has argued, for example, that it is precisely because of the simplifications of language and the reduction of harmonic relations and figures to striking and easily remembered formula in the *Rite* that the "decisive recapture of a long-neglected element," rhythm, was permitted.[46] Whatever the explanation, and in spite of a similarity of symbolism and propelling agency in *Le Sacre du printemps* and *La Création du monde,* the latter unlike the former became only a momentary emblem of the age and was devoid of any power for future shock.

In a little book entitled *Le Jazz* printed in 1926, two Frenchmen,

André Coeuroy and André Schaeffner, undertook to decipher the historical roots of *musique nègre* and to identify its essential ingredients for the 1920s. Beyond the typical but detailed insistence upon rhythm and percussion instruments as the basis of Negro music—with tambours and balafon receiving separate chapters—they judged the role of the spiritual and the nature of the Negro voice in assessing the support system which gave birth to jazz.

Resonating throughout, however, is a clear and continuing need to invoke Stravinsky as one of the prime generators of the current jazz scene, and they conclude with an extraordinary hypothesis:

> It is possible, in addition, that without the previous arrival of *Le Sacre* in Europe jazz would have had no chance of being understood: the work of Stravinsky, born in full view of the discoveries of *l'art plastique nègre,* in the previously unutilized deployment of the percussion, in the violence of the brass, in the hard insistence of its rhythms, and finally by the brusque and successive reinforcements of the *tutti,* brought us to an appreciation of this hirsute form of music in a manner similar to that by which the Afro-Americans were persistently drawn to modern string instrument makers.[47]

Coeuroy and Schaeffner cite Milhaud's *La Création du monde* (1923) as well as Honegger's *Concertino* (1925) for piano and orchestra in their book's final section, entitled "Le Jazz devant les juges" ("Jazz Encounters the Critics"). But it is Stravinsky who repeatedly looms as the new mythical guardian of *musique nègre* in the concert hall, providing an imperial liaison with the makers of contemporary jazz. Yet, one of the critics whom they cite, the art historian Maurice Brillant, reverses the proportions of the Stravinskian formula with a bemused speculation. "But you see what the art of a Stravinsky, so original nevertheless—and especially his rhythms—owes to the influence of the jazz-band. I wonder whether the orchestra of *Noces* could have been born, such as we know it, without jazz."[48]

Not only had a shuffled music history forsaken chronology, but *Le Sacre*'s attendant myths had multiplied and had found a distended base of sponsorship. For musical Primitivism, originally defined in terms of a Russian folk culture rooted in prehistoric times, had now forged an alliance with the themes of a Romanian sculptor and a *musique nègre* imported from the Americas, both North and South, in the company of a scenario, set, and score by a trio of French artists in response to a commission by a Swedish ballet company.

— 6 —

Josephine and Jonny

Musique nègre! How many times I heard it during the past year. How many times I got up in order to be near it! No pitches, just rhythms; no melodic instruments, nothing but percussion instruments; long drums, tamtams and crotales.

In threes, they performed veritable pieces just from rhythm: an uneven rhythm, oddly cut up by syncopations, that bewitched and provoked all to move the body with abandon.

Musique nègre! How many times, far from Africa, have I thought I heard you, and suddenly the entire South was recreated through you.

André Gide

I like jazz when it is the simple expression of *la musique nègre*.

Igor Stravinsky

Josephine Baker

After the Ballets Suédois disbanded in 1925, Rolf de Maré remained on as director of the Théâtre des Champs-Élysées, and according to Josephine Baker his invitation to Caroline Dudley to bring her black troupe from New York to Paris was made at the suggestion of Fernand Léger. *La Revue nègre* opened on October 2, 1925, and during the two weeks of its run turned Baker into a star. Formerly she had appeared in Noble Sissle's and Eubie Blake's black revue *Shuffle Along* and later their *Chocolate Dandies*. Whatever attention she had won had been not because of her dancing, however, but rather because of her irreverent and comic antics on stage. Soon after the arrival of the *Revue nègre* in Paris, it was decided that Maude de Forest, initially billed as the star, could use some support, and Baker, the entertainer, was pressed into service.

The extent to which anything associated with *art nègre* could still stake claims to vogue status could be judged by the clientele who soon clamored for tickets. Fernand Léger, Blaise Cendrars, and Darius Milhaud all attended the opening night performance, as did Jean Cocteau, Janet Flanner, and Jacques-Émile Blanche. Colette, F. Scott Fitzgerald, and Erich Maria Remarque caught later ones, and Cocteau, who totally succumbed to her charm, attended six times. Man Ray photographed her, and she posed repeatedly for Picasso, who called her the "Nefertiti of now." F. Scott Fitzgerald speaks of her in *Babylon Revisited;* Hemingway was dazzled by her and later claimed to have danced the night away with her;[1] Alexander Calder's first wire sculpture of 1926 attempted to capture the vitality of her figure (Figure 6.1); in 1928 the Viennese architect Adolf Loos designed a house for her that seemed to conjure up the stripes of an African zebra more than the black and white marble striations of Siena's Cathedral (Figure 6.2); and in 1929 aboard the *Lutetia* on their way back from South America, the architect Le Corbusier honored her, and in the process created something of a stir, by appearing at a costume ball in blackface and with a circle of feathers around his waist.

Baker's versions of the charleston and shimmy, which gave her audience a memorable visual massage, and her concluding savage dance with Joe Alex proved that *la danse nègre* or *step afro-americaine* was capable of engendering controversy (Figure 6.3). At the Théâtre des Champs-Élysées and later at the Folies-Bergère, where she introduced her famous banana costume, audiences were at first startled, then riveted before ultimately capitulating to her audacity and charm. If the charleston now seems to epitomize the "flapper era" of the 1920s, the shimmy, originating among American blacks, had surfaced earlier in the teens and had become a genuine national craze following the *Ziegfeld Follies* of 1922.[2] Though Baker capitalized on the energy of this popular American phenomenon, she had not been the first to introduce it to Paris or Europe. For as early as April 1921 Milhaud had written a shimmy, entitled "Caramel mou," for an *orchestre de jazz* (clarinet, trumpet, trombone, saxophone, piano, percussion, voice ad libitum) which may have been suggested by the seven-piece ensemble of Louis Mitchell's Jazz Kings. And Hindemith had introduced the shimmy along with a boston and a ragtime in his *Suite: 1922* for piano.[3]

Jacques-Émile Blanche, who painted several portraits of Stravinsky and other notables of Parisian high society of the time,[4] also recorded an intimate verbal glimpse of the impact of the *Revue nègre* and a clarification of the degree to which *Le Sacre* was seen as a logical companion piece without any sense of ethnic confusion. His appraisal is worth quoting at some length:

> This Josephine Baker, this Maude de Forest, Mistinguetts of the tropics, with their hair highly brilliantined and pasted down; these splendid creatures, fleshy and muscular with faces of a rouged androgyne, who are the "Girls" of the *troupe nègre;* these large-buttocked mother figures, with breasts shaped like goatskin bottles; all of this tribe—fren-

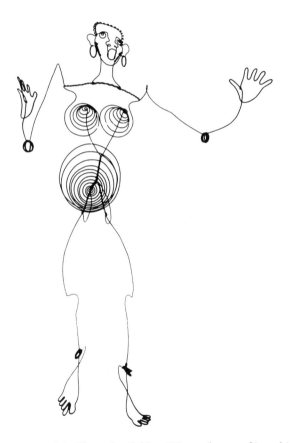

Figure 6.1. Alexander Calder, Wire sculpture of Josephine Baker, 1926.
© 1994 ARS, New York / ADAGP, Paris.

zied, shrieking, chuckling with a sinister laughter—would be as terri-fying *au naturel* in their native village among the straw huts and the banana trees as those unforgettable ladies in the *Le Sacre du Printemps* who appear to want to lie with the earth, to unleash the reservoirs of a stormy, black sky which the fields parched by winter anticipate. Both of these creatures, either by the craft of the costumier or by their peculiar nature, of an ethnic character sweetened by misery, carry us back to prehistoric times, just like the *Sacre* of Igor Stravinksy. An American revue, with its black bamboulas, today seems to reconnect the origins of the human race with the centuries of social convulsions, this art of the savages to the painting, to the music, to the choreogra-phy of the Occident.

And I, who ought to be offended on several counts by this spectacle which exhibits so little of our tradition of decorum and taste, not only did I appreciate all the novelty, but I experienced a kind of fulfillment and satisfaction of the spirit that one feels in the presence of perfection. I found there a manifestation of the *esprit moderne* which I have never witnessed at the Exposition.[5]

Figure 6.2. Adolf Loos, house for Josephine Baker, 1928.

Figure 6.3. Joe Alex and Josephine Baker, "Danse sauvage," *Revue nègre,* 1925. Photo.

Both music and dance critics of the day found in Baker a provocative and pyramiding symbol: she was a sensation largely because of a communicative uninhibitedness that appealed to the French; she was an entertainer, but more particularly she was a dancer—not of ballet but rather of emblematic steps representative of Afro-American culture; and, finally, as a sometime seminude woman she garnered a response that no male could have aspired to in the city of the Folies-Bergére, where the female striptease had achieved vogue status by 1894 and continued as its most sensational aspect through the period of World War I. The reasons behind the sociologists' later deconstruction of this vivacious lady into a victim of social prejudice and sexual manipulation as well as an example of early "cross-over" artistry are not difficult to determine. But it is no myth that in Paris she escaped the feelings of racial prejudice with which she had grown up in St. Louis. Later returns to America, where she encountered inevitable discrimination in hotels and clubs (including an incident at the Stork Club that was witnessed and unsympathetically reported by Walter Winchell), drove her to renounce her American citizenship, to return to France, and to form her "Rainbow" orphanage, which ultimately bankrupted her.

The knowledge that her funeral at the Madeleine in 1975 was attended by more people than any other in French history not only dramatizes her affiliation with that country but confirms with rare poignancy the role of color in a scenario that was played out in France during the decade of the 1920s. For in addition to the justifiably recurrent polemic regarding issues of prejudice, and the more recent analysis that has projected Baker as a "female female impersonator" whose "identity as a transvestite begins with race as well as with class and gender,"[6] there remains the central story that was initially launched through the intricate auspices and multifaceted phenomenon of *art nègre* as it was being played out on both sides of the Atlantic.

As the preceding chapters of this book have made clear, the musics of foreign cultures had appealed to the Western musician over a long period of time. Their technical areas of attraction, however, had resided largely in the scalar and the timbral—that is to say, the pitch modes other than the major and minor familiar to Westerners and instrumental colors, singly or in combination, that assumed the status of an exotic code. The principal element that helped to define Primitivism as it was constituted by *musique nègre,* however, was rhythm. Yet this rhythmic element in its African setting has been properly described as a constituent of corporeal dance, which stands at the center; rhythm is only one of its attributes.[7]

That dance and rhythm were potent allies to the concept of Primitivism was apparent in Matisse's powerful and seminal *Danse* of 1909–10, which soon invited comparison with Stravinsky's "The Dance of the Adolescents" in his *Rite of Spring* of 1913. One version of Matisse's painting had been installed in the Moscow home of the art patron Sergei Shchukin by 1911 and was reproduced in the next year together with Russian folkprints in the *Blaue Reiter* almanac of 1912. The issue of rhythm continued to figure in discussions of Baker's revue, and the journalists, who understandably found a gold mine of copy in her story, as well as at least one notable ballet critic, introduced it in their reviews. Among the former, the American Janet Flanner was just beginning to send home her "Letters from Paris," but her initial report was decidedly tame. Later, in the foreword to *Paris Was Yesterday,* a collection of her Paris essays, she sought to improve upon the original, describing not only the costuming but the concluding movement of the principals.

> She made her entry entirely nude except for a pink flamingo feather between her limbs; she was being carried upside down and doing the split on the shoulder of a black giant. Midstage, he paused, and with his long fingers holding her basket-wise around the waist, swung her in a slow cartwheel to the stage floor, where she stood like his magnificent discarded burden, in an instant of complete silence. She was an unforgettable female ebony statue. A scream of salutation spread through the theater. Whatever happened next was unimportant.[8]

At the time, however, Robert de Flers, a highly regarded reviewer for *Le Figaro* and a member of the French Academy, characterized Baker's performance as "lamentable transatlantic exhibitionism which has us reverting to the ape in less time than it took us to descend from it." His clearly racist judgment continued with a declaration that the troupe of performers epitomized degeneracy more than Primitivism. Paul Guillaume was affronted by de Fler's assault, and he responded not only with a list of contemporary artists who had taken succor from African art but with the conclusion that contemporary sensibility had taken a fundamental orientation from Negro art that was irrevocable. His exhibition "L'art nègre et d'art océanien" had already appeared in 1919, followed by his "Opinions sur l'art nègre" in 1920. The year following Baker's revue, Guillaume's *Primitive Negro Sculpture* appeared in English.[9]

More cautious, more knowledgeable, and more concerned with discussing Baker within the context of Parisian cultural developments was André Levinson. In 1929 he retouched and published what he considered the most important of his reviews in a collection, *La Danse d'aujourd'hui,* and in it preserved his reactions to Josephine Baker.[10] Levinson methodically catalogued the numerous energizing forces that Paris had witnessed in the world of dance in recent years, and spoke knowingly not only of exotic dance but of other spectacles from the circus and music hall. The current rage for Baker and jazz he saw as part of the same impulse, and in fixing the "primitive" note common to both he placed the emphasis upon *rhythm* and its relation to bodily movement. Noting that the classic dance of the ballet secured a rapport with the phraseology of the music by analogy in a series of muscular tensions and relaxations, he concluded that all Primitive dance, from the Russian "hopak" and the bourrée of the Auvergne to the Scottish "reel", the Aragonese jota, and now *le step nègre,* was based upon a spontaneous direct expression of rhythm. He saw each of these dances as based upon a "staccato" of feet scanning the measure, and believed that "the savage or folk dancer" was "essentially an instrument of percussion."[11]

Openly disdainful of the vogue for black art, Levinson nonetheless accorded Baker her due and claimed that she had transcended her sources. The degree to which everyone, critic and foe alike, was willing to endorse some aspect of *art nègre* was clear from his review, which, at least momentarily, amounted to total capitulation:

> Entirely lacking in nobility, prehuman if not bestial, the negro paroxysm can attain to grandeur: Josephine Baker, who inaugurated the charleston rage in Paris, is a stunning creature of simian suppleness— a lascivious idol with the face of a street urchin.
>
> Thanks to her sensual splendor and its spirited impetuosity, her dissolute exhibition borders on the *pathétique.* Here is what we said of her the day following her appearance at the Théâtre des Champs-Élysées: "With Miss Josephine Baker everything seemed to change. From her strained and fluttering body, her reckless dislocations, her springing movements, emanated a rhythm. She seemed to dictate syllable by syllable to the spellbound drummer, as well as the saxophonist ardently bent toward her, the fantastic monologue of her body caught in madness. The music is born of the dance. And what a dance!
>
> "The gyrations of this cynical yet merry juggler, the grin which she affected on her large mouth, are suddenly replaced by visions completely lacking in good humor. The brief *pas de deux* of the savages at the finale with Joe Alex achieved a frenzied brilliance and extraordinary animality. Certain of Miss Baker's poses, back arched, rump protruding, arms entwined and raised as a phallic symbol, the mimicry of the face, evoked all the power of the best Negro sculpture. The plastic sense of a race of sculptors and the ecstasy of the African Eros caught us in its grip. We no longer believed that we saw a comical dancing girl before us: it was the 'black Venus' that haunted Baudelaire. Her personality had surpassed the genre."[12]

Recalling the dance's tendency to renew itself by going back to its historical roots, which could be most readily identified in distant places, Levinson noted the degree to which the Ballets Russes had relied upon the vogue for the Oriental and its appropriation or invention of a whole roster of visual and aural components. And immediately following his appraisal of Baker, he was so bold as to compare the bent knees, the stamping, the tumultuous use of the drums, and climactic jump of a group of dancers from Ceylon with a notable event in the Russian troupe's history:

> Oh yes! The spasmodic jumps of the sacrificial virgin, set once upon a time by Nijinsky, spoke the same anguish and the same sensuality. The obscure, primitive hysteria was only interpreted and exalted by an Occidental intelligence. For the actors from Ceylon, as for the Stravinsky of *Le Sacre,* rhythm is an elementary force which subdues, molds, and sculpts man now turned into a dolorous resonator, an instrument of percussion. What other astonishing thing can equal this hypnotic quality of rhythm?[13]

Baker's appeal, however, clearly stemmed from one very crucial factor. Unlike *Le Sacre du printemps,* which confected mythic scenes from pagan Russia, and *La Création du monde,* which turned to Africa at the time of initial chaos, Baker did not model herself after anything. Although she was clearly symbolic of a class of contemporary black American entertainer, she was in the most general sense not an impersonation. She was Josephine Baker, an original, an American Negress in person. Her steps may have been learned, but when she danced the charleston, it was obvious that they were not imported or appliquéd; they were part of her cultural heritage. She may have dubbed her finale "Danse sauvage" to satisfy the current Parisian appetite, but, like the Javanese dancers at the 1889 Exposition, she was the genuine article, and her claim to cultural authenticity was the source of her power.

More than one American black revue in the period around 1910 had included a jungle number.[14] But Baker's comic antics, her exaggeration of facial and body language that combined spiritual and sexual frenzy with the demeanor of a "cynical, merry juggler," was clearly derived from the American minstrel traditon of the nineteenth century. There, in shows populated as well as applauded by blacks, potentially degrading caricature melded with the "near indispensability of exaggeration and grotesque elements in oral-culture entertainments."[15] Although the seemingly pejorative magnification of physical attributes visible in Paul Colin's poster announcing the *Revue nègre* led some later critics to charge that the Negro had been drawn to look like a baboon, it is surely no sanitized report that traces caricature in this instance to minstrelsy's own venerable tradition of parody and burlesque. Though multiple masks had obviously been put into play, it should be recalled that Colin had designed Jean Börlin's costume for *Sculpture nègre* in 1920, and that his work in the theatre characteristically reflected an interest in ethnological and historical perspectives rather than racist portraiture (see Figure 6.4).

The Exposition Internationale des Arts Décoratifs et Industriels Modernes, held in Paris, April–October 1925, just prior to Baker's arrival, was essentially an emblem of the success of France's postwar recovery.

Figure 6.4. Paul Colin, *La Revue nègre at the Théâtre des Champs-Élysées,* 1926. Poster. © 1994 ARS, New York / ADAGP, Paris.

Germany, typically identified as an emblem of barbarism, was excluded from participation. The various regions of France were all represented, emphasizing regional crafts, wines, and materials, together with samples from France's colonial empire in a Pavillon de l'Asie française, which incorporated Vietnamese styles, and a Pavillon de l'Afrique française which employed a "mock-African mud architecture."[16] France, proclaiming itself once more a leading purveyor of taste among nations of the world, openly, and some thought callously, played to the upper middle-class's desire for a return to the good life.

But if one were to believe the Exposition, civilization could now claim "Primitivist" themes as emblems of taste and chic. Midst the names familiar even today, Baccarat crystal, Christofle silver, and Lanvin perfume could be spotted as appeals to prewar aesthetic preferences, now refurbished through generous applications of *luxe*. Jean Puiforcat, whose silver was the very epitome of Art Deco, for example, wrapped sterling circular filaments on his cutlery redolent of spear bindings or the neck rings of Benin bronzes and introduced ivory and ebony handles on his costliest pots and trays that recalled materials from the African tribal lexicon (Figure 6.5).

Primitivism, both folk and tribal, had now been absorbed by urban rites, and in the world of music Afro-American jazz had become the standard bearer. If the reconstitution of jazz as an emblem of Primitivism was a myth, it only joined hands with the myth of Primitivism itself. At the same time jazz provided the long-delayed arrival of a musical analogue to the tribal sculpture that had served the Parisian painters and sculptors for over a decade. The reality of an Afro-American music was not contestable, but the accommodations and modifications of tribal practice to Western systems which had already taken place at the birth of jazz in America were no less significant than those to which it was now to be subjected at the hands of European artists.

The ultimate reputation of a work like *La Création du monde* obviously came to rest upon issues that transcended musical and pictorial style analysis. The interpretation of African art as "the oldest" undoubtedly stemmed from anthropological discussions, already current at that time and continuing to the present day, of Africa as the cradle of civilization. Visual idealizations of the Noble Savage from Gauguin to Picasso now found a counterpart in the world of sound. For the Western European the image of the African was one of naturalness laced with a spirituality that potentially transcended Christianity, Judaism, Islam,

Figure 6.5. Jean Puiforcat, sterling silver spoon and fork, "Cannes" pattern, 1929.

and other institutional religions, and also came to be associated with the ability of certain performers such as Louis Armstrong to "enter the trance."[17] It was a performance demeanor openly discussed a few years later by Zora Neale Hurston with respect to the practice of "shouting," which she attributed to the survival of African traditions involving "possession" by the gods.[18] Paired with this vision of the African was the symbol of America as energetic, vital, and modern. Recalled now through the sounds of jazz, which was contemporary but purportedly of ancient stock, the mixture was infused with overtones of sexual permissiveness, and the resultant art was deemed to be natural and freely born of a miraculous coupling of two continents.

The mythic recovery of the origins of Western art by such circuitous means seemed to many more than a stunning coincidence. American vitality, which had been musically equated with urban energy by John Alden Carpenter in his *Skyscrapers* of 1923–24, was now re-read and merchandized by Josephine Baker as well as Milhaud and Léger as contemporary Primitivism. The fact that their vision was purveyed in the realm of dance emphasizes the debt which both factions owed to noteworthy predecessors: to Diaghilev and the Primitivist program of modern ballet of the teens; to free-spirited female dancers such as Ruth St. Denis and Isadora Duncan; and to Börlin, who shared Rolf de Maré's concern for anthropological verification. In addition, however, the groups of black jazz musicians who toured Europe in the immediate postwar period were also coming increasingly to the notice of the classically trained musician. Now, critics and composers alike, flirting with the heretofore undreamed-of possibilities of crossover, began to sense the power of invoking popular musical images and sounds in tandem with current social messages.

"High-Brow" Critics of Early Jazz

The period of *La Création du monde* (1923) and the *Revue nègre* (1925) and several seasons thereafter witnessed the appearance of a number of assessments of jazz by the critics. Though the assertion of one American that "to our shame, Europeans realized the importance and the value of jazz many years before the Americans who originated it"[19] may be somewhat overstated, the idea and value of a *musique nègre* analogous to *art nègre* and in tune with its aesthetic and societal goals was sorted out by a number of Frenchmen, including Hugues Panassie, Charles Delaunay, and Robert Goffin, and by others frequently resident in Paris, such as the Swiss conductor Ernest Ansermet. The expression "black music," its English equivalent, seldom appeared, though "le jazz" and later "le jazz hot" found a secure place in the French vocabulary.[20] Well before Baker and the *Revue nègre* had arrived in Paris, the city had had its appetite stimulated for ragtime, blues, syncopated dance music, and New Orleans jazz by people like James Reese Europe and Will Marion Cook, and as early as 1917 Louis Mitchell was to be seen with his Jazz Kings at the Casino de Paris. The degree to which American popular styles had already become the fashion not only of the clubs but of high society helps us to understand how Baker could have been so ecstatically received.[21]

The comments of contemporary critics regarding jazz were frequently appreciations that suggested not only the value of the music for its own sake and the performance artistry involved, but its relevance for composers of "high" art. The first writer of international distinction to record his views was Ernest Ansermet, friend of Stravinsky and conductor of several of his premieres. In an article in *La Revue romande* of 1919, he emphasized in descriptive detail the role of timbre, rhythm, scale, and performance practice, and concluded that the essence of jazz must be clearly credited to an American-Negro conscience whose roots predated its appearance in the United States. This attempt to establish the African base of an Afro-American popular music was in harmony with developments of the past decade in French art and literature, and Ansermet, like most commentators on jazz in the next few years, seemed to relish the opportunity to identify a black music that could stand proudly alongside the burgeoning repertoires of *art nègre* in painting, sculpture, and literature.

Expectedly, the emphasis upon rhythm is apparent from the second sentence of Ansermet's article:

This is not about African Negroes but about those of the Southern states of the U.S.A., who have created the musical style commonly known as the rag. Rag music is founded essentially on rhythm and in particular on the qualities of syncopation in rhythm. Rag music first came to Europe in the form of the cake-walk, as I recall, and then with the one-step, two-step, fox-trot, and all the American dances and songs to which the subtitle of rag-time is applied. America is full of small instrumental ensembles devoted to rag-time, and if the national music of a people is none other than its popular music, one can say that rag-time has become the true national popular music of America. Today, rag-time has conquered Europe; we dance to rag-time under the name of jazz in all our cities . . . Rag-time is even passing into what I will call for lack of another name, the field of learned music: Stravinsky has used it as material for several works, Debussy has already written a cake-walk, and I well believe Ravel will lose no time in giving us a fox-trot.[22] But, under the name of Southern Syncopated Orchestra, there is an ensemble of authentic musicians of Negro race to be heard in London.

Ansermet speaks of Will Marion Cook, the conductor of the Southern Syncopated Orchestra, as "a master in every respect," and of the group's arresting ensemble, fervor, and taste. His principal observation, however, concerns a distinction between source material and perfor-

mance style. Noting ragtime performances based on the "Wedding
March" from Mendelssohn's *Midsummer Night's Dream,* a celebrated
Prelude of Rachmaninoff, and a Debussy chord progression, Ansermet
concluded:

> Thus, all, or nearly all, the music of the Southern Syncopated Orches-
> tra is, in origin, foreign to these Negroes. How is this possible? Be-
> cause it is not the material that makes Negro music, it is the spirit . . .
> The Negro population of North America is African in origin . . . All
> the traditional Negro songs are strewn with syncopes which issue from
> the voice while the movement of the body marks the regular rhythm
> . . . syncopation itself is but the effect of an expressive need . . . in
> a word, the genius of the race.[23]

Turning to questions of timbre and performance practice, Ansermet
praises the Negro by noting the ability of trombonist, clarinetist, and
saxophonist alike to vibrate each note with a perpetual quivering of the
slide or the magic of lip work in discovering the expressive quality of
the "slightly inferior appoggiatura." He praises the finesse of their instrumentation, which he compares to that of Ravel, and also the
mournful quality of their blues. He concludes his panegyric with a salute
to the artistry of the ensemble's clarinet player, whom he mentions by
name, Sidney Bechet, and predicts that the whole world will soon follow the path which he is setting out.

Sidney Bechet, a clarinetist and soprano saxophonist, was born in
New Orleans in 1897. In a memoir of the 1960s Bechet spoke of his
grandfather Omar's days as a slave and fantasized his African roots in a
warm and wonderful way, claiming that the slave dreamed and remembered the old chants, dances, and drum calls, and then reinvented his
African legacy.[24] Later in Chicago, Bechet met Will Marion Cook, who
studied first at Oberlin and then in Berlin, where he became a pupil
of Joachim and Dvořák. Cook took pains not to describe the music
played by his Southern Syncopated Orchestra as jazz, in the hope of
more lasting acclaim. But with Bechet aboard he not only highlighted
his jazz expertise in *Characteristic Blues* but showcased him as the penultimate number on the show.

Speaking of Cook and his offer to take him with him to London,
Bechet remembered his exposure to Ansermet with obvious pleasure;
he noted that a Swiss conductor, Ernest Ansermet, had attended all of
their performances and continually quizzed about how he played his

instrument: "Many a time he'd come over to where I was and he'd ask me all about how I was playing, what it was I was doing, was I singing into my instrument to make it sound that way? . . . This man, he was trained for classical, but he had a real interest in our music. There was just no end to the questions he could think to ask about it."[25] Ansermet ultimately wrote a review of the orchestra, and stated that he was moved by "the astonishing perfection, the superb taste, and the fervor of its playing." In conclusion, he singled out Bechet as the "the first of his race to have composed perfectly formed blues on the clarinet" and labeled him an "artist of genius."

The accolades of the high priests of classical music were one thing, but when Cook's orchestra was invited to play at Buckingham Palace in August 1919, Bechet was suddenly made aware of the social cachet that had begun to accrue to *art nègre* in both London and Paris. His memory of the event is totally disarming:

> Well, I didn't know what to say to a thing like that, walking right into a King's palace. I didn't know what to expect, but the way it turned out, it was just bigger than another place; it was like Grand Central Station with a lot of carpet and things on the walls. Only it had more doors . . . Once we got started we had the whole royal family tapping their feet. There was over a thousand people there. Will told me later that he'd asked them what it was they'd enjoyed most, and the King said it was that blues, the *Characteristic Blues*. But there was a funny thing I was thinking there between numbers when I was looking at the King. It was the first time I ever got to recognize somebody from having seen his picture on my money.[26]

It was not the first time that Cook had played to British royalty, however, for following a popular success in New York with his show *In Dahomey,* he had taken it to London in April 1903, where he found a similar public response following its requested presentation as part of a birthday party celebration for the young Prince of Wales.[27] This time around, however, even Edward J. Dent, musicologist and Cambridge don, signaled his capitulation to Bechet's rendition of *Characteristic Blues* in an article which appeared in *The Athenaeum* of September 26, 1919. Bechet had conquered the academy (Dent), the podium (Ansermet), and the palace (King George V). During the 1920s Bechet recorded with Louis Armstrong, played with Duke Ellington (1924–25), and continued to tour Europe over a number of years. He was there at the time of Josephine Baker's *Revue nègre* in 1925, but his later recollection of it, though positive, is brief: "The show was a great success. Josephine and Louis [Douglas], I remember, danced the Charleston and nobody in Europe had seen that dance before, and that really started something. That show really had Paris going. All the critics and all the papers were writing it up, and the house was full every night."[28] There are several reasons for the terseness of his report. Will Marion Cook had offered advice to Mrs. Caroline Dudley in the initial stages of the production, but Bechet, who participated in the revue, was ultimately limited to backing up some of the special dances and to a big feature number as a jazz-playing fruit seller. Dudley later regretted that she had not featured him more prominently. As the wife of the commercial attaché at the American Embassy, she had entrée to Parisian high society, which could, and did, flock to the production and turn it into a roaring success—a success with the smart set it should be added, though not with the hoi polloi.[29] Its run of two weeks led to other engagements, however, including the Moulin Rouge for the band and Baker, and later for Baker alone when the Folies-Bergère recalled her from Berlin, where the revue had booked an engagement. The *Revue nègre* was not Bechet's final brush with Paris, however. Following a period in the United States during the New Orleans revival in the late 1930s, he returned to Europe in 1949, and it was in France that he died in 1959.

Jonny Strikes Up

The continuing juxtaposition of social questions, racial claims, and questions of artistic evaluation in the growing infatuation with the blend of "high" and "low" were soon tested in the realm of opera with Ernst Krenek's *Jonny spielt auf* of 1927. Krenek's initial brush with jazz lacked the richness of Milhaud's personal confrontation, but the pianist Artur Schnabel was to Krenek what Ansermet had been to Stravinsky in providing sheet music and perhaps recordings. Justly considered the first example of a genuine *Zeitoper,* both with respect to its topicality and its handling of the popular musical elements (jazz ensemble, blues, gramophones), *Jonny* gave Krenek his first success by pitting the anxieties of the artist-composer, Max, symbolic of the inhibited Central European intellectual, against the uninhibitedness of Jonny, the American negro jazz fiddler. At the end of the opera the composer catches the train on the first leg of the journey to America, land of dreams. Such a vision of America was shared by many Europeans in the post–

World War I period and helps to account for the growing craze for its popular music. In contrasting Max with Jonny, Krenek appropriated the jazz idiom only for the latter, and for Max and Anita, the opera singer, he wrote in an openly Romantic idiom "occasionally touched up with dissonant spices and Italianizing Pucciniesque vocal exuberance."[30] The popular note was spelled aurally by a heady mixture of "Shimmy," "Blues" ("Leb wohl, mein Schatz"), and "Tango" ("O rêverie, doucement infinie"). But Krenek made other notations in the score, such as "im Ton eines Niggerliedes, im Ton eines Neger-Spirituals," and borrowed musical materials which vivified Jonny's ethnic character, including the same quotation of "Swanee River" used by Irving Berlin in his "Alexander's Ragtime Band," now labeled an "Altes amerikanisches Negerlied."

But citation does not guarantee stylistic authenticity, and Krenek's approach to jazz is but another example of good intentions being mislead by what the composer perceived as an Ur-text. For Krenek's model would appear to have been of the kind offered by Sam Wooding's orchestra in Berlin. One of the finest of the mid-twenties, Wooding's group was one of innumerable New York ensembles who flooded Europe, playing all the way from Spain to Russia. On their tours, however, they were part of the revue *Chocolate Kiddies,* and Gunther Schuller informs us that rather than showcasing their most original manner they played " 'sophisticated' revue music, a hodge-podge of 'symphonic' introductions and modulations, interspersed with the big tunes from the show and an occasional improvised solo."[31] But, if Wooding's group was in some respects Harlem's answer to Paul Whiteman and Krenek's model therefore distorted, the composer's familiarity with other carriers of jazz is verifiable not only in the music but in the libretto. Finally, whatever the source and range of the ingredients, they constituted a message that had been brought to Europe by black American musicians themselves, and as such were part of an evolving and composite tradition.

Jonny was critically well received in Germany, even tumultuously so in some quarters. But because of the timely libretto joined to jazz and dance idioms, critics concocted numerous terms to skirt the idea of its being an opera: *Opernrevue, Musikkomödie, Buffo-Opera, Jazzoper, Gegenwartsoper,* and *Zeitopernrevue.* It was the last term that survived in abbreviated form.[32] Alfred Baresel, friend of American jazz and a renowned critic of the *Neue Leipziger Zeitung,* hailed the hero as "Neue Sachlichkeit in Schwarz" and dubbed the work the first *Jazzoper.* His opinion was echoed by the Berlin critic Oskar Bie, who claimed *Jonny* was "one of the most fantastic works of all opera history." Yet *Jonny* would probably not have been possible without the mixture of Parisian developments and Dada's devotion to *art nègre*. Nevertheless, through juxtaposition as opposed to fusion, Krenek's opera projected the contrast between high and low art more vividly than before, and in this it struck a new note.

But there were problems at the social level, not so much through the contrast of high and low music as through the contrast of black and white on the same stage with various romantic-sexual overtones. Furthermore, the opera was clearly vulnerable in its inclusion of familiar stereotypes: Jonny is a black, popular entertainer, intuitive rather than rational, not a composer of "high" art music, and is portrayed as both licentious and a thief. Rather than casting the role with a black singer, however, he was played in blackface, which carried potential connotations of a patronizing minstrelsy. Reports in the press prior to the Munich premiere on June 16, 1929, conspicuously misrepresented the theme of the opera and erroneously reported that the title role was to be sung by a black singer. Alfred Jerger, who performed the Munich Jonny, reported that when he commenced "Jetzt ist die Geige mein," stinkbombs went off, fights broke out, the manager stopped the performance, and the police were required to restore order. A large crowd assembled backstage and threatened to lynch him until his white identity was revealed. Aware of their error, they hoisted Jerger to their shoulders and carried him back to their hotel.[33] Fear of a similar reaction at the Metropolitan Opera premiere in New York led to recasting Jonny as a white bandleader in blackface, and Olin Downes noted that the issues of race had been "tactfully avoided."[34]

Although the African component, by comparison with that in *La Création du monde* or the *Revue nègre*, was now reasonably submerged, the alliance between Afro-American jazz and Primitivist mythology's claims to aesthetic relevance in the here and now—lavishly developed over the past two decades—was clear. Nothing could more vividly demonstrate the reality of such a confederation than the knowledge that it was on a visit to Paris in December of 1924 that Krenek first conceived the idea of writing *Jonny*. It has even been claimed that Sidney Bechet was the obvious model for the principal character given the time and place, though the composer has gone on record that he had no particular performer in mind. Krenek did admit, however, that

Jonny spielt auf was written for Paris, and portions of the opera are located there, accompanied by appropriate infusions of French in the libretto. Consequently, it must have been disappointing to him that, though the opera enjoyed a resounding success with forty-five different performances during the 1927–28 season in Berlin, Zagreb, Ljubljana, and Antwerp, Paris responded unenthusiastically to it at its premiere at the Théâtre des Champs-Elysées on June 21, 1928.

Other *Zeitopern* and orchestral works which followed made periodic use of references to jazz. But the jazz impulse tended to be accommodated to newly developing techniques of expression, and its essential blackness began to disappear. William Grant Still's *Afro-American Symphony* of 1930 is an obvious exception; Gershwin's *Porgy and Bess* another. And Thomson's opera *Four Saints in Three Acts* garnered the forces of negritude as an afterthought, though with specific virtues in mind. The capacity for this kind of virile transformation deserves to be momentarily explored.

Thomson and Copland: Composers as Jazz Critics

Retracing the history of opera, Virgil Thomson forwarded the insightful opinion that the vocal line in most operas from Monteverdi to Berg and Stravinsky had remained the same; it was, he believed, the instrumental accompaniment that defined an opera's relation to its age. The truth of Thomson's assertion can be tested by comparing the last act of Stravinsky's *Le Rossignol* with the earlier acts, composed some years before: the progressiveness of the last act is achieved almost solely by means of the orchestral writing, the vocal style remaining virtually unchanged (see Example 2.2). Thomson's own *Four Saints in Three Acts,* completed in short score in 1928 and premiered in 1934, was set to a plotless, highly discursive, and openly hermetic libretto by Gertrude Stein that virtually demanded special treatment. Thomson was specific and analytical about the solution which he offered:

> Now the *Four Saints* accompaniment is as odd as its text, so odd, indeed, that it has sometimes been taken for childish. In fact, many persons not closely involved with either poetry or music but mildly attached to all contemporary artwork by the conviction that it is thrifty to be stylish have for more than thirty years now been worried by my use of what seems to them a backward-looking music idiom in connection with a forward-looking literary one. That worry can only

be argued against by denying the assumption that discord is advanced and harmoniousness old-fashioned.[35]

What Thomson constructed was a relationship between voice and accompaniment that allowed the perception of new relationships precisely because of the simplicity of the constituent materials. Thomson buttressed Stein's method and language through a collection of familiar components whose matter-of-factness was matched by the irrationality of unforeseen juxtaposition.[36] He may also have taken satisfaction in noting the compatibility of such an approach with the improvisatory techniques that stood at the heart of jazz as well as Dada.

In his discussion of *Four Saints* John Cage mischievously calculated that Thomson used 111 tonic/dominants, 178 scale passages, 632 sequences, 38 references to nursery tunes, and one quotation of "My country, 'tis of Thee."[37] Such an analysis, for all its whimsicality, fails to convey the thrust of Thomson's remark. It is the relation of voice to accompaniment visible in the opening measures of the opera that constitutes the radical component: a four-square chorus part receives a mismatched harmonization due to the latter's triple metric organization in a style not unrelated to that in Thomson's *Variations and Fugues on Sunday School Tunes* for organ (1926). (See Example 6.1.)

Now this is not jazz, nor was Thomson given to incorporating the jazz mode into his music to any appreciable degree; his was more a heady mixture of tango from the dance hall, accordion from the cabaret, reed organ from the country church, and recitation tone derived from liturgical chant. Nonetheless, he was an early critic of jazz; indeed, he later claimed to have been the first to subject it to musical analysis in an article which appeared in *Vanity Fair* as early as 1924. Later Thomson noted, however, that the

> journalists kept licking their chops over the "jazz age" long after the Charleston had become a standard feature of American life. This dance coming up in 1925 was quite without relation to the real "jazz age," which since 1912 had practiced a slow, almost motionless dancing in close position. On the contrary, the Charleston's alert tempo and Caribbean beat (of 3/8–3/8–2/8) led not to petting in public but to the jitterbugging that was to mark the late 1930s, even to disengaged elegance, as in the Lambeth Walk.[38]

In light of Thomson's observations concerning the rhythmic component of the charleston and the musical evidence at the opening of *Four*

Example 6.1. Virgil Thomson. *Four Saints in Three Acts,* "Prologue," mm. 1–6.

Copyright © 1933, 1948 (renewed) by G. Schirmer, Inc. (ASCAP).

Saints, it is of some interest to note Aaron Copland's description of the evolution of the charleston rhythm in an article which appeared in 1927 entitled "Jazz Structure and Influence."[39] Here Copland, while allowing that jazz may well have originated on "some negro's dull tomtom in Africa," argued against an intuitive judgment of its characteristic features and for "a study of the mechanics of its frame."

Copland describes the rhythmic foundation of ragtime as an unchanging 4/4 time with accents on the first and third beat in the bass. Over this bass he locates two mandatory rhythms, either or both of which may be used: dotted eighth followed by sixteenth or the ordinary syncopation (sixteenth–eighth–sixteenth). He goes on to claim that

> modern jazz began with the fox trot. For this new dance the four-quarter bass was used as in ragtime but at a considerably slower pace and miraculously improved by accenting the least obvious beats, the second and fourth . . . With this was combined another rhythmic element . . . which is generally supposed to be a kind of 1–2–3–4 and is always written [as eight eighth notes with the fourth and fifth tied].

This notation, however, is deceptive, as Mr. Knowlton has pointed out . . . He was the first to show that this jazz rhythm . . . contains no syncopation; it is instead a rhythm of four quarters split into eight eighths and is arranged thus: 3 + 5 . . . or even more precisely 3 + 3 + 2. Put this over the four-quarter bass [musical example] and you have the play of two independent rhythms within the space of one measure. It is the beginning, it is a molecule of jazz. Whatever melody is subjected to this procedure comes out jazzed . . .

The next step infinitely complicated these, in fact it produced poly-rhythms. In employing two rhythms within one measure jazz after all merely did something that had been done before, if we remember, for instance, the use of older composers of 3/4 against 6/8. But the next era in the jazz age—typified by the song *Stumbling*—saw inde-pendent rhythms spread over more than one measure, over a series of measures: That is, while the conventional 4/4 bass was retained, the melody was put into 3/4 time.

A comparison with the opening of Thomson's *Four Saints in Three Acts* reveals that the metric relationship of accompaniment to melody is the same as in "Stumbling," only reversed. Thomson's claim that its essence could be characterized by this melody-accompaniment rela-tionship clearly promotes its affinity with contemporary developments involving the interface of "high" and "low" musical repertoires. It was an issue that Stravinsky had begun to explore in the teens before his exposure to American popular styles, but that in the early 1920s was undoubtedly further clarified under its aegis.

Copland finished his observations by pursuing the topic as it related to Gershwin and the charleston:

George Gershwin was the composer who took most advantage of the discovery made with *Stumbling*. His *Fascinating Rhythm* is rhythmically not only the most fascinating but the most original jazz song yet com-posed.

With the introduction of the Charleston the most tyrannical ele-ment of our popular music—the evenly rhythmed bass—was elimi-nated for the space of a few measures at least. The Charleston consists of the upper fox trot rhythm: 3 + 5 (eighths) used below as well as above instead of the formerly unflagging 1–2–3–4 bass [musical example].

The charleston was danced by every flapper of the 1920s, and its reconstruction as an emblem of *musique nègre* may appear strained. But it is of no small interest that many years later the venerable musicologist Curt Sachs, in *The Wellsprings of Music,* located the presence of additive meters in numerous cultures in India and the Middle East, and concluded with an opinion that may well have been based upon a reading of Copland: "Africa also favors the ubiquitous meter $3 + 3 + 2$ . . . This 'Fascinating Rhythm'—title of one of Gershwin's piano pieces—has an important key position in nearly every chapter of music history, from the Orient way up to our twentieth century with hot jazz and the Charleston."[40]

Now Copland's view of the subtlety of jazz rhythms is commendable enough, but his attempt as a composer to sort out its technical foundation got him into trouble with several later critics.[41] Yet this analysis of the "mechanics of the frame" of jazz by a composer in search of an American signature was clearly tuned to contemporary compositional interest in folk-based metric structures articulated by Bartók and others. The continually shifting set of relationships common to secondary ragtime rhythms was also a feature undoubtedly familiar to Copland through numerous scores of Stravinsky.[42] The pedagogy of Nadia Boulanger, Copland's teacher from 1920 to 1924, leaned heavily upon Stravinsky's example, and it is difficult to escape the feeling that Copland's 1927 article was in some large measure written in an attempt to credit a burgeoning national expression with qualities analogous to both ethnically based avant-garde practices in Europe and indigenous African-American repertoires.

The search for an authorial model could have sent Copland to a study of the Pléiade in sixteenth-century French literature as well as to the contemporanous anacreontic meters of Claude le Jeune's *musique mesurée.* But, unlike Olivier Messiaen, who was to tap both sources only shortly thereafter, Copland realized that the function of the rest in the charleston along with its tempo and insistent instrumental support invited endorsement of a non-European lineage instead. Listeners were happy, too, to learn of the possibility of a non-Western model, and when Josephine Baker danced the charleston in her Paris review, she quickly established it as an emblem of Afro-American culture. Its power was fixed when it made its way onto the high-society dance floors.

True, it had become so customary for contemporary fashion to embrace black culture that distinctions between black and white, high and low may now have appeared compromised. Let there be no mistake, however. If the multiplicity of societal allusions seemed to camouflage

Figure 6.6. Fernand Léger, costume design for *La Création du monde,* 1922–23.

Collection Kay Hillman, New York. © 1994 ARS, New York / SPADEM, Paris.

Figure 6.7. Chokwe figure of angola wood. Published in Carl Einstein, *Negerplastik,* 1915.

The Pushkin Museum, Moscow.

the categories, the thrill of the charleston and jazz in all their guises continued to stem from the belief that in essence they were black music. American blacks took pride in claiming the music as their own; American whites relished in asserting its Americanness in lieu of an internationally recognized folk repertoire;[43] and Europeans of all stripes devoured it as exotica, as a belated *musique nègre.* Finally, for *le beau monde*—museum goers, artists, collectors, and high-society dancers on both sides of the Atlantic—the bent knees and protruding derrière of

Figure 6.8. Jean Börlin's costume by Paul Colin for *Sculpture nègre,* 1920.
Photo, Dansmuseet, Stockholm.

the charleston itself suggested an affinity with many an African sculpture. Indeed, the juxtaposition of a Chokwe figure, a Léger design, and photographs of Börlin and Baker does not falsify the intimacy of a verifiable lineage (Figures 6.6–6.9). Its genealogy and pedigree were also undoubtedly well known to Martha Graham, who from 1934 on began to develop a vocabulary of American visual metaphors that relied upon the "vigor and sparseness of Shaker and American Indian design . . . [and] the syncopated rhythms and mobile hips of black American styles."[44]

The decade of the 1920s was a turning point in the relationship between the music of black and white Americans: for the first time, black

Figure 6.9. *La Revue nègre:* Percy Johnson (drums), Louis Douglas, Josephine Baker, Bass Hill (tuba), Claude Hopkins (piano), Joe Hayman (saxophone), and Daniel Day (trombone).

musical culture was endorsed as an essential part of the collective American expression. In the process the role of black music was increasingly romanticized to a degree that vied with the sentiment of the Europeans. The diverse reflections of this romanticization can be seen in Virgil Thomson's infatuation with discrete aspects of American black culture and his simultaneous endorsement of the Dadaist infatuation with European *art nègre. Four Saints in Three Acts* sported an all-Negro cast, though the opera is purportedly set in the Spanish Baroque. On the surface the casting may be dismissed as irrelevant, but John Houseman, who directed the first production, made a revealing observation when he told Thomson that "this could have been for Etienne de Beaumont's Soirées de Paris." Furthermore, Thomson's own observations regarding the value of using a Negro cast clearly reflect the pervasive Dadaist infatuation with the Primitive as constituted by black culture. Observing that the Negroes did not resist Stein's obscure language but adopted it and and even conversed in quotations from it, he also remarked on the grace and lack of self-consciousness in their movement, speech, and song.

A review of the terms which marked the original productions of *Four Saints* and *Jonny* should assist in removing the taint of a racist manifesto that has been periodically charged to both and perhaps encourage their return to the stage today. The two-pronged dismissal of *Jonny* in particular—stemming from the portrayal of a black as an intuitive and not particularly admirable jazz musician on the one hand and from the glorification, unacceptable to the Nazis, of black popular styles on the other—is enough to give pause to all.

European Postscripts and Farewells

It would be wrong to suggest, however, that the "high" taste for jazz was forced underground solely by the political pressures of a changing world order. The reevaluation of the power of jazz for the composer of art music is epitomized in the writings of Darius Milhaud in the period 1925–26. His original comments of 1925 are both analytical and laudatory of the Afro-American spirit. He notes that the force and novelty of jazz's technique stems principally from the employment of syncopation by a small but versatile ensemble[45] and a harmonic vocabulary that was gradually assimilating the most recent developments of contemporary music. Citing use of chords of the dominant seventh and ninth in all the latest dances as well as the simultaneous use of major and minor in Zez Confrey's "Kitten on the Keys," he predicted that "in a few years polytonal and atonal harmonies will be routine in those dances which are successor to the shimmy of 1920."[46]

Beyond technical matters, however, and following the taste of the day, Milhaud continued to insist on attributing the essence of jazz to the primitive soul of the North American Negro: "The primitive African side remains profoundly anchored in the blacks of the United States, and it is there that we must find the source of this formidable rhythmic force as well as their expressive melodies, which possess a lyricism such as only oppressed races can produce."[47] Reviewing the use of the jazz idiom in the theatre, Milhaud cited Noble Sissle, Eubie Blake, and others, noted the security yet seeming abandon of their jazz improvisations, and concluded with a set of familiar subscriptions: "Among them the dance preserves an African and savage character, the insistance and the intensity of their rhythms and their melodies being based upon tragedy and despair."[48]

These comments, in the main insightful and appreciative, were originally made in an article which appeared in German in 1925. It is something of a surprise, therefore, to read Milhaud's announcement of jazz's waning fashion in 1926, wherein he states that the recipe for jazz has been reduced to a set of condiments and is being served up in various method books of the time, especially the three recently published volumes of the Winn School of Popular Music: the breaks, the passing discords, the broken harmonies, arpeggios, trills, ornaments, variations, cadences, trombone glissandos, the quivering movement of its slide. Recently returned to Paris from Russia in 1926, Milhaud announced the end of the jazz craze. The original appeal of Harlem for Milhaud on his first visit there in 1922 had resided not only in its novelty for him but in what he sensed as the genuineness of its musical expression; by 1926, however, in the face of a social exchange that had promoted Harlem to vogue status and placed it on the tourist circuit, Milhaud's interest had dissolved. The seasonal fickleness of fashion had spoiled his show.[49]

In retrospect, however, it is clear that Milhaud's response was a tardy one. For Georges Auric's fox trot "Adieu, New York!" of 1919 had been quickly followed by an article "Bonjour, Paris!" that appeared in the May 1920 issue of *Le Coq* in which he suggested that he had intended "Adieu, New York!" as "a final tribute to jazz, a work that would close the period of American influence."[50] Nonetheless Auric's personal example in the elimination of blue notes, syncopations, and other signifiers of jazz was not quickly followed; clearly there were more than a few spasms of consequence that remained to be played out.

For despite the unarguable urge to invoke a call to order with the Armistice of 1918, the vitalizing qualities of Primitivism would not readily disperse, and they not unoccasionally wedded with prevailing Neoclassic aspirations—Ravel's Violin Sonata of 1927 and his two piano concertos, both begun in 1929, being only the most obvious examples. Indeed, it was precisely at the end of World War I that Western European audiences, who had never had the musical equivalent of African-inspired painting, sculpture, clothing, and design at their disposal and who had therefore been obliged to search out touchstones of the musical Primitive through reconstitutions of the Folk and the Orient, were unexpectedly confronted with a powerful black imagery for the first time through the importation of jazz. Now a genuine black music had miraculously materialized, unhypothetical, "real," and updated, and for many it was too potent a source to consign to a brief flirtation.

Among the purveyors of "high" art, not only Milhaud and Ravel, but Stravinsky, Hindemith, and Copland had early recognized its potential as a somewhat ancillary, if natural and compelling, ally. Among the performers involved in shaping the parameters of the "low," too, there began to surface an awareness that their audience was increasingly drawn from across a vastly enlarged social spectrum. Indeed, for a significant number their venue had shifted from Chicago and the Harlem clubs to Buckingham Palace and the Théâtre des Champs-Élysées. American black musicians and performers no doubt soon realized that the European exhilaration over American jazz lay in its potent role as a companion to the fashion of *art nègre*. While James Collier has rightfully taken pains to show America's interest in jazz virtually from its inception and to disclaim the notion that Europe discovered American jazz,[51] sight ought not be lost of the fact that the passion for jazz in Europe—which was based on totally different social perspectives from those operative in America—brought more than a little cachet to Negro jazz artists. In turn this no doubt intensified America's perception of a native art and encouraged a steady escalation of claims for it.

As the taste for black themes and music continued to prosper in London, Paris, and Berlin from the mid-1920s through the early 1930s, back in America a newly proclaimed Harlem Renaissance had affirmed heightened aspirations in art, literature, and music for the New Negro. The story of music's response to this call is somewhat more complex than in the visual and literary arts, and must be judged in the light of an expanded range of social perspectives. But as the Harlem Renaissance struggled to prolong its voice both at home and abroad and the Third Reich moved to surpress it; as American white authors and musicians explored black themes on the legitimate stage, in musical theater, and in opera—frequently in tandem with black stars; an English lady living in Paris named Nancy Cunard sought to complement the work of the most articulate spokesman for the New Negro, Alain Locke, to expand their common frame of reference, to proclaim a contemporary awareness, and to offer a momentary ray of hope for the future.

— 7 —

The Cunard Line

Some modern poets contend that jazz and music-hall songs are
the folk art of our time, that we should mould our art upon
them; we Irish, modern men also, reject every folk art that does
not go back to Olympus. Give me time and a little youth and
I will prove that even "Johnny I hardly knew ye" goes back.

William Butler Yeats

Negro

Nancy Cunard (1896–1965) was born into the life of the English privileged class. Her mother, Lady Cunard, brought her as a girl to Paris
and introduced her to Gertrude Stein, "and very solemnly bade her
never forget the visit."[1] By exposure, event, and temperament she ultimately turned her back upon her family, openly attacked her mother
in a pamphlet which she sent to everyone of social and political station,
took a black lover, Henry Crowder, paraded him in white society,
flirted with Communism, and ultimately tried to enlist the best of her
thoughts and friendships into the production of an anthology entitled
Negro. Unlike Blaise Cendrars's *Anthologie nègre,* a collection of African
tales and myths published earlier in the decade, this was meant to praise
contemporary black culture through the glorification of its art, music,
and literature, and to engage in a war against bigotry.

On the surface, her ambition and agenda were noble; in practice,
she was as capable of hurt as those she complained about. There can
be no doubt, however, that her outrage over racial prejudice of all kinds
was genuine, and her willingness to suffer alienation and risk disinher-
itance was extraordinary.

Her whirlwind escapades belong to another story, but the degree to
which she mirrored the infatuation of high society with black culture

164

belongs to the present one. Yet there was a difference. Rather than using her passion for black culture strictly as an emblem of chic, she took the plight of Negroes to heart and embraced their struggle against discrimination. Beginning in 1920, when she moved to Paris, she systematically developed a rapport with the talented and the powerful, making a procession of friends and enemies along the way, and taking pride in her residency in a city whose newspapers were capable of displaying the headline "Paris, Coeur de la Race Noire."

Cunard's fascination with black culture, like that of many of her class, had come increasingly to dominate her personal life, but by her thirtieth birthday in 1926 it had become a crusade. In that year she formed an amorous liaison with the Surrealist poet Louis Aragon. Two years later in 1928 she and her cousin happened to hear a group of American jazz musicians playing at the Hotel Luna in Venice. The pianist, Henry Crowder, whom Nancy met that night, was to change things forever.[2] Back in Paris, Aragon now out of her life, Cunard not only took Crowder as her lover and assistant in the operations of her Hours Press, but through troubled times and endless separations she forged with him a series of personal campaigns and clarified her devotion to issues of race. Crowder's appearances with her in public places and as hotel companion raised eyebrows and provoked outrage as well as permanent estrangement from her mother, Lady Cunard. Her Black Crusade had begun, and her devotion to Africa was visible to all in the display of her sizable collection of thick African ivory bracelets, two to four inches wide, which frequently adorned her arms in great number. A photograph of ivory bracelets of diverse regions from the collection of Nancy Cunard appears in *Negro,* and the underlying caption clearly suggests their role as fetishes in her personal life:

> Amongst the Ibo people in Nigeria the most valuable and the most prized of all forms of adornments are the anklets and bracelets of ivory. These can only be worn by rich women or by such as are of high rank . . . The anklets are about 9 inches in depth by from 2 to 3 inches in thickness; the bracelets vary in size . . . Once they are on the limbs (they are forced over feet or hands after a course of powerful massage with oil) they are not removed till death.[3]

A photograph of 1930 by Cecil Beaton discloses not only the dramatic flair with which she wore her bracelets but also a black skullcap, which for all its haute couture origins, clearly approximated the brilliantined hair of Josephine Baker and other black entertainers (Figure 7.1).

Figure 7.1. Nancy Cunard, 1930s.

Photo by Cecil Beaton. Courtesy of Sotheby's London.

Cunard acknowledged that her sympathy with African Americans had begun with music, and it was in 1931 that she made the first of two visits to Harlem. But by this time the Harlem Renaissance—epitomized by Alain Locke's *The New Negro* of 1925 and a group of writers, including Langston Hughes, Sterling Brown and Claude McKay, all of whom had located publishers thanks to the support of white patrons like Carl Van Vechten—had begun to flounder. Cunard was puzzled by the American Negro's lack of interest in his African heritage, was troubled by the white man's commandeering of Harlem night spots that no longer admitted black customers, and came to reject the world of Van Vechten's *Nigger Heaven,* which portrayed Harlem as "nothingmore whatsoever than a round of hooch-filled night clubs after a round of snow-filled boudoirs."[4]

Ultimately Locke was to make a contribution to Cunard's *Negro* with a brief entry entitled "Sterling Brown: The New Negro Folk-Poet," in which he sounded a warning against imitation of the false-Negro dialect of Paul Dunbar and other early Negro poets. The authority of Locke's voice was much greater, however, than the dimensions of his entry might suggest. Educated at Harvard, where he was elected to Phi Beta Kappa, he was the first American Negro to be awarded a Rhodes scholarship, in 1907. Following Oxford, he studied for two years at the University of Berlin, and in 1912 he returned to America as a professor of education and later philosophy at Howard University.

The catalytic role of Locke's *New Negro* can hardly be exaggerated. Like Nancy Cunard's *Negro,* for which it provided a model, it was an appreciation of the contributions and more especially a heralding of the potential of a people. Like *Negro,* Locke's volume was also an anthology, and his name appears on the title page as editor, though he made contributions throughout. There were critical essays but also generous samplings of fiction, poetry, and drama, as well as a section on music that included an article by Locke himself called "The Negro Spirituals," another by J. A. Rogers labeled "Jazz at Home," and two poems by Langston Hughes titled "Jazzonia" and "Nude Young Dancer." Although to my knowledge its author never verified the meaning of the last of these, readers of the volume when it first appeared in November 1925 could hardly have kept the image of Josephine Baker from coming to mind. Regardless of whether the model was specific or generic, Hughes paints a compelling portrait of a Negress whose dances—powerful alternatives to both the traditional and the acceptable—are viewed as latter-day companions to Nijinsky's memorable scandal in *Prélude à "L'Après-midi d'un faune."* The poem reads as follows:

> What jungle tree have you slept under
> Midnight dancer of the jazzy hour?
> What great forest has hung its perfume
> Like a sweet veil about your bower?

> What jungle tree have you slept under,
> Dark brown girl of the swaying hips?
> What stark-white moon has been your lover?
> To what mad faun have you offered your lips?

When Cunard returned to Europe from Harlem, she began to visit the ethnological museums, especially the Tervueren Museum near Brussels, in search of material and began to address endless letters to literary friends asking for their contributions to her own projected anthology. The plan called for a documentary book about "what is Negro and descended from Negro" and a circular produced in April 1931 plotted its potential contents: (1) writings and photographs of contemporary Negroes in Europe, the Americas, and the West Indies: (2) a musical section to be organized by the composer George Antheil which would include reproductions of nineteenth- and twentieth-century compositions, including spirituals, jazz, blues, and African tribal music; (3) ethnographical studies including reproductions of African art, ivory carvings, explorers data, and recent photographs; and (4) political and sociological studies by French, English, and American writers including reports on the colonial system, accounts of lynchings, persecution, and racial prejudice.[5]

The book was also to contain poems by and about Negroes, a list of museums containing African art together with reproductions, and documentary articles by Englishmen and Americans concerning the question of color in the United States and Europe. Cunard invited contributions from Negroes and whites alike, and counted on the sympathy and offerings of old friends such as Ezra Pound, Norman Douglas, Harold Acton, and the French Surrealists. Her initial introduction to the themes of *Negro* has been attributed to her meeting and ensuing friendship with Tristan Tzara, one of the inventors of Dada, who dedicated his play *Mouchoir des nuages* to her and introduced her to Brancusi, who made a sculpture of her entitled *Jeune fille sophistiquée.* Not only had Brancusi's *Beginning of the World* of 1924 dramatically reflected the contemporaneous themes of Milhaud and Léger, but his *White Negress* of 1923, the year in which Nancy Cunard moved permanently to Paris, uncannily, if unconsciously, mirrored the black–white fusion which she personified. His specific portrait of Cunard (1925–1927), a dark-toned wooden sculpture in which the face is elongated and reduced to a blank, reflects Brancusi's continuing preoccupation with ovoidal forms more than a search for personal characteristics. Yet something of Nancy's gaiety is captured in the crowning whorl, which appears to represent a more vivacious version of the topknot in *The White Negress* (Figures 7.2, 7.3).

Figure 7.2. Constantin Brancusi, *The White Negress,* 1923.

Philadelphia Museum of Art; Louise and Walter Arensberg Collection. © 1994 ARS, New York / ADAGP, Paris.

Figure 7.3. Constantin Brancusi, portrait of Nancy Cunard, 1925–1927.

Mr. and Mrs. Raymond D. Nasher, Dallas. © 1994 ARS, New York / ADAGP, Paris.

Oskar Kokoschka also painted Cunard's picture, and Wyndham Lewis created a memorable drawing of her ringed in her collection of ivory bracelets. She was photographed by Man Ray with Tzara on his knees kissing her hand before the Bal Beaumont of 1924 and by Cecil Beaton in the most classic pose of all. Ultimately she was spotted as the heroine in Michael Arlen's novel *The Green Hat,* and Aldous Huxley openly modeled Lucy Tantamount after her in *Point Counter Point.* Throughout the twenties she followed the Parisian avant-garde scene with interest and became intrigued by the influx of black entertainers and musicians there. In emulation of Janet Flanner, by that time a personal friend, she even wrote a "Letter from Paris" for *Vogue* in which she extolled Dada, Surrealism, and Josephine Baker.[6]

The publication of *Negro* in 1934 was heralded in some quarters and dismissed as a rambling compilation in others; and from the beginning her motives were not universally above suspicion even among blacks. The book's length, which approached nine hundred pages, and its organization were alternately found disconcerting or heralded as an enormous collage of related materials whose richness of association was left to the reader-browser to discover. Realizing that the final product was anything but a neatly integrated organism, she could only hope that its central thesis was clear, namely "that there was no superior race, merely cultural differences, that racism had no basis whatsoever, and that nations which claimed to be uncontaminated by racism (*viz.,* England) were guilty of hypocrisy as repulsive as the racism they denied."[7]

The section entitled "Negro Stars" opened with a full-page picture of Duke Ellington and his orchestra and a lengthy article entitled "The Best Negro Jazz Orchestras" by Robert Goffin, a Belgian, translated by Samuel Beckett in an effusively lyric style: "Oh you musicians of my life, prophets of my youth, splendid Negroes informed with fire, how shall I ever express my love for your saxophones writhing like orchids, your blazing trombones with their hairpin vents, your voices fragrant with all the breezes of home remembered and the breath of the bayous, your rhythm as inexorable as tom-toms beating in an African nostalgia."[8]

Further on he extols Louis Armstrong as "the king of rhythm" and Duke Ellington "as the most extraordinary phenomenon in the whole development of jazz." Noting that the latter's instinctively "hot" style had begun to evidence a tighter sense of form, he concluded that "this unique conductor has gradually placed intuitive music under control."[9]

Full-page photographs were included of Louis Armstrong, Cab Cal-
loway, Bill Robinson, and Florence Mills, the comely star of *Blackbirds,*
a revue which was seen in London by the Prince of Wales "no less
than twenty times," and which also played for sixteen weeks in Paris
in 1926 hard on the heels of Josephine Baker's success.

George Antheil and Other Musicians

Interestingly, just as Milhaud and Copland were describing American
jazz as a vital and powerful phenomenon—though passé if not defunct
for the composer of art music (1927–28)—Nancy Cunard was beginning to assemble her magnum opus. Her choice of George Antheil to
organize the music section of the book was made to order. Antheil,
for all of his stylistic oscillations, had from the beginning courted a reputation as the "bad boy of music," and the titles alone of his earlier
compositions provided sufficient credentials with respect to the issue
at hand.

Manifestations of African Primitivism had already appeared in Antheil's *Jazz Sonata* and *Sonata Sauvage,* both of 1922. The three movements of the *Sonata Sauvage* carry the titles "Niggers," "Snakes," and
"Ivory" and were premiered in Berlin on January 1, 1923. The audience for a performance in Budapest in February or March, which included Bartók and Kodály, were apparently so enthusiastic following
the first movement that "they thundered and clapped for five minutes"
and, according to Antheil, demanded its repetition before continuing
with the second.[10] Then, following his first trip to Africa in the summer
of 1923, the Paris premiere of *Sonata sauvage* took place at the Théâtre
des Champs-Élysées on October 4 along with his *Airplane Sonata* as a
prelude to the seasonal opening of Rolf de Maré's Ballet Suédois. Erik
Satie, Ezra Pound, James Joyce, Fernand Léger, and Darius Milhaud
were all in the audience, and the "riot" which ensued following the
first movement was repeated upon request and captured on film for a
Georgette LeBlanc movie, *L'Inhumaine.*

The musical language for both sonatas was essentially the same, and
cemented the relationship between prevailing tastes for both primitivism and "musico-mechanics."[11] Léger must have been startled as well
as pleased by the confirmation of such affinities, and the event may
have provided an added impetus for his collaboration the next year
(1924) on the scenery and costumes for Milhaud's *La Création du monde*

as well as a film for Antheil's *Ballet mécanique*. Antheil's manipulation of independent ostinato structures and abrupt sectional demarcation was prominent in both sonatas and betrays an intimate knowledge of the music of Stravinsky, who for a time Antheil claimed as a close friend.

The force of *Le Sacre* as a Primitivist icon still stirred the breast of many composers as late as 1927–28, and it is of no little interest that just prior to the publication of *Negro* George Antheil made the following testy remarks:

> Do we necessarily need to link all new rhythmic experimentation with Stravinsky's "Sacre," or Rimsky-Korsakoff's "Scheherazade"? At the least sign of a break from the four Gods of music; 3/4, 2/4, 6/8, 4/4, do we need to run to Stravinsky like little cry-babies, and call Father? . . .
>
> Aha! Igor Stravinsky, you Rimsky-Korsakoffist! Aha Rimsky-Korsakoff, you Moussorgskyist! Aha Moussorgsky, you swiper from the Russian peasants. What about the music from the campfires of a thousand, no! a million years [ago]! What about the tom-toms. What about the neggers down in Africa. What about the Mongols sweeping over Europe in the middle ages. Do we have to track everything back to the courts of Louis and Napoleon? Do you forever have to stilt about in court dress to 4/4 time, or waltz in the evenings to 3/4? Is there nothing else to your measly little European culture of the last few centuries?[12]

Here Antheil was obviously decrying an automatic acknowledgement of Stravinsky in matters rhythmic, and given the resounding influence of *Le Sacre,* it is not surprising he would have wanted to verbalize a need to escape its force with some sense of urgency. Yet it is also clear that Antheil sensed the value of advertising his attraction to a mythical *art nègre* carrying Primitivist credentials potentially older and more authentic than those brandished in the Russian formula. Antheil's negative reference to waltzes and court dress openly maligns the fashionableness of a currently rising Neoclassicism, which, in its espousal of eighteenth-century form and manners, was capable of promoting a rhythmic deportment far removed from the raw energetic propellants of Bartók, Prokofiev, and Stravinsky in the preceding decade.

The importance of the role of music for Nancy Cunard's story was further reinforced in the music section, which opened with an article by Antheil entitled "The Negro on the Spiral." Antheil's earlier impatience with the Stravinsky cult, in contrast with his attraction to "tom-

toms . . . and the neggers down in Africa" sounded a few years before, now dissolves in the construction of a sweeping historical fiction with respect to music's pancultural metamorphosis over the centuries. The opening sentence reads: "Since Wagner, music has had two gigantic blood transfusions; first the Slavic, and in recent times the Negroid. The Russian Five, leading gradually into young Debussy, and eventually into young Strawinsky, seemed to pass naturally into the present Negroidian epoch, especially after the great and world-shaking events of the *Sacre du Printemps* and *Noces*."

Antheil is ablaze with enthusiasm for the almost unfathomable antiquity of Afro-American jazz, which he proclaims as the ready and natural successor to the Primitivist forces unleashed by Stravinsky. Only a generous sampling of his message will convey the extent and passion of his beliefs:

> The Negro music, like the Negro, has been living for a number of million years under terrible heat; Negro music has, in consequence, been baked as hard and as beautiful as a diamond; it was the only thinkable influence after the *Sacre* and *Noces* had exhausted once and for all every last drop of blood that the primitive Slavic music had in it. The first Negro jazz band arriving in Paris during the last year of the great war was as prophetic of the after-war period immediately to come as the *Sacre* was prophetic of this selfsame war, declared only a year after the stormy scenes at the Champs Élysées Théâtre in 1913 . . . Likewise the *Sacre* left music sunbaked, parched, without a drop of water, and without a blade of green grass; the famine was here; there was no hope; a cataclysm; a great work marking a finality. Nothing could survive underneath this dense heat and smoke except Negro music. It absorbed this period so naturally that in 1919 we find the greatest Slavic composer living writing "Piano-rag-music" and "Ragtime" almost without knowing it, and a whole school of young composers springing up in Paris deeply influenced by American Negro music . . . By 1920 the gigantic Slavic influence of the past 40 years ended; not even the long-delayed performance of *Noces* could call it back . . . Stravinsky himself began to forsake Slavic music. Then, frightened at the gigantic black apparition, each European people scurried hurriedly towards their own racial music . . . From 1920 to 1925 we see one definite trend . . . no matter how absolutely Latin the Latins might become . . . or how Germanic the Germanics might become . . . deep down (or perhaps not even concealed at all) . . . is *ever* present the new *note* of the Congo. This *note* has erroneously been

called "American," but this note belongs no more specifically to the North American Negro than to those of the West Indies or South America. It is *black* . . . not white, nor yellow.[13]

Antheil argues, however, that in his turn to Neoclassicism Stravinsky took the "classic sound and intention, but tightened [it] as hard and fast as a piece of Negro sculpture," and in the process abandoned the "development" section, "which for a hundred years had been the pet insanity of the Germans."[14] He concludes his article with a sweeping and remarkable remapping of influence in world music:

> I called the Americas an enormous détour, but perhaps indeed they were no détour at all, but absolutely upon the path of this gigantic spiral now throwing out its enormous circle over the South Atlantic, taking in South America, the West Indies, and North America in one gigantic swing. Then in 1919, the line, still swinging clockwise, comes back over the North Atlantic and hits Europe. Wagner at the very height of his northern music culture succeeds to Strawinsky who, at the very height of his eastern Tartar culture, succeeds to the Congo. Clockwise the Viking passes on to the Slav, and again the Slav passes on to the African.

In closing Antheil attempts to secure the natural kinship between Slav and African and the power of such a coalition by referring to the fact that the great Russian poet Pushkin was mulatto and to Cocteau's recent remark, "Les premiers grands rag-times (1918) furent l'oeuvre des musiciens russes chez les Nègres de Harlem, à New York. Le Rythme intraduisible de Pouchkine ne viendrait-il du sang noir?"[15] Antheil was not alone in brandishing Stravinsky's Primitivism as Negroid, but perhaps no one approached Antheil's sentiments more directly than Constant Lambert, who publishing his own *Music Ho!* in the same year as *Negro,* spoke unequivocally of Stravinsky's "peculiarly African use of rhythm" and of "an antiphonal use of melodic phrases reminiscent of primitive African singing" in *Les Noces.*[16]

Other articles that follow Antheil's in *Negro* include Edward G. Perry's "Negro Creative Musicians," which denies that the spiritual is "based upon or derived from African rhythms or tribal songs," it being the creation of a group of people "now long removed from the native land of their black ancestors—as the folk-songs of the Russian peasants."[17] Zora Neale Hurston's "Spirituals and Neo-Spirituals" also rejects the idea that the spiritual is confined to the period of slavery and suggests that they "are being made and forgotten every day."[18] In an earlier section, "Characteristics of Negro Expression," Hurston decries the failure of the white musician to assimilate the true Negro accent in song and dance, judges George Gershwin as a *faux* Negro rhapsodist—"just about as Negro as caviar"—and complains that "the Negroes themselves have sinned," including the Fisk Jubilee Singers, whom she accuses of "musicians' tricks" in presenting spirituals to white audiences.[19]

Lawrence Gellert's "Negro Songs of Protest" is devoted mostly to the presentation of song texts with only two musical examples. "Hot Jazz" by Robert Goffin reviews the prehistory of jazz from the cakewalk, ragtime, and blues; decries the exploitations of Paul Whiteman, Jack Hylton, and others "who industrialised jazz to such an extent that nothing remained but a weak dilution devoid of all real musical character"; and noting that hot jazz has replaced melodic jazz, proudly announces its appeal to the most notable composers of the day—Ravel, Milhaud, and Stravinsky. At the close he lays claim to analogies between the discoveries of the humble Negro around 1910 and Surrealists such as André Breton and Louis Aragon around 1920, and further postulates the role of "hot jazz" as a new and potent pseudo-religion for present-day youth.[20]

Other articles include Maud Cuney Hare's "Folk Music of the Creoles" and "Negro Music in Porto Rico" as well as additional essays entitled "The Biguine of the French Antilles" and "Is the African Musical?" The music section concludes with a brief anthology of nine West and East African songs and ten songs from the Congo transcribed by Antheil himself. The source for his tunes is unknown, but their presentation not as engraved examples but as manuscript facsimiles carries the connotation, surely intentional, that he had retrieved them *in situ* on a field trip.

Negro was finally released on February 15, 1934, to mixed reviews and a few raves by intimates. It was a very large book and very expensive, but its organization unfortunately diluted its message. The book reappeared in an abbreviated version in 1970 to generally more favorable response. Anne Chisholm has articulately summed up its ultimate impact: "Perhaps what strikes a modern reader most powerfully is that it is still impossible to regard *Negro* simply as a piece of history or a collection of voices from the past; too many of the ideas and questions it contained remain painfully unresolved."[21]

The Harlem Renaissance and Music

Though the 1920s may have represented an apogee of *art nègre* euphoria, Afro-American jazz retained its vitality throughout the 1930s in Europe and America alike, with Bechet, Ellington, Armstrong, and others leading the way. But in the world of art music, interest in further absorbing its basic ingredients typically led to the diffusion of its rhythms, colors, and harmonies in the fabric of ballet and symphonic and chamber music on both sides of the Atlantic.

William Grant Still (1895–1978) was emblematic of this process among black musicians in America. Trained at Wilberforce College from 1911 to 1914, where he came particularly under the influence of Coleridge-Taylor, Still began to play with a dance orchestra in 1914 and in 1916 joined Harry Pace's and W. C. Handy's music publishing company in Memphis. Here he became familiar with the blues, honky-tonks, and dance halls, played oboe and cello, and made arrangements for Handy's newly organized band.[22] Pace and Handy relocated their publishing house to New York in 1918, and following periods of study at the Oberlin School of Music in 1917 and 1919 Still joined their staff in New York. In 1921, he played the oboe in Eubie Blake's *Shuffle Along*—one of the genuine smash hits among early black musicals on Broadway that launched such stellar personalities as Florence Mills, Josephine Baker, and Hall Johnson—staying with the show until the summer of 1923.[23] During this period, which took him to Boston, he studied composition with George Whitefield Chadwick at the New England Conservatory of Music, and from 1923 to 1925 he studied with Edgard Varèse. That his contact with Varèse may have been viewed as anything but marginal can be guessed from Alain Locke's article "The Negro Spiritual," which appeared in *The New Negro* of 1925, wherein he made the following extraordinary judgment: "Edgar Varèse's *Intégrales,* a 'Study for percussion instruments,' presented last season by the International Composers' Guild, suggests a new orchestral technique patterned after the characteristic idiom of the African 'drum orchestra.' "[24] Though Still resisted Varèse's affinities for avant-garde exploration, it was through Varèse that he was introduced to Eugene Goossens and Howard Hanson, who in turn was responsible for the first performance of the *Afro-American Symphony* (1930), on October 29, 1931, with the Rochester Philharmonic Orchestra—"the first symphony by a black American to be played by a leading orchestra."[25] This was the culmination of a decade of serious, concert-hall composition reflective of the Harlem Renaissance—one that had spawned a series of Still's own orchestral works, such as *Darker America* (1924), *From the Black Belt* (1926), and *Levee Land,* prior to the *Afro-American Symphony*—wherein African-Americans bore witness to their cultural heritage through reference to the spiritual, the blues, and dance music.

If Still was not a conscious participant in the Negro Renaissance, his example promoted its spirit as well as the essence of Dunbar's poem "Be Proud, my Race, in Mind and Soul," which served as the inspiration for the final movement of his symphony.[26] Beyond the *Afro-American Symphony,* which became his most widely recognized work, Still's career encompassed an association with Black Swan Records, devoted principally to the distribution of the music of black composers, as well as with the writing of music for film, including *Lost Horizon* (1935), *Pennies from Heaven* (1936), and *Stormy Weather* (1943). Yet, although he was a role model for the black composer who aspired to the writing of "serious" music reflective of the infusion of native idioms and though he directly helped pave the way for Florence Price's Symphony in E Minor of 1932 and William Dawson's *Negro Folk Symphony* of 1934,[27] he was not even a marginal figure to the Europeans who had fathered the craze for *musique nègre.*

Few black Americans, including the writers of the so-called talented tenth, had journeyed to Europe before the 1920s. Some black musicians had been there as members of ensembles, but it was the rare individual, like Frederick Douglass or Booker T. Washington, who had undertaken what Henry James had portrayed in his novels as a spiritual voyage to the cradle of American civilization. Washington, the recognized leader of his race, had traveled to Paris as early as May–June 1899 and had visited the American painter Henry Ossawa Tanner. Tanner, convinced that his color would prevent recognition at home, had chosen exile in France, where his painting *The Raising of Lazarus* had been acquired by the French government and exhibited at the Luxembourg Galleries and later at the Louvre. Encompassing but not limiting his paintings to black themes, Tanner voiced his desire to be known as a first-rate artist regardless of race. Though his stature throughout the twenties as the most celebrated black artist of his generation may have given spiritual succor to black artists in America, his insistence upon dissociating questions of race from art disqualified him from recognition among Alain Locke's New Negroes.[28]

Despite critical attempts to dilute its force, the French connection with artists of the Harlem Renaissance is no myth and has been elaborately detailed.[29] Alain Locke was the first of the black writers to arrive in Europe in the 1920s, followed by Langston Hughes in February 1924, and Countee Cullen, "the greatest francophile" of them all, in 1926.[30] Faith, however misplaced, in Paris's greater tolerance in racial matters was wedded to an admiration of its claims as a citadel of culture, and in the aftermath of World War I both contributed to a steady movement of black artists—painters, writers, musicians—to the City of Light. Retrospectively it seems clear that France's greater openness to artists of color was based less upon a lack of social prejudice than upon a feeling of French superiority in matters of culture and the endorsement of such a view which the black artists's pilgrimage to Paris seemed to imply. Whatever the proportions of the mix, the interchange served the contemporary aspirations of both parties.

Among musicians, a few black artists made it to the concert hall in both Paris and London, and Roland Hayes had a resounding success in a Wigmore Hall recital of April 23, 1921, that concluded with a gathering of spirituals—a feature soon to become de rigueur for black concert singers. But though Hayes, like Sidney Bechet, was invited to sing for King George V at Buckingham Palace and though Marion Anderson achieved her initial recognition in Europe, Samuel Coleridge-Taylor and for a moment Edmund Thornton Jenkins from South Carolina—prior to his premature death in Paris in 1926 at age thirty-two—were virtually the only black composers to achieve recognition in the Western classical tradition.[31] For most Europeans, Afro-American music was both black and basic, and this meant primarily jazz and to an extent spirituals. Mindful of the European craze, in the article "Jazz at Home," written for Locke's *The New Negro,* J. A. Rogers reminded his readers that "it follows that jazz is more at home in Harlem than in Paris, though from the look and sound of certain quarters of Paris one would hardly think so. It is just the epidemic contagiousness of jazz that makes it, like the measles, sweep the block."[32]

It was more than an epidemic, however. Europe, and France in particular, had not only recognized the virility of Afro-American jazz but had viewed it in some fundamental way as a genuine art form, neither vulgar nor lowbrow. The struggle by historians to understand why composers like William Grant Still were not in Paris alongside their American compatriots in literature, such as Langston Hughes, Alain

Locke, Countee Cullen, and Claude McKay, or a painter such as Henry O. Tanner—all of whom took up extended or repeated residences there—is surely explained by the fact that early on the French, in their passion for *art nègre,* had not only identified a black musical expression but had canonized it in the name of jazz.[33]

Considering jazz in some fundamental way inimitable (although widely imitated), the Europeans initially promoted the concept that genuine black music could only be written by those born and nourished in its culture. It was obvious, however, that the one thing that those of other ethnic roots could aspire to was emulation, and not surprisingly new hybrids appeared swiftly and to considerable applause. At a time when Cocteau was completing *The Cock and the Harlequin,* for example, and long before his pronouncement of 1932 (cited by Antheil in *Negro*) that "the first great rag-times (1918) were the work of Russians at home among the negroes of Harlem in New York," he had recorded a related sentiment in a letter to Albert Gleizes: "Bring me back as many Negro ragtimes and as much great Russian-Jewish-American music as you can."[34]

Though in the late teens Cocteau's reference to Russian-Jewish-American music was undoubtedly to Irving Berlin and Jerome Kern, the ethnic mix was preserved for Europe throughout the twenties in the work of composers like Louis Gruenberg (1884–1964). Born in Russia of Polish Jewish parentage, he arrived in New York at age two. At age nineteen he went to Berlin, where he studied piano as well as composition with Ferruccio Busoni, and in 1912 at age twenty-eight he was appointed to the faculty of the Vienna Conservatory. After returning to the United States in 1919, he became one of the founders of the League of Composers. As one of its most vociferous champions, he tirelessly promoted the belief that the American composer's best chance of finding an individual expression would come through the development of native source materials such as jazz and spirituals. The implications of his pronouncements are clear: two black repertoires had transcended their racial origins and were now in a position to serve the aspirations of a nation at large.

Vachel Lindsay, a prominent American poet from the Midwest who was committed to the integration of art and society through entertainment, invented a "Higher Vaudeville" for this purpose based upon readily recognizable ingredients of popular entertainment. At least a surface affinity between his aspirations and those of Cocteau at the very same time is worth noting. Between 1915 and 1920 Lindsay went about the country attracting large audiences through the recitation of his poetry, which flirted with a broad cultural mix of themes ranging from "General William Booth Enters into Heaven" to "The Congo" and "The Chinese Nightingale." His *The Daniel Jazz* is a good-humored parody of a Bible psalm laced with intonations of the spirituals, and Gruenberg made a setting of it in 1924 for tenor, clarinet, trumpet, and string quartet. The musical version is an alternately perky and soulful, if somewhat lame, fusion of Viennese chromaticism with ragtime and the blues. Yet in promoting vernacular repertoires in tandem with classical formats, Gruenberg not unexpectedly mirrored the practice of and netted products similar to those of the Europeans more than he showed the way to an indigenous American language.

The Daniel Jazz was followed the next year by *Jazz Suite* for orchestra and *Jazzberries* for solo piano, both of which enjoyed a degree of popularity.[35] Living once again in Germany Gruenberg now spoke of his recipe as well as his aspirations for music in an article, "Der Jazz als Ausgangspunkt" ("Jazz as a Jumping-Off Place"), in the April 1925 issue of *Anbruch*—the same issue that contained Milhaud's landmark article on the development of the jazz band. Countering Erwin Schulhoff's claims that the heart of jazz lay in its affiliation with the dance, he proposed that the composer search out its other characteristics, including especially the propelling and variegated role of the soloist.[36]

Throughout the twenties and early thirties Gruenberg continued to compose numerous works with "jazz" in the title, but his most ambitious effort was the opera *The Emperor Jones,* produced at the Metropolitan Opera in 1933 with Lawrence Tibbett in the title role. Although an impressive aria based on the spiritual "Standin' in the Need of Prayer" marks the culminating point of the opera, the symbolic tom-toms that haunt Jones to death have caused the work to be characterized as more like a play with sound effects than an opera.[37] However one summarizes Gruenberg's career—a career that took him to Hollywood as a composer of film scores and produced a notable violin concerto for Heifetz in 1944 that once more attempted to appropriate the soul of black music—he stands as an emblem of a Russian Jewish immigrant's infatuation with the African-American musical legacy. Interestingly, the reception accorded these works in Europe was more favorable than that for the concert works of the Harlem Renaissance, and his various attempts at cultural fusion were widely applauded.

John Alden Carpenter, the other important American symphonic composer to tap the resources of Negro music, was neither Jewish nor from Tin Pan Alley. Son of a wealthy Chicago industrialist, Carpenter showcased a sophisticated and craftsmanlike blend of Afro-American tunes and timbres with Western attitudes and forms in a series of works: the jazz pantomime *Krazy Kat* of 1921; *Skyscrapers* (1923–24), a ballet employing tenor banjo, six saxophones, traffic lights, minstrel tunes and offstage chorus; *Jazz Orchestra Pieces* (1925–26); and the four *Negro Songs* on texts of Langston Hughes (1926). Drawing from another part of America's heritage, he also wrote *Young Man Chieftain,* an Indian prayer with a text by Mary Austin. *Skyscrapers,* an impressive and still viable orchestral piece, was originally commissioned by Diaghilev for production in Monte Carlo. It ultimately premiered, however, at the Metropolitan Opera House on February 19, 1926, and two years later was well received in Munich.

This was hardly surprising in light of Germany's obsession with *Amerikanismus*—a strange amalgam that combined the urban and the primitive as paradoxical cohorts. Negro jazz may have been seen as up to date and nurtured by city life, but it was also bathed in a primitive aura. Similarly, the American Indian held a special attraction for the Germans, as demonstrated by their fondness not only for James Fenimore Cooper, Buffalo Bill, and the *Völkerschau* ethnographic exhibits but also for their own Karl May, whose novels fueled the fantasies of many a child from the 1890s on. Now in the 1920s the American Indian was not so much rediscovered as redefined as an emblem of America. Just as the Negro had conjured up the image in jazz, so Weimar culture, much like Carpenter, adopted two other metaphors for the jungle in America: the Indian Wild West and the modern cityscape. The degree to which the intricate social collage inherent in *Asphaltcowboys* and *Stadtindianer* appealed to a host of German artists at the time is epitomized by the entry submitted by Heinrich Mossdorf, Hans Hahn, and Bruno Busch for the Chicago Tribune Competition in 1922 (Figure 7.4).[38] And just as George Grosz in 1915–16 had recalled his *Memory of New York* through an assemblage of tall buildings, hotels, electric lights, night clubs, cactus, palm, and American Indians, and as Paul Citroën, a student of the Bauhaus and Berlin Dada, had sought to demonstrate America's vitality in a 1923 series of skyscraper photomontages entitled *Metropolis,*[39] so Carpenter clearly understood that the American skyscraper was more than a tall building.

Figure 7.4. The 1922 Chicago Tribune Competition entry by Heinrich Mossdorf, Hans Hahn, and Bruno Busch.

Gruenberg was not the only transplant to America who somewhat predictably found his way back to Europe during the twenties, nor did his and Carpenter's views on black music as a national resource go unchallenged. Varèse, for example, had already won Alain Locke's earlier approbation for his recognition of the power of percussion independent of the jazz mode, which Locke correctly or not continued to associate with African drumming. Having returned to Paris from America in 1928, Varèse now clearly played to current French anti-Semitic attitudes in reporting that: "Jazz is not America. It's a negro product, exploited by the Jews. All of its composers from here are Jews."[40]

Calling for a wider purview of what constituted American music, Henry Cowell also reported in 1934 that jazz had been born of a "strange fusion of the minstrel Negro and the Tin-pan-alley Jew." Noting that jazz had attained an "almost ludicrously high reputation in sophisticated European circles," he lamented that "sometimes new and really very characteristic American scores are turned down in Europe because they are not built on jazz!"[41] The thoughts and aspirations behind Cowell's expressed sentiments are not difficult to judge if we consider a work such as *The Banshee,* composed in 1925, wherein he conjures up the Irish spirit associated with the wailing announcement of a family member's impending death. Impounding folklore in a manner suggestive of Yeats's call to the primitive in the epigraph at the opening of this chapter, Cowell extracts a new sonic art from the innards of the piano while avoiding Stravinskian primitive propellants or the stereotypical inflections offered by jazz.

Ravel in the late 1920s was on several notable occasions seduced by the African-American musical vocabulary in works as varying as the "Blues" from his sonata for violin and piano of 1927 and the two piano concerti of 1930–31. But he also realized that the primitive note could be incised without recourse to the new musical fashion. In the second of the *Chansons madécasses* of 1926, for example, Ravel provided stunning evidence of the power of music not only to evoke issues attendant to *art nègre* but to sermonize on the evils of colonialism. Speaking a musical language that shunned African-American developments and openly admitted to the influence of Schoenberg,[42] Ravel turned the cry of the peacock in his own earlier *Histoires naturelles* (1906)—"Léon! Léon!"— into a chilling warning: "Aoua! Aoua! Méfiez-vous des blancs, habitans du rivage" ("Aoua! Aoua! Do not trust the white man, inhabitants of these shores"). The song was premiered by Jane Bathori before the cycle was completed in the fall of 1925 in a concert sponsored by Elizabeth Sprague Coolidge. Reaction to it by Léon Moreau, a minor composer of the day, was anything but positive. Interrupting attempts to encore the work, he shouted that he was leaving the hall in protest over such anticolonialist sentiments at a time when French soldiers were fighting Abdel-Krim in Morocco. Evariste-Désiré de Parny's original text of 1787 may have predated the French Revolution, but its relevance for modern times was unmistakable. Apparently, however, Ravel was completely stunned by the incident, which was followed by a letter of protest from Moreau.[43]

Another powerful example of the call to blackness in the service of pancultural as well as spiritual accounts was Poulenc's *Litanies à la vierge noire* (1936), written following a pilgrimage to the Black Virgin at Rocamadour. It was here that the composer of *Rapsodie nègre* discovered a new musical dimension, later pursued in a series of sacred choral works that would become models of their kind. The cult of the Black Virgin is an ancient one and Poulenc's response to it may not be separable from his earlier encounters with African-American repertoires.[44] Ultimately, however, the appreciation spoke to the universal sufferings and aspirations of humankind—as did Countee Cullen's *The Black Christ,* written in Paris in 1929—and not of Poulenc's indebtedness to *musique nègre.*

Such enrichment of the musical options in approaches to themes of black culture, then, did not so much spell the elimination of jazz as a potential element in music for the concert hall as it signaled an amplification of the means of expression. But as we have seen in statements made by Milhaud as early as 1926, by the time of Nancy Cunard's *Negro* the initial attraction of jazz for the classical composer had clearly begun to wane in France, and in spite of the momentary appeal of *Zeitoper* and the establishment of a jazz curriculum at the Frankfurt Hoch Conservatory, political developments in Germany by 1934 conspired to restrict further cross-overs between high and low music.[45] The first verbal assaults by the Nazis against *Kulturbolschewismus,* which appeared in the same year as Cunard's anthology, were directed against modern art generally. Then gradually the spectre of Jewish and black American patronage condemned jazz to the lists of degenerate art, and Germany's lengthy infatuation with African-American dance was finally suppressed with the banishment of jazz from German radio in 1935.

If potential misreadings of both *Four Saints* and *Jonny* as racist manifestoes continue to impede their access to the stage today,[46] it is a paradox that in 1938 a "Degenerate Music Exhibition" in Düsseldorf singled out Krenek for disapproval and also condemned the jazz records and scores of Stravinsky, Hindemith, and Kurt Weill for their glorification of unacceptable source materials. It has been noted that the pamphlet distributed in conjunction with the exhibition sported a black saxophonist "striking the same pose as the one on the cover of the piano-vocal score of *Jonny spielt auf.*"[47] In addition to exaggerated racial features, however, a Star of David has been appended to the performer's lapel.

It is another paradox, only recently clarified, that in spite of the Nazi's denouncement of "Nigger-Jew jazz," as a practical matter relating to questions of morale and the need for entertainment Goebbels made repeated concessions to the formation of German swing groups who toured and made radio broadcasts throughout most of the course of the war. The confusion of policy and the final realization of the impossibility of completely suppressing jazz in the Third Reich during the war years constitutes one of the most fascinating chapters of the period.[48]

A different but related re-reading concerns the origins of the word "Mahagonny" as used by Brecht and Weill in their opera of the same name. The testimony which claims that Brecht applied the term "Mahagonny" to the "hordes of brown-shirted petty bourgeois" at a Nazi party meeting in Munich,[49] may have been accurate as a retrospective comment by the composer. But recent research has shown that the original source is to be found in a song, "Komm nach Mahagonne!" with words by O. A. Alberts, a popular lyricist of the early German cabaret, and music by Leopold Krauss-Elka (1891–1964), whose cabaret songs were widely known. The work is subtitled an "Afrikanischer Shimmy," and the refrain begins with the words "Komm nach Mahagonne, Dort in Afrika" followed by word play with barely concealed sexual allusions. Although the music is anything but an authentic Afro-American shimmy, the word "Mahagonne" clearly "takes its name from the skin color of the people native to that continent . . . where sexual attitudes were thought to be unshackled by a Victorian moral code."[50] Thus *Mahagonny*, written between 1927 and 1930, addresses issues related to the search for freedom in civilized society and ultimately the dilemmas entailed in such an attempt, while paradoxically carrying a title that can be traced to a cabaret song reflecting stereotypical attitudes.

In retrospect it is clear that the aspirations of the Harlem Renaissance were supported, even if somewhat obliquely, by the French, the Germans, and other Western Europeans who, recognizing the power of black vernaculars in the late teens and early twenties, gave many Americans pause with respect to a rich and not fully tapped resource. The oft-repeated judgment that the Harlem Renaissance was a failure has recently been subjected to considerable reinterpretation; and, indeed, viewed as a beginning rather than a culmination, it may be promoted as a success story.[51] For if after 1934 fewer works openly advertised the goals promoted by the movement, the virility of the African-American musical lyric and pulse was regularly proclaimed not only in Still's film scores but also in numerous configurations from the Broadway musical to a variety of composed vernaculars. In addition to the lengthy and notable lists of black artists and composers such as Duke Ellington, Louis Armstrong, Dizzy Gillespie, Ella Fitzgerald, Sarah Vaughan, Miles Davis, Oscar Peterson, and Charlie Parker there were also white musicians, such as Bix Beiderbecke, Benny Goodman, Dave Brubeck, and Gunther Schuller, who explored jazz terrain in a manner totally different from that of Paul Whiteman in an earlier decade. In the interest of trying to assess the various ways in which the momentum of the Renaissance did not completely dissipate but, indeed, found a series of new and compelling expressions, the achievements of two American artists of the early 1930s—one black, one white—deserve to be momentarily reviewed with respect to the central impetus of the movement. They are names known to virtually all who profess a love for music: Duke Ellington and George Gershwin.

— 8 —

Take the "A" Train

> Duke Ellington is the pioneer of super-jazz and one of the persons most likely to create the classical jazz toward which so many are striving. He plans a symphonic suite and an African opera, both of which will prove a test of his ability to carry native jazz through to this higher level.
>
> *Alain Locke*

> [I want to] write an opera of the melting pot, of New York City itself, with its blend of native and immigrant strains. This would allow for many kinds of music, black and white, Eastern and Western, and would call for a style that should achieve out of this diversity, an artistic unity.
>
> *George Gershwin*

Ellington: From the "Jungle" to the Classics

Although in speaking of a *musique nègre* the European critics may have assumed that they were talking *about* blacks instead of *to* them, not surprisingly black musicians and performers had been eavesdropping and responded to what they heard from the very beginning. That Duke Ellington was not unaware of the critical reaction to Sidney Bechet and Josephine Baker in the *Revue nègre,* for example, may be inferred from the inclusion of a "jungle number" in his shows at the Cotton Club in New York, which began in December 1927. Ellington, who had been born in Washington D.C. and had never resided south of that city, quickly came to be regarded as the musical master of jungle sounds emanating from the heart of darkest Africa, and "East St. Louis Toodle-Oo" and "Black and Tan Fantasy" became the first signature "jungle" pieces. These pieces had been conceived and recorded in March and

April of 1927 before Ellington ever arrived at the Cotton Club. The so-called jungle effects, involving the use of the growl and plunger mutes, were largely developed by the trumpeter James "Bubber" Miley—Ellington's collaborator on several early compositions—and the trombonist Joe "Tricky Sam" Nanton. Differences in effect between the plunger and straight mute can be more readily comprehended than the growl, which Mercer Ellington has described lucidly: "There are three basic elements in the growl: the sound of the horn, a guttural gargling in the throat, and the actual note that is hummed. The mouth has to be shaped to make the different vowel sounds, and above the singing from the throat, manipulation of the plunger adds the *wa-wa* accents that give the horn a language."[1]

"Black and Tan Fantasy," which introduced the cry, the field-holler, the Easter church piece "Holy City" played in the minor mode, a profusion of blue notes, and a coda citing Chopin's renowned "Funeral March," epitomized the remarkable and somewhat strange arsenal of source materials capable of being summoned to such an assignment. Beyond the mutes and growling effects, Mark Tucker has identified other pseudo-African effects, which the jungle style enlisted, including "pounding tom-toms, unusual harmonies," and "'primitive' scales (usually pentatonic and whole-tone)."[2]

Carl Van Vechten's recent novel *Nigger Heaven* (1926) had promoted interest in Harlem and black life in general, but its success hardly prepares us for Marshall Stearns's eyewitness account of one of the Cotton Club floor shows which captures with rare clarity both the fashion and the force for America of the contemporary European view that held Primitivism, Africa, and American blacks as natural cohorts:

> I recall one where a light-skinned and magnificently muscled Negro burst through a papier-mâché jungle onto the dance floor, clad in an aviator's helmet, goggles, and shorts. He had obviously been "forced down in darkest Africa," and in the center of the floor he came upon a "white" goddess clad in long golden tresses and being worshipped by a circle of cringing "blacks." Producing a bull whip from heaven knows where, the aviator rescued the blonde and they did an erotic dance. In the background, Bubber Miley, Tricky Sam Nanton, and other members of the Ellington band growled, wheezed, and snorted obscenely.[3]

Although the implications of a scenario that reports the rescue of a white goddess from worshipping primitive blacks by an urban Negro aviator are patently complex and capable of multiple interpretations, incorporation of such themes today would be censorable on any number of levels. Yet the seeming lack of embarrassment in showcasing them in the name of entertainment for an audience of gangsters, whites, and Negro celebrities suggests that Ellington and other blacks in some measure simply mirrored the circular trajectory of the cakewalk history. From a strictly technical perspective Ellington, while acknowledging that the jungle sound was due principally to Miley's and Nanton's use of mutes, later judged that "this kind of theatrical experience, and the demands it made upon us, was both educative and enriching, and it brought about a further broadening of the music's scope."[4]

Although various instrumental ingredients of the jungle style may have been introduced by Will Marion Cook in his "March of the Caboceers" from *In Dahomey* (1902) as well as in a 1924 recording of *Africa* by the Original Memphis Five,[5] it is clear that a taste for "jungle" numbers had also been characteristic of the previous decade's black revues, such as the Black Patti Troubadours' productions of *A Trip to Africa* (1910) and *In the Jungles* (1911). In the former, Sissieretta Jones, a fine singer renowned for her "operatic kaleidoscope" in black shows between 1896 and 1910, played an African princess in a skit about the rescue of a missionary from a tribe of Zulus—a show which prompted a Boston critic to speak of a "boisterous humor that colored companies carry off much better than do their white rivals."[6] In the latter show, once more involving a rescue in Africa, Jones appeared as Queen Le-Ku-Li of the Gumbula Tribe.

Thus Ellington's seeming concessions to jungle evocations—including pieces such as "Jungle Jamboree," "Jungle Blues," and "Jungle Nights in Harlem"—were less an obligatory response to white racial stereotyping or a simple sop to Harlem tourism than a perpetuation of attitudes subtly balanced in the history of American minstrelsy, black musical theater, and revues. Yet such pieces were more than an appendage to local history and in some real measure were a reflection of the more recent phenomenon of the French-sponsored *Revue nègre* aimed at Parisian high society. In its transfer home, however, more than a patronage system had been exchanged. Something that had begun as indigenous to America, that had flourished and then settled abroad, had now returned home tagged with an import label. Evidence of this dual sponsorship appears not only in Baby Cox's Cotton Club jungle outfit, which clearly mirrors Josephine Baker's costume for the *Revue nègre* (Figures 8.1 a and b), but also in Copland's first ballet, *Hear Ye! Hear*

Figure 8.1a. Josephine Baker's "Danse sauvage" in the *Revue nègre* of 1925.

Figure 8.1b. Baby Cox, a dancer and singer featured on a few Duke Ellington records, in one of the jungle costumes which she wore at the Cotton Club.

Ye! written in 1934. Essentially a satire of the American legal system centering on the murder of a night club dancer, the most protracted musical episode in Copland's piece witnesses chorus girls doing a "Jungle Jazz Dance," and no doubt was meant to recall both Josephine Baker's Parisian revue and Ellington's more recent success with such numbers at the Cotton Club.[7]

If the resulting elevation in cachet was insufficient to satisfy the highest aspirations of the Harlem Renaissance for a new breed of black poets, novelists, and symphonists, the jungle repertoires provided Ellington with a forum that encouraged experimentation with "weird" harmonies and sonorities, including extended "talking" solos.[8] This in turn promoted the move from improvisation to written masterpieces such as "Ko Ko" (1940)—often referred to as a crystallization of his jungle style—and the more extended *Black, Brown, and Beige* (1943) that increasingly identified Ellington as a composer as much as a performer. In this shift it was understandable that elevated claims were made for Ellington's progressive tuning to the spirit and ambitions of the Negro Renaissance in a fashion that eclipsed the strictly improvisatory genius of Louis Armstrong.[9]

If—Ellington's artistic claims and social evasion notwithstanding—many of the New Negroes of the Harlem Renaissance did not initially applaud his jungle repertoire, it could nonetheless be countered that they were for the most part not Ellington's clientele and that he understood as well as Josephine Baker the proven ingredients of black entertainment for white patrons. Samuel Floyd has suggested that Ellington's sheer status in the world of entertainment coupled with an aristocratic charm and an undeniable support of the aspirations of the Harlem Renaissance "probably made him an acceptable New Negro."[10] But beyond expressions of pride in the accomplishments of Paul Robeson, Roland Hayes, and Coleridge-Taylor, by 1931 Ellington's own development as a musician allowed him to endorse the ambitions of the movement directly. Expressing the opinion that "what is being done by Countee Cullen and others in literature is overdue in our music," he announced his intention to show the way himself by composing a rhapsody that would "portray the experience of the coloured races in America in the syncopated idiom . . . I am putting all I have learned into it in the hope that I shall have achieved something really worth while in the literature of music, and that an authentic record of my race *written by a member of it* shall be placed on record."[11] While with respect to Ellington's announced desire to make a portrait of his people the "rhapsody" in question has been reasonably identified as *Black, Brown, and Beige,* written some twelve years later,[12] it would be possible to claim that one of Ellington's articulated goals was achieved with the "Creole Rhapsody," written during that very year, 1931. For Europeans at the time could already be heard to tout it as "the first real jazz composition,"[13] and by 1936 Locke was citing it as evidence of Ellington's potential eminence as a composer.[14] In his increasing turn to composed music, Ellington not only contributed to the Renaissance's stated mission but pointed the direction of his own future career.

In spite of Goffin's ridiculing remarks concerning Paul Whiteman in Nancy Cunard's *Negro,* most serious writing about jazz in the American press from the early 1920s on had favored symphonic versions over other categories. A *New York Times Book Review and Magazine* article of 1922 specifically extolled Whiteman and already judged that "jungle music is undergoing a refining process under the fingers of sophisticated art." Even so, in 1924 Olin Downes, the venerable music critic of the *New York Times,* put in a bid for the virility of the original dixieland form of jazz when he praised Paul Whiteman's opening "Livery Stable Blues" over the symphonic versions which followed in his renowned Aeolian Hall concert.[15] Then, in turn, the mid-decade saw a move from small dixieland groups to the enlarged ensembles of King Oliver and Louis Armstrong that clearly prefigured the big band sound. The trail of this transformation has naturally been open to interpretation, but it has been speculated that while Ferde Grofé and Whiteman showed the way to notated and carefully worked out arrangements that came to be known as symphonic jazz, Fletcher Henderson, Ellington, Jean Goldkette, and others invigorated this model with jazz solos, virile rhythm sections, and their own composed music that captured the essence of jazz but at a hotter temperature than Whiteman and his kind were capable of.[16]

Robert Donaldson Darrell, a knowledgeable jazz critic who contributed to *Phonograph Monthly Review* from 1926 through the early years of the Depression, had come across a recording of Ellington's "Black and Tan Fantasy" and had found his growling effects humorous. Fascination quickly turned to respect, however, and by 1930 he had stepped up his claims. Speaking of the keyboard gifts of Earl Hines on a Louis Armstrong recording, he praised *Monday Date* as an extraordinary thing and concluded that "Strawinskites (*sic*) and Bartokians will find more than a trace of their cherished modern feeling right here."[17]

The next year Darrell pursued the issue, and speaking of Ellington's

Jungle Band rendition of "Dreamy Blues," one of Ellington's own compositions, offered a comparison familiar to our present story:

> It is a poignantly restrained and nostalgic piece with glorious melodic endowment and scoring that even Ravel and Stravinsky might envy. Indeed it actually recalls those hushed muted trumpets of the beginning of the second part of the "Rite of Spring." . . . "Jungle Nights in Harlem" contains some more amazing piano and orchestral effects (Rimsky-Korsakow would rub his ears on hearing some of the tone colors here!).[18]

Darrell's criticism clarifies, however, that regardless of how Ellington's achievements may have squared with the aspirations of the Harlem Renaissance, his music was tuned to the basic beat of dance rhythm, drawing out "its full juice, dissipating none of his forces in vain heaven-storming," and without resorting to "excursions into Negro Rhapsodies and tone poems."[19] Though some later commentators charged that it was precisely after the English critics Lambert and Hughes encouraged Ellington to move in that direction that "his work began to falter,"[20] others found that the period of his full maturity lay just ahead in such shorter works as "Concerto for Cootie" (1940) and "Ko Ko" (1940), and the more developed *Black, Brown, and Beige* (1943).[21]

Whatever the judgment of his contribution after this turn, Ellington's enthusiastic reception at a party for the Prince of Wales on his first European tour in 1933 not only recalled similar earlier events for Will Marion Cook and Sidney Bechet but specifically validated the appeal of the "Duke" both for European royalty and the classical music establishment. Confirmation of his glamour for the latter group was finally and overtly asserted in a 1934 review by Constant Lambert that seemed intent on outstripping the claims of Darrell a few years before:

> The real interest of Ellington's records lies not so much in their colour, brilliant though it may be, as in the amazingly skilful proportions in which the colour is used. I do not only mean skilful as compared with other jazz composers, but as compared with so-called highbrow composers. I know of nothing in Ravel so dexterous in treatment as the varied solos in the middle of the ebullient *Hot and Bothered* and nothing in Stravinsky more dynamic than the final section. The combination of themes at this moment is one of the most ingenious pieces of writing in modern music. It is not a question, either, of setting

two rhythmic patterns working against each other in the mathematical Aaron Copland manner—it is genuine melodic and rhythmic counterpoint which, to use an old-fashioned phrase, "fits" perfectly.[22]

The high-low, black-white fusion attempted in the works of European composers and from another angle by white American composers of symphonic jazz had now found a third, totally different, and critically acclaimed response in the composed work of a black American jazz original. But it is surely no accident that Ellington, in later voicing his claim to a genuine racial expression, fell back on some of the most stereotypical clichés of *art nègre* fashion in its prime: "Roaming through the jungle of 'oohs' and 'ahs,' searching for a more agreeable noise, I live a life of primitivity, with the mind of a child . . . Living in a cave, I am almost a hermit, but there is a difference, for I have a mistress . . . She is ten thousand years old. She is as modern as tomorrow . . . Music is my mistress, and she plays second fiddle to no-one."[23] Using a language no white critic would have dreamed of invoking, Ellington not only appreciated the force of metaphor but clearly understood the power of myth and played to it.

Gershwin and *Porgy*

About the same time that Ellington made his first appearance at the Cotton Club, DuBose Heyward's play *Porgy* opened in New York under the auspices of the Theatre Guild on October 10, 1927, and the next year he completed a novel, *Mamba's Daughters*. It was more than a little reminiscent of Israel Zangwill's play of 1908, *The Melting-Pot*, which relates the tale of a Russian Jewish composer living in New York whose ambition was to write a symphony "expressing the vast, harmonious interweaving of races in America," and concludes with strains of "My Country, 'tis of Thee" at the final curtain.[24] In a similar vein, Heyward foresaw a new musical expression that would be indebted to the spirit of his own novel *Porgy,* of Gershwin's *Rhapsody in Blue,* and of Laurence Stallings' and Franke Harling's *Deep River*—a Broadway all-black musical that was tagged a "native opera" in its brief run on Broadway in 1926, and that would include a final scene centered on the performance of an all-Negro cast stepping forward to the footlights on the stage of the Metropolitan Opera to sing the "Negro National Hymn." One of the characters summed up the imagined effect of the whole: "God! What music! Primitive!—Sophisticated?—neither—both. Savage, tender, reckless. Something saved from a whole race's beginnings and raised to the nth degree by Twentieth Century magic—a blues gone grand opera." Obviously, traces of the antebellum Southern master's attitude that took pains to note the essentially "primitive" qualities of the Negro as a way of proclaiming cultural difference[25] had been openly impounded in the service of a new, twentieth-century, artistic myth. But such a collection of themes also spoke of broader societal aspirations in Europe as well as America during the preceding two decades, and the popular and critical success which followed was clearly due to the genuine strain of idealism that overshadowed stereotypical calls to smugness or bigotry.[26]

It is of no little interest that Gershwin had read Heyward's novel *Porgy* as early as 1926, had loved it, and even before Heyward turned it into a play had contemplated the prospect of using it as the basis of an opera (see the epigraph at the opening of this chapter). In the period between the inception of the idea and the work's completion, Gershwin received a commission from the Metropolitan Opera to write a Jewish opera, *The Dybbuk,* in 1929. But the fact that the project languished—was in fact never really launched—signals that his interest in African-American music, from the time he was a teenager through the little opera *Blue Monday* (1922) and *Rhapsody in Blue* (1924), provided the fundamental focus for his musical personality. Not until January 1934, however, following a trip to Charleston, South Carolina, was Gershwin in a position to announce to the press that he would be writing an opera "about blacks" and that, having earlier rejected Heyward's initial offer of collaboration in a revue based upon *Porgy* starring the white singer Al Jolson, he hoped that it would feature Paul Robeson as the lead. By February he had written "Summertime," but in the same month Virgil Thomson's *Four Saints in Three Acts* had opened in Hartford, Connecticut, to enthusiastic acclaim and was projected to open in New York the next year. Both Heyward and Gershwin were understandably worried that the black casting of the Thomson-Stein collaboration might take something off the edge of their show. Yet a prevalent perception that Thomson's opera was really about literary life in Paris in the twenties with Gertrude Stein masquerading as Saint Teresa and James Joyce as Saint Ignatius coupled with the generally oblique nature of the text allowed for few comparisons.

Eschewing quotation of genuine spirituals and folk songs in the manner of the play *Porgy* (1927) or Marc Connelly's *Green Pastures* (1930), both Heyward and Gershwin conspired to create an original voice for both the spiritual and the work song. The discovery of the talents of Todd Duncan and Anne Brown belongs to another story, but an understandable effort was involved in locating suitable recruits for the very large all-Negro cast. The Russian-born Alexander Smallens, who had been the conductor of *Four Saints in Three Acts,* was a natural choice for the musical director, and Eva Jessye's black choir, which had also appeared in the Thomson-Stein production, won the assignment handily with a performance of the shout "Plenty Good Room" at the audition.

Reactions to the out-of-town opening in Boston on September 30, 1935, were positive, and claims to the opera's uniqueness—including the judgment that it was destined to be remembered as the first American opera—were registered. Following substantial pruning even prior to Boston, *Porgy and Bess* opened in New York on October 10 at the Alvin Theatre. Understandably, given its initial success and the renown of the composer, the New York critics approached their evaluation a bit soberly. Olin Downes was complimentary but not overwhelmed, and Brooks Atkinson and Samuel Chotzinoff were both vexed by the protracted, and they felt unnecessary, use of recitative.

Beyond the musical and performance values, however, a series of questions loomed, and ultimately the issues of category and intention could not be forestalled. The spectre of a New York Jewish composer treating a story of Southern blacks written by a white novelist that associated African Americans with crime, violence, and shiftlessness in the alternating presence of tenderness and drugs could only have been seen as a perpetuation of racial stereotypes. And with respect to the musical language Virgil Thomson was less than kind and perhaps more than a little envious when he judged that "Gershwin's lack of understanding of all the major problems of form, of continuity, and of straightforward musical expression is not surprising in view of the impurity of his musical sources and his frank acceptance of them."[27] He concluded with the opinion that Gershwin's opera was "at best a piquant but highly unsavory stirring-up-together of Israel, Africa, and the Gaelic Isles." Earlier European opinions familiar to Thomson regarding the Russian Jewish adoption of African-American ragtime had once again been convened with less than laudatory implications and aligned now with concerns over authenticity and further potential ethnic confusion via the playwright.

Even among blacks reaction was mixed, though for reasons different from those that animated the white critics. Duke Ellington, whose willingness to partake in a certain degree of black mythologizing—even ethnic stereotyping—has already been reviewed, spoke somewhat bluntly, if obviously sincerely, in an interview printed in December 1935 shortly after *Porgy*'s premiere. Appearing in the leftist magazine *New Theatre*, Ellington's reponse to Edward Morrow's questions followed the latter's introduction, which chastized the "cult of critical Negrophiles" who "went into journalistic rhapsodies" over this new opera that purportedly caught the "child-like, quaint," and "primitive" spirit of the Negro people. Knowing that Ellington had seen the opera, Morrow asked him what he thought of it. "Grand music and a swell play, I guess, but the two don't go together—I mean that the music did not hitch with the mood and spirit of the story . . . The first thing that gives it away is that it does not use the Negro musical idiom. It was not the music of Catfish Row or any other kind of Negroes."

Ellington also charged that Gershwin had borrowed not only from Liszt but also from Dickie Well's kazoo band. Turning to the piano, he then cited passages from *Rhapsody in Blue* and claimed that they had been taken from the Negro song "Where Has My Easy Rider Gone?" The observation is especially provocative in light of Gunther Schuller's claim that Ellington's "Creole Rhapsody" contains "some subtle 'borrowing' from Gershwin's *Rhapsody in Blue*"[28] and the evidence of "Cotton Tail," which takes off from another Gershwin standard, "I Got Rhythm."[29] The interview proceeded with Ellington playing what he called a "gut-bucket waltz" that he himself had written, and pointing out that it was a waltz but that it still had the Negro idiom. "I have taken the method," he continued, "but I have not stolen or borrowed."

The remark is so pointed that it is amazing that Ellington failed to notice that in adopting external features and turning them to personal account Gershwin had done virtually the same thing. Ellington was no Johann Strauss and Gershwin was no W. C. Handy. Both, however, understood and traded on the venerable practice of discovering an original voice through transformative emulation as opposed to surface imitation. Morrow finished the interview, however, with a resounding homily to the effect that "the times are here to debunk such tripe as Gershwin's lampblack Negroisms, and the melodramatic trash of the script of *Porgy*," and judged that the future of black musical expression should be entrusted to Ellington and others who would "take their themes from their blood."[30] Yet Ellington's knowledge of as well as admiration and respect for Gershwin is evident from the time of Ellington's tellingly titled *Rhapsody Junior* of 1926 and the slightly later "Creole Rhapsody" of 1931.[31]

Ellington's basic reaction, however, was far from unique either in its tone or in its reasoning. Hall Johnson, writing in the Negro magazine *Opportunity,* spoke of the excellence and pliability of the cast, which he felt had infused the whole with genuine qualities of race. Yet he judged that it had understandably not been a perfect Negro opera, and expressed concerns that the necessary intuitions and experience needed for such a venture were probably beyond the reach of any white composer.

Such guarded assessments were natural enough at a time when the aspirations of the Harlem Renaissance, though fading, were still clearly within memory. Indeed, in a panoramic review of the musical history of his race registered in *The Negro and His Music* of 1936, Alain Locke decried the "pseudo-Negroes" in minstrelsy's Age of Caricature (1875–1895) as well as the more recent manifestations in Al Jolson, Eddie Cantor, and Amos and Andy. He also denounced the stereotypical, pathetic, and romantic docility of the earlier Stephen C. Foster era and the later "wide-grinning, loud-laughing, shuffling, banjo-picking, dancing sort of being" who performed to a barbershop chord and a pseudo-Negro dialect. It was not until the age of jazz, he contended, that the genuine Negro voice reappeared.[32] Alongside this assessment, Locke noted that while the Negro was performing his musical wares on the stage, white pioneers were early cashing in on the popularity of ragtime in Tin Pan Alley.[33]

Yet despite Locke's claims that the success of William Grant Still and William Dawson in capturing the essence of a Negro musical language in their *Afro-American Symphony* and *Negro Folk Symphony* respectively were traceable to their ancestry, his analysis failed to spot the technical means which distinguished their solutions from those of non-blacks.[34] Copland, Carpenter, and Gruenberg were all applauded by Locke, and Gershwin's contributions appropriately noted. But the reasons behind his resentment of Gershwin's successes in his approaches to Afro-American themes, both narrative and musical, are masked in Locke's appraisal, made shortly after *Porgy*'s premiere: "From the '*Rhapsody in Blue*' in 1923 to last year's *American Folk Opera, 'Porgy and Bess,'* he has feverishly experimented, with increasing but not fully complete success. Discerning critics detect too much Liszt in the '*Rhapsody*' and too much

Puccini and Wagner in 'Porgy'; and it is not certain how well such musical oil and water can be made to mix."[35] In his appraisal of Gershwin's reliance upon exalted models, however, Locke clearly pinpointed one of the dilemmas inherent in the aspirations of the Harlem Renaissance. In retrospect, it was no doubt inevitable that concerns over Gershwin's borrowing of African-American material would sooner or later be addressed by black musical circles and reservation registered along with the applause.[36]

Compositions—all carrying the title *Negro Rhapsody*—written by Henry Gilbert (1915), by John Powell (who used the French *Rapsodie nègre,* 1917, for a work composed in the same year as Poulenc's identically titled score), and by Rubin Goldmark, the teacher of Gershwin and Copland, could be accorded their due,[37] and the accomplishments of Les Six in adopting elements of the jazz idiom sympathetically recalled even in preference to the jazz concertos of Americans Copland and Gershwin. But, in speaking of William Grant Still's *Afro-American Symphony* (1931) and Edmund Jenkins' *Negro Rhapsody,* premiered in Brussels and Paris in 1924, Locke claimed each to have been written by a "graduate of the jazz ranks" and judged that "the fruits of that apprenticeship have deepened the skill and racial character of their more formal music."[38] Locke's invocation of Jenkins, one of the most genteel of all black composers, as a "graduate of the jazz ranks" clearly speaks to Locke's skewed perspective in the service of a cultural agenda.[39]

It is of no small interest, in this regard, that Zora Neale Hurston, a black herself and widely respected as a sociologist, had already warned against claims of purity in Cunard's *Negro,* and analyzed charges of mimicry among blacks in terms of the time-honored view that originality, even in the works of Shakespeare, resided in the modification and treatment of received materials. Noting that the Negro, living and moving in the midst of a white civilization, had reinterpreted everything from language, food preparation, religion, and medicine to a Rudolph Valentino sheik haircut, she observed that he had also adopted and modified the whites' musical intruments and musical vocabularies. The circular path of such transfusions was further manifested, she recalled, when Paul Whiteman in turn provided "an imitation of a Negro orchestra making use of white-invented musical instruments in a Negro way."[40] Gershwin was obviously aware of such cultural progressions and their familiar habitation in the arts. Indeed, that his deepest aspirations encompassed such a point of view well before he ever began to write

Porgy is clear from the opening epigraph of this chapter, wherein he speaks of his hopes of writing an opera that would invoke the "clashing and blending" of multiple source materials and his desire to fashion "a style that could achieve out of this diversity, an artistic unity."

Some years later Ellington recalled that Gershwin "once told Oscar Levant that he wished he had written the bridge to 'Sophisticated Lady,' and that made me very proud."[41] And by the time of Robert Breen's revival of *Porgy* in 1952 Ellington could unabashedly wire the producer, "Your Porgy and Bess the superbest, singing the gonest, acting the craziest, Gershwin the greatest."[42] Numerous black critics, however, agreed with James Hicks's review of the production for the Baltimore *Afro-American,* which judged *Porgy and Bess* to be "the most insulting, the most libelous, the most degrading act that could possibly be perpetrated against the Negro people."[43] Though in the same season President Truman endorsed *Porgy*'s selection as a State Department tour offering and the opera played throughout Europe to rave reviews and became the first American work ever performed on the stage of La Scala, many of the original concerns would not go away.

But beyond the stereotypical characterizations of the play, Harold Cruse spotted another equally important dimension in his *Crisis of the Negro Intellectual* of 1967, wherein he asserted that *Porgy and Bess* was symbolic of the American black's lack of control over his artistic and cultural destiny, and concluded that "*Porgy* is surely the most contradictory cultural symbol ever created in the Western world." Cruse recommended that, as an emblem of cultural paternalism, "*Porgy and Bess* should be forever banned by all Negro performers in the United States."[44] Not surprisingly, such an injunction failed to materialize as *Porgy and Bess* continued to serve as a testing ground for evolving social attitudes toward race and gender.[45] And numerous African-American singers not only performed but garnered notable critical successes in revivals during virtually every decade following the premiere—Leontyne Price, William Warfield, Grace Bumbry, Roberta Alexander, and Simon Estes being only some of the more readily recognizable names.

Ultimately, individual pieces from Gershwin's opera settled in as classics, the whole remembered for what it was as well as what it was not, and the basic expression recognized as a musical marvel. But the component parts continued to puzzle the critics even as it delighted audiences, both black and white. In some real measure *Porgy and Bess* was an inverted product of the Harlem Renaissance in its response to the movement's central aspiration of putting Negro folk expression to classical account. Inverted, however, because it was penned not by a black composer but by a Tin Pan Alley Jew. Today, while concerns regarding fusion of jazz, blues, and spirituals with classical traditions as well as questions of ethnic authenticity have dispersed and relocated in a new critical terrain that still entertains charges of exploitation, Gershwin's guileless devotion to the thorny questions of race and musical expression is affectionately remembered in a large and familiar repertoire. And Ellington—though many of the issues that originally fueled his compositions have faded from view—continues to speak with a seemingly ever brighter resonance.

Noguchi and Friends

The New York gallery owner Julien Levy, whom the renowned sculptor Isamu Noguchi (1904–1988) had portrayed in 1929, said of the artist in an article of 1933 that "he is always attempting a nice balance between the abstract and the concrete, the relating of fact to meaning."[46] Whether, as Levy suggested, this combination was attributable to Noguchi's mixed parentage (a Japanese father, an American mother of Scottish descent) and international upbringing and education, his capacity to incorporate multiple readings is exemplified in his portrait, reduced to a mask, of the Japanese pioneer of modern dancer, Michio Ito (1925–26); in the portrait of Diaghilev's first Parisian choreographer, Michel Fokine (1926); and in the heads of Buckminster Fuller, Martha Graham, and George Gershwin, all executed in 1929 (Figure 8.2). Though most of these heads were initially sculpted for economic reasons, Noguchi confessed that "The problems of portraiture interested me: the confluence of personality and sculpture where the concentration of characteristics and identity, of sensibility and type, of style, even, belonged, I thought, more to the sitter or his race, than to the sculptor. Or if to the sculptor only as the medium of expression, limited in form, as is a sonnet."[47]

Noguchi had returned to New York at the end of 1928 from a two-year stay in Paris, where he had worked for some months with Brancusi. The 1929 head of Ruth Parks, a waitress whom Noguchi had only recently met, discloses in its ovoidal distillation of the face as well as the topknot a clear reflection of the influence of Brancusi's *White Negress* (1923) and of *Nancy Cunard* (1925–1927). Lincoln Kirstein, too,

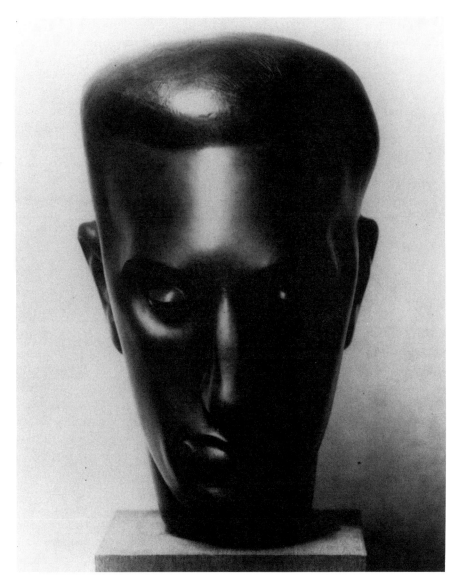

Figure 8.2. Isamu Noguchi, portrait of George Gershwin, 1929.

Courtesy of The Isamu Noguchi Foundation, Inc.

recognized the force of Brancusi in the portrait Noguchi made of him in 1929. Yet Noguchi's sculpture portraits of his friends Martha Graham, Buckminster Fuller, and George Gershwin, executed in the same year, additionally emphasize his capacity for effecting distinctions within the framework of such abstract tendencies. In his portrait of Graham, for example, he seems to have caught the dancer's firmly held conviction that bodily movements reveal inner states of being. Having left her apprenticeship (1916–1923) with Ruth St. Denis and Ted Shawn behind, in 1923 Graham danced in Michio Ito's *Garden of Kama* in Greenwich Village; and though she was not yet the legend she was later to become, she had begun to sense the expressive and ritualistic power of Ito's immobile mask-like face as an adjunct to dance. Her *Primitive Mysteries* of 1931, described by one critic as employing "angular, cold, stylized movement,"[48] featured Noguchi's sister, and in 1935 the dancer and sculptor initiated a collaboration that was to extend to 1966 in a series of twenty-one productions.[49]

In his portrait of Gershwin there were other perspectives that were open to Noguchi. Gershwin had also recently returned home from France in the fall of 1928, at which time Noguchi heard a new work, *An American in Paris,* premiered at Carnegie Hall. Sculptor and composer met and established a friendship that was to endure until the composer's death in 1937. At the time of their initial introduction Gershwin's Afro-American interests were already clearly in evidence in works such as *Rhapsody in Blue,* the Piano Concerto in F, and the projected *Porgy and Bess.* Spotting the communality of their interest and experience, Noguchi achieved in his portrait of Gershwin a cunning fusion of the art of Brancusi, the African mask, and Art Deco stylization. Noguchi's awareness of the range of "primitivist" themes during the preceding two decades is supported by more than critical fancy, being secured not only by his direct exposure to the themes of Brancusi's art but through associations confirmed in two other portraits of 1929: a head of Nicolas Roerich, co-author of the scenario and designer of costumes and sets for *Le Sacre du printemps,* as well as another of Marussia Burliuk (1932), the wife of the Russian painter David Burliuk, who had contributed an article entitled "The 'Savages' of Russia" to the *Blaue Reiter* journal in 1912.[50]

By 1930, however, the lure of folk cultures and even specifically the attraction of *art nègre* was heightened by a new set of social perspectives for many American artists. Noguchi, for example, knew the pain of racial prejudice first-hand. His father had left his mother before he was born, had returned to Japan, where he developed a reputation as a poet in English, and had initiated a correspondence with both Yeats and Pound. When the young Noguchi, having studied in Japan from the age of two to thirteen, again came to Japan in 1931, he encountered the rejection of his father, who wanted to be spared the embarrassment of acknowledging a half-breed child. In the wake of the "long, silent conversations" which he finally effected with his father over a period of two months, a heightened social conscience was inevitable.[51] Noguchi was aided in turning such personal feelings to artistic account by conversations in the home of David Burliuk, and his first statements, *Birth* and *Death (Lynched Figure)* (Figure 8.3), executed after a retreat to Woodstock, New York, in the summer of 1934, were calculatedly sensational. *Birth* spoke not only of the pain of the mother's labor but, autobiographically, of the birth agony of the child. *Death* was prompted by a photograph he had seen of a Negro man, hanged and burned, published in *International Labor Defense*. The outrage expressed by the sculpture's "sinewy limbs that curl in like the edges of charring paper . . . heightened by suspending the figure from a metal armature by a real rope knotted around its neck"[52] was born of lifelong personal concerns beyond its specific subject.

Similarly, his contemporaneous *Black Boy* (c. 1934), sculpted from ebony—now lost, though originally in the collection of George Gershwin—patently spoke to a similar collection of issues of time, place, and person and to a palpable communality of concerns on the part of the composer and his friend. A sculptor of Japanese and Scottish ancestry and a composer of Russian Jewish heritage both now living in New York, who despite their successes knew the power and the hurt of racial prejudice, responded in their individual ways to the predicament of the American Negro. If Gershwin's attempt to underscore the humanity, the joy, and the sorrow of a people was variously interpreted, Noguchi's *Death* was dismissed at the time in at least one quarter as "a little Japanese mistake."[53]

Noguchi's later devotion to stone and rock, materials which he observed were to be found everywhere—even in planetary explorations—provided a conduit to universals beyond the anxieties of the contemporary world. Like Brancusi and many other artists of the twenties, he began to address those themes of the Primitive dealing with the fundamental myths of creation and a search for the beginnings of things.

Figure 8.3. Isamu Noguchi, *Death (Lynched Figure),* 1934.
Courtesy of The Isamu Noguchi Foundation, Inc.

No sculpture more clearly encapsulates this fundamental preoccupation than *Momo Taro* (1977), a folk-hero the circumstances of whose birth from a peach are known to every Japanese child (Figure 8.4).[54] But looking at the central, hollowed-out portion of this nine-piece granite sculpture of his late maturity after it was finished, Noguchi saw the potential for amplified readings. Was it a cry, a cavern, a peach and its pit, or a space capsule capable of hurtling its way through the heavens?[55] Noguchi had effortlessly transformed the indefiniteness of the tale's beginning in a distant past—"Mukashi, mukashi, aru tokoro ni . . ." ("Once upon a time in a certain place . . .")—into a contemporary preoccupation with mankind's interplanetary aspirations and dreams. Similarly, in his numerous portraits of the late twenties as well as in such later works as the craggy and pensive head of Léger from 1941,[56] Noguchi not only ratified his relation to other kindred spirits working in different media but also hinted at a connection between immediate concerns at the time of conception and a retrospective, more universal resonance. The social relevance of his original confrontation with Gershwin also resurfaced in a particularly poignant fashion at the time he was carving the Billy Rose Sculpture Garden out of a Jerusalem

Figure 8.4. Isamu Noguchi, *Momo Taro*, 1977.

Storm King Art Center, Mountainville, New York. Gift of the Ralph E. Ogden Foundation, 1978.4.
Photo by Jerry L. Thompson.

hillside for the Israel Museum between 1960 and 1965. Symbolically, he sought and received permission from the Gershwin family to make a second cast of his 1929 portrait to present as a gift to the newly opened museum.

Primitivism Revisited

In 1959 a film of *Porgy and Bess* starring Sidney Poitier, Dorothy Dandridge, Sammy Davis, Jr., Pearl Bailey, and Diahann Carroll was criticized by black writers as a perpetuation of racial stereotypes, and an article appeared in *Ebony* magazine entitled "Why Negroes Don't Like *Porgy and Bess*." Both helped prepare the climate for the resurrection of old concerns. But coincidentally in the late 1960s an unexpected and somewhat paradoxical revival and reinterpretation surfaced when the ragtime craze once again hit with full force. As Scott Joplin climbed to the top of the charts, the pianist and musicologist Joshua Rifkin was joined by composers like William Bolcom and William Albright, all white, in a coalition that in part recalled the past in an attempt to renew the present but that, more important, continued to challenge the interrelationship of black and white, high and low art. By the 1960s, however, Bolcom and Albright thought little about the Africanness or Primitiveness of their source materials and commandeered ragtime as a vital and inherently natural part of their American heritage, as a link, even, between the native popular and imported classical traditions of American music. Mindless nostalgia or confrontational politics had much less to do with their appropriation than homage, visceral attraction, and musical respect.[57]

In the late 1960s and early 1970s the first serious study of African music by Westerners to achieve a degree of dissemination was undertaken by white Americans: by such figures as Steve Reich, whose investigation of African drumming served as the basis of his own minimalist compositions, and the ethnomusicologist John Chernoff, whose researches in Ghana were reported in an influential monograph, *African Rhythm and African Sensibility*. Chernoff's characterization of African music with respect to "multiple meter and apart-playing, of handclapping and 'metronome sense,'"[58] and Marius Schneider's clarification of the premium that this music places upon the juxtaposition of repetitive patterns "which continuously change their accents until they return to their initial pattern"[59] have contributed to a delayed recognition of the affinities between African rhythm and the processes discovered by Stravinsky between 1912 and 1914.[60]

The idea of trying to recover the oldest non-Western cultural traditions prior to the European conquests has, however, come to be seen as an impossibility. In retrospect, no attempt "to describe Africa's difference—as 'primitive,' 'animist,' 'prelogical,' 'collective,' 'rhythmic,' or whatever, seems immune from connotations and taints of ethnocentrism."[61] Yet, while verification of the nature of our beginnings and a genuine understanding of alien cultures both seem permanently out of reach, the quest for origins and the promotion of fusion continue to combine in a potentially noble, if mythic, crusade by poet, painter, and musician alike. Spurning any sense of guilt in our inability to establish "authenticity" in such matters, the artist acknowledges the ethnocentric dilemma even as he announces his need to perpetuate it in reenacting the eternal fantasy of self discovery. Undoubtedly Picasso, Braque, Vlaminck, Apollinaire, Guillaume, Léger, Milhaud, and Poulenc would all have understood Christopher Miller's assessment of one of the predicaments of contemporary literary criticism:

> Europeans have been making "theories" of Africans for centuries. My feeling is that the most fruitful path for the Western critic of African literature—the *Theor*—is not to play it safe and "stay home," nor to "leave home without it" and pretend to approach African literature with a virgin mind, but to balance one against the other, by reconsidering the applicability of all our critical terms and by looking to traditional African cultures for terms they might offer.[62]

The same might be said about all the cultural sources tapped under the banner of Primitivism, which we must finally remind ourselves was not limited to Africa or Oceania. For Russian artists relied upon archaeologists and connoisseurs of peasant culture in resurrecting, as well as in part confecting, an ancient civilization to which they could lay claim. Similarly, Manuel de Falla and Federico García Lorca, while heralding the purity and antiquity of the *cante jondo primitivo,* pursued the search for "truth without authenticity." Ferruccio Busoni, too, obtained Native-American musical materials through his former pupil Natalie Curtis for use in his *Indian Fantasy* (1913) and *Indianisches Tagebuch* (1915). And the recordings of Native-American music permitted by the development of Berliner and Edison recording technologies proved to hold an irresistible fascination for American composers such as Arthur

Farwell and Charles Wakefield Cadman, who saw in them materials providentially rescued from the brink of extinction. But for Busoni as well as for Farwell their interest in the certification of these materials was obviously secondary to the imaginative flight to an elusive culture which they permitted, and surely not far removed from the natural curiosity attendant on the appearance of "bona fide" Native-American villagers at the Dresden zoo in 1906 or the members of Buffalo Bill's show who pitched their tepees in Rome's Colosseum in the same year.[63] Similarly, Gershwin's creative passage toward an idealized African-American expression completely muted thematic quotation while joining experience with intuition in confecting a derivative but highly original magic of its own.

Aided by Europe's acclamation of an African-American music abroad, consensus as to what constituted a recognizable American musical diction had begun to be achieved. Once again, however, America's claims to developments independent of Europe were frequently premature and excessive. For even in matters of rhythm, the energy and example of other folk-based expressions coined by such figures as Bartók and Stravinsky under the banner of Primitivism were to prove essential to the American profile of a Copland or a Bernstein. Perhaps it was even predictable that, despite a keen analysis of ragtime and the charleston in the late 1920s, Copland turned in the 1930s and 1940s to other quarters in search of a different brand of Americana with *Billy the Kid, Rodeo,* and *Appalachian Spring.* Such scores probably attested less to Copland's evasion of black music and subjects per se than to the desire to find an alternative to the early European craze for jazz and to the Europeans' definition of the American voice almost exclusively through it.

If *art nègre* was not the only conduit to the Primitive or the American, in the twenties it was momentarily the richest,[64] and scrutiny of its potential was zealously carried out over a wide range—visual, literary, and musical. Yet the breadth of the encounter, rather than providing a more articulate focus, only sanctioned the formation of more extravagant and varied myths about ourselves and our origins. As with all such excursions, the possibilities for misunderstanding, purposeful or accidental, were considerable. In light of the demonstrated capacity of the colonialist, the dictator, and both contemporary liberal and conservative to perjure aesthetic evidence in the service of personal social agendas, the impulse behind mankind's cultural appropriations and the tendency to impound them in the formation of new myths invites perpetual scrutiny.

Yet, the composite evidence of cross-cultural, multi-media inter-change and the proliferating connections between Primitivism, begin-nings, cultural myth, and ethnic difference as well as similarity makes it difficult to accept those retrospective verdicts that judge the Primitivist impulse or the vogue for *art nègre* as merely "a manifestation of fashion" and lacking in any genuine force as a current of contemporary thought.[65] For despite the reasonable warning that prior to the Euro-pean colonization of Africa the Negro did not create works of art but rather fetishes for the purpose of housing the spirit of his ancestors,[66] the alliance of artifacts from black cultures with the aspirations of West-ern society ultimately implied recognition of a vital human resource that clearly transcended issues of clan or class. Its force not only in spell-ing out the meaning of European Modernism but in facilitating the formation of what might constitute a verifiable American musical voice can hardly be overestimated.

Understandably, Native Americans and African Americans alike have periodically expressed alternating rage and regret at the most blatant and stereotypical perspectives evident in Modernism's recruitment of their cultures. Even if Nancy Cunard and Europeans like Milhaud eventually could not escape such charges, it was surely the American, George Gershwin, who posed the central enigma. Like Ellington, Gershwin aspired to forms of expression that for numerous reasons seemed out of reach. A touching letter from Maurice Ravel to Nadia Boulanger as late as March 8, 1928, discloses Gershwin's communicated sense of inadequacy for the task ahead. Speaking of the American's pro-found talent and worldwide success, which "no longer satisfies him, for he is aiming higher," Ravel stated that "he knows that he lacks the technical means to achieve his goal." Rightly concerned that instruc-tion might tarnish Gershwin's natural gifts and fearful of his incapacity to guide, Ravel asked Boulanger if she would be willing "to undertake this awesome responsibility."[67] Like Ravel, Boulanger resisted the as-signment, and though late in life Gershwin did take lessons with Henry Cowell, Joseph Schillinger, and Wallingford Riegger, by that time not only were his voice and the technical means to express it in place but a major portion of his compositions were already penned.

Gershwin never went to college but found a powerful alternative classroom when he chose to "Take the 'A' Train" to Harlem. There he found himself open to censure not for having journeyed to a destina-tion that was off limits but, once he was there, for claiming entrée to its societal voice in an attempt to identify a larger American cadence.

As with all such coalitions, the larger Modernist–Primitivist alliance—of which this was a late but clear manifestation—was retrospectively capable of being vilified, deconstructed, and rejected as an untenable venture. Ultimately, however, an appraisal of its individual achievements reveals troubling assertion and insatiable inquiry, opportunism as well as nobility of outreach, that still makes us wonder if the world will see the likes of such a time again.

In such reviews a contemporary paradox inevitably surfaces to the effect that the richness of *diversity,* historically applauded as one of the central and enriching conditions of American civilization, may in some fundamental sense be incompatible with the concept of *integration;* that the noblest values of the one may preclude a fostering of the other. How best, the question persists, can one preserve the notion of America's independence from foreign models and the sense of a fresh start, for example, and at the same time acknowledge a people's natural yearning to claim multiple roots in a culturally diverse society. The dreams of Ellington and Gershwin registered in the twin epigraphs of this chapter pose both the ideal and the dilemma.

— CLOCKWORK —

— 9 —

The Valley of the Bells

A building occupying, so to speak, a four-dimensional space—
the fourth being that of Time—. . . seeming to conquer and lay
claim, not just to a few square yards, but to successive epochs
from which it emerged victorious.

Marcel Proust

The inner eye opens to visions of time and space which overstep
what the laws of the physical world around us permit.

Karlheinz Stockhausen

Time is the most elusive and perplexing concept in human existence.
Existence itself implies a before and after—pre-birth and post-death—
about which we can consciously know nothing. Even in our daily
rounds a look at the heavens places us in a dilemma if we ponder that
what we presently observe is a light whose energy and path were initiated millions of years ago. We understand why it is that to look out
into space is to look back in time, but we struggle to comprehend its
significance. To wrestle with such questions is not only to entertain
the notion of relativity but also to risk a supreme sense of alienation.

Beyond such metaphysical concerns, the musician is obliged to confront the issue of time constantly in both its linear and simultaneous
dimensions, and to invoke a memory with respect to each that surpasses
the function of melody and harmony and includes their interaction in
the horizontal/vertical moment. The issues are vast and in music involve the aural partitioning of a single linear whole into digestible
phrases, motifs, or smaller moments; the comprehension of lines simultaneously in motion; of harmonic, durational, and timbral sequence; of
stasis and motion, ellipsis and anastrophe. The ability to take in multiple

simultaneous events or to remember musical events recalled or transformed over a large time span poses significant challenges for the listener. Recognition may improve with familiarity or instruction with
respect to listening strategies, but the idea of multiple layers of sound
moving at different speeds has always intrigued the composer as a constructive gambit far beyond the ability of most listeners to register it
aurally. This is as true of isorhythmic and cantus firmus practices of the
Middle Ages and Renaissance as it is of Messiaen's time grids in *Quartet
for the End of Time* (1940) or the gigantic formschemes of Stockhausen's
Inori (1974), *Sirius* (1977), and the opera cycle *Licht* (1981–).[1]

A concern for such issues eventually dissolves in the conclusion that
it is impossible to define how a piece of music ought to be heard. Both
composer and listener are always striving toward a possibility. Our attention to details typically sharpens and relaxes in unpredictable patterns, a factor that carries the power of seduction in anticipation of
fresh discoveries on repeated hearings—even of familiar works. In a
polyphonic environment the various lines may tend to confirm one
another's identity and character or they may operate almost totally independently. While a proclivity for the latter condition is observable in
polyphony of the Middle Ages and the Renaissance, to a lesser degree
throughout later periods, and continuously in specific non-Western
musics, a conscious movement toward simultaneous non-alliance in
matters of harmony, rhythm, phraseology, and cadence appears as an
increasingly observable musical fact of life in the early years of the present century. This tendency, interestingly enough, is observable not only
in music written by those figures typically associated with the avant-
garde of the first decades (Schoenberg, Stravinsky, Ives) but in more
familiar music of the same period routinely encountered by present-
day concertgoers (works by Debussy, Ravel).

Although reflections on the relativity of time and space were entertained well before the twentieth century, Einstein's name looms as a
familiar icon in any retrospective view of the issue. Our collective interest in him is due in large measure to the fact that the notion of relativity
has been lavishly explored outside the scientific domain. In painting,
the positioning of objects typically implies a spatial relationship that in
turn may suggest temporal values. In the twentieth century, however,
numerous forces have conspired to attempt a new depiction of time
on the canvas and to flirt with the notion of portraying dislocations in
time as well as simultaneity on a two-dimensional surface. The first

approaches to Cubism around 1908 were fundamentally centered on an investigation of this very issue.

In literature the difficulty in fixing the coordinates of time in real experience was also a seductive theme for many writers. None struck its ineffable note with greater impact than Proust, who brought the reader face to face not only with the sensation of suspended time but also with the difference between childhood time and the adult mixture of voluntary and involuntary memory based upon accumulated experience and reverie.

Beyond Proust's nostalgic time-fracture, hinted at in the opening epigraph of this chapter, literature in the early decades of the twentieth century also explored realms more complex, as well as more fashionable, in both philosophy and painting. The intellectual basis of art was contemplated at length, and while the period in general fell somewhat short of a return to the age of Descartes, concern for the physical properties of sound as well as factors involved in its perception achieved vogue status. Such discussions were frequently led by personalities only peripherally trained as musicians but whose interest was consuming. Paul Valéry's fascination with the technical problems of a single poem, "La Jeune parque," for example, occupied him over a period of five years from 1912 to 1917, sealing the link between poetry and geometry on the one hand and between poetry and music on the other.[2] Like music, literature is premised on temporal linear values, and it was natural that these two arts would share a particular intimacy in their attempts to explore new orders of time and space.

More attuned than Proust and Valéry to the extreme avant-garde implications of such discussions was Blaise Cendrars, who claimed to have written the first simultaneous poem in his *Prose du transsibérien,* published in 1913, the same year as the opening volume of Proust's *À la recherche du temps perdu.* With it he also achieved a *petit succès de scandale.* It stirred a polemic largely because of its physical appearance, a seven-foot sheet with parallel text and abstract painting by the artist Sonja Delaunay. The poem was printed in an edition of 150 copies, which, if placed end to end, it was claimed would reach the top of the Eiffel Tower. Cendrars, Sonja Delaunay, her husband, Robert, and Apollinaire all became engaged in a public dispute over the origins of the term *simultanéisme, simultanisme,* or *le simultané,* an issue very close to the heart of the Futurists, the Cubists, and later the techniques of Dada.

Cendrars's *Prose du transsibérien* was printed in ten different type faces and sizes as well as in different colors, and as such claimed lineage with Mallarmé's renowned *Un Coup de dés* of 1897. The various types help the reader locate repetition and variation in the formal network of the piece even as they interface with Delaunay's parallel colors. That her contribution was not conceived as an illustration of a text was made explicit by Apollinaire: "Blaise Cendrars and Madame Delaunay-Terk have made a first attempt at simultaneous writing where the contrast of colors trains the eye to read at once the multiple aspects of the poem; just as a conductor reads at a single glance the superimposed notes of an orchestral score, or as one takes collective note of both the visual and printed elements of a poster."[3] Delaunay's painting is totally devoid of narrative, does not compete with the story of the text, but rather directs the eye in a vertical movement as it follows the horizontal/vertical layout of the poem, which seems to float in the wash of Delaunay's colors (Figure 9.1). The text itself is, indeed, a journey on the trans-Siberian railroad to Moscow and ultimately Manchuria. Like Cendrars's other poem, *Le Panama,* it begins and ends in Paris, city of modernity and of the poet.[4] It was the city of the painter and the composer as well.

The introduction of the "fourth dimension," referring to time, in the discussion of the painters during this period was clearly an appropriation of an issue currently in vogue in the world of physics. In such attempts, the visual artists openly sought alliance with a dimension inherent to the world of organized sound, whether literature or music. But while music held the natural capacity to project materials simultaneously as well as linearly, this was more difficult for literature. Mallarmé had begun the search for such a solution with his *Un Coup de dés* (1897), and Apollinaire became obsessed with the same exploration in his *Calligrammes* (1914). Although Apollinaire, following his own typographical experiments, ultimately rejected the concept of simultaneity for poetry in an article of the same year, Blaise Cendrars's adoption and promotion of the idea was not to be easily dismissed. It was an issue that would continue to intrigue the avant-garde in literature for years to come, and Joyce, Eliot, and Dos Passos all played with and occasionally floundered in their preoccupations with the time factor—including not only simultaneity, but intercut and other alternatives to linear time. Testimony to the continuing fashion of Cendrars and his most famous poem among the musicians appeared as late as December

Figure 9.1. Blaise Cendrars and Sonja Delaunay, *Prose du transsibérien,* 1913. The original publication, unfolded, was seven feet in length.

22, 1924, in a collage concert of Jane Bathori and Marcel Herrand at the Salle Huygens, at which passages by Tristan Tzara and Blaise Cendrars were interspersed with texts by Cocteau and Apollinaire.[5] Herrand recited from Cendrars's *Prose du transsibérien* and Bathori sang excerpts from his *Paques à New York* set by Honegger. And only the month before, on November 29, the Ballets Suédois had premiered Satie's *Relâche,* an idea originally concocted by Cendrars, advertised as a "ballet instantanéiste."

Manifestations of the abiding infatuation with time, space, and narrative were apparent in the cinema from its inception. The classic early example is D. W. Griffith's pathbreaking film *Intolerance* of 1916, where four stories simultaneously recalling pre-Christian Babylon, the life and crucifixion of Christ, the St. Bartholomew's Day massacre of the Huguenots in sixteenth-century France, and a modern story of a young man wrongly condemned to death, are accompanied by a score confected by Joseph Carl Breil characterized by pastiche, intercut, and allusion. From that time forward the most popular of all the entertainment media has relied heavily and even fundamentally upon the power of collage. Indeed, the cinema was a central agent in promoting the comprehensibility of fracture, and in turn conditioned Western society not only to accept it but to demand it as a compelling ingredient in all branches of communication, including radio and ultimately television. At the same time, the cinema has insistently promoted concepts of simultaneity with respect to the musico–dramatic relationship, vividly demonstrating a capacity to contradict and surpass predictable synchronism between gesture and sound.

Literary critics, frequently reflecting upon their experience with the cinema, have been busy developing theories of spatiality as opposed to temporality in contemporary literature for decades, and have typically focused their attention on a new dimension judged to have been introduced with the lowering of the narrative quotient and increased fragmentation observable in such landmarks of early modernity as Joyce's *Ulysses,* T. S. Eliot's *The Waste Land,* Ezra Pound's *Cantos,* and to a lesser degree Proust's *À la recherche du temps perdu.* It is not surprising that attempts have been made to link developments in literature to those that had taken place in the movement from a Newtonian world to Einstein's relativistic cosmos. The idea has been posited that there was an attempt to overthrow literature's former narrative domain, defined as temporal, and to replace it with disjunctive syntactic arrangements that promote concepts of simultaneity, described as spatial. The argument has at least temporarily subsided with the rejection of the notion that spatial forms are static and temporal forms are dynamic, the reconstitution of Einstein's claim that the two are intimately interrelated, and the corollary acknowledgment that they have been present in the literatures of all ages and cultures—"that we literally cannot 'tell time' without the mediation of space."[6]

Mark Roskill has similarly summarized the several tenets of Cubism as viewed by Apollinaire, Jean Metzinger, and their circles around 1912, noting their fascination, which was obsessive, with recent discoveries in non-Euclidian geometry and physics and the world of Einstein in particular.[7] The principal frustrations of the painters Gleizes and Metzinger centered on the desire to experience "all the angles of a prism simultaneously." New technologies, including the automobile and the airplane, permitted new angles, vistas, and temporal observations; and the infatuation with the Eiffel Tower was symbolic of these new technologies and the resulting transformation of perspectives. Evidence of the Tower's force can be seen in Robert Delaunay's multiple Cubist canvases, which in turn suggested to Apollinaire a new physical arrangement for one of his poems in *Calligrames* that approximated a view of it from the top.

Simultaneity had already been introduced as a specialized term in color theory by Michel-Eugène Chevreul as early as 1839,[8] in a book that was to have an enormous influence upon the work of Seurat and the Neo-Impressionists and later Robert Delaunay; and it appeared with awesome consequences in the philosophy of Henri Bergson,[9] wherein he attempted to define simultaneity as "the intersection of time and space." Contrasting intuition and intellect, he claimed that it was the former that perceived the reality of time, which is duration. This, he argued, was sensed from the life experience, was not divisible or measurable, and was demonstrated by the collective phenomena of memory. The Futurists' later adoption of the term combined aspects of both of these nineteenth-century points of view, promoting its use to encompass the interpenetration of objects with surrounding space and by 1912 its significance for emotion and memory. Delaunay's specific concerns ultimately revolved around the simultaneous contrast of color and its optical reception.[10]

Léon Werth had introduced the idea of "duration" in a review of a Picasso exhibition as early as May 1910. Like Metzinger and Gleizes he proclaimed the right of the artist to "transfer onto the plane of a picture the sensations and reflections which we experience with the passage of time." Finally, the combination of simultaneity and relativity was addressed by Metzinger in an article, "Cubism and Tradition," of August 1911, and the point of view was ultimately crystallized in the first important theoretical statement about Cubism, which Metzinger made with Gleizes in their *Du Cubisme* of 1912. They asserted that movement around the object allowed the painter to "seize from it several successive aspects" (or appearances) which, when "fused together into a single image, reconstitute it in time."

Now, in the world of music many of these ideas were hardly novel, and, indeed, had been elaborately addressed in Western music in compositions dating back to the Middle Ages and the early Renaissance, where the fourteenth-century isorhythmic motet and fifteenth-century cantus firmus mass provide vivid testimony to the challenge that such questions posed. In non-Western repertoires, too, heterophonic folk practices, which implied the non-synchronous alliance of multiple improvisations of the same idea, provided a reasonable analogy. It need hardly be doubted that Debussy's and Ravel's fascination with the gamelan ensembles of Java and Bali, which appeared at the Paris universal expositions of 1889 and 1900, was also as much inspired by temporal considerations as scalar and timbral ones. Admission of the relevance of both the painterly perspective of Paul Klee, which was similar to that of Gleizes, and Indonesian heterophony as a compositional *point de départ* was still being voiced by Pierre Boulez many years later.[11] We are reminded of the impact of transcultural exposure on the musical perspectives not only of Debussy around 1905 but of Bartók as early as 1908 when he promoted polytonality (the simultaneous projection of two or more "keys") as an extrapolation from performance practices of Hungarian folk music. It is clear in retrospect that in the early years of the twentieth century, music, along with literature and the visual arts, contributed fresh solutions to the issues of time, space, and narrative. In some ways music held the ideal position of the three for entertaining such a fundamental encounter.

Critics and historians have debated Adorno's admonition that "difficulty" in some measure was a prerequisite for membership, and surely for canonization, in the avant-garde. The basic assertion can readily be confirmed in numerous works of the early twentieth century. Yet while difficulty is typically taken to connote lack of ease in assimilation upon initial confrontation, it is intriguing to note that even relatively chaotic temporal behavior in music can be readily accommodated if other parameters are controlled in such a fashion as to afford compensatory orientation.

Ravel's "La Vallée des cloches" ("The Valley of the Bells") from his *Miroirs* (1904–5) provides an ideal locus for savoring the ways in which the fundamental aspects of spatial and temporal coordination were addressed by a Parisian composer almost a decade prior to the time of Cendrars's and Apollinaire's publications described above. It is well to recall that beyond its concrete and picturesque reality, the bell's primary fascination for Symbolists of all persuasions had resided in its multilayered richness as a psychological and aural symbol. Among the Russians, Tchaikovsky *(1812 Overture)* and Musorgsky *(Boris Godunov)* invoked its sounds to resurrect the memory of events from war and coronation, while in his choral cantata *The Bells* of 1913 Rachmaninov set poetry of the figure most idolized by the French Symbolists, the American Edgar Allan Poe. Rimsky-Korsakov was also keenly aware of the overtone structure of bells and spoke lucidly of it as a principle of orchestration. Their later compatriot Igor Stravinksy acknowledged its potency in fashioning his haunting conclusions to both wedding and funeral rites in *Les Noces* (1922) and *Requiem Canticles* (1966).[12]

The most influential of these works written prior to Ravel's *Miroirs* was Musorgsky's *Boris Godunov,* an opera not only known to young Parisian artists at the time but enshrined as a cult object of study along with Debussy's *Pelléas et Mélisande.* Ravel's fascination with the symbol of the bell and its acoustical properties had been manifest in two early works. The *Ballade de la Reine morte d'aimer* for voice and piano (1893) was a setting of Roland de Marès' *Complainte de la Reine de Bohême.* The allusion to the "small bells of Thulé" at its conclusion calls forth Ravel's first sonic excursion into this domain, which was pursued shortly thereafter in his "Entre cloches" from *Sites auriculaires* for two pianos (1895–1897). These somewhat tentative sketches, which joined a prominent use of harmonic fourths characteristic of bells with tolling repeated notes, propelled Ravel into a deeper investigation of the properties of bells in two works written shortly thereafter and in close proximity: "La Vallée des cloches" (*Miroirs,* 1903–5) and "Le Gibet" (*Gaspard de la nuit,* 1908).[13]

Although there is no need to claim for Ravel an overriding concern in these works for philosophical notions concerning time and existence or to stress unduly an interdisciplinary awareness on his part with respect to the formation of avant-gardes, a Symbolist orientation clearly led Ravel to the discovery of a construction in *Miroirs* that was perceived by the composer as a breakthrough in his development. Ravel stated that *Miroirs* "marked a rather considerable change in my harmonic evolution, which disconcerted even those musicians who had been accustomed to my style." It should be stressed that the harmonic language of "La Vallée des cloches" was clearly as important in establishing the multiple temporal-spatial planes as the element of rhythm. Ravel's sonic landscape was purportedly prompted by the tolling of Parisian church bells at noontide, now reset through its title to a valley wherein neighboring villages simultaneously and uncoordinatedly sound the Angelus.

Ravel's technical solution to his poetic charge is sure, directly perceivable, and in its intricacy and control an extraordinary achievement in the world of Western art music.[14] While it postdates the philosophical disquisitions of Bergson on the question of simultaneity, it antedates by half a decade the first Cubist and Futurist manifestoes on the subject in the plastic arts.[15]

A glance at the complete score of *Miroirs* reveals that Ravel uses three staves—rather than the traditional two—in only a single movement, "La Vallée des cloches," where it is employed throughout (Example 9.1). This notational gambit makes its first appearance here in the piano works of Ravel, and had yet to appear in the works of Debussy. Although accommodation to three staves in his *Préludes* of 1910–1913 is familiar to pianists, this layout makes its first tentative appearance in the works of Debussy in the second series of *Images* of 1907. Here, beyond reasons of clarity, Debussy chooses a three-system notation in order to highlight, although somewhat timidly, the registral layers, which in turn suggest hand placement at the keyboard. Ravel's solution, while subscribing to all of these factors, moves well beyond such a limited utilitarian purpose. For the notational layers are the vehicles for discrete temporal and tonal ideas, installed in such a fashion as to suggest an analysis of the work.

A glance at the opening section of the music even by readers unfamiliar with musical notation should readily reveal five layers of ostinati, or repeated patterns, of unvarying pitch and register, whose beginning measures are 1, 3, 4, and 5 (low G and middle voice e♯'). Yet the magic stems from the fact that whenever an exact repetition occurs in the

Example 9.1. Maurice Ravel, *Miroirs,* "La Vallée des cloches," mm. 1–13.

opening eleven measures, mutation is achieved through the introduction of a new pattern or the rhythmic displacement of an old one. Though numerous pairs approach identity, analysis reveals that no two of them are the same. Furthermore, while the harmony is seductive and emphasizes the quartal structures characteristic of bells, the layering emphasizes tonal ambiguity. The pentatonicism that dominates the opening of the piece and suggests compatibility with E major/C♯ minor in accordance with the key signature is quickly compromised in measure six with the introduction of two new, single-pitched bells, the low G_1 and the middle e♯'. Analysts will note that, in spite of their dissonating effect, these two insistently sounded pitches function as an augmented sixth sonority and ultimately expand to the octave F♯ at measure twelve in a totally classic, if somewhat delayed, resolution.

The final effect of the piece involves a temporal and spatial narrative understandable to all. And it is precisely because the anticipation which the ostinato incites is perpetually foiled that any listener can follow the sonic fantasy of Ravel's musical landscape. Dedicated to Maurice Delage, a favorite pupil who would remember this very work in a piece written at the end of World War II,[16] it must also have brought him many admirers among other composers of the day. Indeed, the registral separation for discrete and conflicting ideas, both tonal and temporal, is something that can be spotted in the work of numerous composers of the next half decade. It would even be tempting to suggest that it provided something of a general model for the first of Stravinsky's *Three Pieces for String Quartet*.[17]

The agencies of polychords, polytonality, and polystylistic reference as employed by the composers in promoting illusions in space and time during the first years of the century reflect a powerful and universal concern. Proust, Bergson, Picasso, Cendrars, Delaunay—they all pondered the imponderability of nonlinear time and intimated their suspicion that the answers were to be found not in science but in art. Yet even the New Physicists were currently proposing ideas that could have appealed only to the painters, the poets, and the musicians. They argued that "access to the physical world is through experience, the common denominator of all experience is the 'I' that does the experiencing. In short, what we experience is not external reality, but our interaction with it."[18] Thus formulated and further fueled by contemporary psychological notions of the "continuous present," such perspectives read like an aesthetic decree.

Related but differently formulated questions were searching for answers in what only appeared to be radically dissimilar terrain in the music of Edgard Varèse and Charles Ives. Varèse spoke openly of his infatuation with the concept of "music as spatial—as bodies of intelligent sounds moving freely in space—" at some point between 1903 and 1907,[19] and pursued the notions of juxtapositional development, projection in space, metrical simultaneity, and sound-mass technique as reflections of the New Physics throughout his career.[20] And for Ives, the competing brass bands converging on the village square, the holiday celebrations with their boisterous collision of national tunes, and the flooding reverie of familiar Sunday School hymns from childhood days all provided a rich resource for his early recognition of the value of temporal/tonal collage in testing the relationships of memory and experience. Ives's investigation of the spatial component as well as his invocation of vernacular styles promoted a rethinking of the forming process in music. Ultimately, the micro-collage principle may be said to have encouraged the unmediated juxtaposition on a larger scale of unconnected styles and structures. The Third and Fourth symphonies, for example, as well as some of the sets of orchestral pieces, "were assembled from individual movements conceived independently and only later gathered together into sets with varying degrees and sources of unity between movements".[21]

At the deepest structural level, too, Arnold Schoenberg retrospectively registered his interest in and concern for the larger issues of musical time in relation to its spatial deployment. Recalling the perspective of his own *Jakobsleiter* (1917–1922) and prefiguring the literary theorists of a later age, he argued in his article "Composition with Twelve Tones" (1941) that such a relativistic view of space and time was based upon classical principles and was valid for all music:

> *The unity of musical space demands an absolute and unitary perception.* In this space, as in Swedenborg's heaven (described in Balzac's *Seraphita*) there is no absolute down, no right or left, forward or backward. Every musical configuration, every movement of tones has to be comprehended primarily as a mutual relation of sounds, of oscillatory vibrations, appearing at different places and times.[22]

It is clear that Schoenberg's concerns were less cerebral than metaphysical, more intuitive than intellectual, and therefore in tune not only with Bergson's disavowal of the notions of "before" and "after" in the world of time but with his feeling that intuition provided the foundation of perception and hence the agency whereby one transcends the familiar veneer of daily facades.[23] The same issues also interested Apollinaire, Picabia, Léger, and Gleizes, and most especially Henri Martin Barzun and Riciotto Canudo, friend of Gleizes and editor of the periodical *Montjoie!* which in 1913 carried discussions regarding simultaneity in music. Paradoxically, quotidian experience which meshed fantasy with reality frequently fed both creative action and the disquisitions of the theorists. In the 1920s George Antheil continued to argue related questions for a new musico–mechanico age.[24] As we shall see, however, no one was more fascinated by the temporal and spatial factors attendant to the issue of simultaneity, more intrigued by their potential, or more convinced of their force than Igor Stravinsky. A personal friendship between the two composers virtually guaranteed Stravinsky's familiarity with Ravel's conquests in *Miroirs*. But it was his awareness of the Cubists, frequently hinted at but never fully articulated, that was to prove equally catalytic.

— 10 —

Stravinsky and the Cubists

The esoteric element was always something which was ingrained in art generally: the esoteric of proportions in architecture and in painting. This occurs especially when science and art are going hand in hand.

Pierre Boulez

In its special mode of handling its given material, each art may be observed to pass into the condition of some other art, by what German critics term an *Anders-streben*—a partial alienation from its own limitations, through which the arts are able, not indeed to supply the place of each other, but reciprocally to lend each other new forces.

Walter Pater

Cubism: Definitions and *Dramatis Personae*

In the opening statement of his fundamental study on Cubism, Robert Rosenblum proposed that the discovery of Cubism around 1910 was as revolutionary and important as the contemporaneous revelations of Einstein and Freud:

For the traditional distinction between solid form and the space around it, Cubism substituted a radically new fusion of mass and void. In place of earlier perspective systems that determined the precise location of illusory depth, Cubism offered an unstable structure of dismembered planes in indeterminate spatial positions . . . no single interpretation of the fluctuating shapes, textures, spaces, and objects could be complete in itself . . . In expressing [this paradox] Cubism offered

a visual equivalent of a fundamental aspect of twentieth-century experience.[1]

The painter now welcomed analysis of his components through emphasis upon the *process* of assemblage and the valuation of simultaneously
exposed perspectives. The result was an art of visual contradictions and
intentional ambiguity.

Among the first generation of artists who initially defined the aesthetic of Cubism, 1881 was a banner year: both the Spaniard Pablo
Picasso and the Frenchman Albert Gleizes, the first Cubist theorist,
were born then. So were, it might be observed, the Russian painters
Larionov and Goncharova; and a musician by the name of Igor Stravinsky was born in the next year, 1882. All were in their early thirties
when they found themselves together for the first time in Paris.

From the first decades of the twentieth century, interdisciplinary
connections between the worlds of art and music have been periodically
drawn in an attempt to elucidate the origins of Modernism. Yet the
link between music and Cubism has invariably been asserted in the most
general terms, and has rarely been subjected to meaningful scrutiny.
Christopher Gray launches his book *Cubist Aesthetic Theories* with the
declaration that "Cubism was more than another artistic 'ism.' It was
something much deeper. Cubism was a vital force which found expression in music and literature as well as in the visual arts of painting and
sculpture."[2] Further observations, however, are limited to the classical
claim of sisterhood between literature and art *(ut pictura poesis)* and even
the contention that connections are to be found in a common concern
for certain aesthetic problems rather than in any technical means, which
are held to be nontransferable.[3]

Despite problems attendant to moving from visual criteria to sonic
ones, from a geometric space to a time space, and potentially representational line and color to essentially abstract tone and timbre, it is possible
to demonstrate that there was a natural affinity between Stravinsky and
the Cubists which antedates Stravinsky's first meeting with Picasso in
1917. That Stravinsky knew of the painter's work can be corroborated
from numerous pieces of evidence and various correspondences—including the letters of Cocteau to Stravinsky, which reveal that the former frequently spoke to Picasso about the Russian musician before that
date.[4]

Besides Picasso, Braque, and Juan Gris, however, there were other artists with a demonstrable Cubist inclination who were in closer proximity to Stravinsky in the period 1913–1915. A lesser-known figure today, but one central to the early definition of Cubism, for example, was Albert Gleizes. The activities of a group of artists known as the Abbaye de Créteil, which Gleizes organized during the years 1906–7, were familiar to the likes of Marinetti, founder of the Futurists, to Brancusi, and to the Muscovites as well. Gleizes's *Les Brumes du matin sur le Marne* was included in a Russian exhibition in 1908, and together with Metzinger and Mercereau he had appeared in the first "Jack of Diamonds" exhibition in Moscow of 1910.[5]

Given Diaghilev's intimate association with the world of the painters from the turn of the century and his initial sponsorship of Stravinsky from around 1909, it is hard to imagine that the composer could have escaped an early knowledge of Picasso, Gleizes, and Metzinger as well as native Russian artists such as Goncharova, Larionov, and Malevich, who were actively at work producing their own Cubo-Futurist canvases from 1909 on.[6] Benois spoke directly of the young Stravinsky's participation in discussions at committee meetings of Diaghilev's Ballets Russes prior to the initial production of *The Firebird*:

> One of the binding links between us, besides music, was Stravinsky's cult of the theatre and his interest in the plastic arts. Unlike most musicians, who are usually quite indifferent to everything that is not within their sphere, Stravinsky was deeply interested in painting, architecture, and sculpture. Although he had had no grounding in these subjects, discussion with him was very valuable to us, for he "reacted" to everything for which we lived. In those days he was a very willing and charming "pupil." He thirsted for enlightenment and longed to widen his knowledge.[7]

While Stravinsky's relation to these Russian artists has frequently been reviewed with respect to their common interest in the radical transformation of the folk heritage, it is possible to demonstrate that their shared commitment to the premises of Cubo-Futurism provides an equally dramatic clarification of the ways by which ideas of the primitive were adapted and absorbed into the modern lexicon. Richard Taruskin has properly noted, for example, that the neonationalist tendencies of Larionov and Goncharova soon manifested a gradual abstraction of the motifs of folk art "to the point where nothing of the subject remained visible."[8] Such developments were totally in harmony with speculations forwarded by Wilhelm Worringer[9] in 1908 and quickly disseminated in Russia by Kandinsky as well as through the consequent pronouncements of T. E. Hulme in January 1914 regarding the establishment of a new theoretical edifice based on a new "tendency towards abstraction."[10]

Goncharova, who was born of the Russian aristocracy (her paternal grandmother was a daughter of Pushkin), had together with Larionov first launched a Primitivist style at the third exhibition of the "Golden Fleece" in December 1909. In addition to the boldness of line and abstractness of color directly traceable to the Fauvists, both painters drew upon embroidery from Siberia, pastry forms, and toys as well as upon icon painting and the *lubok,* or peasant woodcuts.[11] But by 1911 Goncharova had announced her view that Russia's neonationalist strain contained more than folklorism and that it betrayed expressive characteristics compatible with the most modern tendencies. In a letter to the journal *La Parole russe* (*Russkoe Slovo*) of 1911, she had been quite explicit:

> Cubism is a good thing in and of itself, although not completely new, especially in Russia. It is in this style that the Scythians, of precious memory, executed their "Babas" of stone; it is in this style that the remarkably beautiful wooden dolls which one sees for sale at the market are made. They are works of sculpture. In France, too, the Gothic and Negro sculptures were the point of departure for Cubism in painting.[12]

Rosenblum's claim in his book on Cubism for a profound connection between Picasso's *Les Demoiselles d'Avignon* of 1907 and Bartók's *Allegro barbaro* (1910), Stravinsky's *Le Sacre du printemps* (1911–13), and Prokofiev's *Scythian Suite* (1914–1916) is one that has been periodically forwarded. Despite the seeming dissimilarity of their subject matter, the substitution of Slavic or Magyar folk primitive for African ritual primitive was a convention that was accepted at a reasonably early date, as previously noted. More important, there were constructive premises directly traceable to the Cubists that the musicians understood as well. Rosenblum's intuition that Stravinsky's approach to musical structure "might well be called 'Cubist'"[13] is particularly tantalizing in light of Ernest Ansermet's retrospective but unreserved judgment that up to *L'Histoire du soldat* Stravinsky's music was a manifestation of the spirit of Cubism.[14] It could even be argued that a connection between Stravinsky and the Cubists can be traced to the premiere of *Le Sacre du printemps,* as we see in Maurice Touchard's review of 1913: "This style or absence of any style is clearly a forethought. Has Stravinsky intended thus to depict the barbarity and crudity of these people? Or has he simply given in to a tendency, rather notable among Russians as well as in this country, to call attention to himself through harmonic excesses, through a kind of musical *cubism?*"[15]

The question emerges, "In what ways did the late nineteenth-century neonationalist infatuation with folk art, seen as an emblem of societal roots, nourish early twentieth-century concerns for the primitive as a spearhead in the definition of Modernism, and to what newer forces such as Cubism did it exhibit a potential for accommodation?" Much of the avant-garde impulse in Russia in the period 1907–1913 had been identified under the Futurist banner. While in certain particulars the Russian movement was in harmony with the Italian Futurists, in its details it was separable from them and was identified initially in painting before being taken up by the poets. Not only in their adoption of folk-art imagery but in their irreverent attack on conventional use of language—including epithet, street language, and archaic, erotic, or infantile language which promoted a noncontextual jumbling of words until only the sound remained, the Russian Futurist poets such as Mayakovsky, Kruchenikh, Khlebnikov, Elena Guro, and David Burliuk all owed a debt to the example of Larionov and Goncharova during the period 1908–1913.[16]

The degree to which the Russian avant-garde was connected with the developing aesthetic of other progressive centers in Europe has been detailed, including the recognition that from the turn of the century the Russian link was at least as strong with Munich as with Paris. The Blaue Reiter movement is testimony to this assertion. But with the World of Art movement the Russian-Paris axis had been so strengthened by 1914 that the arrival of Goncharova and Larionov in Paris in that year brought an immediate gallery exhibition organized by Paul Guillaume, the catalogue for which was introduced by Apollinaire.

Guillaume and Apollinaire were at this time not only arbiters of taste but promoters of the avant-garde in Paris. Yet neither their writings nor those of Gleizes and Metzinger at the time had laid out the principles of Cubism in a lucid and articulate fashion. Later in 1922 Gleizes did publish a set of demonstration figures as a means of providing a clear explication of both the premise and the process secured verbally in his treatise

Du Cubisme of 1912. A series of diagrams (Figure 10.1), entitled "Movements of Planar Transference toward the Side," disclose the way in which the Cubists sought to define "the schemes of the painter and his laws" using only the most elemental geometric forms. In the discussions that accompanied his diagrams Gleizes pronounced: "To paint is to animate a surface plane; to animate a surface plane is to rhythmicize space."[17]

In addition to current Russian concerns centering on questions of ethnicity, Stravinsky's *Le Sacre du printemps,* written in the period 1911–1913, exhibited an interest in the manipulation and reduction of ingredients to their essence—involving in this instance the technically adroit use of metric dislocation and polytonal juxtaposition of diatonic scraps fragmented from Russian folktunes. Unlike the melodies in *Petrushka,* however, these were now so partial or reconstituted that Stravinsky in later years was able to deny their origins altogether. In their fleeting resemblance to familiar material as well as in their incompleteness Stravinsky promoted a direct analogy with the collage assemblages of the Cubists; and in his flagrant shearing of prior definitions of musical space and time, he proclaimed a new and joltingly ambiguous terrain demonstrably akin to the reassessment of the visual plane. It is also possible to sense that in some measure he may have intuited Ernst Cassirer's distinction between the "qualitative and concrete" conception of time held by people in oral cultures and the linear and "objective" nature of written Western music.[18]

A rethinking of both melodic/harmonic and rhythmic structures began to serve Stravinsky from the time of *Petrushka* (1910–11), and with

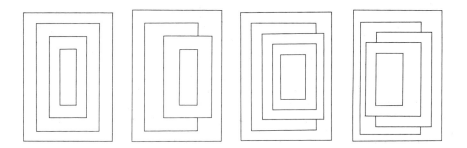

Figure 10.1. Albert Gleizes, *Les Schémas de la peinture et ses lois:* "Mouvements de translation du plan sur un côté."

Le Sacre we begin to see the codification of his preference for the opposition of tonally distant four-note segments (the musical analyst would call them diatonic tetrachords tritonally related).[19] Such pitch factors were typically joined to two principal types of rhythmic-metric construction, with numerous passages betraying characteristics of both: changing meters homorhythmically articulated by registrally and timbrally fixed components; and stable metrics, or consistently varying ones, serving as an ostinato against which other lines are deployed with their own noncoincidental metric life.[20] Both rhythmic relationships are observable in *Le Sacre:* the first in the "Danse sacrale,"[21] and a prefiguration of the second appears in "Jeux des cités rivales," persuasively plotted by Pieter van den Toorn (Example 10.1).[22] Jann Pasler, in noting the extent to which such techniques of superimposition in *Le Sacre* transcended their more limited role in *Petrushka,* has convincingly argued that in *Le Sacre* "they reflect the visual multiplicity on stage and suggest the simultaneity of unrelated actions."[23]

The *Three Pieces for String Quartet* of 1914, a seemingly unambitious work which followed hard on the heels of the premiere of *Le Sacre,* occupies a special place in Stravinsky's output because of its historical position. Signifying anything but a relaxation or reactionary simplification, these brief pieces vivify Stravinsky's need to extrapolate and to synthesize the implications of the most radical rhythmic/harmonic manners of *Le Sacre* and to raise its basic tenets to the level of a total abstraction. The potential function of the first piece of this set as part of a theatrical presentation, *David,* in no way compromises such a claim in light of the nature of Cocteau's proposed scenario. Indeed, a clarification of the role of this exercise as part of a projected collaboration should help to sensitize our understanding of Stravinsky's acute awareness of his relationship to the premises of the contemporary Cubists.

Just as the gradual recognition and separation of an aesthetic orientation and its underlying intellectual premise occurred in the second phase of Cubism, so the need to identify the architectural basis of the highly visceral language struck in *The Rite* was perceived only a posteriori as a kind of response to Hulme's belief that "one must recognize thought's essential independence of the imagery that steadies it."[24] Creative intentionality and critical reaction typically take on separate lives. But though composers or painters may play little or no role in voicing their objectives, the force of criticism not infrequently swings back to affect the artists as they become aware of the verbalized arguments.

For his practical demonstration of the structural consequences of *Le*

Example 10.1. Igor Stravinsky. *Le Sacre du printemps,* "Jeux des cités rivales," nos. 64–71.

Reprinted with permission of Boosey & Hawkes, Inc.

Sacre, Stravinsky chose three planes of utterly simple materials in his *Three Pieces*—the juxtaposition of which causes dislocation and ambiguity, encouraging a new perception of time, space, and proportion. While Schoenberg's contemporaneous flirtations with the world of atonality play no part in Stravinsky's game plan, the latter's challenge to the world of music in this work was as radical as the Cubist challenge to realism and perspective from the time of the Renaissance. And in spite of the seeming familiarity of its ingredients and their tonal centricity, Stravinsky's results were as disconcerting and significant as, and decidedly more intellectually structured than Schoenberg's concurrent expeditions into atonality.

The point of view behind Stravinsky's solutions was, moreover, clearly in accord with that of the Cubists, who treasured African native perspectives in emphasizing what they knew about a subject rather than what they saw. *Idea* reigned supreme, and the artist strove to express this through simplification as well as stylization. Such stylization ultimately led to the confection of non-naturalistic qualities which held the immediate potential of assuming qualities of the symbol. Stravinsky's transfiguration of the Russian folk melos in *Three Pieces* paralleled these developments exactly. The composer's meeting with Jean Cocteau at this very time was ultimately to prove serendipitous as well as frustrating.

1914: Cocteau, Stravinsky, and *David*

Cocteau, according to his memory, met Stravinsky for the first time in Monte Carlo in April 1911, and their preserved correspondence traverses somewhat spottily the arch of their careers from 1913 to 1962. If the most significant collaboration of these two artists came in *Oedipus Rex* (1926–27), their first important interaction occurred as early as 1914. Already by 1913 Cocteau was openly trying to gain Stravinsky's attention by announcing that his new book, *Le Potomak*,[25] was to be dedicated to the composer. On January 22, 1914, Stravinsky played the first two acts of *Le Rossignol* for a group of friends which included Cocteau, Maurice Delage, André Gide, Maurice Ravel, Erik Satie, and Jacques Copeau. Copeau (1879–1949)—organizer of the Théâtre du Vieux-Colombier, an organization of aspiring young artists—had requested that Stravinsky compose a dance suite, though he had not offered a specific commission for the project. He was later to become an important collaborator with Stravinsky on several projects during the 1920s and 1930s, as both performer and director of *L'Histoire du soldat* and as the stager of *Perséphone*.[26] It was precisely at this time, in the spring of 1914, that Cocteau had his first meeting with a Cubist, Albert Gleizes, as the former was having his portrait painted by the latter's wife-to-be, Juliette Roche. Although Cocteau had previously made the Cubists an object of ridicule, he and Gleizes got along famously, exchanging cards and telephone numbers. According to Mlle. Roche: "A few days later, Cocteau was talking of nothing except Duchamp-Villon, Jacques Villon and Albert Gleizes; and Misia Godebska reproached me sharply: 'Why did you put Jean in touch with the Cubists? He is a man of the Right, not the Left . . . He'll be ruined among such people as that.' "[27]

Cocteau's awareness of the celebrity which attended *Le Sacre* has frequently and reasonably been cited as the main impetus behind Cocteau's turn to Modernism. The acceptance at this time of Diaghilev's challenge "Étonne-moi!" ("Astonish me!") as his personal credo can be seen as a manifestation of his desire to cash in on the notoriety surrounding the most recent productions of the Ballets Russes. But Cocteau quickly began to sense that in order to make his own mark he would have to distance himself from Diaghilev. For this purpose he devised a new plan and a project, *David,* for which he hoped to enlist the services of Stravinsky. The same impulses which had attracted Cocteau to *Le Sacre* also brought him to Gleizes and the Cubists.[28]

By February Stravinsky had ensconced himself and his family in Leysin in order to be near his wife, who was ill in a sanatorium, and he began to busy himself with the completion of the final act of *Le Rossignol*. But at precisely this time a brief note to Stravinsky of February 4 suggests that Cocteau had taken control of Copeau's project and made it his own. It would be a ballet entitled *David* with a scenario by Cocteau and music by Stravinsky. Cocteau had already begun to characterize Stravinsky's contribution: "Our plan enchants me. The dance *must not express anything*. The [dancer's] body must arouse itself in a burst, becoming another instrument of the orchestra."[29] In a letter of February 13,[30] Cocteau tells Stravinsky that he has mentioned nothing of the project to anyone,[31] offers to bring the text of his scenario along, inquires as to the contemplated size of orchestra and chorus, and concludes "I am finishing my (your) book [*Le Potomak*]."

On February 15, Stravinsky wrote to Cocteau[32] stating that the project could proceed only if a sum of 6,000 francs could be found, for which he would allow exclusive presentation rights for a period of two years. February 17 brought a reply from Cocteau[33] that he was devastated by Stravinsky's letter, informing him that he would gladly pay the sum himself if he had the money, but also implying that such a liaison with "the theater of the young" might be seen as advantageous. On a more practical level Cocteau also made it clear that Stravinsky's contribution need not be lengthy and that it could properly take the form of two or three brief dances.

By February 19 Stravinsky must "have received the letter of February 17 and telegraphed a positive reply," for Cocteau mentions in telegrams of the nineteenth and twentieth Stravinsky's "marvelous kindness," the observation that "you could not disappoint me. I am happy and embrace you," and on February 21 he projects his March 2 arrival in Leysin, stating: "A female theosophist described one of David's dances to me, according to the Magi: it is prodigious. He danced before the Sacred Ark: *The Dance of the Planets!!!* Imagine the Music!!!"[34] We know from Cocteau's *David Notebooks* that he envisioned a ballet consisting of three scenes taken from the life of David.

> The first, "la danse autour de la tête," would depict David's victorious battle with Goliath, his triumph with the aid of a stone in a sling, his difficulty in cutting off the head, and, finally, his dance of victory around it; the second was "la danse autour du javelot," based on the biblical scene where Saul becomes jealous of David when the women sing, "Saul slew his thousands, and David his ten thousands." Saul hurls his spear at him; but David, dancing, evades it. The third and last situation was "la danse autour de l'arche," where, after having become King of Israel, David dances ecstatically around the Ark and is reproached for his unseemly dancing by Saul's daughter Michol. David proudly replies that the Lord Jehovah has chosen him over all others and that he will play before the Lord.[35]

David's battle with Goliath occurred in his youth, his dance before the Ark of the Covenant when he was a mature leader of his people. All three dances outlined by Cocteau attend early Judeo-Christian stories, to which he joins a cosmic "planetary" element (see Figure 10.11). Hoping, perhaps, that if one angle did not fire Stravinsky's imagination, another would, he confects a potpourri of potentially seductive ingredients. The resulting hodgepodge is not unlike that for his immediately forthcoming *Parade*. Although Cocteau later laid the failure of his projected ballet to the fact that it was "uselessly complicated by the Bible and a text," [36] some have attributed the confusion to the fact that Cocteau's analysis of David's relation to Goliath, Solomon, and the Ark was fueled by autobiographical details.[37]

Shortly after his arrival, Cocteau wrote Gide describing "the intensity of Stravinsky's work," and revealed that Jacques Copeau was expected to present *David*. Cocteau must have left Leysin after a few days. In any case, Stravinsky wrote to Copeau on March 15 that there were still a few remaining details which he hoped to be able to arrange with him when he came to Paris around April 2 for Monteux's concert performance of *Le Sacre*.[38]

On March 18, Cocteau wrote to his mother that "*David* will be something very, very important" and later in an undated letter that "Stravinsky played something of the future *David* and it is impossible to say how beautiful it was . . . *David* will be short (20 minutes) but, as Igor says, this drop will poison an elephant of five acts."[39] Other references to *David* occur in a letter of May 15: "*David* will be the great work of the era . . . *David* is essential. One awaits *David* as the sand thirsts for fresh, heavy water."[40] Then a letter from Cocteau to Stravinsky dated "Sunday" at the end of May 1914 reflects Misia Sert's report that there had been a misunderstanding between him and Stravinsky, and brings protestations from Cocteau that he did not want to publish his forthcoming *Le Potomak,* which "was dedicated to you from its conception, . . . while there was a cloud between us. I will come tomorrow morning at about eleven and embrace you among the tennis courts, the roses, and cocatoos."[41]

In spite of an intermittent correspondence over the next year between various parties which suggested that *David* was still a viable project, May 1914 effectively signaled the end of the Cocteau-Stravinsky collaboration.[42] In retrospect it has been assumed that Stravinsky was annoyed at Cocteau's assumption that he would be willing to lend his name to a fledgling company by scribbling a "few measures," and yet at the time Stravinsky's letters to Copeau indicated his continuing interest even after the question of inadequate funding had surfaced. In later years, however, we have it from Stravinsky himself that "I never did know exactly what Cocteau had in mind about *David* . . . Cocteau pestered me. He pestered me about *David* and had to be driven away. He was an embarrassing young man at that time, utterly persistent. One soon had enough of his wheedling and his flattery."[43]

In light of positive production hopes, which lingered until May, and the report from Cocteau in March that Stravinsky had been working "like a dynamo" on the score and had actually played some of the music for him, it remains to determine just what this music might have been. It may be postulated that the first of the *Three Pieces for String Quartet,* composed during March and completed on April 26, 1914, was the dance originally intended for *David.* The second and third pieces of what later was to become a set were composed in July, following not only Stravinsky's falling out with Cocteau in May but also an inquiry on June 14 from the second violinist of the Flonzaley Quartet saying that rumor around Paris had it that the composer had just written a dance for string quartet.[44] The group was especially interested in a set of three pieces for their American tour, scheduled for the next year.

More than a year later, however, the project of *David* was seemingly still being held in abeyance, and Misia Sert wrote to Cocteau at the end of the summer of 1915, showering her enthusiasm over a new work, *Les Noces,* which Stravinsky had played for her, and adding, "He is preoccupied at this moment with another work . . . and he will not commit himself to *David* just now."[45]

That the idea of *David* was not only on the wane but definitely discarded in the minds of the principals is made clear in a letter from Cocteau to Stravinsky of October 4, 1915: "*David* does not matter to me. Never speak to me about *David. David* is already banished from my head. *David* is you, the *Sacre,* the *Noces villageoises. David* is a moment of us, which was no doubt necessary to our union. What must be retained of *David* is a pact of long and fraternal friendship."[46]

A lengthy letter filled with veneration and self-pity followed, but a more upbeat letter of reconciliation came on August 11, 1916, in which Cocteau reported that Gide took him to hear a performance of the *Three Pieces for String Quartet* at Darius Milhaud's. He expressed delight at Stravinsky's new opus, conveyed the information that Misia Sert, who was there, "understood nothing," and announced that he was working constantly with Satie and Picasso on a new vehicle to be ready by October.[47]

Already a year before, sensing that *David* was probably not going to come to fruition, Cocteau had begun to bid Albert Gleizes to join him in another enterprise also ultimately destined not to materialize, *A Midsummer Night's Dream*—a potpourri of clowns, cinema, and the circus—with costumes and sets by Gleizes and music by Satie to be conducted by the young Varèse.[48] At the same time he had started to angle for an introduction to Pablo Picasso, which Varèse arranged in November 1915. Cocteau was beginning to assemble the necessary ingredients for a future production, as yet unnamed. It would involve the retention of many features originally conceived in connection with *David* and the *Dream:* music stripped to its barest essentials (the "new simplicity" of Satie), acrobats and the circus (emblems of the "everyday" which the Surrealists were soon to subject to a distancing technique and transform into a new iconic vocabulary), non-narrative theater, Cubist costumes and decor, and an illusory frontal exterior of sample performances which contrasted with the real show inside the tent. It would also lead him back to Diaghilev in the production of what was to become *Parade.* Stravinsky, for his part, had moved ahead to the composition of *Les Noces.* Larionov's caricature of 1917 reveals the history of intrigue behind both works (Figure 10.2)

Figure 10.2. Michel Larionov, caricature of Stravinsky, Diaghilev, Cocteau, and Satie, 1917. With the failure of his plan for collaboration with Stravinsky on *David,* Cocteau turned to Satie and *Parade.* Stravinsky returned to Diaghilev and *Les Noces.*

In *The Cock and the Harlequin* of 1918, Cocteau confirmed that the idea of a collaboration with Stravinsky in *David* was hatched immediately after the premiere of *Le Sacre,* and more specifically that

> an acrobat was to do the parade for "David," a big spectacle which was supposed to be taking place inside; a clown, who subsequently became a box, a theatrical version of the phonograph at a fair, a modern equivalent of the mask of the ancients, was to sing through a megaphone the prowess of David and implore the public to enter to see the piece inside. It was, in a sense, the first sketch of *Parade,* but uselessly complicated by the Bible and a text.[49]

The ingredients of Cocteau's aesthetic code are clear: retention of the "fair" from *Petrushka* and use of "the mask of the ancients" contrast with allusions to phonographs and megaphones in order to interpret a biblical subject for modern times.

Although Cocteau may have had to abandon *David,* in *Parade* he achieved not only a produceable vehicle but also a *succès d'estime,* about which Stravinsky spoke candidly in his *Autobiography* of 1936: "*Parade* confirmed me still further in my conviction of Satie's merit in the part he had played in French music by opposing to the vagueness of a decrepit impressionism a language precise and firm, stripped of all pictorial embellishments."[50]

Seven Portraits of Stravinsky, 1913–1916

Stravinsky's memory in later years of his association with painters was unusually clear. Even more important is the fact that, while the early Fauve and Cubist painters were deeply involved with the irregular forms and spatial relationships of landscape painting, they realized that one of their most fundamental problems centered on how to paint convincingly a human figure in an abstract fashion. Gertrude Stein had remarked pointedly, "If you do not solve your painting problem in painting human beings you do not solve it at all."[51] The stylistic range of a series of portraits made of Stravinsky between 1913 and 1916 is thus of more than passing interest with respect to Stravinsky's unarguable awareness of the most forward-looking trends.

Two portraits of 1913 include an ink portrait by Pierre Bonnard, now lost, and one in oils by Modigliani only recently discovered. Remembering discussion surrounding a similar project by Modigliani,

Stravinsky thought the whole thing had come to nothing. He told Robert Craft, "I don't remember the circumstances very clearly but I visited
him in company with Léon Bakst in 1912 or 1913 because either he
or I or Diaghilev had conceived the project of his doing a portrait. I
don't know why it wasn't realized—whether Modigliani was ill, as he
so often was, or whether I was called away with the ballet. At that time
I had an immense admiration for him." Surprised in 1957 to learn of
its resurfacing, Stravinsky commented, "Modigliani must have done it
from memory. I regret to have to admit that it does resemble me."[52]

Two further paintings from the same period, one of 1913 and another
from 1915 (Figure 10.3), were executed by Jacques-Émile Blanche
(1861–1942), an intimate of the Ballets Russes circle and a hanger-on
of the rich and the famous. The pictures are traditional, realistic, and
typical of the type of conservative society portrait for which he became
justly celebrated.[53] Blanche's admiration for Stravinsky continued for
many years, and together with Gabriel Pierné he was to nominate Stravinsky in 1935 in an unsuccessful bid for his membership in the Institut
de France.[54] Stravinsky later reflected upon these portraits and their
painter in his *Conversations* of 1959:

> Jacques-Emile Blanche was another friend of my early Diaghilev years.
> He painted two portraits of me that are now in the Luxembourg. I
> remember sitting for him, and how he drew my head and features
> only after a great amount of modeling, while everything else, the body
> and the background, was added *in absentia*. This meant that one's legs
> might turn out too long and one's middle too capacious, or that one
> might find oneself promenading on the beach at Deauville, as I am
> made to do in one of my portraits. However, Blanche's faces were
> unusually accurately characterized, and that was the important thing.
> Blanche was a *fine mouche* for celebrities; he came to make my portrait
> almost the morning after the premiere of the *Firebird*.[55]

Blanche mixed with the fashionable, the famous, and the soon-to-be-
famous, and his representational style endeared him to those in search of
a likeness. Janet Flanner, who knew him, penned a terse but telling
verbal portrait of the man and the age:

> Blanche was negligible as a creator, but as a young-man-about-town
> and a society reporter he was a genius. His true vogue and social com-
> prehension ended with 1914; his period thus coincided with Proust's,
> when the Champs-Élysées was the scene for the fashionable drive,

Figure 10.3. Jacques-Émile Blanche, portrait of Stravinsky, 1915.

Dieppe was all the go, and ladies in evening dress wore black feathers in their topknot.[56]

Though Blanche knew the avant-garde personally, he was troubled by them, and Gertrude Stein tells a story that conveys his pervading confusion over current developments:

> It was about this time that the futurists, the italian futurists, had their big show in Paris and it made a great deal of noise. Everybody was excited and this show being given in a very well known gallery everybody went. Jacques-Émile Blanche was terribly upset by it. We found him wandering tremblingly in the garden of the Tuileries and he said, it looks alright but is it. No it isn't, said Gertrude Stein. You do me good, said Jacques-Émile Blanche.[57]

In contrast to Blanche's portrait is another completed about the same time by Léon Bakst, a painter who worked in an ornate curvilinear style typically infused with brilliant colors that conjure up Hellenic, Oriental, and other exotic motifs. As recently as 1912 he had designed costumes in this fantasy style for *Le Dieu bleu* with music by Reynaldo Hahn and scenario by Jean Cocteau (Figure 1.3). The preserved correspondence between Bakst and Stravinsky confirms that, while friendly, the two artists did not share a common bond in artistic matters generally. A lengthy letter of October 25, 1917, regarding a proposed collaboration on Gide's *Antony and Cleopatra* gives the best evidence of their aesthetic distance.[58] With respect to the *Three Pieces for String Quartet,* for example, Bakst wrote the composer on November 17, 1916, stating that Violette Murat had been in such a state of excitement about these pieces that she wanted to cover the expense of having them engraved. Bakst concluded, "I pass on her kind suggestion. (I myself understand nothing in the music.)"[59]

It is somewhat surprising, then, to find the fashion of emerging Cubist ideals so clearly in evidence in Bakst's portrait of Stravinsky (Figure 10.4). Here his adoption of a Cubist approach is extraordinary, and the work would not typically be taken for a painting of the artist.[60] One can only assume that Bakst's portrait was executed in the spirit of a caricature, and that its Cubist tone was adopted as a pointed allusion to an aesthetic which was both current and fashionable. That this may have endeared him to the Cubists is suggested in two letters from Cocteau to Stravinsky dated August 11, 1916, and January 19, 1917, in the

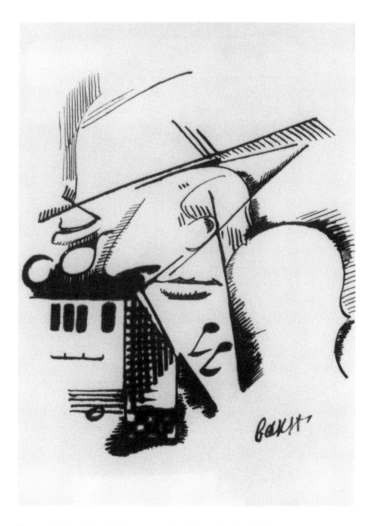

Figure 10.4. Léon Bakst, portrait of Stravinsky, 1915.

latter of which Cocteau, speaking of Bakst, states, "I take him to the Cubist vanguard where he is adored."[61]

Michel Larionov (1881–1964) is a somewhat different matter. Both he and his companion Goncharova had been brought to Paris by Diaghilev in June 1914 from Moscow where they had earlier defined a Futurist-Primitivist-Cubist-Rayonist movement in Russia. Beyond a neonationalist interest in their ethnic heritage, their subscription to the dynamics of urban society placed them close to the Futurists. And in the portrayal of simultaneous movements in time, such as in Malevich's renowned *Scissor's Grinder* (1912) and Goncharova's *The Cyclist* (1912–13)[62] or *Aeroplane over Train* (1913),[63] we have evidence of an interest in the simultaneous portrayal of motion in time by the Russian avant-garde prior to their arrival in Paris.

Stravinsky dedicated his *Cat's Cradle Songs* of 1915–16 to Larionov and Goncharova at a time when he was already at work on *Renard* and *Les Noces*. Larionov designed the costumes and scenery for the former in 1917, Goncharova for the latter in 1921, and a picture of them to-gether as early as 1915 confirms the intimacy of their contact (Figure 10.5). Stravinsky described Larionov as: "a huge, blond mujik of a man, even bigger than Diaghilev (Larionov, who had an uncontrollable tem-per, once knocked Diaghilev down). He made a vocation of laziness, like Oblomov, and we always believed that his wife, Goncharova, did his work for him. He was a talented painter, nevertheless, and I still like his *Renard* set and costumes."[64] Stravinsky nowhere makes mention of the fact that Larionov had painted a portrait of him (Figure 10.6). Larionov's portrait of 1916, while nominally in harmony with the heavy

Figure 10.5. Leonide Massine, Natalia Goncharova, Michel Larionov, Igor Stravinsky, and Léon Bakst, August 1915.

Figure 10.6. Michel Larionov, portrait of Stravinsky, 1916.

brushwork and elemental reductiveness observable in the scenery for *Renard*,[65] betrays a vastly more aggressive Cubist quality, and the simultaneous three-quarter and profile views of Stravinsky's head adumbrate the renowned *Girl before a Mirror* (1932) by Picasso, whom Stravinsky had not yet met at this time. Its Cubist demeanor had already been employed in the world of portraiture by Goncharova in her own portrait of Larionov (Figure 10.7). Fokine saw this painting hanging in the

Figure 10.7. Natalia Goncharova, portrait of Larionov, 1913.
© 1994 ARS, New York / ADAGP, Paris.

studio of Larionov and Goncharova in the fall of 1913 when he visited
them with Diaghilev in order to ask Goncharova to design the decor
for *Le Coq d'or*. He later recalled his reaction: "Her paintings shocked
me at first. In a large dark studio of a gloomy suburban house we were
introduced to her work, for some reason by candlelight. The entire
room was covered with paintings all facing the wall. One by one the
canvasses were turned for us to see . . . there was a portrait—the face
almost a metre in diameter. I think it had only one eye."[66]

Goncharova pursued the space-time game with her *Spanish Dancer
with a Shawl and Comb* (Figure 10.8) and *Spanish Woman with a Fan*,[67]
both executed in 1916 as costume designs for Diaghilev's production

Figure 10.8. Natalia Goncharova, *Spanish Dancer with a Shawl and Comb,* 1916.
© 1994 ARS, New York / ADAGP, Paris.

of Ravel's *Rapsodie espagnole*. In the former, the dancer's nose and mouth "are shown in two positions to suggest rapid movement"; in the latter, "the left eye is seen to the right of the head."[68] Goncharova's potentially catalytic role was forecast in her first production for the Ballets Russes, Rimsky-Korsakov's *Le Coq d'or,* as we have seen. Diaghilev brought her to Paris for this very purpose, and both she and Larionov, her lifelong companion whom she married only late in life, soon settled into his milieu. The ease with which she made her entrée is reflected by the fact that Apollinaire wrote the preface to her exhibition of 1914 at the Galerie Paul Guillaume. To the Cubist method she added reminiscences of Iberian art and native Russian icons, demonstrating with rare clarity the process of fusion inherent in the current Parisian avant-garde. Her collaboration with Stravinsky on *Les Noces* in 1922 would be her final testimony to this vision.

Robert Delaunay (1885–1941), celebrated for a series of Cubist views of the Eiffel Tower,[69] also painted Stravinsky's portrait. But this was done a number of years later, in 1921, and its decidedly non-Cubist demeanor is in harmony with a momentary turn away from Cubism by numerous artists previously involved in the movement. Delaunay's jealousy of Picasso and his first antagonistic feelings toward Cubism were already apparent in his wartime letters to Albert Gleizes in New York. By the time of his Stravinsky portrait, when Picasso too had begun to espouse a Neoclassicism based on Ingres and to elevate modeling and control of line drawing in portraiture, Delaunay was still attacking Picasso but now for the neo-traditionalism evident in works like his three portraits of Stravinsky (1919–20), *Mother and Child* (1921), or *Woman in White* (1923).[70] As the Stravinsky portrait illustrates, however, it was a direction in which Delaunay himself was headed. Stravinsky remarked many years later that Delaunay "was another painter I saw very often at one time. He talked too much and too enthusiastically about 'modern art,' but was otherwise quite likable. He did a portrait of me too . . . I don't know what has become of it [now in the collection of Marian von Castelburg], but it was certainly better than Albert Gleizes' cubist one, which is my mustache plus what-have-you."[71] Here it seems clear, however, that Stravinsky's memory has momentarily confused Gleizes's portrait (no perceivable moustache) with the caricature by Bakst, which features a prominently dislocated one.

Two other portraits of Stravinsky were executed nearer to the time when Cocteau importuned the composer to collaborate on the *David* project. They more than the others help us to sense the potential immediacy of the Cubist aesthetic for Stravinsky at the time he composed the first of the *Three Pieces for String Quartet*. The first is by Paulet Thévenaz, who accompanied Cocteau on his visit to Stravinsky in Leysin as he prospected for *David* (Figure 10.9). Born in Geneva in 1891, Théve-

Figure 10.9. Paulet Thévenaz, portrait of Stravinsky; signed, "A Igor Stravinsky, Paulet Thévenaz, Leysin 1914."

Collection H. de Beaumont.

naz was known as a portrait painter as well as a dancer and a specialist in Dalcrozian movement, which Cocteau had studied with Thévenaz from 1911 on. The technique of eurhythmics fascinated Cocteau, and the emphasis which Dalcroze placed upon the notion of polyrhythms in contrasting the gestures of the individual and the crowd has been held to be influential in Cocteau's formulation of stage movement; it had also contributed fundamentally to Nijinsky's choreographic solutions for *Le Sacre du printemps*. Now Thévenaz collaborated with Cocteau in drafting a choreography for *David* which incorporated these very Dalcrozian techniques, and it was even projected that he would create the leading role in the premiere.[72] Thévenaz's portrait of Stravinsky is inscribed to Stravinsky and dated 1914. The picture's planar structure is clearly Cubist, and promotes the virility as well as the fashion of the aesthetic for portraiture of contemporary artists allied with the avant-garde.

The portrait of Stravinsky by Albert Gleizes (1881–1953) is also signed and dated 1914 (Figure 10.10). Daniel Robbins' introduction to a catalogue of Gleizes's works states: "For the *Portrait of Stravinsky* there exist half a dozen pen and ink studies, such as no. 55 (dated Paris, Juin, 1914), as well as a large oil sketch which bears the inscription, 'Étude pour Stravinsky, Petroushka, Théâtre des Champs-Élysées.' "[73]

Unlike Bakst's caricature of 1915, Albert Gleizes's rendering of his

Figure 10.10. Albert Gleizes, portrait of Stravinsky, 1914.
© 1994 ARS, New York / ADAGP, Paris.

subject was totally predictable. Together with Metzinger, Gleizes had become the undisputed theorist for the Cubists by virtue of their tract *Du Cubisme* in 1912, and his name was unavoidably linked with developments on that front. Eschewing the monochromatic, earthy matte-colors of the first, or *analytic,* phase of Cubism, Gleizes boldly used primary colors together with a hint of collage in the musical staff with four notes in a way characteristic of the second phase, known as *synthetic* Cubism. Stravinsky's choice of a string quartet clearly forwards an *analytic* color component, and his emphasis in the *Three Pieces* on the simultaneous presentation of complementary but temporally disassociated parts is totally in harmony with Gleizes's and Metzinger's view: "today painting in oils allows us to express notions of depth, density, and duration supposed to be inexpressible, and incites us to represent, in terms of a complex rhythm, a veritable fusion of objects, within a limited space . . . the fact of moving around an object to seize several successive appearances, which, fused in a single image, reconstitute it in time, will no longer make thoughtful people indignant."[74]

Stravinsky may or may not have seen Gleizes's newly published tract *Du Cubisme* in 1912. But we do know that Cocteau's initial meeting with Gleizes and his enthusiastic reaction to the Cubists in March–April 1914 coincided precisely with Cocteau's attempts to lure Stravinsky into the spectacle of *David* and Stravinsky's composition of the first of his *Three Pieces for String Quartet.* The second and third pieces were written later during the summer, undoubtedly under the stimulus of satisfying the commission for the Flonzaley Quartet. While there are ingredients of all three pieces that could be profitably discussed under the rubric of Cubist sponsorship, the first of the *Three Pieces* surfaces as a virtual demonstration piece, a *reductio* of Cubist premises. Therein Stravinsky distilled rhythmic and harmonic points of view only sporadically apparent in *The Rite,* and in harmony with Gleizes's and the Cubists' infatuation with the power of reconstitutions in time, promoted, like them, both the ambiguity and the force of unsuspected relationships among the simplest materials while rejecting all decorative preoccupations.[75]

Gleizes had followed the development of modern music since his association with Albert Doyen at the Abbaye in 1906–7, where the young Edgard Varèse is known to have been a frequent guest. With his introduction to Cocteau in the spring of 1914 his awareness of Stravinsky was undoubtedly escalated. And with the first concert performance of *Le Sacre* by Pierre Monteux in April 1914, which brought with it a new wave of exposure to audiences which had missed the original ballet the year before, and the premiere of a new opera, *Le Rossignol,* on May 26, Stravinsky's image had been further secured. It is doubtful, however, that Stravinsky sat for Gleizes's portrait, as he does not speak of it, while he does verify such sessions with Picasso and Giacometti.

Cocteau and the Simultaneists

Cocteau's *David Notebooks* disclose the tenor of the thoughts which he must have placed before Stravinsky on his visit to Leysin in March 1914. Cocteau's plan that the viewer would perceive a "parade" frontstage, "while behind the curtain a hidden performance is going on as if another world—*Le spectacle intérieur*—is reinforced by a device on the visible frontstage through which spoken text and singing resound as if coming from behind or 'beyond.'" These forerunners of the megaphones originally intended for *Parade* and the pairs of phonograph speakers in Cocteau's *Les Mariés de la Tour Eiffel* underscore a fundamental and recurring device in virtually all Cocteau's ballets: projection of an illusory external performance behind which lies the "real" show.[76] Cocteau's opening text for *David,* which survives, reads:

> Enter, ladies and gentlemen to see in ourselves the first event:
> Everything—both interior and exterior—takes place at the same time.
> Enter inside—enter ourselves!
> On the other side! In the interior!
> . . . . .
> Outside one sees only my poor comrade the acrobat who, for the eye, is like
> an instrument of the orchestra for the ear.[77]

As late as 1915 Cocteau continued to emphasize this psychological duality in a space-age costume for the principal character which included a mask that was more than a shield (Figure 10.11).[78] Given the knowledge that Cocteau's plan for *David* ultimately proved to be a preparation for *Parade,* Cocteau's remarks of 1917 which judge Satie's music as a simultaneous representation of the interior/exterior dimension clearly imply the nature of his original hopes for Stravinsky's contribution: "Gradually there came to birth a score in which Satie seems to have discovered an unknown dimension, thanks to which one can listen simultaneously both to the 'Parade' and the show going on inside."[79]

Cocteau's temporal/spatial conception also found contemporary reinforcement in the work of painters and littérateurs. This was true not only of Apollinaire's *Calligrammes,* some of whose contents were composed as early as 1912, but also of his poem "Fenêtres," of 1912, which was inspired by and published together with Robert Delaunay's *Fenêtres simultanées.* Apollinaire's association with Gleizes's circle as early as 1913 is confirmed by Gleizes's portrait of the poet's editor Eugene Figuière of 1913,[80] which incorporates the titles of Apollinaire's *Les Peintres cubistes* (1913) as well as Gleizes's *Du Cubisme* (1912). The portrait also speaks

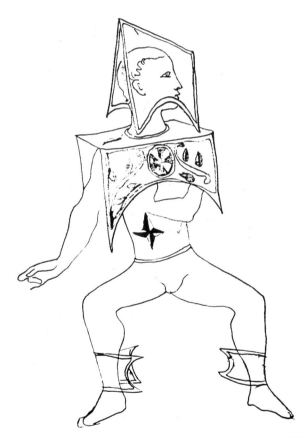

Figure 10.11. Jean Cocteau, design for a dancer for the ballet *David,* ca. 1915.
The University of Texas, Institute for the Humanities. © 1994 ARS, New York / SPADEM, Paris.

symbolically of fractured time with the partial clock in the upper left-hand corner, and of simultaneous rhythms as an adjunct to this new view with the expression "rythmes simultanés" at the lower right.

Other evidence of the wide-ranging appeal of "simultaneism" during the years immediately preceding the First World War is readily visible in numerous tracts and works of art by painters and literary figures, each with a somewhat different interpretation of the term. These include, in addition to statements made by Bergson and the Futurists, Robert Delaunay's "Simultaneism in Contemporary Modern Art, Painting, Poetry" (October 1913) and Blaise Cendrars's "simultaneous poem" *Prose du transsibérien* (1913) as well as his later article "Simultaneity" (1924).[81]

Further confirmation of an interaction between the poets and musicians appears in a set of poems written by Amy Lowell in 1916 in which she attempted to "reproduce the sound and movement of the [*Three Pieces for String Quartet*] as far as is possible in another medium." Capturing the fantastic air of the second piece in a Pierrot poem worthy of Giraud and the liturgical mood of the third through allusion to the groaning of a church organ, for the first of the pieces Lowell evokes Futurist/Cubist values with opening words ("Bang! Bump! Tong!") evocative of Marinetti's *Zang, Tumb, Tuum* of 1914.[82] And the lines "Red, yellow, blue / Colours and flesh weaving together / In and out with the dance" are in tune with both the synthetic Cubists' adoption of primary colors and the dance quality which Stravinsky attributed to the first piece.[83]

Such a collection of evidence clearly confirms Blaise Cendrars's declaration of 1954 concerning the appeal and liveliness of the interaction among the arts: "At this time, about 1911, painters and writers were equal. We lived mixed up with each other, probably even with the same preoccupations. It could be said that every writer had his painter. I myself had Delaunay and Léger, Picasso had Max Jacob, Reverdy; Braque and Apollinaire had everybody."[84]

The unescapable observation from such a multiple conjunction of personalities is that specific values, verifiably and properly referred to as Cubist, had been identified in art and literature, attributed to *Le Sacre* from the time of its premiere, and endorsed in such variable and numerous quarters in 1914 as to constitute a vogue. But vogue is the proper word, and many artists undoubtedly sensed more of the socioeconomic fashionableness of Cubism than its potential relation to universals through its access to Primitivism or other attendant intellectualisms. Membership in the avant-garde was a very seductive prospect, and by definition its rallying point required seasonal change or nuancing. Thus by June 1915 Cocteau was already saying, "Cubism was convenient for a large public. Cubism was convenient and a little simple, as Impressionism was, in its time. Let's hope that the postwar will bring the death of the 'ism.' "[85] Yet only a few months later, after his initial meeting with Picasso, a rendezvous which he described as "written in the stars," Cocteau proclaimed, "Don't fool yourself . . . Cubism was a classicism after the romanticism of the Fauves."[86] Even as late as 1918 the continuing appeal of the idea of Cubism as a replacement for a moribund Impressionism and as the purest emblem of modernity was made explicit by Cocteau: "The Impressionist painter looked at nature through eyes squinting at the sun; today Cubism rediscovers that austere discipline of the great epochs, renounces charming games, and the universe again becomes the pretext for a new architecture of the sensibility."[87]

Attempts to speak of *Parade,* the only project which Cocteau brought to fruition during this period, as a Cubist ballet have been made with considerable caution: reasonably with reference to Picasso's "fragmented cityscape and skewed proscenium arch"[88] as well as the costume constructions for the Managers; selectively through reference to Cocteau's scenario;[89] somewhat marginally with respect to certain aspects of Satie's score;[90] and only debatably with reference to Picasso's preludial "Red Curtain."[91] Yet the term was invoked from the beginning, and Massine claimed that Cocteau defended the sound effects of the clicking typewriter, the wail of the ship's siren, and the droning airplane engine as well as the originally intended but later discarded megaphones as "in tune with the cubistic concept of the production."[92] However, Huntley Carter, who reported on the premiere for an English publication, argued that the term "cubist" was incorrect and that "the proper description for *Parade* was 'simultaneity.' "[93]

Nonetheless, in the early teens Cubism was perceived not only as avant-garde but as *the* quintessential artistic discovery of a new age, and in some miraculous way a mirror of recent discoveries by Einstein (relativity) and Freud (the conscious and subconscious). Although its basic tenets may have been only partially understood by some, numerous artists in painting, literature, and music vigorously began to play with a new sense of time and to upset the old notions of rectilinear motion with experiments in simultaneity.

Analytical Observations

Let us proceed to a closer view of the structure of the "Dance," the first of Stravinsky's *Three Pieces for String Quartet,* in search of a constructive principle potentially in harmony not only with Cocteau's multidimensional stage text for *David* but with the painters who were busy painting Stravinsky's portrait at the time.[94] The piece is a reasonable, if not very complex, demonstration of some of the fundamental "schemes of the painter and his laws" later forwarded in the diagrams of Gleizes.

In spite of the limited pitch and rhythmic content and the consistent diatonic stepwise motion of Stravinsky's materials (Example 10.2), their potential origins in a hypothetical folk melos is seemingly subverted at every turn. The run-on character of the first violin, for example, would appear to be too long to remember as a melodic unit, especially in light of its pitch-class redundancy. Yet it is clearly reflective of a well-defined group of Russian folk instrumental "dance-until-drop" tunes called *nai-gryshi,* which "typically consist of a short (often three-measure) phrase repeated *ad infinitum* as the basis and framework for an open-ended series of extemporized variations, played by wedding bands, or simply by a *'muzhik'* on a balalaika or a concertina, to accompany a strenuous and often *competitive type of male dancing*" (italics added).[95] Further, the indication *avec toute la longueur de l'archet,* which appears over the first violin part in the revision of 1918, not only coincides with its contemporaneous appearance in the "Petit Concert" of *L'Histoire du soldat* but also announces Stravinsky's desire to confirm retrospectively its origins in folk practice. For, in describing the genesis of the idea in *Histoire,* Stravinsky related how a young gypsy came to him in a dream: "She had a child on her lap, for whose entertainment she was playing a violin. The motive she kept repeating used the whole bow or, as we say in French, *avec toute la longueur de l'archet.* The child was very enthusiastic about the music and applauded it with his little hands."[96]

The fragmentary nature and unpredictable appearances of the second violin tetrachord, however, are as ambiguously referential as the painted four-note collage in Gleizes's Stravinsky portrait. Their collective mission is apparently to perform a continuous search for a new context— or to use the words of Gleizes's Abbaye circle, to promote *collectivity, multiplicity,* and *simultaneity* as ideals.

The details of the interaction of the several parts of Stravinsky's piece can be summarily graphed but only somewhat prolixly verbalized:

Example 10.2. Igor Stravinsky. *Three Pieces for String Quartet*, no. 1, mm. 1–11.
Reprinted with permission of Boosey & Hawkes, Inc.

(1) The two outer voices, first violin and cello, lay down the basis for the piece: the cello repeats a 7-beat ostinato pattern against which the violin plays a lengthy 23-beat melody fashioned from four contiguous pitches (C, B, A, G). The cello states its pattern 14 times; the first violin plays its complete melody 4 times plus a quickly abandoned 5th statement;

(2) Against this the second violin plays a tetrachord (F♯, E, D♯, C♯), which stands in a tritonal relation to the tetrachord of violin 1 with respect to their lowest and highest pitches (C♯, G; F♯, C), and in semitonal conflict with respect to the extreme outer pitches (C♯, C). The cello pitches relate to both: E♭–D♭ are enharmonic to the D♯–C♯ of violin 2 and the C fundament is the highest pitch of violin 1. The potential of tritonally related tetrachords in asynchronous juxtaposition had already been demonstrated in notable sections of *Le Sacre,* such as the "Jeux des cités rivales" (Example 10.1). Here, however, a favored relationship becomes the exclusive premise for an entire piece.

(3) Beyond this the two violins gradually establish a relationship against the grid of viola/cello as follows:

(a) Violin 1: In the initial statement the first beat of the 23-beat pattern coincides with the first beat of the cello's 7-beat ostinato pattern ($7 \times 3 = 21$), but thereafter commences predeterminably on the 3rd, 5th, and 7th beats of this ostinato. Having reached the end position of a 7-beat pattern, it can only double back beginning on 2, and it appears to do so for a single turn. Here the piece quickly ends, however, the brief beginning transformed into an abbreviated coda.

(b) Violin 2: The tritonally related tetrachord alternates single (4-note) and double (8-note) statements in a seemingly unpredictable manner. The single statements are sporadically introduced, but the double statements always begin on the 5th quarter note of the 7-note ostinato and occur at the 3rd, 6th, 9th, and 12th statements of the 14 that constitute the cello part. To continue the pattern would place it in the 15th statement of the cello, but the cello has stopped at the 14th statement. The final statement of violin 2 is a *single* statement and its beginning coincides for the first time in the piece with the beginning of violin 1.

In sum, three essential layers (vn 1, vn2, va/vc) establish their independence through different phraseological lengths, variable periodicity, and independent tonal orientation until they locate a logical terminating point. Having exposed a number of changing relationships, the piece wraps itself up with a symmetrical three-bar postlude that mirrors the three-bar prelude that had announced the beginning.[97] The potential circularity, which is only emphasized by the seemingly arbitrary frame of prelude and postlude, is clearly reflective of an increasingly familiar literary gambit of the time. It is to be found in Proust's *Recherche,* purportedly modeled in this regard after the *Thousand and One Nights,* as well as later in Joyce's *Finnegans Wake*. And in the world of music Satie's "perpetual" tango in *Sports et divertissements* (also of 1914) as well as a series of allusions to circularity in Berg's *Wozzeck, Der Wein,* and the Violin Concerto command interest less as demonstrations of symmetricality or endless form than as reflections of contemporary disquisitions on relativity in the time-space continuum.

The possibility of a magical controlling element embedded in the work at a highly esoteric level beckons in one further calculation: the seemingly arbitrary pattern of the double eighth-note statements of the second violin recurs every 21 beats. This encourages the possibility that a governing Fibonacci number (1, 2, 3, 5, 8, 13, 21, 34, 55 . . .) has been introduced as a secret controlling agent directly relatable to the ostinato grid (7 beats) of which it is a multiple.[98] Now the "process" portion of the piece (that is, the part without the 3-measure prelude and postlude) contains 98 quarter-note beats, and the nearest beat to the "Golden Section" point ($98 \times .618 = 60.564$) is 61. It is precisely on this beat that the third of the four double statements of the second violin enters, effectively signaling the mid-point of this form-determining figure. Jonathan Kramer has rightly characterized Stravinsky's piece as "a deliberate exploration of proportional control," and although he has warned that "Stravinsky's proportional consistencies are never exact, which implies that he did not consciously calculate sectional durations," he has allowed that "the first movement of Three Pieces is probably an exception."[99] An exact duplication of the same proportional qualities in *In Memoriam Dylan Thomas* of 1954, however, provides tantalizing evidence regarding Stravinsky's continuing attraction to such properties.[100]

There are, in fact, special reasons to assume that Stravinsky was aware of the Fibonacci series and its relation to the Golden Section by 1914, in light of the appeal of such properties to a group of Cubists who labeled themselves the "Section d'Or." An exhibition of their paintings had been held in Paris between October 10 and 30, 1912. Works by Juan Gris, Fernand Léger, Albert Gleizes, Jean Metzinger, Robert Delaunay, and Jacques Villon were shown. During this period the group typically met on Sunday afternoons to discuss problems of rhythm and proportion, and they took their name from a treatise of 1509 entitled *Divine Proportion* written by Luca Pacioli and illustrated by Leonardo da Vinci which discussed the Golden Section. The Golden Section, "while not the only constant to which the Cubists referred for the mathematical organization of their canvasses, did reflect their profound need for order and measure."[101]

Theories and Postmortems

Stravinsky might well be amused at such an intricate detailing of the backgrounds and observable relationships in the first of the *Three Pieces for String Quartet*. At the same time, he would clearly recognize the *dramatis personae* (Gleizes, Metzinger, Larionov, Bakst, Cocteau, Copeau, Sert, Cendrars, Delaunay, Picasso), and admit their proximity to him at this point in his life as well as knowledge of their work. It is also virtually a certainty that analogies between music and the work of the painters would not offend him. For his immediately preceding scores not only had involved an intimate interchange with Benois *(Petrushka)* and Roerich *(Le Sacre du printemps)* but had also brought the admission that the *Three Japanese Lyrics* (1912–13) had been undertaken in an attempt to solve musical problems analogous to the questions of perspective in Japanese painting.[102]

More specifically, in light of the fact that the first of the *Three Pieces for String Quartet* was conceived precisely at the time of Cocteau's discussions for the ballet *David,* Stravinsky's music may be plausibly seen as a direct response to Cocteau's call for a music that mirrors: the frontal (exterior) action of a clown/acrobat (violin 1); the backstage (interior) action of David's battle with Goliath, symbolized by means of preparatory gestures culminating in the seemingly unpredictable but highly controlled unleashing of his sling ("the magic bullet"), allied with David's difficulty in removing the head of his enemy (violin 2); and the simultaneous dance of victory (the cello/viola ostinato). Furthermore the tritonally related and apparently irrationally spaced material of violin 2 possesses a psychological quality precisely because its not readily audible metric foundation is demonstrable a posteriori as the proportion in nature known as the Golden Section. Owing to its proportional logic, the Golden Section readily functions as a fetishistic emblem of victory against difficult odds. It is of no small interest that many years later in 1962, following the completion of his "dance drama," *The Flood,* Stravinsky affixed to the cover of his notebook of sketches a picture of David instead of Noah![103] Stravinsky obviously recalled the Scriptural reference to David's dance before the Ark of the Covenant, an event ecstatically proposed by Cocteau in his letter to Stravinsky of February 21, 1914, as the final scene of the original *David* scenario.

Analogies between Stravinsky's new time/space world in the first piece for string quartet and the Cubist painters' attempts to obliterate notions of illusionist depth are inviting.[104] For just as the discovery of perspective in Renaissance painting had been paralleled in fifteenth-century music by the revelation of a simultaneous (as opposed to consecutive) approach to harmonic counterpoint, so now Stravinsky and a few of his contemporaries mirrored the action of the painters in the contravention of the old harmonic/contrapuntal laws through a radical new definition of musical time. If Schoenberg's atonal disorientations undertaken in these very years can be seen as a challenge of the same time-honored premise, it is important to emphasize that his solution was totally different from Stravinsky's in that it was less fundamentally defined with respect to a control of temporal planes and less concerned with the reconstitution of the rhythmic/metric element.

Although David's battle and dance of victory, if we may now call it that, was initially served up in the monochromatic colors of a string quartet akin to the palette of the analytic Cubists, it was later "colorized" into the hues of the synthetic Cubists when Stravinsky arranged these pieces for orchestra, a task begun in 1914 but completed only in 1918. At this time, when they were relabeled *Études* for orchestra, the first of the quartet pieces was also given the title "Dance" by the composer (the second and third movements, "Eccentric" and "Canticle" respectively). It was as though Stravinsky wished to leave behind the final clue to the genesis of his little piece—a work at once enigmatic and perplexing, whose multiple views of the simplest materials extracted the essences of the literary and visual Cubists in a disarming distillation of traits previously discovered in a more intuitive fashion in *The Rite* and tentatively allied to matters of prosody in *Three Japanese Lyrics*.[105]

Having demonstrated in a virtually theoretical fashion the capacity of simultaneously presented patterns of unequal length to generate a form, Stravinsky never again employed such a network in so extended and rigorous a manner. But the essence of the discovery remained at the ready as a detail technique, and together with the *personnages rythmiques* (to use Messiaen's later terminology) plumbed in the second and third pieces for string quartet, it was to serve as one of the most recognizable features of Stravinsky's later music.

Potentially even more striking "continuities"[106] reflective of Stravinsky's Cubist encounter may be interpreted in virtually every phase of his career. A recognition of its formal consequences does not supplant theories of prosody with respect to the composer's legendary fascination with noncoincidental accents between text and music, from *Three Japanese Lyrics* (Russian) to *Oedipus Rex* (Latin), *Perséphone* (French), and numerous English-texted works from the late period (for instance, *Cantata, Three Shakespeare Songs, In Memoriam Dylan Thomas*). But it does add a new and complementary dimension to it. Indeed, a part of Stravinsky's "rejoicing discovery" with respect to non–accentual alignment in native repertoires such as the *pribaoutki* may also have resided in his joy at sensing the compatibility of folk melos practices with contemporary artistic theory.

The issue, once identified, encourages the recognition and reconsideration of other manifestations of Stravinsky's lifelong habit of planar shifting. Typically, when he was engaging in such realignments, Stravinsky remained loyal to a tonal center. And a similar pairing of an orderly relocation of the pitch element with an extended sense of tonal "centricity" is observable even in the late serial works.[107] Is it possible that echoes of Stravinsky's Cubist encounter, long since fused into a natural component of his thought, surface once again at the end of his career?

In an attempt to answer this question, let us return to a consideration of early Cubist theory and its language. Gleizes's approach to planar realignment was not restricted to the level of his most elemental demonstration, shown in Figure 10.1. Although he may have launched his "schemes of the painter and his laws" with this diagram, the two immediately ensuing sections are entitled "Simultaneous Movement by Rotation and Transference of the Plane Leading to the Creation of Spatial and Rhythmic Plastic Organism," and are accompanied by a final series of eight figures (Figure 10.12). In Gleizes's Fig. VIII we can already begin to see how the more complex manifestations of Cubism could quickly lead not only to intricate patterns but to configurations that clearly resemble some of Gleizes's own mature compositions.[108]

Is it reasonable to sense in Stravinsky's late-style infatuation with the consequences of "rotation" and "verticals" (however he may have approached them, via Krenek or not) a residue of his "Cubist experience" earlier in the century?[109] Indeed, may it not be possible to read in one of the seemingly most obscure, and to some one of the most obtuse, statements that Stravinsky ever penned, a reflection of his capacity for viewing the concept of variation at a Cubist angle? Stravinsky's serial matrixes for the composition of his *Movements for Piano and Orchestra* (Figure 10.13)[110] were later given the verbalization quoted below. It

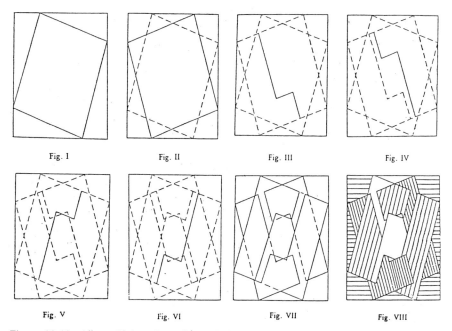

Fig. I   Fig. II   Fig. III   Fig. IV

Fig. V   Fig. VI   Fig. VII   Fig. VIII

Figure 10.12. Albert Gleizes, *Les Schémas de la peinture et ses lois:* "Mouvements simultanés de rotation et de translation du plan aboutissant à la création d'un organisme plastique spatial et rythmique."

clearly suggests less a capitulation to Schoenbergian serial orthodoxy than a personal reinterpretation more than slightly redolent of Stravinsky's attraction to Cubist premises at the zenith of his Russian period and a late-style compositional approach totally in harmony with the composer of *The Rite* and the *Three Pieces for String Quartet:* "Every aspect of the composition was guided by serial forms, the sixes, quadrilaterals, triangles etc. The fifth movement, for instance, uses a construction of twelve verticals. . . Five orders are rotated instead of four, with six alternates for each of the five, while at the same time the six work in all directions, as though through a crystal."[111]

"Movements," "rotation," "in all directions," "at the same time": even the vocabulary is identical with Gleizes's terminology. The formulation of such a context for Stravinsky's late works highlights potential continuities not only with his handling of the diatonic folk melos of the Russian period but also with the potential origins of certain of his Neoclassic techniques, especially those involving the critique of

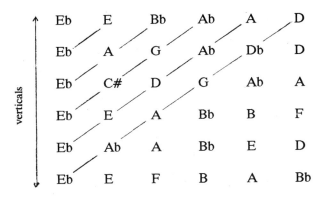

Figure 10.13. Hexachordal rotation in Stravinsky's *Movements for Piano and Orchestra*.

adopted materials. And in the hexachordal rotation to "ground zero," which in the case of the *Introitus* for T. S. Eliot involves tritonally related hexachords, Stravinsky promoted tonal centricity among familiarly colliding opposites.

The question at hand thus concerns the most fundamental single ingredient in Stravinsky's attitude toward composition. It would, of course, be irresponsible to suggest that Stravinsky's discovery of this important view was made solely through his exposure to Cubism. It seems fair to contend, however, that Cubism reinforced personally evolving proclivities at a decisive point in Stravinsky's career. And to the extent that his awareness of the ferment and importance of the Cubists' activities was heightened through personal association with some of the movement's most famous practitioners, the role of extra-musical solutions in the definition of musical Modernism around 1910 may have been more direct than previously thought.

Diaghilev's *World of Art* had from its inception at the turn of the century nurtured interdisciplinary associations—which were patently Symbolist inspired—as one of its most fundamental goals. In fact, Diaghilev initially discovered Stravinsky at a musical concert sponsored by his organization. And Benois's presence, as indicated earlier, was especially catalytic in the promotion of this interdisciplinary view. Stravinsky's awareness of the activity of literary and visual artists was therefore extraordinarily acute from the beginning. It seems clear that the interface of Cubism with music helped to secure fresh and ultimately basic attitudes with respect to time and space in the world of sound. Significantly, the impact of such a confrontation helped to seal a point of view that would resound and be subject to reinterpretation throughout the long arch of Stravinsky's career.

It is almost certain, for example, that in the early teens Stravinsky was innocent of the obvious analogies between the planar proportions of his own music and the basic properties of the fourteenth-century isorhythmic motet. Yet his friendship throughout the 1920s and 1930s with the musicologist Jacques Handschin, whose speciality was medieval music, and his increasing interest in the "idea" of this music—as opposed, no doubt, to an intimate familiarity with an extensive repertoire of pieces from the period—may be attributable in considerable measure to a delayed recognition of the constructive affinity between medieval music and his own.[112] The genesis of a startlingly similar point of view with respect to music of the Middle Ages in the works of Olivier Messiaen and other composers of a later generation may in some measure be reasonably attributed to Stravinsky's role as an important intermediary.[113] Finally, one can hardly fail to observe that the constructive appeal of the Fibonacci series in the twentieth century has been as powerful for analysts as for composers, and that while impressive arguments and calculations have been adduced by both sources, fascination with its properties has clearly taken on a life of its own. The reason for this may be no more complex than the compulsive search by both parties for an external order in an art originally fueled by unorthodox yet highly expressive internal convulsions.[114]

Although it may seem odd that Stravinsky never spoke directly of the experience of Cubism or of an attraction to its properties during the crucial years, 1909–1915, when he was in Paris, it is well to remember that Picasso was equally silent on the subject during this very time, and that he left all theoretical explanations to the likes of Gleizes and Metzinger and aesthetic arguments to critics such as Apollinaire and Pierre Reverdy. Gertrude Stein, noting Juan Gris's preference for exactitude and mathematical precision, tellingly remarked that "Picasso by nature the most endowed had less clarity of intellectual purpose" and that he was dominated almost exclusively by ritual.[115]

Although the ritualistic element was equally strong in the works of Stravinsky, it would be surprising, in light of the greater scope of Stravinsky's preserved verbal testimony, if he had failed to address directly the more general question of proportion in music and its relation to mathematics and painting if such issues were, indeed, relevant to the creative process as he viewed it. Thus it is of no small consequence that as late as 1960, in the second of the conversation books, Robert Craft posed the question, "Has music ever been suggested to you by, or has a musical idea ever occurred to you from, a purely visual experience of movement, line, or pattern?" Stravinsky's answer begins, "Countless times, I suppose," and, even more significantly for the present argument, concludes with a single illustration, the second of the *Three Pieces for String Quartet*.[116]

Evidence of Stravinsky's attraction to visual analogies with music can be adduced in his willingness to record a brief history of music through a set of line drawings. At first glance this may be interpreted as a simple assertion that music possesses beyond its aural qualities a spatio-temporal dimension which can be symbolized in ways other than its traditional notation. But the configuration which he confected to represent his own music is astonishingly similar to a set of drawings made by Picasso in 1924 as a sequel to *Still Life with Mandolin*. Here Picasso "reduced his vocabulary of marks to the dot and the line alone"[117] in what retrospectively appears as almost a direct prefiguration of the personal logo which Stravinsky drew in the early 1960s to represent his own music (Figures 10.14, 10.15).

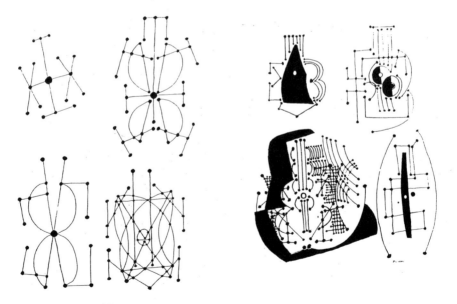

Figure 10.14. Pablo Picasso, *Drawings*, 1924. As published in *La Révolution surréaliste*, January 15, 1925, pp. 16–17.

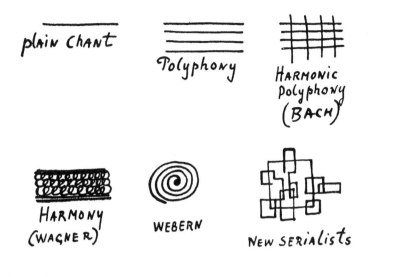

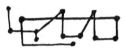

I.S. This is *my* music:

Figure 10.15. Stravinsky's response to Robert Craft's question "Would you 'draw' your recent music? For example . . ." From *Conversations*, 1959.

Elsewhere Stravinsky left no doubt that for him visual proportion was akin to aural proportion and that mathematics was music's natural domain.

Q. Do you regard musical form as in some degree mathematical?
A. It is, at any rate, far closer to mathematics than to literature—not perhaps to mathematics itself, but certainly to something like mathematical thinking and mathematical relationships. (How misleading are all literary descriptions of musical form!) I am not saying that composers think in equations or charts of numbers, nor are those things more able to symbolize music. But the way composers think—the way I think—is, it seems to me, not very different from mathematical thinking. I was aware of the similarity of these two modes while I was still a student; and, incidentally, mathematics was the subject that most interested me in school. Musical form is mathematical because it is

ideal, and form is always ideal . . . But though it may be mathematical, the composer must not seek mathematical formulae.[118]

If an awareness of Stravinsky's extra-musical orientation and a knowledge of its crucial importance for his art in the period between 1909 and 1914 offers a vital base for our current critical assessment, the force of such a broadly constituted federation must have been apparent to Stravinsky from the beginning. It was a point of view that obviously resonated in the mind of the young George Antheil, who, writing home from Paris to Mary Curtis Bok in August 1922, stated that the composer, rather than looking to Beethoven or Stravinsky, should find his sense of organization in the works of Picasso, his sense of form and time-space in the sculptures of Brancusi and Lipchitz, and his psychology in James Joyce and Gertrude Stein.[119] The allusion to Stein is especially provocative in light of her prose style in *The Making of Americans* (1909–1911), where repetitive sentences of limited vocabulary convey a sense of process, which she likened to a dog drinking. In the recurring snippets of minimal information now stretched from sentence to paragraph length, Stein, like Stravinsky in the first of his quartet pieces, created a sense of psychological difficulty more through a resulting monotony that bordered on aphasia than through the obscurity of the materials. She also openly acknowledged a debt to the analytic Cubists, whose social circle was her own.[120]

It could be argued that with the first violin performance indication *avec toute la longueur de l'archet* Stravinsky also intended to note a paradoxical link between such run-on repetitions and folk fiddling practices. However, in forging a simultaneous interdisciplinary alliance with a new and vital avant-garde, Stravinsky had gradually diffused the link with folk repertoires and severed a powerful musical claim to the authority of the past. There can be little doubt that he, and others of his contemporaries, quickly recognized and responded to this paradox. The reconstitution of a more recent and identifiable legacy soon became their primary concern. For Stravinsky and a host of his contemporaries, the decades of Neoclassicism lay just ahead. With such attempts to relocate and distance the present—which was one of the primary concerns of the Surrealists and a group of Parisian composers who developed under the auspices of Satie and Cocteau—the history of music was soon to be reviewed, reinterpreted, and enlarged. The preparation of editions of older music from the Middle Ages to the Classic period—already well launched from the turn of the century by the composers themselves as well as by scholars in the newly forming discipline of musicology—gained increasing momentum and provided a new resource capable of competing with, if not replacing, the folktune anthologies. The purview of the past was in the process of being dilated to an extent hardly imaginable in 1882, when Stravinsky was born. Composers of his and a younger generation were now quick to recognize the opportunity, to seize the resource, to proclaim its vitality, and to manipulate its potential authority.

Though in the post-Armistice period Cendrars could express the conviction that Cubist pictures were "as potent as savage fetishes,"[121] he no longer believed that pre-1917 Cubism could show the way to the future. Cendrars protested that young artists, in an attempt to reconstitute a world blown apart by war, now sensed a need to emphasize "precisely the point which was left out of the Cubist experiment: the study of depth. The young have a sense of reality. They abhor a vacuum; they abhor destruction . . . They are alive. They want to construct; and one can only construct in depth."[122] Similarly, the layered flatness of Stravinsky's solutions in *Three Japanese Lyrics* and *Three Pieces for String Quartet* was soon to be compromised through a reconsideration of phraseology and the vertical from the time of *Pulcinella* and the *Octet* onward. Like Picasso, who in *Three Musicians* (see Figure 11.3) reconciled the experience of Cubism to a relatively conventional perspective, Stravinsky began to effect adjustments that made his music resonate with a sense of history.

It seems clear that Stravinsky was aware of and responded to the Cubist vision in the period around 1912–1914. But, like the painters, he quickly became cognizant of the crisis which he had helped to ignite. In the interest of its resolution, rather than the overthrow of newly discovered values, he confected a brilliant and discerning accommodation in the early postwar period. In the 1920s Stravinsky would still have been capable of sharing Gleizes's newly pronounced veneration of the murals in the medieval cathedral and the universally communicative rhythm of its flat shapes.[123] But unlike Gleizes, who in spite of certain pronouncements was to remain steadfastly Cubist to the end, Stravinsky, Picasso, and others of a slightly younger generation had now moved on from the consequences of Cubism to a fresh terrain. A shift in Picasso's orientation visible from the time of his introduction to Cocteau and his involvement with *Parade* (Satie)[124] was later confirmed with two ballet productions, *Le Tricorne* (Falla) and *Pulcinella* (Stravinsky). In all three instances Picasso's reintroduction of the figure and perspective confirmed a Neoclassic realignment of the forces of Cubism. The fracture of analytic Cubism that had been partially healed in the synthetic phase around 1912–1914 was now subject to a new degree of integration, loudly proclaimed on the critical front as a kind of reclamation of tradition over the avant-garde. Similarly, after 1920 the constructive bias of Stravinsky's *Three Pieces for String Quartet* did not disappear but, as in the art of Picasso, began to accommodate to a new language and a new task.

— MASQUERADES —

— 11 —

Obsessions with Pierrot

A masked character . . . posits himself as an enigma, and he defies all others to decipher his language. He thus places himself outside common law, claiming for himself the use of a freedom all the larger for not being limited, momentarily, by social conventions.

Jean-Louis Bédouin

Man is least himself when he talks in his own person. Give him a mask and he will tell you the truth.

Oscar Wilde

Edward Gordon Craig and the Über-marionette

What passed for Oriental-Neoprimitivist alchemy at the hands of Goncharova in *Le Coq d'or* and for Cubist-inspired visions of time and space in Cocteau's plans for *David* can, in retrospect, also be seen as a reflection of broadly based concerns in the contemporary theater. But the theatrical avant-garde movements of the early twentieth century also had their roots in numerous historical precedents, and the leaders seldom tried to conceal the debt. Following their aborted projections for a collaboration, as Cocteau moved toward *Parade* and Stravinsky toward *Les Noces,* the traditions of the Orient and the *commedia dell'arte* continued to be reviewed, modified, and pressed into service.

The planar aspects of *interior* and *exterior* action forwarded with respect to *David* and the separation of body from voice in *Coq d'or* both had an ancient ancestry in various kinds of theater, especially from the Orient. While the origins of puppetry, for example, are considered to be prehistoric, a high level of sophistication developed at an early date in the East, and a perceptible East-to-West trend has been alleged. Puppetry brought with it the idea of supernatural forces with potentially religious associations, and in Japan it borrowed from the ancient traditions of No drama and Kabuki theater in achieving its zenith in the Bunraku puppet theater of the seventeenth century.[1]

Crucial to an understanding of the Bunraku theater is its physical arrangement. The puppet itself is roughly two-thirds life-size, operated by a chief puppeteer who controls the head and right hand; a second puppeteer, standing somewhat back, controls the left hand; and a third puppeteer controls the feet. All puppeteers are totally neutralized by black clothing. Performed on a full-size stage with scenery, the story is told and lines are spoken by the reciters, who occupy the right of the stage together with the samisen musicians, who provide an accompaniment to the action.[2]

In the aristocratic and much more ancient No drama the chorus frequently sings the lines of the central figure, who mimes or dances the action, and there is a pervasive trading between articulation source and character. One of No drama's most striking features involves the dressing of the actors with succesive kimonos in full view of the audience. The mask is taken out of its box with ritualistic gestures, and the actor adorns himself with a mask made not for him but for his ancestors who performed the first No dramas, and he feels invested with its force.[3] The effect of the whole is to objectify and promote the recognition of universals and to sense their link to ancestral tradition.

The conventions of puppetry, endorsed by the Japanophile Judith Gautier even for performances of Wagner, as well as the role of the Japanese mask were increasingly studied in the period of the fin de siècle, and in the early decades of the new century were adopted by a number of notable figures of the theater. As early as May 1900, the Englishman Edward Gordon Craig had employed masks in a production of Purcell's *Dido and Aeneas* at the Hampstead Conservatoire, for which he prescribed an unusual use of light and bodily dismemberment to accompany Dido's death at the conclusion of the opera: "One dance I'll make a dance of arms—with *white* arms—the rest of the scene dark—and out of it, the voices—with arm accompaniment—exciting if done well."[4] Such lighting experiments were to find a clear echo in the theatrical developments at the Bauhaus in the 1920s.

Then in his first announcement concerning the idea of the super-marionette of 1905 Craig presented a series of designs for complete and neutral demi-masks as well as a more expressive variety for which he acknowledged the influence of Walt Whitman's poem "Faces."[5] Finally, in a classic article of 1908, he pressed his ideas to their conclusion in proclaiming the idea of the Über-marionette, a life-size puppet, to replace living actors: "The actor must go, and in his place comes the inanimate figure—the über-marionette we may call him, until he has won for himself a better name . . . The Marionette . . . appears to me to be the last echo of some noble and beautiful art of a past civilization."[6]

Beyond the compelling tradition of mask and marionette in various societies, the primary interest for the contemporary twentieth-century theater concerned the relationship of the voice to the actor. Although Craig was preeminent among those early innovators of the modern theater who preached the value and function of puppetry and mask, he was fundamentally opposed to its antiquarian aspects, refusing to copy the Greek mask or those of the *commedia dell'arte* and Nō drama, and seeking only nourishment for the future in all of them.[7] Craig put it bluntly in *The Mask:* "There is a stage expression of the actor 'getting under the skin of the part.' A better one would be getting 'out of the skin of the part altogether.' "[8] In the same article he fashioned a fantasy conversation between an actor, a poet, and a musician, acknowledging the superiority of the musician because he is forced to allow abstract sounds to speak for themselves.

Craig was no lover of contemporary music. But his passions were deep, and his liaison with Isadora Duncan was so urgent that virtually all actors and dancers were compared unfavorably with her. For him she was the source for the whole modern movement, and he continually reviewed her impact upon Fokine, Nijinsky, and Diaghilev's Ballets Russes, even as he decried the accomplishments of the Russians in general.[9] His concerns touched upon many of the familiar topics of the day, including beyond Duncan and Diaghilev, Jaques-Dalcroze, the *commedia dell'arte,* and ethnic dance, especially that of the Japanese and the Javanese. He spoke with equal fascination of the function of Ashanti funerary masks and the masks of the Nō drama,[10] noting their power to draw attention to spiritual essences and to suppress the personal ego of the performer.

For the painters the vogue of the mask was attributable in part to the affinities of *art nègre* for tribal artifacts. But Emil Nolde, for example, employed the "primitive" mask for the purpose of excluding the psychology of the individual and discovering expressions of a more universal nature, appropriating the grimacing forms typical of folk art and especially the Tyrol rather than exotic models.[11] In this we see a parallel with the interest in *arts primitifs* of Eastern Europe and Russia from the turn of the century, which was accompanied by a concern for the "minor" arts of made objects, especially those with a ritualistic potential. The objects which the ethnologists scrutinized for their social markings fascinated and nourished both the art historian and the artist who, "searching to pierce the veil of mystery, discovered therein forms forgotten by traditional academicism."[12]

August Macke, painter and decorator for the theater, also defended not only folk art and the artistic trends of secret African societies, but the masks and puppet plays of the Greeks, the Japanese, the Siamese, and the mystery plays among the heathens and the first Christians.[13] At the conclusion of his article entitled "Masks" in *Der Blaue Reiter,* he summed up the force of the mask of various cultures for contemporary society from Ceylon, New Caledonia, Benin, and Chichén Itzá.[14]

Craig's concerns like Macke's mirrored those of the musician of the first three decades. The potential interdisciplinary nourishment which the musician began to sense as he became increasingly involved in musical-theatrical works himself was richly interpreted and ultimately led to the development of a glossary of modifications and transferrals.

Vsevolod Meyerhold and the *Commedia dell'arte:* *Pierrot* and *Petrushka*

The geographically dispersed reaction against the naturalistic theater implies that its origins were not nationalistic. Among those who made the most memorable contributions were Adolphe Appia (1862–1928), a Swiss who rejected painted scenery and experimented with light and shade, color and intensity in his probe of the three-dimensionality of the stage—especially in his productions of Wagner. Appia viewed Wagner's music and text as a product of the "first primordial idea of creation," free of all conventions in the real world, and it was through his music that he sought to work out his ideas of the modern theater. These included his belief in the central role of the actor, whose actions "preformed by the score, transfer the music on to the stage," newly conceived as an open space upon which lighting could assume a powerful function and replace all need for the painted backdrop. His ideas were brought to fruition and demonstrated in cooperation with Jaques-Dalcroze in the production of *Echo und Narzissus* (1912) and Gluck's *Orfeo ed Euridice* (1913).[15] In his probe of an anti-realist, non–illusionist approach to theater, Appia formed theories that clearly complemented the work of Gordon Craig. Both were driven by a desire to move away from the prevailing histrionics of contemporary actors. In *Madama Butterfly* and later in *Turandot* even Puccini must have felt something of the power of the mask and the Orient to diffuse the heightened passions of *verismo* and at the same time to support a nobility of expression.

In addition to an Englishman and a Swiss there was also a Frenchman in the figure of Jacques Copeau, the founder of the Théâtre du Vieux-Colombier. Cocteau was obviously knowledgeable about Copeau's movement toward a new kind of spatio-temporal theater when he sketched his ideas about *David* to Stravinsky and suggested Copeau's collaboration in the project. But it was the Russian Vsevolod Meyerhold who perhaps stands in closer proximity to the tale unfolding in the musical theater than any other person. The force of Oriental theatrical traditions had been appropriated and implanted in Russian experimental theater early in the twentieth century. In 1911 at the Alexandrinsky Theater in St. Petersburg, Meyerhold, one of the important prophets of contemporary theater and one of the first advocates of the theater of the absurd, was deeply absorbed in the conventions of both Chinese and Japanese drama, and continually decried attempts to create a sense of reality on stage. He believed that both the Kabuki traditions of Japan and the Kathakali dance theater of India showed the way in that they both appealed to the audience to invoke their imagination.[16] For Meyerhold the mask also permitted a paradoxical union of contradictory extremes, the aristocratic carnival and the *commedia dell'arte*.

By the middle of the sixteenth century, when the *commedia dell'arte* was flourishing in Italy, puppets were already an established fixture, and soon developed an independent life in various countries: the Italian Pulcinella, for example, became Polichinelle in France, Punch in England, Kasperle in Germany, and Petrushka in Russia. Composers were attracted only incidentally to these figures, though operas for puppets in the form of Venetian burlesques were staged as early as 1679 at the Teatro S. Moisè, and Gluck and Haydn actually composed puppet operas in the eighteenth century for performance at the summer palace of Nikolaus Esterházy.

Of all figures in the *commedia dell'arte* it was Pierrot whose popularity was ascendant during the nineteenth century. A buffoon attired in a loose white tunic with huge buttons, loose sleeves, white pantaloons, and white face, he became increasingly subject to mood swings that emphasized a psychological fragility. Pierrot as portrayed by the mime

Jean-Gaspard Debureau (1796–1846) became for Baudelaire "le vrai pierrot actuel, le pierrot de l'histoire moderne," and before long other Symbolist poets and musicians recognized his capacity for striking varied poses. The Belgian Albert Giraud wrote his *Pierrot lunaire,* subtitled *Rondels bergamasques,* in 1884, and Debussy began his *Suite bergamasque* a few years later in 1890, capturing the moonstruck note of Pierrot from Bergamo in his renowned "Clair de lune." Similarly, Verlaine's *Fêtes galantes* of 1864 conjured up the figure of Pierrot, and Debussy introduced Scaramouche and Pulcinella in the first line of "Fantoches" ("Marionettes") from his first set of *Fêtes galantes* of 1892. Debussy's fascination with Pierrot continued in the guise of a sonata for cello and piano as late as 1915, for which Debussy proposed the subtitle *Pierrot fâché avec la lune (Pierrot Vexed with the Moon).*[17] The Decadent Pierrot of the late nineteenth century had always been a figure drawn to multiplicity rather than singularity, given to fusion as well as confusion, and assisted by Sarah Bernhardt as well as Félicien Campsaur's *Lulu,* published in 1901, he finally achieves a morphological rebirth as a *clownesse.*[18]

Meyerhold's devotion to the *commedia dell'arte* and the attendant conventions that built directly on these Symbolist ambiguities appeared for the first time in St. Petersburg on December 31, 1906, in *Balaganchik* (*The Puppet Booth*). The fifteen-page verse-play by the poet Alexandre Blok conjures up the figures of Pierrot, Harlequin, and Columbine in order "to conceal behind the masks the profound desperation of wise men who doubt."[19] Meyerhold played the role of Pierrot himself, and one critic described his characterization thus: "This white Pierrot is an absolute stranger to all Pierrot's that I have ever known, whimpering and full of affectation. This one is full of acute angles, he whispers in a strangled voice words which speak of a distant sadness. He is mordant, penetrating the soul; he is tender and at the same time impertinent."[20] Meyerhold's means for underlining the contrasts of gaiety and despair were especially remembered as relying heavily upon dry and artificial intonations of the voice, which causes one to wonder if Schoenberg had been made aware of the director's interpretations at any time prior to the premiere of his own *Pierrot* on October 12, 1912. Schoenberg's first visit to St. Petersburg, however, came only two months later, on December 12, 1912, in conjunction with a performance of his tone poem *Pelleas und Melisande.* Interestingly, Meyerhold had produced his own version of Maeterlinck's *Pelléas et Mélisande* only shortly before in 1910, treating it as a fairy tale from a children's book.[21]

In numerous ways Schoenberg's *Pierrot lunaire* involves a set of masks joined to a cluster of conventions that invites visual and sonic comparison with Meyerhold and Campsaur even more than does Stravinsky's *Petrushka,* whose only voice is orchestral. In the premiere performance of Schoenberg's cycle the Viennese actress Albertine Zehme, dressed in Pierrot costume and powdered face, delivered her text in front of a black Spanish screen behind which Schoenberg conducted the instrumentalists. More particularly Pierrot is intoned by a soprano, thus perpetuating the newly sprung tradition concerning gender transferral. And Schoenberg's invention of *Sprechstimme*—a kind of speech-song that avoids sustaining a given pitch and advocates the continual use of portamento—not only parallels Meyerhold's whimpering affectations but promotes confusion of sexual identity in the androgynous expression of a masked *clownesse*.[22]

In addition there are textual and musical issues which reinforce the idea of a congestion of facades. Consisting of an arrangement of twenty-one poems from an original cycle of fifty, Schoenberg's cycle lacks a genuine narrative progression. Endorsing the psychological component above all, he subscribes to a "playing at fear" that leads from pretense to anxiety, then surprise and laughter at the deception involved.[23] Furthermore, the formal rigidity of the *Pierrot* texts creates expectations which are not confirmed by the musical response. For Schoenberg's music eschews exact recall in setting Albert Giraud's rondeaux, each of which involves three quatrains containing repetition between lines one, seven, and thirteen as well as between lines two and eight. Although in the first and last of the twenty-one numbers he brings back musical ideas from the initial refrain in both of its repetitions, in the remainder the literary pattern is more vaguely suggested or ignored altogether.

Against this unyielding textual form Schoenberg applies a freely atonal language marked by a series of musical devices familiar to tonal music, from rhythmic and pitch motives to insistent ostinato to contrapuntal games involving triple canon and retrograde diminution, as in "Moonspot." Even here, however, there is a ruse. For although follow-the-leader formalisms may be clearly audible, the canon, which historically presented one of the highest challenges in tonal music of the preceding centuries, is devoid of any intimation of contrapuntal conquest in a world without harmonic laws such as governs Schoenberg's score.[24]

One further detail beckons as an emblem of the whole. Of the twenty-one pieces that Schoenberg chose for his *Pierrot lunaire* cycle, concession to singing—that is the use of sustained tones—occurs in only a single number, "Nacht," and on the three pitches that constitute the prevailing motif of the piece, mysteriously dubbed a passacaglia in the score. The accompanying text is the three-syllable word *verschwiegen* ("concealed"). The mask of *Sprechstimme*, or inflected speech-song, is thereby revealed, calling attention to the original premise that proposed *singing* as artificial and *Sprechstimme* as more naturally expressive. One brief moment of abandon measured against stratagems worked out over the entire cycle, and the artificiality of Schoenberg's invention is exposed.

Otto Eric von Hartleben's anything but straightforward translation of Giraud's French into German not only continued to mirror the taste for Baudelairean themes of decadence, but also introduced a note of irony missing in the original. Furthermore, alongside avant-garde attitudes drawn from the *commedia dell'arte*, Hartleben's experience as a German cabaret littérateur encouraged him to introduce a hint of Orientalism in the taste of the day, and some have seen Schoenberg's players as performing "in the shadow of a 'shadow theatre.' "[25] Such prevailing diversity of sponsorship helps to clarify Schoenberg's verbalizations of regard for *Petrushka* and Stravinsky's for *Pierrot* in Berlin during October 1912, and, indeed, helps legitimize their expressions of admiration beyond mere protocol in spite of the seemingly chasmic aesthetic distance between the two works.

For the Russian interest in the *commedia dell'arte* from the turn of the century was also clearly inspired by the French Symbolists, and Meyerhold queried Apollinaire repeatedly about the tradition. It was not only the strange masks of the fair booths which intrigued him, but especially their function in a carnivalesque structure and the potential collaborative roles of painting, music, and ballet in the larger tradition. Thus, beyond the temptation to connect Schoenberg's *Pierrot* with Meyerhold, it is indispensable to be aware that in addition to Benois, whose interest in puppet theater is typically considered crucial to the conception of *Petrushka*, Meyerhold loomed as a forceful protagonist of the subject, style, and methods invoked in Stravinsky's ballet. In Blok's *The Puppet Booth (Balaganchik)* true and counterfeit love, innocence and guile, heartfelt and superficial emotion—all of the contrasts of *Petrushka*, including the stylized gestures attendant to each character—were laid out by Meyerhold. Not only did Meyerhold's interpretation prefigure the grotesquerie of Nijinsky's puppet, but, we are informed, his Pierrot "sighed and flapped his arms the same way every time, much as Petrushka would do five years later."[26] Finally, in *Petrushka,* beyond the *maslenitsa* or pre–Lenten carnival entertainments populated by barkers, puppet shows, masked mummers, and trained bears,[27] the title character, the dancer, and the Blackamoor are a collective and direct reflection of the story's *commedia dell'arte* triangle of Pierrot, Colombine, and Harlequin that appeared in Blok's play.[28]

Reinforcing the behavior of the characters themselves, Stravinsky's musical solutions were in harmony with attempts to contrast the naturalistic with the mechanical. As a basic gambit, the composer alternates an advancing personal musical language periodically tinged with bitonality (the "Petrushka chord" itself, for example) with the vocabulary of familiar vernaculars in a direct reflection of the story's naturalistic (the fair, the crowds) and illusory (the puppets, the entertainers) components.

The first of these pairs is identified by an energetic, folk-based music, and the second by a variety of means. The Ballerina's music has been described as "simple, repetitive, 'balletic' in a dim, Minkus-like, rehearsal-piano style,"[29] and the mild syncopations that accompany the Moor deserve to be entered in the archives as Stravinsky's earliest attempt at *musique nègre.* Both contrast vividly with the characterization of Petrushka, whose pathos and agony are portrayed by the composer's most advanced language and device. The simple, diatonic cornet arpeggios of the Ballerina are replaced by Petrushka's C major and F♯ major, which, though equally basic and subject to arpeggiation, jangle simultaneously in dissonating cascades and tremolos.

Such tactics, which involved a momentous step beyond the diatonic-chromatic/natural-magic conventions of *Firebird* inherited from Rimsky-Korsakov, made their first appearance in Stravinsky's music in *Petrushka,* and were destined to be reworked and reinterpreted once again in *Pulcinella* in the service of Neoclassicism. However, the collective lineage constitutes a legacy for Stravinsky so varied and filtered that he may have been only partially aware of the range of the sponsoring agencies.

Renard, Pulcinella, and *Les Noces*

Cataloguing the various brands of Russian preliterate theatre which served as models for Stravinsky's theater pieces from *Petrushka* to *Les*

Noces, Simon Karlinsky has identified *Renard* as "a modern revival of the spirit of the *skomorokhi,*" itinerant folk entertainers "who also doubled as buffoons, musicians, and animal impersonators."[30] By the time of *Renard* Stravinsky had left behind the overt folk-music base of *Petrushka,* or its fractured residue as in *Le Sacre,* and had confected a musical style distilled from his earlier experience. The text of *Renard* was based upon a selection of episodes from Alexander Afanasiev's collection of Russian stories surrounding the trickery of Reynard the Fox. Undoubtedly mindful of the difficulties which he had encountered in setting Andersen's fairy tale, *Le Rossignol,* Stravinsky made plans from the beginning to avoid direct identification between singer and actor. The result was the continuance of a series of hybrids, traceable or not to the textual obsessions of Alexander Dargomyzhsky's *The Stone Guest* or Musorgsky's *Boris Godunov,* involving speech and/or singing now joined with mime. The work was composed in 1915–16 as a commission from the Princesse Edmond de Polignac. Lacking a proper space, she failed to introduce it at one of her renowned *soirées musicales,* and the work, conducted by Ansermet, premiered at the Paris Opéra only in May 1922, with costumes by Larionov and choreography by Nijinska, who also danced the title role. At the time, however, there was a general consensus that the work would have fared better under the more intimate conditions offered by Polignac than in the oversized spaces of the Opéra.

Perhaps it was in light of foreseeable delays and the desire to protect the work's need for intimacy that Stravinsky had earlier encouraged the performance of *Renard* as a puppet show. A letter to his mother of August 11, 1916, states that his new *Renard* was a play for "dancers or marionettes, the musicians and singers being in the orchestra pit,"[31] and in the note prefixed to the score published in 1917, Stravinsky appended the following remarks:

> Renard is to be played by clowns, dancers or acrobats, preferably on a trestle stage with the orchestra placed behind. If produced in a theatre, it should be played in front of the curtain. The players remain all the time on the stage. They enter together to the accompaniment of the little introductory march, and their exeunt is managed in the same way. The roles are dumb. The singers (two tenors and two basses) are in the orchestra.

The actualization of the first of these options, involving a trestle stage, was entrusted to Larionov for the premiere in 1922 and extended to an even more exaggerated dimension in a production of 1929.[32] In the latter version, the roost on which the cock was perched was enlarged to the proportions of a platform capable of alternately accommodating four dancers and three acrobats who doubled in the same costumes. Both the use of platforms and the acrobats, who soared effortlessly from the wings by executing giant leaps aided by hemp ropes, were meant to recall the circus, and Renard's appearances and disappearances were accomplished through the aid of suspended Venetian blinds. Each of these elements emphasized dimensionality and motion, which were totally in keeping with Constructivist aims. They were natural allies as well of both the story and the cimbalom flourishes of Stravinsky's score, which were coordinated with the action. Listeners ignorant of the Russian language are denied access to another dualism. As André Schaeffner has put it:

> Behind the stage and as though in a cage are four voices, sounding from amidst some twenty instruments. The buffoonery is as much in the onomatopaeics of the text or the timbre of the instruments as in the actors' gestures. Two separate plots are acted simultaneously and join at times. In mid-song *Renard* unites religious and profane chant: in the Russian version Stravinsky switches from common to orthodox Church Slavonic.[33]

In later years, at a time when he recalled his "rejoicing discovery" that in Russian popular verse "the accents of the spoken verse are ignored when the verse is sung," Stravinsky also spoke of its importance for *Renard:*

> We all know parlor games in which the same sentence can be made to mean something different when different words are emphasized . . . In *Renard,* the syllable-sounds within the word itself, as well as the emphasis of the word in the sentence, are so treated. *Renard* is phoneme music, and phonemes are untranslatable . . . The players are to be dancing acrobats, and the singers are not to be identified with them; the relationship between the vocal parts and the stage characters is the same as it is in *Les Noces* and, also as in *Les Noces,* the performers, musical and mimetic, should all be together on the stage, with the singers in the center of the instrumental ensemble.[34]

In the matter of costumes, Larionov refurbished the potentially neonationalist ring of the tale by denuding the folkloric note of its Orientalism, and took full advantage of Futurist developments by employing heavily padded constructions stiffened with cardboard. Their character was heightened by colorful geometric makeup, anthropomorphizing demi–masks, and conspicuous headdresses.[35] In the sets and stage business, Larionov clearly joined the Cubists and the Futurists in their love of street language and graffiti as well as Cocteau and Les Six in their love of the circus, and transformed its spatio-temporal aspects in order to underscore the element of farce and, at the same time, to reject both historical and ethnographic alliances (Figure 11.1). In doing so, Larionov nonetheless drew directly from the Russian turn of the century fascination with the circus and magical entertainments of various kinds, just as Stravinsky had adopted the preliterate tradition of the *skomorokhi*.[36]

The ongoing manipulation of such a consortium of ingredients in a musical theater sponsored by the most renowned ballet company of the day understandably gave the conservative critics of the dance increasing consternation. André Levinson, noted for his ambivalence about current developments and for his dedication to the principles of the *danse d'école,* registered his feelings about *Renard* in an unequivocal but laconic voice that lamented the passing of the dance as he knew and loved it. Proceeding to a consideration of *Les Noces,* he noted the increasing divergence between the musical and scenic elements as well as an opposition between dancer and musician now pushed to an extreme by *l'esprit géométrique* of Mlle. Nijinska. Rejecting the colorful scenic tendency of the Ballets Russes in general and *Le Coq d'or* in particular, Levinson nonetheless praised Goncharova for a "wondrous malleability, as feminine as it is Slav." Levinson compares Goncharova's call to monastic austerity through her reduction of all color to black, brown, and white and her enjoinment of Russian folklore denuded of all color to the *Ingriste* aims of Picasso. Furthermore, he saw Stravinsky's reduction of forces to voices and an ensemble of two double-pianos and percussion as a transformation of the mysterious spiritual forces of millennial rites and demi-heathens into the solemn expressions of rustic life through which shines the soul of a people. By way of conclusion, however, Levinson offered an uneasy judgment: "In *Petrushka* the puppet moves toward the incarnate, to becoming a living being; in *Noces* living people are reduced to the mournful emptiness of a mannequin."[37]

There can be no doubt that a sense of the mechanistic and mannequinesque is promoted in *Les Noces* by the relentless propulsion of the music, which proceeds with hardly a rest from beginning to end and is accentuated by the instrumental ensemble's essentially percussive character and the choral chanting. Furthermore, the abdication of a

Figure 11.1. Michel Larionov, costume of Renard the Peasant with demi-mask.
Victoria and Albert Museum, London. © 1994 ARS, New York / ADAGP, Paris.

narrative text for a series of tableaux de-emphasizes any sense of plot as well as the individual roles: the soprano of the opening scene is not the bride but merely her voice, and is associated with the goose in the final scene; and the fiancé's words are sung by a tenor in the grooming scene, but at the end by a bass. Solutions at virtually every level under-score the ceremonial disposition of the work, about which Stravinsky remarked:

> *Les Noces* is a suite of typical wedding episodes told through quotations of typical talk. The latter, whether the bride's, the groom's, the par-ents' or the guests', is always ritualistic. As a collection of clichés and

quotations of typical wedding sayings it might be compared to one of the those scenes in *Ulysses* in which the reader seems to be over-hearing scraps of conversation without the connecting thread of dis-course. But *Les Noces* might also be compared to *Ulysses* in the larger sense that both works are trying to *present* rather than to *describe*.[38]

In retrospect, and despite their demonstrable sponsoring roles, Ori-entalism, Neoprimitivism, and folklorism emerge as wholly inadequate terms to suggest the range and vitality of these developments, even as described by contemporary observers of the scene.[39] During the period 1914–1922 a collection of patronages had been absorbed and tran-scended. Furthermore, the figure of the acrobat and the world of the circus, which had dominated the production of the painters from 1905 on, had surfaced in the theater as an ally.[40] Cubist spatial perspectives had been picked up by Cocteau and his circle in the early teens, and had been initially tested in the aborted spectacle *David*. Then, in *Parade* several devices were introduced to bring them to their first musico-theatrical fruition, but Cocteau emphasized their relation to a range of metaphysical concerns, including the role of the mask and the tradition of the puppet:

> In the first version the managers did not exist. After each music-hall turn an anonymous voice, issuing from a kind of megaphone, sang a type-phrase, summing up the different aspects of each character. When Picasso showed us his sketches, we realized how interesting it would be to introduce, in contrast to the three chromos, unhuman or superhuman characters who would finally assume a false reality on the stage and reduce the real dancers to the stature of puppets.[41]

A series of productions which traded upon both the failed and realized experiences of *Parade* followed in quick succession.

Special relationships between narrative, direct speech, dance, and musical accompaniment appeared, for example, in *L'Histoire du soldat* of 1918. This time, however, all participants were to be placed on stage in full view, much as they were later in *Les Noces* (Figure 11.2), a work with which Stravinsky was already occupied when the idea of *Histoire* first came to him. It was planned that the Soldier and the Devil would appear as actors, alternately speaking or miming, but the function of the participants was not immediately ascertained, and Stravinsky has clarified the metamorphosis:

> The narrator device was adopted to satisfy the need for a two-way go-between; that is, for someone who is an illusionist-interpreter be-

Figure 11.2. Natalia Goncharova, sketch for a set of *Les Noces,* 1922.
Wadsworth Atheneum, Hartford, Connecticut. © 1994 ARS, New York / ADAGP, Paris.

tween the characters themselves, as well as a commentator between the stage and the audience. The intercession of the narrator in the action of the play was a later development, however, an idea borrowed from Pirandello. I was attracted by this idea, but then I am always attracted by new conditions and those of the theater are, to me, a great part of its appeal. The role of the dancer was a later conception, too. I think we must have been afraid that the play without dancing would be monotonous.[42]

Although at about the same time Stravinsky readily acknowledged his indebtedness to Satie's achievement in *Parade,* here his specific reference to Pirandello instead of Cocteau in theatrical matters carries with it a clear hint of revisionism.

But beyond such issues of fusion in the developing theater, we cannot forget that in *L'Histoire du soldat* Stravinsky also claimed to have bade a musical farewell to his Russian past and to have embraced a new vernacular repertoire in the guise of Afro-American jazz. This fusion of high and low in the world of music and theater had already been prefigured by the Cubists and by Picasso in particular with a series of collages executed between 1911 and 1914 that incorporate pasted sheet music. They are conspicuously drawn from the café-concert/music hall repertory, and include *Trilles et Baisers (Trills and Kisses), Sonnet,* and *Ma jolie,* all of which resonate with the artist's personal experiences at the Cabaret du Lapin Agile. Popular music thus took its place alongside other ephemera including newspaper articles, advertisements, wallpaper, and playing cards, and like them contributed not only to dislocation but to verbal punning.[43]

Stravinsky's *Pulcinella,* which once again brought an alliance between Diaghilev and Picasso, who designed the sets and costumes, pursues the tactics of the immediately preceding works but with a new array of conventions. Just as Proust introduces the Baron de Charlus in *Remembrance of Things Past* with a set of social masks calculated to camouflage his sexual orientation and initially allow the reader to be misled, so Stravinsky commences *Pulcinella* with an adoption of the music of Pergolesi with only the subtlest hint that the music is anything but a straightforward rendition of eighteenth-century music. Like Proust, Stravinsky also refuses removal of the disguise but rather in time renders it transparent.[44] Indeed, in later years Stravinsky maintained that he attempted not so much to forge Pergolesi's signature as to use his voice with a new accent, and concluded that "the remarkable thing about *Pulcinella* is not how much but how little has been added or changed."[45]

Years later it was determined that the musical attributions were false and that Pergolesi was not the sole author of the borrowed music.[46] That Stravinsky was unaware that Pergolesi and pseudo-Pergolesi had been appropriated in tandem must be seen as completely inconsequential. Though various levels of integration are achieved, integration is not the watchword, and in the final analysis the original identity of the author is not at issue. For a more generalized deception is the name of the game, and it is one whose nature is only gradually clarified.

Few besides the connoisseur would pick up the evidence of an intruder in the opening section, for example, and in the "Serenata" that follows, Stravinsky's addition of an appropriate Neapolitan symbolism through a strumming guitar figure is so circumspect that a twentieth-century composer's involvement might still pass undetected. Little by little, however, the camouflage is lifted, and by the time of the vivo duo for trombone and double-bass, some two-thirds of the way into the score, Stravinsky's presence is unmistakably evident even to the unsuspecting. The finale, which protracts the *cadence obligée* to the point of a Satiean absurdity, once again retains ingredients of an eighteenth-century formula but so inflates and distorts it that the listener is left in no doubt as to who is in control of the whole operation.[47]

Such descriptions regarding musical manners are totally in harmony not only with the theatrical conventions of the *commedia dell'arte,* which include stereotypical use of the mask in tandem with the element of surprise, but with the scenario of the Neapolitan comedy *Four Identical Pulcinellas,* used as the basis for the Stravinsky-Diaghilev collaboration: four imposters masquerade as Pulcinella and the real Pulcinella disguises himself as a magician. Furthermore, Stravinsky follows the tradition recently laid down in *Le Coq d'or, Le Rossignol,* and *Renard* by placing the *Pulcinella* singers, a soprano and a tenor, in the pit with the orchestra. Accentuating this physical displacement, the original texts of their arias carry only a marginal relationship to the action which is developing on the stage.

The persistence of Harlequin, Pierrot, and Pulcinella in diverse aesthetic terrain during the first two decades of the twentieth century raises the question of their appeal. For Picasso, Gris, Derain, Metzinger, and Severini, as well as many other painters of the time, the *commedia dell'arte* figures provided a backdrop against which they could display their changing aesthetic positions. In his *Harlequin* of 1915, generated from the rotating planes described by Gleizes, and the refined *Harlequin* of 1917 in the guise of a ballet dancer placed against a set from *Parade;* in his line drawing of Harlequin (1918) for Cocteau's *Le Coq et l'Arlequin,* predictive of his cover for Stravinsky's *Ragtime* of the next year; and, finally, in the guitar-playing Harlequin and clarinet-playing Pierrot of *Three Musicians* (1921); Picasso addressed more than stylistic questions and autobiographical details (Figures 11.3–6).[48] Indeed, it has been suggested that in the period of Stravinsky's *Pulcinella,* for which Picasso created the sets and costumes, many artists sensed in the *commedia dell' arte* the possibility of restructuring a model of normalcy for postwar times in contrast to the anxiety-laden and aberrant behavior that had characterized much prewar theatre.

The French scholar Pierre Ducharte, in his *La Comédie italienne* of 1925, recognized with rare clarity the force of the tradition to which numerous contemporary artists were then making their contribution. Pointing to the painters as well as the poets, the Fratellini clowns, and the Ballets Russes, he concluded: "Poets, musicians, writers, painters of talent or genius, [otherwise] the most strongly opposed to each other,

Figure 11.3. Pablo Picasso, *Three Musicians,* 1921.
Museum of Modern Art, New York. © 1994 ARS, New York / SPADEM, Paris.

meet in their common love for the *commedia dell'arte*."[49] Even more
fundamentally, however, owing to the Italian origins of the *commedia*
it could serve in the immediate postwar period as an ideal forum for
extolling Latin, non–Germanic virtues, and especially for claiming them
as the source of a developing Neoclassicism. It was a claim that involved
a healthy set of fictions, and one that did not go undisputed. But in
some very important ways, it was honored, as Stravinsky became the
embodiment of a Latin-based Neoclassicism with its love of eighteenth-
century forms and manners,[50] while Schoenberg, first adopting Pierrot
and then reclaiming the classic forms of his own inheritance in the

Figure 11.4. Pablo Picasso, *Harlequin,* 1917.

Museo Picasso, Barcelona. © 1994 ARS, New York / SPADEM, Paris.

1920s, denied his relation to the aesthetic altogether. Schoenberg's position is understandable, for he saw in the subscription of the French to Neoclassicism an attempt to gloss over the mediocrity of their achievement in the nineteenth century by turning to the eighteenth, a period of undeniable riches. Refusing to relinquish claims to the continuing superiority of German music through such a historical ruse, Schoenberg denied a "return to" anything and steadfastly proclaimed the notion of continuing German hegemony.[51]

Figure 11.5. Pablo Picasso, *Harlequin*, 1915.
Museum of Modern Art, New York. © 1994 ARS, New York / SPADEM, Paris.

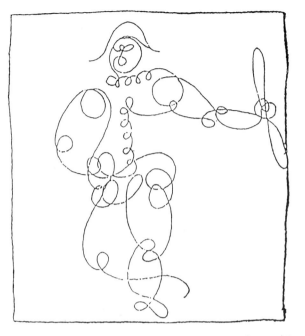

Figure 11.6. Pablo Picasso, figure of Harlequin for Jean Cocteau's *Le Coq et l'Arlequin* (1918).

Ballets Suédois: Dolls, Oxes, and Weddings

The French perspective received a series of endorsements during the brief seasons of the Ballets Suédois, including a little-known work by Debussy, *La Boîte à joujoux* (*The Toy Shop*). The ballet was planned and composed as early as 1913 in collaboration with André Hellé, widely known as a cartoonist and illustrator of children's books, who provided the libretto, the costumes, and the scenery. In the preface to the score he explained: "Toy-boxes are really towns in which toys live like real people. Or perhaps towns are nothing else but boxes in which people live like toys." (Figure 11.7)

Debussy's response was a musical companion to his earlier *Children's Corner*. A work more diverse, mature, and natural than its predecessor, it is nonetheless highly calculated in its reflection of the box's potpourri contents: French folktunes, Hindu chant (atypically identified in the score), music-box effects, themes from *Carmen* and *Faust,* arguable ref-

Figure 11.7. A scene from the Ballets Suédois production of *La Boîte à joujoux* (1923).
Photo, Dansmuseet, Stockholm.

erences to *Petrushka* through tritone materials and secundal figurations and to *Le Sacre* through insistently repeated eighth-note chords, to *Pelléas et Mélisande* through thematics and timbral reference (an oboe figure clearly recalls the child Yniold amidst a flock of sheep in *Pelléas*), to Mendelssohn's "Wedding March," to his own ballet *Jeux,* to "Golliwog's Cakewalk," and to an English folktune, "The Keel Row," recalled from Debussy's orchestral *Gigues*—all are served with a subtle irony and projected onto the fantasy scrim of a child's make-believe world. Debussy's collage citations invoke Stravinsky's game plan in *Petrushka* on numerous levels, but the advantage of tune recognition has now been transferred from a Russian audience to a Parisian one.

Debussy had written in a letter of October 31, 1913, that "only puppets could understand the text and the expression of the music properly," and elsewhere he suggested that the principal roles should be acted by children and that dance should not be introduced. Because of the war, the premiere of the work had been delayed until December 1918, six months after the composer's death. It was afforded an undistinguished production at its premiere, but the conductor Inghelbrecht was attracted to the score, whose orchestration had been completed by André Caplet, and he recommended the work to Börlin, who produced it on the Ballets Suédois bill for February 15, 1921. Börlin's choreography underscored the puppet imagery of Hellé's dancing dolls with angular, mechanized movements, and the whole had the effect of a ballet for marionettes.[52]

Other manifestations of the French perspective followed in a series of productions largely under the guidance of Jean Cocteau. His first stage work following the collaboration with Diaghilev on *Parade* was *Le Boeuf sur le toit,* which premiered on February 21, 1920, at the Comédie des Champs-Élysées. The tradition of the revue, which could be traced back to the eighteenth century in France, was already enjoying a full-blown revival when Robert Dreyfus penned his monograph, *Petite histoire de la revue de fin d'année,* in 1909. Calling largely upon items from the daily press, such revues could also incorporate, as Dreyfus' title suggests, a review of the past year's events. Cocteau's jumbled scenario for *Parade,* which he passed along to Satie, had stressed these very qualities. Now, with music by Milhaud blended from the maxixes and tangos drawn from his Brazilian experience, Cocteau provided an answer to the critics of *Parade:* "Having seen the word 'farce' erroneously employed with respect to *Parade,* the idea came to me to make a farce, a genuine farce of the Middle Ages, with masks, men playing the roles of women, pantomime and dance."[53]

Eschewing both the Italian *commedia dell'arte* and French literary traditions, Cocteau wedded characters drawn from the music hall and circus, including the Fratellini clowns, to a world recently charted by Charlie Chaplin. An American bar was furnished with a Negro boxer, a bartender, a pool-playing Negro dwarf, a cop, a bookmaker, and red-haired, busty women played by transvestites. Each was outfitted with a cardboard head three times normal size and naturalist theater was thrown to the wings. Picasso later got Cocteau to admit that the proportions were off, resulting in an appearance of dwarfs with enormous heads rather than artists outfitted with false ones. But Cocteau confirmed their value and function in *Le Boeuf,* laid the groundwork for other shows that he would soon prepare, and joined some of the most important figures of the theater in the 1920s in probing the versatility of the mask for modern times. The disconcerting effect of the component parts was exacerbated through a new relationship between music and movement. Unlike *Parade,* which conveyed a natural correspondence between action and sound, *Le Boeuf* forwarded a fresh perspective closely allied to Cocteau's fascination with the contemporary cinema. As Milhaud put it: "In contrast to the rapid music, Jean retarded the movements to resemble a slow-motion film. This gave to the entire cast an unreal character which suggested a dream sequence."[54]

With *Parade* and *Le Boeuf* behind him, Cocteau saw his *Les Mariés de la Tour Eiffel* premiere on June 18, 1921, under the auspices of the newly formed Ballets Suédois. His defection from Diaghilev was clearly prompted by the company's claims to be an avant-garde alternative to the Ballets Russes. The setting of a middle-class Parisian family wedding at the Eiffel Tower on the fourteenth of July identified the culture in question, but Cocteau's original thought to call the work *La Noce* and later *La Noce massacrée* clearly hinted at a challenge to the Diaghilev-Stravinsky aesthetic. Cocteau changed the title at Stravinsky's request, since the composer had been at work since 1917 on a stage piece which bore the title *Les Noces villageoises*. Cocteau finally settled on *Les Mariés de la Tour Eiffel,* which he described as "a title in the style of the old vaudeville shows that ultimately serves to signal the very French side of a work and to introduce to the stage some essential emblems of our culture."[55]

In *Les Mariés* the central emblem of culture was no longer the Russian *lubok* as practiced by Goncharova and Larionov but the vernacular *image d'Épinal*. Épinal, a French village in Lorraine, had been producing these somewhat crude but brilliantly colored broadsides as woodcuts since the sixteenth century and after 1850 as lithographs. The *image d'Épinal* attracted early twentieth-century avant-garde artists because, though figurative, it was free of Beaux-Arts associations, and also because it possessed a naiveté that "partook of a kind of primitivism which was congenial and even familiar to late nineteenth- and early twentieth-century artists."[56] Building upon the Futurist model of Fortunato Depero (1892–1960), who had collaborated with Giacomo Balla in his "mechanical" theater and sound poems and who had updated the *commedia dell'arte* through mask, costume, and megaphone, Cocteau found in the *image d'Épinal* a fresh and distinctively French flavor which he first utilized in *Parade* and then in *Le Boeuf sur le toit*.[57] Now in *Les Mariés* a popular French tradition of ancient stock was appropriated in the service of caricaturing bourgeois rites, big game hunters, sideshow entertainers, and flatulent generals.

Cocteau's instinct for both shock and simplicity also directed him to test new relations between speech, music, and dance. His experiences with *Parade* and *Le Boeuf sur le toit* were near at hand—as well as the productions of the Ballets Suédois in *La Boîte à joujoux* and *L'Homme et son désir,* premiered only twelve days before on June 6, 1921. Auric was to have composed the music, but lacking sufficient time Cocteau divided the assignment among five members of Les Six: Auric composed the overture, "Le 14-Juillet," and the "Ritournelles de liaison," which connected the various scenes; Milhaud composed the "Marche nuptiale" and "Sortie de la noce"; Poulenc, the "Discours du Général" and "Baigneuse de Trouville" ("The Trouville Bathing Beauty"); Tailleferre, the "Valse de dépêches" ("Waltz of the Telegrams") and a "Quadrille"; and Honegger concluded with a "Funeral March." The parceling out of the music to multiple composers obviously fostered a sonic patchwork redolent of a music hall revue. Between the framing marches only three pieces were genuine dances: "La danse de la baigneuse de Trouville," "La danse des dépêches," and the "Quadrille." Jean Börlin was named as the sole choreographer in Cocteau's advance comments, appearing in the June 1921 issue of *La Danse,* but later in the twenties equal credit was given to both Cocteau and Börlin, and in 1948 Börlin's name was omitted altogether. Notices and claims aside, the initial spirit behind the whole was clearly summarized by Auric when he called it "un spectacle très à l'image de Jean Cocteau."[58]

Milhaud's opening "Wedding March" struck the parodic note from the beginning by having the bridal couple enter "marching like dogs in a dog show," to quote Cocteau's stage directions. The General's wedding speech follows, but it is without words: "The General's speech is in the orchestra. He only gesticulates."[59] Poulenc's music is a perfect piece of pompous "blah-blah-blah," and Paul Witzansky, who performed the role, brought the rich Danish mime traditions of Auguste Bournonville to the task. The "Waltz of the Telegrams" was danced by ladies with oversized bosoms wearing light-blue tutus, *sur les pointes* but with noticeably wobbly ankles in a highly exaggerated imitation of Tchaikovsky's swans. Classical ballet was overtly parodied, and the music aided in deflating the entire business. In "The Trouville Bathing Beauty" Poulenc served up an artificially stylish promenade music that was alternately twittering and coy, blatantly tonal, and worthy of a contemporary Parisian revue.

Although Carina Ari danced the bride in the premiere performance, on numerous later occasions Börlin took the role incognito. This was possible because of the concealing costumes, created over a wire frame with a bulk that precluded gracious movement, and the masks, which drew upon the traditions of Japanese No drama and the *image d'Épinal* but with facial expressions that bespoke caricature (Figure 11.8). To this Cocteau added another sphere of layered reality through the reintroduction of the megaphone idea originally projected for *Parade,* now represented by a pair of huge phonograph speakers behind which two readers recited the text (Figure 11.9). Cocteau's comments at the time of the production hint at the desired effect:

> Ballet? No. Play? No. Revue? No. Tragedy? No. A sort of clandestine marriage, rather, between classical tragedy and the end-of-the year revue, between the chorus and the music hall number. The whole thing already viewed at a distance, in perspective, modern antiquity, characters from our childhood, wedding party with a tendency to vanish into thin air, episode on the Eiffel Tower which, after being discovered by the painters, becomes once more what it should never have ceased to be: a lovely young woman in mittens, whose sole former employment was that of reigning over Paris and who, today, is simply the telegraph lady. What happens? Nothing that can readily be described. The sort of people one meets on a Sunday outing come and go while human gramophones, to right and left of the stage, comment on their actions.[60]

Cocteau aimed at confecting a "truth greater than the truth"[61] by looking around, behind, over, or under familiar facades, and his two human gramophones, rejecting naturalistic speaking, "spoke very loudly, very quickly, and pronounced each syllable distinctly."[62] Kenneth Silver has proposed that Cocteau's Dadaist entertainment was in effect a postwar celebration party, whose seeming note of frivolity wedded figures drawn from the *images d'Épinal* to the spirit of *Grand Guignol.*[63] However one characterizes the final show, it was Cocteau's intention not just to lampoon naturalistic theatre and classical ballet but to confect a thoroughly French product that mirrored both the absurdity and the poetry of life. Yet, if the show also served to introduce a group of young French musicians to the public, their music could no more be judged as concert music independent of the original background than could Minkus' music for *La Bayadère* or Satie's for *Parade,* and the risks in presenting the music without the visual counterpart were common to all.

A few years later Poulenc's *Les Biches* (1924) served to revive the assertion that Goncharova's and Diaghilev's earlier solution separating voice and body had honored traditions of the French opera-ballet—a claim that had never been introduced with respect to Cocteau's *Les*

Figure 11.8. Masked bride and groom in the Ballets Suédois production of Cocteau's
Les Mariés de la Tour Eiffel, 1921.

Photo, Dansmuseet, Stockholm.

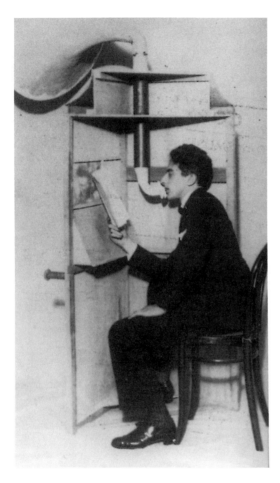

Figure 11.9. Jean Cocteau as the First Phonograph in *Les Mariés de la Tour Eiffel*.
Photo, Dansmuseet, Stockholm.

Mariés. The issue was obviously resurrected now because *Les Biches* employed invisible choruses singing eighteenth-century texts. But the argument, however much in harmony with Poulenc's later claims of affinity for the world of Watteau in his *Concert champêtre* for harpsichord and orchestra (1927), clearly invited examination.[64] A 1924 article by André Schaeffner entitled "The Singers in the 'Pit,'" written with the recent experience of both *Les Noces* and *Les Biches* in mind, recalled Goncharova's accomplishments in *Le Coq d'or,* reviewed the history of the French opera-ballet, and characterized the Poulenc work as a compromise between the solutions of *Pulcinella* and *Les Noces*.[65]

Figure 11.10. Stage set for *L'Homme et son désir* showing the four tiers and cardboard figures for the musicians.

Photo, Dansmuseet, Stockholm.

Schaeffner also identified two scores by Milhaud, for *L'Homme et son désir* and *Salade,* as further accomplices in the current exploration. In the first of these both the lingering specter of Cubist theater à la *David* and Dalcrozian eurhythmics were held to be palpably evident.[66] Seeing Paul Claudel supervise the preparation of characters cut out of cardboard and the tiered arrangement of the participants (Figure 11.10), Milhaud later recalled the joining of stylized movement with the forces of simultaneity, both visual and sonic:

> I could visualize several independent groups: on the third tier, to one side a vocal quartet, and on the other, oboe, trumpet, harp, and doublebass. On the second tier, on either side, the percusssion. On one side of the first tier, the piccolo, the flute, the clarinet, and the bass clarinet; on the other, a string quartet. I wanted to preserve absolute independence, melodic, tonal, and rhythmic, for each of these groups. I realized my desire, and in order to facilitate the execution of my score, written for some instruments in common time, for others in

triple time, and for others in six-eight, and so on, I inserted an arbitrary bar-line every four beats, adding accents to preserve the authentic rhythm.[67]

Milhaud's use of a textless chorus also necessitated review of the function of the voice both as textless instrument (as in Debussy's "Sirènes" from *Three Nocturnes* and Schmitt's *La Tragédie de Salomé*) and as a purveyor of text—with or without intimate connection to the action on stage. In sum, a whole roster of cohorts was now reassessed in light of the dramatic and symbiotic metamorphosis taking place between music, dance, and theater. It is not surprising that some missed the cues of the turnover, however, and Janet Flanner's views, expressed in 1929, the last season of the Ballets Russes, must have been commonly held:

> Among the intellectuals who justly acclaimed the ballet two decades ago—during the riots attendant upon the launching of iconoclasts like the *Sacre*—there has been of late, and perhaps equally justly, a tendency to sniff at the troup. The Ballet is not what it was, but neither are the sniffers . . . It is the passing of time which has weakened the authority of the Ballet—that and the later Stravinsky. For *Reynard,* his last contribution to the Ballet repertory, is not ballet music. This year's best bet . . . was *Le Fils Prodigue* by Prokofiev.[68]

As far as her remarks went, Flanner was right on all counts.

Petrushka, Pierrot, La Boîte à joujoux, Renard, Parade, Pulcinella, L'Homme et son désir, Les Mariés de la Tour Eiffel, La Création du monde, and *Les Biches,* as well as Manuel de Falla's *El retablo de maese Pedro* and Stravinsky's *Oedipus Rex:* each of these works written in the fifteen years between 1912 and 1927 reflects in one way or another the individual or collective force of a stylized theater drawn from both ancient and folk practices joined to the perspectives of Cubism and the contemporary revue. The ways in which these related traditions aided the musician in projecting his view of the contemporary are varied, but capable of illuminating the premise behind some of the early twentieth century's musical landmarks. The relation of each of these to the musical theater of the same period, as we have just seen, is both demonstrable and powerful—aiding the musician to sense new relationships in the revitalization of his art rather than serving as direct models for imitation. But if many of the works in this list are currently judged as period pieces which fail to find any urgency for present times, it is imperative to note that the initial stage component has almost completely disappeared. *Renard, Pulcinella, L'Homme et son désir, Les Mariés de la Tour Eiffel, La Création du monde,* and *Les Biches* no longer hold the boards today as theater pieces, and are familiar principally from recordings or occasional performances in the concert hall. As a consequence, the impact of and the issues attendant to the original productions have faded from view.[69]

Similarly, recall of the original aesthetic behind Schoenberg's disturbing masterpiece *Pierrot lunaire* may prove essential in deciphering its puzzling message. Attempts to vivify the work for modern audiences have generally proven elusive, though Rudolf Nureyev's solo choreography of *Pierrot* in 1977 probably came closer to reclaiming the miming and shadow-play effect of the original than any other production of recent times.[70] But beyond questions surrounding the projection of Schoenberg's work, recognition that the *Pierrot* legacy found a larger audience in works by other composers than did the original itself forces consideration of the surprising degree to which this "unloved" masterpiece served as a kind of authority figure for composers of vastly differing orientations over the remainder of the century.[71] From Stravinsky's *Three Japanese Lyrics* (1912–13) and Ravel's *Trois poèmes de Stéphane Mallarmé* (1913), both of which use the *Pierrot* instrumental ensemble, to Poulenc's *Rapsodie nègre* (1917) and William Walton's *Façade* (1921), which employ modifications of both the instrumental and vocal premises of *Pierrot;* from Boulez's *Le Marteau sans maître* (1954) to Peter Maxwell Davies' *Eight Songs for a Mad King* (1969), the allure of an early modern masterwork has repeatedly sprung from two quite discrete characteristics: instrumental color and timbral rotation; and the sonic/psychological heart of the matter, which resides in the *Sprechstimme.* Both factors were capable of being emulated from a strictly technical point of view. Yet it proved impossible to completely dissociate them from their original context as a pair of newly designed conventions in the service of a *commedia dell'arte* updated for modern times. Ravel's penetration of the obscurity of Mallarmé, Stravinsky's recondite approach to a set of Japanese haiku, and Walton's playful interpretation of Edith Sitwell's whimsical lines tinged with madness all flourish under an identical patronage.

More recently, the force of the *Pierrot* legacy for *Le Marteau* has been verified by Boulez in a surprisingly protracted comparison,[72] and Davies has confirmed that his psychological probe of King George III is incomprehensible without an awareness of Schoenberg's example.[73] Even more recently, literally dozens of works have endorsed the continuing legacy of the *Pierrot* ensemble, and in the music theater piece of the 1960s and 1970s the *commedia*'s potential as a psychosis-bearing host has been repeatedly acknowledged, as in R. Murray Schafer's *Requiem for a Party Girl* (1972). Here a modified *Pierrot* ensemble of flute, clarinet, horn, piano, harp, percussion, violin, viola, and cello accompanies Ariadne, the heroine, whom the composer describes as "the prototype of those strange harlequinesque creatures one meets occasionally at parties, beneath whose furious demonstrations of gregariousness and *joie de vivre* one detects obscured signs of terror and alienation." In each instance, emulation has disclosed its capacity for deviation as well as confirmation. Thus, the seemingly ad hoc nature of the original *Pierrot* instrumentation is seen to have congealed into a new standing ensemble, subject to modification without loss of identity; and the attendant *Sprechstimme* has become a natural companion to a variety of singing practices in the ongoing pursuit of vocal expression and its psychological potential.

In light of the subject and time of composition of the piece, Schoenberg's choice of Pierrot forces a consideration of the meaning and function of the mask, less in relation to primitive societies and Greek theatre or waning Symbolism and emergent Neoclassicism than to *commedia dell'arte* as an emblematic host for the most divergent stylistic expressions. Hofmannstahl's libretto for Strauss's *Ariadne auf Naxos,* a play within a play incorporating a *commedia* troupe, was conceived in the same year as Schoenberg's *Pierrot,* for example. And the theater from Wedekind, Jarry, Pound, Eliot, O'Neill, and Pirandello to Andreyev, Meyerhold, Copeau, Piscator, Kaiser, Kokoschka, Yeats, Apollinaire, and Cocteau repeatedly announced the allure of the metaphor residual in both puppet theater and the mask. Even the rudimentary theater of the Zürich Dadaists relied heavily upon extravagant combinations of mask, costume, dance, and declamation.[74] Hugo Ball, who costumed himself in a quasi-priestly cardboard robe for one of his sound-poem incantations at a soirée on April 14, 1917,[75] recorded the appeal of the mask for the Dada theater:

> Janco had made for the soirée a number of masks that were more than just inspired. They were reminiscent of the Japanese or ancient Greek theater and yet were absolutely modern . . . What fascinated all of us about the masks was the fact that they embodied not human, but over-life-size characters and passions. The horrors of the day, the paralyzing background of things, were made visible.[76]

Here we are allowed to sense the continuing appeal of a tradition not just for a series of ephemeral aesthetic shifts but for a war-weary society at large. In this light it is understandable that experiments in the theater at the newly forming Bauhaus in Weimar in the early 1920s would build upon many of these multiple perspectives of the preceding decade. A collection of features previously resident in Greek and Oriental drama, Parisian and Dada revue, *lubok* and *image d'Épinal,* Russian lamenting practices and preliterate theater, African tribal ritual, *commedia dell'arte,* and a sequence of productions that incorporated aspects of each in a rapidly evolving "ballet" tradition that strained the meaning of the word were now to be further tested in a world totally enamored with all aspects of the *mécanique*. Hindemith, Antheil, and Varèse, frequently encouraged by Stravinsky's example, were to surface as the composers centrally atuned to the challenges of such a distillation; but Oskar Schlemmer and Fernand Léger were to prove crucial allies in providing a background conducive to the formation of their ideas.

— 12 —

Masks and Machines

In our large cities, the population is godless, materialized—no bond, no fellow-feeling, no enthusiasm . . . There is faith in chemistry, in meat, and wine, in wealth, in machinery, in the steam engine, galvanic battery, turbine wheels, sewing machines, and in public opinion, but not in divine causes.

Ralph Waldo Emerson

If today's artists love the machine, technology, and organization, if they aspire to precision and reject anything vague and dreamy, this implies an instinctive repudiation of chaos and a longing to find the form appropriate to our times.

Oskar Schlemmer, 1926

Hindemith, Schlemmer, and the Bauhaus

Composed in 1920 and premiered in Stuttgart in 1921, Hindemith's *Das Nusch-Nuschi* was conceived for a specifically Burmese brand of marionette theater; and between 1919 and 1922 Manuel de Falla composed a puppet opera, *El retablo de maese Pedro,* which premiered in Paris in 1923. In a series of engagements involving a variety of distancing techniques, Poulenc, Milhaud, Stravinsky, Hindemith, Weill, and others helped not so much to promote myths about the primitive or the Orient, or to promote the cause of the anti-naturalistic theater per se, as to suggest alternating layers of consciousness in the modern psyche and to clarify the dilemma inherent in the daily rites of human existence. For a world recently numbed by war, the appeal of the mask and the puppet, not as escape mechanisms but as spiritual probes, was no doubt centered in their appeal as perennial authorities with a capacity for mutation.

Milhaud recorded his love for the puppet theater in an article entitled "Marionettes" that summed up the fascination of an age. Noting its force in the work of Falla, Stravinsky, and Claudel, he reminisced about evenings with the puppets in Lyons and Naples and especially at the Piccoli in Rome. Stating that for him this was the ideal theater, where the puppets were capable of a precision equal to live actors and yet more readily capable of taking on diverse representations, he concluded: "Everything that is unreal and impossible in the theatre becomes easy and possible in this little temple of unbridled and exorbitant fantasy."[1]

Puppet theater addressed issues of concern to composers in other ways as well, especially with respect to an ongoing consideration of correspondences between color and sound. Building upon the Symbolist interest in synesthesia from the second half of the nineteenth century, a few innovators in the theater had begun to contemplate replacing actors not with marionettes, as Craig and Meyerhold had proposed, but with bodies and colors accompanied by sound. Kandinsky's *The Yellow Sound* (1907), Schoenberg's *Die glückliche Hand* (1911–1913), and Kazimir Malevich's *Victory over the Sun* (1913) are classic, if not necessarily totally successful, illustrations from the first years of the century. The effect of the lighting and of the disembodied faces of a chorus peering through openings in a scrim in *Die glückliche Hand* can be inferred from a reading of Schoenberg's libretto as well as from a series of watercolors by the composer. And Benedikt Livshits has described how the use of a console-controlled lighting system in *Victory over the Sun* "cut up the bodies of the actors into geometric sections . . . presumably because of the absorption of similar colors by the colored spotlights." The geometrical shapes of the costumes themselves, however, obviously also promoted the ease with which the figures, "broken up by the blades of light," alternately lost arms, legs, and heads in a fashion that was soon to be emulated by the Bauhaus theater.[2] Finally, a 1917 Futurist production of *Fireworks* in Rome eliminated the human body altogether in a ballet of lights playing on abstract geometrical forms by Giacomo Balla to the accompaniment of Stravinsky's music (Figure 12.1).

In some ways the most abstract endeavor in the direction of what has been called the "painters' theater" was Oskar Schlemmer's *Das Triadische Ballett (The Triadic Ballet)*, envisioned as early as 1912.[3] When Schlemmer's association with the Stuttgart Landestheater and the Wei-

FUTUR BALLA 1915

Figure 12.1. Giacomo Balla, set for *Fireworks,* a Futurist play of lights, with music by Stravinsky, 1917.

mar Bauhaus began to offer the possibility of mounting his project, he solicited the cooperation of the young Paul Hindemith, who arrived in Stuttgart at the beginning of July 1920 and announced that he was prepared to write the music for the entire production. After hearing Schlemmer's ideas Hindemith set to work immediately and in a few days' time announced that he had completed the music for three of the dances. Schlemmer traveled to Frankfurt to hear it and his verdict was direct: "a quicksilver young fellow, works like a demon . . . the right man, although not the perfect one; too bad I don't have his ability—I know what would be just right. For that we might wait forever."[4]

Owing to lack of time to finalize details and Schlemmer's ongoing responsibilities at the Bauhaus in Weimar from December 1920 on, the *Triadic Ballet* was performed in the Small Theater of the Stuttgart Landestheater on September 30, 1922, to music by Handel, Boccherini, Mozart, Bossi, and Debussy instead of by Hindemith; the original plans were not to come to fruition until 1926. In the meantime the Schlemmer-Hindemith collaboration found another outlet in a double-bill of two one-act operas by the young composer: *Mörder, Hoffnung der Frauen* (*Murderer, Hope of Women*) to a text of Kokoschka and *Das Nusch-Nuschi* (*The Thingamagig*) to a libretto by Franz Blei. It was Schlemmer's first stage production, and he not only designed the scenery and costumes but also collaborated on the choreography of both dancers and singers.

Hindemith had completed *Mörder* in the summer of 1919, *Das Nusch-Nuschi* on August 14, 1920, and *Sancta Susanna,* the third of a planned triptych, on February 5, 1921. The premiere performance of the first two, in which Schlemmer participated, took place in Stuttgart on June 4, 1921, and created a sensation.[5] Troubled equally by text, music, and production, the press reviewed the issues which had surfaced in the 1907 premiere of Kokoschka's play, and deemed Blei's text not only absurd, but tasteless and obscene.

Hindemith had chosen his three texts with the intention of addressing sexuality from three different angles: in *Murderer, Hope of Women,* the classic battle of man and woman as filtered through the psychological perspectives of Otto Weininger's *Geschlecht und Charakter (Sex and Character);* in *Das Nusch-Nuschi,* a parodistic burlesque involving the castration of an emperor in a Burmese marionette play; and in *Sancta Susanna,* institutional repression in which a nun is entombed alive. All three subscribed to the non-realistic atmosphere of Expressionistic theater. But beyond the original impetus of Kokoschka's mythic probe and Blei's oriental puppet show, other issues played a role in Hindemith's first approach to the stage. Wrestling with the possibility of using war as a theme and the "complete abandonment of reality as an artistic reference point,"[6] two of Hindemith's friends, the sculptor Benno Elkan and a Frankfurt theater critic, recommended both Japanese and Indian puppet plays as models. This proved to be prescient in light of the Burmese marionette tradition that ultimately accompanied Hindemith's second choice, Blei's *Das Nusch-Nuschi.*

That Schlemmer intended a contrast between the heroic–pathetic style of *Murderer* and the grotesque color fantasy of *Nusch-Nuschi* he made clear in a letter to Otto Meyer of May 16, 1921: "My theatrical projects: two operatic one-acters, one in grand theatrical style, the other 'for Burmese marionettes,' with an idiotic text—comical, erotic, Indian. One of them (the Kokoschka) can be done in dull or earth tones, the other very bright."[7] Hindemith's musical response to *Das Nusch-Nuschi,* projected through the largest orchestra Hindemith had used to that time, pursued the updating of an inherited Oriental code in the second scene with an atmospheric use of harp, celesta, mandolin, and English horn against a backdrop of strings in a manner which, aided by the presence of a pair of shrieking monkeys, has reminded some of Mahler's *Das Lied von der Erde.*[8] Other more incontrovertible allusions are to Wagner's *Tristan und Isolde* at the moment of castration of the emperor by the field marshal: "This to me, Kyce Waing, this to me! Where loyalty, now betrayed, where now honor and true kind . . ." and to Strauss's *Till Eulenspiegel's Merry Pranks* following the response of one of the dancers to a poet's marriage proposal: "When the banana branch sprouts and the dove lays eggs in the water; when the eel climbs the tree to make his nest, then perhaps . . . (all laugh)." Other parodistic intentions lie behind Hindemith's inclusion of a chorale fugue presented as an obligatory offering to the new tide of Neoclassicism. Hindemith's note in the score is unexpectedly protracted and polemical:

> The following "chorale fugue" (with all the comforts: augmentation, diminution, stretti, and basso ostinato) owes its existence to an unfortunate accident: it happened to occur to the composer. It has no other purpose than this: to fit into the stylistic framework of this scene and to give all the "experts" the opportunity to complain loudly about the monstrous tastelessness of its creator. Hallelujah! The piece really ought to be danced (waddled) by two eunuchs with enormous naked bellies.[9]

Not only the conjunction of multiple authorities but the uncertain intention behind them served the young Hindemith well in confusing his audience and making an unmistakable bid for membership in the world of the musical avant-garde. The encoding of Expressionism as heroic-classicism in *Murderer* and as grotesque Oriental puppetry in *Nusch-Nuschi* presented a dialectic between a pair of works that was ultimately confronted in Schlemmer's *Triadic Ballet.* Too, in light of Alban Berg's recently premiered opera, *Wozzeck* (December 1925), Schlemmer could hardly have failed to note that Georg Büchner's *Woyzeck,* upon which the opera was based, portrayed character types more than individuals and advanced the proposition, within the context of a fractured plot that risked incoherence, that all people are essentially madmen or puppets. Schlemmer further depersonalized his "actors" through an emphasis upon the mechanistic and upon geometric figure and color, and his final devotion to a single concept, Man in Space, was worked out through costume design and scenery, but always with an awareness of the architecture of the stage and of bodies in motion.[10]

Xanti Schawinsky, stage designer, writer, dancer, and assistant to Schlemmer, later recalled his Bauhaus days and spoke of its rich musical heritage dependant upon diverse folk repertoires, homemade compositions, improvisation and jazz, as well as "chairs, gunshots, hand bells and giant tuning forks, sirens and pianos prepared by means of nails, wires," and other kinds of tone-modifying materials. Such an assortment clearly suggests an awareness of the current productions of Henry Cowell and George Antheil. But Walter Gropius, director of the Bauhaus, predictably concluded, "My own great impression of Schlemmer's stage work was to see and experience his magic of transforming dancers and actors into moving architecture."[11]

The Triadic Ballet was in some ways merely an ultra-modern *commedia dell'arte,* and Schlemmer was explicit about the relationship:

> Costume and mask emphasize the body's identity or they change it; they express its nature or they are purposely misleading about it . . . The native costume, as produced by the conventions of religion, state, and society, is different from the theatrical stage costume. Yet the two are generally confused. Great as has been the variety of native costumes developed during the course of human history, the number of genuine stage costumes has stayed very small. They are the few standardized costumes of the *commedia dell'arte:* Harlequin, Pierrot, Columbine, etc.; and they have remained basic and authentic to this day.[12]

Schlemmer was not alone in sensing the force of the *commedia* for modern times. During the summer of 1922, for example, Sergei Eisenstein, the young film maker, joined Sergei Yutkevich in writing a Constructivist satire, *Columbine's Garter,* intended for the use of Nikolai Foregger, one of the most innovative Soviet directors of the day. Pierrot was cast as a Bostonian capitalist, Columbine as an erotic dancer and daughter of Russian émigrés (costumed as an Automat restaurant and a flush toilet), and an American hotel jazz band played in the background.[13]

Schlemmer's approach was more analytic and more abstract; he elucidated the genesis of his costumes in a series of diagrams and clarified their relationship to issues of space and movement in a set of sketch analyses (Figures 12.2, 12.3). The appeal of Schlemmer's explorations for musicians in a decade that had unveiled Stravinsky's *Pulcinella* (1919–20), Nikolai Foregger's *Good Treatment for Horses* (1922)—a highly eccentric dance theater/agitprop production that combined three hundred cartoon-like gestures with poses taken from a manual on American jazz published in Berlin[14]—and Antheil's *Ballet mécanique* (1923–1925) within a few years of each other is apparent.

Having staged his *Triadic Ballet* on numerous occasions in previous seasons, Schlemmer initially entertained the notion that for his 1926 version he might divide the music into three parts, each written by a different composer—Stuckenschmidt, Toch, and Hindemith.[15] Later, having decided on a single score by Hindemith, he was extremely candid in a letter to his wife about the cachet he believed the young com-

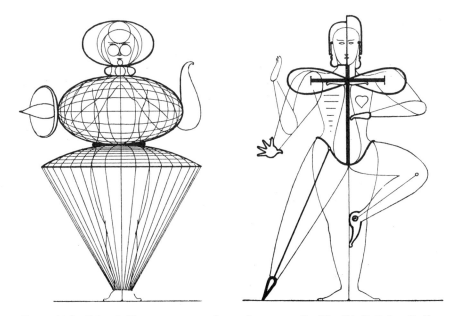

Figure 12.2. Oskar Schlemmer, two analyses of costumes for *The Triadic Ballet:* (Left) *The Laws of Motion of the Human Body in Space.* Here we have the various aspects of rotation, direction, and intersection of space: the spinning top, snail, spiral, disk. Result: a *technical organism.* (Right) *The Metaphysical Forms of Expression,* symbolizing various members of the human body: the star shape of the spread hand, the [infinity] sign of the folded arms, the cross shape of the backbone and shoulders; the double head, multiple limbs, division and suppression of forms. Result: *dematerialization.*

© 1994 The Oskar Schlemmer Theatre Estate, Collection UJS, Badenweiler, Germany.

Figure 12.3. Oskar Schlemmer, *Figurines in Space,* study for *The Triadic Ballet,* ca. 1924.

poser would bring to the production. "Since a noted composer, Paul Hindemith, has taken over the musical side and is writing mechanical music for it—that is to say, music for a player piano—through his name and one-tenth through mine and a few tenths through that of a famous woman dancer we hope to engage, the desired triumphal progress of the ballet is practically assured."[16]

Hindemith had worked intimately with Schlemmer in 1921 and was thoroughly familiar with Bauhaus theatrical philosophies by 1926 when he returned to *The Triadic Ballet* project, which he now outfitted with a score prepared directly on punched paper rolls for mechanical organ.[17] Though sketches for a score version are preserved, it is understandable that Hindemith's music was never published.[18] Schlemmer made an entry in his diary for July 5, 1926, in which he addressed four "whys" concerning the production: why ballet, why triadic, why Hindemith, why a player piano? The first question he answered as follows:

> Because the heyday of ballet may be long since past, and the old courtly ballet is certainly dead, but today's entirely changed circumstances give good cause to believe that this particular art form can be revived. Now we have eurythmics, the chorus of movement developed out of them, and a new cult of strength and beauty; one is thus justified in reviving their opposites: the brightly colored masquerades once so popular with the people; theatrical costume dance; and also ballet, to be born in a new form. For human beings will always love bright games, disguises, masquerades, dissimulation, artificiality, as they will always love any festive, eye-catching, colorful reflection of life. This speechless theatrical dance, this non-committal Muse who says nothing yet means everything, contains possibilities for expression and articulation which an opera or a play could not offer in such purity.[19]

Schlemmer answered the second question by observing that the triadic idea contained numerous symbolic messages: transcendence of the egoistic one and the dualistic two in a collective three; and the threesomes of form, color, space / height, depth, breadth / ball, cube, pyramid / red, blue, yellow / dance, costume, music. In Hindemith he sensed a composer who, beyond his capacity to wed the mechanistic with popular dances and Neoclassic counterpoint, claimed a mastery of the spiritual dimension ranging from the "cheerful grotesque to full pathos." Finally, he favored the idea of the player piano or organ because their "music provides a parallel to the costumes, which follow the mathemat-

ical and mechanical outlines of the body. In addition, the doll-like quality of the dances corresponds to the music-box quality of the music
and this should furnish the unity implied by the concept of 'style.' "[20]

Schlemmer's career was associated primarily with the Bauhaus in
Weimar and then at Dessau, and though the school had originally been
devoted to the arts, crafts, and architecture, it gradually expanded its
base to include the theater. A variety of music programs were presented
during his tenure there, including performances of Schoenberg's *Pierrot
lunaire* in 1922.[21] And prior to Schlemmer's collaboration with Hindemith on *The Triadic Ballet,* a *Mechanical Ballet* by Kurt Schmidt with
music by H. H. Stuckenschmidt had been performed in August 1923
as part of a program entitled *Mechanischen Kabaretts.*[22] Stuckenschmidt
has spoken of the genuine interest in the new music among members
of the Bauhaus, and how he talked to them about Satie, Cocteau, Milhaud, Poulenc, Auric, Stravinsky, and especially Antheil. "Everyone
had already heard of 12-tone music," he said, "and I had to explain
what I thought about it." Stuckenschmidt also vividly recalled prepara-
tions for the *Mechanische Ballett* with Kurt Schmidt:

> After the first collective dinner, I went with Kurt Schmidt to his atelier
> . . . Then [at rehearsal] these strange geometric figures danced . . . In
> the corner stood an old piano. It had no voice and rattled monstrously.
> I improvised a few chords and rhythms, and with this the cardboard
> figures began to respond. An abstract dance of Square, Circle, and
> Triangle was extemporaneously invented. After perhaps a quarter of
> an hour Kurt Schmidt rose somewhat breathlessly but contentedly
> from his perch. I had instinctively guessed and realized what he had
> imagined: a primitive accompanimental music, that reflected some-
> what the basic geometric forms. The harmony was made up only of
> triads, the melody of folksong, and the rhythm of dance and march
> elements. I treated the piano in the manner of George Antheil, with
> fortissimo-explosions and glissandos.[23]

Stuckenschmidt also made contact with virtually all the Bauhaus Masters, including Moholy-Nagy, Paul Klee, and Lyonel Feininger. Feininger apparently would have nothing whatsoever to do with modern
music, though he was keenly partial to the Baroque composers, whom
he invoked in his own academic composition. Paul Klee, however,
was openly smitten with Schoenberg's *Pierrot lunaire,* and, according to
Stuckenschmidt, Moholy-Nagy "was interested only in the most modern music. Above all the possibility fascinated him of reproducing music

mechanically, about which Walter Benjamin had earlier set down his ideas. Moholy-Nagy saw in the phonograph record the music of the future. But he protested against the notion that it should be used only as a means of reproducing a performance rather than as a means of investigating new orders of sound."[24]

The architectural historian Sigfried Giedion, who attended performances at the Bauhaus at that time, reported on the importance of theater and music there, including performances of Stravinsky's *Histoire du soldat* conducted by Hermann Scherchen and another production of Schlemmer's *Triadic Ballet* at Jena.[25] A few years later Scherchen's graphic rendering of Beethoven's "Great Fugue" stimulated Schlemmer to envision a ballet based upon the conductor's reductive notation. Although the music was originally conceived as imagined only in the dancers' heads, Schlemmer reported that Scherchen finally concluded "that the whole thing should be done not with human dancers, but with mechanical shapes . . . More important than the forms themselves is their color; he conceives of a construct of form and color in space, mechanically propelled, which would act out the fugue."[26]

Of the complex of ingredients that had recently accrued to the theater and contributed to its metamorphosis, Schlemmer spoke affirmatively and with expectation. Noting the human transformation from naked to costumed man, to puppet and marionette, and now to the larger-than-life fantasy figure clearly indebted to Craig's Über-marionette; aware of the promise of the poets who were looking for new sculptural and architectural formats of expression beyond the printed page; and recalling Busoni's dreams for organizing ether waves and mechanically produced sound in unheard-of intensities, Schlemmer was clearly dazzled at the future's potential.[27] Indeed, Schlemmer's confrontation with the world of music did not stop with Hindemith, Scherchen, Busoni, and Beethoven. Only a month after his excitement over the Beethoven fugue project, he wrote to Otto Meyer on September 15, 1927: "the work I am doing with the conductor has advanced to the point that we are adapting a piece by Igor Stravinsky, *Les Noces,* with the idea of illustrating what happens in music by means of continuous color projections; we hope this will produce a more intense effect and avoid the complications of pantomime performed by human actors."[28] Stravinsky may never have learned of their project, but he knew of the work of both men, had visited the Bauhaus along with Busoni in August 1923, and was personally acquainted with the conductor. Furthermore, his own immediately preceding concerns for theatrical solutions as well as his willing experimentation in the theater of the Futurists in the *Fireworks* production of 1917 and his own recent confrontation with the problems attendant to *Oedipus Rex* (unstaged premiere May 30, 1927) is sufficient to suggest that the Bauhaus experiments could only have intrigued him. But Stravinsky's general sense of alienation from their efforts, as well as a specific antipathy to Hindemith's music which he heard there, are made explicit in a letter to Ansermet of September 1, 1923. He speaks of hearing interminable and boring *Lieder* of Hindemith, relays Scherchen's claim that this young German composed too much, and professes admiration only for some new piano pieces of Busoni.[29]

In the event Schlemmer not only completed some *Noces* sketches[30] but managed to bring one Stravinsky work to completion, a production of *Le Chant du rossignol* performed at the Stadttheater Breslau on December 11, 1929, where the abstractions of the Bauhaus theater absorbed the exotic colors of the Orient in a fusion with *De Stijl* objectives (Figure 12.4).

Regardless of Stravinsky's ambivalence about the Bauhaus, his personal involvement with the machine aesthetic was anything but casual. And both the authority of Stravinsky's *Le Sacre* via *Les Noces* as well as their combined and continuing relevance to the issue at hand is made clear in Richard Hammond's 1929 review of *Les Noces,* which speaks of Prokofiev's *Pas d'acier* as "almost a *Sacre Mécanique.*"[31] Clearly, the mask's capacity not only to recall the various received traditions but also to accomplish the depersonalization of the human figure in pursuit of universals—all of this in the company of the newest developments of the theater, the poet, and the musician—is a factor that stretches from *Petrushka* and *Parade* to *Pulcinella* and *The Triadic Ballet.* From the *faux pathétique* puppet world of the first of these to the implied facade of all entertainment in the second, we come to the pasteboard figures of *Pulcinella* and the outright mechanism of *The Triadic Ballet,* wherein each figure is given a plastic formalization, eliminating human emotion, refusing joy or terror, and reclaiming the costume mask as a reality.

The musical languages of Stravinsky, Satie, and Hindemith in each of these provide different but direct counterparts to the theatrical message. Stravinsky's techniques in *Petrushka* differ from Satie's only in detail; both employ vernacular and pseudo-vernacular sources projected by overlap and intercut, and both embrace a nostalgia without tears. *Pulcinella*'s modish Neoclassic game also involves a deception: a score which on the surface sounds more like the music of the eighteenth century

Figure 12.4. Oskar Schlemmer, set for "The Emperor of China's Bedroom, The Death," Act III, *Die Nachtigall* (*Le Chant du Rossignol*), 1929, music by Igor Stravinsky, 1914. It was performed at the Stadttheater, Breslau, on December 11, 1929.

© 1994 The Oskar Schlemmer Theatre Estate, Collection UJS, Badenweiler, Germany. Photo Archive C. Raman Schlemmer, Oggebbio, Italy.

than the twentieth but which depends on the projection of Pergolesi to the forefront as the legitimate author in order that the composer of *Le Sacre* can play from behind a scrim. And in his work for mechanical organ Hindemith disguised the human element through the elimination of the live performing musician as a counterpart to Schlemmer's use of geometric figure and color. Behind the sound, however, is a human paper puncher, beneath the mask there is a man. And the union of the two creates a new type.[32]

De Stijl and the Mécanique

Theo van Doesburg (1885–1931), painter, theoretician, and friend of Mondrian, founded and financed the Dutch journal of aesthetics and art theory, *De Stijl,* from 1917 to 1928. In it he sought to offer a forum for discussion among all creative artists of the avant-garde, whom he felt should be self-consciously aware of their artistic beliefs. The aesthetic promoted by *De Stijl* that came to be known as Neoplasticism was characterized by the rejection of representation and the reduction of expression in painting to the straight line, the right angle, and the three primary colors together with the non-colors black, white, and gray. This ascetic rigidity developed in a general way from the experience of the First World War, and Van Doesburg and his followers felt that societal problems were largely a reflection of unbridled individualism, the cure for which was to be found in collectivization and depersonalization. The abstraction and precision of machine technology was prized above craftsmanship, and it was their hope to eliminate subjective expression from art altogether. Van Doesburg's *Rhythmus eines russischen Tanzes* (1918) and the seven attendant studies are a remarkable demonstration of his philosophy and method, which are not unakin to Gleizes's Cubist demonstrations a few years later (Figure 12.5). From such premises Mondrian deduced ethical principles promoting the suppression of subjective individualism and the discovery of a universal harmony which could in turn signal the direction for a future utopian life.

The objectives of *De Stijl* were widely shared beyond the Netherlands, and Mondrian's ultimate removal to New York in 1940 at the beginning of a second world war sealed his international reputation and brought alliances with both Constructivism and Frank Lloyd Wright in the emergence of a modern style of architecture. In the world of music, two figures in particular shared the group's objectives, and left a virile documentation of their sympathies: Edgard Varèse and George Antheil.

Varèse studied with Albert Roussel and Charles-Marie Widor in Paris between 1904 and 1907 and then in Berlin with Busoni. By 1913 he had returned to Paris, leaving behind all of his music, which was destroyed by fire, and in 1915 he left for New York, where he quickly became engaged with the newly formed International Composers' Guild. Though Varèse never explored the mechanical theater in the manner of the Schlemmer-Hindemith collaboration, his admiration for Busoni sealed a connection with Bauhaus objectives, and his infatuation with mechanized urban life ratified a natural alliance with the world of Mondrian and Léger. Both directed his search for new sound sources and ultimately led him to fundamental electronic explorations in tandem with architecture in the company of Le Corbusier and Iannis Xenakis in the 1950s.[33]

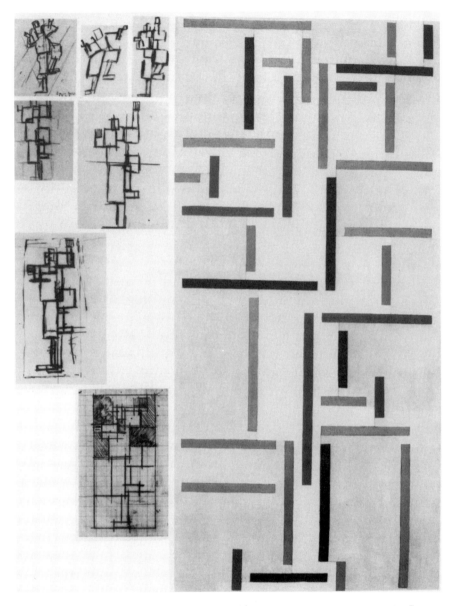

Figure 12.5. Theo van Doesburg: (left) seven studies for *Rhythmus eines russischen Tanzes*, 1917–18; (right) *Rhythmus eines russischen Tanzes*, 1918.

The title of Varèse's first published score, *Hyperprism,* already announced an architectural-sculptural affinity, and the premiere performance in New York on March 4, 1923, followed by additional ones on November 7, 9, and December 16, 1924, secured the impression of a new musical force. Even the American composer Charles Martin Loeffler, who inclined toward a kind of mellow Impressionism, expressed amazement more than discomfort:

> It would be the negation of all the centuries of musical progress, if I were to call this music. Nevertheless, I seemed to be dreaming of rites in Egyptian temples, of mystic and terrible ceremonies which history does not record. This piece roused in me a sort of subconscious racial memory, something elemental that happened before the beginning of recorded time. It affected me as only music of the past has affected me.[34]

Such perceptions of a connecting thread between Modernist Primitivism and a new Urban Utopia were to surface repeatedly. But in its refusal of thematicism and its emphasis upon a plasticity of expression born of fluctuating tempi, a coagulation of revolving sound masses, and a new role for percussion, winds, and an imaginary electronic world, Varèse's slender output surpassed all attendant theologies and was ultimately seen to constitute one of the noblest achievements of twentieth-century music.

Although Varèse's music is too rich and variegated to encapsulate summarily, numerous attitudes persisted throughout his career. He was one of the earliest regular guests of the Abbaye du Créteil, where he was befriended by Gleizes, Mercereau, Picabia, and Duchamp.[35] Later associations with Apollinaire, Cendrars, Max Jacob, Joseph Stella, Le Corbusier and others confirmed his claim that "during the greater part of my existence my friends have tended to be painters, poets, architects, and scientists, rather than musicians."[36]

Already intrigued by the potential of a dawning machine age, by 1916 Varèse had called for "new ears for new music," and by 1917 he was contributing to the Dada periodical *391,* wherein he advocated the expansion of musical vocabularies beyond the rudimentary explorations of the Futurist *intonarumori.*[37] He believed that the machine offered the composer a new hope for the future, and he became enthusiastically involved, like Duchamp, with questions of science, mathematics, and especially the fourth dimension.[38] It was a direction that had already

been prophesied by T. E. Hulme, who believed that an alliance between Cubism and the machine offered greater possibilities than one
with Kandinsky's imaginative abstractions.[39]

Varèse defined the three dimensions of music as horizontal, vertical,
and dynamic swelling or decreasing; to that he added a fourth, that of
sound being projected like a beam of light with no hope of being reflected back. Asked in 1953 to describe his *Intégrales* of 1924–25, he
simply encouraged listeners "to visualize the changing projection of a
geometrical figure on a plane, with both plane and figure moving in
space, but each with its own arbitrary and varying speeds of translation
and rotation."[40] Prefiguring Stravinsky's recapture of a similar perspective a few years later, Varèse pointedly accorded the language of Gleizes
and the Cubists an updated endorsement.

In many ways Varèse was as much a pacemaker as a producer. The
long, arid stretches and brief catalogue of compositions betray the lot
of the visionary. But if this is so, an important group of composers were
privileged to know him and ultimately to share his achievements as well
as his frustrations. In the 1920s his natural alliance with the world of
George Antheil and Fernand Léger was as much spiritual as practical. In
the combinative aesthetic of George Antheil as expressed in the 1920s,
however, we spot a new ingredient joined to the Parisian note that
spells recognition of a vital new force. Antheil believed that the Banal
and the Mechanistic offered the basis for a new music of the immediate
future, and he judged that ragtime embraced both properties.[41]

In 1922, Antheil published a "Manifest der Musico-Mechanico" in
Van Doesburg's *De Stijl* that echoed Varèse's sentiments of the late
teens. He predicted that

> not far in the future there will be no more orchestras, only orchestral
> machines with a thousand new sounds, and a thousand new sonorities,
> in contrast to the simple ones now produced by present-day fiddles,
> brass, and woodwind instruments. These machines will, of course,
> have nothing in common with the foolish Futurist machines of the
> Italian Futurists which had no mathematical dimensions or pretentions
> to space, but were only and sheerly improvisations of noise intended
> to imitate automobiles, airplanes, etc., which is ridiculous, and has
> nothing to do with music.[42]

Recalling Stravinsky's infatuation with the player piano, Antheil's primary interest centered on the possibility of establishing control over
every nuance of the music, including the inaccuracies of performance.

Years later Antheil amplified his view of *Ballet mécanique* beyond the initial assertion that it had been the first music composed for machines and the first to incorporate the fourth dimension. In a perceptive analysis included in a letter to Nicolas Slonimsky, Antheil addressed the importance of time, as opposed to tonality, in the ballet, and drew a protracted parallel between his method and Picasso's approach to painting:

> In the *Ballet Mécanique* I used time as Picasso might have used the blank spaces of his canvas. I did not hesitate, for instance, to repeat one measure one hundred times; I did not hesitate to have absolutely nothing on my pianola rolls for sixty-two bars; I did not hesitate to ring a bell against a certain given section of time or indeed to do whatever I pleased to do with this time canvas as long as each part of it stood up against the other. My ideas were the most abstract of the abstract. Still I was totally misunderstood.[43]

But if Antheil called on Picasso for a time-space analogy and in so doing sympathetically embraced Léger's and the cinema's celebration of the object through a willingness to isolate the musical moment, it was surely Stravinsky's *Les Noces* which served him with a ready-made sonic model. Antheil recorded that it was not by chance that he arrived in Paris precisely on June 13, 1923, a date that coincided with the premiere of Stravinsky's *Les Noces*, to which Antheil had received Stravinsky's personal invitation. The new work was performed on a double-bill with *Pulcinella*, by Antheil's own admission his first exposure to Neoclassicism. The next day he met Stravinsky at the piano warehouse rooms at Pleyel, where he played the rolls of *Les Noces* on an electric pianola (Figure 12.6). Comparing that rendition with the live performance, Antheil claimed: "I like the second version even better than the one which we had heard last night; it was more precise, colder, harder, more typical of that which I myself wanted out of music during this period of my life. 'It is wonderful!' I cried."[44]

Stravinsky's first introduction to the player piano had come in 1914 when he visited the Aeolian Hall in London, at which time his *Four Études*, op. 7, were transferred to pianola rolls. Two years later his orchestral *Fireworks* and the "Chinese March" from *The Nightingale* were similarly transferred and performed in public. Then following a trip to Madrid in the same year, 1916, Stravinsky wrote his *Étude for Pianola*, which he incorrectly claimed in a letter to Ansermet of June 6, 1919, to be "*the first in the world!*"[45] Difficulties with synchronization of the pianola in live performance ultimately led Stravinsky to abandon its use

Figure 12.6. Stravinsky at work with the Pleyela, Paris, 1923.
Photo, Vera Sudeikina.

in the second version of *Les Noces* of 1919. Rex Lawson, who prepared the player roll for its world premiere in 1981, has identified the problem: "Synchronization of a Pianola with other instruments is quite demanding but not impossible, although the difficulty is all the greater when the tempo is strict. Sheltering the odd late note under the wing of a slight rubato is only too easy, but not in *Les Noces!*"[46] The degree to which instrumental mechanization in *Les Noces* still intrigued Stravinsky as late as 1921 can be seen in a letter of November 22 to Ansermet: "As for Racz, the cimbalomist, I would like to hire him full-time and pay him by the month. He would be a kind of secretary, assisting me in the copying and in all sorts of things in my musical work. He will also play the cimbalom in *Noces* if we do not succeed in mechanizing the instrument, which we are now trying to do."[47]

Stravinsky's involvement with mechanical piano players from the late teens throughout the 1920s was clearly the catalytic force that drew Antheil to them in his *Ballet mécanique*. Although it has been noted that Antheil's First Violin Sonata moved toward an even more percussive style than the Berlin piano sonatas in direct emulation of *Les Noces,* the composer claimed that "a strange twirling music" which he heard on a hasty trip to Tunisia in July 1923 made an indelible impression upon him and left its imprint on the final version of the work.[48] Antheil also later alleged that with the sonata he had finally rid himself of the sound of *Les Noces*. This was not to be the case, however; for *Ballet mécanique,* the score most stylistically derivative from Stravinsky's wedding cantata-ballet, lay just ahead and was to occupy most of his energies during the remainder of 1923 and 1924.

Other encounters had contributed to Antheil's approach as well. Antheil had met Hans Stuckenschmidt at the Donaueschingen Festival in July 1922. By late spring 1923 in Berlin, Stuckenschmidt and Antheil were frequently in each other's company, and Stuckenschmidt wrote in *Der Kunstblatt* that "Antheil's piano sonatas make all the rest of our contemporary music writing in Germany seem unimportant."[49] While the report may be somewhat exaggerated, in later years Antheil was happy to cite Stuckenschmidt's approval of his music.

> Stuck almost wept over the "Death of the Machines" sonata, which was his favorite. Afterward he wrote: "Music must be abstract, yet be the legitimate language of all of those parts of human thought and feeling which exhaust words. Music is the language of beyond the beyond, so to speak. One must now, as does Antheil, use all kinds of new methods in order to trap these new-old emotions into musical sounds."[50]

At the Dresden Opera in the early months of 1923 Antheil also saw the Schlemmer-Hindemith production of *Murderer, Hope of Women,* which made an enormous impression on him, and he came to feel that Hindemith's music was the only German music of the period worth listening to. Antheil even claimed that because of this experience he decided to give up all ambitions of a career as a concert pianist and to concentrate on composing.[51]

Antheil's announcement immediately following his sonata recital at the Théâtre des Champs-Élysées on October 4, 1923, that he was looking for a film and not a dance troupe to go with his upcoming ballet ultimately brought a collaboration between the composer and Dudley Murphy, who agreed to the venture only under the condition that he could obtain the cooperation of Fernand Léger. Léger's film was shown for the first time in October 1924 in Vienna as part of an exhibition of new theater techniques, but Antheil's score was not heard, even privately in Paris, until the summer of 1925.

Léger's recognition of the power of the cinema to detach and enlarge the object or to fragment had been stimulated by his friend Blaise Cendrars, whose manifesto "ABC du Cinéma" appeared in 1921,[52] by Abel Gance's film *La Roue,* which he saw being shot during 1920–21, by the film criticism of Jean Epstein and René Clair, and by his own collaboration on Marcel L'Herbier's *L'Inhumaine* (1923).[53] The latter movie incorporated not only extravagant Futurist sets by Léger and Alberto Cavalcanti but also editing procedures involving precipitously shifting shots of a car's engine and wheels that clearly forecast Léger's contribution to *Ballet mécanique.*[54] Though the temporal issues which film introduced with respect to splicing techniques and rhythmic sequencing may have had little effect on Léger's easel painting, something of the realism of the film frame as well as the capacity of the close-up to isolate and explode did find its way into numerous works. In retrospect it is clear that Antheil's working method, which he claimed to have extracted from Picasso, also directly mirrored Léger's approach to the making of the film. Léger put the matter thus:

> Ballet Mécanique dates from the period when architects talked about the machine civilization. There was a *new realism* in that period that I myself used in my pictures and in this film . . . [I] was doing painting in which the active elements were *objects* freed from all atmosphere, put in new relationships to each other . . . Contrasting objects, slow and rapid passages, rest and intensity—the whole film was constructed on that.[55]

Léger's enthusiasm for the close-up led him to discover the object, the fragment, even fragments of the human body as subjects in their own right. A collar stud or a fingernail magnified a thousand times, which he compared to "a nascent planet," a syphon whose enveloping hand is cropped by the picture frame—all heralded the intrinsic interest of the object apart from meaning. The traceability of Léger's painting of a syphon to a Campari advertisement which was appearing in the French magazines during 1924 (Figures 12.7, 12.8) has led Robert Rosenblum to make "comparisons with Lichtenstein and Warhol's adaptation of commercial illustrations within the domain of high art." But he has also rightly stressed the commonplaceness of such emblematic "machine-made facts that defined the urban world" in early twentieth-century Cubist still lifes.[56]

Comparisons between Stravinsky and Antheil were automatic and numerous from the first public performance, which took place at the

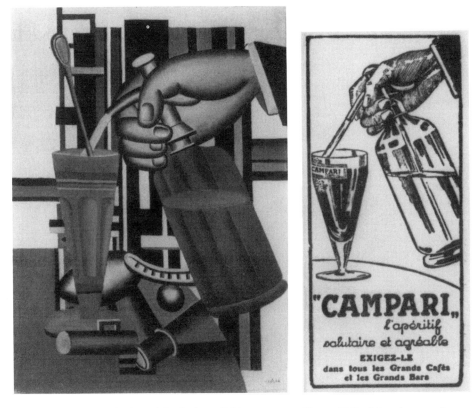

Figure 12.7. Fernand Léger, *The Syphon,* 1924.

Albright-Knox Art Gallery, Buffalo, New York. Gift of Mr. and Mrs. Gordon Bunshaft, 1977. © 1994 ARS, New York / SPADEM, Paris.

Figure 12.8. Advertisement for Campari from *Le Matin,* September 12, 1924, p. 3.

Théâtre des Champs-Élysées with Vladimir Golschmann conducting on June 19, 1926. The sixteen pianolas of the original version, run from an electronically controlled single roll together with various percussion including airplane propellers and electric bells, had been reduced to one pianola, two pianos, and percussion. A performance with eight pianos and a variety of percussion followed on July 16 at a concert arranged by Antheil and Virgil Thomson at the home of Mrs. Christian Gross, wife of an American diplomat. Although Antheil's original is filled with repetitions and silences theoretically included in order to promote the music's role as a cinematic accompaniment, the first version of the score was, by Antheil's own admission, almost twice as long as the film.

From the beginning Léger abdicated any responsibility for effecting a simultaneous alliance, which he left to Antheil. Quickly, however, the music and the film disclosed an incompatability with respect to both internal synchronization and overall length, and the two ultimately took on independent lives. In 1952–53 Antheil made a final revision for four pianos, two xylophones, airplane propeller sounds, and a sizable battery, at which time Antheil commented, "Repetitious measures, intending to synchronize only with the film, have been cut abundantly, reducing the playing time from the original of more than a half hour to less than eighteen minutes."[57] Ironically such pruning adjusted the playing time of the music in relation to the running time of the film only marginally, and all questions of synchronization remained unaddressed.

In live performance Antheil's *Ballet mécanique* brought visual quotations redolent of Léger's mechanical world with a recognizable airplane propeller on a tall stand in lieu of Strauss's wind machine and a brightly painted fire siren in anticipation of Varèse. Noting that the subject had already been destroyed in painting, Léger claimed that the avant-garde cinema had now destroyed the script.[58] Antheil, not to be outdone, claimed that he was the first person on earth to compose a music "*out of* and *for* machines"; that it had nothing to do with tonality; that it contained "absolutely no 'forte' or 'piano' moments" and was "*merely played loud enough to be heard*"; and that he had now reduced music to the "principal stuff of music—*time-space*" permitting future construction of "larger and almost endless forms."[59]

Such investigations confirmed numerous attitudes developing in the 1920s under the banner of *Die Neue Sachlichkeit,* a German designation for "the new objectivity," which carried connotations of detachment, decried both Impressionist vagaries and Expressionist angst, and meshed naturally with the rising tide of Neoclassicism.[60] At the same time it reflected the French infatuation with the art of the everyday, the French love of the circus and cabaret, and embraced evolving technologies as symbolic theatrical cohorts. Such technologies appeared from the mid-twenties on, both in the theater of Piscator and on the stages of *Zeitop-ern*. If such an emphasis upon the present seemed to renounce the past as subject matter, there was a paradoxical alliance with the Expressionist painters, whose earlier Primitivism now clearly began to mesh with the propulsive, raw energies of urban life.[61]

In light of the fact that the rising popularity of film increasingly threatened the financial solvency of the legitimate stage, opera, and ballet during the Weimar Republic, it was perhaps inevitable that concessions to bourgeois taste should have been made through appeals to a new machine age epitomized by the Bauhaus, which Walter Gropius opened in Weimar in 1919. The Bauhaus itself helped sponsor the Kabarett format, which we have seen moved beyond pure entertainment to the showcasing of current issues of the day with Kurt Schmidt's *Mechanische Ballett* to music by Stuckenschmidt. But the playwright Ivan Goll had used slides and film clips in his *Die Unsterblichen* as early as 1920, the same year which saw his collaboration with Léger. And although Erwin Piscator is typically cited as one of the pioneers in the use of slide projections and cinema on the legitimate stage, his first use of film came with *Trotz Alledem* in 1925, a "Historical Revue of the Years 1914–1919 in Twenty-four Scenes with Interspersed Films." The year before, the French had also been busy exploring the power of the film in a production for Rolf de Maré's Ballets Suédois, *Relâche*. Here Satie's music-hall ensemble for the cinematic Entr'acte crossed the line from banality to boredom by mechanically projecting a series of four- or eight-measure ostinati totally lacking in continuity, and arbitrarily recalling musical materials without narrative consequence. The momentary hint of a waltz tune and an appropriate allusion to Chopin's "Funeral March" were not intended to save the day through an appeal to narrative relevance but rather to emphasize the absurdity of realist theater.

Later in the twenties a number of works followed in quick succession reflecting these new attitudes and techniques. Weill's opera *Royal Palace* (1927) with a libretto by Goll used a film sequence, and Hindemith's *Hin und Zurück,* a brief domestic opera with a libretto by a leader of the *Kabarettrevue,* Marcellus Schiffer, employed music and action that moved forward to midpoint followed by a retrograde presentation of both elements in a fashion that clearly mirrored film's capacity for reversal. Later Antheil's opera *Transatlantic* (1930) projected captions and a film clip playing in the middle of a four-tiered set redolent of Milhaud's solution for *L'Homme et son désir* and forecast the incorporation of film in Berg's *Lulu,* an opera already well under way. Film's compatability with the richest aspirations of the *simultanéistes,* the collagists, and a new social order had been demonstrated and secured.[62]

From the time of D. W. Griffith's simultaneous tetralogy in *Intolerance* and the montage techniques of Eisenstein which juxtaposed and fused objects and actions to produce a new and separate meaning, the potential of the cinema was irresistible. Eisenstein's demonstration in the Odessa steps sequence of *Potemkin* (1925) of the power of film to prolong real time through splicing and repetition may have served to heighten a highly charged moment within a narrative sequence. But Lèger's *Ballet mécanique,* shown for the first time in October 1924 and ceremoniously announced as the first film without script, had already probed the possibilities of similar techniques in the service of a range of observations well outside narrative structure of any kind. Here the woman's recurrent and mechanical climbing of an identical flight of stairs, for example, borrows on the cinema's power not only for temporal stalling but for allegorical allusion, in this instance to the relevance of the Myth of Sisyphus for modern times. Antheil's repetitious and non-narrative chunks, which pursue a life of their own independent of but psychologically attuned to the film, similarly subscribe to the filmlike montage techniques which have been claimed for Joyce's *Ulysses.*[63] Such comparisons do not appear idle in light of the fact that at the very time Antheil was at work on *Ballet mécanique* he projected, and actually began, a setting of the "Cyclops" episode from *Ulysses.* It was never completed, but in 1925 a three-page fragment was published of the work, which Antheil predicted would be "the *Sacre du Printemps* of the future which all composers to follow will have a hard time scrambling over."[64]

Behind the technical aspects of film making and the new emphasis placed upon the object in its own right stood a variegated social program which ranged from Cendrars's belief in the cinema's power to effect mass social revolution to the utopian, if elitist, social programs of Ricciotto Canudo and Élie Faure, which aspired to the creation of a "new humanity." For all of Léger's anchor in the aesthetic of Purism and his continuing hopes for the theater's capacity to transform life, he was suspicious of the impresario mentality. In film he saw an opportunity to pursue his populist ideals, and in *Ballet mécanique* he not only countered the bourgeois desire for narrative cinema but attempted to encourage the recognition of beauty beyond the frame and the gallery. "The beautiful is everywhere; perhaps more in the arrangement of your saucepans on the white walls of your kitchen than in your eighteenth century living room or your official museum," he stated.[65] The primary forms of geometry were to replace the old forms, and the artist was to search for the discovery of the universal laws of proportion that underlay them. This unmediated emphasis upon pure form and primary shape stood at the heart of the new humanity and bonded naturally to the Purist's celebration of the technological transformation of existence. At the same time, Léger differed from the early precursors of film by abdicating any role as social reformer even as he pondered the function of a new medium that in some ways was capable of being viewed as a new, mass folk expression.

The inherent paradox of this dichotomy was forwarded in the introduction to *Ballet mécanique*. A painted mechanico-cubist wooden model of an abstract marionette in direct imitation of Charlie Chaplin had been completed by Léger in 1920 for use as an illustration in Iwan Goll's *Die Chaplinade,* and Léger opened his new film with a sequence, "Charlot Cubiste," based upon it that had originally been fashioned in 1921 as part of a project that was never completed (Figure 12.9).[66] Just as George Grosz, Lux Feininger, and Paul Klee all executed self-portraits in the likeness of Charlie Chaplin, so the "Little Tramp" was seen as a decoder of the absurd and the visionary and as such the encapsulation of the contemporary dilemma in all its manifestations: the hero of a cultural revolution but also the engineer/machine man who was his technological counterpart.[67] Richard Brender has suggested that "*Ballet mécanique* held up an optimistic mirror to mass culture, channeling back to the masses all the energy they generated. Only by showing them what they had accomplished could Léger turn them into agents of their destiny responsible for creating a new society. Seen in these terms, *Ballet mécanique* takes on the poignancy of a relic of a civilization that never was, or the blueprint for one that would never be."[68]

On the musical side, too, while Antheil's *Ballet mécanique* created a *scandale* both in Paris and especially later on in New York, rather than launching a career it was to remain the work by which the composer

Figure 12.9. Left: "Charlot Cubiste," opening film sequence for *Ballet mécanique,* 1924. Right: Fernand Léger's wooden model (1920–1923) after his own illustration for Iwan Goll's *Die Chaplinade,* 1920.

would be most prominently remembered. At the same time, the musical diction of *Ballet mécanique* was too close to that of *Les Noces* to permit sustained adoption in a new venue. Nonetheless, Antheil's association with both *De Stijl* and Stuckenschmidt, and by extension the Bauhaus and Léger, aided in casting the work at the time as an emblematic host for many of the aesthetic aspirations of an era.

Indeed, in classifying his work as a ballet and jettisoning live dancer and mask of whatever design for a film, Antheil had confirmed the most radical assertions of an age—including Stravinsky's admonition forwarded to Cendrars and Ansermet as early as 1919 that music ought not "express" the film, as some critics advocated, and his wonderment that preoccupation with such goals kept them from understanding "the charm of music played parallel to a film."[69] In the end, Antheil abandoned the film, and the ballet, shorn of any visual component whatsoever, was reduced to a sonic industrial mimesis of an imaginary film scene. If the score was later capable of being interpreted as a mirror of the internal combustion of contemporary urban life or as akin to the fateful clockwork energies of the Oedipus story as told by Cocteau in his contemporaneous *The Infernal Machine,* its ultimate reputation was largely devoid of social inference. Rather it congealed into a historic artifact, a footnote to the art of noises originally promoted by the Futurists, and was only somewhat nostalgically recalled as an attendant accessory to an avant-garde film confected in the service of defining the societal aspirations of modern man.

Early in the next decade Martha Graham reacted strongly to what she felt was the European sentimentalization of the machine in the theater and in dance, and by 1934 she voiced her concerns explicitly: "The dance today does not express a machine. How can a man be a machine or imitate a machine? There has been a change of tempo brought about by the machine. We can only express this tempo."[70] Like Antheil's, Graham's search for a new expression was not totally devoid of a social conscience. But in trying to ferret out an American expression independent of European models, she undoubtedly felt the need to sidestep their veneration of American urban life through jazz and the *mécanique.* It was only natural, therefore, that she turn to frontier life as the preferred locus in search of a genuine American diction. Even here, however, Graham retained the force of the mask in the visage of many of the principal characters which she created;[71] relied upon nonlinear concepts of time as well as gestures familiar to her from No drama and other Asian theater arts; and chose an American sculptor of Japanese ancestry, Isamu Noguchi, to provide a stark sense of space through the summary use of a rope, a simple fence, or sheet-metal abstractions. Graham undoubtedly understood that Antheil's *Ballet mécanique* had not so much helped to sound the death knell of ballet per se as to force recognition of a new realm of possibilities in the alliance of sound and motion. She also acknowledged Léger's emphasis upon pure form and primary shape as central to the discovery of a new humanity not only in her choice of Noguchi but in her own developing vocabularies of modern dance as well.

From Adorno to Ligeti

The more overt manifestations of a mechanical age that had prospered on the European stage in the 1920s were to have profound and direct consequences for the remainder of the century. Adorno, active throughout the period and in contact with many of the central cast of characters, continued to argue both the aesthetic values and the philosophical underpinnings of film and recording, the twin discoveries of technological reproduction that were to impact persistently on the world of music in the decades to come. Showing awareness of the strides made by Alfred Stieglitz and others since photography's infancy, and of John Philip Sousa's warnings at the turn of the century regarding the dangers inherent in proliferating phonographs and player pianos,[72] Adorno's initial opinions reflected his interest in questions of popular culture and technology and were recorded in *Musikblätter des Anbruch* from 1925—presumably through the offices of his teacher Alban Berg, who was one of the first editors of the journal. Encouraging an expanded focus of its scope to include both "light music" and kitsch, Adorno dubbed the latter reactionary, anything but modern, yet not dismissible and even necessary as a battle topic, *pro* and *contra,* in the interest of a reading of all mass cultures. In tandem with such topics he called for a consideration of the role of technology in the dissemination of music, both light and serious, and proposed reactivation of a column devoted to the discussion of "Mechanische Musik" originally introduced by H. H. Stuckenschmidt in *Musikblätter.*

Adorno was concerned with the transformations of the original, formulating event that occur as the result of mechanical mediation, and with the recognition of the destruction of its original aura which brings a paradoxical liberation of music from the confines of notation. But unlike the views of Walter Benjamin, who in 1936 also bemoaned the loss of uniqueness in the plurality of all mechanical reproductions,[73] Adorno's underlying philosophy of recording is involuted and consistently given to having it both ways out of an interest in its indexical status: "music deprived of its best dimension" is oddly "not significantly altered by it." And though he initially denied the possibility of a gramophone-specific music, like Moholy-Nagy he presciently foresaw and called for the transformation of the gramophone from a reproductive to a productive technology. *Musique concrète, Elektronische Musik,* "Scratch," "mix," sample, and soundbite were just around the corner.[74]

In some mysterious way Adorno, not unlike Varèse, held out the possibility that through the gramophone record nature's Ur-alphabet might be discovered; that rather than re-creating a previous acoustic event a music might be inscribed without ever having sounded: a primordial language requiring no code, where hieroglyphs do not carry meaning but are the meaning currently lost through man's alienation from nature.[75] The idea may be traceable to the German Romantics but it is surely in harmony with the incantations of the Dadaists as well.

Adorno's recognition of the power of recording and radio led him to glorify the authority of citation in a program entitled "Beautiful Moments"—a montage of musical excerpts with running commentary broadcast on July 15, 1965, that ran almost two hours and was constructed from fifty-two musical examples from thirty-seven different compositions by fourteen composers.[76] In Adorno's call upon the new technologies to confect a selection of best takes, to rely upon the element of chance inherent in live performance, to expose the falseness of so-called inspiration, and to allow the observer to contemplate and even complete potential interrelationships, he charted a provisionary list of possibilities that had already been envisioned in some dimension by the collagists and the Simultaneists as well as by D. W. Griffith, Antheil, Varèse, Léger, Moholy-Nagy, and others. The Age of the Machine and the Mask had not so much disappeared as it had been metamorphosed into a complex scenario that remained to be played out.

Numerous connecting links in the guise of turntables, wire and tape recorders, and then proliferating electronic studies and their subsequent histories became increasingly audible in studios developed in Europe, America, and Japan from the late 1940s through the 1950s. Following rudimentary explorations, both discrete and in juxtaposition with live performers, it became gradually apparent that the list of combinations and venues was virtually limitless. Though charges periodically surfaced that electronic music would ultimately prove to be analogous to finger-painting on the one hand or the natural receptacle of intricate structures incapable of being heard on the other, belief in the riches that were to surface in some future maturity virtually never faltered.

By the 1980s and 1990s, electronic ventures were widespread, varied in nature, and frequently redolent of an earlier age's infatuation with collage. In *Cat O'Nine Tails* (1988), for example, John Zorn (b. 1953) utilized fifty-one distinct musical "moments" drawn from five broad categories "that include directed improvisation and collages of other composers' string-quartet writing," and steered his performers to reflect the sado-masochism inherent in the classic cartoons of the 1940s and 1950s. More controlled were the energetic series of pieces by Michael Daugherty (b. 1954) carrying Pop titles like *Snap* (1987), *Bounce* (1988), *Firecracker* (1988), *Strut* (1989), and *Superman Suite* (1988–1993) that made imaginative use of synthesizers and samplers and mirrored his interest in film, including the silent classics. Demonstrating that audience appeal could come in different guises, Daughtery's freshness seemed to cast both Roy Lichtenstein, to whom he has been compared, and the Minimalist movement as decaying relics. With *Beat Boxer* (1991), written for the Kronos Quartet and performance tape, Daugherty composed a work that was virtually emblematic of the new and simultaneous alliance of popular culture, concert music, and the new technologies. Daugherty put it this way:

> Beat Boxer takes its title from the vocal technique used by rappers to imitate the drum machine rhythms used in rap. I recorded the two voices "beat boxing" to words I had written down. Using computer technology, I composed the tape part by reconfiguring and editing the phrases. I wanted to create an active interplay between Kronos and the rappers so that rap and concert music might energize each other.

Extracting echoes from rap's rhyming lines set to an insistent beat, the words *pizzicato* and *sul ponticello* are parlayed into a word game that ironically invokes the names of Beethoven, Mozart, Tchaikovsky, and Stokowski against the perseverating musical presence of the "Dies irae." Once again manipulation of a series of icons drawn from the Western canon virtually guaranteed multiple critical reactions.[77] For just as Lichtenstein delighted in finding patterns in the soles of a pair of Keds sport shoes that clearly mimed the geometric abstractions of a Victor Vasarely and left open all questions of interpretation,[78] so Daugherty insists that in his invocation of avant-garde string techniques alongside modern technology and Pop titles he bids the listener to find his own meanings and that he intends no sermon. Predictably, however, invitations to intertextual reading could not neutralize potential charges of exploitation by the dominant culture.[79]

Once again the earlier visions of Ellington, Gershwin, Copland, Graham, and Noguchi as to what might constitute a bona fide American expression had been updated and transcended. And Adorno, regardless of his abstruseness or proclivity for contradiction, now appeared to have presaged the relevance of the Machine Age as it was spelled in the twenties for an Age of Aquarius yet to come. He had also identified a complex of issues concerning communication, mass culture, and evolving technologies that resounds more clearly every day.

One can point not only to Pierre Boulez's specific invocation of the 1920s Bauhaus as both technical and interdisciplinary model for a new center that was baptized IRCAM (Institute de Recherche et de Coordination Acoustique/Musique) at the Centre Pompidou in Paris in 1977,[80] but on more practical terrain to the advent of the Yamaha Disklavier in the 1990s. Combining a mechanical acoustical piano with sophisticated digital electronic controls, this player piano for modern times can re-create the performance of others or one's own with an unsuspected fidelity to sonority, articulation, and pedaling.[81]

In another quarter the continuing legacy of an earlier machine age for present times has received vivid confirmation from György Ligeti in his piano *Études* written between 1985 and 1993. Claiming both the Renaissance proportional layering techniques of Johannes Ockeghem and the twentieth-century player piano polyrhythms of Conlon Nancarrow as prototypes, Ligeti further dramatized the relevance of the machine aesthetic in the early 1990s by synthesizing a performance of the ninth of these *Études*, "Vertige," as a demonstration of its inhumanly fast but ideal speed, currently obtainable only on an electronic sequencer. No fanciful heir to Robert Schumann's marking *So rasch wie möglich* followed by *Noch schneller,* the result was held up as but momentarily utopian—a model that Ligeti predicted would be attainable in live performance in a decade's time. Hindemith and Nancarrow, the paperpunchers, had been superseded by a computer tutor to a future generation of performing artists.

— 13 —

Oedipus and *Agon*: "Husks of Style?"

My instinct is to recompose, and not only students' works, but
old masters' as well. When composers show me their music for
criticism all I can say is that I would have written it quite differently. Whatever interests me, whatever I love, I wish to make
my own.

Igor Stravinsky

So the danger lies not in the borrowing of clichés. The danger
lies in fabricating them.

Igor Stravinsky

Wherever mystery prevails, explanations are typically sought, and the
attempt to identify the Russian base of Stravinsky's music is a perfect
example of the perennial search for secret principles. At a more specific
level, however, the periodic compulsion to demonstrate such a base for
Stravinsky has been prompted by the anxiety attendant to a series of
radical stylistic turnovers and the need to establish a point of reference
in the face of what appeared to some to be a discontinuous development. The composer's admission of only a single folktune in *Le Sacre
du printemps* (1911–1913) long seemed improbable to many in light of
the recently and contemporaneously composed *Firebird* (1909–10) and
Petrushka (1910–11). Yet it was not so much Stravinsky's silence about
such matters as his denial of further reliance upon such materials that
proved perplexing.

Stravinsky's reticence may, however, be related to a dilemma that
Rimsky-Korsakov had addressed in his autobiography, *My Musical Life*,
posthumously published in 1909. Here he recalled at length the music

critics who, "having noticed, both in *The Snow Maiden* and *May Night,*
two or three melodies borrowed from collections of folksongs (to notice
many they were powerless, as they were ill-acquainted with folk creation), proclaimed me incapable of creating my own melodies."[1] His
dismay obviously stemmed from the fact that his strategy for addressing
the anxiety of influence through recourse to the twin prongs of tradition
and adoptive transformation had gone unrecognized.

In later years, Stravinsky's retrospective need to claim a special role
for *Le Sacre* at the birth of musical Modernism was natural enough, and
he may well have thought, like his teacher, Rimsky-Korsakov, that to
acknowledge extensive derivation of his materials might place undue
emphasis upon the source rather than the transformation. Or, to put it
another way, it was understandable that he would have wanted to encourage recognition of the details of his Russianness independent of
borrowed materials. Nonetheless, since Stravinsky's death the compulsion to clarify his Russian character has brought numerous significant
finds and has lead to the realization that it was not restricted to the so-
called Russian period. Additional melodies and motifs have been traced
to the nineteenth-century folktune collections;[2] the "coalescence of
high emotional intensity and . . . personal detachment" in *Les Noces*
has been traced to peasant village wedding rituals;[3] the sonority of his
Latin *Mass* has been linked to the harmonies of Georgian male-voice
choirs rather than to Machaut; and the supremacy of parallel major sevenths, seeming heterophony, and empty melodic spaces completed in
hocket-like fashion have been attributed to a celebration of folkish out-
of-tuneness, a failed unison, and to street marchers catching a breath
in the middle of a phrase.[4]

Assuming that many of these techniques and sources were ultimately
absorbed into a personal language and their presence maintained
throughout his career, how, then, does the perspective change with
Stravinsky's first overt appropriation of non-Russian musical material
in the ballet *Pulcinella?* The idea was purportedly prompted by the suggestion of Diaghilev—a Russian, too—that they should enlist the music of Pergolesi, and the turn has been attributed to their collective
disaffection for a revolution at home. Later Stravinsky confessed that
Pulcinella marked the beginning of a long love affair with the past but
claimed that it was a look in the mirror, too. For all the later critical
claims of a momentous stylistic turn, however, the mirror needed to
reflect no further back than *Petrushka.* Whatever the complex of ingre-

dients that now encouraged him to look to the Italian origins of the *commedia dell'arte,* it was, indeed, a turn that melded nicely with Russian traditions on the one hand and the French inclination toward Neoclassicism nourished from the 1880s on the other.[5] It is a factor that in his late years Stravinsky also related to his youth in St. Petersburg: "I have often considered that the fact of my birth and upbringing in a Neo-Italian—rather than in a purely Slavic, or Oriental—city must be partly, and profoundly, responsible for the cultural direction of my later life."[6]

Following the purloining of Pergolesi and pseudo-Pergolesi for *Pulcinella,* Stravinsky persisted in summoning up the eighteenth century and especially in promoting the notion of Bach and Mozart as ideal models in a series of works that continued to take note of contemporaneous developments. By the early 1930s Arthur Lourié, musician friend, confidant, and some would say quasi-spiritual mentor of Stravinsky's in the 1920s, was in a position to make a judgment of the new alignment. Ultimately, he may have been more interested in forwarding his own procrustean Neo-Thomism than in trying to explain the composer's new orientation, but he nonethless clearly invoked and contrasted an earlier Primitivism with an emerging Neoclassicism in the following remarkable assessment: "Stravinsky, after playing the role of the bellicose king of the underbrush, of the steppes and the jungle, of the nonconformist . . . restores [the canon] of Johann Sebastian and utilizes it as a polemic against modernism."[7]

A polemic against Modernism or a revivification of same via a new alliance that now embraced Apollo instead of Dionysus?[8] The chronology of Stravinsky's various acts of embrace have been responsibly and richly recounted and analogies drawn with Picasso's Neoclassic turn at about the same time. The issue that has received the most careful examination, however, has been the appeal of two composers, Mozart and Beethoven, whose German nationality alone might well have robbed them of potential model status for a Parisian composer in the years immediately following World War I. Although Egon Wellesz had comfortably taken note of the prevailing "return to Mozart" as early as 1911, the French view of the matter had to be more carefully stated. Debussy, just before the war in 1913, and Ravel, not long after the armistice in 1920, both observed that while for all his genius Beethoven was capable of lapses of taste, Mozart was the embodiment of elegance and refinement—qualities which allied him with French national artistic goals and somehow allowed him to escape his German origins.[9]

Clearly, despite Bach's and Mozart's Germanness, both composers could claim a decidedly Italianate streak widely recognized as an important ingredient of their greatness—for which the *Concerto in the Italian Style* and *Le Nozze di Figaro* may stand as familiar examples.

French anti-German sentiments, which played long and loudly throughout the decade of the 1920s, could hardly have eluded the notice of Stravinsky who, for all his familiarity with German musical culture and his command of its language, increasingly felt the pressure to ally himself with Gallic proclivities in such matters. It is of no little interest, however, that some critics saw other forces at work in *Mavra,* an opera dedicated to Glinka, Pushkin, and Tchaikovsky. Ansermet, speaking "On Russian Music" in *Melos* (July 1922), designated *Mavra* as "the beginning of a new period, one in which music is divested of everything that has cramped it," but Boris de Schloezer in an article entitled "Les Ballets Russes" written in the same month wrote:

> In *Mavra* Stravinsky did not succeed, and the general impression is that of a pastiche, of a sort of musical joke that is not sufficiently amusing. Stravinsky's idea is probably involved with the question of renovating his forms, of creating a new comic-opera style. In this case, the subject is too thin, too fragile, and the Italo-Russian and black-American styles do not mix.[10]

Although Stravinsky openly identified the Neo-Italian strain as a prevailing voice throughout his career, the critic's designation of a black-American component in *Mavra* says a great deal more about the period than the music. Indeed, the opinion clearly prefigures the notion played out in the remaining years of the decade that the most rudimentary syncopations were capable of being automatically heard in light of the new forces of jazz.

Regardless of the critical view of the role of popular American sources in the formulation of this new aesthetic equation, however, Stravinsky's opinion regarding his allegiance to Mozart is poignantly projected in a letter of August 15, 1922: "Here I am at the head of modern music, so it is said, and as I willingly believe. Here I am, forty years old, and ignored in the grand prizes of the 'Great International Congress' of Salzburg—the capital of Mozart, who is for me what Raphael was for Ingres and is for Picasso."[11] Varying exterior perceptions aside, in the composite Franco-Slav view Mozart was in, Wagner was permanently out, and Beethoven, when invoked, was tapped only in the briefest Neoclassic guise, as in the appropriation of his piano sonata op. 54 for the last movement of Stravinsky's piano sonata of 1925.[12]

Though Stravinsky's music continued to exhibit affinities for the eighteenth century and, surprisingly to many, to the nineteenth century as well, there was another less prominent but equally resilient ally of the Neoclassic movement. It was Greece, and its initial appeal in the twenties was remarkable, in art and literature as well as music. Because the shadow of *Oedipus Rex* (1927) and *Apollo* (1928) was ultimately to fall again on *Orpheus* (1945) and finally on *Agon* (1953–1957), recognition of the Greek revival invites scrutiny with respect not only to the generating sponsorship but to the reasons for its continuing appeal.

Oedipus

Interest in Greek drama hardly faltered from the time of the Renaissance to the twentieth century, despite periods of intense revival and refurbishing. After 1900, the Neoclassic movement brought periodic endorsements of the Greek in ways that have already been discussed in connection with the dance and the theater—the work of Craig, Benois, Bakst, Duncan, Dalcroze, and Nijinsky, for example. But beyond the world of frieze and movement, Hellenic subject matter prompted numerous composers to a reconsideration of their art. Despite the fact that little Greek music had survived, and then in a largely undecipherable notation, a preserved body of Greek music theory did offer the possibility of a touchstone for the contemporary composer much as it had in the Renaissance. Even where a specific link beckoned, however, as with Greek tetrachordal structure, it is doubtful that Stravinsky was ever emboldened to consider its affinity with venerable folk practices invoked from the beginning of his career.

In the period immediately prior to Stravinsky's first two Greek pieces, the opera-oratorio *Oedipus Rex* of 1927 and the ballet *Apollo* of 1928, Milhaud had provided a trilogy of works to texts of Paul Claudel: music for *Agamemnon* (1913–14), *Les Choëphores* (1915), and *Les Eumén-ides* (1917–1922). Claudel was not alone in his fascination with Aeschylus, and the immediate tradition for translation was strong both in France and in England.

But the appeal of Sophocles' *Oedipus* was even richer, and in the period immediately surrounding Stravinsky's approach to the text its pervasive favor ultimately achieves the status of a broadly constituted fashion. Musical interest in the classic tale had persisted from Andrea Gabrieli's music to Giustiniani's text at the Teatro Olimpico in 1585[13] and Henry Purcell's for a text of Dryden and Lee of 1692 to Mendelssohn's *Oedipus in Kolonus,* published in 1852, John Knowles Paine's *Oedipus Tyrannus,* published in Boston in 1895, and the Swiss composer Frank Martin's incidental music to *Oedipus Rex* in 1923. Fascination among literary figures had been equally strong from the time of Seneca's tragedies,[14] which included a reworking of the *Oedipus* story, to the age of Voltaire.[15]

Yeats had begun to search in 1904 for an *Oedipus* to produce at the Abbey Theatre, initially soliciting the well-known translator Gilbert Murray, who refused on the grounds that

> it is a play with nothing Irish about it: no religion, not one beautiful action, hardly a stroke of poetry. Even the good things that have to be done in order to make the plot work are done through mere loss of temper. The spiritual tragedy is never faced or understood: all the stress is laid on the mere external uncleanness . . . Sophocles . . . was in a trance and his body was possessed by a series of devils—Sardou, the Lord Mayor of London, Aristotle, the Judicious Hooker, and all the Editors of the Spectator from its inception to the present day.[16]

Times change; tastes change. But it is clear from the record that one reason Yeats was originally attracted to *Oedipus,* as Murray's remarks obliquely intimate, was the English censorship in the theater that prohibited its performance because it dealt with the theme of incest. Even more poignantly, on an American lecture tour in 1903–4 Yeats learned while in South Bend, Indiana, that *Oedipus* had been produced at Notre Dame University, an institution with a proud Irish Catholic tradition, and he felt that a performance of this work in Ireland could stand as the symbol of a new freedom in the Irish theater. Murray's transcultural objections had been dissolved.

Plans for using translations by Sir Richard Jebb and Robert Whitelaw continued throught the 1909 season and included communication with Edward Gordon Craig, with whom Yeats had been familiar since 1901, regarding use of Craig's methods and stage screens for the production. English censorship of *Oedipus* was removed in 1910, and Gilbert Murray finally composed his own translation in 1911. First produced in 1912, it coincided with Yeats's first attempt to make a translation of his own. For whatever reason, after an auspicious beginning Yeats's project was soon dropped and was resurrected only in 1926, when he returned to the writing of the choruses and revision of the dialogue.

The first performance of Yeats's *Oedipus the King* took place on December 7, 1926, at the Abbey Theatre, Dublin. Buoyed by the success of the first productions, Yeats contemplated extending his project to include versions of the other two of Sophocles' Theban plays, *Oedipus at Colonus* and *Antigone*. Only the first of these was ultimately realized, but Yeats's accelerating familiarity with Sophocles forced him to revisions and improvements of *Oedipus the King* following work on *Oedipus at Colonus*. Yeats's completed version was published in 1928 together with monophonic music for the choruses composed by the producer, Lennox Robinson. Noting that the main function of the chorus was not so much to project the text clearly as to "relax the tension" of the drama, Yeats concluded that in light of the fact that "the chorus could not move, I told Mr. Lennox Robinson, producer & musician, that his music & liturgical singers had to do the dancers' work as well as their own."[17] Robinson's music, it should be noted, is modally rich and anything but formulaic, and it was included along with the initial publication of the play in 1928.[18]

Although the prominence which Yeats accorded the role of music in his discussion of the productions is understandable, the absence of any record that incidental music written for *Oedipus* by George Antheil ever joined hands with Yeats's text is surprising in light of the following details: it is recorded that an Antheil score accompanied a production of *Oedipus Rex* in 1928 while he was Assistant Music Director of the Berlin State Theater; Antheil had known Yeats from 1924 on; in 1929 Antheil wrote a detective story, *Death in the Dark,* bearing the *nom de plume* Stacey Bishop, in which he was assisted by T. S. Eliot, Yeats, Ezra Pound, Franz Werfel, and Gerhart Hauptmann; and in the summer of 1929 Antheil collaborated with Yeats on his play *Fighting the Waves* by providing background music.[19] The conclusion is virtually inescapable that Antheil's music for *Oedipus,* now lost, was in some measure prompted by his association with Yeats and by the desire to directly challenge Stravinsky, whose aesthetic he was struggling to leave behind.[20]

In light of the long period of gestation for Yeats's *Oedipus,* the closeness of its premiere on December 7, 1926, to that of Stravinsky's and Cocteau's opera-oratorio on May 30, 1927, is striking. Given Yeats's periodic presence on the Parisian scene in the immediately preceding years and his familiarity with the Diaghilev ballet and the literary circle there, it is hard to imagine that as Cocteau undertook his translation of *Antigone* he could have been unaware of Yeats's involvement with Sophocles. Finally, the keen impression that Nikolai Gnedich's Russian translations of Sophocles had made upon Stravinsky in his teens notwithstanding, it was Cocteau's translation of *Antigone*—for which Honegger (1921) and later Carlos Chávez (1933) prepared incidental music and which served as the libretto for Honegger's opera (1924–1927)[21]— that ultimately piqued Stravinsky's interest in turning to the Frenchman for the first time since the aborted *David* project more than a decade earlier.[22]

Thus, fascination with Greek theater texts on the part of both literary figures and musicians set the stage for Stravinsky's approach to *Oedipus Rex* in 1927. But if the source of Stravinsky's text meshed favorably with the current and pervasive fashion of Neoclassicism at the time and seemingly signaled the setting aside of Russian subject matter, his musical manners pointed more toward inclusion than exclusion, toward an expanded rather than an alternative base of operations. For in *Oedipus* Stravinsky retained use of Primitivist ostinati and vocal patterns derived from both folk and liturgical practice, coupled Greek subject matter to a Latin text, joined chorus and mask to musico-dramatic stasis, continued to toy with matters of prosody, wedded cinema fanfares with allusions to Handel and Verdi, and in the process forged a musical language that the composer must have viewed less as pastiche than as an approximation of T. S. Eliot's belief that the poet can possess the great tradition only through great labor, that it cannot be inherited, and that it can be obtained only through a developed historical sense that "compels a man to write not merely with his own generation in his bones, but with a feeling that the whole of the literature of Europe from Homer and within it the whole of the literature of his own country has a simultaneous existence and composes a simultaneous order."[23]

Reactions to Stravinsky's *Oedipus* were mixed, though frequently predictable. We know that even before the premiere Prokofiev was taking note of the assemblage of ingredients in a letter to Miaskovsky of May 26, 1927: "Stravinsky has been delivered of *Oedipus Rex,* a scenically static opera–oratorio in 2 acts . . . The librettist is a Frenchman, the text is Latin, the subject is Greek, the music is Anglo-German (after Handel), it will be produced by a Monegasquan enterprise and on American money—the height of internationalism."[24] Poulenc wrote to Stravinsky shortly after the premiere in a far more approving, indeed highly laudatory, voice,[25] and Ravel declared that with *Oedipus* Stravinsky had demonstrated that "while he plays with old forms, he is actually finding something new."[26] Schoenberg, however, dismissed the orchestra of *Oedipus* as sounding "like a Stravinsky-imitation by Krenek . . . I still believe this work is nothing—even though I really liked *Petrushka.* Parts of it very much indeed."[27] And as late as 1973 in the Charles Eliot Norton lectures, Leonard Bernstein continued to express amazement at the invocation of Verdi:

> Why Verdi of all people, who was so unfashionable at the time *Oedipus* was written, someone for the musical intellectuals of the mid-twenties to sneer at; and *Aida,* of all things, that cheap, low, sentimental melodrama, the splashiest and flashiest of all the Verdi operas— why? . . . Was Stravinsky having a secret romance with Verdi's music in those supersophisticated mid-twenties? It seems he was.[28]

The ghost of Verdi? Well beyond the role of Jocasta and Bernstein's reasonable if debatable proposal that *Oedipus'* pivotal diminished seventh-chord and four-note motif stem directly from *Aida,* Stravinsky's affection for Verdi has been confirmed by numerous evidences ranging from the presence of a portrait of Verdi hanging on the wall in a well-known photograph of Stravinsky taken at his player piano in the Salle Pleyel in the 1920s to the clandestine references to Verdi's *Requiem* in Stravinsky's *opus ultimum,* the *Requiem Canticles* of 1966. Further nods to Verdi can be argued throughout the *Oedipus* score, including recall of the bumptious "Zitti, zitti" male chorus at the moment of Gilda's abduction in *Rigoletto* (one of Stravinsky's favorites) in the construction of a "mortuary *tarantella*" for "Mulier in vestibulo." Stravinsky answered charges of inappropriate gaiety anchored in regular rhythms potentially applicable to both choruses by claiming that they created a tension "greater than any tension that irregular, upset rhythms could produce."[29]

However, while in Berlin in 1931, the composer, somewhat exasperated with the critics' "I spy" mentality, encouraged caution with respect to the issue: "What shall I do? One part of the press says that I should continue to shock. Another part says that I am now making the right music since I have started to compose like Verdi. They are actually unable to hear that I am doing something different altogether."[30] But in Bologna in 1935 all defenses are down: "Verdi! Verdi! The great mighty Verdi. How many beautiful things there are in his early works as well as in the final ones. I admire him unconditionally, a truly great composer! I prefer Verdi to all other music of the nineteenth century!"[31]

Verdi may not have been the only composer on Stravinsky's mind when he composed *Oedipus,* however. For in addition to Bernstein's roster of derivations from Rameau/Gluck, Mozart, Beethoven, Handel, Musorgsky, and Russian and Greek dance, the spectre of another less likely nineteenth-century personality makes an appearance at one of the crucial moments of the drama. In the Shepherd and Messenger's scene wherein the fateful news of the King's incestuous, murderous relationship to Jocasta is announced, a persistent rhythmic figure in the accompaniment and a triplet vocal figure on *kekidi* corresponds directly to the opening pages of Mendelssohn's *Oedipus in Kolonus* (Examples 13.1, 13.2). The reference is so protracted—well beyond the excerpts included here—that only our current unfamiliarity with the score can account for its not having been previously noted. But why Mendelssohn? Stravinsky's acknowledgment that the scherzo of his Symphony in E-flat (1906), written while he was a pupil of Rimsky-Korsakov, was overtly derived from Mendelssohn via Tchaikovsky is sufficient to establish an early knowledge of and natural affinity for the composer. Dredged up twenty years later, however, the reference comes as a surprise. Yet, although the figure appears in the opening pages of Mendelssohn's score where Stravinsky's likelihood of noticing it would have been greatest, Stravinsky's own addiction to precisely this figure in numerous contexts from *Fireworks* to *Pulcinella* ("Serenata"), the Violin Concerto (first movement), and numerous other works throughout his career, argues basically for serendipitous collusion between a nineteenth-century source figure and a durable personal signature.

A similar set of perspectives applies to the exclamatory figure which Stravinsky joins to "Laius!" at the epic moment of recognition. On the surface it would appear that Stravinsky's proclamation of affection for Purcell in later years[32] deserves to be retrodated to the period of *Oedipus* in light of the Englishman's incidental music to the play. Although Stravinsky's use of a diminished seventh chord for the instrumental arpeggiation in lieu of Purcell's major triad underscores the sonority's foundational role throughout *Oedipus,* the additional use of a key signature of two flats, a change of meter (from duple to triple for Stravinsky; from

Example 13.1. Felix Mendelssohn, *Oedipus in Kolonus* (1852), Part I, "Wo weilt, entschwunder, gescheucht von dieser Stätte, der schamlose, der freche Mann?"

Example 13.2. Igor Stravinsky, *Oedipus Rex* (1927), Act II, "Natus sum quo nefastum est, concubui cui nefastum est, kekidi quem nefastum est. Lux facta est!"

Reprinted with permission of Boosey & Hawkes, Inc.

triple to duple for Purcell), and the repeated pitch and identical rhythm on the text "Laius!" (Examples 13.3, 13.4) collectively make a compelling argument not only for the advertisement of a specific source but simultaneously for Stravinsky's dictum that ultimately "true tradition lies in the contradiction."[33] Stravinsky's continuing appropriation of such gestural figures—frequently of extreme brevity, as in his borrowing of an instrumental flourish to Ferrando's "Un' aura amorosa" in *Così fan tutte* for the opening of Rakewell's Act I cavatina, "Love, too frequently betrayed," from *The Rake's Progress* (Examples 13.5, 13.6)—signals that their role is principally that of a catalytic starter.[34]

Recognition of the validity of such connections only corroborates Stravinsky's boundless capacity to be energized by a range of musical authorities. In turn, a key is offered not so much to the mystery of *Oedipus* as to the centrality of Stravinsky's curiosity about the grand tradition in all its diversity and a need to face the potential anxiety of influence full face. The consequent acts of ventriloquism, which map naturally with gestures of self-referentiality, are only a natural corollary to this fundamental orientation.

In tandem with proliferating bases of allegiance, in *Oedipus* Stravinsky also continued his prosodic habits of nonalignment between text and music, first worked out in *Three Japanese Lyrics* and the *pribaoutki* of the teens. Even in the face of a suggestion in 1937 by the conductor Bernardino Molinari, whom he respected, that the accent in *kekidi* should properly be on the second syllable, not the first, the passage remained unchanged in a new edition of 1947 which announced revisions, corrections, supplements, and alterations.[35] The earlier "rejoicing discovery" which Stravinsky had made in setting Russian peasant folk texts was now joined to his rediscovery of Ciceronian Latin while in search of a "pur langage sans office."

But why was *Oedipus* not set in Greek? Or if the sonority of Latin was required, why not Seneca's version of the story? And why commission a Frenchman, Cocteau, whose libretto would then require translation once again by the Abbé Daniélou? From one angle, Stravinsky could be seen to be merely perpetuating the fashion for translations of Greek plays for modern times—however palimpsestically arrived at—that had been fostered by the English, French, and Germans alike. From another, it is evident that his main objective coincided with both Yeats's and Eliot's desire to demonstrate the relevance of history for the present in a composite and serendipitous cultural assemblage of *objets trouvés*. And, like Eliot, Stravinsky was now increasingly drawn to the notion of poetic invisibility and transcendental subjectivity, which placed a premium upon an escape from the expression of personality.[36]

Furthermore, the growing frustration that Stravinsky had experienced in the translation of his Russian-texted pieces with respect to matters of prosody could be dissolved in the choice of Latin, the one language that seemed to be immune from any need for recasting. And the constructive order from French to Latin was, to Stravinsky's mind, in tune with the idea that the "music might be endowed with a certain monumental character by translation backwards, so to speak, from a

Example 13.3. Henry Purcell, *Oedipus* (1692), "Laius!"

secular to a sacred language."[37] Finally, Stravinsky claimed that in *Oedipus* "the word is pure material," and concluded that he preferred "Latin to Greek and Slavic because Latin is definitely fixed—as well as universal, thanks to its diffusion by the Church."[38]

Thus, perhaps even more central than Stravinsky's recognition that Latin offered him "a medium not dead but turned to stone and so monumentalized as to have become immune from all risk of vulgarization"[39] was the fact that the choice of Latin carried undisguisable ecclesiastical overtones which promoted fusion between the antique and the pan-Christian as an intimately allied pair of perennial authorities. Indeed, it is remarkable that the genesis of the idea behind both *Parade* and *Les Mariés de la Tour Eiffel* had originally rested in a biblical scenario. Obviously, in this light Cocteau's later dismissal of the antecedent and aborted *David*—"a story uselessly complicated by the Bible" that he had nonetheless intended to be accompanied "by Gregorian chant

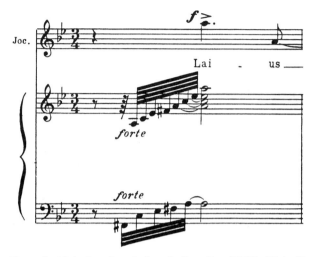

Example 13.4. Igor Stravinsky, *Oedipus Rex* (1927), "Laius!"
Reprinted with permission of Boosey & Hawkes, Inc.

rather than modern music"[40]—does not quite wash, and Honegger's *King David* of 1921 is indicative not so much of a fashion as of the acknowledgement of a vital resource and its continuing utility in addressing the dilemmas of a weary postwar world.

This transformation of the appeal of biblical tales and Latin texts generally throughout the 1920s was part of the postwar psychology that found numerous artists—including both Cocteau and Stravinsky—toying with issues of spirituality and even conversion or reconversion. The first articulate signs came naturally enough in the world of literature, where, among works in the English language, T. S. Eliot's *The Waste Land* (1922) combined something of the raw edge and force of Ezra Pound, to whom it was dedicated, with a style rich in classic allusion and the expression of modern man's lust and fears. The underlying story of the search for the Grail mirrored a concern for personal salvation that soon became an obsession on the part of many artists in the 1920s. Stations along the way for Eliot included his confirmation in the Church of England in 1927, followed by his *Ash Wednesday* of 1930 and *Murder in the Cathedral* of 1935. Analogously, Cocteau's struggle for personal esteem and against an addiction to opium led first to the

Example 13.5. Wolfgang Amadeus Mozart, *Così fan tutte,* "Un' aura amorosa."

Example 13.6. Igor Stravinsky, *The Rake's Progress,* "Love, too frequently betrayed."
Reprinted with permission of Boosey & Hawkes, Inc.

health clinics and then to his open *Letter to Jacques Maritain,* written in 1925, wherein he sought a momentary salvation in the Neo-Thomism of the philosopher.

In musical matters Arthur Lourié's knowledge of Russian Orthodox music as well as his keen interest in questions of modality and the repertoire of Byzantine chant were all near at hand for Stravinsky's consideration. But this does not quite account for Stravinsky's literal reconversion to Orthodoxy as the result of a religious experience on the occasion of the seven hundredth anniversary of St. Anthony in the Basilica at Padua in 1926. The first musical reflection of this conversion was an a cappella setting of the *Pater noster* in Slavonic, his first religious work and the only one composed simultaneously with *Oedipus*. After the Russian Revolution, Stravinsky's turning away from Russian themes and toward a Western-oriented Neoclassicism undoubtedly left a sense of void, which the use of his childhood language for prayers now addressed. The eventual association of this new orientation with a spiritual turn, which was by definition supranational, was also natural and led quickly to his preference for Latin as the language best suited to the expression of universal truths. The specific resonance between Antiquity and the Scriptures, beyond the obvious issue of perennial authorities, is a topic that still remains to be clarified. But it is incontestable that the dual experience of *Pater noster* (1926) and *Oedipus* (1926–27) led Stravinsky directly to the composition of the *Symphony of Psalms* (1930).

Late in life Stravinsky's capacity to perform an autopsy on his earlier works varied, but at his best, as with *Oedipus,* he parsed in an unusually lucid fashion the various issues of language, music, staging, and criticism that spelled the essence of the piece as well as the composer's working habits.[41] The recognition of a specific *Oedipus* manner that goes beyond the Russian markings of choral chanting and instrumental ostinato is identified by the composer in such large details as an arching recitative-aria scheme "in which each aria was to mark a crucial development in the story" as well as in such smaller details as the clarinet trill at "Lux facta est." Although admission is made that manner may quickly turn into mannerism, Stravinsky provides the cautionary admonition that the approach is not new and that he had "worked and thought in exactly the same way in Russia." His simultaneous attraction to the Baroque idea that dramatic progression can be accompanied by "a downward pull of the key center," to Wagnerian seventh chords, to a Folies-Bergère tune, to an Alberti bass, and to Verdi all at the same time, led Stravinsky to confess that "much of the music is a *Merzbild,* to borrow Schwitters' term, put together from whatever came to hand."

In the staging of *Oedipus,* many of the theatrical explorations of the first three decades of the century are also clearly in view. The notion of a chorus without faces seated singly in a row across the stage reading from scrolls ultimately gave way to actors appearing on elevated platforms at different heights behind the chorus.[42] Yet the composer admonishes that the actors do not "act," that they do not listen to one another. Indeed, in the original version he did not even allow them their exits and entrances and felt that their static representation supported the fatalistic development which, for him, was the meaning of the play. That the force of other theatrical developments of the teens and twenties also colored his conception of *Oedipus* Stravinsky made clear in the following extraordinary recollection:

> I have also been asked why I failed to take one more step and use puppets, as my late friend Robert Edmond Jones once did for a performance of my *Oedipus* in New York. This notion did occur to me, in fact, and I had been impressed by Gordon Craig's puppets when he showed them to me in Rome in 1917. But I am also fond of masks, and while composing Oedipus' first aria, I already imagined him wearing a roseate, ogival one, like that of a Chinese sun god—just as, when I composed the Devil's music in *The Flood,* I imagined a singer made to seem transparent, like a scorpion.

Thus like Yeats, Stravinsky also thought of Craig, though predictably not so much for his screens as for his puppetry, and like both of them he was also attracted to Japanese No drama.[43] And like Eliot, he pursued classical allusion in the interest of confecting not illusion but a new sensibility of the modern spirit conditioned by a reawakening of the panoramic richness of multiple traditions. When in *The Waste Land* Eliot writes a passage like

> London Bridge is falling down falling down falling down
> *Poi s'ascose nel foco che gli affina*
> *Quando fiam uti chelidon*—O swallow swallow

or

> Under the brown fog of a winter dawn,
> A crowd flowed over London Bridge, so many,
> I had not thought death had undone so many.
> Sighs, short and infrequent, were exhaled,
> And each man fixed his eyes before his feet

invoking in quick succession the directness of a child's world of games, the contemporary Londoner, and the agony of Dante's "Purgatory," he invites the listener to recognize the collage aspect of his assemblage and to hone his sense not of history but of the pastness of the present.

Beyond any precise recognition of the sources involved, however, Eliot's main call was upon James Frazer's invitation in *The Golden Bough*[44] to search for the underlying, original story behind all myth. Frazer's principal thesis centered on the belief that primitive man's explanation of the annual withering and rebirth of vegetation was akin to the rise and fall of kings, whose weakness or death is mirrored in the land becoming wasted and whose health or resurrection returns it to fertility.[45] In drawing attention to the combination of the priestly with the kingly office in Africa and other primitive societies, Frazer unknowingly prepared a natural conduit between the mythic life–death struggles of *The Rite* and the ancient tale of *Oedipus*. Claiming that *The Golden Bough* was as important for modern times as Freud, Eliot had also sensed from his first exposure to *The Rite of Spring* in October 1921—beyond the choreography, which he deplored—the power of Stravinsky's fertility rites "to transform the rhythm of the steppes into the scream of the motor horn, the rattle of machinery, the grind of wheels, the beating of iron and steel, the roar of the underground railway, and the other barbaric cries of modern life; and to transform these despairing noises into music." In this Eliot saw the clarification of the lesson that "in art there should be interpenetration and metamorphosis."[46]

In *Oedipus Rex*, as in *The Rite* and *The Waste Land,* quotations fall naturally into place either from the composer's stockpile of memory or from a review of his cultural inheritance; and, like the poet, the composer's later conversation books provided a highly intriguing and provocative gloss. Finally, just as Eliot's hero of the twenties, John Dryden, had written an *Oedipus,* so Eliot was to create his own version in his last play, *The Elder Statesman* (1959).[47]

Of all the stagings of *Oedipus* the ones that pleased Stravinsky least were the first performances at the Kroll Opera, Berlin, which he acknowledged were musically well prepared by Otto Klemperer. But the speaker wore a black Pierrot costume, and despite Stravinsky's complaints of its irrelevance, the director prevailed. The composer also recalled that "Hindemith and Schönberg were in the audience at the Berlin performance, the former *hingerissen* [charmed], and the latter—who must have heard in it nothing but empty ostinato patterns and primitive harmonies—*abgekühlt* [chilled]."[48] The reaction of the two composers could have been predicted: although the musical language and the libretto of *Oedipus* were seemingly far removed from Schlemmer-

Hindemith's *Das Nusch-Nuschi* of 1926, it shared numerous aesthetic details; and Schoenberg's thoughts about the theater at the time were mostly negative, reflecting his jealousy of Berg's *Wozzeck* on the one hand, his repudiation of Krenek's *Jonny* on the other, and ultimately capable of spawning only a lame satire in the guise of his own opera *Von Heute auf Morgen* (1928–29). Not surprisingly, the performance of *Oedipus* that pleased Stravinsky most was Cocteau's in the Théâtre des Champs Élysées in May 1952, a production once again characterized by the use of huge theatrical masks.

While much of the wording of the libretto the composer later found pretentious, in the early 1960s Stravinsky still professed to love the music.

> . . . *all* of it, even the Messenger's fanfares which remind me of the now badly tarnished trumpets of early 20th Century Fox. Neo-classicism? A husk of style? Cultured pearls? Well, which of us to-day is not a highly conditioned oyster? I know that the *Oedipus* music is valued at zero by present progressive-evolutionary standards . . . I know, too, that I relate from an angle to the German stem (Bach-Haydn-Mozart-Beethoven-Schubert-Brahms, Wagner, Mahler-Schoenberg), which evaluates solely in terms of where a thing comes from and where it is going. But an angle may be an advantage.

Agon

There is no unified history of the mask in rite or theater, and obviously its function as well as the source of its appeal have changed through the centuries. Yet the perpetual return of the mask in various cultures implies a perceivable utility for all times and places.[49] What was its inherent appeal to the Modernists?[50] One interpretation might propose that an emotional base had been so pressurized that the mask and ultimately the machine provided a scrim behind which the dramatist and composer could once again take command, control their message by means that prized directness and convention, and simultaneously recognize the force of a perennial authority. Just as the masks of the *commedia dell'arte* were always half-masks, allowing an interaction with part of the face, so the contemporary search for personal identity has continued to be "closely linked to the metaphor of the theater," whether in Sophocles, the Renaissance *theatrum mundi* of Shakespeare, or the "theater of the unconscious" of Sigmund Freud.[51] In the depersonalization which attends use of the mask the potentially ominous consequences for the artist in the impersonation of self-effacement are typically avoided through their transfusion into a tension-bearing system that allows the playing out of the artist's innermost desires and secrets.[52]

As previously noted, one of the dominions perennially appropriated in such a scheme was the world of Mozart, who, playing in the wings throughout the twenties, continued to appear periodically through Stravinsky's Neoclassic valedictory in *The Rake's Progress* of 1951. With Stravinsky's turn from Neoclassicism, many critics gave a sigh of relief that the flirtation was ended, even if that meant, as some soon feared, a new marriage with the rigors of serialism. But was it ended? What continuities did seeming closure now illuminate? A spotlight had suddenly been thrown on the basic posture of Stravinsky's creative process, which had somewhat more understandably escaped detection in the turn from a Russian to a Neoclassic base at the time of *Pulcinella* and the *Octet*.

Cantata, In Memoriam Dylan Thomas, Canticum Sacrum, Agon, Vom Himmel Hoch Variations, Threni, Monumentum pro Gesualdo, Movements for Piano and Orchestra. These were Stravinsky's principal works from the fifties, a troubled decade for many of the younger generation of European as well as American composers, when Neoclassicism collapsed and the heralded arrival of total serialism only seemed to clog the machinery of composition before it could ever engage. The emphasis upon contrapuntal games in the first half dozen works listed above suggests the continuation of a constructive gambit familiar from the twenties but one also now in harmony with a gradual move toward the world of composing with twelve tones.[53] Similarly, the antiquarian angle continued to be explored in approaches to Bach, Gesualdo, medieval verse, and ecclesiastical office. But melodies punctuated by rests and hocket-like colorations, formerly attributed to folk and medieval practice, were now charged to an amiable use of *Klangfarben* techniques à la Webern in the service of defining a new and illuminating approach to counterpoint. Such an interpretation was obviously enjoined in order to promote the idea of a probing synthesis of modern and old techniques. At the same time, however, other factors proclaimed the continuing promotion of multiple ingredients in a manner clearly redolent of the citation-collage practices of earlier years.

Thirty years after *Oedipus*, Stravinsky's juxtapositions in *Agon* (1953–1957), though familiar, continued to surprise in large measure because the constituency of the assemblage could not have been predicted. At a more fundamental level Stravinsky's admonition that "the danger lies not in the borrowing of clichés. The danger lies in fabricating them" remained only partially understood. As with *Le Rossignol* a momentous stylistic turn, undertaken after the inception of the work, was allied to the task at hand without thought of stylistic ambiguity. The composer, exploring new terrain, thus characteristically betrays his fascination with a new perspective and simultaneously reviews and recapitulates the habits of an entire career to that date.

Seen in this light, *Agon* is not a fleeting document of taste or the unfortunate reflection of an artist caught in the mire of a stylistic shift, but the statement of an artistic credo, of a *modus operandi* for a lifetime. Thematic quotation from folk or classic repertoires may be absent, but virtually every parameter of the work proclaims the composer's deliberately self-conscious appraisal of music history as he knew it placed in tandem with the winning of fresh perspectives: tonal and atonal live side by side two decades after Berg's Violin Concerto (1935) and Schoenberg's *Kol Nidre* (1938) but a decade and a half before George Rochberg's Third String Quartet (1972); angular projections of twelve-note series alternate with or are projected against diatonic scalar patterns and ostinati that demonstrate an overt tendency to seek out C major as a tonal goal; and tonality is further endorsed by cadential melodic figures molded from so-called Landini sixths recalling the fourteenth and fifteenth centuries. Furthermore, Baroque dance designations herald expectations of tempo and metrics which are alternately endorsed or obscured; and canon and ritornello, periodically familiar throughout his career, assume a heightened role as formal functionaries. The final product is less an uneasy alliance than a masterly convergence of the materials of the composer's musical craft honed over a career.

Agon is the Greek word for "game" or "contest," and Stravinsky's work was initially described as a ballet for twelve dancers (four male and eight female) and twelve notes, whose duodecimal connection extends to the partitioning of the whole into twelve movements arranged in four sections of three. But it is a game with multiple rules, based upon physical distinctions of gender common to both ballet and athletic competitions. For the first time, Stravinsky wrote a full-length ballet with no story, and his dancers are dressed in rehearsal costume. As Schlemmer had correctly observed, though the institutions of religion, state, and society had historically developed a wide variety of costumes, the range of genuine stage costumes, which notably includes those of the *commedia dell'arte,* had remained extremely limited. In *Agon* Stravinsky and George Balanchine appropriated an obvious addition—rehearsal dress, which is analogous to athletic clothing. But this reduction of costume is also a symbol that not only projects an abstraction and confirms the absence of a narrative but serves as a ritual body mask that announces the presence of multiple identities. It also prompts recall of the role of Dalcrozian *gymnastics* in Stravinsky's earliest successes, *Petrushka* and *Le Sacre du printemps.*[54]

Though ballet had traditionally promoted distinctions in function based upon the physical reality that defines gender, it was an issue that had increasingly been abdicated behind the mask and the machine. Yet the critic André Levinson was correct in noting that even in those classic repertoires that embraced clearly defined gender roles, the *danseur* had been neglected by critics and historians alike.

> Ballet is taken by so many to be simply an emanation in movement of the feminine principle, its secret emotional essence—wherein visually perceived lines and colors are permeated with a refined—almost dematerialized—sexual appeal. By others . . . it is taken to be one of the embodiments of the Eternal Feminine whose charms transcend the merely sensual, that is to say, as an allegory, a code.[55]

Levinson argued that the *danseur,* who was denied the possibility of dancing on *pointe* (only *demi-pointe* was allowed), was enjoying a renaissance in the early decades of the century and that, beyond his muscular presence in the service of the ballerina, he could also lay claim to a set of virtuosic moves, including *grands jetés, entrechats, pirouettes,* and turns in the air.

In light of Levinson's disaffection for tendencies first observed in *Petrushka,* pushed further toward a Dalcrozian solution in *Le Sacre,* and mechanized outright in various productions of the twenties, it is of no small interest to consider the relationship between dance and music and the range of conventions reintroduced by Balanchine as early as *Apollo* (1927) and then later addressed by Stravinsky in notable fashion in a pair of works which the composer saw as completing a trio: *Orpheus* of 1945 and the last full-length ballet, *Agon* of 1953–1957—works that even Levinson, had he seen them, might have termed *dansant.*[56] The idea of a trilogy was first suggested by Lincoln Kirstein in a letter to

Stravinsky of April 29, 1948, immediately following the premiere of *Orpheus*. In a long letter of August 23, 1950, Kirstein indicated that he had even talked to T. S. Eliot about collaboration in such a project. A specific commission *sans* Eliot was offered on February 16, 1951, and by November of that year Kirstein began to speak of introducing the terms "pavane, rigaudon, menuet, waltz, tarantella, polka . . ." Only on August 13, 1954, having already started to compose the music, does Stravinsky announce that he has settled on the title *Agon*.[57]

The opening male quartet in *Agon* makes a formal pronouncment of gender: four men, backs to the audience, turn and execute a *pas de quatre* loosely reflective of the imitative but non-canonic fanfare. The cinema garishness of the opening *Oedipus* fanfare, only partially moderated in the recent overture to *The Rake's Progress,* has been further tempered and contrapuntalized. The men are immediately joined by four women in a double *pas de quatre* and then by the full complement of eight women in a triple *pas de quatre.* Here, with the women firmly anchored to the ground throughout, the four male dancers take simultaneous flight in a series of leaps that can hardly fail to recall the memorable *grands jetés* at the opening and close of *Le Spectre de la rose*—a final acclamation en masse of the masculine. Cocteau's recall of Nijinsky's performance in *Le Spectre,* both verbally and in a caricature following a gala charity performance at the Opéra in December 1911, provided certification for both the elegance and the attendant athleticism: "After lightly kissing the girl, the Spectre of the Rose leaps out her window . . . and lands among the stagehands, who squirt water into his face and scrub him with towels, like a boxer between rounds. What grace coupled with what brutality!"[58]

But in the group leaps of *Agon* are we meant to see a team of modern athletes clearing the high hurdles? Or is it nature's ballet of the primitive, a herd of gazelles? Indeed, invitation to multiple readings persists at every level of the work. Does the allusion to a dodecaphonic series later in the piece, for example, reflect Stravinsky's current infatuation with Webern, or does its ultimate capitulation to the harmonic-tonal perspectives of the whole provide a sermon regarding his lifelong views about tonality?[59] Is his use of the mandolin intended as a ready reference to its associations as a Viennese timbral signature (Mahler, Schoenberg, Webern); as an approximation of the Russian balalaika, of "Tchaikovsky's harp, just back from the Viennese dry-cleaner";[60] as a new companion to the harp, frequently directed by Stravinsky to play *près de la table* as a kind of orchestral guitar;[61] or is it a specific reflection of his interest in John Dowland's lute galliards, with which he familiarized himself in a version for guitar at the time he was writing *Agon?*[62] Similarly, do the aerated pointillisms and immiscible projection of piano and harp in the Coda to the "Pas de deux" direct us to Webern or to a review of the concertante role of the piano throughout the composer's career and specifically of the discrete role of piano and harp in the *Symphony in Three Movements?* Does the feminine dancing on point confirm an orientation to the classical ballet or recall its role as a *masque mécanique* for the dancing dolls of *Coppélia, Petrushka,* and *La Boîte à joujoux?*

Agon is a game, but it is more than an athletic contest. It is a riddle posed under the guise of a diverse set of musical clues: framing Olympic fanfares; antique French group dances;[63] a Webern series;[64] canonic structures with historical as well as contemporary implications;[65] and variable tonal orientations attributable to circumstances much like those attending the composition of *Le Rossignol* in that the work was begun, interrupted, and resumed in tandem with a momentous stylistic deflection. The consortium of ingredients, in typical Stravinskian fashion, fails to explode in a stylistic mishmash but rather congeals in a precocious, if somewhat precarious, balance of materials which honors the vitalizing force of Modernist collage. The result is an enigmatic and multilayered mask that invites removal.

Luciano Berio has described *Agon* as "the hyper-intelligent parable of a 'short history of music' that performs a lucid, but tragic autopsy on itself under the pretext of a game."[66] For Stravinsky's and Balanchine's dancers offer not only a compelling abstraction but a juxtaposition that tells a story, both personal and historical: eschewing narrative in the sequence of numbers, it offers an articulate review of the composer's beginnings with the Russian ballet, his flirtation with Neoclassicism, and his adaptiveness to the latest musical trends.

A ready test site comes with the imitative but non-canonic trumpet duo that accompanies the opening "Pas de quatre" of *Agon* and the later canon for two trumpets, absolutely strict with respect to pitch, rhythm, and register, in the "Bransle Simple."[67] Balanchine's choreography rigorously registers this technical distinction. For just as the trumpet figures in the opening "Pas de quatre" are free and not strictly canonic, so the imitation of the male dancers, one dancer following another, overlaps the music and resists a note for note illustration. The rigid canonic structure of the "Bransle Simple," however, is appropriately mirrored by a rigorously reflective choreography.[68] Beyond this audiovisual correspondence, both of Stravinsky's passages can claim a musical lineage that reaches back to the canonic trumpet pair that introduces Stravinsky's youthful *Fireworks*.[69] It is an idea that in turn clearly recalls the figure, sonority, and texture of principal material in Tchaikovsky's incidental music to *The Tempest*.

Yet at the time Stravinsky claimed that he got the specific idea for the instrumentation in *Agon* from an illustration in De Lauze's *Apologie de la danse* (1623), and something of its spirit from the world of jazz,[70] and that the initial idea of invoking three bransles for the second "Pas de trois" ("Bransle Simple," "Bransle Gay," and "Bransle de Poitou") was attributable to a reading of Mersenne's *Harmonie universelle* of 1636.[71] Lincoln Kirstein, who brought these sources to Stravinsky's attention even before he had started to compose, suggested in a letter of August 31, 1953, the appropriation of "a series of historic dances, the correct tempi of which you can quite ignore, but they are called courante, bransle, passepied, rigaudon, menuet, etc. etc. It is as if time called the tune, and the dances which began quite simply in the sixteenth century took fire in the twentieth and exploded."[72] But if historic dances were sought, why choose those whose origins, except for the bransle, are traceable only to the seventeenth century, and in any case invoke nothing even remotely Greek? Indeed, why no mention of the Greek lyra, kithara, or aulos, not to mention genera, tonoi, or nomos? Failure to summon any claim to Greekness is countered not so much by an imaginary historicism as by a practical and opportunistic invocation of the earliest dances about which we have reasonable choreographic evidence. Other timbral associations—flutes with women dancers and trumpets with men—appear less arrowed to any heightened contemporary sensibility surrounding the issue of gender in music than to venerable traditions of instrumental rhetoric in the world of music well beyond the world of ballet.

Given the multiple alternatives, most listeners will wonder if the "Bransle Gay," typically in triple meter, is best construed as a reference to Stravinsky's earlier Baroque attitudes (Example 13.7). Or does the pronouncement of its ostinato rhythm on the castanets hint at historical Russian-Moorish associations, noted on more than one occasion by the composer himself, or at his own occasional Spanish flirtations in the teens? As one reviewer commented at the time of the premiere, Stravinsky's invocation of French Baroque court dances refers to its models about as much "as a Cubist still–life recalls a pipe or guitar."[73] Ansermet, who had a falling out with Stravinsky at this very time over his turn to serialism, was even less courteous with respect to his contrived metrics: "Here we touch on the defect of 'intellectual' creative activity, which consists in manufacturing and elaborating structures that are *unnecessary* and add nothing to the musical substance of the work."[74]

Of the two assessments the allusion to Cubism is nearer the mark, and recall of the argument concerning the first of the *Three Pieces for String Quartet* will allow easy recognition of Stravinsky's ostinato habits of the teens still actively at work.[75] Ansermet's concern over the seemingly capricious rhythmic notation of the upper parts undoubtedly reflects his sense of discomfort at Stravinsky's move toward serialism following the death of Schoenberg in 1951. Despite an early association between conductor and composer from the late teens onward, Stravinsky's embrace of serialism was seen virutally as an act of betrayal as well as a potential move toward intellectual sterility.

All charges of proliferating complexity in the juxtaposition of measures of 7/16 and 5/16 against a consistent 3/8 in the castanets can be clearly accommodated, however, through reference to Stravinsky's early compositional practice. For against the triple metrics of the ostinato reflective of the designation "Bransle Gay," Stravinsky constructs upper parts that give only the illusion of independence and are far from irrational. In fact, though Stravinsky's calculation may be compared to that in the first of the *Three Pieces for String Quartet,* the patterning in *Agon* is even more readily perceivable: since only measures of 7 and 5 sixteenths are used throughout, adjacent combinations at the beginning (7 + 5, 5 + 7) invariably combine to a sum of 12, which is a multiple of the ostinato's 6 sixteenths. Further confirmation of alignment occurs when the instruments stop and the castanets play alone for a single measure of 3/8 with the ballerina continuing to mark her pattern. In that the isolated castanet measure also opens and closes the piece, its formal function is unambiguously announced. The final two statements involve longer multiples of 6: 30 sixteenths occupying six statements of 5/16; and finally $(7 \times 5) + 7 = 42$ sixteenths, which is another multiple of six. The following chart indicates where the ostinato pattern aligns

Example 13.7. Igor Stravinsky, *Agon,* "Bransle Gay," complete.

with the upper parts (>), and illustrates the genesis of multiple perspectives from restricted materials. Cubism and French court dance join in a symbiotic embrace:

310	311	312	313	314					
(3/8)	7/16	5/16	5/16	7/16					= 12 + 12
>	>		>						

315	316	317	318	319					
(3/8)	5/16	7/16	7/16	5/16					= 12 + 12
>	>		>						

320	321	322	323	324	325	326			
(3/8)	5/16	5/16	5/16	5/16	5/16	5/16		= 30	
>	>								

327	328	329	330	331	332	333	334		
5/16	5/16	5/16	5/16	5/16	7/16	5/16	5/16	= 42	
>									

335
(3/8)
>

Metric alignment aside, elements of reprise also appear throughout the work, in the manner of both the *personnages rythmiques* in *The Rite* (m. 311 = m. 313 contracted by two sixteenth notes) and the cut and paste techniques of *The Five Fingers* (311–312 = 318–319; 313–314 = 316–317; 332–334 = 311–313). The solo castanet measures (310, 315, 320, 335) and the reprise of the opening material for flutes and bassoons at 332, which does not align with the castanet figure as in the beginning, also identify the larger sections and ultimately the form of the piece: A (a^1 = 311–312, a^2 = 313–314); A′(a^2 = 316–317, a^1 = 318–319); B (320–331), A″ (A minus 314).

An acute awareness of number's relation to musical form and movement remained a constant throughout Stravinsky's career. He never spoke more lucidly about it, however, than at the time he was writing his Violin Concerto (1931). Speaking to the violinist Samuel Dushkin, who served as a consultant, he voiced a perspective that applies equally to the "Bransle Gay" from *Agon:*

> In mathematics there are an infinite number of ways of arriving at the number seven. It's the same with rhythm. . . it makes no difference if you say five and two or two and five, six and one or one and six, and so on. With rhythm, however, the fact that they add up to seven

is of secondary importance. The important thing is, is it five and two or is it two and five, because five and two is a different person from two and five.[76]

Just as such changing perspectives confirm a preoccupation with rendering the formal dimension audible while thematic, technical, and historical references together carry the allusion of multiple attendant masks, so pitch and tonality contribute to the polyfocal nature of the piece. For if the ballet as a whole consistently demonstrates an attraction to C major, its capacity to entertain tetrachordal, hexachordal, and dodecaphonic collections in tandem with serial and nonserial, octatonic and diatonic C-scale pitch elements clearly compounds the Janus-faced nature of the work, which continuously operates under the simultaneous exposition of multiple authorities.[77] The "Coda" to the "Sarabande" and "Galliard" provides a perfect demonstration: the tonal orientation announced by the sustained c-g of the trumpets at the opening and corroborated by the parallel sixths which intermittently return to the c-e dyad of the solo violin is counterbalanced by the dodecaphonic projections of the surrounding strings, whose shifting weight seems to proclaim a continuing search for the perfect balance of a Calder mobile (Example 13.8, mm. 185–189, P: A, B, B♭, C, D♭, E♭, E, G♭, F, G, D, A♭; mm. 190–200, I: A, G, G♯, F♯, F, E♭, D, C, C♯, B, E, B♭). This concern for balance is reflected in the formal scheme of the work at large, where the interjection of essentially identical music under the title of "Prelude" (not the first movement of the work) and two "Interludes" suggests a formal function well beyond the designations for "Sarabande" and "Galliard." It is a factor that has also been demonstrated as a constructive principle guiding the proportions of the whole.[78] Finally, the choreography which Balanchine devised as a cohort to this ensemble of relationships was anything but an arbitrary and ancillary overlay of the composed music; rather it served as a partner in elucidating both the details and the overriding arch of the work.[79]

Understandably the call upon such a broadly constituted aesthetic in *Oedipus* and *Agon* has not escaped criticism, especially by the realists, who see in it the basis as well as the Achilles heel of Modernism. Its defenders, however, have argued its power and charged that the removal of relativism leads to the inevitably futile attempt to express reality in a single optimum form.[80] Left to divine the meaning of Stravinsky's seeming random access to culture—hinted at in a thousand leads both true and false—we are encouraged to sense his subscription to the tenet that "everything has been prewritten, and so what is said in the

Coda

(One male and two female dancers)

Example 13.8. Igor Stravinsky, *Agon*, "Coda" to "Sarabande" and "Galliard," mm. 185–199.

past determines the real to come when that past is remembered."[81] The power inherent in such a pluralistic resonance, however, also carries the attendant dilemma of *The Waste Land,* which hovers around identification of the authorial voice, namely "Who is speaking?" as an essential preamble to the question "What does it mean?"

The feeling that the search for the new ought to be free of entangling alliances with the past can be spotted in the declarations of many serialists of the 1950s who expressed a fundamental alignment with the pronouncements of Boulez. Boulez openly charged that, following the "brilliant fireworks display" of the period 1909–1912, the creative energies of both Schoenberg and Stravinsky had ossified in the compulsive search for order based upon absolute models. Haunted by history, he claimed, they lost their instinct for the "wild" discovery and settled into sterile manipulation. Yet, however one may characterize the final result, neither in his turn to Neoclassicism in the 1920s nor in his accommodation to and assimilation of the series in the 1950s was Stravinsky's approach academic or historical in the narrowest sense. No prisoner of tradition, he was invigorated, rather, by the potential for perpetual renewal through confrontation with it.

Near the end of his life, Stravinsky made it clear that he was acutely aware that his agglutinative approach to composition was a cause for concern even among audiences who claimed to be friends of the contemporary scene, but concluded:

> Composers continue to be generated in and by traditions, nevertheless, however vestigial, splintered, and self-fabricated (by the free adoption of ancestors and the choosing and pasting together of assorted bits and pieces of the past). All works of art, and anti-art, must have antecedents, though these may not be readily apparent, and though connection may be created and discovered only after long periods of time.[82]

Clearly Stravinsky's affinity for the layered disguise, his desire to contemplate more than a single perspective was promoted by literary, visual, and theatrical developments over a lifetime. Acknowledged or not, it was a feature shared by many of the most prominent European composers of his age. Yet the agony that a host of analysts and philosophers have experienced over Berg's Violin Concerto, for example, is symptomatic of an ongoing contemporary dilemma. Noting the opposition of Carinthian folktune, Bach chorale, and dodecaphonic series, the young Boulez deemed their juxtaposition a "serious error."[83] He also expressed dismay at the interrupting banality of the military march and cradle song in *Wozzeck* as well as the "exasperating sentimentality" of the *trio estatico* from the *Lyric Suite*.[84] Later, however, he would find Berg's appropriation and overloading of forms more compelling and, though still intoxicated with history, ultimately capable of dissolving the original state of ambiguity.[85]

The question of the need for integration in the presentation of systems of potential conflict has spawned a lively literature that has debated qualities of antagonism versus antithesis and the possibility of stalemate wherein the contestants are judged of equal strength. Stravinsky's *Agon* has been regarded as a "complex unity, breaking down either-or distinctions,"[86] but also, unlike Berg's works, as reflective of a period of stylistic turnover.[87] We should bear in mind, however, Stravinsky's own counter to objections over his *Oedipus* manner to the effect that he had "worked and thought in exactly the same way in Russia," which suggests that the essence of his compositional attitude is not located at, but only dramatized in, moments of dramatic stylistic shift such as *Le Rossignol* and *Agon*.

Though such questions have typically been argued within the framework of the European tradition, their relevance for American musical developments has been addressed less frequently. Interestingly, it was in America that Stravinsky discovered Webern, refueled his antiquarian interests (*Mass; Cantata; Vom Himmel Hoch; Threni; Monumentum pro Gesualdo; A Sermon, a Narrative, and a Prayer; Requiem Canticles*), made a momentous realliance with the world of dance, and once again confronted the theatrical mask in *Agon* and *The Flood*. It was the Rockefeller Foundation that commissioned *Agon* for the New York City Ballet, but it was another displaced Russian, George Balanchine, who choreographed it. The transferral of artistic personalities to American shores which made this a natural coalition in 1954 had been set in motion fifteen years before, however. For it was in 1939—Diaghialev now ten years deceased and war clouds forming—that Stravinsky, together with a host of other artistic refugees, immigrated to America and adopted a new homeland. The Slav transplanted as a Frenchman was soon to become an American. The reasons behind Stravinsky's two geographical relocations may have been different, but Russia's historic infatuation with French culture and France's fascination with America in the 1920s facilitated a pair of similarly critical removals and dissipated, in both instances, the potential bitterness of exile.

— CUT AND PASTE —

— 14 —

Exodus: 1939

> The wave of migration reached its peak when Germany, ruled
> by the National Socialist Party, set out to absorb neighboring
> territories; it reached its conclusion with the collapse of France.
> Even while these events were in process, an interest arose in
> their bearing on the creative work of the composers affected by
> them. The question was raised to what extent this work was
> influenced by their more or less forcible, unplanned departure
> from customary surroundings and by their new living condi-
> tions.
>
> *Ernst Krenek*

In 1939 the middle section of Chopin's *Fantasie-Impromptu* was widely
known throughout the United States as a revived popular song from
the teens, "I'm Always Chasing Rainbows." It was an age which invoked the image frequently in song, and Judy Garland's rendition of
"Somewhere over the Rainbow" in *The Wizard of Oz,* also of 1939,
intoned another fantasy—that of a better world, a happier life beyond
the Depression. Reflecting America's continuing isolation and resistance to any sense of obligation to participate in settling Europe's problems, both songs were marked by an innocence light years away from
the virile pacifist irony of Terry Riley's *A Rainbow in Curved Air,* written in 1970 at the height of the Vietnam conflict. Similarly, WPA,
PWA, NRA, CCC, and the radio fireside chat, all emblems of Roose-
velt's first two administrations, were familiar societal logos reflecting
strictly domestic concerns and a national resolve to combat a harsh period of economic blight.

But the United States was also suffering from societal and spiritual
ills that were not solely economic. Like Josephine Baker before her,

Marian Anderson had gone to Paris in 1930 in search of a platform and had achieved her first recognition there. Yet before the decade was out Sol Hurok would persuade her to return home under his management. In 1939, having been denied permission by the Daughters of the American Revolution to sing in Constitution Hall in Washington, Anderson sang to an overflow crowd at the Lincoln Memorial on Easter Sunday, and gave a poignant signal to Americans that all was not right in the land. Nonetheless, the warning went largely unheeded. Unthinkable as it may seem at this distance, World War II, whose beginning lay only four months ahead, would be fought by American armed forces that were racially segregated.

At the same time a handful of artist-intellectuals who felt sympathetic toward world socialist aims was flirting with international Communism in what amounted to a dress rehearsal for *Scoundrel Time*. That a virus was perceived to be loose in the land was made clear in 1938 when Congressman Martin Dies brought his investigating committee to Hollywood and heard testimony charging that ten-year old Shirley Temple was a Communist. Simultaneously in Europe plans for a "final solution" of another kind of "problem" were being hatched. Although the ovens of Auschwitz and Dachau had not yet been turned on, as American children listened to the radio with their Captain Midnight decoders in hand, Hitler's Jugend were being programmed for a more realistic adventure. It was the beginning of the end of an era. Paradoxically, the declaration of war on September 1, 1939, signaled that the end of the Depression in America was imminent; for Europe it was the beginning of the daily horrors of World War II. The flight from Europe, begun earlier in the decade, now reached fever pitch as some of the finest artists and intellectuals began moving in increasing numbers to American shores.

Among composers, one of the first to arrive was Arnold Schoenberg. Raised in the Orthodox Jewish faith in Vienna, he converted to Lutheranism in 1898 at the age of twenty-four, but his increasing awareness of the growing wave of anti-Semitism in Germany as well as in Vienna now led to his flight from Germany and his reconversion to Judaism in a private ceremony in Paris in July 1933. Schoenberg's journey to Boston in October of that year provided vivid testimony to the musical community in America of the serious problems facing the Jewish artist in Europe. Once in the United States he soon moved to Los Angeles, taking up residence in the fall of 1934.

Living in the cinema capital of the world, Schoenberg expressed his feelings about the movies in an openly hostile article of 1940 entitled "Art and the Moving Pictures." Although Schoenberg's earlier interest in the potential of talking pictures had been made clear in an address that was put on film in 1929, his own *Begleitungsmusik für ein Lichtspielszene* of 1929–30 was music for an imaginary film scene. Now attempts on the part of Hollywood to solicit Schoenberg's cooperation in a real film venture dissolved when he was told that the studios reserved the right to cut and arrange his music in whatever manner they might deem necessary, and he must have begun to wonder, at least momentarily, to what extent artistic freedom existed in America after all.

On the positive side Schoenberg pursued his interest in the Jewish national cause, though only intermittently owing to ill health. His 1938 setting of the Kol Nidre, the most solemn of the prayers of atonement chanted on Yom Kippur Eve, was intended for synagogue use and pointed to Schoenberg's passionate and continuing attention to his previously announced concerns—concerns which were later to be mirrored in different ways in such works as *Ode to Napoleon Bonaparte* (1942) and *A Survivor from Warsaw* (1947). Concurrently, however, Schoenberg was undertaking an intensive self-examination with respect to the issue of communication. The two principal works written at this time, *Kol Nidre* and the Chamber Symphony No. 2, both have a retrospective character: the completion in 1939 of his second chamber symphony, begun in 1906, forced a reconsideration of his current musical language and its compatibility with an earlier one; and Schoenberg's announced hope that the message of *Kol Nidre* would be comprehensible to the public at large promotes the conclusion that his confrontation with Hollywood played a significant role in a momentary stylistic realignment. This is readily audible in the music which accompanies the opening of *Kol Nidre,* where the anxieties of atonal, Expressionist text painting (lines 1–4) nestle comfortably alongside overtly tonal and chorale-like piety (lines 5–8).

> The Kabalah tells a legend:
> At the beginning God said: "Let There Be Light."
> Out of space a flame burst out.
> God crushed that light to atoms.
> Myriads of sparks are hidden in our world,
> but not all of us behold them.
> The selfglorious, who walks arrogantly upright, will never perceive one;
> but the meek and modest, eyes downcast, he sees it.

At the precise moment this score was being composed at Schoenberg's North Rockingham home in Brentwood, Shirley Temple lived in a house directly across the street. With the clouds of international conflict forming, and the declaration of war just around the corner underscoring the prudence of Schoenberg's earlier flight from Europe, a Jewish expatriate was addressing musical and moral matters of deep personal concern in the shadow of a child movie star whose optimism and musical talents of a totally different nature had helped a nation to weather the Depression of the 1930s. The voice of the "bright-eyed, curly topped, poor little rich girl" which had done much to help stay America's gloom over the past five years was still very much in everybody's consciousness, and the sheet music from her films rested on many an American piano. Attempting to sustain the optimistic cinema psychology of the Depression, America continued to pretend that, if it acted right, "Santa Claus *was* comin' to town." In retrospect, the juxtaposition of Arnold Schoenberg and Shirley Temple epitomizes with rare poignancy the somewhat oxymoronic conditions of time, place, and personality. Indeed, the view from North Rockingham Avenue in 1939 Brentwood, California, might well have been characterized as that of "The Gathering Storm on the Goodship Lollipop."

Numerous other Viennese were also in Hollywood with Schoenberg. Max Steiner had come to America much earlier, in 1914, and to Hollywood as early as 1929 with the advent of talking pictures. A decade later in 1939, the hit of the year along with *The Wizard of Oz* was *Gone with the Wind,* and talk of Scarlett O'Hara and Rhett Butler was on lips everywhere—a condition which television, the video recorder, and now literary sequels suggest may go on forever. But it is good to remember in assessing America's musical taste and values of the time that while the author, Margaret Mitchell, was from Atlanta, the composer of the film score, Max Steiner, was from Vienna. In *Gone with the Wind* and *Dark Victory,* a Bette Davis classic of 1939 which also claimed a Steiner score, the transference of an expressive Romantic Viennese style to the purposes of American movie storytelling had been sealed and accepted. Indeed, the movie industry proved fundamental in setting the musical taste for the general public with respect to popular as well as operatic and symphonic repertoires throughout the decades of the 1930s and 1940s. Artists such as Grace Moore, Lily Pons, and José Iturbi achieved star status, and many an American was exposed for the first time to the tragic lyricism of *La Bohème*'s Mimi, to the pyro-

technic coloratura of Delibe's *Lakmé,* or to the flamboyant energy of
Falla's "Ritual Fire Dance" through their performances on screen.

Further evidence of the Viennese musical occupation of Hollywood
was to be found in the work of Erik Korngold, whose film scores for
1939 included those for Bette Davis's *Juarez* and for *The Private Lives
of Elizabeth and Essex,* starring Davis and Errol Flynn. Two years before,
Korngold had won an Oscar for Flynn's *The Adventures of Robin Hood,*
and two years later he was to write the film score for *King's Row,* starring
a rising young American actor named Ronald Reagan. One of the most
astonishing wunderkinds of the early twentieth century, Korngold,
born in 1897, was the son of Vienna's most powerful music critic, Julius
Korngold. His father's anti-Schoenbergian stand was legendary, and the
talents of the precocious young son naturally ran toward an opulent
Romantic idiom. In 1920 with the ecstatic reception of his opera *Die
tote Stadt* Korngold was, at the age of twenty-three, the rage of Europe.
Like Schoenberg, Korngold arrived in Hollywood in 1934. By 1939
his musical language had changed little, a factor which accounts for the
fact that his violin concerto of 1942 was written for and played by Jascha
Heifetz, while Schoenberg's violin concerto of 1936 remained on the
shelf. Korngold had found not only a source of income but a continuing
creative outlet in the films. In the movie *Deception* of 1944, for example,
Bette Davis simulated a performance of Beethoven's *Appassionata* while
Korngold's full-fledged cello concerto, fictively performed by Paul
Henreid, was unveiled to the world as the work of the composer Ho-
lenius, portrayed by Claude Rains. In one sequence, Davis, having just
murdered the composer as part of a love triangle, arrives at the concert
hall for the concerto's world premiere. The time given over to this
scene, which is some four minutes in length, not only fulfills the requirements for a pause before the denouement but reflects the clout
that Korngold had in showcasing his own music in the movies.

Franz Waxman, a Berliner and friend of Bruno Walter, also fled to
Hollywood with the rise of Nazism, and soon became one of its most
respected composers. With a style indebted to both Strauss and Prokofiev, he wrote scores for such prominent titles as *Magnificent Obsession*
(1936), *Rebecca* (1940), *The Philadelphia Story* (1941), *Dr. Jekyll and Mr.
Hyde* (1941), *Suspicion* (1941), *Sunset Boulevard* (1950), *Rear Window*
(1953), and *The Spirit of St. Louis* (1957). Having founded the Los
Angeles Musical Festival he also promoted the music of Prokofiev,
Honegger, von Einem, Orff, and Britten, increasingly developed a "se-

rious" musical language that was Jewish in inspiration, and won the respect of Stravinsky.

Other sources of the film music idiom of the time were to be found in a style associated with the aesthetic of the Russian Primitivism which had flourished at the beginning of the second decade of the century, especially in works such as Stravinsky's *Rite of Spring* and Prokofiev's *Scythian Suite*. Indeed, many an Indian war dance in American cowboy and Indian movies of the time mirrored, unconsciously or not, the musical manners of both composers. It would make a fascinating study to sift through the various ethnic sources as well as the "high" and "low" repertoires at hand for the movie studio composer in order to determine the potential contributors to Hollywood's view of American Indian music. Native Americans today smile at Hollywood's ubiquitous 1-2-3-4 drumming with a primary accent on the first beat and wonder at the genesis of this confected cinema code.[1]

Sergei Rachmaninov also lived in California in 1939. His familiar *Rhapsody on a Theme of Paganini* had been written in Hollywood only a few years before, and his last important work, the *Symphonic Dances,* op. 45, was completed the next year. And Igor Stravinsky was en route to Los Angeles, where he was to maintain a home almost to the end of his life. The city was fast becoming the musical expatriate capital of the world, and it made for some interesting, if strange, bedfellows.

Stravinsky left France for America on the *S.S. Manhattan* in September 1939, shortly after the outbreak of hostilities. He had accepted the Charles Eliot Norton Chair at Harvard and immediately found himself busy delivering the lectures, originally written and delivered in French, which were later published in English as the *Poetics of Music.* Stravinsky had already finished the first two movements of his Neoclassic Symphony in C in France by August of 1939; the third movement was completed after his arrival in Cambridge during the autumn and winter of 1939–40; and the concluding movement was written in Beverly Hills in August of 1940. The appearance of both the *Poetics* and the Symphony in C not only announced that both Neoclassicism and a resuscitated tonality had continued to flourish in Europe but hinted that they could be expected to thrive in America as well.

Among the Americans who studied with Schoenberg in California at the time was David Raksin, who later "developed" the music of Kurt Weill for the film *Where Do We Go From Here?* and composed the memorable title music for the film *Laura.*[2] John Cage, born in California, had gone to New York in 1933, where he studied with Henry Cowell. Returning to California in the fall of 1934 at the very moment of Schoenberg's arrival there, he also began studies with him, composing various works which disclose an interest in twelve-note serial manipulations, such as his *Metamorphosis,* written as late as 1938. By 1939 however, Cage was already turning his attentions to unimaginable corners of the avant-garde with his *Imaginary Landscape No. 1* for two variable-speed turntables, frequency recordings, muted piano, and cymbal. His *Second Construction* of 1940 reflects a continuing preoccupation with non-Western source materials and "prepared" traditional instruments, an interest which was reinforced by his friendship with Lou Harrison, by his intimate knowledge of Cowell's percussion pieces, and possibly also by a familiarity with the metal and junk collages of Kurt Schwitters. Cage's *Second Construction* of 1940, which reflects the earlier timbral and rhythmic exploration of Henry Cowell, also publicizes the fact that twenty-five years after its premiere the lengthening but propelling shadow of Stravinsky's *Le Sacre* had not completely faded.

Cage left for Chicago in 1940 and thence for New York the next year, but his early exposure to such variable materials is a fascinating thing to observe. Yet his early output, unlike that of Ives, contains no variations on "America" or quotations of "Jesus, Lover of My Soul" and "Nearer, My God, to Thee." Cage may have been unaware of Ives's use of the second of these tunes in his "Concord" Sonata, premiered in 1939 by John Kirkpatrick, but he could hardly have been unfamiliar with Jeanette MacDonald's recent heart-rending performance of "Nearer, My God, to Thee" in her film *San Francisco* of 1936. Cage's refusal of this source material and overt sympathy for Oriental philosophy and European Dada gradually contributed to the international view of the possibility of a musical avant-garde of American origins for the first time. The seriousness of such a claim can be judged by the vehemence with which some of his European colleagues, including Stockhausen and Boulez, later protested their independence from his example.

In 1939, however, Europe's fascination with music in the Western Hemisphere, as in the 1920s, continued to reside largely in an admiration of its popular culture. Such a point of view had originally gained momentum in the teens, as witnessed in the tango teas in London and Paris before the outbreak of World War I; and the fascination with American blues and ragtime, the shimmy, charleston, and fox trot all reflected not only an interest in keeping with the fashionableness of *art nègre* among the painters and the canonization of the "art of the every-day" espoused by Cocteau and Les Six, but a fascination with the vitality of American life and its urban bustle. Maurice Ravel's and Alban Berg's attraction to Gershwin illustrates the extent to which the king of Tin Pan Alley was considered relevant for a Parisian dandy and a Viennese serialist as late as 1930.

By 1939 Berg, Ravel, and Gershwin had all died—recently and pre-maturely—and much of the vitality of their symbiotic interchange had dissipated.[3] Hindemith, who had similarly displayed his interest in the adoption of ingredients from popular idioms in the 1920s, found himself faced with issues of more pressing concern in the 1930s. By 1933 it was apparent that he would have to leave Germany, and the 1934 pre-miere of three important orchestral interludes from *Mathis der Maler,* an opera which openly discussed the relation of the artist in periods of political upheaval, achieved only a momentary success. Hindemith was soon branded a "cultural Bolshevik," and a radio ban on all his music was imposed. In 1939, having been labeled an undesirable artist by Goering, Goebbels, and Hitler himself, Hindemith was busy composing a large group of solo sonatas (including those for horn, trumpet, clarinet, and harp), but he was also planning to leave Europe for America. He arrived in Buffalo the next year. There followed a residency at Yale that lasted until 1953, at which time he returned to Switzerland for the remainder of his life. But his impact upon both music and musical education in America was immense, and during his residency his stock was never higher. In the 1940s not only did many young American composers fall under the spell of Hindemith—at the time a viable and attractive alternative to Schoenberg or Stravinsky—but his force as a teacher, from the education of the young to his espousal of medieval and Renaissance music in the Yale Collegium Concerts, was keenly felt throughout the land.

In 1939 the young British composer Benjamin Britten, having just finished his important vocal cycle, *Les Illuminations,* to texts of Rim-baud, also followed the wave of composers who were emigrating to America. He was joined on his voyage by the tenor Peter Pears, and in America Britten penned the first of a series of scores written especially for Pears's voice, the *Seven Sonnets of Michelangelo* (1940). Curiously enough, Britten's first encounter with the music of the Orient took place in America, through a meeting in 1939 with Colin McPhee, who introduced him to the pattern and sonority of the Balinese gamelan. The full fruits of this confrontation were destined to simmer for another decade and a half, however, before finding an outlet in *The Prince of the Pagodas* (1956–57).[4]

Among the most renowned musical pedagogues of her time, indeed of the century, Nadia Boulanger had an enormous following in America dating back to the 1920s. Her first classes at Fontainebleau had included Aaron Copland, Roy Harris, and Virgil Thomson, and in her pedagogy, which continued to attract an important American contingent, Boulanger repeatedly championed the music of Igor Stravinsky. In 1938 she traveled from France to Washington to conduct the premiere of his latest work, the "Dumbarton Oaks" Concerto, which had been commissioned by Mr. and Mrs. Robert Woods Bliss. She returned to America in 1939 for a highly successful series of conducting engagements with both the New York Philharmonic and the Boston Symphony. While in Boston she also gave courses at Radcliffe. Arriving back in Paris, she immediately began to persuade Stravinsky that the imminent dangers of war dictated that he move to America for the duration. With an offer of the Norton lectureship from Harvard in hand, Stravinsky left for America in September 1939. Boulanger followed him in 1940 and began teaching at the Longy School in Cambridge. The extent to which many aspects of European musical life were being transferred to America became especially evident when the Fontainebleau Schools were re-formed in exile in Newport, Rhode Island, in 1941, under the directorship of the pianist Robert Casadesus, who had also fled France by this time.

In addition Krenek was now in America. The composer of the opera *Jonny spielt auf* (1927), a work more than any other reflective of the European infatuation with American popular manners, was now also involved in teaching, though from a totally different angle: Jonny's tangos and blues were soon to be replaced by an interest in the Renaissance composer Johannes Ockeghem and the contemporary Viennese serialists. Krenek's own personal style was also to take a permanent turn toward the Schoenberg camp. But Krenek has also recorded that his initial discovery of "rotation," a recondite serial principle that he was to pursue only in the later 1950s, was momentarily laid aside after the completion of an unaccompanied choral work, *Lamentatio Jeremiae Prophetae* of 1941, out of a concern for public comprehensibility—a concern similar to Schoenberg's in the music written during his first years in America.[5] After teaching in numerous locations, including Vassar beginning in 1939, then Hamline University in St. Paul, Krenek ultimately migrated to Hollywood, where he became a permanent fixture in California's cultural landscape.

Owing to the exigencies of war, American musical education had been taken securely under the wing of a European elite now transported across the Atlantic. It was a pedagogical dominance that was to last for a considerable time, and one that was in some very real measure responsible for the tenor of musical training in institutions of learning throughout the country. For in 1939 the vast majority of the most influential music professors in America either were of foreign birth or had received their advanced training abroad. In 1981 the German composer Karlheinz Stockhausen reminisced about the state of affairs in post–World War II America:

> I was there in 1958, if you can still call that after the war, and before that had been aware of what was going on in America through friends and contacts from about 1952. Boulez was there that year . . . As for an absence of tradition, what I encountered on my tour of America in 1958 was a musical life and intellectual climate entirely dominated by German and Austrian immigrants. I found myself having to defend the young American school and their more free and aleatoric music against these extraordinarily strict and dogmatic professors and teachers who had moved to America and whose influence still pervaded the atmosphere of the music faculties. It was the same wherever I went: the climate was strongly deterministic, as a result of the influence of European scientists, and the musicologists were of the same orientation. It was against the domination of music by powerful academic forces that small groups of intellectuals reacted, stimulated by abstract expressionism, dadaism and surrealism.[6]

However one might care to critique Stockhausen's observations, there can be no arguing that in the graduate disciplines of composition, music theory, and musicology foreign dominance was pervasive. The search for a distinctive American voice, however, was perhaps most discernible in composition, promoted as it was by Howard Hanson's annual festivals of American music at the Eastman School of Music, by conductors such as Serge Koussevitsky, who regularly commissioned and performed works by American composers, and even by Arturo Toscanini, who championed Ferde Grofé's *Grand Canyon Suite* and Samuel Barber's *Adagio for Strings*. It should be noted, however, that

Koussevitsky was a Russian, that Toscanini was an Italian, and that Hanson himself had studied with Respighi in Rome. American musicology, however, was in the first throes of its existence and struggling to demonstrate a standard. It was understandable that the models and the training for the discipline had been found in Europe, and 1939 was a time of turning.

Otto Kinkeldey, an American trained in Berlin as early as 1902–1909, had been appointed to the first chair in musicology at Cornell University in 1931, and in 1934 Glen Haydon arrived home from the University of Vienna, where he had recently taken his doctorate, in order to accept an appointment at Chapel Hill. With the imminent prospect of war increasingly visible, a steady stream of European-born musicologists now headed for America and quickly took up academic posts, assembling in the process a veritable Who's Who of the founding fathers of American musicology: Curt Sachs, who had left Germany in 1933, came to the United States in 1937 to take a position at New York University, and in 1939 Alfred Einstein, who had also left Germany in 1933, arrived to assume teaching duties at Smith College. Before another decade was out both Sachs and Einstein would accept visiting professorships at the University of Michigan, where a new graduate program in musicology was forming. Otto Gombosi, a Hungarian trained under Sachs in Berlin, also left for the United States in 1939, settling first in Seattle, then at Chicago and Harvard. Similarly, Manfred Bukofzer, who had studied in Heidelberg under Heinrich Besseler, moved to America in 1939, first to Case Western Reserve and then to Berkeley; Leo Schrade arrived at Yale in 1938; and in that year, the American Helen Hewitt, back from her work with Besseler in Heidelberg and Yvonne Rokseth at the Sorbonne, was the first woman to receive the Ph.D. in musicology at Radcliffe. The International Musicological Society also met for the first time in America in 1939, mirroring not only the beginnings of academic training in the discipline in our universities, but the flight of numerous music historians from Europe to America.

A similar roster can be claimed in the world of art historians and artists. George Grosz, the brilliant satirist associated with Dada and *Neue Sachlichkeit* in the late teens and twenties, arrived in New York in 1932. With the closing of the Bauhaus, the designer Josef Albers arrived at Black Mountain, North Carolina, in 1933; the architect Mies van der Rohe came directly from Germany in 1938 to establish a new institute in Chicago; and Walter Gropius, who had spent three years in London, arrived in 1937. The list of art historians was as rich as that of the musicologists: Erwin Panofsky, who came to Princeton and the Institute for Advanced Study from Hamburg in 1933, later claimed, "I was expelled into Paradise"; and H. W. Janson eluded the Nazis by accepting a German government fellowship for study in the United States, where he remained for the rest of his life. An entire faculty had been assembled for the inauguration of a new discipline in American higher education.

Of the prominent composers who fled to the United States— Schoenberg, Stravinsky, Milhaud, Britten, Hindemith, Bartók, Rachmaninov, Krenek, Korngold—Kurt Weill, who had been in America since 1935, found an audience with the greatest ease, turning the experience of his Brechtian years in Berlin to new account with surprising success. In 1937 he was drawn to Hollywood, and in 1938 he had his first big Broadway hit with *Knickerbocker Holiday,* to a book by Maxwell Anderson. It opened October 16, 1939, at the Barrymore Theatre for a run of 168 performances. Krenek's observations regarding the émigré composer's concerns for communication in a new land reflect, at least in his own mind, the anxiety of artistic transplantation:

> If Kurt Weill in America seemed to exchange the aggressive, bald, and sarcastic style of his Brecht period for the sumptuousness, the mundane sentimentality, and the, if at all, circumspect irony of the Broadway manner, he was probably hardly aware of the fact that in so doing he descended in our eyes below the level of his tradition and his earlier works. Rather he did, as he himself told me, what seemed necessary to comply with that natural, invincible urge of his to communicate via the musical theater: he adapted this communication to the only vehicle at his disposal, namely, the Broadway stage.[7]

In July of the next year the Weills would welcome their close friends Darius and Madeleine Milhaud on their arrival in New York. Milhaud was to head for Oakland, California, where he taught at Mills College from 1940 to 1947. In November 1940, after the fall of France, the internationally renowned Léger had also come to New York, where he established a studio and lectured about his own work at Yale University. Then in the summer of 1941 he went to California to teach at Mills College, where he found Darius Milhaud and André Maurois in residence. No country in the world had ever played host to such a stellar array of musical and artistic talent. As it turned out, their visits were in most instances protracted, and in many cases permanent, involving American citizenship. While the collective presence of the European composers may not have done very much to promote the emergence of a later, postwar avant-garde (which is the point of Stockhausen's and Krenek's quite different observations), their very proximity encouraged students to study their scores with care, and their best music assumed almost textbook status.

Giancarlo Menotti, Italian-born, had been in America since 1928, and the premiere in 1939 of his *The Old Maid and the Thief*, a worthy successor to his *Amelia Goes to the Ball*, gave a clear signal that *verismo* was not yet dead, and that there were viable alternatives to opera as written by Schoenberg, Berg, Hindemith, and Krenek. But there were also native Americans vigorously at work in search of an indigenous expression. Copland, having in the 1920s flirted with the European view of adapting American jazz rhythms to concert-hall music as well as with the angular cellular manipulations of Schoenberg and Webern, turned in the 1930s to a style that was both simpler and more direct. In 1939 he had just finished *Billy the Kid* and was composing *A Quiet City*. In 1939 America also heard the premiere of what many felt was the first great American symphony, Roy Harris' Symphony No. 3. Was there a European heritage here? Some have attributed the development of Harris' natural gifts for the grand line to Boulanger, Celtic folksong, and Protestant hymnody. But Harris' energetic rhythmic style, however much it may have shared with Copland via Boulanger, did not seem to pose important questions of lineage. Hear what you will in it, most Americans were content to regard it as a new voice, and one whose energy and breadth encouraged them to claim it as their own.

From another perspective, Edgard Varèse, a Parisian by birth who had come to New York in 1915 and returned to France in 1928, staying until 1933, was now back in America but in the throes of a personal depression—at a creative impasse and on the threshold of what was to be a further decade of silence. The depression had surfaced in large measure because of his momentarily stilled aspirations for a new technology which he believed America was in an ideal position to sponsor. He had already thrown a challenge to the notion of what an American music could be with his initial arrival in New York and the composition of a work provocatively entitled *Amériques* (1918–1921). This in itself was more than a little startling in light of the fact that he had been an intimate of the Parisian circle of artists and musicians from 1906 on, and had helped fan the fierce fires of French nationalism through the early years of World War I. Yet he was also conversant with the French admiration for American urban vitality and especially the Gallic capitulation to the Afro-American fusion that seemed to epitomize in some mysterious manner the societal dreams of an age. That *Amériques* called upon the rhythmic virility and swollen percussion of *Le Sacre* points not so much to a confusion of language as to the capacity for metamorphosis of a powerful language born under different auspices.

Although the French would later be the first to promote the high standing of American vernacular music, Varèse's charge to Americans stemmed principally from the fact that he believed there were other challenges that awaited them in the realm of cultivated art music. For all his Communist leanings and personal beliefs regarding the role of music in constructing an ideal and openly visionary society, his views of America, no less than the Americans' views of Europe, were clearly prompted by the perennial search for a vitalizing quality in other cultures. Indeed, having been involved in French nationalist aspirations earlier in the century, Varèse now encouraged American composers to look beyond their vernacular inheritance and to join him on an uncharted journey in search of a new world of sound.

With the New York Armory Show of 1913 many Americans may have been made aware of the vitality of European Modernism for the first time. But though awareness of developments in the visual arts and literature came relatively quickly and with immediacy, notice of events in the world of music lagged behind, in large measure owing to delayed or infrequent performances. The American premieres of Stravinsky's *Le Sacre du printemps,* for example, took place in New York, Boston, and Chicago as late as 1924, and difficult as it must be for us to imagine today, the work was unavailable on any recording.

Too, for all of their American origins, both Gertrude Stein and Ezra Pound had taken up residency abroad in the first and second decades of the century, and the progress of their art centered almost exclusively on European developments, to which they made fundamental contributions. Contrarily, Ives, denying any knowledge of contemporary European models, was busy at home staking his claim to a new perspective. But Ives and a few minor figures like Leo Ornstein stood virtually alone among musicians before the end of World War I, and though beginning with the twenties they were joined by Ruggles and Cowell and complemented by a rising group of native American composers who traveled to France to study with Nadia Boulanger in search of the European perspective, it was only with the flood of Europeans to American shores in 1939 that the mix became so rich and awareness of the artistic options of the time so heightened as to forever prohibit American musical isolationism again.

Among this company, Ruth Crawford stands out as something of an exception: she was a Modernist and a woman; she did not travel to Europe but found her training first in Chicago and later in New York; she was aware of Skriabin and Stravinsky, Honegger and Hindemith, but reacted principally to the example of Cowell, Ruggles, and Charles Seeger; she knew Whitman and the American Transcendentalists but also traded on the spiritualist strain of the Theosophists shared by artists from Chicago to Moscow. Disclaiming innocence of European examples as well as dependency upon Ives, she was nurtured by a small group of composers who had heeded Varèse's invocation to establish a Modernist American voice independent of jazz and folk idioms.[8]

Yet, though Varèse's vision was utopian and his quest was designed "to encompass everything that is human, from the primitive to the farthest reaches of science,"[9] by 1939 America, the land of dreams, had at least momentarily let him down in his effort to establish a " 'progressive' musical Americanism known as the so-called American Experimental Tradition."[10] Despite Varèse's challenge, the pervasive European emphasis on the popular side of America's musical voice undoubtedly contributed to the prevailing notion that American music was somehow defined by, perhaps even limited to, such a base. But from a larger perspective the ongoing dialectic between universalist and nationalist ideologies typically attributed to Varèse's generation was plainly not limited to composers of a Socialist or Communist orientation nor exclusively confined to proponents of cultivated or vernacular expressions. Indeed, by 1939 concern for such larger issues had already become the mark of an age now at a critical juncture and on the eve of a new world conflict.

It is clear that increasingly vocal demands to incorporate American studies into university curricula over the next half century were not only culturally responsible but retrospectively capable of being diagnosed as a reply to issues well beyond nationalism. The idea that a consideration of "American music," for example, would by definition incorporate colonialist religious music on the one hand, vernacular musics on the other, and that it would be crowned by a consideration of fusions inherent in Afro-Asian alliances signaled a powerful sense of social imperative inherent in such studies. At the same time it endorsed a tendency to soft-pedal, if not outright deny, the European legacy and to claim a newly emerging voice "rooted in the soil" even in the face of overt emulative practices. Such an attitude was, perhaps somewhat predictably, commensurate with the Puritan call to "first times," and in harmony with the aspirations of those eager to locate America's cultural footing in a time that preceded the first emigrations to the North American continent, to sidestep in some measure those Occidental foundations which had been left behind, and simultaneously to assert the possibility of cultural revelation.[11]

Nonetheless, the commanding presence of some of Europe's finest talents quickly left a mark upon America's developing musical taste and manners. In the season 1938–39, for example, Bartók gave the musical world a series of pieces that were to become classics of the repertoire: the *Sonata for Two Pianos and Percussion;* the final volume of his *Mikrokosmos,* Book VI; the *Divertimento for Strings;* the Violin Concerto No. 2; the sixth and last of his string quartets; and *Contrasts* for violin, clarinet, and piano. Bartók's arrival in America at this time explains the American component in the premiere of *Contrasts,* given by Bartók in collaboration with Joseph Szigeti and Benny Goodman. In this connection it should be observed that the prolonged presence in America of numerous instrumentalists and singers had helped set new standards of performance as well. Russian artists such as Heifetz, Piatigorsky, Rubinstein, and Horowitz were all recognized as a familiar part of the musical scene, as were other Europeans such as Toscanini, Flagstad, Melchior, and Lotte Lehmann.

But in addition to the standard concert repertoire performed by these virtuoso artists, the period also witnessed a search for contemporary values in the performance of earlier music, discussed today under the rubric of "authenticity and early music" or, more recently, "historically informed performance." In 1938–39 a composer-son and a composer-wife team, Igor and Soulima Stravinsky and Béla and Ditta Bartók, recorded performances of Mozart four-hand piano music with vastly different approaches: Stravinsky's rendition was "pure, simple, dry, geometric, and hard" (to invoke Richard Taruskin's judgments), a dramatic contrast with Bartók's interpretation, which was laced with crescendi and diminuendi, accelerandi and ritardandi.[12] The aesthetic foundations of Neoclassicism sounded in Stravinsky's *Poetics of Music,* published in

1939, were being tried out in an unsuspected venue, carrying with it signals of contemporary taste as unmistakable as a new work by the composer. The flight of the harpsichordist Wanda Landowska from Paris to America the next year followed immediately by her dazzling public performances of the Goldberg Variations helped underscore Stravinsky's orientation in an extraordinarily dramatic fashion. It is perhaps not too much to claim that something of their collective example continues to resonate to the present day in the early music movement, in the continuing investigation of performance practices, and in the resuscitation of early instrumental models.

Thus America, traditionally a host to émigrés from all over the world, in the late 1930s experienced an unprecedented infusion of artistic and intellectual talent due to recent political events. Yet, the momentary sense of personal security which many European artists and scholars must have felt in their flight was undoubtedly accompanied by a sense of loss. If the zeal of a Schoenberg, Hindemith, or Schrade in pointing out a perceived standard to their adopted country was sometimes messianic and occasionally accompanied by the wag of a finger, more often than not they can be said to have worked tirelessly in the transference of the best of their musical culture to a new land. In addition, Europe's long-standing infatuation with America's cinema and popular music was now played out in person in Hollywood and on Broadway. It would be difficult to maintain that the resultant transformations in both spheres compromised or halted the development of a burgeoning desire for an identifiable American music or thwarted the discovery of whatever might be said to constitute bona fide American values. For it was in some large measure due to this accident of world history that America prospered and discovered new patterns in the patchwork quilt of its art and society.

In the writing of *The Making of Americans* Gertrude Stein set out to describe the creation of the American people, following a representative family in its emigration from the Old World to a new land and their trek across the continent to California. Ultimately, she had difficulty trying to decide what it meant to write such a history: "Were the descendants of German immigrants to stand for the American experience, or did she wish to describe types of people more fundamentally conceived than nationalism would allow? The answer was that she was doing both."[13] It seems that much the same thing happened with respect to American musical manners. Most of the European émigré composers brought with them ideas for a music that had developed under patently national sponsorship, and the circumstances behind their removal to America could only have exacerbated this sense of national identity. Thus it is understandable that the search in the 1930s for an American musical profile surfaced not so much through a direct scrutiny and review of national goals and idioms as in the natural playing out of the talent of the principal players of diverse origins who came together during the course of world events.

The year 1939 was an end as well as a beginning in many ways, and the new musical energies that were amassing in America had counterparts not only in art and art history, science and social science, but along a whole technological range: John Atanasoff and his computer; Chester Carlson and the Xerox copier; jet-powered planes as well as microwave technology—all made their appearance in that year. But the implications of these breakthroughs were only dimly perceived, and in some instances they were ignored or rejected as impractical dreams. Like the inventors, however, composers in tandem with performers stuck with their investigations, and because of world events an enlarged range of options was near at hand. American musical higher education made a dramatic shift in its announced goals as well as in the quality of its training. Schoenberg, Stravinsky, Hindemith, and Bartók collectively proved to be a powerful force in the formation of a sense of musical identity—not so much for a nation as for an age. Both Schoenberg and Hindemith assumed an important and sustained pedagogical role; Stravinsky and Bartók did not. Yet their aggregate presence in America seemed to encourage the belief that henceforth it would be possible for an aspiring musician in any discipline to train and develop at home. Talents, small and large, could engage the composers in dialogue, confront their scores, ponder their alchemy, and commandeer their most trenchant aphorisms in the service of self-discovery.

In spite of these prevailing winds, America's discovery of its musical voice was patently not limited to a Eurocentric orientation. For if many Americans had long taken pride in the vitality of black American jazz in its various guises and had taken note of the European infatuation with it, an increased interest in those musical roots centered in national folk musics, also observable in virtually all European cultures during the nineteenth century, had begun to take hold in America. Charles Seeger (1886–1979), one of the founding fathers of American musicology and ethnomusicology, spoke to the issue in 1939 in studies entitled

"Grassroots for American Music" as well as "The Importance to Cultural Understanding of Folk and Popular Music,"[14] and busied himself with transcriptions of Appalachian folksong. The latter were ultimately published with the assistance of his second wife, Ruth Crawford, and John and Alan Lomax. And a singer and player of the guitar, harmonica, and fiddle named Woody Guthrie, who had felt the sting of the Depression and had experienced the Dust Bowl of 1935 from Oklahoma to California, was recorded at length by Lomax for the Library of Congress in 1940. Joining Charles Seeger's son, Pete, in a folksong sextet called the Almanac Singers, Guthrie was to become a legend and one of the most vigorous influences in the folksong revival of the 1950s. From the beginning such activity did not escape the attention of American composers like Aaron Copland and Roy Harris, who realized that while citation of America's folk balladry could not assure the birth of a vital American music any more than it had done for Scotland in the nineteenth century, knowledge of indigenous folk repertoires offered the same potential previously recognized by Stravinsky and Bartók, Berg and Hindemith, Holst and Vaughan Williams.

But beyond European and native repertoires, other angles beckoned as well. Because of the war many American citizens traveled and returned with new perspectives; many migrated and settled in different parts of the country—Southerners came North, Easterners discovered California; and the ethnic diversity of Europe, Central and South America, the Caribbean, and the Orient spilled across the land and became a permanent part of the social landscape. During the thirties musical visits and exchanges by composers like Copland, Carlos Chávez, and Villa-Lobos brought an increasing awareness of the music of Mexico, Brazil, Argentina, and the Caribbean and promoted the ideal of a musical Pan-American union. World War II, which was fought in the Pacific and North Africa as well as on the European continent, also took many Americans to Asia for the first time, and their return brought a new sense of the East to the national conscience on all fronts. Even before the war, Californians such as Cowell, Cage, and Harrison, as well as the Canadian Colin McPhee, who also eventually ended up in California, had looked westward across the Pacific for inspiration. Finally, and fundamentally, the African-American musical sensibility, which had been developing since the turn of the century, continued to fuel the composite nature of America's musical resource, which was clearly a mirror of its ethnic diversity.

Thus, the exodus by European composers to America in the thirties as well as the first-hand observations by American performers and composers at home and in lands south of its borders and in the Pacific encouraged not only an enlarged perspective but a diversity of expression hardly imaginable at the turn of the century. Although all these factors played a role in the formation of whatever it was that was to constitute American music, the magic was to be explained not by any formula but by the recognition of a Grand Collage of the social, artistic, and political events that occurred between 1900 and 1950. If the force of multicultural interaction was not new, the range and immediacy were. Too, if intermittent expressions of regret persisted regarding America's perceived Eurocentrism, such adjudications rang hollow to those who realized that neither of the adjectives "European" and "American" had ever been culturally pure, unified, or uncontaminated by exposure to global perspectives; that, indeed, their respective histories were in large part the tale of multicultural interchange. Finally, the advantages of inclusion were obvious unless the aim was to locate a mythic Ur-expression with no possible claim to authenticity. And by 1939 the pluralism of America's culture had become too pronounced to tempt many to such an adventure.

Nineteen thirty-nine, which saw the publication of Joyce's *Finnegans Wake,* has in the eyes of some been claimed as the year that brought the end of Modernism as an international movement and, hence, signaled a time of turning to a new age of Postmodernism.[15] Others would contend that for America Modernism has continued to serve as the dominant culture from the end of World War I to the present day.[16] If we accept James McFarlane's view of an incipient Bohemian phase of Modernism that placed a premium upon rebellion and embraced fracture, a secondary stage that witnessed the restructuring of the parts and an attempt to re-relate the fragments which it had initially separated, and a closing period characterized by "a dissolving, a blending, a merging of things previously held to be forever mutually exclusive,"[17] then it is possible to assert that by 1939 ingredients had been assembled in America sufficient not only to proclaim a diverse cultural expression but to position a young society well within the embrace of Modernism's final maturity.

It was not until the early 1950s, however, that the impact of these developments was sufficient to allow the sense of fruition necessary to any perception of closure and an ensuing quest for a new and empowering aesthetic. Understandably, virile confrontation and occasional co-operation between trans-Atlantic musical avant-gardes occurred, even as attempts to formulate a postwar schedule quickly promoted a continuing struggle with the formalistic arguments of the twenties: serialism (total order) squared off with Dada (chance) even as Neoclassicism was momentarily confined to a rattling cage. By this time, Americans—home from the wars and no longer reliant upon the stories of their fathers about World War I or upon the Lost Generation for a portrait of Paris—commanded an increasingly secure voice in the definition of new agendas, both high and low, to which the Europeans now clearly began to pay heed.

If it is proper to state that "Modernism was an affair of many movements, of a common avant-gardizing tendency with international origins, a massive and constant change of personnel, and considerable capacity for transit,"[18] then we may fairly argue that with the intellectual and artistic exodus that immediately preceded the first declarations of World War II not only had all of the conditions been met on American soil for confrontation with a new aesthetic but they had become so incorporated within the social and political fabric as to render mute any and all demands for capitulation to a label. The dialectic of "old authority" and "new culture" circumspectly announced the passing of an age and beckoned the dawn of an era as yet unnamed. In retrospect it seems clear that the wake of 1939 was not only for Finnegan.[19]

— 15 —

Tristan's Scissors

In the shops in Barcelona instead of post cards they had square
little frames and inside it was placed a cigar, a real one, a pipe,
a bit of handkerchief etcetera, all absolutely the arrangement of
many a cubist picture and helped out by cut paper representing
other objects. That is the modern note that in Spain had been
done for centuries.

Gertrude Stein

Cutting and Pasting: 1900–1925

From the first decades of the century the ancient power of invoking
familiar material was accorded fresh recognition in music, literature,
and art. Indeed, bipartisan appropriations of folk and classic repertoires
familiar in the works of Stravinsky were conspicuous in most composers
of the day. Hungarian, Bulgarian, Romanian, and Arabic folksong together with the music of Domenico Scarlatti, Debussy, Schoenberg,
Liszt, and Beethoven were candidly announced as the foundation of
Bartók's art as early as his Piano Concerto No. 1 of 1926.[1] And we
know that Hindemith's affinity for the shimmy and the fox trot as well
as for Gregorian chant and German folksong was as central to his art
as Carinthian tune and polka, tango and chorale were for Berg. In each
instance a personal style was coined not so much through the appropriation of ingredients from a particular cultural or historical model as
through a mode of critique.

It was a posture that was also familiar to the French in such fin-de-
siècle composers as Emmanuel Chabrier and Erik Satie. Debussy and
Ravel, too, early showed an interest in exploring the issue not only
through allusions to the Orient and Spain but in the citation of the
masters and folktunes alike. Yet beyond typical claims of respect inher-

ent in the marriage of high art and the *Volk* of multiple cultures throughout the history of music and art, there is another way of viewing such a resplendent game: the musical object may be moved outside the realm of aesthetic function into the arenas of social and political discourse. The collage principle now passes to a different level of criticism.

From such an angle Debussy's "Et la lune descend sur le temple qui fut" might well be viewed as a perfumed attempt at sanitizing colonialist perjuries, and "Feux d'artifice" of 1913, in its scintillating resonance of a citation from the "Marseillaise" in a distant key, as a celebration of French imperialism on the eve of impending world conflict with the Germans. From this perspective, Satie's abortive "Le feu d'artifice" of 1914 could then be perceived not so much as a spoof of Debussy's aesthetic grandeur but as a prefiguration of the collapse of national aspirations: the composer invites the dismissal of his own music, and the anti–masterpiece mentality of Dada is just around the corner. In an even more startling juxtaposition, Debussy cited both American and German musical manners in his "Golliwog's Cakewalk" from the *Children's Corner* suite (1906–1908). Employing cut and paste techniques in a series of flip-flop citations of American ragtime and Wagner's *Tristan*, Debussy's seemingly slight piano piece could hardly be dismissed as simple fashion or blatant parody given the growing importance of *art nègre* for contemporary French culture and of the master of Bayreuth for Debussy's personal musical development to that time.[2]

Taking another work premiered in 1913, how should we read *The Rite of Spring*: as a neonationalist pronouncement; as a seminal voice in the construction of a transcendental Primitivist vision for the twentieth century; as a useful agent in defining a contemporary view of the individual and the present-day aspirations of the historical tribe; or, in more Freudian terms, as an illumination of the link between the distant dreams of childhood and the immediate pressures of daily experience?[3] If so, what use do we have for the technical observations of Bartók, Messiaen, Boulez, Allen Forte, and Pieter van den Toorn regarding the work's structure that were elaborated over the three-quarters of a century following the work's premiere? It is possible in turn, of course, to interpret the investigations of each of these authors not as formalist documents at all, but rather as politically charged statements: Bartók in order to forward his own views regarding the rich potential of synthesizing the folk resource and to promote his own nationalist objectives; Messiaen to validate his theories of scalar systems and rhythm, which stood at the heart of his own compositional approach, and perhaps to bolster claims to an enhanced French legacy; Boulez not only to notarize the "birth certificate of modern music" but to register a constructive interpretation that could buttress his own relation to the developing tradition; and Forte and van den Toorn not only to bring rational order to perceived chaos but understandably to validate their own evolving theories through application to an acknowledged masterpiece.

In America, too, Charles Ives demonstrated the power of multiple messages in searching out the possibilities of a speech worthy of a young but maturing nation. His *Flanders Field* (1917) sets the openly maudlin text of John McCrae in the company of ingenious combinations of the "Marseillaise," "America," and "Columbia, the Gem of the Ocean." McCrae's text was known to many a school child at the time, and the tunes chosen by Ives were known to them as well. Memory, nostalgia, and fantasy potentially flood the listener, and composite citation encourages intertextual interpretation without freezing the message. Ives's surface symbolism, though not difficult to read, is less obvious in its reference to Debussy, who had also placed "God Save the Queen" ("America") in octaves in the bass of his "Hommage à S. Pickwick Esq., P.P.M.P.C," and had used the identical interior snippet from the "Marseillaise" in the soprano of his "Feux d'artifice," both *Préludes* from Book II published only a few years before. Notice of the relationship brings to mind Ives's boldly stated opinion that Debussy might have been a better composer had his spiritual premise been stronger and his "form," "perfume," and "manner" less obviously in control. Ives's manipulation of identical source materials in the same registers therefore invites comparison, and his avoidance of Romantic sentimentality or Impressionist mists (Ives was capable of both) carries the ring of an aesthetic challenge. Indeed, Ives's song contains a double-edged message. For if the work can be described as subtextually anti-Debussy, it was on the surface pro-French in a way that was not characteristic of Ives. This is explainable, however, not only by the historically shared aspirations of America and France with respect to questions of *liberté* and *fraternité* but by the immediate involvement of both countries as allies in a world then at war.

These several test cases only confirm the force as well as the dilemma of an increased reliance upon the technique of collage: cut and paste techniques from multiple sources not only provoke an expanded awareness of the time-space factor on the technical front but invite, even

demand, multiple assessments without claim to priority from the interpretive angle. The plurality of materials in the original assemblage exacts
a critical explosion.

The power of collage was explored along only partially new frontiers
in the immediate post–World War I years. Following the earlier lead
of Marcel Duchamp in his *Erratum musical* of 1913,[4] Tristan Tzara
clipped words from a newspaper article in 1919, tossed them into a
paper bag, and copied them anew in the order in which they were
removed. Chance discovery now mixed with an anti-art stance that
decried expression and sentimentality, and at the Cabaret Voltaire in
Zurich Emmy Hennings sang to the accompaniment of Hugo Ball on
programs that included the music of Skriabin and Varèse, simultaneous
poetry readings, the noise-music of the Futurist Luigi Russolo's *intonarumori,* and the improvisation of Negro rhythms on drums.

Having been blackballed by Richard Huelsenbeck from membership
in the Berlin Club Dada, Kurt Schwitters established his own chapter
in Hanover after the war under a new logo, "Merz." The word had
no meaning and had been discovered by Schwitters quite by accident
in the act of fitting a letterhead of the Commerz- und Privatbank into
a collage.[5] Schwitters sought to free art from traditional materials and
techniques as well as from socially motivated expression both in his
junk-art concoctions, which he called "Merzbilden," and in his *Sonate
in Urlauten,* a study in meaningless linguistic sounds recited at the Bauhaus in 1924. An easy and natural transfer of the principles of collage—
both in the work of the Cubists and in the music of Stravinsky and
Satie—to the work of the Dadaists can be reasonably claimed. And
Schwitters himself reinforced the potent agency of the found object in
exploring the boundaries between speech and music by acknowledging
that the rondo-like manipulation of sounds in his *Sonate in Urlauten* had
its genesis in proof sheets for the selection of typefaces.[6] The work was
begun in 1922, and the first part appeared in the *Internationale Revue* in
November 1927, but the completed work in four movements, with an
introduction, a conclusion, and a cadenza in the fourth movement, was
published in Hanover under the title *Ursonate* with typography by Jan
Tschichold only in 1932 (Figure 15.1).

Beyond their abstract qualities the creations of Schwitters and the
Dadaists also meshed naturally with and were supported by the trans-
forming aesthetic of Primitivism in the 1920s. In *Flight Out of Time*
Hugo Ball quoted his poem "Gadjiberibimba":

EINLEITUNG:

Fümms bö wö tää zää Uu,	**1**
pögiff,	
kwii Ee.	

Ooooooooooooooooooooooooooooooooooo,	
dll rrrrrr beeeee bö, **(A)**	**5**
dll rrrrrr beeeee bö fümms bö,	
rrrrrr beeeee bö fümms bö wö,	
beeeee bö fümms bö wö tää,	
bö fümms bö wö tää zää,	
fümms bö wö tää zää Uu:	

ERSTER TEIL:

Thema 1.

Fümms bö wö tää zää Uu,	**1**
pögiff,	
kwii Ee.	

Thema 2.

Dedesnn nn rrrrrr,	**2**
Ii Ee,	
mpiff tillff too,	
tillll,	
Jüü Kaa?	
(gesungen)	

Thema 3.

Rinnzekete bee bee nnz krr müü?	**3**
ziiuu ennze, ziiuu rinnzkrrmüü,	
rakete bee bee.	**3a**

Thema 4.

Rrummpff tillff toooo?	**4**

ÜBERLEITUNG.

Ziiuu ennze ziiuu nnzkrrmüü,	**3**
Ziiuu ennze ziiuu rinnzkrrmüü:	
rakete bee bee? rakete bee zee.	**3a**

DURCHARBEITUNG.

Fümms bö wö tää zää Uu,	**U1**
Uu zee tee wee bee fümmmms.	
Rakete rinnzekete **(B)**	**U2**
rakete rinnzekete	
rakete rinnzekete	
rakete rinnzekete	
rakete rinnzekete	
rakete rinnzekete	
Beeeee	
bö.	

fö	**1**
böwö	
fümmsbö	
böwörö	
fümmsböwö	
böwörötää	
fümmsböwötää	
böwörötääzää	**395**

Figure 15.1. Kurt Schwitters, "Meine *Sonate in Urlauten*," *Internationale Revue,* November 1927. It is the first part of Schwitters' *Ursonate,* here under the title *Sonate in Urlauten.*

> gadji beri bimba
> glandridi lauli lonni cadori
> gadjama bim beri glassala
> glandradi glassala tuffm i zimbrabim
> blassa galassasa tuffm i zimbrabim.

and spoke of its effect in performance, noting that his voice involuntarily took on a ceremonious cadence akin to the priestly lamentations handed down in the liturgical chants of Occident and Orient. He claimed that such sound-poems were intended as a rejection of "the corrupted language made impossible by journalism," and that the search for the "innermost alchemy of the word" necessitated giving up the word entirely.[7]

Preference for the sound and rhythm of language over meaning and etymology can be observed in a wide range of venues from the Russian and Italian Futurists to numerous ethnic groups including the American Iroquois,[8] but also in the work of Mallarmé and especially Stravinsky from *Zvezdoliki* (1911) and *Renard* (1915) to *Les Noces* (1914–1923) and *Oedipus* (1927) and more recently in the work of Luciano Berio (*Circles*, 1960; *Visage*, 1961) and Milton Babbitt (*Phonemena*, 1974). Furthermore, the possibilities for wordplay in both polyglot pun and neologism had been repeatedly demonstrated in the works of Joyce and his contemporaries. But Richard Huelsenbeck, while noting that sonic discoveries had been made in the juxtaposition of phonemes and syllables that were denied to coherent poetry, left no doubt that in the recitations of the Dadaists he heard "one of the many manifestations in our time of the primitivistic tendency." He was reminded, he said, of the rediscovery of Negro art, the drawings in the caves of Altamira and Lascaux, children's art and folk art, and saw in them a common impulse for aesthetic and moral renewal. He concluded, however, that "the roaring of the Ashanti and the babbling of an infant are interesting rhythmically—Gershwin and Stravinsky are the ones to use such sounds—but babbling is not language."[9]

The ultimate demonstration of a tendency toward a nihilistic meta-collage was made by the Dadaists in their only theatrical experiment, the ballet *Relâche,* performed on December 4, 1924. Commissioned by Rolf de Maré, director of the Ballets Suédois, it had a scenario by Francis Picabia and music by Erik Satie. It opened to a stage covered with circular metal discs with an electric bulb shining from each. Cast in two acts with a cinematic entr'acte, it celebrated the Art of the Everyday in an absurdist romp patently indebted to the music-hall variety revue. A fireman chain-smoked cigarettes in contravention of city fire ordinances and throughout the evening poured water from one bucket to another. An anonymous figure periodically measured the stage, and "quotation" was introduced through the brief illumination of a naked couple posed as Cranach's *Adam and Eve,* Adam being portrayed by Duchamp. *Relâche* can mean "No Performance" as well as "relaxation," and both inferences were honored: amusement and annihilation of the theater took place simultaneously.

Satie's exasperatingly minimalist music, whose repetitions recall nothing so much as a needle stuck in the groove of a phonograph record, accompanied the entr'acte and was claimed as the first music written expressly for a film; the film itself was made by Duchamp and Picabia in collaboration with a young cameraman, René Clair. The *danseur* Jean Börlin, dressed in a ballerina's skirt, was filmed from below as he jumped up and down on a glass pane—recalling for those in the know his disguised performances as the Trouville Bathing Beauty in Cocteau's *Les Mariés* three years before; a chess game between Marcel Duchamp and Man Ray with Satie as kibitzer took place on the roof of the Théâtre des Champs-Élysées; and a funeral procession with a hearse drawn by a camel ended with the appearance of a grinning corpse that makes all of the mourners disappear through the magic of film. The second act contained more of the same kind of provocation, including a sign which announced "Satie is the greatest musician in the world," and the whole spectacle was brought to a conclusion with the authors driving on stage in a 5-h.p. Citroën. They were greeted with catcalls, and the Ballets Suédois was dissolved forever. As Rolf de Maré put it: "*Relâche* was too much for all of us."

Nonetheless, Vsevolod Meyerhold's agitprop production *D.E. (Give Us Europe)* of the same year not only traded on the earlier Russian Futurist wing in placing a high premium upon street language and graffiti but epitomized the continuing rage for social collage in the search for a relevant eccentric theater. In retrospect it is apparent that the range of images clearly reflects the age: "Chaplinesque routines of cannibalism conducted by British lords in rocking chairs alternated with vigorous displays of biomechanical etudes by Red sailors . . . followed still by wild apache dance numbers to the music of Moscow's first live jazz band."[10] Yet, despite Paris' momentary exhaustion and Moscow's turning away from the avant-garde as an agent for social progress by decade's end, the taste for paste and scissors was destined to return with a vengeance at century's close.

Samplings: Postwar and Postmodern

Modernism's purported effort to escape the dominant culture and to promote artistic autonomy has now been declared an illusion by the Postmodernists. In such a critical stance, *deconstruction* was born: not only were all texts now seen to conceal the seeds of their opposite as well as all intermediate grounds, but the notion of a creative construction or discovery that certifies the self's power to act autonomously was held to be a fiction.[11] This loss of constructive power leads inevitably to the disappearance of the category of the masterpiece. And it now seems clear that at least for a time society not only ceased expecting masterpieces from the entire generation of composers who surfaced immediately after World War II, but also, perhaps somewhat subliminally, viewed any presence of politics in the arts as an unattractive alliance in light of memories of the notable repressions of the Third Reich and practices still continuing in the Soviet Union at that time.[12] The decade of the 1950s was allied, however, with developments in music composition that were perceived as anything but frivolous. Indeed, the dual advent of total serialism and aleatory techniques, locked in a deadly struggle for survival, characterized a period of aesthetic political conflict during which, as Boulez later suggested, the paralyzing prominence of theory and polemic virtually ruled out composition.

In Britten's *War Requiem* of 1961 collage played a handy role in momentarily resurrecting the idea of the masterpiece, addressing in the process society's need for a type of canonization long dormant. In the process a retrospective spotlight was thrown upon the unwillingness to confer such status on most works written during the 1950s. World War II had been finished for over a decade, but problems of a divided Germany and a hostile Soviet Union made the spectre of World War III a horrifying possibility. In this light the textual solution of troping the Requiem Mass with the World War I poetry of Wilfred Owen was a masterstroke, and early performances, which showcased an English tenor (Peter Pears), a German baritone (Dietrich Fischer-Dieskau), and a Russian soprano (Galina Vishnevskaya), were calculated to dramatize the intentions behind the composer's creation with rare poignancy. But beyond the circumstances surrounding the genesis of the *War Requiem,* the collection of ingredients which formed to make such a statement also spoke of the age's taste for pluralistic commentary: the antiquity of the mass is counterbalanced by a poetry written in World War I and set to music by an English composer fifteen years after the end of World War II; Ralph Vaughan Williams' *Dona nobis pacem* (1936) served as an unmistakable prewar textual model and Berlioz in part an instrumental one; the locus of the premiere was the new Coventry Cathedral standing next to the bombed-out shell of the old one; and international implications reflective of the 1960s were soon added through the choice of performers for a recording that was widely circulated.

From the 1950s on, however, other agencies had surfaced to offer liberation from the paralyzing polemics issuing from Darmstadt that regarded serialism as the only possible language of the future. Though a working model of a tape recording machine had been developed by 1935, it was not commercially available until after World War II. At that time Cage composed his first tape piece, *Imaginary Landscape No. 5* (1952), using the new technology in a manner clearly dependent on Dadaist practice: forty-two phonograph records were transferred to tape, which was then sliced into segments of varying lengths, the reassemblage being accomplished according to chance operations. But prior to Cage's contribution the French had already embarked on a systematic investigation of the possibilities of tape in connection with the cataloguing of a repertoire of sounds in nature. Dubbed *musique concrète,* its fascination was dependent as much upon modes of manipulation as it was upon the source of its materials, and Tristan Tzara's scissors were readymade for the task at hand. Pierre Schaeffer's *Étude aux chemins de fer* (1948), a three-minute early classic of its kind, assembled and juxtaposed the sounds of railway trains for a "concert of noises" that was broadcast over French radio. Though many, with some reason, declared a preference for the idealized locomotive of Honegger's *Pacific 231,* continuities between the new technology and both Futurism and Dada had been clearly demonstrated.

The early history of electronic music was closely allied with tape, and editing techniques involving splicing and overlay were by definition akin to notions of collage investigated in painting, literature, music, and the cinema in the early decades. From Earle Brown to the intuitive scores and performance options of Stockhausen, Boulez, and Witold Lutosławski, the power of collage was soon echoed in ways well beyond the initial infatuation with Dada as inherited directly from the experience of Cubism. Collage also served numerous other composers in their initial approaches to electronic composition such as Stockhausen's *Gesang der Jünglinge* (1955–56) and Varèse's *Poème électronique* (1958).

In its search for abstract formalizations and its investigation of the power of serialism and chance, the period of the fifties was frequently preoccupied with the elimination of all references to the known and preformed. Although *musique concrète* was premised upon the manipulation of sounds from nature and the everyday, transformation typically removed the sources beyond ready recognition. Beginning with the sixties, however, Stockhausen and others once again appropriated and integrated "not only 'found *sound*-objects'. . . , but also fragments of 'found *music*-objects' (from all possible epochs and lands)" in the exploration of a new sound world. Stockhausen's *Hymnen,* an integrated treatment of snippets from national anthems heard as though over a shortwave set, testified to the lure of such repertoires: "Naturally, national anthems are more than that: they are 'loaded' with time, with history—with past, present and future. They accentuate the subjectivity of peoples in a time when uniformity is all too often mistaken for universality."[13] In 1970 Stockhausen attempted to distinguish between his compositional process and the notion of musical collage as practiced earlier in the century. Noting that the collages of Berg, Stravinsky, and Varèse "were pasted over, under, or next to one another," he claimed that with the introduction of electronic techniques such as intermodulation in works like *Momente* (1961–1964), *Telemusik* (1966), *Hymnen* (1965–1967), and *Kurzwellen* (1968–1970) he had attempted to remove all the glaring dualisms of time and culture in a new synthesis.[14]

The decades of the seventies through the nineties continued to explore the power of familiar metaphors and to propose unsuspected affinities with earlier collage practices. The Soviet composer Dmitri Shostakovich, who returned repeatedly to the symphony in his last years, completed his legacy in the form with Symphony No. 15 of 1971, a work that has continued to perplex the program annotators as much as the deconstructionists. The first movement, purportedly located in a toy shop, recalls both the venue and metaphor of Debussy's *La Boîte à joujoux:* alternating between light-hearted and sardonic moods, it plays host to a citation from Rossini's *William Tell* and a bassoon figure from Tchaikovsky's Fifth Symphony. The opening of the last movement in turn is devoted to an expansive recollection of the "Fate" motif from Wagner's Ring cycle and the opening measures of *Tristan and Isolde.* Few listeners were content to view the symphony as a potpourri of familiar tunes, however, or as a concession to public taste; rather it was heard as the autobiography of a persecuted artist in a police state that pointedly called upon highly recognizable musical symbols of irony and death.

The American Christopher Rouse, who in turn cited Shostakovich's own musical signature D–S–C–H (D–E♭–C–B) in his Symphony No. 1 of 1986, took as a more fundamental point of departure the "Adagio" of Bruckner's Symphony No. 7. But Bruckner's work, which was a memorial to Wagner as well as a testament to the idea of the cultural hero, is stood on its head: Rouse, like Bruckner, employs Wagner's tubas, but in a direct thematic reference Rouse exchanges the order of the model's opening intervals and the tonal dialectic of the whole is maneuvered (E, D, d, E♭) in a symbolic negation of Bruckner's intent.

Similar relocations of material and meaning surfaced in David Gompper's celebration of the five hundredth anniversary of Columbus' voyage in a work entitled *Transitus* (1992) for large wind ensemble. Ignoring postcolonial indictments, the young American composer focused instead on the voyage as metaphor. For beyond the serene evocation of vast oceanic expanses at the outset, the ringing climaxes in the approach to the point of no return, and the pacific conclusion attendant to land's unexpected appearance, the work carries multiple cultural and constructive messages well beyond narrative concerns: Gompper has adopted specific harmonic skeletons and timbral flashes from Lutosławski's orchestral *Postludium* (1960) and recast them as a preludial port of debarkation that soon disappears from sight in a metaphorical journey to a new land.

Other modes of manipulating received material were explored by the Argentinian composer Mauricio Kagel, whose music typically rests on the sophisticated treatment of the banal and the absurd or conversely on the positioning of sublime materials in hackneyed contexts. In a work called *Quodlibet* he explored the potential of a group of fifteenth-century French chanson texts, and in another piece entitled *Dance School (Tanzschule),* based upon an eighteenth-century dance textbook, Kagel appropriated some seventy different dance scenes and supplied them with commentary, pictures, and corresponding dance tunes. Authenticity in the execution of dances ranging from court ballets to folk and peasant varieties was not at issue, only the confection of what Kagel called "the first systematic attempt to achieve an all-comprehensive dance theater. In consequence, one might consider it to be *a guide to total collage,* with frame structures so porous that further discoveries (from the immediate surroundings, from history, fiction, literature) can be inserted, 'mounted in.' "[15] Kagel's plan recognized humanity's random non-chronological accession of culture and confirmed that the need to look everywhere, to reassemble, and to catalogue in the name of art had become epidemic. But it also clearly endorsed the hope that such cultural outreach could rejuvenate the very process of music, that henceforth it might be possible "to consider a composition purely in the category of 'becoming.' "[16]

Another type of collage with a strong historical resonance also flourished in virtually every decade from the 1920s on in works by numerous composers that completed music left unfinished: realizations by Hindemith, Orff, Krenek, Berio, and Henze of unrealized continuos in operas or opera scenes by Monteverdi; or Stravinsky's addition of only a single missing line to Gesualdo's canonic motets *Assumpta est Maria* or *Da pacem Domine* (1959), for example. A kindred fascination also surfaced with music that has come down to us absolutely intact. Bernard Rands's *Madrigali,* for example, uses pieces from Monteverdi's eighth book of madrigals as a point of departure. Obviously what the composer does with the adopted material quickly becomes an issue as important as the source itself, and in this particular instance Rands's principal gambit focuses on a dramatic slowing of the harmonic rhythm in the interest of clarifying a complex of surface details: a twentieth-century X-ray of a seventeenth-century masterwork, if you will.

Beyond such technical solutions, combinations of social, political, and aesthetic messages resounded in a great deal of music written from the seventies through the nineties. Hans Werner Henze repeatedly addressed contemporary issues attendant to the contemplation of a social world order in his stage works. But in a work for piano, orchestra, and tape of 1973, he also symbolically invoked a fourteenth-century instrumental "Lamento di Tristan" alongside a citation from Wagner's study for *Tristan,* "Im Treibhaus," and a textual quotation from Gottfried von Strassburg. In such conjugations Henze emphasized less the erotic aspect of Wagner's music than the enduring power of one of Western civilization's greatest love stories. Similarly, if Jakob Druckman's *Lamia* for soprano and orchestra of 1975 initially appeared to point to the composer's specific infatuation with the seventeenth century and Cavalli, the very range of his references—from Ovid, French folk texts, Wagner, and Cavalli to bird song, *Sprechstimme,* and in the final section a Malaysian folk text—suggested that Druckman was attempting a statement that broadly hints at universals. It also placed listeners in a position where they had to be familiar with the references or be cut off from the message. Now, in fact, few listeners would know or be able to identify Cavalli specifically, but it is reasonable to expect that many would recognize the style as pre-modern, and for some it would register as pre-Mozart. With a note from the composer that its music originally accompanied a legendary figure such as Dido, the listener's memory is activated and cannot be prevented from forming its own fantasy discourse.[17]

From the late 1960s on an increasing awareness of the possibilities of collage was audible along an expanded base of operations. Colgrass's *As Quiet As* (1966) took a simple Beethoven sonatina and served it up à la Haydn, Stravinsky, Webern, and Count Basie. And in *Ancient Voices of Children* (1970) George Crumb set texts by Lorca concerned with " 'ur-concepts' . . . embodied in a language which is primitive and stark." His search for an appropriate musical response led him to include numerous devices: "bending" the pitch of the piano with a chisel applied to the strings, paper-threaded harp, mandolins tuned a quarter-tone low, Tibetan prayer stone, Japanese temple bells, and tuned tom-toms. In addition, he professed a naturalness in calling upon a host of unrelated stylistic elements: "a suggestion of Flamenco with a Baroque quotation . . . or a reminiscence of Mahler with a breath of the Orient."[18]

Compulsion to citation has frequently been prompted, however, by circumstances that do not appear readily on the surface. Alfred Schnittke, whose music first became widely known outside the Soviet Union in the late 1970s and 1980s, showed a particular disposition to play the collage game throughout this period—not via his native Russian repertoires but through an obsessive exploration of Western European traditions, both high and low. In this it is possible to view him as an agent provocateur in the dissolution of the Iron Curtain mentality. In his Symphony No. 1 (1969–1972), which cites passages from Beethoven, Chopin, Strauss, Grieg, Tchaikovsky, the "Dies irae," Haydn, jazz, and previously written music for theater and film, the Soviet composer demonstrated that the principle could prove operative even within the confines of a form with powerful constructive implications. The possibility of a genuine polystylistic music had been forwarded, and Tristan's scissors had found not so much a new champion as a new role.

Schnittke's initial contact with the West came in 1946–1948, when his father was employed in Vienna, during which period he studied there privately, but his principal training took place in Moscow (1953–1961), where he remained as a teacher until 1972. Originally drawn to the music of Webern—probably in some degree because it was prohibited in the Soviet Union—Schnittke later displayed a fascination with the classic Viennese style and with Mahler, though in "bits and pieces."[19] His attraction to Mahler as well as fragments from unfinished works surfaces in the second movement of his Concerto Grosso No. 4/ Symphony No. 5 (1988) based on the incomplete second movement of Mahler's early Piano Quartet. But the retrospective nature of this movement and a concerto grosso–like first movement that sets the spectre of Bach à la Hindemith against an alternating dream landscape ultimately yield to the composer's personal symphonic voice in the extended third and fourth movements, which conclude in a vivid and compelling funeral march. Other pieces, such as his String Quartet No. 3 of 1983, also pursue the opportunities for reworking received material—in this instance a *Stabat mater* of Orlando di Lasso, the main theme of Beethoven's *Grosse Fuge,* and a sequence of four notes D-E♭-C-B (in German D-S-C-H, the musical signature of his compatriot Dmitri Shostakovich). Despite the tapping of such a range of sources, throughout the 1980s Schnittke's addiction to polystylistics gradually began to promote integration. And in his Third (1981), Fourth (1983), and Fifth symphonies (1988) he pursued a desire "to find the general in the dissimilar"—in the Fourth through a stylization of the intonation systems of the ritual music of three religions: Orthodox, Catholic, and Protestant. A turn to opera in the 1990s saw the steady confirmation of this orientation.[20]

Something of this new composure as well as the force of Western repertoires for a composer living in a society that for decades had imposed musical isolation was pointedly demonstrated in a work entitled *Offertorium,* a violin concerto written in 1980 for Gidon Kremer by the Soviet composer Sofia Gubaidulina (b. 1931). The title refers to the citation and manipulation of the royal theme from Bach's *The Musical Offering,* projected in a *Klangfarben* orchestration similar to one confected by Anton Webern in 1935. Gubaidulina has stated that she chose this material because it served "to unite the two personalities who have produced, in the history of music, the greatest impression on me."[21] On the surface stands a patent intellectualization that is readily audible: a set of variations are announced through the systematic shortening of the theme by one note from the beginning and one from the end until at the climax it is reduced to a single note. A final section rebuilds the theme, "from the middle outwards and in reverse."[22]

Such observations, however, are formalistic and technical and, beyond detailing the metamorphosis of a theme, convey limited information regarding the sound of the work. For in addition to the initial references to Bach, Webern, and *Klangfarben* techniques and the subsequent attention to a formal process connoting sacrificial "offering," Gubaidulina runs the gamut from tonal to atonal, from monophony to tone cluster, from chaos to chorale, from snarling horns to the ethereal chiming of the celesta—all served up in the guise of a virtuoso violin concerto for which a grand intuition appears to be the only steadying hand. By the conclusion of the work, the formalistic premise of the title has been totally absorbed and dissolved. Yet both the stylistic range and the special recognition accorded to Bach and Webern carry a message as powerful as the tumbling of the Berlin Wall given the suppression of both pre-classic (Bach) and avant-garde (Webern) music in the Soviet Union during the Stalin years. With the cultural thaw of the 1960s Gubaidulina, together with Andrey Volkonsky, Edison Denisov, and Schnittke, began to develop a musical language that found freshness of inspiration in both local and imported sources, and their collective reclamation of repertoires formerly suppressed constitutes a powerful chapter in the social-political history of a nation. The same marriage between an initial infatuation with Webern and the later softening influences of folk and other Western cultures might be noted in numerous pieces written during the 1980s by the Polish composer Henryk Górecki: his impressive Trio for clarinet, cello, and piano ("Lerchenmusik," 1984), for example, melds materials ranging from plainchant to Beethoven's Fourth Piano Concerto with passages whose repetitions alternately signal an indebtedness to minimalism and to Messiaen.[23]

The guidance requisite to an understanding of the appropriated ingredients in a work like *Offertorium* should not lead to the conclusion, however, that such referential qualities are intellectualisms incidental to the listening experience. For a seemingly casual preparation of the listener by a performing ensemble or composer through program notes or disc liners can dramatically alter the way a piece of music is received. All protests to the contrary that music should be able to stand the test of an autonomous existence, such preconditioning holds the possibility of seduction for a lifetime. For new repertoires in particular there may not be a second opportunity without it.

Packaging and Messaging

Record jackets and liner notes, which typically accompanied the long-playing record and which continue to grace the compact disc, hold an enormous potential for influencing the listener's reception well beyond the original intentions of either designer or composer, who normally work independently of each other. John Walker has lucidly demonstrated how the visual dimension of Pop music has rejuvenated itself "by interacting with and feeding off fine art." On a 1985 British ZTT label titled *I Q 6 Zang Tumb Tumb sampled,* carrying an obvious allusion to the Futurist Marinetti,[24] he has noted an alliance with the most obscure references to high art, both with respect to the abstract geometric designs of its covers and the formidable series of sleeve notes, which clearly enter the arena of literary and social criticism. The contrast between the 1950s, when an album typically carried only a photo of the rock star and a listing of the song titles, and the 1980s, when sophisticated socio-psycho-babble invaded the packaging of Pop, is remarkable.[25]

In numerous venues and repertoires, from the Beatles' *Sgt. Pepper's Lonely Hearts Club Band* album (1967)—which forwarded an amalgamation of blues, jazz, electronics, Indian music, and a sizable orchestral sound—to Terry Riley's *Salome Dances for Peace,* a work for string quartet of 1989, study of the album cover beckons. Though Riley was in no way involved with the graphic art which accompanies the recording, its provocative title and format, which like the *Sgt. Pepper* album carry numerous visual allusions to cultural diversity, encourage listeners to become social critics as they contemplate this quartet of two and a half hours duration without text.[26] But the general impression of a collection of fetishes on the cover is supplemented by the interior notes, which stimulate other perspectives. For just as the Beatles experimented in the mid-1960s with string quartet accompaniments, Eastern religion, and drugs, traveled to India with the prospect of exploring fresh spiritual frontiers, and flirted with the idea of composition as a controlled product of the electronic studio, so Riley's travels to India and study with the vocalist Pandit Pran Nath, it is claimed, stirred the composer to a world view married to recent realignments concerning the potential of a classical string chamber ensemble. *Salome Dances for Peace* was commissioned by IRCAM in Paris and dedicated to the Kronos String Quartet, an American group that has repeatedly promoted global perspectives, and Riley states that in this work he set out to write a ballet about Salome, evil seductress from antiquity now reincarnated as a sorceress who uses her alluring powers to create universal peace.[27] Drawing on Native-American mythology as well as the legend of Orpheus and the Underworld, Riley confects a fleeting musical landscape out of materials with seemingly little or no relation to one another: jazz, blues, North Indian raga, Middle Eastern scales, minimalist pattern, and the vocabulary of traditional Western art music.[28]

Riley claims that such multicultural perspectives arise naturally, not from a premeditated compositional angle but, as he put it, "because I've listened to a lot of music from all over the world for 30 years."[29] Such ingenuous and patently ecumenical remarks may not have been calculated solely to sidestep frequently expressed claims of cultural ownership or increasingly familiar charges of postcolonial exploitation on the part of members of the dominant culture, but Riley's remarks implicitly suggest that he wished to avoid the problems surrounding the reception of Gershwin's *Porgy and Bess*. To the extent that the congregation of such varied materials is central to the message of the work, however, a parsing of its ingredients is ultimately essential in light of the fact that the net effect is far removed from any kind of popular entertainment that might be inferred from the composer's commentary. Somewhat paradoxically the record notes repeatedly encourage acknowledgment of the work's scope and grandeur in a manner that may come as a surprise to the listener-reader prepared to detect an anti-Eurocentric bias in Riley's global orientation: "Unlike any quartet ever written, *Salome Dances for Peace* is long, triple the length of Beethoven's longest quartet. And it is a narrative epic, grander in scope than the medium—traditionally favored for its intimacy—has previously known . . . Like a late Beethoven quartet, *Salome Dances for Peace* is a spiritual journey."[30] Beyond the appeals to multiculturalism, the authority of the past, the difficulty of escaping the canon, and the continuing relevance of the masterpiece idea for our times continue to lurk in the shadows.[31]

That a totally different kind of message lies behind Peter Maxwell Davies' equally lengthy and textless ballet, *Salome,* of 1978 may be inferred by listeners who confront, either before or during their encounter with the music, the photographs that grace the cover of its album. While Riley's work includes the image of a somewhat neutral, if nude, female torso in the center of the front cover, Davies' album exhibits a much more erotic semi-nude Salome in a brilliant red cape on the front, and a crouching, decidedly menacing one on the back—both far removed from the almost serene Art Nouveau decadence of Beardsley's *Salome of the Peacock Skirt* that graces a Leinsdorf-Caballé recording of Strauss's opera, for example. The final impression of new works in particular may ultimately center as much on such factors as the sound of the music or the accompanying scenario, except in the most general terms. Interpreted solely on the musical evidence, neither Riley's or Davies' work would automatically call up the figure of Salome. With the introduction of her name, however, we begin to fantasize before we ever embark on the act of listening, and memory of the various transformations of her story, musical character, and even gender over the past century in particular are sufficient to trigger a variety of responses. Only the year before Riley's quartet, for example, Ken Russell packaged Salome anew in his "triumph of postmodern trash cinema," *Salome's Last Dance* (1988), redefined the mask in terms of cross-dressing with the substitution of a transvestite boy in the title role, and in so doing recalled ancient and venerable Oriental traditions and practices.[32]

Something of this pervasive force of history, subject to recall and transformation with respect to extra-musical association or constructive bias, is prominent throughout the work of Peter Maxwell Davies (b. 1934). Stressing the importance of a knowledge of early music and chiding British conservatism and lack of technique, Davies launched a career that quickly caromed through a series of unpredictable orientations. Yet for all his avant-garde posture, his compulsion to protest his relation to a tradition provided the foundation for the discovery of a language. His interest in the work of Monteverdi was made clear in a series of works from 1961 to 1962, all of which took their formalistic starting point from a study of Monteverdi's Vespers of 1610 even as they eschewed citation or surface similarities to the model altogether. A decade later he drew upon a totally different musical facade from the same time period in his *Tenebrae pro Gesualdo* (1972), based upon a Holy Week responsory of the Italian chromaticist initially published in 1611. As with *Salome,* however, elements of Gesualdo's personal biography—including his reputation as a murderer and psychopathic genius—provide an unavoidable backdrop to the work that may resonate as strongly as Davies' collage score, whose basis stands in a series of statements drawn from Gesualdo's "O vos omnes" transcribed for voice and guitar. These in turn are set against an alternating group of glistening instrumental meditations in Davies' most advanced manner that force recognition of Gesualdo's tortured maze as a model of rationality.

Throughout his career Davies' working method has to an extent perpetuated these two approaches to a model, which may be audible in surface details or submerged in technical details. In both instances acknowledgment of the source is typically announced in the title or through accompanying commentary. Familiar examples include *Taverner,* an opera based upon the music and life of one of the most important English composers of the Renaissance, and *Worldes Blis,* an orchestral work in which a brief English song from the Middle Ages serves as the source for an extended symphonic work of forty minutes. And in *Eight Songs for a Mad King,* Davies packages the whole as a Pierrot ensemble in both the vocal and instrumental component, calls into question the sanity of George III, parodies Handel, cites flamenco rhythms, and transforms *Messiah* into a fox trot imported as a symbol of 1920s decadence. For Davies the history of English music contrasted with that of world repertoires frequently serves as his playing ground; at the same time a respect for tradition serves only as the starting point for a whole range of observations. Madness and blasphemy are channeled through ancient myths and rituals, both musical and literary, and the totality of the received tradition from the banal to the sublime is summoned in a retrospective gloss, a formalistic adaptation, or an expressive outrage.

Recognition of such a smorgasbord of source materials encourages scrutiny of the changing function of the composer's intention and the audience's perception during the period 1960–1990. Though the Postmodernist mentality has been blamed for placing a premium upon endless, runaway quotation or allusion, both catholicity and simultaneity of embrace increasingly surface as the ongoing benchmarks of an age clearly moored to a previous tradition. Postmodernist criticism's periodic denial of specific extra-referential meaning has in turn sponsored charges of mimicking self-reference compulsively celebrating the overload of a multimedia age that has flung the doors wide open to world culture. It should be noted, however, that such a conclusion virtually demands a new criticism and in the process elevates its role: multiple readings are now forwarded not as a luxury or a footnote but as a necessity, and the assertion is made that the "text" is only understandable through, is in a sense completed by, a series of such interpretations.[33]

Some composers have added weight to this argument by forwarding the notion that a composition is only completed by another composition. In the search for a new angle in viewing music's canonical repertoires, Berio's voyage aboard the scherzo of Mahler's Second Symphony in the third section of his *Sinfonia* (1968) emerges with increasing clarity as a seminal work. Here quotation is not the *essence* but is ancillary to the central skeleton, which is Mahler's symphony. Berio has indicated that the multiple quotations from Bach, Berlioz, Brahms, Strauss, Schoenberg, Stravinsky, Stockhausen, and Boulez, should be thought of as *markers* which signal the harmonic countries that are traversed on his journey: "little flags in different colours stuck into a map to indicate salient points during an expedition full of surprises." He also requests that they be thought of not as collage, but rather as agents which recall bits of the "history of music" as an accompaniment to the underlying scherzo—a perspective that forces recall of Stockhausen's structural confrontation of the whole history of music within the framework of a Japanese prayer ritual in his *Inori* of 1974.[34]

More recently Berio has underscored the function and power of re-working fragments from the past in the completion of another Schubert "unfinished" symphony, which he has entitled *Rendering* (1988–1990). The sketches which serve as the basis of Berio's reconstruction and am-plification are those for a tenth symphony in three movements dating from "Frühjahr-Sommer 1828."[35] Since Schubert died on November 9 of that year, the sketches come from the last months of his life. That the symphony can thus be identified as Schubert's "last" as well as "un-known" and "unfinished" can hardly have failed to have been a precipi-tating factor in Berio's original choice. Yet, though the Schubert sym-phony, unlike the Mahler Second utilized by Berio for his *Sinfonia,* was left as a sketch and therefore invites completion, the idea of a gloss is common to both. That Berio sensed other affinities as well is betrayed by a note accompanying the score in which he states that "the expres-sive climate of the second movement is stunning: it seems inhabited by Mahler's spirit." Furthermore, the fact that both works use the genre of the symphony as a *point de départ* underscores the dilemma of the continuing appeal of the Classic-Romantic generic revivals which be-gan in the 1970s on the one hand and their potential *irrelevance* for present times on the other—an issue openly discussed by Schnittke re-garding his own Symphony No. 2. Yet, rather than approaching the received formalisms of sonata, rondo, and variation as ideals from with-out, Berio makes alternately predictable and unexpected completions of a master's fully imagined but unfinished design from within: the sur-viving torso completed "in the style" is presented in tandem with dis-crete and prominent inserts à la Berio. Berio has nuanced his intentions:

> *Rendering* with its dual authorship is intended as a restoration of these sketches, it is not a completion nor a reconstruction. This restoration is made along the lines of the modern restoration of frescoes that aims at reviving the old colours without however trying to disguise the damage that time has caused, often leaving inevitable empty patches in the composition (for instance as in the case of Giotto in Assisi) . . .

In the empty places between one sketch and the next there is a kind
of connective tissue which is constantly different and changing, always
"pianissimo" and "distant," intermingled with reminiscences of late
Schubert (the *Piano Sonata in B flat,* the *Piano Trio in B flat* etc.) and
crossed by polyphonic textures based on fragments of the same
sketches. This musical "cement" comments on the discontinuities and
the gaps that exist between one sketch and another and is always announced by the sound of a celesta, and must be performed "quasi
senza suono" and without expression.[36]

Attempts to differentiate such late twentieth-century perspectives
from those of earlier avant-garde movements and to relocate them in
an elaborate criticism have become chronic. Yet the debt remains clear
even when distinctions are made with respect to intention and significance: the need for perpetual and mutating guidance in reading such
a mixture of the playful and the technical, the narrative and the abstract,
is common to both. Stravinsky offered a particularly vivid illustration
of the underlying premise of diverse collage practices in a conversation
with Nicolas Nabokov in which the composer elaborated on cut and
paste procedures in the Epilogue of his ballet *Orpheus* (1947):

> "Here, you see, I cut off the fugue with a pair of scissors." He clipped
> the air with his fingers. "I introduced this short harp phrase, like two
> bars of an accompaniment. Then the horns go on with their fugue
> as if nothing had happened. I repeat it at regular intervals, here and
> here again." Stravinsky added, with his habitual grin, "You can elimi-
> nate these harp solo interruptions, paste the parts of the fugue together,
> and it will be one whole piece."[37]

Yet what on the surface appeared to be a callous exercise in Modernity
was in reality a forceful agent of the drama. For Stravinsky concluded
that he intended the interruptions of the harp to be heard as a reminder
of Orpheus' earlier song. "Here in the Epilogue," the composer added,
"it sounds like a kind of . . . compulsion, like something unable to stop
. . . Orpheus is dead, the song is gone, but the accompaniment goes
on."

— 16 —

Pyramids at the Louvre

> To combine the lustre of your Name with the splendour of the
> Monuments of Egypt, is to associate the glorious annals of our
> own time with the history of the heroic age.
>
> *Dedication to Napoleon Bonaparte by Vivant Denon, 1803*

> For most of its 4,600 years, the Sphinx has been falling apart . . .
> Restoration after restoration left the monument with new rocks
> that didn't fit with the old. This century, as major portions of
> the statue threatened to pull apart, restorers used concrete, and
> water and salt oozed in and out of the stones. Egypt has just held
> the first global conference on how to save the Sphinx.
>
> *Associated Press Release, March 6, 1992*

Cultural Borrowings and Inserts

Familiar obelisks stand on the banks of the Thames in London, in Central Park in New York City, and at the Place de la Concorde in Paris, the first two of which are familiarly referred to as Cleopatra's needles. The circumstances behind their journeys from Egypt to their present locations constitute independent stories, but the London and Paris obelisks resonate with a special history in light of the Egyptian campaigns of Lord Nelson and Napoleon Bonaparte in 1798–99. The systematic descriptions and drawings which Napoleon charged Vivant Denon to record vividly suggest the moment when this chain of future actions was put into motion:

> We came afterwards to the obelisk, named Cleopatra's needle: another
> obelisk thrown down at its side, indicates that both of them formerly

419

decorated one of the entrances of the palace of the Ptolemies, the
ruins of which are still to be seen at some distance from thence . . .
They might be conveyed to France without difficulty, and would
there become a trophy of conquest, and a very characteristic one, as
they are in themselves a monument.[1]

Denon's report on the pyramids was even more ecstatic, and after admiring the accuracy of their structure and the mystery of their construction, he concluded that "these gigantic monuments may be considered
as the last link in the chain of the colossi of art and nature."[2]

It is of more than passing interest that following his assignment with
Napoleon, Denon became director of the Louvre, and that on the Paris
Métro, the city's subway system, the stop which serves the Louvre,
Palais-Royal, immediately follows one designated Pyramides. For between 1985 and 1989 the idea of the pyramid was resurrected with
more jolting effect in the construction of a set of such forms in the
Louvre's courtyard, known as the Cour Napoléon. At first they created
shock, then debate, and finally at least momentary celebration as the
project was completed and its function, both practical and aesthetic,
realized. Designed and engineered by the internationally renowned architect I. M. Pei, an American of Chinese ancestry, they were introduced not only as a new mode of access to the Louvre but, by way
of totally revamping the exhibition spaces, to something which was
henceforth to be dubbed the Grand Louvre. The Cour Napoléon,
where the pyramids were placed, is one and a half times the size of the
Piazza San Marco in Venice; the largest of Pei's crystalline objects stands
seventy-one feet high, reaching a point just below the top floor of the
Louvre; three smaller ones, sixteen feet tall, are placed around a reflecting pool. Thousands of lights which play at night with the fountains
and the structures old and new now redeem the Louvre as a new focus
of interest for Parisians and tourists alike.

Egypt, the French in Egypt, the Pyramids: all once again emerged
as symbols of Westerners' fascination with the beginnings of their civilization. Earlier in the century the Russian Constructivist Ivan Leonidov
had forecast the power inherent in the juxtaposition of antique shape
with new material in his project for a Palace of Culture Sports Pavilion,
and had even highlighted the dialectic of old authority with modern
culture by placing a floating dirigible over a pyramid and a palm tree
(Figure 16.1). Yet, it is of interest to note that Pei soft-pedaled the
Egyptian connection and chose to emphasize instead the importance

Figure 16.1. Ivan Leonidov, project for a Palace of Culture Sports Pavilion, Proletarsky area, Moscow, 1930.

A. Shchusev Museum of Architecture, Moscow.

of classical French landscape design and its greatest exponent, André Le Nôtre. A square pattern divided diagonally, a form persistently visible in the adjacent gardens of the Tuileries, provides the same design as the floor plan of a pyramid viewed from above, and Pei claimed his love of such pure geometrical forms as the guiding force. All denials notwithstanding, Pei's use of three smaller pyramids in the manner of what Marie Christine Loriers has called an "attenuated echo"[3] (Figure 16.2) to the central emblem cannot fail to recall the satellite pyramids at the Great Pyramid of Cheops (Figure 16.3). And even if the name of the open space in which the new pyramids were placed (the Cour Napoléon named for Napoleon III, not Napoleon Bonaparte) provides little or no historic justification of the formal choice, the conjunction of images was surely nothing less than a felicitous cultural ploy and one that patently invites interpretation as well as future mythologizing.

Other related architectural solutions involving modern appendages to classical structures had been carried out by Pei before he approached the Louvre, including the East Wing to the National Gallery in Washington. Both there and in an initial version, later abandoned, of the Kennedy Library in Boston, Pei introduced truncated glass pyramids.[4] In restructuring the interior spaces of the Louvre, Pei early ruled out what he saw as the simplest solution, namely, to have no visible entrance. He added, "I wanted to give the entrance symbolic dignity and

Figure 16.2. I. M. Pei's pyramid entrance to the Louvre, contrasting with the Napoleon III architecture behind it.

Photo, S. Courturier / Courtesy of Pei Cobb Freed & Partners.

architectural excitement. You have to have an emergence. The pyramid was chosen as the most respectful form."[5] Having considered and rejected both explicitly classical and Postmodern schemes, Pei decided that the Modernist application of glass and steel to a classical form provided the ideal complement to the classical facade of the Louvre.[6]

Similarly, in the world of music the removal and relocation of materials has been practiced with such frequency throughout the twentieth century by Western composers that what once carried the unexpected force of a cultural or chronological loan has been increasingly received as an accustomed gambit. From the last fin de siècle to the present one, the newness of the angle for the composer has continued to be constituted in a variety of approaches including timbral, rhythmic, and scalar

Figure 16.3. General view recorded by Vivant Denon of the Great Pyramid of Cheops, its satellite pyramids, and the Sphinx of Giza.

codes or in spatio-temporal relocations. The invoked materials have ranged geographically to all parts of the globe, have been extracted from folk and popular repertoires and their hybrids, and have been recalled from the major and minor classics of musical literature of the past thousand years.

The force of Pei's pyramids at the Louvre stems principally from the integral insertion of an object into a surrounding that remains untouched on the exterior except for the arrival of the new objects and the adjustments of perception and perspective which inevitably follow. This quality of "insert" on classic terrain has become an increasingly perceivable dimension of Postmodernist collage and one that can be distinguished, say, from Stravinsky's gloss of Pergolesi in *Pulcinella,* though it is clearly akin to the insertion of folktunes in *Petrushka* and

Wozzeck with respect to the discreteness of the juxtaposition. A pair of questions immediately arise: How can we best characterize an analogous type of Postmodernist collage in music, and how is it best distinguished from Modernist habits which surfaced in the first quarter of the century? Yet the question is no sooner asked than the hypothesis emerges that continuity between the Modern and the Postmodern may be as operative as severance. Issues of continuity aside, the variety of definitions accorded the term Postmodernism and the patent sophistry surrounding much of its literature has alienated numerous artists, even those whose works might typically be sequestered as examples of the aesthetic. In light of Stockhausen's stated belief that "the future will judge the retrospective exploitation of traditional music as signs of decadence," his judgment that "I really think that the term 'Postmodern' is terrible" ought come as no surprise.[7] But Luciano Berio, whose *Sinfonia* has been frequently forwarded as one of the early icons of musical Postmodernity, has also signaled his position unequivocally: "I am constitutionally allergic to Postmodernism."[8]

As a test of the proposition concerning perceivable continuities, let us confront two examples from the 1980s. Both are by well-known composers with some claim to leadership in the avant-garde—if, indeed, such a concept still holds any meaning. Both are cadenzas to standard instrumental concertos by venerable composers of the Classical period: Schnittke's cadenzas to the first and third movements of the Beethoven Violin Concerto in D major, and Stockhausen's cadenzas for Haydn's equally familiar Trumpet Concerto. However, in order not to misconstrue their contributions, a brief review of the concerto cadenza is essential.

Historical Prototypes for the Modern Cadenza

As a mark of virtuoso display, the instrumental cadenza evolved directly from the vocal cadenzas of the Baroque, typically limited to the extent of a single breath. Later extensions in length were apparently inevitable, prompted not only by virtuosi anxious for public esteem but by the composers themselves, who were not infrequently the protagonists. By their very nature such virtuoso intrusions, which took on various forms and functions, all betray the character of an insert in performance.[9] In his *Versuch einer Anweisung die Flöte traversiere zu spielen* (1752), the first treatise to devote an entire chapter to the question, Joachim Quantz defined the cadenza as an extempore embellishment on the fifth in the bass. When cadenzas were not only written out but actually obbligato, as those for C. P. E. Bach's set of six concertos, they were generally addressed to amateurs, and Quantz makes no allowance for the category. He locates the origin of the classic cadenza in the waning years of the previous century with the establishment of its most salient feature, namely, the pause by accompanying musicians, in the period 1710 to 1716.

To the extent that concision was not the order of the day, proportional distortion was capable of contributing to the essential foreignness of the introduced material as much or more than the absence of thematic relationships. It is noteworthy in this regard that virtually all the cadenzas provided by other composers to Mozart's concertos are very much longer than Mozart's preserved ones. Although both stylistic and thematic *heterogeneity* was a potential problem when the cadenza was not specified by the composer, J. S. Bach, Haydn, and Mozart all composed non-thematic cadenzas.

These problems inherent in the unspecified cadenza mushroomed in the nineteenth century, though Beethoven's approach to the concerto cadenza became increasingly circumspect. For although he composed five piano concertos (op. 15, 1795; op. 19, 1798; op. 37, c. 1800; op. 58, 1806; op. 73, 1809), cadenzas to the first four were all written as late as 1809 and under special circumstances which have recently been tied to his relations with the Archduke Ferdinand.[10] In the same year, Beethoven's concern for formal integration, which was always potentially threatened by the introduction of cadenzas, also prompted him to introduce the following indication in the first movement of his final piano concerto (the "Emperor"): "Non si fa una cadenza, ma s'attacca subito il seguente" ("Do not play a cadenza, but attack the following at once"). Here Beethoven provides an obligatory written cadenza that segues with a concluding coda.

The year 1809 constituted a banner year for Beethoven during which the issue of the cadenza was subjected to intense review. For in this year the composer wrote cadenzas not only for his first four piano concertos and his own transcription for piano of the Violin Concerto, op. 61 (1806, trans. 1807)—all of which had originally been published without cadenzas—but for Mozart's D minor piano concerto, K. 466, as well. In the latter, Beethoven's additions have been characterized as a violation of the ground rules of the Mozartean cadenza, as a repudiation of the Classical ideal of cadential elaboration, and by Richard Kramer even as a "revealing indiscretion," "an act of artistic impropriety," situating a moment in history "in which the past is vilified and a precarious future glimpsed."[11] Indeed, there can be no arguing that Beethoven's additions to Mozart evidence the same distancing individuality that characterizes the cadenzas that he wrote for his own piano concertos.

Formally positioned in a sonata design between the end of the recapitulation and the beginning of the coda and indicated by a fermata over a tonic six-four chord, the cadenza was typically viewed as the prolongation of a single sonority which found resolution and closure in the dominant. And Mozart, like his contemporaries, rarely investigated remote tonal terrain but focused, rather, on the exploration of pattern and figure. Yet while Beethoven's shift from E♭ minor to B major in his cadenza to K. 466—the harmonic gesture that lies at the heart of Kramer's characterization—stands patently outside the traditional behavior of Mozart's approach to the cadenza, its harmonic and figural context is candidly and pitch specifically spelled out in the opening of Mozart's *Fantasia,* K. 475 (Examples 16.1, 16.2a). Rather than pointing

Example 16.1. Ludwig van Beethoven, Cadenza, WoO 58/1, for Mozart, K. 466, mvt. 1, opening.

to demonstrable harmonic links with his own *Eroica* Symphony as Kramer proposes, Beethoven's E♭ minor–B major shift in conjunction with further references to Neapolitan relationships as well as right-hand arpeggiations against left-hand motivic triplets followed by leaping quarter notes secure the impression that Beethoven's references to K. 475 are explicit and offered in the spirit of emulation (Example 16.2b). It does seems clear, however, that Beethoven is intent upon making a functionary reallocation of Mozart's expository or developmental materials and tonal relationships to the formal terrain of the cadenza.[12] Thus in his cadenzas for Mozart as well as for his own piano concertos, all of which were composed in 1809, Beethoven offered a series of specimens that virtually constituted a sermon regarding the unsuspected potential of an aging convention.

Schnittke, Stockhausen, and the Cadenza

In approaching Schnittke's cadenzas to the Beethoven Violin Concerto and Stockhausen's offerings for a series of Classical concertos we are

Example 16.2a. Wolfgang Amadeus Mozart, *Fantasia* in C minor, K. 475, mm. 137–140.

Example 16.2b. Wolfgang Amadeus Mozart, *Fantasia* in C minor, K. 475, mm. 8–10.

now prepared to note that the disruptive potential of the cadenza had been alternately exacerbated and controlled by Beethoven himself in fabricating vehicles both for his own concertos and for works by other composers. But in addition, as Kramer has wisely stated, Mozart's own cadenzas to his concertos had introduced another issue that was destined to haunt the genre. "That Mozart should have bothered to write out his cadenzas must give us pause. To ask why he did so is to question whether the improvisatory ground rules of cadenza, even in the hands of a composer who would have had supremely little trouble complying with those rules, were perceived as a mask held up at the fermata: a mask that signifies improvisation but conceals composition."[13]

The legacies of both Mozart and Beethoven are initially somewhat timidly manifest in the opening minute and a half of Schnittke's first movement cadenza, where his objective appears to be primarily integrative and emulative through the recognition and reworking of previously heard themes from the concerto together with allusions to textures present in Joseph Joachim's and Fritz Kreisler's well-known cadenzas for this work. Then suddenly Schnittke announces his intention to draw from sources outside the Beethoven Violin Concerto through two brief citations from the symphonic repertoire, the second movement of Beethoven's Seventh and what at first hearing sounds like the third movement of Rachmaninov's Second Symphony. The latter, however, is identical with the opening theme of Bartók's Violin Concerto No. 1, and the conclusion of Schnittke's citation soon invokes the more complete figure as it appears in the development of the first movement of Bartók's concerto (see Example 16.3).

This in turn spawns a series of borrowings that invites the listener to review the history of the instrumental cadenza since Beethoven. The first of these references is to the solo violin presentation of the twelve-note series in Berg's Violin Concerto, which discloses an unsuspected relationship to the Bartók citation made only seconds before, and this is immediately followed by a secondary theme from the first movement of Bartók's Violin Concerto No. 2 which segues immediately from the top note of the Berg citation. A series of rhythmic statements pronounced in quick succession involving triple and quadruple stops extracted from the Shostakovich Violin Concerto No. 1, the Bartók Concerto No. 2, and the Berg Concerto is immediately followed by an unexpected appearance of the timpani. Here Schnittke's historical perspective is conspicuous and his instrumental choice pointed. For not only does the third movement of Beethoven's "Emperor" Concerto contain a notable dialogue between piano and timpani, but even more pertinently Beethoven's Violin Concerto opens with five solo strokes of the timpani which through the course of the movement attain to a striking symbolism.[14] Finally, and even more conspicuously, while Beethoven did not compose a cadenza for his Violin Concerto in its original version of 1806, he did make an arrangement of the entire concerto for solo piano and orchestra the next year, and both versions were published at the same time in 1808. For the piano version Beethoven then wrote cadenzas for both the first and third movements in 1809, incorporating, as it happens, a prominent use of the five-note timpani motif in consort with the piano in the first of them. It will be noted that it is a rhythmic idea which Beethoven also borrowed in his cadenza to Mozart's K. 466, written in the same year (Example 16.1, mm. 6–9).[15] With Schnittke's specific incorporation of the timpani into the first movement cadenza he displays a pronounced awareness of the history of the cadenza as it pertains to Beethoven, and in his restriction of its function to the opening motif of the concerto he also emphasizes its integrative potential.[16]

But beyond the introduction of the timpani, the sheer length of the cadenza which Beethoven appended to his Violin Concerto in its adaptation for piano is striking and invites examination. Reasons for Beethoven's provision of such an expanded commentary can be traced not only to the composer's own keyboard prowess but also to a reasonable desire for compensation in light of the undemanding nature of the violin part in its transferral to the piano.[17] For the single melodic line of the right hand in the perpetual company of a routine left-hand accompaniment is finally and only released with the entrance, one might say explosion, of a full-blooded cadenza of 125 measures that qualifies as a genuine dramatic *scena* in four parts, the final three of which receive individual character or tempo markings: Marcia, Meno allegro, and Presto.

Thus, Schnittke's first movement cadenza for violin of 1985 provides the counterpart not only to Beethoven's cadenza to the same concerto transferred to the piano by virtue of its length, sectional quality, and especially the introduction of the timpani, but also to Beethoven's cadenza to Mozart's K. 466 by virtue of the introduction of harmonic transgressions and the citation of music extraneous to the concerto. For the rhythmic component, once introduced by Schnittke via the tim-

18'52": Cadenza begins, developing ideas of 1st mvt.

20'18": Rhythmic motto à la Joachim and Kreisler cadenzas

20'32": Beethoven, Symphony No. 7, 2nd mvt. (a)

20'49": Beethoven Violin Concerto motif (b) altered to prefigure Berg-Bach citation (g)

21'09": Bartók, Violin Concerto No. 1, mvt. 1, mm. 48-51 (c)

21'23": Berg, Violin Concerto, mvt. 1, mm. 15-18 (d)

21'27": Bartók, Violin Concerto No. 2, mvt. 1, mm. 62-64 (e)

21'36": Shostakovich, Violin Concerto No. 1, mvt. 2, No. $57^{+5,6}$, mm. 5-6 (f)

21'40": Berg, Violin Concerto, citation of Bach chorale, "Es ist genug" (g)

21'53": Shostakovich, Violin Concerto No. 1, mvt. 3, cadenza, "Più mosso" (h)

22'01": Bartók, Concerto No. 2, mvt. 1, coda, mm. 373-373 (i)

22'12": Berg, Violin Concerto, mvt. 2, mm. 41-42 (j)

[Cut in recording: Berg, Violin Concerto, mvt. 2, mm. 110-114, 121, 16-22.]

22'19": 5 timpani strokes à la Beethoven Piano Concerto arrangement and Busoni cadenza (k)

22'23": Brahms, Violin Concerto (rhythmic motif) (l)

22'24": 5 timpani strokes (m)

22'28": Berg, Violin Concerto, mvt. 2 (rhythmic motif), mm. 36-38 (n)

The timpani strokes and the Brahms and Berg citations appear as follows in the original score. In the recording by Kremer, m. 2 (Berg) is replaced by m. 4 (Brahms), and mm. 4-5 are performed from the *ossia*.

22'33": 8 timpani strokes

22'39": Berg, Violin Concerto, mvt. 2, mm. 33-34

22'45": Berg, Violin Concerto, mvt. 2, mm. 61-64

22'51": Berg, Violin Concerto, mvt. 2, mm. 58-60

23'07": Cadenza ends

Example 16.3. Citations in Schnittke's Cadenza to the first movement of Beethoven's Violin Concerto as they appear in real time on Philips. CD 410549-2 performed by Gidon Kremer.

pani, immediately segues into a review of the rhythmic motto and its potential force through a revealing quotation from the Brahms Violin Concerto. Now Brahms had written cadenzas for Beethoven's Piano Concerto No. 4 and, like Beethoven, also for Mozart's K. 466. Also, like Beethoven, Brahms wrote no cadenzas for his own Violin Concerto, leaving the task to the dedicatee, Joachim. As a consequence Schnittke focuses on the most prominent rhythmic motif of Brahms's first movement, a motif which can be seen to be embedded in Berg's rhythmic motto. In Schnittke's original version he even juxtaposes the two, placing an *ossia* passage from Berg directly above the Brahms citation, thereby telegraphing the kinship. Numerous further allusions to the Berg cadenza appear shortly and force recall of the fact that the Berg "cadenza" (marked "Frei, wie eine Kadenz" at the beginning of the second movement) is no traditional heir to the designation in its psychological appropriation of Mahler's death rhythms—an obsession repeatedly invoked throughout Berg's career from *Wozzeck* to *Lulu*— and in its utilization of the orchestra as a partner throughout. The materials cited above are shown in Example 16.3 in the order of their appearance along with their location in real time as they occur in the recording by Gidon Kremer.[18]

In Schnittke's cadenza to the third movement, cyclic integration once more takes place through the recall of the timpani motive of the first movement. But in a cadenza that otherwise contains routinely conservative passage work, toward the end Schnittke conjures up a demonic whirlwind from a string section of ten violin *soli* that simultaneously recalls the tone clusters of the fifty-two *solo* string ensemble in Krzysztof Penderecki's *Threnody for the Victims of Hiroshima* (1961), thus invoking a new brand of late twentieth-century string virtuosity light years beyond the Beethoven-Brahms-Berg succession and one tuned to the task of social and political pronouncement.[19]

By way of review note that Schnittke, in a manner characteristic of many of his earlier works, calls upon five well-known violin concertos in addition to Beethoven's in fashioning his gloss: those of Brahms, Berg, Bartók (two), and Shostakovich. By virtue of medium and nationality Brahms and Berg are, of course, direct spiritual descendants of the Beethoven concerto in question. And in spite of his Soviet citizenship, Schnittke's family name, it should be recalled, is of East German origin. Thus in his juxtaposition of Beethoven, Brahms, and Berg, Schnittke defines a personal and historical legacy. Furthermore Bartók, like Brahms, had also written a cadenza to a Beethoven piano concerto, the third, and, like Schnittke, he invoked the spirit of the marginal Eastern European. And with Shostakovich Schnittke calls on a revered fellow countryman who struggled throughout his life to maintain artistic independence in the face of official censure—a state of affairs which Schnittke himself faced in his early career.

Far from being a simple assessment of the materials of the concerto itself, Schnittke's striking inserts in the grand tradition of twentieth-century collage invite the listener to review the history of the violin concerto in terms of the authority of the past—not only with respect to the particular issue of the cadenza but in relation to the pervasive forces of emulation, personal biography, and social history. Finally, rather than an endorsement of current assertions of Beethoven's irrelevance for present times, Schnittke's contribution must be seen as a mirror of humanity's unremitting and mystical infatuation with him, and especially his capacity for continuing metamorphosis and mythologizing.[20]

Stockhausen's cadenzas to Haydn's Trumpet Concerto can similarly be heard on one level as a respectful reworking of Haydn's musical materials, as an emulative parody of the conventions of tonality and the cadenza, or, equally correctly, as a companion piece to the extended scene for solo trumpet, "Oberlippentanz" ("Upper Lip Dance") from the opera *Samstag aus "Licht"* (1984), which in fact accompanies the recording which Stockhausen has made of the Haydn trumpet concerto with his son Markus. In the first movement cadenza, not only do thwarted expectations with respect to Haydn's language promote surprise but they ultimately lead the knowledgeable listener to a realization that the uncanny silences, isolated tritones, registral play, and timbral variety speak not only to the late twentieth century in general but to Stockhausen's original contributions to the trumpet literature in particular (Example 16.4). In an open embrace of the virtuoso potential of the instrument and its natural outlet within the framework of a cadenza to a classic concerto, Stockhausen has annexed materials from the original and embued them with ingredients of his own language.

Finally, in the third movement Stockhausen has also *parodied* the virtuoso premise of the traditional cadenza in a repeated series of approaches to a high E♭, never achieved (Example 16.5).[21] Stockhausen's message is anything but a humorless academic commentary, however.

Example 16.4. Karlheinz Stockhausen, Cadenza to Haydn's Trumpet Concerto, mvt. 1.
© Stockhausen Verlag.

For even as he eschews external citation à la Schnittke, he constructs a series of puns on the vocabulary and syntax of tonal music by presenting virtuoso elements in tandem with the unarguable force of the leading tone and its suppression through register and the rest. It is of more than passing historical interest that such grammatical features with an uncontestable humorous component had already been introduced in the thwarted expectations of "false-start cadenzas" used by Mozart in the finale of the Sonata in F, K. 332, and Haydn in the third movement of the Symphony No. 68.[22]

In retrospect it is clear that the dilemma over the nature and quality of harmonic prolongation as well as the issue of the composed versus the improvised cadenza has a lengthy history. Even more provocative is the recognition that Beethoven's preoccupations of 1809 and the current attraction to the cadenza betray a kindred sensibility. And, as in earlier times, both Stockhausen's and Schnittke's contributions were prompted by their intimate involvement with contemporary virtuosi with whom they have previously and repeatedly worked. For in addition to the cadenzas to the Haydn trumpet concerto, which were written for his son Markus, Stockhausen has written cadenzas for the Mozart clarinet concerto, the flute concertos, and one of the piano concertos as natural responses to the protracted artistic liaison of Suzanne Stephens, Kathinka Pasveer, and his daughter Majella, respectively, with performances of his music. Similarly, if somewhat differently, Schnittke's cadenzas to the Beethoven violin concerto are a reflection of his continuing artistic involvement with the violinists Mark Lubotzki and Gidon Kremer. Schnittke has reviewed the genesis of the cadenzas thus:

Example 16.5. Karlheinz Stockhausen, Cadenza to Haydn, Trumpet Concerto, mvt. 3, excerpt for trumpet in E♭.

© Stockhausen Verlag.

My cadenzas to Beethoven's Violin Concerto were composed gradually—initially to the first movement (for Mark Lubotzki), then to the second movement in cooperation with Gidon Kremer, and then to the third movement (for Gidon Kremer). Kremer also played them for the first time in a definitive version. But the most important—the cadenza to the first movement—had already been performed (Mark Lubotzki!).[23]

Kremer was also the dedicatee for Schnittke's *Paganiniana* and his Violin Concerto No. 4—the latter containing an extraordinary passage for the soloist, who is asked to improvise against the accompanying orchestra in a gradual diminuendo to the point of inaudibility, after which the soloist continues to perform passionately: *poco a poco senza suoni, ma molto appassionato (Cadenza visuale!).*

To the extent that the complete subtext of these cadenzas is discernible only to those who have been privy to analysis of an order comparable to Robert Rosenblum's typographical dissections of Picasso's collages,[24] the average listener is faced with an interpretive riddle analogous to the enigmas which surface in the confrontation of visual collage in the "historic avant-garde" around 1909–1914. To be sure, collage, in the sense of grafting onto acknowledged masterpieces that were otherwise left unaltered, had taken place within the visual arts from the time of Duchamp's *L.H.O.O.Q.* of 1919. Duchamp not only outfitted the Mona Lisa with a moustache and goatee but furnished her with the caption *L.H.O.O.Q.*, which when pronounced would be understood by a Frenchman to mean "She has a hot derrière." But rather than misogyny, Duchamp's intention was the opposite, namely, parody of an essentially male art "as pseudo-religion: Sensibility worshipping the Culture-Hero, the great dead artist in his posthumously appointed role as a divine creator."[25] Those who were eager in the early 1990s to announce the formation of a new and binding alliance against the "Dead, White, European Male" in the reconstitution of the artistic canon should take note of the tardiness of their claim. Stockhausen has voiced similarly ambivalent feelings about worship of the dead culture-hero from a somewhat different angle. In throwing a challenge to performing organizations to assume a greater sense of responsibility in programming the music of our own time, he has bluntly condemned "the machinery of composer stripping" and the "financial exploitation of dead composers through established gangs of cultural manipulation and 'music marketing.' "[26]

Yet, realizing that there is no hope of replacing the concerto repertoire of the Classic masters and that programs of one's own music may benefit from cohabitation with these repertoires in the concert hall, Stockhausen in recent years not only has scheduled the Mozart and Haydn concertos on the same program with his own *Tierkreis* (in a version employing clarinet, flute, trumpet, and piano), but has promoted the notion of a peaceful and prosperous coexistence through the insertion of his own cadenzas in these concertos. Commenting on the genesis of his cadenzas, the composer has articulated their meaning:

> The only reason for writing the cadenzas of Haydn's and Mozart's concertos is my collaboration with Markus, Suzanne and Kathinka. Dr. Ruzicka, Director of the Radio Symphony Orchestra Berlin, offered a chance to give the world premiere of *Lucifer's Dance* in Berlin (in the version for symphony orchestra) in case I would be willing to conduct the classical concertos with these three soloists. So: friendship! The same will happen again with these soloists and Majella Stockhausen (piano) this November in Vienna (I will have to write another cadenza for a piano concerto of Mozart).[27]

Having said that he "wanted Susee, Markus, and Kathinka to play these concerti because people had the false idea that these interpreters were not able to play traditional works masterfully,"[28] Stockhausen also stated that he prefers not to think of his cadenzas as collage or insert, and proclaimed that his intention had been "to pull the 18th century a moment into the 20th century and release it again (Humour being the main aspect)."[29] Semantic concerns regarding the word "insert" dissolve in light of the composer's clear articulation of the feeling for historical "pull and release" and especially the overriding objective of humor. The composer's role is dramatized in the telling cover of the published score, designed by Stockhausen, which shows his hands holding a magnifying glass over the cadenza fermata of the original (Figure 16.4).[30]

Retrospectives, Overlays, and Restoration

From the time of Duchamp's anti-masterpiece attack on the Mona Lisa (1919) and Stravinsky's "beginning of a love affair" with the past in *Pulcinella* (1919–20) to the present day, the wholesale retention of an original masterwork as a point of departure has been periodically observable in both painting and the world of music. Some of the most notable examples are Picasso's post–World War II parodies of Manet, Delacroix, and Velásquez, an artist who also attracted Francis Bacon in his psychological *Study after Velásquez's Portrait of Pope Innocent X* of 1953.

Claes Oldenburg's "Cpin = Kiss" lithograph of 1972 (Figure 16.5) offered another provocative assemblage that on the surface forced recall of his *Late Submission to the Chicago Tribune Architectural Competition of 1922: Clothespin (Version Two)* of 1967 on the one hand,[31] advertised the role of non-art in the world of art on the other, and forecast the achievement of a forty-five-feet high sculpture in the shape of a clothespin in an outdoor Philadelphia piazza that was to appear in 1976. However, for those who would read it as an affirmation of Duchamp and Schwitters a half century before, as the triumph of mass culture's taste for parody and the artist's bid for immediate economic success over ultimate immortality, Claes Oldenburg's 1972 lithograph, *Design for a Colossal Clothespin Compared to Brancusi's "The Kiss,"* forwards claims well beyond its obvious themes of dominance and wit. Here Brancusi's primordial stone sculpture of 1907 and Oldenburg's Pop colossus would seem to be far removed from each other, even though the duality of an embracing organism is instantaneously verifiable as common to both.

Figure 16.4. Karlheinz Stockhausen, title page for Cadenzas to Haydn's Trumpet Concerto.

Photo, Markus Stockhausen. © Stockhausen Verlag, 1984.

While it could be argued that the clothespin presented by itself may be more susceptible to ridicule than when it is placed in juxtaposition with an icon of early twentieth-century art, the viewer is left to wonder if it is the lithographer's intention to hint at the universality of seemingly diverse tension systems or to defend the potential nobility of Pop Art. Resolution of the question may come from the simple recognition that

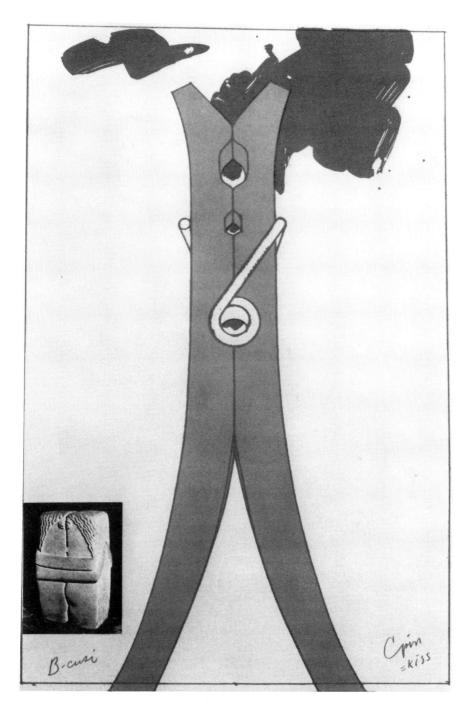

Figure 16.5. Claes Oldenburg, *Design for a Colossal Clothespin Compared to Brancusi's "The Kiss"* ("Cpin = Kiss"), 1972.

not unlike Stockhausen, philosophically speaking, Oldenburg accepts tradition not as belonging to the past but, rather, as constituted by everything that is available to him, and that he has simply found pleasure in taking humorous note of an unsuspected affinity. Both artists' reliance upon the tactic of "insert" dramatizes the comparison.

In the two concertos under consideration it was clearly neither Stockhausen's nor Schnittke's intention to deface or parody in the manner of Duchamp nor, in light of other available cadenzas, to render them performable in the manner of Berio's *Rendering*. At the same time the idea of resurrecting from the sacred vaults an acknowledged masterpiece which invites the "paste-in" through the established convention of the cadenza was undoubtedly viewed as an opportunity for an unorthodox solution well beyond a Modernist collage exhibition or the simple fulfillment of a commission. Introducing a voice seemingly far removed from, but to a degree ascertainably indebted to, the cadenza solutions of Beethoven, and reflecting an attitude no less respectful but stylistically more alien than Schoenberg's arrangement of the G. M. Monn harpsichord concerto as a cello concerto (1932–33),[32] both Stockhausen and Schnittke have interpolated a localized, affectionate, and telling critique that reveals a central contemporary attitude. That these cadenza contributions may have identified a new and potent contemporary access to the classics is suggested by even more recent cadenzas for the Mozart oboe concerto by Charles Wuorinen as well as for Mozart's piano concertos K. 467 and 491 by Philip Glass.[33] Yet as with Duchamp, in all of these instances no actual defacement of the original took place: the original Mona Lisa survives as a *virgo intacta* in the Louvre, and the unsullied Ur-texts for Haydn, Mozart, and Beethoven are readily retrievable.

Whether Schnittke's and Stockhausen's cadenzas to standard concertos of the past are interpreted as part of the New Pluralism of the 1980s and 1990s, as a current and fashionable revivification of collage practices from the early decades of the century, or as a symptom of our residency in an age of Postmodernism wherein the potential for multiple readings of a prior legacy are obsessively mined, the taste for a fundamental musical habit in our time has been isolated.

The challenge that Schnittke's and Stockhausen's cadenzas are not comparable to Pei's pyramids in either scope or effect is worth countering. Though it can be argued that the playing time of a cadenza in comparison to that of the concerto as a whole is usually comparatively small, Schnittke's two cadenzas are an extraordinary four and two minutes in duration. Yet beyond all calculations concerning real time, there is an even more important psychological factor. For, when attending to performances by Gidon Kremer of the Beethoven concerto or by Markus Stockhausen of the Haydn, one listens specifically in anticipation of the cadenzas, and invariably audience commentary following such performances focuses almost exclusively on this issue. Perception and memory invert the relative temporal dimensions. The reasons are multiple and not hard to find: initially, the unavoidable recognition of an intrusion of the unfamiliar on familiar terrain; affection and some anxiety for tradition; self-identity for our times; the virtuosity of the performer; and, ultimately, relief from the numbness which can set in from repeated hearings of such ritualized repertoires.

Figure 16.6. Illuminated at dusk, the pyramid and fountains in front of the Louvre now claim parity with the Eiffel Tower and Arc du Carrousel.

Photo, Serge Sautereau / Courtesy of Pei Cobb Freed & Partners.

Obviously in the composition of cadenzas to Classic concertos Stock-hausen and Schnittke, Wuorinen and Glass have all asserted their relationship to the grand tradition, much as Pei did at the Louvre. But if such claims have been made by artists of virtually every age, the sense of insert that accompanies the writing of such cadenzas—much like the abutment of architectural additions to a classic edifice—forcefully conscripts new perspectives in the ongoing contemplation of the ancient-modern relationship. For if I. M. Pei has graced the Louvre with a set of crystal pyramids that function as welcoming conduits to the museum, there is more than one way of viewing his solution. From two angles, it stands in contrast with the Louis XIII or Napoleon III architecture behind it; from a third, and especially by night, the lighted pyramid and fountains greet other noble illuminations such as the Eiffel Tower, the Arc du Carrousel, and the Arc de Triomphe which have familiarly marked the city of Paris and claim parity with them (Figure 16.6). Regardless of our vantage point, we cannot forget the fact that the new pyramids are resident in a city that has played host to the art of the world—including specifically the art of Egypt and the Orient on numerous and historic occasions, and that the shape of Pei's additions is anything but ambiguous. Ultimately, recognition of both geographical and temporal dislocation is as unavoidable as with Stockhausen's and Schnittke's cadenzas, which can also be reviewed with respect to national pedigree, questions of aesthetics, form, and language, and prior cadenza guests in these very concertos. Yet there is a difference. I. M. Pei has provided a compatible and efficient but stylistically alien addition to the Louvre in a courtyard that was never intended to be filled in. With the Haydn and Beethoven concertos, however, the original architects had thoughtfully prepared the foundation for and invited such an insertion. Too, music's ready portability allows the cadenzas to be offered as an option, while the pyramids now stand as obligatory companions.

— 17 —

Envoi: The New Cartography

Every man possesses the whole of mankind within him. A European can experience Balinese music, a Japanese that from Mozambique, a Mexican Indian music.

Karlheinz Stockhausen

Many musical languages are spoken in order to make the larger statement convincing . . . tonal and atonal can live side by side.

George Rochberg

I am often haunted by the thought that all of the many musics of the world are coming together to form one music.

George Crumb

Cultural Relativism and Contemporary Arts

Simulating attitudes current among anthropologists in the United States and Germany in the period around 1900, ethnomusicologists in the first half of the twentieth century typically subscribed to the notion that non-Western music was essentially static, in stark contrast to Western music, which was dynamic. Although by the 1930s anthropology had begun to investigate the processes of cultural change, through the period to around 1970 ethnomusicology continued to foster the notion that because of the stasis and isolation of non-Western musics generally, not only were their underlying systems codifiable but their origins addressable. This hermetically sealed view of musical expression found the discipline disregarding "the most prominent kind of music in the world's cultures, music in which Western and non-Western elements were combined, and in which the musical practices and concepts from the West were used in various ways to modify non-Western traditions."[1] Not surprisingly it was an attitude that had mirrored anthropology's inability to contemplate a non-Western anthropology about the West.[2] Though it was the Western tradition that had promoted the value of seeing things from all sides, that had fostered the idea of cultural relativism, that had invented the notion of anthropology itself, and that had insistently asserted interest in the art and music of distant cultures, the very openness which claimed to foster objectivity quickly brought with it anxiety and the suspicion that it is impossible to assume genuine knowledge of another culture without giving up part of one's own.

The career of the Canadian Colin McPhee offers a classic example of this dilemma. Though the impact of Southeast Asian dance upon Diaghilev's troupe may have faded notably after 1910, a resuscitation of interest in Javanese dance followed the Paris Exposition of 1925.[3] At about the same time, McPhee, trained in Toronto, Baltimore, and Paris as a pianist and composer in the Western tradition, was attracted to the sounds of the Balinese gamelan through recordings which he heard as early as 1929. By the spring of 1931 he was already a member of a group called the New York Polyhymnia, whose purpose was "to foster international exchange of unknown musical cultures and of unknown works, old and new."[4] By the summer of that year he had arrived in Bali, where he was to remain for the next four years. His involvement with and ultimate rapture over the culture gradually led him to feel that his role as a Western composer was momentarily irrelevant, and in 1934 he announced that "the urge to write music had left." A similar experience befell Mantel Hood, who also traveled to Bali not as an ethnomusicologist but as a composer. "I took a stack of score paper three-feet high and all my black pencils. I came back after two years with the same blank score paper. I couldn't write a note. I didn't write again for ten years."[5] The comment by Boulez that "too great a knowledge of things inspires respect in us and prohibits spontaneous usage" springs to mind.[6]

Yet, in a manner not unlike Debussy's delayed response to Javanese music in "Et la lune descend," McPhee's study of the gamelan ultimately found an outlet in his own composition. On his way back to New York in the spring of 1935, McPhee wrote to Henry Cowell that his mind was brimming with ideas both for a book on Balinese music and for several orchestral works, including a fantasia for piano and orchestra on Balinese melodies and rhythms. McPhee characterized the fantasia as "authentic stuff and not dished-up impressions à la Eichheim," referring to Henry Eichheim's orchestral *Java* and *Bali,* written in 1929 and 1933.[7] McPhee's reputation ultimately rested on his important study *Music in Bali,* which was not published until two years after his death in 1966, and an impressive toccata for orchestra and two pianos, *Tabuh-Tabuhan* of 1936, which was promoted in large part by a recording. It is symptomatic of the period that the latter work was completed in Mexico with the encouragement of Carlos Chávez at a time that also saw Copland there and that found Chávez himself involved in the composition of a *Sinfonía India* based upon native Mexican materials. It would be another half century before scholars and composers alike would be in a position to acknowledge the importance of both Chávez and McPhee, and to sense that their impact was larger than the sum of our familiarity with their scores.

Concrete evidence that McPhee's story is less parochial than it would initially appear is dramatized by a meeting in 1939 between McPhee, recently returned from Bali, and the English composer Benjamin Britten, who had just arrived in America, where he was to remain until 1942. McPhee introduced Britten first to his *Balinese Ceremonial Music,* a transcription of Balinese gamelan music for two pianos, and the two performed and recorded it in 1941. Back in England Britten performed it again, this time with the English pianist Clifford Curzon in a Wigmore Hall recital of 1944. Some twelve years later on a concert tour of Southeast Asia with Peter Pears, Britten found himself in Bali, where once again he was transfixed by the richness of the musical culture. In time-honored practice, he began to make a set of his own manuscript sketches of gamelan performances, and shortly thereafter arranged a recording session of the finest gamelan ensemble in the town of Ubud. Ultimately McPhee's transcriptions and possibly even his *Tabuh-Tabuhan* together with Britten's own sketches and recordings provided important source material as well as a general catalytic influence in the composition of one of Britten's most important and least known scores, *The Prince of the Pagodas.*[8]

Britten's approach to his ballet, premiered on New Year's Day 1957 at the Royal Opera House in London, conspicuously transcended McPhee's desire to write "authentic stuff" or to avoid "dished-up impressions." For beyond the citation of Balinese musical material and allusion to the seductive sonority of its gamelans, Britten pursued the

Stravinskian aesthetic of cohabitation, which was finding its most recent expression in his currently produced *Agon* (1953–1957). Numerous features even appear to lay express claim to the authority of Stravinsky's persistent manner for the task at hand: repeated trumpet fanfares; reference to the "Danse chinoise" and "Valse des fleurs" from Tchaikovsky's *Nutcracker;* several citations from Stravinsky's *Apollon musagète* and one from Prokofiev's *Fiery Angel;* a march announcing the arrival of an Oriental emperor at his court; invocation of waltz, tango, and gavotte; an allusion to Strauss's celestial figure at the presentation of the silver rose; a variety of orchestral sonorities capable of claiming multiple sponsorship; and the overriding sense that Britten's exploration of the Middle Kingdom involved a respectful recognition of other pagodas from *Estampes* and *Ma Mère l'oye* to *Le Rossignol* and *Turandot*.[9]

Whether or not we are aware of it, our current fin-de-siècle promotion of multiculturalism is in no small measure a continuing reflection of the role played by Debussy and Stravinsky, Copland and Cowell, McPhee and Britten, Chávez, George Crumb, Steve Reich, and many others in periodically refueling interest in world repertoires and in encouraging study, performance, and ultimately appropriation. In the process such interests have also nourished the fitful Western preoccupation with eliminating cultural parochialism. From the time of the Renaissance, which brought the first self-conscious awareness of its cultural identity, Europe has struggled with its own claims to superiority and has typically encouraged self-criticism as a norm in paradoxical union with colonialist ambitions and perjuries. The West's development of the discipline of anthropology is frequently judged as the classic assertion of this tendency. But the conclusion inevitably follows that though the anthropologist may attempt to suspend judgment of other cultures, tolerance and criticism are anything but neutral ideals and are themselves clearly reflective of cultural attitudes.[10]

The disciplines of ethnomusicology and historical musicology have just begun to measure the nature and force of cross-cultural collusion, both in the past and in the twentieth century, and in the process they have sketched preliminary evidence regarding not only the allure of the exotic for the Eurocentric communities but the reverse appeal—that of Western thought, high and low, for non-Western societies.[11] This juggling of cultural values, especially evident in the programming and commissions of a group like the Kronos String Quartet, is symptomatic not so much of thoughtless entanglement as of the continuing appropriation of values that were lively at the last fin de siècle—now expanded to include a purview of the entire century: blues, Pop, and rap flourish as companions to atonality, electronics, and minimalism; Gershwin and Ellington time-share with Kevin Volans, Reich, Riley, Michael Daugherty, and John Zorn, who are played side by side with Bartók, Webern, and Górecki.[12]

Virtually all repertoires, "cultivated" and popular, offer the same potential for cross-over.[13] But what in the 1950s and 1960s amounted to a relatively limited interest in global references, in the 1970s, 1980s, and 1990s burgeoned to a commonplace well beyond the initial impact of Colin McPhee's Bali or Steve Reich's Ghana. Indonesian gamelan and West African drumming were increasingly claimed as familiar musical expressions by Westerners even as American popular idioms were reciprocally absorbed. A formerly somewhat esoteric interest in the cultures which spawned these musics progressively became a Western preoccupation, and it was even suggested that there could be moral benefits in attending to such repertoires.

The degree to which the pace quickened in the second half of the century is exemplified in the work of Olivier Messiaen. His use of Greek modes in the 1940s ostensibly reached back to the beginning of Western civilization, but by the end of that decade he was already broadening his perspectives to incorporate manifestations of Hindu culture alongside the medieval Tristan legend and even a gamelan-like ensemble in his *Turangalîla-Symphonie* (1946–1948) for large orchestra. Then in the 1950s his highly intellectualized adaptation of Hindu ragas wedded Eastern rules to Viennese serialism in a fashion that retrospectively spelled Debussy's view of the Javanese *slendro* as a superficial fantasy. By the 1960s Messiaen, like many others, had been attracted to Japan, and he sympathetically falsified a courtly Gagaku ensemble in tandem with a miniature *catalogue des oiseaux* for his *Sept haikai* of 1962.

Stockhausen has related an even more elaborate and multi-directional interchange. In his *Telemusik* of 1966 he claimed that "the crass dualism between old and new, traditional and modern, primitive music and art-music—yes, even Asian and European music was dissolved" and announced "the beginning of a genuine 'symbiosis' of European, Asian, African, and South American music: *Tele-Musik*."[14] While such prescient remarks were destined to resound in numerous quarters to the end of the century, Stockhausen's attempt to integrate "an extinct Japanese musical style with folkloristic elements of many other cultures in a unified electronic–*musique concrète* composition" found an even more immediate response. For confronted with Stockhausen's example, native Japanese composers, who had previously been drawn almost exclusively to the music of the European avant-garde of the 1950s, "now combined European and Japanese musical instruments and sought out a stylistic symbiosis between modern European and old Japanese music."[15]

By the time of the Olympic Games held in Munich in 1972, the association between "World Culture and Modern Art" was sufficiently commonplace that a vast exhibit was set up as a complement to the parade of athletes from around the world. The visionary fraternity that had empowered the modern notion of these games was extended to include exhibitions that tested the notion of Orientalism and Primitivism in painting, theater, and music. Even the "Chinese Emperor's March" from Stravinsky's *Le Rossignol* was piped daily through the loudspeakers![16]

Redefining High and Low

If a tributary of musical-theatrical Orientalism as an adjunct to world sports contests reflected a capacity for transfer both between cultures and between high and low repertoires, similar shifts within the popular categories themselves rendered increasingly elusive the notion of source purity. Noting how the intermingling of rhythms from various ethnic groups and cultures had vitalized Caribbean music for centuries, Daisann McLane has highlighted the quickening pace at which events unfold today. Because of improvements in recording technologies and increased mobility among Caribbean peoples as well as the executives of the northern media centers such as New York, London, and Paris,

> a rhythm developed in one end of the region can rip up dance floors a thousand miles away in a matter of months, even weeks . . . A soca record from Trinidad makes a splash in northern Brazil, where a local musician who likes the beat modifies it, then adds it to a popular Bolivian melody. The new sound is a hit in Bahia, where a French record company executive on vacation hears it, buys the rights and takes it to Paris. And everything comes up lambada.[17]

But beyond cultural fusion among vernaculars, recent calls for parity between "high" and "low" in all the arts reflect a further dimension of the contemporary infatuation with cultural criss-cross.[18] A great deal of the Postmodernist argument has centered on the destruction of traditional differentiations between categories: high and low, artist and critic, signified and signifier. As John McGowan has put it, "In each case, the goal is to unsettle a privilege that accrues to one side of the pair and that can be maintained only by a logic of separation."[19] Indeed, in the decades of the seventies, eighties, and nineties, numerous composers, even those only obliquely concerned with the distended critical base, appeared intent on making this precise point.

William Bolcom, for example, has effectively asserted not only the force of both cultivated and vernacular repertoires but also their fertilizing capacity through juxtaposition, claiming the power of memory for all musics in works such as the *Songs of Innocence and Experience* (1984). Served up in the context of a traditional oratorio, Bolcom's work of three hours' duration employs an orchestra, chorus, and soloists, as well as a children's choir, a madrigal group, a boy soprano, and a rock ensemble. Sometimes Bolcom utilizes the sound world of Stockhausen and Berio as the connective tissue to a mixture of cradle song, tavern tune, waltz, reggae, and disco beat. Yet the in-and-out movement from dissonant chromaticism to overt tonality not only provides contrast but helps to shape the drama of the whole. Both eye and ear shift constantly with the spotlight. Recalling the mixture of ritual and theater in Leonard Bernstein's *Mass,* the multiplicity of musical languages presents not so much an integrated vision or authentic allusion to the age of Blake as a powerful meditation upon the prevailing authority of variable musical vocabularies and sonic overrun in contemporary life. In his even more recent opera, *McTeague,* commissioned by the Chicago Lyric Opera and premiered in 1992, Bolcom tuned some of the same ingredients to a different task, and playing the master of synthesis as much as eclecticism, he demonstrated once more the appeal of his approach for an age.[20] Philip Glass's *Low* Symphony, based on themes from David Bowie's rock album *Low* and premiered only a few weeks after Bolcom's opera, offered evidence of a similar perspective from a minimalist quarter.[21]

William Albright, one of Bolcom's colleagues in the 1960s rag revival, also demonstrated not only the accruing authority but the compelling vitality of criss-cross in his "neo-everything" *Concerto for Harpsichord and Strings* of 1991. Falla's, Poulenc's, and Stravinsky's sensitivity to the genre and instrument may be in the wings, but the work is less an update or a nostalgic backward glance than a post–Postmodern love letter to the world of music. Recapitulation, cadenza, and coda; Baroque sound source and articulation; funeral march and smokey jazz lament; the texture and tonality of Beethoven's Fourth Piano Concerto; Middle Eastern heterophonic incantantion and hoopla—"part boogie, part fandango corrected mid-course by a 'Valse triste'"—collectively proclaim the recurring homily of the twentieth-century composer: past and present, high and low, East and West are all his natural domain and in skillful hands may be joined in a powerful embrace.[22] Indeed, the blank parody and inherent neutrality attributed to Postmodernist pastiche by Fredric Jameson is nowhere in sight, and the claim that the "new age" aesthetic has brought not only the death of the subject but the dissolution of personality is laid bare as a myth.[23]

At the same time, such works force recall of the fact that composers on one side or another of the so-called vernacular/cultivated divide have been crossing back and forth during the greater part of the twentieth century: Scott Joplin penned the opera *Tremonisha* (1915) as well as "Maple Leaf Rag"; Duke Ellington gave us "Sophisticated Lady" but also the torso of an opera, *Queenie Pie;* Gershwin, "I Got Rhythm" (*Girl Crazy,* 1930) as well as *Porgy and Bess* (1934), the Piano Concerto in F, and *An American in Paris;* Leonard Bernstein composed works like the *Jeremiah* Symphony and *Chichester Psalms* in tandem with *On the Town, Candide,* and *West Side Story;* Kurt Weill gave us *Lady in the Dark* but also *Mahagonny* and a violin concerto.

More recently Frank Zappa, of "Valley Girl," penned an attractive but thoroughly highbrow work called *The Perfect Stranger,* released on a compact disc conducted by Pierre Boulez; and David Byrne of Talking Heads fashioned a ballet, *The Catherine Wheel,* for Twyla Tharp as well as an orchestral work, *The Forest,* for the Chicago Symphony and a small vocal ensemble which sings "haunting syllables and dirges throughout its 60-minute duration."[24] Stewart Copeland, founder and drummer of the Police, in late 1989 received a world premiere of his minimalist-inclined opera *Holy Blood and Crescent Moon;* and even hardcore punk artist Glenn Branca has written six "symphonies" for a large ensemble of electric guitars as well as a purely orchestral piece, *Freeform,* premiered in June 1991 by the New York Orchestra of St. Luke's. Is it any surprise, then, that Eric Clapton has recorded a Concerto for Guitar and Orchestra written for him by the film composer Michael Kamen, or that Prince provided the music for *Billboards,* a work premiered on January 27, 1993, in Iowa City on a commission from the Joffrey Ballet? Or that Beatle Paul McCartney, who had in another era co-composed

"I Want to Hold Your Hand," co-wrote the eight-movement *Liverpool Oratorio,* which secured the services of the Royal Liverpool Philharmonic Orchestra and Chorus as well as Dame Kiri Te Kanawa and other stellar soloists for its televised world premiere in June 1991? McCartney, who to the present day is innocent of music notation, confessed, "I've always had half an eye on going in this direction."[25] Totally confounding the categories was the reception of the Third Symphony (1976) by Henryk Górecki, which achieved an unprecedented crossover in its ascent to the top ten of the British Pop charts in the spring of 1993.

Though, like the Dadaists, many of the Darmstadt generation of the 1950s and 1960s gradually rejected the thoroughly Western idea of the masterpiece, some critics began to voice the possibility of reappropriating the category in non-traditional terrain. For if a masterpiece presumes a guiding genius, then there should be no reason to exclude Duke Ellington, for example, or other masters of jazz.[26] Or the Beatles, the Jefferson Starship, Elvis Presley. Arguments that had centered on the high-low relationship from the turn of the century had once again begun to force a reconsideration of the canon and the masterpiece syndrome.[27] The arguments were not very different from the discussions surrounding the Art of the Everyday in the teens or the struggle to define the nature and power of jazz in the twenties. Popular musical expressions which had traditionally spoofed the very idea of critical respectability and, consequently, held the notion of the masterpiece to be irrelevant were now enjoined in a controversy that appeared largely to be of concern to the critics, not to the swelling roster of admirers, whose numbers were already legion.

In pursuit of the continuing elimination of cultural borderlines, it has been repeatedly noted that elite culture today aspires to mass popularity, popular cultures resounding from the mass media seek intellectual upgrading and emotional enrichment, and both high and low draw from a similar stockpile of violence, sexuality, and societal confusion with varying claims to historical relevance.[28] "Cross-over" artists like Laurie Anderson,[29] the punk world of the Sex Pistols,[30] and Madonna[31] have all begun to attract a critical following whose deconstructive jargon is as far removed from the interests of the typical audience listening to these musics as that of the theorists who expound on classical repertoires, and recent trends point to a similar development in the world of jazz.

A 1990 show at the Museum of Modern Art, entitled "High and

Low: Popular Culture and Modern Art,"[32] pressed a related contemporary, even specifically all-American, dream by honoring the comic strips alongside easel painting. We were reminded that in 1960 Andy Warhol bled patches of a crossword puzzle against a blank cutout of Popeye, whose contrast was said to promote less an idealization of mass culture than a sense of isolation and iconic presence in the recognition that "the very highest and very lowest visual elements in the culture—Mondrian and a crossword. . .—had already a punning similarity"[33] (see Figure 17.1). The lineage of Lichtenstein's *Okay, Hot-Shot* (1963) was now retraced to Degas and especially Gauguin (*Vision after the Sermon,* 1888) in the use of looming foregrounds counterposed against a theatri-

Figure 17.1. Andy Warhol, *Popeye*, 1960.

Collection Mr. and Mrs. S. I. Newhouse, Jr. © The Andy Warhol Foundation of the Visual Arts, 1994.

cal recession, and rather than surrendering to the forces of mass culture the Pop artists of the 1960s and 1970s were judged to have been hanging on for dear life; "it was high art that had the live ammo, and it recreated popular culture in its own image."[34]

If the lingo seemed fresh, the underlying relationship was clearly capable of being spotted at other crucial moments in both American and non-American venues in earlier decades. Robert Rosenblum has also reviewed for us how Cubism's alliance with Pop culture constantly invoked "a juggling act between, on the one hand, an arcane visual language that was legible only to an elite group of artists and their audience and, on the other, a profusion of popular references that, while often obscure to us, could be understood by any resident of Paris on the eve of World War I."[35] Similarly, Stravinsky's voracious appetite for the vernacular in his three early ballets as well as Goncharova's and Larionov's reliance upon the broadsheet style of the *lubok* in their earliest Diaghilev productions directly invoked the power of the high-low constituency. And just as Toulouse-Lautrec mediated the force of commercial advertisement and high art in his cabaret posters well before Andy Warhol, so his contemporary Erik Satie appropriated the world of the café-concert in a fashion that later served Cocteau in his transferral of this vision to local French traditions of the *image d'Épinal* and breathed life into a new generation of musicians dubbed Les Six.

A kindred phenomenon surfaced not only in the ragtime revival of the 1960s but repeatedly in the late 1980s and early 1990s with the cross-over artists and composers mentioned above as well as with composers like Michael Daugherty (b. 1954). Inspired by Pop personalities like Desi Arnez, Buddy Rich, and Liberace and tuned to the power of the comics, he has noted the fascinating and troubling contradictions in our culture and sought out a metaphor for them in the appropriation of formerly taboo subjects. His orchestral *Superman Suite* (1988–1993) has separate movements entitled "Lex" (an orchestral chase scene highlighted by police whistles), "Mxyzptlk," "Oh Lois!" and "Bizarro." Frankly in search of options beyond the abstract, he develops his view of Superman less from the comic strip than from the film versions, where the rate of speed is very fast, the episodes are brief, to the point, and, as he puts it, "without much fat." Analogously, his compositional technique aims at melding cinematic practices with the contemporary freedom provided by the television remote control. Yet, rather than confecting a highbrow imitation of popular culture, like Warhol and

Lichtenstein he harnesses the "ammo of high art," assembling an array of procedures and clichés drawn from Stravinsky to the minimalists as receiving hosts for a smorgasbord of sounds extracted from Pop.

The current venerators of Pop would include few, however, who would remember John Alden Carpenter's comicstrip ballet *Krazy Kat* (1921), Hindemith's mechanical organ music for a film, *Felix der Kater im Zirkus* (1926), or, conversely, Louis Armstrong's infatuation with opera evident in the extensive borrowings from this repertoire in his pioneering trumpet improvisations of the same period.[36] A later generation is therefore now free to infer and embellish a whole new set of corollaries. In retrospect it is clear, nonetheless, that many of the issues that were audible as well as visible in the opening decades of the twentieth century are still around, though the proportions have been adjusted and the message has been retouched. As in *Finnegans Wake,* the last sentence connects with and seemingly completes the first. Yet on the return journey there is little sense of a circular trajectory, since memory of those conditions which attended the outward voyage is slim.

For along the way the categories of highbrow and lowbrow have continually been reshuffled. True jazz—reviewed via recordings, hybrid imitations, or updated transformations that frequently move a considerable distance from the original—is less popular than it was in the 1920s, is still music for the connoisseur, perhaps more elitist than ever, fostered by the academy, increasingly subjected to cultural critique, and enjoyed now by an audience probably no larger than that for Mahler. In the meantime, however, other popular musics have materialized, prospered, and found themselves designated as social reference points. In a world that has never heard of Daugherty's *Beatboxer* (1992)[37] or Morton Gould's *The Jogger and the Dinosaur* (1993)—a symphonic rap narrative for children—rap has been canonized as an innovative art form among blacks and as source material for whites. But just as Gershwin found resistance to his appropriations and Elvis Presley was blamed for the cross-cultural commandeering of rock-and-roll, so the arbiters of hip hop culture struggled to determine the possible role of a white presence. Conversely, and somewhat predictably, rap's familiar television imagery also served the country music executives as a negative stereotype in an attempt to sell a new traditionalism and a return to homespun values.[38]

From another quarter in 1992 Michael Jackson pursued a celebration of the virtues of brotherhood among blacks, Orientals, and Native

Americans in the company of a Western European canonic text long celebrated for its promotion of global fraternity: a 1966 George Szell recording of Beethoven's Ninth Symphony. In this instance, however, the spectre of copyright infringements not unexpectedly loomed and threatened to spoil his show. It was not a problem that the nineteenth-century black minstrel had to face in his repeated citations of and co-nundrums based upon Shakespeare;[39] that the earlier jazz performer had to contend with in appropriating Mendelssohn's "Wedding March," Rachmaninov's C♯ minor prelude, the minuet from Ravel's *Sonatine,* or C. P. E. Bach's "Solfeggietto";[40] or that caused any problems for Barry Manilow in his citation of a Chopin prelude in "Could It Be Magic," for Emerson, Lake, and Palmer in their appropriation of Mu-sorgsky's *Pictures at an Exhibition,* or for Paul Simon in his parody of Bach's "O Haupt voll Blut und Wunden" in "American Tune."[41]

Beyond questions of ownership or copyright, such borrowings con-firm a continuing awareness of and ready access to high culture by mak-ers of popular music throughout the twentieth century as a counterpart to the much more widely discussed reverse phenomenon. Just as Shake-speare and opera served as cornerstones of both popular and elite culture in nineteenth-century America,[42] so the appropriation of a Beethoven symphony by a popular entertainer today would make little sense unless its recognition could be assumed by a large segment of society.

It is sobering to discover that today the Igbo people of southeastern Nigeria routinely indulge in a kindred type of communicating with quotations reflective of their multicultural exposure that could with rea-son fill Modern and Postmodern artists with envy. Their easy accession in daily speech of a rich collection of local proverbs as well as biblical references and citations from classical English literature reflects the ad-vantages analogously sensed by musicians from Boston to Bali: a call upon the authority of the past through polylingual reference; the atten-dant capacity to confront if not resolve multiple points of view; and a depersonalization that promotes the sense that universals have been tapped in the formation of idealized models for daily behavior.[43]

The practice of both allusion and quotation, therefore, is rich, vola-tile, and of ancient stock. Just as members of Igbo society and listeners to Western art music take a measure of cultural pride in being able to recognize a rich parade of citations, so popular musical repertoires everywhere regularly operate under a similar premise that one must be "in the know" in order to comprehend the relationship between various "cover" versions of the same tune and text as well as recondite allusions to both well-known and generally unfamiliar repertoires. Recognition of a subtext, a sense of "getting it," carries a note of satisfaction to listeners in virtually all repertoires. The response is as to the story teller, whose art is contingent upon both memory and modification. Though the alternate embrace and dismissal of a knowledge of texts and subtexts in the appreciation of a work of art has been subject to deliberate exaggeration in recent criticism, a single, incontrovertible proposition ultimately surfaces: appreciation of art, as of life, is not only enhanced by but, indeed, allowed solely through the invocation of memory at every turn.

A problem with no easy answer in sight, however, has recently surfaced in the world of Pop music with the surfeit of opportunities in an age of digital reproduction. Electronics, computers, sound-bites, and sampling have reduced the field to a state of chaos, where storage, reproduction, transformation, even so-called deconstruction of repertoires have provided a wealth not only of opportunities but of confusion with respect to authorship, performer, and materials. Collage has achieved a new meaning in a runaway organism that virtually defies identification of origins in any parameter, and the notion of authority virtually disappears at the hands of the technical producer, who is free to juxtapose and manipulate at will in the creation of the final product. Pop has plundered its archives and in the process has become so self-referential that it has been remarked that songs frequently sound like copies of parodies. In 1988 Andrew Goodwin made the following observation: "On his recent solo LP *Now and Zen,* former Led Zeppelin vocalist Robert Plant samples from his old recordings, having spent the last few years listening to new bands sample his old records. Plant decided it was time to pastiche from his own pastiche."[44]

Not surprisingly, the complex issues surrounding the permissiveness of the new technologies have spawned a cluster of Postmodernist theories for popular music that invoke Walter Benjamin, Peter Wollen, and other cultural analysts, complete with a critical vocabulary and recondite argumentation that protest their relevance for high art. In light of music's perennial advancement through seductive and sympathetic technologies, it should come as no surprise if such predictions soon prove to be accurate. Yet in such extreme tendencies the critics have attempted to justify further telling distinctions between Modern and Postmodern habits: though heterogeneity and simultaneity are common to both, claims abound that the Postmodern mode has gradually yielded to a telling transition from resonating parody to faceless citation. Such judgments, however, have seldom been put to a meaningful test in the world of music and tend to linger stillborn in the world of cultural criticism.

Media, Maps, and Time-Space Fusion

Collectively, the various media have helped to promote cross-over between high and low and dissolution of ethnic and chronological boundaries as well, in what is alternately viewed as a grand alliance or an exalted confusion. A combination of such possibilities was forwarded as a fundamental premise of Peter Sellar's 1990 productions of a series of Mozart operas on PBS. In *Le nozze di Figaro* Hapsburg Vienna and Prague are relocated in New York's Trump Tower. Tide and Crest stand on the shelf, and Batman earrings and video Camcorders attest to the currency of the message at hand. Have the directors undertaken such transferences and rejuxtapositions in order to underscore Mozart's continuing validity? Or is there perhaps a subliminal desire not so much to disenfranchise Mozart or to reclaim the opera's masterpiece status as to vivify through parody, in the emulative sense, a work that otherwise teeters on the brink of banality through excessive repetition?

Whatever the composite of reasons, it seems clear that, like the Early Music movement's persistent vivification of aging or unknown repertoires for the present through the application of a newly designed set of "performance practices," the late twentieth-century fascination with reconstructing opera from Monteverdi to Wagner reflected current investments in promoting novel perspectives on familiar terrain even as it identified a prevailing disdain—or at best antipathy—for contemporary opera per se through the period of the 1980s.[45] Three American operas premiered in the fall of 1992, William Bolcom's *McTeague,* Philip Glass's *The Voyage,* and John Corigliano's *The Ghosts of Versailles,* appeared to attempt redress of this state of affairs while remaining mindful of the tastes of an age. Calling up Beaumarchais, Marie Antoinette, and Figaro and company in a panoramic revisitation of familiars, Corigliano's music ran the gamut from Mozart and Rossini to Ravel and the most recent Neoromantic and intergalactic sound worlds. *Ghosts* was offered as fantasy, as high-camp comedy, and, quite pointedly, as an opera that could make claims to Postmodernity.

It is possible to sense in both Corigliano's and Sellar's work a confirmation of literary criticism's current devotion to the notion of inter-
textuality: the sense that a given text discloses its collective meaning
only through perpetual and obsessive re-reading in relation to other
texts. Corigliano's position can also be related to the notion of *misreading*
as forwarded by Harold Bloom and interpreted in musical contexts by
Joseph Straus and Kevin Korsyn.[46] Their shared perspective implies not
only intentional and purposeful transformation of a model in the initial
creative process but the recognition that, while criticism may further
a sense of completion of the work, the meaning of any given piece of
music can ultimately be expressed only as another composition.[47] Yet
regardless of how one tunes the argument, contemporary criticism must
inevitably be haunted by the fact that the search for originality through
recognition of a concealed or announced model is not a discovery of
late twentieth-century hermeneutics but, indeed, is enfolded in an ancient and venerable tradition of both theory and practice.[48]

Whatever the history or pedigree of the idea and our contemporary
claims for it, it is clear that the recruitment and revivification of works
from the past, frequently as a companion to more current languages,
persistently surfaced as a principal habit of the 1980s and 1990s. But in
contrast with contemporary concerns for "authenticity" in matters of
musical text and performance practice, tampering with the visual component has assumed a fresh and vital new role. What the still camera
initiated and the cinema promoted, television and the VCR have now
escalated to an unprecedented and perhaps irreversible domination—
some would say contamination—of our daily lives. With the assistance
of a new breed of vocal superstar whose show biz potential in a few
instances has approached, if not equaled, that of the rock star, opera
has become the supreme playing field: *Tosca* has been relocated in Nazi
Germany and Scarpia recast as a member of the Gestapo; Wagner's *Nie-
belungenlied* has been transferred to the Industrial Revolution; and Stravinsky's *Rake* has abandoned Hogarth's eighteenth century for a world
of leather jackets and Sony Walkmen. That such "misreadings" are essentially visual and cannot be projected on an audio recording provides
little cause for concern in light of the ubiquity of the VCR and the
ready availability of laser video recordings of a swollen roster of operas
in multiple versions.

It might be noted, however, that the social power of such willful
kinds of deception is verifiable throughout the history of cartography,

which provides one of the surest reflections of humanity's changing perspectives. More than geographical records, such charts are frequently maps of the mind as well. Indeed, from the medieval "T-O" maps (Figure 17.2)—which showed the earth as a flat disc, divided into the three continents of Europe, Asia, and Africa with the top of the map being east and the center of the earth located at Jerusalem in accordance with Scripture—to Renaissance maps reflecting the Age of Discovery, ever-changing cultural biases have been recorded.[49] Perhaps no one, however, ever eclipsed the overtness or whimsicality of the Surrealists' map of the world published in *Variétés* in 1929 (Figure 17.3). Here distortion does not so much fly in the face of available information as register a consortium of current values. One quickly notes the Surrealists' esteem for Easter Island ("Ile de Pâques"), much enlarged, and their dismissal of the United States of America, totally suppressed.[50]

Yet a credo of the late twentieth century that would center on the deconstruction of each and every text in search of a concealed opposite and note the strategies employed in the cover-up[51] not only had been envisioned and preempted by the Dadaists[52] but by definition had served artists and historians of every stripe throughout the ages. The search for the new characteristically transcends its original mission and perpetually clears the path to a new standard; the classics are inevitably born of those impulses that fueled the avant-gardes. Whatever the constituent

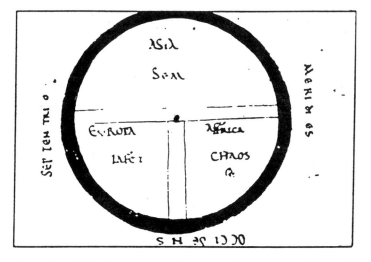

Figure 17.2. T-O Map, from the *Etymology* of Isidore of Seville (ca. 560–636).

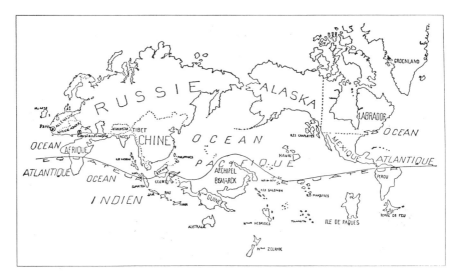

Figure 17.3. Surrealist map of the world, from the magazine *Variétés*, 1929.

elements, in the late twentieth century *authenticity* is no longer confused with *authority* in music, and the contemporary artist, with an ease that makes Debussy's imaginary excursions into Java appear timid, has taken the world as his oyster in an affectionate, if somewhat compulsive, embrace.

Art and Colonialism Revisited

The current drive to reevaluate the whole of Western European history and the ready willingness on the part of some Americans to flagellate themselves for their genetic connections to Europe and its colonializing attitudes has now led to a joyless discrediting in some quarters of all art and music potentially reflective of such encounters. Columbus, on the eve of quincentennial celebrations of his voyage, was seized upon as the historical figure most susceptible to charges of multiple contemporary heresies—Eurocentrism, imperialism, elitism, and phallocentrism.[53] Appropriately, the new perspective argued for a recounting of the Spanish conquest of the Americas, of enforced Christianity, of the abuse and enslaving of Native Americans, and continued deception and pillage following the birth of a nation. For most Native Americans the quincentennial was celebrated as five hundred years of cultural survival in the face of enormous odds.

Thus by 1992 world social history had been so broadly reevaluated and rewritten that many of the perspectives attendant to the Paris Expositions of 1889 and 1900 as well as the Chicago Exposition of 1893 had largely disappeared from view. For despite the acceleration of ecumenical and global values in the arts generally, the discipline of anthropology and by extension ethnomusicology had been subject to such realignment that some began to wonder how long it would be before the Javanese gamelans, present at all three expositions and long familiar to several American university campuses, were expelled as politically incorrect. For following renewed charges of material plunder and spiritual violation against Columbus and his successors, uncertitude and disquiet began to reign among the ranks of Western ethnomusicologists who had gone to China, Japan, and Java, had studied and preserved their classical repertoires from "inevitable extinction," and had brought them home where they were "marginalized"—subject no longer to modification, but only to loss of function and cultural-spiritual atrophy.[54]

That the phenomenon was observable in reverse, however, is worthy of momentary consideration. Eta Harich-Schneider, a German harpsichordist and musicologist who lived the years of World War II in Tokyo and who was one of the first Westerners to be given access to the traditions of courtly Gagaku, has noted that

> for a century, thousands of Japanese have made their musical studies in the West, and for the rest of their lives preserved the musical style prevailing in the West at the time they studied. The method is accumulative, comparable to the agglutinative structure of their language. Because of this strange traditionalism (to which we owe the precious survivals from remote times) all trends of Western music of the past sixty or more years, long obsolete in the place of their origin, survive in Japan.

Noting a tendency of the Japanese students to form distinctive French, Viennese, or German groups reflective of the site of their studies, she observed groups dedicated to *nouveau-classicisme,* Les Six, and the like. But she also found the copying of the satirical, negative style typical of Auric, Satie, and Milhaud to be inadequate "because they poked fun at a romanticism which they, the Japanese, had never had."[55]

The new technologies which have shrunk our globe have irrevocably brought the tribes of mankind face to face in all their diversity. Left conscience-stricken about an appropriate stance with respect to world cultures, we now seek to satisfy curiosity about our brethren and yet remain free of any taint of colonialism—now redefined to include artistic and intellectual appropriation. Having formerly charged Eurocentrism and elitism against Western historiographers, the ethnomusicologist has begun to sense a similar plight. Noting ethnomusicology's mounting crisis of confidence and a loss of faith in its objectivity, Judith Becker has stated the dilemma with rare candor: "Most painfully of all, we have come to see ourselves as a part of the enemy, the colonialists, the imperialists, the exploiters . . . We have found the enemy, and she is us . . . We've lost, in our own eyes, something of our superior position vis-à-vis what we think of as the elitist study of Western classical music. Our own elitism has emerged."[56]

The ethnomusicologists' new sensitivity now appears due less to a failed mission or improper behavior per se than to the recognition of the similarity of their own presumptive anthropological fantasies to the colonial mythologies of Western artists and historians. Looking back at the time which attended the birth of Modernism, however, it is difficult for us to imagine that any other than the most hardened critic would deny to Debussy and Ravel, Holst and Stravinsky, Bartók and Milhaud, Louis Benedictus and Louis Laloy those discoveries that surfaced as the result of such a compelling cultural interface. Though the art of the twentieth-century composer may in some degree be seen as a by-product of the Age of Columbus and the ensuing Age of Colonialism, Modernism's pancultural outreach, while undoubtedly reflecting varied societal values, was rarely constituted from the basest political and social motives. The story is rather less simple than that. It is also more interesting and, in general, more benevolent. Indeed, the Western musician has continuously looked to the East—and conversely the Orient has frequently, if intermittently, viewed the Occident—with an affection that seems to elude society at large. In retrospect the same claim may surely be registered for the Western ethnomusicologist as well.

We note evidence of the continuing proliferation of such attitudes in the world of music in unlikely places. Denise Hamilton's 1990 report in the *Los Angeles Times,* for example, took note of the fact that the taste of Japanese youth for the Rolling Stones and Madonna has been enlarged to embrace "Buraku-con," or black contemporary artists such as Bobby Brown, Janet Jackson, and Bell Biv Devoe as well as Prince and George Michael—and this in a society where ethnic diversity is shunned. We know that something of this same capacity for ecumeni-

cism is also true of the art music of contemporary Japan, where alongside the continuing traditions of No, Bunraku, and Gagaku, the composer Toru Takemitsu has produced sympathetic blends of East and
West for symphonic orchestra with hichiriki and samisen soloists, and
other composers continuously and openly address the aesthetic questions currently being debated by Americans and Europeans.[57] In Java,
too, the gamelan today willingly adopts and transforms the chimes of
Big Ben and in a work like Evan Ziporyn's *Filling Station* has invited
the participation of the Western composer, providing an inverted complement to the work of McPhee *(Tabuh-Tabuhan),* Boulez *(Le Marteau),*
Britten *(Prince of the Pagodas),* Crumb *(Ancient Voices of Children),* Stockhausen *(Inori),* Hartke *(Pacific Rim),* and a host of others.

Generally speaking, however, the contemporary Western composer
has tended not to envy but rather has sought to transcend the curiosity
of the ethnomusicologist who studies the music of Japan, transports it
to America, and cultivates its traditions with a respect that disallows
tampering, only to find that he has marginalized a repertoire that still
undergoes transformation in its native land.[58] Far from feeling guilty of
a kind of cultural imperialism or of acting as an agent for the diminution
of the communities that have supplied him with the touchstones of his
art, the composer today knows that he cannot give up his own identity
following such encounters. Turning over the memory of the music and
the context in which he first chanced upon it, the composer will be
content to use Tristan's scissors, to rearrange Stein's bits and pieces, to
use or resist an airbrush in order to conceal or accent the framing edge
of his appropriation, to discover for himself undreamed-of conjugations, and to confect a new story. Realizing that to avoid the politics
of art completely is a political act itself, the composer also knows that
in the great works of the past political issues tend to cancel one another
out. In the enduring repertoires, black and white, male and female,
imperialist and native—all dichotomies—inevitably serve the quest for
a larger story that illuminates the human dilemma common to all.[59]

As a consequence, "acculturation," which has variously been defined
as adoption and adaptation of a different culture or negatively as a loss
of culture, has lost its former Eurocentric colonialist connotations and
is now seen to be working in reverse. "Musical transculturation" has
been proposed as an acceptable expression to signify the "complete cycle of positive musical processes set in motion by culture contact" in
order to avoid a term loaded with an ethnocentric etymological his-

tory.[60] With the realization that analysis concerning parentage will not yield all the pertinent information, new approaches which emphasize the role of fusion and transformation have recently emerged. Notions of hegemony begin to fade and the natural permeability of adjacent cultural borders is increasingly acknowledged. Interest in invoicing African drum rhythms as well as European developments which may have served as the basis for the syncopations of jazz has given way, for example, to a consideration of their musical and extra-musical meanings in a new context.

Wynton Marsalis' *Citi Movement,* written for the Garth Fagan dance group in 1991, not only allows but encourages such a perspective. Like Ellington's review of his people in *Black, Brown, and Beige,* Marsalis' 132-minute opus is charged with history. Unlike Ellington, he has "taken collage seriously as an esthetic," blending circus music, New Orleans polyphony, Afro-Caribbean beat, Ellington's piano figures and reed writing, European concert music, and the cacophony of the city in an optimistic celebration of a place typically characterized by noise, poverty, and homelessness. Like Ellington's, his music embraces composition as much as free soloing, but now in order to participate the players of Marsalis' group have to be "as familiar with ragtime and New Orleans marches as be-bop and the music of John Coltrane."[61]

Lest we think that such perspectives and actions are the discovery of a Postmodern age, however, it is sobering to recall Ralph Waldo Emerson's judgment concerning what he already understood to be the ongoing and historic nature of such conjunctions: "We are as much informed of a writer's genius by what he selects as by what he originates. We read the quotation with his eyes, and find a new and fervent sense; as a passage from one of the poets, well recited, borrows new interest from the rendering. As the journals say, 'the italics are ours.' "[62]

Identity: Beginnings and Endings

The indifference or even antagonism of both Dada and Postmodernism to the concepts of genius and masterpiece has been regarded in some quarters as indicative of a restless, if so far unsuccessful, search for a spiritual substitute in a highly secular age. Indeed, the Postmodernist venture has been described as a turn to the most empty abstractionism of the Modern period, now convened in a playful assemblage of objects stripped of all cultural context and of history. Citation has now been held to resonate not as a momentary reference but as a genuine incorporation of substance.[63] Such adjudications have seldom involved reference to specific repertoires, however, and while a comparison between Stravinsky's several X-ray rags from the late teens and Bolcom's "Graceful Ghost Rag" (1970) might allow general corroboration of such a claim, a consideration of Corigliano's interrupting citations of Albéniz's tango in his symphony of 1990 alongside Stravinsky's substantive "Tango" for piano of 1940 would seem to destroy it, perhaps even argue that the perspective ought to be reversed. Yet, whatever the vulnerability of Fredric Jameson's contention that Postmodernism's adoption of Modernist codes has rendered it faceless, replacing parody with pastiche that lacks bite or inference, he is surely correct when he forwards the claim that in music "not Schoenberg . . . but Stravinsky is the true precursor of postmodern cultural production."[64]

The critics of Postmodernism's basest side have charged nihilism, kitsch, banality, Disneyland culture, cheap imitation, and a delight in a kind of decadence redolent of the last fin de siècle.[65] Yet, somewhat paradoxically, as was true for the Dadaists—who deplored the masterpiece along with banality, praised the intellect and bemoaned the academy—the idea of the masterpiece is anathema to many present-day academics eager to promote the cause of Third World musics and popular arts of every stripe. The cry has come: "Roll over, Beethoven."[66] Despite the potential nobility of such a crusade, the argument fails to acknowledge that the Western canon has always been in a state of flux, and that the European musical tradition may be viewed as the paradigmatic example of cultural ecumenicism. With the addition of new repertoires our estimates of the old have always been revised to some degree. Such adjustments, it should be clear, are by-products of the same cultural relativism which the multiculturalists now claim to have discovered.[67]

For the second half of the twentieth century has been witness to the accession of vast quantities of earlier repertoires with their own hierarchies as well as the realignment of more recent ones. The steady glorification of Gustav Mahler from 1950 to the present and the quick shifts of interest in Anton Webern's music—ranging from dismissal to enthronement to neglect in the twenty-five-year period 1945–1970—are vivid examples of recent memory. This very reevaluation, as it turned out, was a reasonably accurate mirror of what the new generation of composers was about as well. Further, less likely subscriptions to Romanticism have recently come from some of the most vocal proponents of enlarging the canon who now, perhaps somewhat surprisingly, find themselves back in the quagmire of the old top 50 with their deconstruction of Schubert's *Unfinished* Symphony as a testimony to the composer's homosexuality or even as a document of pederastic rape.[68]

Thus, in the perennial recharacterization of familiar composers in the light of new social, aesthetic, psychoanalytic, and performance dicta, as well as in a swelling repertoire of early music and a widening interest in world musics, many of the perceived enlargements to the canon have drawn as much from attitudes primed eighty to one hundred years ago as from recent events. The banishment of Modernism to the curio cabinet, or worse yet the claim that it was an ignoble fiasco simply because the values which it initially embraced no longer precisely coincide with current ones may make for a brand of ethics or sociology compelling to some. But it surely impoverishes our broadest notion of what history can be and sorely tries our abilities as prognosticators if in the telling we felt we had to be sure of the function of such repertoires for all time. For behind the many masks of Modernism reside those impulses common to most ages: the exotic and the home-grown, the noble and the savage, the old and new, the high and the low, the black and the white, the passionate and the cool. Twentieth-century music embraced them all in varying alignments and juxtapositions and in the process left behind a sometimes puzzling but frequently compelling art. Even if it seldom offered final answers, the coloration, diversity, and vibrancy of the questions which it posed have thrown an unequivocal challenge to an age now forming.

Despite persistent claims concerning the impending death of Postmodernism,[69] the term as concept may endure yet awhile. In this light Frank Kermode's verdict regarding historic periodicity and aesthetic labels offers a sober judgment and helpful reference point with respect to the usefulness of such terms: "*Ism* is indeed a fiery particle; it can add or take away value, suggest adulation or disparagement—it all depends on how the user feels about novelty."[70] Clearly, the dilemma of Postmodernism is self-induced in an attempt to vivify the present. But beyond the *ism,* the word's prefix is equally troubling in light of a growing suspicion that we are not post-anything, only passengers unsuspectingly consigned to a spiral trajectory.

Correspondingly, any redefinition of the Western canon surfaces as an issue less dramatic than it has been made to seem in light of the canon's traditional malleability and the confusing brilliance and pluralism of world cultures, which are equally unsusceptible to framing. The danger that one canon might merely be substituted for another has prompted return to an expanded conception of the original which views a resonating plurality of experience as the ideal. The occasionally clarifying, frequently circular Postmodernist debate over the idea of the canon as outlined by T. S. Eliot, E. H. Gombrich, Northrup Frye, Frank Kermode, and Edward Said has clearly begun to abate with the realization that while recent curricular renovations in the academy may have solved nothing, they have encouraged the activation of a latent willingness to entertain multiple points of view.[71] Thus, openness of presentation rather than a mandatory consideration of specific new repertoires has now surprisingly achieved an escalating endorsement. As a consequence the currently modish suppression or contraction of studies relating to European repertoires, in favor of the investigation of non-Western and American popular musics on the one hand or gendered social studies on the other, ultimately appears as a seasonal and necessarily ephemeral choice extracted from a cornucopia of options.

Indeed, the perception grows that the American social historians' previous failure to deal with the spirit of minority cultures fairly may in some large measure be attributed to a tendency to treat each of them in isolation rather than as part of a reciprocal mosaic. In their renowned *The Rise of American Civilization* (1927), for example, Charles and Mary Beard's shrinkage of black achievement to a single phenomenon, the invention of ragtime,[72] may appear regrettable in part because of its reductiveness, but principally because of their seeming ignorance of the richness, the roots, and later multiple consequences of an issue of their own choosing. Today, the appeal of considering cultures in combination rather than through their discrete histories or repertoires increasingly looms as an attractive starting point. Even Said has been heard to assert that

> by linking works to each other we bring them out of the neglect and secondariness to which for all kinds of political and ideological reasons they had previously been condemned . . . *Worldliness* is therefore the restoration to such works and interpretations of their place in a global setting, a restoration that can only be accomplished by an appreciation not of some tiny, defensively constituted corner of the world, but of the large, many-windowed house of human culture as a whole.[73]

No call for the reduction of a thousand islands of difference to a global platform of communality, the invitation to such a mode of discourse promotes more than the recognition of a set of cultural mirror images, and recognizes that while there are numerous incommensurable worlds, the duality of sameness and difference in the company of reciprocity inevitably conscripts uncertainty in the location of a boundary line.[74]

Acting on the essence of such critical prescriptions and demonstrations, Stockhausen has dramatically summed up his perspective for the creative artist by stating the he no longer views tradition "as having occurred 'previously.' Tradition is everything that is available to me, that has already been formed." In the act of deploying such an expanded base, however, Stockhausen warned of a new sense of responsibility:

> If a European is moved by a piece of Indian music, he discovers the Indian within himself. If a Japanese is touched by some European music, he finds within himself a European from the period when this music was born out of the inner pressures of an absolutely specific historical moment. The serpent always lurks within exotic charms, leading people to lose the protective paradise of self-assurance. The great shock occurs when someone who approached an unfamiliar culture with harmless curiosity is so moved by this experience that he or she falls head over heels in love with it. Music, a temple ceremony, or a dance can't be taken home. Either you must stay where you experienced that, or you are overtaken by unexpected yearnings when you are "back home" again . . .
>
> Those are discoveries of the deeper self in which there slumbers everything that has ever existed in this world or will come into being at any future time. Once this primal ground has been touched, a yearning to *experience the whole,* bringing to life the entire range of diversity, can no longer be stilled.[75]

All postcolonial theories that view cross-cultural appropriation as potential exploitation are clearly out of view.

In 1960 Stravinsky, who had sought to touch a primal ground himself near the beginning of his career, offered a somewhat different perspective on the issue when asked if he had "a special theory of, or meaning for, tradition."

> No, I am merely very prudent with the word . . . the true tradition-making work may not resemble the past at all, and especially not the immediate past, which is the only one most people are able to hear. Tradition is generic; it is not simply "handed down" . . . but under-

goes a life process: it is born, grows, matures, declines, and is reborn, perhaps. These stages of growth and regrowth are always in contradiction to the stages of another concept or interpretation: true tradition lives in the contradiction . . . At the same time, however, the artist feels his "heritage" as the grip of a very strong pair of pincers.[76]

Modernism's recall of the variable past—both chronological and geographical: the Orient, the Primitive, the Neoclassic, the Everyday (which is the familiar continuance of the past)—is thus defined not as an escape from the present nor a flight toward obscurity but as an attempt to discover a radical vision based upon cultural memory, both fleeting in its daily transmutations and fixed in its reliance upon myth and legend.[77]

Yeats felt that Modernism's "apparent incoherence" in the eyes of the general public was attributable to the fact that, like the poetry of the coterie, "it depends upon the acceptance of a use of language not guided by utilitarian principles."[78] But Eliot steadfastly argued that the human mind contained "all the past," that the poet should be conversant with his art from its beginnings in order to sense his current mission,[79] and forwarded what is now read as the elitist conclusion that to neglect Greek "means for Europe a relapse into unconsciousness" because to do so would be to break the chain that links us to our beginnings. Despite repeated warnings, the appeal of such a perspective has appeared in numerous updates, geographical transferrals, and critical inversions. Allan Bloom's attempt to imagine "an unbroken 'natural' tradition running from Socrates to the Declaration of Independence," for example, ended in thoroughly Americanizing first times.[80] Once again the seduction of searching out continuities had thrown the mechanics of social criticism into reverse gear and had illuminated the enduring if elusive search for origins and tradition in a variety of agendas.[81]

Attempts to incorporate the cultural and historical as well as aesthetic sense in patterns of art lay at the core of Modernism.[82] And it is understandable that in them we detect Modernism's affinity with the Sophists' compulsion to test the *pro* and the *contra* of every issue; with the Renaissance emulative attitude that emphasized the necessity of contemplating a model as well as alternatives to it in constituting either an artistic or an intellectual frame of reference; and with the Postmodernist stance, as expressed by Roland Barthes, which insists that literature consists of "texts" not "works": "This does not mean just that it has several meanings, but rather that it achieves plurality of meaning, an irreducible plurality. The Text is not coexistence of meanings but passage, traversal; thus it answers not to an interpretation, liberal though it may be, but to an explosion, a dissemination."[83] The premium which Barthes places upon plurality of meaning, for all its Postmodernist resonance, must nonetheless be identified as a Modernist predilection par excellence. Indeed, Modern art and literature's simultaneous pursuit of exaggerated objectivity and subjectivity in tandem with rampant cerebralism and irrationalism has provoked notice of striking parallels with the bizarre world of schizophrenia on the one hand and a joyous affirmation of the range of life's experience on the other.[84] The condition that sent a Postmodern age scrambling in search of diversity and its companion multiculturalism would appear to be symptomatic of far more fundamental paradoxes than its criticism has implied.

From a different angle Edward Rothstein has judged that "multiculturalism's obsession with diversity of representation is perverse,"[85] principally because the laudable perspective that began by promoting respect for other cultures inevitably led to a revisionism that would, in its push for relativism, reduce the Western tradition to a footnote—a possibility earlier noted and warned against by Eliot. If there is some cause for optimism, however, it is due to the realization that the interface of time past with time present has historically forced consideration of the terms of cultural relativism and the reasonable conclusion that "the dialectic of 'old authority' and 'new culture' matches the dialectic of modernism itself."[86]

In a 1971 assessment of Stravinsky and his age, Boulez had already resurrected the notion attributed to Klee of the possibility of "too much culture." He further hypothesized the prospect of escaping memory completely: "How good it would be to wake up and find that one had forgotten everything, absolutely everything!" At the same time Boulez understood as clearly as anyone that art is incapable of discovering essences without recourse to experience or memory, and that the force and value of the model resides not in its call for simple imitation but, as with all authorities, in its perennial invitation to the artist "to shrink history by making a transfer of it."[87] Nonetheless, in the repeated registration of his indebtedness to non-musical models—to Baudelaire, Mallarmé, Kafka, and especially to Paul Klee[88]—Boulez implied that he had taken note not so much of a source book for a tune or a topic as of a set of formal, cultural, and psychological perspectives. Boulez ultimately confirmed that "just as Klee feared, there is no escape from the knowledge of our own culture, nor nowadays from meeting the cultures of other civilizations—but how imperious a duty we have to volatize them!"[89]

A growing number of Western composers, whose human concerns are reflected in their extended investigations of world musics, have continued to sense the relevance of cultural collage in varying degrees of synthesis, and have relished the vibrancy that it has brought to their own work. The ingredients summoned to the formation of this musical mosaic have been drawn from a vastly distended base that includes not only the music of Java and Japan or rock and reggae, but the whole of Western music from the Middle Ages to the present day. Yet neither Christopher Rouse's claims for Led Zeppelin and Canned Heat as backgrounds to his orchestral work entitled *Bump* (1984) nor Ned Rorem's suggestions of an underlying and more universal resonance of seasonal cycles in his piano trio, *Spring Music* (1991), can explain the visceral propulsion of the first or the lapidary and compelling diction of the second. For each age is obliged to find a touchstone, postulate its relation to a continuing tradition, and leave to the future to make of it what it can.

Alfred Schnittke has been so bold as to predict, however, that "contemporary reality will make it necessary to experience all the musics one has heard since childhood, including rock and jazz and classical and all other forms, combining them into a synthesis. This has not happened in my generation . . . The synthesis must arise as a natural longing, or through necessity."[90] How far we have come on this projected path, let alone the inevitability of the prediction, would be difficult to assess. But we sense that the nourishment, the power, and the pull of history that Claes Oldenburg felt in juxtaposing Brancusi's *The Kiss* (1907) with a *Design for a Colossal Clothespin* (1972) could not have been totally unlike Berio's sentiments in his abutment of the Swingle Singers chanting utter banalities against a background of Mahler's *Resurrection* Symphony (1894) in his *Sinfonia* of 1968. Both used recall less for the reasons that accompanied rock's tapping of the imagined prehistoric in the confection of contemporary primal Pop on the one hand or for the veneration attending exhalted repertoires on the other, than from an enlarged sense of the authority of the past, the grand tradition as Stockhausen defined it: everything available to them, everything already formed. And this everything, it is well to remember, includes not only recent additions to an expanded cultural inventory but icons from the Western canon as well. Try as we might to dismiss Shakespeare, Beethoven, or Michelangelo, each attempt at devaluation brings a shock to the encoded stockpile of cultural memory and jump-starts the next round of rediscovery. Kathleen Brandt, who worked with the team charged with the restoration of the Sistine Chapel Ceiling and who witnessed the varying reactions, put it thus: "The controversy . . . illuminates a poignant episode in our own cultural life, telling us that a sudden change in our image of the past can still be profoundly unsettling today."[91]

Although the contemporary artist as well as the historian have been brought face to face with the impossibility of tracking down a presuppositionless, totally undistorted view of world or local cultures, the elusive search for fraternity that fueled so many of society's revolutions has continued to haunt them and to propel explorations that are both utopian and respectful—respectful of tradition and experience, and deferential to an unknown future. In the process, however, both are inevitably faced with the old dilemma framed by E. M. Forster in *A Passage to India* of 1924 with the question, "How can the mind take hold of such a country?" Recognizing that in building his towns and garrisons many miles from home the colonialist-invader is inevitably consigned to his own exile and to quarrels and dissatisfactions born of his inability to find his way back, Forster concluded that the invitation to travel to the far country is a lure not a promise, and as enigmatic as it is irresistible.[92]

It was undoubtedly predictable that both colonial and postcolonial debates were destined to be superseded by new perspectives born of developing circumstances, and the artist's proclaimed world view fated to be spotted as a mirage much as in the age of Forster. For politicians and historians involved in a centennial review found themselves forced to recognize that resurgent ethnic conflicts were already witnessing their third wave in this century—the first following the end of World War I, the second reflected in the eruption of anticolonialist movements in Africa and Asia following World War II. But as the Cold War gave way in the 1990s to dozens of smaller wars over issues of local ethnic dominance in Bosnia, Croatia, Spain, Germany, Russia, Somalia, Israel, Ireland, and India—indeed, in every corner of the globe—older issues of multiculturalism and diversity took on a new resonance and prompted the United States Senator from New York, Daniel Patrick Moynihan, to warn that "the defining mode of conflict in the era ahead is ethnic conflict. It promises to be savage. Get ready for 50 new countries in the world in the next 50 years. Most of them will be born in bloodshed."[93]

What constitutes a reasonable hope for the role of music in such a climate? Will the prospect of Global Fraternity, the proclamation of a World Beat, or the expressed hope of Total Fusion prove to be a mere fantasy or only momentarily démodé? Is a new wave of neonationalism with its accompanying musics—more intensely parochial, more narrowly circumscribed than before—fated to wipe out the perceived ecumenical advances? Such questions invite the natural response that the idea of cultural blend in the arts has always been tethered to an audaciously utopian vision anchored to patently practical developments. For, as Mikhail Bakhtin has so wisely noted, there is a paradox inherent in all notions of societal coexistence that resides in the very nature of language—resting ambiguously, as it does, on the borderline between self and other. All words in all languages carry the accumulated weight of successive generations, are retrieved not from a dictionary but from the mouths of others, and achieve personalization only through adaptation to a new expressive requirement. Typically, such cultural relays are triggered by an infinite variety of personal experiences, are neither narrowly ideological nor inflexibly formalistic but rather intuitive fusions of the two.[94]

Today we have come to realize with increasing clarity that the perpetual grafting inherent in any developing language—in the arts as in politics—typically results in a gradual realignment of features previously in view rather than what may at first appear to be an erasure of previous tradition. Neither George Gershwin's *Rhapsody in Blue* nor Andy Warhol's *Brillo Boxes* brought art to an end; both gave notice, instead, that a liberating pluralism was at hand.[95] Similarly, despite current millennial pronouncements of the end of culture, the intensity of a Postmodern age's subscription to multiculturalism is surely best read not as a naive and fatal attraction to cultural overload but as the advertisement of newly sighted possibilities and an impending fresh start. For just as the perennial nature of such cycles had already been noted by the fourteenth-century French composer and poet laureate Guillaume de

Machaut in a remarkable rondeau, "Ma fin est mon commencement, et mon commencement est ma fin," so T. S. Eliot's later gloss can now be read not as a Modernist manifesto or as sheer nostalgia for the last fin de siècle, but as a sage valedictory at century's close:

> We shall not cease from exploration
> And the end of all our exploring
> Will be to arrive where we started
> And know the place for the first time.
> (*Four Quartets*, "Little Gidding," *IV*)

Notes

Bibliography

Index

— Notes —

Preludes and Postulates

1. The volume of twenty essays to which Levin's remarks are appended, Hoffman 1989, covers the whole range of collage techniques from those of the Cubists ca. 1910 to those of the 1980s, and in the process primarily identifies the issue of collage as it pertains to the plastic arts. Stemming from a series of seminars at Harvard in 1987 on concepts of the avant-garde, the collection for the most part provocatively skirts references to the world of literature and music.
2. "Stravinsky: Style or Idea?" in Boulez 1986b: 356.
3. Ibid.: 358.
4. Critical reactions to the formalistic approach in the Museum of Modern Art exhibition "Primitivism in Twentieth-Century Art" in 1984 proved in retrospect to be a time-of-turning for many of the arts. See Rubin 1984 for the essays attendant to the exhibition; Ashton 1984, Kramer 1984, McEvilley 1984, and Clifford 1988 for the tenor of the ensuing debate.
5. Norris 1982: 93.
6. Rubin 1984; Varnedoe and Gopnik 1990b; Baer 1992.
7. White 1973: 371–372. See also "The Question of Narrative in Contemporary Historical Theory" in White 1987.
8. Virgil Thomson, *The New York Times Book Review,* September 26, 1968.
9. Alan Bennett, "102 Boulevard Haussmann," BBC TV production, 1990.

1. "And the Moon Descends over the Temple That Was"

1. See especially Said 1978.
2. Wolf 1982: 6.
3. Said 1978: 252.
4. See Pfrogner 1953: 63–88, 184–232; Covach 1990: 218.
5. See Lipsey 1977, Huxley 1945, and Campbell 1990: 93–94.
6. It is not coincidental that Perrault (1627–1703), the author of *Histoires ou contes du temps passé* (alternative title, *Contes de ma mère l'Oye*), was renowned

in his time for the role he played in the *Querelle des anciens et des modernes,* wherein he argued for the idea of human progress. He believed that a nation's literature reflects its cultural position, and claimed refinements for the modern over the barbarous ancient. By choosing the realm of myth, which stands outside of history, for his fairy tales he established a locus beyond time. The attraction of his world for the Symbolists is understandable.

7. Said 1993.
8. For the increasing distinction attendant to various ethnic musical references in the nineteenth century, see Ralph Locke, "Exoticism in the Nineteenth Century" (in progress). See also Balardelle 1981.
9. See Ringer 1965 and 1984.
10. During the composition of *Madama Butterfly* Puccini wrote to Giulio Ricordi: "I have had a visit today from Mme. Ohyama, wife of the Japanese Ambassador. She told me a great many interesting things and sang some native songs to me. She has promised to send me some native Japanese music" (Adami 1931: 146). Regarding Puccini's use of Japanese materials in *Madame Butterfly,* as well as of the American national anthem in the same opera, see Carner 1936: 45–67 and Schatt 1986: 22–40. Concerning the generalized impulse behind such appropriations, see Felber 1925: 726.
11. See Stamper 1989.
12. See Jay 1987.
13. A. Pougin cited in Devriès 1977: 33. Unless otherwise indicated, all translations are mine.
14. Devriès 1977: 26.
15. Ory 1989: 19–21.
16. See Benedictus 1889 and 1900.
17. Lesure 1980b: 70.
18. For a thorough discussion of Javanese melodic models see Mueller 1986: 157–186; for the impact of the Siamese upon the Russian scene prior to Diaghilev's Paris seasons see Misler in Baer 1988: 78–83.
19. Godet 1926: 59–61, as translated in Mueller 1986: 159.
20. For a discussion of the instrumentation and tuning of the Conservatoire's gamelan see Pillaut 1887: 244–245. Although Debussy may have had access to a gamelan prior to 1889, in the absence of performers and a repertoire the encounter was destined to be without issue.
21. Tiersot 1889: 32, 33–34.
22. Debussy, "Du goût," *S.I.M.* (February 15, 1913).
23. I am grateful to Susan Walton for assistance in identifying the gamelan instrument most closely approximated by Debussy's solution.
24. Laloy 1906: 64. Tiersot (1889: 12), speaking of the music which accompanied the Annamite (Vietnamese) theater, betrayed similar feelings that Oriental music was in general not harmonic. Laloy also published some fragments of Cambodian melodies in *Mercure musical* (August 15, 1906).

25. See Mueller (1986: 170), who first noted the connection between Debussy's opening sonority and Benedictus' example.
26. See Lockspeiser 1951: 151.
27. Laloy (1912: 122–126) includes a group of "Mélodies notées." Laloy was later to provide Roussel with the libretto for his opera *Padmâvatî* (1914–1918).
28. Lesure 1980b: 233. Debussy himself remarked in a letter to Stravinsky of November 8, 1913: "Our reading at the piano of *Le Sacre du printemps* at Laloy's house, is always present in my mind. It haunts me like a beautiful nightmare and I try, in vain, to reinvoke the terrific impression" (Stravinsky and Craft 1959: 52).
29. Laloy 1944: 95–96.
30. Godet 1918, reprinted 1962: 117.
31. See Debussy 1942: 81.
32. See Boulez 1986b: 422.
33. See Watkins 1988: 17–20.
34. See Schatt 1986: 63 for a telling appreciation of this issue in *Das Lied von der Erde*.
35. For a detailed investigation see Newbould 1975: 228–231.
36. *Comoedia* (May 15, 1921), translated in Stravinsky and Craft 1978: 143.
37. The steady eighth-note motion, the changing metrics at each measure, and the independent phrase-rhythm of the melody which is introduced at the opening of the curtain, m. 12, and subject to immediate realignment at m. 16, should be reviewed in light of the evidence of Chapter 10. For a useful overview of the opera, see Prost 1990: 65–81.
38. Silver 1989: 260–261.
39. Other lesser-known works which reflect Debussy's infatuation with the Orient include *Tarantelle styrienne* (1890); two Verlaine songs, "Clair de lune" (1891) and "L'Échelonnement des haies moutonne à l'infini" (1891); the *Rapsodie* for saxophone of 1903–5, at one point entitled *Rapsodie orientale;* and *Khamma,* an Egyptian ballet of 1911–12.
40. Said 1978 dominated a great deal of the commentary and critique on the subject in the decade following its publication.
41. See Honour 1973 for the rich details regarding Western emulation of the East from the seventeenth century to the present in matters of dress, furnishings, ceramics, and painting.
42. Olkhovsky 1983: 39–41.
43. Levinson 1982: 39.
44. See Levinson 1982: 46 for an appraisal of this state of affairs.
45. See Bowlt in Baer 1988: 63.
46. Nijinska 1981: 292.
47. See Karlinsky in Baer 1988: 21 and Alexandre 1913: 2.
48. See Misler in Baer 1988: 78–83.

49. See Ries 1986: 183 for the scenario of *Le dieu bleu.*
50. Van Holt 1911, reprinted in Rood 1977: 75–76.
51. This point of view was established as a *World of Art* tenet before Diaghilev came to Paris. See "Notes" in "Chronicles," *Mir Iskusstva* 7 (1902): 42.
52. See Diaghilev 1899: 59, 66; Baer in Baer 1988: 60.
53. Stravinsky and Craft 1960: 77.

2. Of Nightingales and Ukiyo-e

1. Stravinsky 1936: 45.
2. Stravinsky understandably also acknowledged a similar pattern in Musorgsky's song cycle *Without Sunlight.*
3. See V. Stravinsky and Craft 1978: 114.
4. See White 1966: 226, ex. 17.
5. Cf. Albright 1988: 116.
6. See White 1966: 227, ex. 18.
7. Stravinsky 1981: 148.
8. Robert Craft, notes to the recording of *Le Rossignol,* Columbia KS 6327.
9. Nancy Van Norman Baer, "Design and Choreography: Cross-Influences in the Theatrical Art of the Ballets Russes" in Baer 1988: 69.
10. Later Soviet productions capitalized upon the idea of the *lubok* in Leonid Leontiev's 1920s production of Stravinsky's *Petrushka,* where the mummers' and revelers' dance in the next to last scene was characterized by André Levinson as "a dance *lubok* with comically stressed accents and broken movements" (Souritz 1990: 60). And in Fedor Lopukhov's 1927 production of Stravinsky's *Renard,* which followed the composer's directions that the four singers should not participate in the action, "the style of a primitive popular print *(lubok)* . . . was emphasized by such details as the multi-colored sun, decorated with designs, and an ornate cloud, which the buffoons carried out on poles" (Souritz 1990: 290). For more about the history and importance of the *lubok* see Michel Larionov, "Icones et loubki," extract from a preface to the catalogue for the exposition organized by him for Bolchaï Dmitrovka, IIe Salon d'Art, Moscow, 1913, in Loguine 1971: 33–35; and Goncharova, "Le Loubok hindou et persan," ibid.: 36. Hundreds of "icons and *loubki*" from various countries, including Persian, Chinese, French, Tartar, and Japanese woodblock prints, were presented from Larionov's private collection.
11. Michel Larionov, "Icones et Loubki" in Loguine 1971: 34–35.
12. Natalia Goncharova, "Le Loubok hindou et persan" in Loguine 1971: 36.
13. Serge Grigoriev, "Gontcharova et Larionov, peintres-décorateurs des ballets de Diaghilev" in Loguine 1971: 105–106.
14. Benois 1939: 101, translated in Bowlt 1988: 53.
15. Serge Volkonsky, *Otkliki teatra* (Petrograd, 1914): 57.

16. *Le Ménestrel,* 80.23 (June 6, 1914): 179. See Beaumont 1939: 127.
17. See Julie Sazonova, "La chorégraphie des ballets de Diaghilev," *La Revue musicale,* special no. (December 1, 1930): 73.
18. Noverre 1803: 160–161. I am grateful to Roland John Wiley for bringing this notice to my attention.
19. See Chapter 10.
20. See Brunella Eruli, "Masques, acteurs, marionettes: objets 'transitionnels' " in Aslan 1985: 216.
21. See Louÿs, "Marionettes," *La Revue blanche* (June 1894): 573–574; translated in Richardson 1986: 162.
22. Translated in V. Stravinsky and Craft 1978: 124–125.
23. Virgil Thomson, "Stravinsky's Operas," *Musical Newsletter* (Fall 1974), reprinted in Thomson 1981: 505.
24. Ravel's and Bartók's reports are translated in V. Stravinsky and Craft 1978: 120.
25. See Chapters 11 and 12.
26. Camille Mauclair, "Le Sense du Lied," *Le Courrier musical* (October 15, 1906): 604–605; translated in Schwab 1991: 13.
27. Richardson 1986: 150.
28. See Chapter 1, n. 15.
29. Ibid.
30. *Les Musiques bizarres à l'Exposition de 1900:* 9; translated in Richardson 1986: 175.
31. Funayama 1986: 276.
32. See Schatt 1986: 81–82.
33. I am indebted to William Malm for this interpretation. In the present example, however, Benedictus records the lowest D in the opening two measures and again in m. 7. For a modern transcription of the same song in a different key that also includes periodic sevenths where the lower range is exceeded, see Tani 1970: 174–175.
34. Stravinsky 1936: 45.
35. Translated in Funayama 1986: 274. Funayama also considers the original Japanese texts and the background for these songs.
36. Richard Taruskin, "Stravinsky's 'Rejoicing Discovery' and What It Meant: In Defense of His Notorious Text Setting" in Haimo and Johnson 1987: 162.
37. See Said 1978: 115–117.
38. For another musical analogue drawn from Japanese art, see the discussion of Stravinsky's "Huxley" Variations in n. 116 to Chapter 10.
39. See Hall 1989: 99–100.
40. Stravinsky 1939: 82.
41. Flanner 1972: xvii.

42. See Chapter 9.
43. See Chapter 10.
44. Boulez 1986b: 341. Boulez's article "Speaking, Playing, Singing" originally appeared as "Dire, jouer, chanter," *Cahiers Renaud-Barrault,* 41 (1963): 300–321.
45. Translated by Elaine Brody in "Louis Bourgault-Ducoudray," *New Grove Dictionary of Music and Musicians,* vol. 3 (1980): 111. I am grateful to Scott Messing for bringing Bourgault-Ducoudray to my attention.
46. See Stravinsky and Craft 1959: 23–24 and Boulez 1986b: 424.

3. Out of Africa and the Steppes

1. Lloyd 1991; Rubin 1984; Laude 1968; Goldwater 1938.
2. It is omitted from the *New Grove Dictionary of Music and Musicians* (1980), ed. S. Sadie; Paul Griffiths, *The Thames and Hudson Encyclopaedia of Twentieth-Century Music* (1986); *The New Harvard Dictionary of Music* (1986), ed. D. Randel; *The Norton/Grove Concise Encyclopedia of Music,* ed. S. Sadie (1988).
3. Guillaume and Munro 1926: 11.
4. Coleridge-Taylor 1904, Preface.
5. See Schuller 1968: 38–43 concerning harmonic practices and 6–26 for a clear discussion of African polymetrics.
6. Wallaschek 1893, reprinted 1970; Junod 1897; Krehbiel 1914, reprinted 1962, was originally dedicated to Horatio Parker.
7. Stravinsky and Craft 1960: 77. The expression "massacre du printemps," indeed, appears repeatedly in the early reviews. The first to confect this pun was probably Gustave de Pawlowski, "Au Théâtre des Champs-Élysées: *Le Sacre du printemps,* ballet de deux actes de M. Igor Stravinsky," *Comoedia,* 7 (May 31, 1913): 1. See Bullard 1971: vol. 2, 39.
8. See Varnedoe, Preface to Rubin 1984: x.
9. Jean Cocteau, "Opinions sur l'art nègre," *Action,* 3 (April 1920): 20. The opinion is echoed and amplified by the Viennese Erwin Felber in "Exotismus und Primitivismus in der neueren Musik," *Die Musik,* 21 (1925): 724–731.
10. Marcel Proust, *À la recherche du temps perdu, La Prisonnière,* vol. 3 (Paris, 1987–): 237.
11. Garafola 1989: 32.
12. Johann Wolfgang von Goethe, *Westöstlicher Diwan* (1819; rep. Munich, 1958): 8–12.
13. White 1978: 183.
14. See Cro 1990.
15. Ellis 1991: B1.
16. See Hughes and Allen 1988 and Bozeman 1988.
17. See Leighten 1990 for the suggestions that Picasso's *Les Demoiselles d'Avignon*

of 1907 was less a sexual autobiographical confession than a virulent sermon protesting colonialist abuses in the French and Belgian Congos.

18. Guillaume and Munro 1926: 12–13.

19. For the role of Primitivism in the early twentieth-century avant-garde's promotion of abstraction, see Isaak 1986: 7–9.

20. White 1978: 170.

21. Falla 1922.

22. Stein 1946: 174–175. Picasso "was in his creative activity dominated by spanish ritual, later by negro ritual expressed in negro sculpture (which has an arab basis the basis also of spanish ritual) and later by russian ritual. His creative activity being tremendously dominant, he made these great rituals over into his own image."

23. Translated in Morgenstern 1956: 403.

24. Judith Gautier, *Le Journal officiel* (October 14, 1875): 8,655.

25. Falla claimed that, unlike Bizet's, Debussy's music was "not written *a la española* but *en español*" although he had never visited Spain. Falla 1922: 407.

26. Goldwater 1986: 89.

27. Ellis 1992: B2.

28. Burke 1978: 16.

29. Laude 1968: 118.

30. For an amplification of the spirtual dimension of Schoenberg's art, see Covach 1991.

31. In 1906 a Batwa pygmy named Ota Benga, initially brought to America by the white missionary Samuel Phillips Verner and showcased at the St. Louis Exposition of 1904, was displayed in a cage with orangutans at the Bronx Zoo. Similarly, when the two returned to Africa, Verner submitted to being placed in a caged enclosure for viewing by the natives. For the incredible series of events that surround this story see Bradford and Blume 1992.

32. See Feest 1987, Wegner 1983, and Lloyd 1991: x, 191.

33. See Freud, *Totem und Tabu* (1911) and "Psychoanalytical Notes on an Autobiographical Account of a Case of Paranoia (The Case of Schreber)" in *The Complete Psychological Works,* ed. J. Strachey, vol. 12 (London, n.d.): 82.

34. Wassily Kandinsky, *The Art of Spiritual Harmony* (London, 1914): 1.

35. See Stoecker 1986 and Pakenham 1991 for a rich overview.

36. Compare with Said 1991: 72–73, where he speaks of the *retrograde* behavior among "advanced writers and artists, of the working class, and of women, groups whose imperialist fervor increased in intensity and perfervid enthusiasm for the acquisition of and sheer bloodthirsty dominance over innumerable niggers, bog dwellers, babus, and wogs, as the competition between various European and American powers also increased in brutality and senseless, even profitless, control."

37. Hegel 1956: 91.

38. See Watkins 1988: 174.
39. See Chapter 11.
40. See Bridgman 1988.
41. Rimsky-Korsakov 1942.
42. Gerald Abraham, "Rimsky-Korsakov," *New Grove Dictionary of Music and Musicians* (London, 1980): xvi, 29.
43. See Taruskin 1986: 20.
44. Ibid.: 28–29.
45. See Rubin 1984: 242.
46. See Bowlt 1988: 46.

4. "Massacre" and Other Neologisms

1. For a rich series of documents and eyewitness accounts in the period 1810–1910 see Wiley 1990.
2. Stravinsky 1936: 56. See also Baer 1988: 60, Pasler 1986: 74, and Garafola 1989: 52–58 for a consideration of the various forces at work in *L'Après-midi d'un faune.*
3. The analogy was picked up a few weeks later in Touchard 1913: "Or has he simply given in to a tendency rather notable among Russians as well as in this country, which is to call attention to himself through harmonic excesses, through a kind of musical cubism?" See Bullard 1971: vol. 2, 198.
4. See Wiley, *Ivanov and Dance,* forthcoming. Rimsky-Korsakov had become progressively antagonistic to the classic *danse d'école,* and in an opera-ballet, *Mlada,* of 1892 his anthropological bent, already tested in a series of operas tuned to the solar cycle, found a fresh ally.
5. See Pozharskaya and Volodina 1990: 38.
6. A single, albeit oblique, exception would be Fernand Gregh's appreciation of the dances in *Prince Igor* shortly after the premiere of *Le Sacre.* See *La Revue musicale* for July-August 1913: 8–11. Translated in Bullard 1971: 205–207. In addition to *Danses polovtsiennes du "Prince Igor,"* *Les Sylphides* and *Le Spectre de la rose* were also performed at the premiere of *Le Sacre,* all choreographed by Fokine.
7. Boschot 1913: 6; original reproduced in Lesure 1980a: 15–16. Translation by the author with appreciation for numerous felicitous expressions in Bullard 1971: vol. 2, 12–13; Boschot was known not only as a critic of *L'Écho de Paris* from 1910 to 1938 but as a biographer of Berlioz.
8. Chantavoine 1913: 6, complete translation in Bullard 1971: vol. 2, 19.
9. Pawlowsi 1913: 1. Reproduced in Lesure 1980a: 18–22, translated in Bullard 1971: vol. 2, 39–46.
10. Vuillermoz 1913: 49–56, translated in Bullard 1971: vol. 2, 165–166.
11. Spector 1990: 160 gives the date January 1912. Garafola 1989: 60 speaks of "the demonstrations by Dalcroze's pupils in St. Petersburg early in 1911."

12. See Spector 1990: 162.
13. See Chapters 11 and 12.
14. Louis Laloy, "Stravinsky," *Comoedia* (Autumn 1913); translated in Bullard 1971: vol. 2, 236.
15. Louis Laloy, *La Grande Revue* (June 25, 1913): 612–613, translated in Bullard 1971: vol. 2, 179.
16. Touchard 1913, complete translation in Bullard 1971: vol. 2, 196.
17. See Hodson 1985. See also Peter Hulme and Neil L. Whitehead, ed., *Wild Majesty: Encounters with Caribs from Columbus to the Present Day. An Anthology* (Oxford, 1992).
18. See "*The Rite* at Seventy-Five" in Craft 1992 for a review of the production and p. 238 for confirmation that it produced "the impression of watching Indians at a pow-wow in a kitsch Western."
19. See Honour 1975, fig. 298 for Delacroix's sketch.
20. George Sand, *Le Diable à Paris* (Paris, 1846). See Honour 1975: 329 for an extract.
21. Cited in Létay 1987: 378. Like Budapest, Dresden, Vienna, and other East European cities played host to numerous *Völkerschauen* including Samoyed, black African, and Bedouin groups.
22. Adami 1931: 62. Interestingly, William F. Carver, the cofounder of the troupe with William Cody, had originally proposed the name "The Golden West" for the show in 1883. See Rosa and May 1989: 71–72.
23. "Buffalo Bill in London," *Harper's Weekly* (September 3, 1892), cited in Rosa and May 1989: 155–156.
24. See Honour 1975: 316–17; Berkhofer 1979: 88; and Fiorentino 1987.
25. Pushkin even spoke of the hypocrisy of the American government policy regarding Indians in his review of *A Narrative of the Captivity and Adventures of John Tanner,* published in 1836.
26. See Vaschenko 1987: 307–310.
27. See Rosa and May 1989: 66–73 regarding Carver and p. 158 for a reproduction of the 1893 poster; Blackstone 1986: 81–82 for a discussion regarding claims that the Russian riders were not really Cossack soldiers but Georgians from the Caucasus.
28. Cody made a single foray across the Russian border in 1906, but it was too brief to elicit significant reaction.
29. Thorp 1957: 180–190. He also visited Australia in 1890 and 1891.
30. Wiley 1985: 310, n. 12.
31. *Vsemirnaya illyustratsiya* [*World Illustrations*], 53.26 (January–June 1890), issue for 23 June 1890: 439, 442 (text), 441 (illustrations). I am indebted to Roland John Wiley not only for knowledge of this notice but for its translation.
32. Yost 1979: 224, Walsh 1928: 278, and Rosa and May 1989: 179.
33. See Rosa and May 1989: 116–125, 174; Fiorentino 1987: 408; and Clerici 1987: 420–421, which also includes an artist's rendition of Buffalo Bill's

troupe in front of St. Peter's Church in the Vatican and with their tepees erected in the Roman Colosseum.

34. Karl May, *A Small Yes:* 5 as cited in Tower: 33, n. 14.

35. Tower 1990: 30.

36. Bowlt 1988: 48 and Fokine 1961: 109.

37. Levinson 1982: 56. Cf. Bridgman 1988: 30 with respect to the sentiments of Benois and the art critic Igor Grabar.

38. Rambert 1972: 63.

39. Friar 1972: 69, 80, 89, 92, 95. Even Cecil B. De Mille's first film—and some claim the first feature made in Hollywood—was *The Squaw Man* of 1913.

40. See Perloff 1991: 27 regarding the Sioux and Pasler 1982 with respect to the Apaches. Even earlier an English group of "aristocratic ruffians" dubbed themselves the Mohawks following a London visit in 1710 of the "Four Kings of Canada." See Feest 1984: 88. See also Mariani 1987.

41. Garafola 1989: 63. For the reactions of the Russian critic André Levinson to *Le Sacre,* see Levinson 1982: 51–57 and Levinson 1991: 35–41.

42. Cited by Taruskin in Pasler 1986: 26. Robert Craft spoke incidentally of Stravinsky's interest in American Indians in a letter to the author of March 8, 1993: "Like all Russians of their class they were fascinated by American Indians, and before I knew them had read Cooper and anything else on the subject they could find. They knew Twain, of course, and our crossings of the Mississippi on our transcontinental trains were thrilling experiences for them. They would be awakened early in the morning, or stay awake during the night in order to see the river from the long trestle. We drove across at Natchez in 1950 and, returning west, at Bemidji, after which we visited a reservation in Montana and the site of the Little Big Horn massacre."

43. Bartók 1920, reprinted in Morgenstern 1956: 426–427.

44. Stravinsky's claim that the only folktune quotation in *The Rite* was the opening bassoon melody was never challenged until after his death. Two studies, Morton 1979 and Taruskin 1980, permanently changed this view.

45. Stravinsky and Craft 1959: 82.

46. Stravinsky and Craft 1962: 169.

47. See especially Morton 1979 and Taruskin 1980.

48. See Boulez 1968: 72–145 and especially 125–127; Watkins 1988: 216–217 for a synopsis.

49. Boulez 1986b: 363.

50. See Peltier in Rubin 1984: 109; also André Salmon, "Negro Art," in translation in *The Burlington Magazine* (1920), wherein he traces the development of "Negromania" from the late nineteenth century.

51. That European interest in the Native American was not totally superseded by an attraction to the African American in the period of the 1920s is persuasively addressed in Tower 1990.

52. Astruc 1987: 196–200.

53. Bordman 1978: 159.

54. Bierley 1973: 17, 67.

55. Cocteau 1935: 89–91. Trans. in Ries 1986: 3.

56. V. Yastrebtzev, *Recollections of Rimsky-Korsakov,* vol. 2 (Moscow, 1962).

57. I am indebted to Nancy Milford for this information.

58. See N. Perloff 1991.

59. Stravinsky and Craft 1962: 103–104.

60. Poulenc 1978: 42 confirms the continuing association between artists and musicians at the same venue: "In a Montparnasse studio, under the title 'Lyre et Palette,' we'd become associated with the artists Picasso, Braque, Modigliani and Juan Gris, who exhibited there. Ricardo Viñes played my *Mouvements perpétuels* for the first time in that studio."

61. See Fournier 1952: 130.

62. See Schwab 1991: 135, fig. 5. Charles Koechlin's "Chant de nuit dans le jungle" was also first performed by Jane Bathori on December 3, 1916, and the complete *Trois poèmes,* op. 18, of which it is a part, were first performed November 26, 1917, at the Vieux-Colombier (Schwab 1991: 120). See also Harding 1972: 60–61.

63. See Browning 1979 and Rosenstock 1984: 476.

64. Poulenc 1963: 41. With respect to the French infatuation with Madagascar as an emblem of black culture, see James 1990.

65. Laurent, "The Performer as Catalyst," as cited in Schwab 1991: 169.

66. As translated in Rischbieter 1968: 164. See Hennings 1957.

67. An introduction to the *Fête nègre* by Paul Guillaume together with press notices of both the exposition and the fête are given by Collin d'Arbois, "L'Exposition d'Art nègre et la Fête nègre" in *Les Arts à Paris* (November 1, 1919): 4. For the reproduction of Fauconnet's costume designs, see Allard, "Fête nègre," in *Le Nouveau Spectateur,* 4 (June 25, 1919). See also Philippe Peltier, "From Oceania" in Rubin 1984: 109. I am grateful to M. Peltier of Paris for providing a copy of the November 1, 1919, issue of *Les Arts à Paris,* which is unavailable in any library in the United States, and for many other prompt and courteous responses to my inquiries. He informs me that the exceeding rarity of the periodical can be explained by the notice in the next issue that all copies of the November 1 issue had, for whatever reason, been recalled.

68. *Les Arts à Paris* (November 1, 1919): 4.

69. Ibid.: 4.

70. Ibid.: 11.

71. Ibid.

72. I am grateful to Philippe Peltier for the information regarding Cendrars's "poème dansé" in a communication of April 4, 1991.

73. Häger 1990: 13. The notice of "Music by Francis Poulenc" could only refer to *Rapsodie nègre* at this date.
74. Reproduced in Rubin 1984: 157.
75. See Peltier, "From Oceania" in Rubin 1984: 109–110; G. Duthuit, "Cinématographe et fêtes," in *Action,* 4 (July 1920); M. Sanouillet, *Dada à Paris* (Paris, 1965).

5. The Creation of the World

1. Mariz 1970: 12.
2. Both *Amazon* and *Uirapuru* are recorded on Gega GD 102 conducted by Ricardo Averbach.
3. For further discussion regarding the staging of this work see Chapter 10.
4. It should be noted that Villa-Lobos had also been early attracted to the wordless chorus, mouths closed, in Puccini's *Butterfly,* a technique which he was to employ in his *Quatuor* (1921) as well as in *Bachianas Brasileiras No. 5.* See Peppercorn 1989: 33.
5. Milhaud 1953: 119.
6. Ibid.: 136–137.
7. Ibid.: 147–148.
8. Ibid.: 148–149. See also Milhaud 1927.
9. See N. Perloff 1991: 204. The circled figure in Perloff's ex. 6.27 can also be found in Gershwin's *Rhapsody.*
10. Lambert 1934: 218.
11. Milhaud 1953: 120.
12. See N. Perloff 1991: 203.
13. Fernand Léger, "The Invented Theater" (1924) in Rischbieter 1968: 97.
14. Glover 1983: 94–95.
15. It was Milhaud who introduced Cole Porter to Rolf de Maré. Porter's eighteen-minute skit combined the shimmy, "Jazzbaby," and a nostalgic Swedish waltz in its portrayal of the integration of Swedish immigrants into American life.
16. Laude 1968 was the first to note this. See also Rosenstock 1984: 480.
17. Léger's figures are reproduced in Haeger 1990: 194; Larionov's in Rischbieter 1968, fig. 94c.
18. Léger 1924 in Rischbieter 1968: 97.
19. See Chapter 11.
20. Roskill 1985: 29.
21. See Sproul 1980 for examples from Africa, the Near East, India, China and Japan, Siberia and the Eskimos, North America, South America, Australia and the Pacific. See also Maclagan 1977.
22. Blaise Cendrars, "The Scenario of *La Création du monde*" in Rischbieter 1970: 99.

23. Green 1987: 43. Léger's *The Card Game* is reproduced in pl. 56.
24. Häger 1990: 68.
25. Chernoff 1978: 144. See also Robert Thompson, "An Aesthetic of the Cool: West African Dance," *African Forum,* 2.2 (Fall 1966): 93–94.
26. The films are deposited at the Bibliothèque Nationale in Paris. See Häger 1990: 58.
27. Häger 1990: 42.
28. Aschengreen 1986: 104.
29. See Clarke and Crisp 1987: 164.
30. Vuillermoz 1923a: 167. I am grateful to Susan Walton for the location of this review as well as other perspectives on *La Création du monde.*
31. Xavier de Courville, *Revue musicale,* 6.4 (February 1, 1925): 216.
32. Quoted in Häger 1990: 44.
33. *Criterion,* 2.8 (July 1924): 490, a review of *The Growth of Greek Civilisation* by W. J. Perry.
34. See Craig 1982: 133; also Crawford 1987 and Manganaro 1986: 393–421.
35. See Shanes 1989: 29. Another magic bird, Uirapuru, was appropriated by Villa-Lobos as the subject for a ballet after he saw Stravinsky's *Firebird* in 1913.
36. Oskar Schlemmer and the sculptor Lothar Schreyer shared the directorship of the Bauhaus theater workshop in the early 1920s, and the latter's studio was home to a variety of "South Seas statues, masks, and Negro idols, a leopard throne . . . and a large painting by Léger." The year 1922 saw not only their production of an early version of *The Triadic Ballet* in Stuttgart but the presentation of a reflecting-light play by Kurt Schwerdtfeger, entitled *Story of Creation.* The relation of the latter to themes that were concurrently being explored by Brancusi as well as Léger, Cendrars, and Milhaud is apparent. Hans Haffenrichter, "Lothar Schreyer and the Bauhaus Stage" in Neumann 1970: 68–70.
37. Shanes 1989: 76.
38. Barbara Hepworth, autobiographical note for 1931–1934, describing a visit made to Brancusi in 1932, in *Barbara Hepworth* (London, 1952).
39. Milhaud 1953: 134.
40. See Geist 1983: 150 and Shattuck 1968. Geist has even suggested that Brancusi's *Socrate* (1923, Geist fig. 143) is a portrait of Satie based upon a humorous self-portrait by the composer. Satie's opera *Socrate* dates from 1918.
41. See Häger 1990: 42.
42. Milhaud 1953: 152–153.
43. See N. Perloff 1991: 92–93 for details regarding Milhaud's exposure to Gershwin at the Bar Gaya as early as 1921.
44. Fernand Léger, letter to Rolf de Maré, September 12, 1922, Dansmuseet, Stockholm. Cited and translated by McQuillan 1979: 615.

45. See Hepokoski 1991 for an enlightening disentanglement of Adorno's aesthetic.
46. Boulez 1986b: 362.
47. Coeuroy and Schaeffner 1926: 98–99. For an early cautionary assessment of "The Influence of Jazz on European Music" see André Hodeir, *Hommes et problèmes du jazz* (Paris, 1954), trans. David Noakes, *Jazz: Its Evolution and Essence* (New York, 1956/R1979): chap. 16.
48. Coeuroy and Schaeffner 1926: 125.

6. Josephine and Jonny

1. Haney 1981: 67–68, 104.
2. Mae West's claims to having invented the shimmy were obviously contrived. See her *Goodness Has Nothing to Do with It* (Englewood Cliffs, N.J., 1959): 65.
3. See N. Perloff 1991: 176.
4. See Chapter 10.
5. Blanche 1928: 225–226.
6. Garber 1992: 280.
7. Léopold Sedar Senghor, "Standards critiques de l'art Africain," *African Arts / Arts d'Afrique,* 1.1 (Autumn 1967): 6, cited and translated in Chernoff 1979, states: "This organizing force which makes the black style is 'rhythm.' It is the most perceptible and the least material thing. Even in the nightly drumming, black music is not a purely aesthetic manifestation, but brings its faithful into communion, more intimately, to the rhythm of the community which dances, of the World which dances."
8. *The New Yorker* (1925), reprinted in Flanner 1972: xx–xxi.
9. Guillaume 1926. The catalogue for his exhibition "L'Art nègre et l'art océanien" was prepared by Henri Clouzot and A. Level, who also published *Sculptures africaines et oceaniennes, colonies françaises et Congo belge* (Paris, 1925).
10. All translations here are by the author based upon Levinson 1929. Levinson's first notices of Baker appeared as "La Danse. Paris ou New-York? Douglas. La Vénus noire," *Comoedia* (October 12, 1925): 2, and "La Danse. 'Loin du bal.' Joséphine sifflée. Blanc et noir," *Comoedia* (December 7, 1925): 4. An English version, "The Negro Dance: Under European Eyes," which appeared in *Theatre Arts Monthly* (April 1927) and which is reproduced in Acocella and Garafola 1991: 69–75, differs in numerous details.
11. Levinson 1929: 272. For the English version in *Theatre Arts Monthly* (April 1927), see Acocella and Garafola 1991: 71.
12. Levinson 1929: 276–277. The English version, which appeared in *Theatre Arts Monthly* (April 1927) and is reprinted in Acocella and Garafola 1991: 74, illustrates the rephrasing (and elsewhere abbreviation) of original reviews

in these anonymous translations; Levinson's introduction of quotation marks in *La Danse d'aujourd'hui* (1929) clearly indicates his desire to recall the initial wording.

13. Levinson 1929: 286–287.
14. Riis 1989: 87–88, 146–147.
15. See Riis 1989: 5–6; also Graziano 1990: 89; and Levine 1977, chap. 5, "Black Laughter."
16. For a discussion of the exposition, see Silver 1989: chap. 8, "Perchance to Dream."
17. See Gioia 1989: 30. Gioia's Primitivist Myth refers principally to Robert Goffin's potentially racist identification of Negritude in jazz as the ability, such as exhibited by Louis Armstrong, to enter "the trance."
18. See Zora Neale Hurston, "Shouting," in Cunard 1970: 34.
19. Toledano, introduction to Ansermet's essay as reproduced in Toledano 1947: 115. Collier 1988 elaborates on the untenableness of the opinion at some length.
20. See Hugues Panassie, *Hot Jazz,* 1st American ed. 1936; Robert Goffin, *Aux frontiers du jazz* (Paris, 1931); Charles Delaunay, *Hot Discography* (Paris, 1936). See Gioia 1988: 24–32.
21. See Cook 1988, chap. 4, "Jazz: The Sound of the New World," for a rich overview of the personalities and the relationship of jazz to French art music. See also Berlin 1980.
22. Ansermet was right. Ravel included a fox trot in his opera *L'Enfant et les sortilèges* (1920–1925).
23. Ansermet 1919, reprinted in *Écrits sur la musique* (Neuchâtel, 1971/R1983): 171–178; translated and reprinted in numerous languages, including English in *Jazz Hot: International Review of Jazz Music* (Paris), 28 (November-December 1938): 4–9, and in *Frontiers of Jazz,* Ralph de Toledano ed. (New York, 1947): 115–122.
24. Bechet 1961: 7.
25. Ibid.: 126–127.
26. Ibid.: 128.
27. For more about *In Dahomey* see Riis 1989: 103.
28. Bechet 1961: 147.
29. Chilton 1987: 75.
30. Krenek 1974: 26.
31. Schuller 1968: 325, n. 8.
32. For a rich discussion of *Jonny spielt auf,* see Cook 1988: 77–114.
33. Alfred Jerger, liner notes to Krenek, *Jonny spielt auf* (excerpts), Amadeo AVRS 5038. See Cook 1988: 105.
34. Olin Downes, "*Jonny spielt auf,* Opera of This Age," *The New York Times* (January 20, 1929). For a complete review of the "Performance History and

Critical Reception" of the opera both inside and outside Germany, see Cook 1988: 101–114.

35. Thomson 1967: 106.
36. Marcel Raymond, *From Baudelaire to Surrealism* (New York, 1950): 271.
37. Cage and Hoover 1959: 157.
38. Thomson 1967: 113.
39. Copland 1927: 9–13.
40. Sachs, 1962: 118.
41. See especially Sargeant 1938: 59–64. Sargeant's criticism of Copland's thesis was picked up and summarized shortly thereafter by John Pryor Dodge (1939: 322). I am indebted to Richard Crawford for bringing these sources to my attention.
42. See Chapter 9 for a detailed consideration of this issue.
43. Locke (1936: 1) openly confirmed this opinion: "America is a great music consumer, but not as yet a great music producer. Music spreads over the whole surface of American life, but there are few deep well-springs of native music as in the folk music of many other countries. Negro music is the closest approach America has to a folk music, and so Negro music is almost as important for the musical culture of America as it is for the spiritual life of the Negro."
44. Jowitt 1988: 177.
45. Milhaud 1925: 200–205; French version as "L'evolution du jazz-band" in Milhaud 1927: 51–59.
46. Milhaud 1927: 54–55.
47. Ibid.
48. Ibid.: 58–59.
49. Milhaud 1949: 192.
50. N. Perloff 1991: 175.
51. Collier 1988.

7. The Cunard Line

1. Stein 1946: 102.
2. See Crowder 1987.
3. Cunard 1970: 431.
4. Chisholm 1979: 179–180.
5. The complete contents of the circular are given in Hugh Ford's introduction to Cunard 1970: xxi. See Leighten 1990 for a penetrating discussion of colonial abuses discussed in the French press as early as 1905.
6. Chisholm 1979: 98, 101.
7. Cunard 1970: xxii.
8. Cunard 1970: 181.

9. Ibid.: 182.

10. Letter to Mrs. Mary Curtis Bok, March 4, 1923, preserved in the Library of Congress. See Whitesitt 1983: 9.

11. A book under this title was commissioned but never completed. A typescript "Manifesto of the Musico-Mechanics" is part of the Antheil estate. See Whitesitt 1983: 69.

12. Antheil 1927–28: 227.

13. Antheil 1970: 214.

14. Ibid.: 216.

15. Ibid.: 217–218. "The first great rag-times (1918) were the work of Russians at home among the negroes of Harlem in New York. Did not the untranslatable rhythm of Pushkin come from black blood?"

16. Lambert 1934: 190–191.

17. Ibid.: 220.

18. Ibid.: 223.

19. Ibid.: 31.

20. Ibid.: 239.

21. Chisholm 1979: 222.

22. See Southern 1982: 359 and Rae Linda Brown, Notes to Still's *Afro-American Symphony,* Library of Congress Record OMP 106.

23. Bordman 1985: 360. Riis (1989: 182) confirms that the string of black revue successes had dwindled before the war and that *Shuffle Along* ushered in a new vogue. On the role of black musical theater in the Harlem Renaissance movement, see Graziano 1990.

24. Locke 1925: 209.

25. Eileen Southern, "William Grant Still," *New Grove Dictionary of Music and Musicians,* vol. 18 (1980): 146.

26. Brown 1990: 75.

27. Brown 1990.

28. Fabre 1991: 31, 35 and Gordon 1990: 141.

29. The revisionist view promoted in Collier 1988 that French testimony to the power of jazz was a delayed recognition of a repertoire already embraced in America, for all its merits, carries the potential of diminishing the French role in the acknowledgment and support of black American art in general.

30. See Fabre 1991, chap. 5, "Langston Hughes and Alain Locke: Jazz in Montmartre and African Art," and chap. 6, "Countee Cullun: 'The Greatest Francophile.'"

31. See Green 1990: 36–38; also Christ Stapleton, "African Connection: London's Hidden Music Scene," and John Cowley, "London Is the Place: Caribbean Music in the Context of Empire, 1900–60," in Oliver 1990: 87–89 and 61.

32. Locke 1925: 216.

33. See Fabre 1991.

34. N. Perloff 1991: 4, n. 11.

35. Gruenberg also published four volumes of spirituals with his own ingenious harmonizations in 1926.

36. For an informative summation of the dialogue that vivified the periodicals in the 1920s on the issue of jazz in serious composition, see Cook 1988, chap. 4, "Jazz: The Sound of the New World," particularly 64–70.

37. Article on Gruenberg by Carleton Sprague Smith, *The New Grove Dictionary of Music and Musicians,* vol. 7 (1980): 760.

38. See Florian Zimmermann, ed., *Der Schrei nach dem Turmhause* (Berlin, 1988).

39. Tower 1990: 45, 49–51; the Grosz and Citroën illustrations reproduced on pp. 45, 48, respectively.

40. Ruth Phelps and Henri Morane, "Artistes d'avant-garde en Amérique," *Le Figaro hebdomadaire* (July 25, 1928): 8–9; cited and translated in Mattis 1991: 15.

41. Henry Cowell, "Jazz Today," *Trend* (October–November 1934): 162, 164. Cited in Mattis 1991: 15.

42. Ravel (1928: 141) states, "I am quite conscious of the fact that my *Chansons madécasses* are in no way Schoenbergian, but I do not know whether I ever should have been able to write them had Schoenberg never written."

43. See Orenstein 1975: 91. For an informative consideration of potential Malagasy musical influences in Ravel's cycle see James 1990.

44. Concerning the rich history of the cult of the Black Virgin, see Begg 1985.

45. See Cook 1989: 40ff.

46. Cook 1988: 235, n. 33, states, however: "*Jonny spielt auf* has been performed in the last two decades in Florence (1963, 1965), Regensburg (1968), Vienna (1980), Leeds (1984), and most recently, Palermo (1987) without any apparent problems and using black singers in the title role."

47. Cook 1988: 75. The cover is reproduced in Minna Lederman, *The Life and Death of a Small Magazine, (Modern Music, 1924–1946),* Institute for Studies in American Music Monographs, 18 (Brooklyn, 1983): following 142.

48. Kater 1991.

49. Schebera 1990: 80.

50. Hauff 1991.

51. Baker 1991: 123–124 and Floyd 1990.

8. Take the "A" Train

1. Mercer Ellington 1978: 25 and Schuller 1968: 326. For additional clarifications of the "jungle" style and its metamorphosis see Crawford 1992, chap. 6.

2. Tucker 1988.

3. Stearns 1975: 183–184.
4. Ellington 1973: 420.
5. Tucker 1988.
6. Riis 1989: 146–47.
7. See Robertson 1992: 68 for the scenario and number sequence. The blues portion of the scene, which involves numbers 15 and 16 of the original production, eventually became the "Piano Blues No. 2," the only portion of the score that was published.
8. Schuller 1968: 344.
9. See Robert Goffin, "The Best Negro Jazz Orchestras" in Cunard 1970: 181.
10. Samuel Floyd, Jr., "Music in the Harlem Renaissance: An Overview," in Floyd 1990: 8.
11. Ellington 1931: 22; cited in Tucker 1990: 123.
12. Tucker 1990: 124.
13. Collier 1978: 245–246; see also Floyd 1990: 8.
14. Locke 1936: 99. See also Burgett 1990.
15. *The New York Times* (February 13, 1924).
16. Collier 1988: 20.
17. Darrell 1930.
18. Darrell 1931.
19. Darrell 1932: 153–57.
20. Collier 1988: 39.
21. Rattenbury 1990.
22. Lambert 1934: 214.
23. Ellington 1973: 447.
24. Schlesinger 1991: 32–33.
25. Levine 1988: 226–227.
26. Alpert 1990: 69.
27. Quoted in Alpert 1990: 118.
28. Schuller 1968: 354.
29. See Collier 1987: 229.
30. Morrow 1935: 5–6. Alpert (1990: 122) confuses and conflates some of Morrow's comments with Ellington's.
31. Andrew Homzy, review of Rattenbury's *Duke Ellington, Notes,* 48 (June 1992): 1244.
32. Locke 1936: 54.
33. See Rattenbury 1990: chap. 5, "The Influence of Tin Pan Alley."
34. Locke 1936: 114–115.
35. Cf. Locke 1936: 112 with Lambert 1934: 194–195.
36. Beyond the useful assemblage of materials in Alpert 1990, the most perceptive, ongoing criticism of *Porgy and Bess* appears in Crawford 1972 and 1986 and in his article in *The New Grove Dictionary of Opera* (1992).

37. Locke 1936: 107.
38. Ibid.: 110–111.
39. I am indebted to Richard Crawford for this perception.
40. Zora Neal Hurston, "Characteristics of Negro Expression" in Cunard 1970: 28.
41. Cited in Jablonski 1987: 192.
42. Alpert 1990: 183.
43. Ibid.: 181–182.
44. Cruse 1967: 103.
45. *Porgy and Bess* was staged at the Metropolitan Opera Company in the 1980s, at Glyndebourne in 1986, and at Covent Garden in 1992; Hollis Alpert's book *The Life and Times of "Porgy and Bess"* appeared in 1990; and in the early 1990s James Standifer undertook the examination of *Porgy and Bess* from 1920 to 1960 for a film documentary.
46. Levy 1933: 29–30.
47. Noguchi 1967: 19.
48. Quoted in Don McDonogh, *Martha Graham* (New York, 1973): 81.
49. Grove 1989: 34, 46.
50. See Noguchi's "The 'Arts' called 'Primitive,'" *Arts News,* 56 (March 1957): 24–27, 64, and "Noguchi on Brancusi," *Craft Horizons,* 35 (August 1976): 26–29.
51. Noguchi 1967: 20.
52. Grove 1985: 48. See also "Lynching as a Japanese Sculptor Sees It," *The Christian Century,* 52 (February 13, 1935): 197; and Grove 1989: 16.
53. A remark of the influential art critic Henry McBride cited in Noguchi 1967: 23.
54. This tale was also learned and recited from memory in Japanese by dozens of eighteen-year-old GIs—the author included—in the Army Japanese language program at the University of Minnesota in the fall-winter of 1945.
55. Brancusi poses the question thus in the Whitgate Productions videorecording, *Isamu Noguchi* (Chicago, 1980).
56. See Grove 1989: 98–99.
57. William Bolcom, "Ragtime," *The New Grove Dictionary of Music and Musicians,* vol. 15 (London, 1980): 539.
58. Chernoff 1979: 55.
59. Schneider 1962: 207. See also Chernoff 1979: 57ff. and Nettl 1975: 106–107.
60. See especially the discussions regarding Stravinsky's *Three Pieces for String Quartet* (1914) in Chapter 10.
61. Miller 1986: 120–139.
62. Ibid.
63. See Feest 1987 for a drawing. I am indebted to Tara Browner for her investi-

gation surrounding the appropriation of Native-American culture by European and American composers as part of a seminar project.

64. Ezra Pound also tried his hand at composition with an opera on a text of François Villon, *Testament,* and almost got away with it through an appeal to primitiveness. Thomson 1967: 83 put it thus: "In late June of 1926, Ezra Pound's opera had been performed in a stylish execution before a stylish intellectual public at the Salle Pleyel . . . the orchestra contained a *corne,* or animal's horn, five feet long, that could blow two notes only, a bass and the fifth above it, but with a raucous majesty evocative of faraway times. The vocal line, minimally accompanied, was a prosidization of Old French, which Ezra was said to know well. The music was not quite a musician's music, though it may well be the finest poet's music since Thomas Campion."

65. M. P. Francastel, *Nouveau dessin: Nouvelle peinture* (Paris, 1944): 148. "Let us take *art nègre,* for example. If one considers its direct repercussions, one must conclude that they are mediocre . . . *Art nègre* thus appears, for the moment at least, as a manifestation of fashion and not as an important current of contemporary art."

66. See Ladislas Szecsi, "The Term 'Negro *Art*' Is Essentially a Non-African Concept" in Cunard 1970: 413.

67. Orenstein 1990: 293.

9. The Valley of the Bells

1. Concerning Stockhausen's fascination for working in five and more time-layers, see his discussion regarding "Luzifers Traum" *(Samstag aus Licht)* in Stockhausen 1989b: 131.

2. See Roth-Mascagni 1979 and Stimpson 1984.

3. Guillaume Apollinaire, "Simultanisme-Librettisme," *Les Soirées de Paris* (June 15, 1914): 323–324.

4. See Bochner 1978: 122.

5. See Schwab 1991: 146.

6. W. J. T. Mitchell, "Spatial Form in Literature: Toward a General Theory," *Critical Inquiry,* 6.3 (1980): 541. See also Rudolf Arnheim, "Space as an Image of Time" in *Images of Romanticism,* ed. Karl Kroeber and William Walling (New Haven, 1978): 1–12; Robert P. Morgan, "Music Time / Musical Space," *Critical Inquiry,* 6.3 (Spring 1980): 527–538; Joseph Frank, "Spatial Form in Modern Literature," *Sewanee Review,* 53 (Spring, Summer, Autumn 1945); Joseph Frank, "Spatial Form: An Answer to Critics," *Critical Inquiry,* 4.2 (Winter 1977): 231–252; William Holtz, "Spatial Form in Modern Literature: A Reconsideration," *Critical Inquiry,* 4.2 (Winter 1977): 271–283. See also Elizabeth Ermarth, *Sequel to History: Postmodernism and the Crisis of Representational Time* (Princeton, 1992).

7. Roskill 1985: 29.

8. Michel-Eugène Chevreul, *De la loi du contraste simultané des couleurs et de l'assortiment des objets colorés* (1839); English translation by Charles Martel as *The Principles of Harmony and Contrast of Colors* (1872).

9. Henri Bergson, *Essai sur les données immédiates de la conscience* (1889); English translation as *Time and Free Will*.

10. See Roskill 1985: 34.

11. See Boulez 1989: 72–75 and especially the illustrations on 68–69. Klee's displacements, which permit the simultaneous consideration of the same material from multiple angles, are clearly akin to Cubist theory and the demonstrations of Albert Gleizes. See Chapter 10. Compare these visual perspectives with critical theories of "inversion" in the works of Proust as discussed by Dominique Jullien, "Inversion, retournement, indexation" in *Proust et ses modèles* (Paris, 1989): 138–168.

12. Puccini's fascination with bells and the attendant spatial component is revealed in a letter to Don Pietro Panichelli written during the composition of *Tosca*, Act III: "Now please let me know the exact tone of the church bells in the neighborhood of Castel Sant'Angelo and the exact tone of the big bell at St. Peter's." Quoted in Dante del Fiorentino, *Immortal Bohemian* (New York, 1952): 104.

13. The projection of different tempos occurring simultaneously also appears in the orchestral overture to *L'Heure espagnole* (1907–9).

14. The French fascination with the bell sound manifests itself in such early works as Debussy's "Les Cloches" (*Deux Romances,* 1891) as well as in his later "Cloches à travers les feuilles" (*Images,* second series, 1907) and "La Cathédrale engloutie" (*Préludes,* Book I, 1910–1913). Honegger also wrote *Six poèmes,* containing "Les Cloches" (1916–17), and *Trois poèmes,* including "Cloche du soir" (1916).

15. See Antliff 1988.

16. "In morte di un samurai" for voice and piano (1951).

17. See Chapter 10.

18. Zukav: 92.

19. Varèse 1967: 214.

20. See Johnson 1991: 32–33.

21. Burkholder 1985b: 88.

22. Arnold Schoenberg, "Composition with Twelve Tones" in *Style and Idea,* ed. Leonard Stein (New York, 1975): 223.

23. Hoffman, "Collage in the Twentieth Century: An Overview" in Hoffman 1989: 2.

24. "My *Ballet mécanique*" in *De Stijl,* 6 (1924–25): 144, and "Manifest. Der Musico-Mechanico" in *De Stijl,* 6 (1924–25): 99. See also Helga de la Motte-Haber, *Musik und bildende Kunst: von der Tonmalerei zur Klangskulptur* (Laaber,

Ger., 1990), particularly pp. 194–197, regarding the concept of "Simultanei-tät" or "Gleichzeitigkeit"; and Robert P. Morgan, "Musical Time / Musical Space," *Critical Inquiry,* 6.3 (Spring 1980): 527–538, where he discusses phys-ical space as a component in the music of Gabrieli, Berlioz, Wagner, Mahler, Ives, Stockhausen; and notational space as in Crumb, Cage, Brown, Pender-ecki, etc. Compare also with Stockhausen 1989b, particularly pp. 151–161, regarding simultaneous, multiple layers of the *formel.*

10. Stravinsky and the Cubists

1. Rosenblum 1966: 9.
2. Gray 1953: 3.
3. Isaak (1986: 2) openly challenges this notion.
4. Craft 1982: 87.
5. Robbins 1966: 14–15. See also Maur 1985: 360.
6. See Gray 1986: 83–130 and Taruskin 1986: 36–38.
7. Benois 1941: 302.
8. Taruskin 1986: 36–37.
9. Wilhelm Worringer, *Abstraction and Empathy: A Contribution to the Psychology of Style* (1908), trans. Michael Bullock (New York, 1967).
10. T. E. Hulme, "Modern Art and Its Philosophy," an address to the Quest Society, January 1914; published in Hulme 1924: 82.
11. Gray 1962: 97.
12. Loguine, "La Révolution artistique à Moscou au début du siècle" in Loguine 1971: 21–22.
13. Rosenblum 1966: 40.
14. Ansermet 1965: 446.
15. "Ballets russes et français," *La Nouvelle Revue,* 8 (July 1, 1913): 116–125, translated in Bullard: 198.
16. Gray 1961: 108.
17. Extracts from "La Peinture et ses lois," *La Vie des lettres,* October 1922, are reproduced in Alibert 1982, 133–134, 189. The complete caption reads: "Dessin d'un tableau-objet réalisé dans le champ d'un plan octogonal. Selon les déterminants de la mécanique plastique particulière au plan, les aspects de l'évolution dans le temps et l'espace, rythmique et spatiale, ont été fixés par le sentiment propre de l'artiste." See also Green 1987: 88, 146.
18. Cassirer 1955: 108.
19. Taruskin 1986, 34–35. Cf. also Forte 1978 and van den Toorn 1983.
20. Van den Toorn 1983: 139–140.
21. See Watkins 1988: 216–217.
22. See van den Toorn 1983: 140.
23. Pasler 1986: 73.

24. Roskill 1985: 86–87.
25. Written in 1913–14 but not published until 1919.
26. Craft 1982: 74, n. 6.
27. Steegmuller 1970: 115.
28. Ibid.: 117.
29. Craft 1982: 74.
30. Ibid.: 76.
31. Except Delage and a few others, according to Cocteau. The only person whom it was essential to keep in the dark was Diaghilev.
32. Craft 1982: 77.
33. Ibid.
34. Ibid.: 78.
35. Aschengreen 1986: 60–61.
36. See n. 49.
37. Aschengreen 1986: 61. The continuing appeal of David for a postwar age, though from a different musical perspective, was confirmed a few years later with Arthur Honegger's *Le Roi David* (1921), the composer's first important success. Honegger's interest in David also led him to the private purchase of what has been claimed to be the model for Michelangelo's renowned sculpture—a model whose existence has only recently come to the attention of art historians. Hartt's claims of authenticity for the model have been widely debated. See Hartt 1987.
38. Craft 1982: 82.
39. Ibid.: 82, n. 15.
40. Ibid.: 83–84.
41. Ibid.: 84.
42. The *David Notebooks*—four cloth-bound notebooks now at the Humanities Research Center of the University of Texas at Austin—are labeled "*David— Ouverture*," the second and third, "Premier Tour," the fourth "Deuxième Tour." See Stravinsky 1982: 74, n. 10.
43. Steegmuller 1970: 103.
44. Pierre Monteux had heard the same rumor as early as March 14. In a letter of that date Monteux wrote Stravinsky asking for the first performance of a new dance or dances which had been rumored as recently composed: "Nothing could please me more, dear friend, than if you would reserve the premiere of your *Trois Danses* for me. Approximately when do you think that they will be ready? I can hardly wait to become acquainted with them." Robert Craft has properly noted that "by this date, Stravinsky had no more than sketched the first of the pieces, the only one that was to become a dance." Stravinsky 1982: 407–408.
45. Craft 1982: 85, n. 21.

46. Ibid.: 85.
47. Ibid.: 86–88.
48. Brown 1968: 127.
49. Crosland 1972: 326.
50. Stravinsky 1936: 93. See also Steegmuller 1970: 179.
51. Stein 1955: 119. *The Autobiography* was written in 1932 and first published in 1933.
52. Stravinsky and Craft 1959: 96.
53. The 1915 Portrait of Igor Stravinsky by Blanche is reproduced in color in Stravinsky 1984: 57. A study for this portrait was made in 1913, reproduced in color in Stravinsky 1984: 51.
54. See Craft 1984, appendix J.
55. Stravinsky and Craft 1959: 111.
56. Flanner 1972: 54.
57. Stein 1946: 104.
58. Craft 1984: 94–97.
59. Ibid.: 89.
60. Reproduced in Stravinsky 1984: 61.
61. Craft 1982: 8.
62. Reproduced in Gray 1986: 141.
63. Reproduced in Chamot 1979: 53.
64. Stravinsky and Craft 1959: 111.
65. Reproduced in Watkins 1988: 227.
66. Chamot 1979: 48.
67. Reproduced in Chamot 1979: 74.
68. Chamot 1979: 72.
69. See Watkins 1988: 272, for Delaunay's *Red Eiffel Tower* of 1911–12.
70. Silver 1989: 148–149.
71. Stravinsky and Craft 1959: 113. Delaunay's portrait is reproduced in *Stravinsky* 1984.
72. Spector 127: "At the outbreak of war in 1914 Thévenaz returned to Geneva to complete the course in *rythmique* and then left for New York to become an instructor at the new Dalcroze School." Thévenaz also provided drawings for the 1916 French edition, *La Rythmique,* of Jaques-Dalcroze's *Méthode* of 1906 (see Spector: 130–131). See also Aschengreen 1986: 64; Steegmuller 1970: 94, 103, 114; Garafola 1989: 100, 431, n. 13.
73. Robbins 1966: 53.
74. Gleizes and Metzinger 1913: 20, 55.
75. Ibid.: 20, 42.
76. Aschengreen 1986: 61–62.
77. Cocteau's complete opening text appears in Aschengreen 1986: 62.

78. See Pasler 1991: 263–65.
79. Jean Cocteau, "La Collaboration de *Parade*," *Nord-Sud: Revue littéraire*, 4–5 (June-July 1917): 29; reprinted in Cocteau 1926: 50–51.
80. Gleizes's portrait of Eugene Figuière is reproduced in Rosenblum 1966: 169 and Robbins 1966: 51.
81. Henri Bergson expounded on this question from the time of his *Essaie sur les données immédiates de la conscience* (1889) to *Durée et simultanéité, à propos de la théorie d'Einstein* (1922). See also Jacques Maritain, *La Philosophie bergsonienne* (Paris, 1930); Sherry Buckberrough, *Robert Delaunay: The Discovery of Simultaneity* (Ann Arbor, 1982); Bochner 1978: 97–123; Monique Chefdor, *Blaise Cendrars* (Boston, 1980): 41–48; Cohen 1978; Gross 1985; M. Perloff 1986; and Coen 1987.
82. See Watkins 1988: 239 regarding "parole in libertà," whose visual placement toys with the temporal element in the printing of poetry.
83. Lowell's poem is reproduced complete in White 1966: 233.
84. Cohen 1978: 169. Concerning the relation of the painters to the musicians see also Stravinsky 1976, Stravinsky 1980, and Bartsch 1981.
85. Cocteau's opinions through this period are reflected in the wartime journal *Le Mot*, which first appeared in November 1914.
86. Poole 1967: 200–201.
87. Jean Cocteau, *Dans le ciel de la patrie* (Paris, 1918), quoted in Silver 1984: 87.
88. Silver in Anderson and Saltus 1984: 89.
89. See Watkins 1988: 263–264 for Cocteau's proposed scenario for "The Little American Girl."
90. Cf. the principal material of the woodwinds and the accompanying strings in the "Chinese Magician" to the structural premise of the first of Stravinsky's *Three Pieces for String Quartet*. See Watkins 1988: 264. See also Gillmor 1988: 199–200 and Harbec 1987.
91. Reproduced in Watkins 1988: 264, fig. 13.5. For a lucid discussion of the "Red Curtain" see Axsom 1979. See also Cooper 1968 and Marianne Martin, "The Ballet *Parade*: A Dialogue between Cubism and Futurism," *Art Quarterly*, n.s. 1 (Spring 1978): 85–111.
92. Leonide Massine, *My Life in Ballet* (London, 1968): 103.
93. Huntley Carter, "Newest Tendencies in the Paris Theatre," *Theatre Arts*, 2 (December 1917): 35.
94. White 1966, 234, claims that no. 1 is a precursor of a "long series of popular Russian tunes that Stravinsky poured out in profusion during the four years 1914–1917," and proposes that a demonstrable continuity can be illustrated by comparing it to the opening of the first movement of the Symphony in C (also no. 2 with *Symphony of Psalms* and no. 3 with *Symphonies of Wind Instruments*).

95. Taruskin 1982: 191. Noting the presence of the *naigryshi* tradition in Glinka's *Kamárinskaia,* Taruskin also observes that Stravinsky had introduced it in the "Dance of the Earth" in *Le Sacre du printemps* and was to do so later in the fourth tableau of *Les Noces.* No connection is advanced, however, with respect to the initial dance movement of *Three Pieces for String Quartet.*

96. Stravinsky and Craft 1962: 13. I am grateful to Jeffrey Lyman for noting that the bowing indication first appeared in the 1918 revision and for bringing the comparison with *L'Histoire du soldat* to my attention.

97. The third and last movement exposes another kind of constant and variable which had already been exposed in *Le Sacre du printemps,* that is, the *personnages rythmiques* of the "Danse sacrale." Here the relationships are due not to changing relationships simultaneously presented but to a collage effected by the juxtapositions of materials which remain the same, expand or contract in a seemingly indeterminate way, until indeterminacy begins to become predictable.

98. Named for the Italian mathematician Leonardo Fibonacci (ca. 1170–1240).

99. Kramer 1986: 177.

100. I am indebted to Timothy Taylor for his observation as part of a seminar project that a similar relationship exists in Stravinsky's *In Memoriam Dylan Thomas.* Here the third of four statements of the refrain "Do not go gentle into that good night" occurs at measure 34 (the Golden Section) of a piece 55 (Fibonacci number) measures long. See Kramer 1986 for a discussion of other proportional schemes in Stravinsky's late works.

101. *Phaidon Encyclopedia of Art and Artists* (New York, 1978): "Section d'Or," 611. For further material on the use of the Golden Section in Cubist work, see Camfield 1965 as well as Lucy Adelman and Michael Compton, "Mathematics in Early Abstract Art" in *Towards a New Art* (London, Tate Gallery, 1980); and Johnson 1991. Roskill (1985: 58) enriches the issue with respect to time and place by noting that "Gris worked on a series of drawings embodying mathematically calculated proportions, for which he used a ruler and compasses. These served as the basis for paintings of 1914–15." See also Johnson 1991.

102. See Funayama in Pasler 1986: 273.

103. Communication from Robert Craft, June 9, 1989: "In 1961, S. posted a picture of David dancing before the ark on the cover of his *Flood* sketchbook . . . (*not* of Noah.) . . . Your programmatic interpretation is plausible, and the Golden Section is a certainty."

104. See Rosenblum 1966: 72 for a discussion of this important issue.

105. See Taruskin 1987 for an in-depth discussion of planar shifting between musical and textual accent in the first of the *Three Japanese Lyrics.*

106. See Austin 1987 for a provocative discussion regarding the quality and range of "continuities" in Stravinsky's music.

107. A confirmation of this idea (expressed independently of the notion of Cubism) appears in Wuorinen and Kresky 1986: 263.

108. See, for example, Gleizes's *Triptych* (1930–31) reproduced in Robbins 1966: 102–103; or Gleizes, *Composition, dominantes roses et vertes* (1942), reproduced in Robbins 1966: 110.

109. See Covach 1990: 167ff. for a discussion of "rotation" in Hauer's music from 1922–32. Berg's and Krenek's discovery of rotation took place in the 1930s and 1950s, respectively, but the concept was not theoretically discussed before the 1950s.

110. See Babbitt 1986: 252–254. The division of the twelve-note series into two hexachords, each of which is systematically subjected to a rotational plan involving the preservation of interval content from "ground zero" (E♭ and G) had audible tonal consequences in the music. See also Wuorinen and Kresky 1986.

111. Stravinsky and Craft 1960: 100.

112. See Stravinsky 1985: 133–138 for the Stravinsky-Handschin correspondence (1931–1933).

113. In the first movement of the *Quartet for the End of Time* (1940), for example, the cello lays down a changing grid of five pitches projected over a rhythmic pattern of fifteen values while the piano plays a twenty-nine–note ostinato wedded to a rhythmic pedal of seventeen values. Similar constructions, including those based on Greek and Hindu rhythmic patterns, are pervasive throughout Messiaen's career. More audible is simultaneous temporal construction in the first movement, "Amen of the Creation," of the same composer's *Vision de l'Amen* (1943) for two pianos, where chorale-like visions of Creation resound against quivering bell sounds at the introduction of the first light.

114. It would be impossible to make a comprehensive list of those composers whose music has been analyzed for evidence of the Fibonacci series and the Golden Section, but Bartók and Debussy have been subject to such extensive dissection in this regard as to provide a *locus classicus* for an introduction to the associative formal questions. See particularly Howat 1983 and Lendvai 1971. The principles of rotation, familiar to the Cubists and later applied by Stravinsky in his approach to serialism in the 1950s and 1960s, may also be profitably compared to technically related achievements in the 1920s in the serial manipulations of Schoenberg (*Serenade,* op. 24, 1920–1923), Hauer (*Etüden für Klavier,* op. 22, 1922–23), and Berg (*Lyric Suite,* 1925–26).

115. Stein 1946: 174–175; see chap. 3: 12 for a more complete citation of Stein's remarks.

116. Stravinsky and Craft 1960: 89. I witnessed a dramatic demonstration of Stravinsky's alertness to the analogies between the visual arts and music when the composer was in Ann Arbor for the May Festival in 1964, during which

he conducted the Philadelphia Orchestra in a performance of *Perséphone*. On the evening of the day before his concert he, Mme. Stravinsky, and Robert Craft came to my apartment prior to dining out. Above the dining table hung a four-panel Japanese screen whose underlying formal grid was the typical mosaic of four-inch gold leaf squares. At the front door on the way to dinner, Stravinsky noticed the screen, paused momentarily and remarked, "Those are my 'Huxley' Variations!" At the time Stravinsky was in the midst of composing the work, which he had begun the previous July (1963) in Santa Fé but which would not be completed until October 28, 1964.

117. Green 1987: 72. Picasso uses a similar line-and-dot technique in his cover for Poulenc's *Poèmes de Ronsard* (1925), reproduced in Maur 1985: 106. Stravinsky's drawings appear in Stravinsky and Craft 1959: 120.

118. Stravinsky and Craft 1959: 16–17.

119. See Whitesitt 1983: 69–70.

120. See Dubnick 1984: 20–25 and McMillan 1964.

121. Silver 1989: 321.

122. Blaise Cendrars, "Why is the 'Cube' Disintegrating?" (English translation of "Pourquoi le 'Cube' s'effrite?" *La Rose rouge,* May 15, 1919), in Edward Fry, *Cubism* (London, 1966): 155.

123. Gleizes, "La Peinture et ses lois, 'ce qui devait sortir du cubisme,' " *La Vie des lettres* (October 1922): 46. See Green 1987: 146.

124. Roskill 1985: 88–89.

11. Obsessions with Pierrot

1. Named at a late date in its history for the puppetmaster Vemura Bunrakuken (1737–1810).

2. See Eruli 1985: 216. Eruli also takes note of Claudel's marionnette pieces, *Protée,* and Léger's cardboard figures for *L'Homme et son désir* and *La Création du monde.*

3. Stiefel 1985: 81. See also Martzel 1985 and Lamarque 1989.

4. Craig 1968: 9.

5. Bablet 1985: 141. See Eynat 1987: 182–183 as well as Eynat 1980: 171–193.

6. Craig 1908: 3ff.

7. Aslan 1985: 142.

8. Craig 1908.

9. For a collection of Craig's views on the Ballets Russes, and especially Nijinsky and Bakst, whom he deplored, see Rood 1977, Part II: "Gordon Craig on the Classic Dance."

10. Bablet 1985: 137–146.

11. Laude 1968: 487.

12. Bablet 1985: 138.

13. August Macke, writing to Gabriele Münter, September 25, 1911. Quoted in Klaus Lankheit, "*Kommentar:* Die Geschichte des Almanachs" in Kandinsky and Marc 1974: 19.

14. Macke, "Die Masken," in Kandinsky and Marc 1974: 89.

15. Manfred Boetzkes, "Appia," *New Grove Dictionary of Music and Musicians* (London, 1980): vol. 1, 508, which also reproduces the stage design for Gluck's *Orfeo.*

16. Ibid.: 22.

17. For additional information on the force of Pierrot see Watkins 1988: 183–189.

18. Palacio 1990: 42.

19. Blok 1963: vol. 8, 169–170.

20. S. Auslender, quoted by Volkov 1929: 280–281; translated here from the French as cited by Picon-Vallin 1985: 149. See also Taviani 1985: 121.

21. Roose-Evans 1970: 20–21.

22. See Félicien Champsaur, *Pierrot et sa conscience* (Paris, 1889), and *Le Jazz des masques* (Paris, 1928).

23. "Speaking, Playing, Singing: *Pierrot lunaire* and *Le Marteau sans maître*" in Boulez 1986b: 335–336.

24. See Watkins 1986: 243–48.

25. André Schaeffner, "Variations Schoenberg," *Contrepoints,* 7 (1951): 110–129, cited ibid. See Steven Moore Whiting, "Erik Satie and Vincent Hyspa: Notes on a Collaboration" (in preparation) regarding the shadow play in the Parisian cabaret tradition.

26. Garafola 1989: 30. See also Braun 1979: 70. Fokine admired Meyerhold's interpretation so much that early in 1910 he cast him as Pierrot in *Carnaval,* a ballet that similarly owed a large debt to *Balaganchik.*

27. Karlinsky 1986: 4–5.

28. Picon-Vallin 1985: 149, n. 20.

29. Albright 1988: 109.

30. Karlinsky 1986: 4–5.

31. V. Stravinsky and Craft 1978: 140.

32. Goncharova and Larionov, "Serge de Diaghilew et l'évolution du décor et du costume de ballet" in Goncharova 1955: 31–33.

33. Notes to Everest LP 3184.

34. Stravinsky and Craft 1962: 138–139. Regarding the impossibility of translating *Renard* see also Stravinsky and Craft 1959: 36.

35. Garafola 1989: 83–4.

36. Bowlt 1988: 55.

37. Levinson 1929: 84–85.

38. Stravinsky and Craft 1962: 130–131.

39. David Hockney's use of three masks (Oriental, Primitive, and Greek) for a poster to announce a triple bill *(Le Rossignol, Le Sacre du printemps, Oedipus*

Rex) at the Metropolitan Opera in 1981 hints at their role in establishing a familial association that could be expanded to include *Petrushka* (puppet theater), *Renard* (marionette theater), and *Pulcinella (commedia dell'arte)* within the same time frame.

40. See Kahnweiler 1946: 223 and Laude 1968: 444–445.
41. Crosland 1972: 327.
42. Stravinsky 1959: 102.
43. See Weiss 1990: 86–87, 98–99 and Rosenblum 1990: passim.
44. Festa-McCormick 1984: 87ff.
45. Stravinsky and Craft 1962: 112.
46. See Barry S. Brook's discussion of the multiple sources in his notes to Christopher Hogwood's recording of *Pulcinella* on London 425614–2, which also includes separate performances of Gallo's Trio Sonatas 1, 2, and 7 as well as Pergolesi's *Sinfonia*.
47. See Watkins 1988: 314.
48. See Silver 1989: 129.
49. Ducharte 1925: 332, as cited, discussed, and translated in Silver 1989: 160–161.
50. See especially Messing 1991.
51. On this subject, see especially Messing 1988.
52. For a review by Raymond Charpentier, see Häger 1990: 121.
53. *Comoedia,* June 20, 1921.
54. Milhaud 1953: 87.
55. Interview in *Comoedia,* June 18, 1921.
56. Silver 1989: 40–41.
57. Silver (1989: 126) discusses the role of the *images d'Épinal* in *Parade*.
58. Aschengreen 1986: 104–105.
59. Cocteau 1948: 54–55.
60. Häger 1990: 146–148.
61. Cocteau 1950: vol. 9, 327.
62. Cocteau 1948: 52.
63. Silver 1989: 307.
64. See Jones 1984.
65. Schaeffner 1924.
66. See Spector 1990: 175–178 and Milhaud 1949: 63–67.
67. Milhaud 1953: 81–82.
68. Flanner 1972: 55.
69. Nonetheless, it is important to understand that the independent interest in much of Stravinsky's theater music of the period brought an irreversible change of perspective with respect to the issue: interest in *Petrushka, Le Sacre, L'Histoire du soldat, Pulcinella,* and *Les Noces* as concert pieces never faltered from the beginning.
70. The tenableness of such a view of the work had already been summed up

in a letter from Oskar Schlemmer to Otto Meyer on January 5, 1913; see Schlemmer 1972: 8.
71. See Boulez 1986b: 325–329.
72. Boulez 1986b: 330–343.
73. See Watkins 1988: 610–613.
74. See Nicholls 1991.
75. See Chapter 4.
76. Rischbieter 1968: 164.

12. Masks and Machines

1. Milhaud 1927: 76.
2. See Isaak (1986: 79), who quotes Benedikt Livshits, *Polutoraglazyi strelets* (Leningrad, 1933): 187–188. For more information regarding the interrelationship of Bauhaus activities with Russian Constructivism and European avant-garde theater generally, see Baer 1992. Regarding *Victory over the Sun* in particular see Baer, "Design and Movement in the Theatre of the Russian Avant-Garde," in Baer 1992: 38–41.
3. See Rischbieter 1968.
4. Letter to Tut Schlemmer of July 10, 1920, in Schlemmer 1972: 84. The German edition, p. 91, gives the following appraisal not found in the English edition: "gut, sehr neuartige Harmonik, tät am liebsten gleich lostanzen."
5. Maur 1975: 73. See also Laubenthal 1986.
6. See G. Plattke, ed., *Deutsche Bühne: Jahrbuch der Frankfurter Städtischen Bühnen,* vol. 1, season 1917–18 (Frankfurt am Main, 1919): 269ff. See especially Schubert 1986.
7. Schlemmer 1972: 105. For Schlemmer's report on the critical reaction to the premiere performance, see his letter to Meyer of June 14, ibid.: 106–107.
8. See Schubert 1988: 5.
9. Translated in Schubert 1988: 5.
10. For a vivid account of the Bauhaus theater by one of Schlemmer's pupils, Lux Feininger, see Gropius 1961: 8–9.
11. Ibid: 9.
12. Ibid.: 25.
13. See Gordon 1992: 118.
14. See ibid.: 119.
15. Schlemmer 1972: 192, a letter to his wife of March 28, 1926.
16. Letter to Tut Schlemmer of April 22, 1926, in Schlemmer 1972: 193.
17. In the 1960s Stockhausen adapted music from his *Momente* for use with Schlemmer's ballet.
18. The first sketches in score are to be found in the Paul-Hindemith-Institut, Frankfurt am Main. See Maur 1975: 75.

19. Schlemmer 1972: 196.
20. Ibid.: 196–197.
21. Kandinsky wrote Schoenberg on April 15, 1923, regarding the possibility of coming to the Bauhaus, but Schoenberg responded on April 20 declining on the basis of reports of Kandinsky's anti-Semitism.
22. See Stuckenschmidt 1985: 408ff. For one of Schmidt's sketches for the *Mechanische Ballett,* see ibid.: 409, fig. 2.
23. Ibid.: 410.
24. Ibid.
25. Sigfried Giedion, "Bauhaus Week in Weimar, August 1923," in Neumann 1970: 77.
26. Schlemmer 1972: 209.
27. See Tut Schlemmer, ". . . from the living Bauhaus and its stage" in Neumann 1970: 160.
28. Schlemmer 1972: 211–212.
29. Stravinsky 1982: 171. Stravinsky later recorded his memories of the Bauhaus in a conversation with Robert Craft (Stravinsky and Craft 1959: 99), stating that Busoni "seemed to be very much touched by the work [*Histoire du soldat*]. But whether it was the play of Ramuz, my music, or the whole thing, was not easy to determine, especially since I knew that I was his *bête noire* in music. Now, thirty-five years later, I have a great admiration for his vision, for his literary talent, and for at least one of his works: *Doktor Faust.*"
30. See *Bauhaus, 1919–1933: Meister- und Schülerarbeiten, Weimar, Dessau, Berlin* (Zurich, 1988), fig. 245.
31. Richard Hammond, "Viewing *Les Noces* in 1929," *Modern Music,* 6.3 (March-April 1929): 19–24, a review of Victor Belaiev's *Igor Stravinsky's Les Noces: An Outline* (London, 1928). Shortly thereafter the journal *Modern Music,* 8.3 (March-April 1931), devoted an entire issue to the topic of "Music and the Machine."
32. Aslan 1985: 146. See also Schlemmer 1978: 71.
33. See Watkins 1988: 583–589 for a discussion and illustration of the Brussels Philips Pavilion of 1958.
34. Ouellette 1966: 78.
35. Maur 1985: 363.
36. Ouellette 1959: 11.
37. *391* (New York), 5 (June 1917).
38. Maur 1985: 363.
39. Hulme, "Modern Art" in *The New Age* (1914). Despite Hulme's reverence for the machine and his expressed caution with respect to Kandinsky, it is interesting to compare Schlemmer's figure sketches for the *Triadic Ballet* with Kandinsky's figures planned for a performance of Musorgsky's *Pictures at an Exhibition* (see Maur 1985: 192, fig. 313f, and 195, fig. 315).

40. Varèse, interviewed by Fred Grunfeld, December 13, 1953; cited in Bernard 1987: 7.

41. George Antheil, "Jazz," *Der Querschnitt* 1–2.2 (1922): 172–173; published in English.

42. George Antheil, "Manifest der Musico-Mechanico," *De Stijl,* 6.8 (1924): 99–100; translated into German; reprinted in *De Stijl* (Amsterdam, 1968): vol. 2, 406–407. The original English text is from the Antheil Estate type-script, reproduced in Whitesitt 1983: 69.

43. Letter to Nicolas Slonimsky, July 21, 1936, Music Division, Library of Congress, George Antheil Correspondence. Quoted in Whitesitt 1983: 105–106.

44. Ibid.: 104.

45. Stravinsky 1982: 138. Contrarily, Lawson (1986: 288) states, "Thus, the Etude for Pianola, although conceived as a unique entity, was in fact issued as part of a series, along with works by Malipiero, Casella, Eugene Goossens, Herbert Howells, and several others. It was not, however, the first work to be written for the Pianola. The Orchestrelle Company's 1914 catalogue lists several such compositions, although all by minor composers, in addition to many special arrangements of existing works, notably by Busoni, Scharwenka, and Percy Grainger."

46. Lawson 1986: 296.

47. Stravinsky 1982: 153.

48. Letter to Mary Curtis Bok, October 1923. Manuscript in the Library of Congress.

49. Whitesitt 1983: 25.

50. Ibid.: 91–92.

51. Antheil 1945: 81–83.

52. Blaise Cendrars, "ABC du Cinéma," trans. Serge Gavronsky, *Film Culture,* 40 (Spring 1966): 19–20.

53. Green 1987: 112.

54. Fritz Lang's *Metropolis* of 1927 also made abundant use of machine motifs, including their appearance in the confection of a female robot who incites the working class to revolt. See Norden: 109 for other films influenced by the Futurist fascination with the machine.

55. Whitesitt 1983: 106, quoting Léger's words in *Functions of Painting,* trans. Alexandra Anderson (Paris, 1965), in *The Documents of Twentieth-Century Art,* ed. Robert Motherwell (New York, 1973): 48–50. See also Bauquier 1987: 141–142 for Léger's synopsis of *the Ballet mécanique* dated July 1924, in which he reiterates the objective, realist, and non-abstract nature of the film and its reliance upon fragments both figurative and mechanical. "No scenario," he writes. "Some reactions of rhythmic images, that is all."

56. Rosenblum 1990: 120.

57. "Composer's Notes on 1952–53 Re-editing," unnumbered beginning pages, *Ballet mécanique*, rev. 1952 (Delaware Water Gap, Pa., 1959).

58. Schmalenbach 1985: 94.

59. Antheil, "My *Ballet mécanique*," *De Stijl*, 6.12 (1924–25), as it appeared in *Der Querschnitt*, 5.9 (September 1925): 789–791.

60. For a rich interpretation of the term *Neue Sachlichkeit*, see Stephen Hinton, "Weill: *Neue Sachlichkeit*, Surrealism, and *Gebrauchsmusik*," in *A New Orpheus: Essays on Kurt Weill*, ed. Kim H. Kowalke (New Haven, 1986): 61–82.

61. See Lloyd 1991.

62. See Cook 1988: 36–38.

63. See Craig Barrow, *Montage in James Joyce's Ulysses* (Madrid, 1980).

64. Excerpt, "Mr. Bloom & the Cyclops," published in "Antheil Musical Supplement," *This Quarter*, 1.2 (1925): 22–24.

65. Léger, "The Machine Aesthetic, I" (1924) in Léger 1973: 62–63.

66. Norden (1984: 109) states that "perhaps Chaplin returned the favor when he included the now-famous segment in his feature-length film 'Modern Times' (1936), in which his 'Little Tramp' character is pulled by a conveyor belt into a huge machine assembly and is twisted around various cogs and gears." Chaplin's popularity escalated during the 1920s, and he even found his way into Soviet constructivist theater such as the FEKS (Factory of the Eccentric Actor) 1922 production of *The Marriage: A Gag in Three Acts,* a satire based upon Gogol that introduced Chaplin both as a main character and in a film short called "Charlie Chaplin and Little Betsy" projected onto the backdrop. The FEKS manifesto of 1921 had already proclaimed: "We revere Charlie Chaplin's ass more than the hands of Eleonora Duse!" See Gordon 1992: 115, 117.

67. Tower 1990: 72. For more on "Charlie Chaplin as Emblem of American Mass Culture," "The Artist as Robot and Engineer," and "Jazz and Dance as Symbols of the Machine Age" see "Utopia/Dystopia: *Dada-merika* and *Dollarica*" in Tower 1990: 68–72 and 95–99.

68. Brender 1984: 59–60.

69. V. Stravinsky and Craft 1978: 357–358.

70. Armitage 1937: 101.

71. Similarly, the dancer Ruth Page included six masked jurymen and a crowd of marionettes in her first production on an American subject, *Hear Ye! Hear Ye!* with music by Aaron Copland (1934). See Robertson 1992: 58.

72. See Levine 1988: 160–166.

73. Benjamin 1968: 217–251.

74. See Levin 1990: 33–34.

75. Levin 1990: 38–39.

76. The text was published in the *Philharmonischer Almanach II,* ed. Klaus Schultz

and Peter Girth (Berlin, 1983): 101–118, and included in *Gesammelte Schriften,* vol. 18, 695–718.

77. On the etymology of "rap" see William Safire, "The Rap on Hip-Hop" in *The New York Times Magazine* (November 8, 1991): 18–20; on the expression "Hip-Hop" see Greg Rule, *Keyboard* (July 1992): 39.

78. See Varnedoe and Gopnik 1990b: 338–339.

79. For additional issues surrounding rap culture, see Kyra D. Gaunt, "Performance Practice in Hip-Hop Musical Construction: The Concept of the 'Break,'" a paper presented October 3, 1992, at the International Association for the Study of Popular Music Conference, the University of North Texas State, Denton, Texas.

80. See Boulez, "The Bauhaus Model" in Boulez 1986b. Originating as an interview in 1970, it was rewritten by Boulez in 1980.

81. See Edward Rothstein, "Please Don't Shoot This Player Piano," *The New York Times* (June 20, 1993): H31.

13. *Oedipus* and *Agon*

1. Rimsky-Korsakov 1942: 208.
2. See Morton 1979 and Taruskin 1980.
3. Mazo 1990.
4. Andriessen and Schönberger 1989: 223–224.
5. See especially Messing 1988.
6. Stravinsky 1962: 33–34.
7. Lourié 1932.
8. See Andriessen and Schönberger 1989: 81–96, "Poétique musicale," for a rare attempt at clarifying the relationship between Maritain, Lourié, and Stravinsky.
9. See Messing 1991: 10ff.
10. See Stravinsky 1982: 156–157, nn. 83, 87.
11. Ibid.: 160.
12. For Lourié's claims regarding the sonata, see Lourié 1925: 101.
13. See Leo Schrade, *La représentation d'Edipo tiranno au Teatro Olimpico (Vicence 1585)* (Paris, 1960).
14. An English translation of Seneca's *Oedipus* by Frank Justus Miller appeared in 1917.
15. The *Oedipus* of John Dryden (1631–1700) was acted at His Royal Highness the Duke's Theatre in 1692, and a fifth edition had already been printed by 1696. For Voltaire (1694–1778), see *Seven Plays,* including *Oedipus,* trans. William F. Fleming (New York, 1988).
16. Clark and McGuire 1989: 9.
17. Robinson is identified as the producer but not the composer in the published

version of 1928. Two manuscript fragments of the Preface reproduced in Clark and McGuire 1989: 107, however, include the wording above.

18. The music for the chorus is included in Yeats 1928: 55–61.

19. W. B. Yeats, *Wheels and Butterflies* (London, 1934): 70, states "*Fighting the Waves* is in itself nothing, a mere occasion for sculptor and dancer, for the exciting dramatic music of Geroge Antheil." The piano-vocal score of Antheil's music is included on pp. 161–181.

20. See Antheil 1945: 229 and Whitesitt 1983: 130, who offers the following assessment: "Although the score is now lost, its characteristics may be inferred from a letter from Antheil to Ezra Pound in which the composer described the similiarities between his incidental music and the *Symphonie en Fa.* Antheil stated that the two works shared two main themes, the same tragic and heroic style, the same size orchestra and a similar treatment of the string instruments."

21. Honegger's opera premiered on December 12, 1927. The initial production of Cocteau's play, for which Honegger wrote incidental music quite independent of the music later employed in his opera, was provided with scenery by Picasso and costumes by Coco Chanel. Stravinsky attended the premiere performance on December 22, 1921.

22. See Bauschatz 1991.

23. "Tradition and the Individual Talent" in Eliot 1950: 4. The article was originally published in 1919. For an enlightening discussion of Eliot and this issue see the Introduction to Agha 1986.

24. Brown 1986: 48 and V. Stravinsky and Craft 1978: 268.

25. V. Stravinsky and Craft 1978: 269 gives the following French: "Votre art est arrivé à une hauteur qu'il faudrait le langage de Sophocle pour en parler."

26. *The New York Times,* August 7, 1927.

27. Schoenberg 1975: 482–83.

28. Bernstein 1976: 411, 417.

29. Notes to *Oedipus* recording, Columbia MS 6472.

30. Reported in *Börsencourrier* (Berlin), September 1931, trans. in V. Stravinsky and Craft 1978: 204.

31. Reported in *Il resto di carlino* (Bologna), May 1935, trans. in V. Stravinsky and Craft 1978: 204.

32. In Stravinsky and Craft 1959: 36 Purcell and Britten are singled out as the pinnacles of English opera, and in Stravinsky and Craft 1960: 99 Purcell's *Funeral Music for Queen Mary* is acknowledged as a model for his *Epitaphium* of 1959.

33. Stravinsky 1960: 121.

34. I am grateful to Russell Miller for bringing this comparison to my attention. Further points of contact appear in Stravinsky's retaining Mozart's horn and bassoons while substituting a pair of oboes for his clarinets. In the continua-

tion of the aria Stravinsky's offbeat instrumental rhythms also parody Mozart's oom-pah-pah accompaniment. On Purcell see V. Stravinsky and Craft 1978: 160.

35. V. Stravinsky and Craft 1978: 271.

36. Eliot 1950: 21.

37. Notes to Columbia Record MS 6472.

38. *La Veu de Catalunya* (Barcelona), March 1925 (Catalonian), as translated in V. Stravinsky and Craft 1978: 205.

39. See also Stravinsky 1936: 131–132.

40. Cocteau 1970: 47.

41. All of the following quotations regarding *Oedipus* are from the notes to Stravinsky's recording of *Oedipus Rex,* Columbia MS 6472 (1963).

42. For photographs and a discussion of how the first productions of Weill's *Der Zar lässt sich photographieren,* premiered in Berlin on February 18, 1928, openly parodied Stravinsky's *Oedipus* through the use of a chorus of men in long white beards and top hats, see Cook in Kowalke 1986: 83–101. Apparently with Weill's approval, *Der Zar* was paired with Stravinsky's *Oedipus* as a double-bill on numerous occasions.

43. See Sekine 1990. A 1993 film of Stravinsky's *Oedipus* featuring the Butoh dancer Min Tanaka wedded the traditions of mask, mime, and Craig's Übermarionette in a production directed by Julie Taymor, conducted by Seiji Ozawa, with Jessye Norman as Jocasta and Philip Langridge as Oedipus. The narration, always intended to be delivered in the language of the audience, is in Japanese, reflecting the fact that the production was originally designed for the first Saito Kinen Festival in Japan, September 1992. See Edward Rothstein, *The New York Times* (March 31, 1993): B3, for an appreciation.

44. Published in 1890; reissued in 12 vols., 1907–1915; abridged one-volume edition, 1922.

45. See Perkins 1976: 506 for a discussion of this issue with respect to *The Waste Land.* See also Campbell 1960/R1989.

46. In a "London Letter" to the *Dial* of October 1921. See also Robert Crawford 1987.

47. For the rich details of the Stravinsky-Eliot association and correspondence, see V. Stravinsky and Craft 1976: 537–544, "Renard and Old Possum."

48. Stravinsky knew full well Schoenberg's feeling about *Oedipus,* fully recorded in an article of 1928. See Schoenberg 1975.

49. See Aslan 1985 and especially *Contemporary Theatre Review,* 1.1 (1991): "Proceedings of the Soviet/British Puppetry Conference (Glasgow, November 1989)." A partial list of contents of the latter issue includes: George Speaight, "Petrushka and Punch: National Traditions and New Developments in Puppet Comedy"; Inna N. Solomonik, "The Oriental Roots of the Soviet Rod-Puppets"; Anna Nekrylova, "The Leningrad Puppet Theatre and Folk Tradi-

tion"; Inna N. Solomonik, "Home Puppet Theatre in Pre-revolutionary Russia"; and Natalia Raitorovskaya, "The Artists' Puppet Theatre."

50. See Adolphe Appia, *La Musique et la mise en scène* (Bern, 1963): 28–29.
51. Boym 1991: 31, 34, 68.
52. See also Bauschatz 1991.
53. See Watkins 1986.
54. See Chapter 4, n. 23 for a corroboration of Levinson's equation of Dalcrozian movement with *gymnastics*.
55. Levinson 1982: 84.
56. Although *Jeu de cartes* dates from 1936, many of Stravinsky's instrumental scores of the 1930s and 1940s that were later choreographed, such as *Danses concertantes* (1941–1943), were originally intended for concert and not stage performance. *Scènes de ballet* (1944), commissioned as part of a Billy Rose revue wherein only fragments were utilized, also achieved its first complete performance at a concert of the New York Philharmonic in 1945.
57. The Kirstein-Stravinsky correspondence is printed in Stravinsky 1982: 263–295.
58. Phelps 1970: 49.
59. See van den Toorn 1983: 390–414 for a brilliant illumination of the complementary encoding of tonal and serial in *Agon*.
60. Andriessen and Schönberger 1989: 214.
61. See Lyman 1992: 19.
62. V. Stravinsky and Craft 1979: 645.
63. See Andriessen 1989: 210–211.
64. See Pousseur 1972 and van den Toorn 1983.
65. See Watkins 1986 for further information about canon in Stravinsky's late works.
66. Berio 1985: 65.
67. For the various types of "canons" in Stravinsky's late style, see Watkins 1988.
68. Alm 1989: 263, 267. See also Sherr 1988.
69. See Watkins 1986: 217, 226–227.
70. On the issue of jazz, see the epigraph at the beginning of this chapter as well as Stravinsky 1959: 132, and compare with Andriessen and Schönberger 1989: 144.
71. See Andriessen 1989: 210–211.
72. For the Kirstein-Stravinsky correspondence see Stravinsky 1982: 287ff.
73. Quoted in *Stravinsky and the Dance* (New York, 1962).
74. Ernest Ansermet, *Les Fondements de la musique dans la conscience humaine* (Neuchâtel, 1961). Quoted in White 1979: 495.
75. See Chapter 10.
76. Dushkin 1949: 370.
77. See van den Toorn 1983: 390–414 for a rich parsing of the pitch component.

78. See Kramer 1986.
79. For a lucid assessment of the relation between choreography and music in *Agon,* see Robynne Stilwell, University of Michigan Ph.D. diss., 1994.
80. Barthes 1970: 68.
81. Ross 1986: 81, 63.
82. Stravinsky and Craft 1969: 103.
83. Boulez 1966: 238–40.
84. "Incidences actuelles de Berg," trans. as "Present-Day Encounters with Berg" in Boulez 1968. See Jameux 1991: 35–36.
85. Boulez 1976: 17–18, 21.
86. Clifton 1983: 247.
87. Pople 1991: 101; pp. 98–102 advance a lively discussion of the general issue.

14. Exodus

1. See Cronk 1992.
2. See Raksin and Sherry 1992: 6–9.
3. For more on this unlikely trio see Watkins 1988: 302–306.
4. See Chapter 17.
5. Krenek 1970: 116.
6. Stockhausen 1989b: 141.
7. Krenek 1970: 115. See also Taylor 1992.
8. Tick 1992.
9. "Projet pour espace dans une version pour orchestre," typescript, Fernand Ouellet Archive, National Library of Canada, Ottawa, cited by Mattis 1991.
10. Mattis 1991 speaks insightfully on this subject.
11. See Hughes and Allen 1988 and Bozeman 1988.
12. Taruskin 1988: 183.
13. Bridgman 1970: 65.
14. Seeger 1938–39 and 1939.
15. Bradbury 1991: 38–39 and Butler 1980.
16. Singal 1991: 2.
17. MacFarlane 1976: 80–81, 83–84, 92.
18. Bradbury 1991: 35.
19. Butler 1980 and Bradbury 1991: 38.

15. Tristan's Scissors

1. See Watkins 1988: 402–411 for a discussion of the role of these repertoires in the music of Bartók.
2. See Robin Holloway, *Debussy and Wagner* (London, 1979).
3. See Gay 1985: 127.
4. See Maur 1985: 140, fig. 218 for a facsimile.

5. It has been argued that, despite the genesis of the word, for German-speaking peoples "Merz" can suggest the root of *ausmerzen,* "to sort or pick," as well as the obsolete verb *merzen,* meaning "to cast off."

6. See Maur 1985: 20, 142 and catalogue figures 222 and 223 for a reproduction of Schwitters, *Sonate in Urlauten.* See also Henry Cowell, "Vocal Innovators of Central Europe," *Modern Music,* 7.2 (February-March 1930): 34–38.

7. Quoted in Huelsenbeck 1974: 61.

8. See Cronk 1988: 53.

9. Ibid. See also Browning 1979.

10. Gordon 1992: 125.

11. McGowan 1991: 20.

12. See Barry 1989.

13. Notes to *Hymnen für elektronische und konkrete Klänge,* DGG 139421–2.

14. Stockhausen 1970: 224, originally presented as part of six seminars at the Internationale Ferienkurse für Neue Musik, Darmstadt, 1970. The expression "intermodulation" refers to the interference of two signals typically encountered when a radio is slightly mistuned, and Stockhausen applied it to refer to a variety of electronic techniques beginning with *Telemusik,* wherein multiple recordings were made to interfere with one another.

15. Duffalo 1989: 58–59. Kagel's dance text was Lambranzi's *Neue und curiose theatralische Tantz-Schul* (1716).

16. Boulez 1986b: 354.

17. For a discussion of numerous similar works from the period see Watkins 1988, chap. 30, "Uses of the Past: A Synthesis."

18. See the composer's notes to Nonesuch Record H-71255.

19. This orientation was perhaps best summed up in his *Moz-Art à la Haydn* (1977)—"a playful collage derived from a single source—Mozart's pantomime music K. 446 (K. 416d), of which only an incomplete first violin part survives." See David Fanning's notes to Schnittke's *Moz-Art à la Haydn,* DGG 429 413–2.

20. In addition to his first opera, *Life with an Idiot* (premiered April 1992), other operas projected for completion in the 1990s include one on the Faust legend and another on the chromatic madrigalist of the late Italian Renaissance, Carlo Gesualdo.

21. Notes by Steven Ledbetter to Deutsche Grammophon 427 336–2. See also Restagno 1991.

22. Ibid.

23. See also Górecki's String Quartet No. 1 (1988), "Already It Is Dusk," which is recorded with his trio for clarinet, cello, and piano ("Lerchenmusik," 1984) on Elektra/Nonesuch 9–79257–2.

24. See Watkins 1988: 239 for a sample page from Marinetti's *Zang Tumb Tuum* (1914).

25. Walker 1987: 93–94.

26. Elektra Nonesuch 979217–2.
27. Notes by the composer to Elektra Nonesuch CD 79217–2.
28. Notes by Mark Swed to Elektra Nonesuch CD 79217–2.
29. Composer's notes to the recording.
30. Mark Swed's notes to the recording.
31. See Chapter 17 for a further investigation of this topic.
32. See Garber 1992: 338–349.
33. See Habermas on Derrida in Habermas 1987: "Excursus on Leveling the Genre Distinction between Philosophy and Literature," 185–210.
34. Berio 1985: 106–107. In *Coro* Berio further demonstrates his insistence upon the transformation of ingredients in the act of citation by appliquéing a Central African performance technique, for example, upon Yugoslav musical material; see Berio 1985: 152–153.
35. Otto Deutsch, *Franz Schubert: Thematisches Verzeichnis* (London, 1951), Catalogue No. 936A.
36. Composer's preface to *Rendering: Per Orchestra (1988–1990) / Schubert-Berio* (Vienna, 1991).
37. Nicolas Nabokov, *Old Friends and New Music* (London, 1951): 89–90.

16. Pyramids at the Louvre

1. Denon 1803: 105–106.
2. Ibid.: 271.
3. Loriers 1989: 37–38.
4. See Wiseman 1990: 101, 169, 237. The original design projected for the Kennedy library, a form eighty-five feet in height, was interpreted by some at the time as having a potential symbolic value in connection with a martyred President.
5. "French Ferociously Debate the Pei Pyramid at the Louvre," *Architecture: The AIA Journal,* 74 (May 1985): 25.
6. Ibid.
7. Letter to the author of January 22, 1993.
8. Letter to the author of September 14, 1991.
9. See Whitmore 1991, chap. 3, "When Is a Cadenza Not a Cadenza?"
10. Kramer 1992: 125–126.
11. Ibid.: 131.
12. Recognition of a reference to Mozart's K. 475 allows an interpretation slightly different from Kramer's judgment that "the point to be made here is not that Beethoven means to evoke the symphony in the cadenza, but that the rhetoric of the cadenza revives the tensions normally associated with the extreme dissonance of Beethoven's development."
13. Kramer 1992: 122.

14. Bartók's use of the timpani with the piano in his Piano Concerto No. 1 can with reason be related to the same tradition.

15. Brahms also wrote a cadenza for K. 466 which underscores the palimpsestic nature of cadenza history. The original manuscript carries the following autograph note by Clara Schumann: "Cadenza by Brahms for Mozart's D Minor Concerto, making use of a cadenza by me. In turn, in the cadenza which I published later, I used some passages from Brahms's cadenza, etc. Clara Schumann. 1891." See the English translation of the *Revisionsbericht* to vol. 15, Brahms, *Sämtliche Werke: Studien und Bearbeitungen für Klavier* (Leipzig, 1927), ed. Eusebius Mandyczewski, in the Dover edition entitled *Complete Transcriptions, Cadenzas, and Exercises for Solo Piano* (New York, 1971).

16. Timpani had also been incorporated in a somewhat more modest fashion by Busoni in the cadenza which he wrote for this very concerto in 1915.

17. See Hess 1979: ix.

18. Philips CD 410 549–2.

19. I am indebted to Professor Stephen Shipps's review of the Schnittke cadenza with me, which resulted not only in confirmations but identification of the citations at d, e, and f in Example 16.3.

20. For an impressive and wide-ranging overview of the implications of this statement see Comini 1987.

21. The work is written for E♭ trumpet; the unattained goal in the score, therefore, is a high C.

22. Whitmore 1991: 15.

23. Letter to the author of July 25, 1992.

24. Rosenblum 1989.

25. Hughes 1981, 66.

26. Stockhausen 1989a.

27. Personal communication to the author of November 12, 1986. "A few minutes before leaving for our Italian tour this is an answer to your question #11. I conducted in Berlin, Haydn, 2 × Mozart [clarinet and flute concertos], and after the second intermission we performed *Tierkreis*."

28. Letter to the author of January 22, 1993.

29. Letter to the author of March 29, 1990. Despite Stockhausen's disclaimer, the composer's notes to the recording state: "Markus has been regularly performing the Haydn Trumpet concerto at public concerts for several years now. In 1983 and 1985 I wrote cadenzas for him to insert in this work, too." Acanta Records, FonoTem GmbH, Hamburg, 40.23 543 (1985); Radio Symphony-Orchestra Berlin, Markus Stockhausen, trumpet. In the bitextual liner notes, however, the equivalent of the word "insert" is missing in the original German, reprinted in *Texte zur Musik, 1977–1984,* vol. 5 (Cologne, 1989): 661.

30. In a communication of March 26, 1991, Stockhausen wrote: "The covers

are my ideas—as are all the scores of Stockhausen Verlag. These are my hands, and Markus took the photographs." For further discussion of Stockhausen's views regarding citation, see "Integration of Past and Present," "World Music," and "Beyond Global Village Polyphony" in Stockhausen 1989c: 19–34.

31. See Varnedoe and Gopnik 1990b: 352 for a reproduction.

32. Schoenberg's awareness of his transgression of the stylistic limits of the original is apparent in his placating remarks to the cellist Pablo Casals, for whom it was written: "I was mainly intent on removing the defects of the Handelian style . . . I think I've succeeded in making the whole thing approximate, say, to Haydn's style. In harmony I have sometimes gone a little (and sometimes rather more) beyond the limits of that style. But nowhere does it go much further than Brahms; anyway there are no dissonances other than those understood by the older theory of harmony; and it is nowhere atonal." See Reich 1971: 185.

33. Schnittke has also provided cadenzas to Mozart's K. 467 and 491.

17. Envoi

1. Nettl 1985: "Unchanging Music," 14–15. See also Bohlman 1992 and Becker 1972.

2. See Clifford 1989 and Robbins 1991: 369.

3. Evident in Levinson, "Les appels de l'Orient: Réflexion sur une danseuse javanaise," *Comoedia,* 18 (November 1925): 2. Translated in *Theatre Arts Monthly* (December 1930) and reprinted in Acocella and Garafola 1991: 118–124.

4. "New York Polyhymnia Opening Program on April 12," *Musical Courier* (March 12, 1931).

5. See Oja 1990: 82.

6. See the epigraph to Chapter 2.

7. Oja 1990: 93. Compare also with the remarks of Boulez and Bourgault-Ducoudray in Chapter 2, n. 34.

8. A complete recording of the work was made in 1990 by the London Sinfonietta under the direction of Oliver Knussen for Virgin Classics, VCD 791103–2/4. For a colorful introduction to the gamelan's influence, hear disc no. 1, track 30, "The Pagodas."

9. See Mervyn Cooke's rich introduction and synopsis as well as Oliver Knussen's appreciation of the ballet in the booklet accompanying the above recording.

10. See Kolakowski 1990, "Looking for the Barbarians": 18–19.

11. See especially Nettle 1985; also Rothstein 1993.

12. See Whittall 1987 regarding the ramifications of stylistic pluralism for music theory.

13. See Savage 1983 and Walker 1987.

14. Stockhausen 1970: 224, comments originally made as part of six seminars at the Internationale Ferienkurse für Neue Musik, Darmstadt, 1970.

15. See Stockhausen 1978: 475 and Palmer 1990.

16. See John Russell's report from Munich on the exhibition to mark the Olympic Games, "Confrontations," *The Sunday Times* (London) (July 30, 1972), reprinted in Wichmann 1972: 24. See also the following reports contained therein: Dietmar Polaczek, "Vogelgesang und Aufwärtsflug: Die Zuhörer auf Wanderschaft, diesmal zu Cage und Stockhausen"; K. H. Ruppel, "Das Theater des 'Schönen und Sanften': Japanische No-Spiele im Münchner Haus der Kunst"; Harald Vocke, "Schrei, Brokat und archaischer Tanz: Die Noh-Aufführungen im Klangzentrum München"; and Dietmar Polaczek, "Die Kunst der Beraubten: Das 'Ife University Theatre' aus Nigeria im Klangzentrum."

17. Daisann McLane, "A New Caribbean Generation Sets Listeners to Swaying," *The New York Times,* Sunday, May 6, 1990, a feature article on Juan Luis Guerra and Joe Arroyo.

18. For a different perspective see William Schuman's opinions registered in Duffalo 1989: 390–391; and McClary 1989: 57–81.

19. McGowan 1991: 19–20. See also Chambers 1992.

20. For an interview with Bolcom about the *Songs* see Malitz 1992.

21. See Rothstein December 1992.

22. See the composer's Program Note to the score of *Concerto for Harpsichord and String Orchestra.*

23. See Jameson in Brooker 1992: 166–169. For a different angle regarding the power of diverse musical cultures to trigger distinct but related echoes, see Bergstein 1993 on the Miles Davis–Karlheinz Stockhausen conjunction.

24. Polkow 1992: 18.

25. Ibid.: 17.

26. Hodeir 1956.

27. See Morgan 1992 further perspectives on the issue.

28. See Werckmeister 1991: 49.

29. See "Laurie Anderson" in Rockwell 1983; Walker 1987; and McClary 1989.

30. Marcus 1989.

31. Schwichtenberg 1992.

32. Two publications appeared as a result of this show: the text collaboratively authored by Varnedoe and Gopnik (1990a) and a collection of readings edited by them (1990b) with essays by John E. Bowlt, Lynne Cooke, Lorenz Eitner, Irving Lavin, Peter Plagens, Robert Rosenblum, Roger Shattuck, Robert Storr and Jeffrey S. Weiss. See the Bibliography. For a perspective on the exhibition see "The Art World Revisited: Comedies of Similarity" in Danto 1992: 33–53.

33. Varnedoe and Gopnik 1990a: 193.

34. Varnedoe and Gopnik 1990a: 208.
35. Varnedoe and Gopnik 1990b: 119.
36. See Berrett 1992.
37. See Chapter 11.
38. Dave Marsh, "Just What's Being Sold in Country? The Benign Images used to Market Country Music May Conceal a Sinister Undertone," *The New York Times* (May 24, 1992): H20.
39. See Levine 1988, chap. 1, "William Shakespeare in America."
40. The latter two are used as introductions to Bud Powell's "Bud on Bach" and Sinus Newborn's performance of Strayhorn's "Lush Life," respectively. I am grateful to Guthrie Ramsey for bringing recordings of these works to my attention as part of a seminar project.
41. See Finson 1979.
42. Levine 1988, chap. 2, "The Sacralization of Culture." Levine not only provides a masterly and enlightening investigation of the high-low question in the nineteenth-century American concert hall, opera house, and museum but also characterizes the gradual dissolution of "a rich shared public culture that once characterized the United States" (p. 9).
43. Penfield 1983: 1–12, 85–91.
44. Goodwin, "Sample and Hold: Pop Music in the Digital Age of Reproduction" in Goodwin 1989: 260.
45. See Kosman 1992: 117.
46. See Bloom 1973, Straus 1990 and 1991, and especially Korsyn 1991: 14.
47. For Alexander Solzhenitsyn's views on the issue of Postmodernity, expressed in response to the awarding of the medal of honor for literature by the National Arts Club in January 1993, see "The Relentless Cult of Novelty and How It Wrecked the Century," *The New York Times Book Review* (February 7, 1993): 3, 17.
48. Historical musicology has been concerned with precisely this issue for several decades. See, for example, Bianconi 1973, Brown 1982, Burkholder 1985a and 1985b, Dobbins 1969, Haar 1966, Hewitt 1977, Pigman 1980, and Watkins 1973, 1980, 1986, 1991 ("Aggiornamenti"), 1994.
49. See Lanman 1981 and Mignolo 1991.
50. See Maurer 1984: 555.
51. See "Postmodernism, Posthumanism, and Politics" in Gaggi 1989: 164.
52. See Huelsenbeck 1974: 140–141.
53. See Garry Wills, "Goodbye, Columbus" in *The New York Review of Books* (November 22, 1990): 6–10, for a review of the anxieties attendant to the Columbus Jubilee in 1992; and Brian M. Fagan's review of Ronald Wright, *The Americas through Indian Eyes Since 1492* (Boston, 1992) in *The New York Times Book Review* (June 7, 1992): 25.
54. The currency of the issue was reflected in a series of papers on the question

of intercultural reception and fusion in music presented at the Fourth Symposium of the International Musicological Society, Osaka, July 21–25, 1990, under the theme "Tradition and Its Future in Music." The question of "marginalization" was directly addressed by William Malm in his paper, "Japanese Music Performance Groups in America as Marginal Survivals." See also Seeger 1991.

55. Harich-Schneider 1971: 548–549. I recall with pleasure the study of music theory with Harich-Schneider in Tokyo during the fall of 1946.
56. Becker 1991: 393–394.
57. See Heifetz 1987.
58. See Price and Price 1992.
59. See Lehmann-Haupt 1992 and also Taylor 1993.
60. Kartomi 1981: 233.
61. Peter Watrous, "Direct Descendant: New Marsalis Work Owes Much to Duke Ellington," *The Ann Arbor News* (February 21, 1993), reprinted from *The New York Times*.
62. "Quotation and Originality" in Emerson 1876: 172.
63. Jameson 1991: 3.
64. Ibid.: 17. See also Wellmer 1991.
65. Mestrovic 1991: 27–28; Scott 1990: 441.
66. See Rothstein 1991 for a discussion of the phenomenon.
67. See especially Robbins 1991. For evidence of newly developing perspectives among ethnomusicologists, see Becker and McDaniel 1992.
68. See Suydam 1991, Rothstein 1992, and McClary 1992.
69. See Grundberg 1990 and Bradbury 1992.
70. See "Canon and Period," chap. 6 in Kermode 1988: 119.
71. See Gorak 1991 for a brilliant overview and Morgan 1992 for a musical perspective.
72. Schlesinger (1991: 27) also discusses the omissions and distortions of other historians.
73. See Said 1991: 28. See also Schlesinger (1991), who argues that in an effort to increase the self-esteem of minorities, many curricular revisions have only infused the teaching of history with an ideology of racial separatism, and have given too little attention to the common values that transcend groups.
74. Mason 1990: 163, 166.
75. "Beyond Global Village Polyphony," in Stockhausen 1989c: 24–25, 30–31.
76. Stravinsky 1960: 121.
77. See especially Campbell 1990.
78. Craig 1982.
79. T. S. Eliot, "War Paint and Feathers," *Athenaeum* (October 17, 1919): 1036.
80. See Allan Bloom's *The Closing of the American Mind* (1987) and the discussion in Levine 1988; but see also Hughes and Allen 1988: xiii, 226–232, where

Puritan colonial America's claims of connectedness to the "first church" are lucidly forwarded not as a natural historical progression but as an arbitrary reclamation of a time of innocence.

81. See Ermath 1992.
82. Craig 1982: 131, 144, 146.
83. Roland Barthes, "From Work to Text" in J. V. Harari, ed., *Textual Strategies: Perspectives in Post-Structuralist Criticism* (London, 1979): 76.
84. See Sass 1992 and Appel 1992, respectively. Jameson 1991, however, invokes Lacan's theory of schizophrenia as an attribute of Postmodernism.
85. Rothstein 1991: 34.
86. Craig 1982: 249.
87. Boulez 1986b: 358.
88. Boulez 1990. See Chapter 9, n. 11 of this book for a sample of Boulez's testimony regarding Klee. For a reflection of the range of Boulez's interests in literature and art, see *Éclats / Boulez* (Paris, 1986).
89. Boulez 1986b: 359.
90. Polin 1984: 11.
91. Brandt 1987: 400.
92. Forster 1924: 136.
93. *The New York Times* (February 7, 1993): Y12.
94. See Bakhtin 1984: 199–200; Clark and Holquist 1984: 63–94; Morson and Emerson 1990: 133–135; Danow 1991: 26–27; and Gates 1992: 43–44.
95. See Danto 1992: 36–41.

Bibliography

Acocella, Joan. "Vaslav Nijinsky" in Baer 1988: 96–111.

Adami, Giuseppe. *Letters of Giacomo Puccini*, trans. Ena Makin (Philadelphia, 1931).

Adorno, Theodor. "Frankfurt a. M. Die Jazzklasse des Hochschen Konservatorium," *Die Musik,* 21 (May 1929): 625–626.

Agha, Shahid Ali. *T. S. Eliot as Editor* (Ann Arbor, 1986).

Albright, Daniel. "Toy Nightingales and Dancing Dolls: The Origins of Stravinsky's Drama," *The Kenyon Review,* 10 (Winter 1988): 102–119.

Alexandre, Arsène. *The Decorative Art of Léon Bakst* (London, 1913).

Alibert, Pierre. *Albert Gleizes* (Paris, 1982).

Allard, S. N. "Fête nègre," *Le Nouveau Spectateur,* 4 (June 25, 1919).

Alm, Irene. "Stravinsky, Balanchine, and *Agon:* An Analysis Based on the Collaborative Process," *The Journal of Musicology,* 7.2 (Spring 1989): 254–269.

Alpert, Hollis. *The Life and Times of "Porgy and Bess": The Story of an American Classic* (New York, 1990).

Anderson, Alexandra, and Carol Saltus, ed. *Jean Cocteau and the French Scene* (New York, 1984).

Anderson, John D. "Varèse and the Lyricism of the New Physics," *The Musical Quarterly,* 75 (1991): 31–49.

Andriessen, Louis, and Elmer Schönberger. "1957—*Agon*" in *The Apollonian Clockwork: On Stravinsky,* trans. Jeff Hamburg (Oxford, 1989): 209–215.

Ansermet, Ernest. "Sur un orchestre nègre," *La Revue romande* (Lausanne), 3.10 (October 15, 1919): 10–13.

———— *Die Grundlagen der Musik im menschlichen Bewusstsein* (Munich, 1965).

———— *Écrits sur la musique* (Neuchatel, 1983).

Antheil, George. "Manifest der Musico-Mechanico," *De Stijl,* 6.8 (1924): 99–102.

———— "Abstraction and Time in Music," *The Little Review,* 10.1 (Autumn and Winter, 1924–25): 13–15. Republished in *The Little Review Anthology,* ed. Margaret Anderson (New York, 1953): 336–338. A German translation appeared as "Abstraktion und Zeit in der Musik," *De Stijl,* 6.10 (1925): 152–156.

———— "My *Ballet mécanique*," *De Stijl,* 6.12 (1924–25): 141–144.

———— "Mother of the Earth," *Transatlantic Review* (Musical Supplement), 2.1 (1927–28): 227.

———— "The Negro on the Spiral or a Method of Negro Music" in Cunard 1934/R1970: 214.

———— *Bad Boy of Music* (New York, 1945).

Antliff, Robert. "Bergson and Cubism: A Reassessment," *Art Journal,* 47 (Winter 1988): 341–349.

Apollinaire, Guillaume. "Simultanisme-Librettisme," *Les Soirées de Paris* (June 15, 1914): 323–324.

Arbois, Collin d'. "L'Exposition d'Art nègre et la Fête nègre," *Les Arts à Paris* (November 1, 1919).

Armitage, Merle. *Martha Graham: The Early Years* (New York, 1937/R1968).

Aschengreen, Erik. *Jean Cocteau and the Dance,* trans. Patrick McAndrew and Per Avsum (Copenhagen, 1986).

Ashton, Dore. "On an Epoch of Paradox: Primitivism at the Museum of Modern Art," *Arts Magazine,* 59 (November 1984): 76–79.

Aslan, Odette. " 'L'Arlequin serviteur de deux maîtres' au Piccolo Teatro de Milan" in Aslan and Bablet 1985: 173–178.

———— "Du rite au jeu masqué" in Aslan and Bablet 1985: 279–289.

Aslan, Odette, and Denis Bablet, ed. *Le Masque: Du rite au théâtre* (Paris, 1985).

Astruc, Gabriel. *Le Pavillon des fantômes: Souvenirs* (Paris, 1987).

Austin, William. "Fortunate Continuities and Legitimate Accidents" in Haimo and Johnson 1987.

Axsom, Richard H. *"Parade": Cubism as Theater* (New York, 1979).

Babbitt, Milton. "Order, Symmetry, and Centricity in Late Stravinsky" in Pasler 1986.

Bablet, Denis. "D'Edward Gordon Craig au Bauhaus" in Aslan 1985: 137–146.

Baer, Nancy van Norman. "Design and Choreography: Cross-Influences in the Theatrical Art of the Ballets Russes" in Baer 1988.

———— *Theatre in Revolution: Russian Avant-garde Stage Design, 1913–1915* (New York, 1992).

———— et al. *The Art of Enchantment: Diaghilev's Ballets Russes, 1909–1929* (New York, 1988).

Baker, Houston A., Jr. *Modernism and the Harlem Renaissance* (Chicago, 1987).

———— "Modernism and the Harlem Renaissance" in Singal 1991: 107–125.

Bakhtin, Mikhail. *Problems of Dostoevsky's Poetics,* trans. and ed. Caryl Emerson (Minneapolis, 1984); originally published in 1929, revised in 1963.

———— *Art and Answerability: Early Philosophical Essays* (Austin, 1990).

Balardelle, Geneviève. "L'Exotisme extrême-oriental en France au tournant du siècle," *Revue internationale de musique française,* 2.6 ("Dossier: L'Exotisme musical français") (November 1981): 67–76.

Baresel, Alfred. "Jazz als Rettung," *Auftakt,* 6 (1926): 213–216.

Barry, Malcolm. "Ideology and Form: Shostakovich East and West" in Norris 1989: 172–186.

Barthes, Roland. *Writing Degree Zero and Elements of Semiology,* trans. Annette Lavers and Colin Smith (Boston, 1970).

Bartók, Béla. "Der Einfluss der Volksmusik auf der heutige Kunstmusik," *Melos,* 1 (1920): 384ff; rep. as "The Influence of Peasant Music on Modern Music" in Morgenstern 1956.

Bartsch, Ingo, et al. *Hommage à Picasso: Kubismus und Musik* (Bochum, Ger., 1981).

Bauer, Marion. "L'Influence du 'Jazz-Band,'" *La Revue musicale,* 5 (1924): 31–36.

Bauhaus, 1919–1933: Meister- und Schülerarbeiten, Weimar, Dessau, Berlin. Essays and catalogue for an exhibition at the Museum für Gestaltung Zurich/Kunstgewerbemuseum, June 25–August 21, 1988, organized by Claude Lichtenstein.

Bauquier, Georges. *Fernand Léger. Vivre dans le vrai* (Paris, 1987).

Bauschatz, Paul. "*Oedipus:* Stravinsky and Cocteau Recompose Sophocles," *Comparative Literature,* 43 (Spring 1991): 150–170.

Beaumont, Cyril. *Five Centuries of Ballet Design* (London, 1939).

Bechet, Sidney. *Treat It Gentle* (New York, 1961).

Beck, Earl R. "The Anti-Nazi 'Swing Youth,' 1942–1945," *Journal of Popular Culture,* 19 (Winter 1985): 45–53.

Becker, Judith. "Western Influence in Gamelan Music," *Asian Music,* 3.1 (1972): 3–9.

Becker, Judith. *Traditional Music in Modern Java: Gamelan in a Changing Society* (Honolulu, 1980).

Becker, Judith, and Lorna McDaniel. "Call and Response: 'A Brief Note on Turtles, Claptrap, and Ethnomusicology;' and 'A Page on Turtle Relations,'" *Ethnomusicology,* 35.3 (Fall 1991): 393–398.

Bédouin, Jean-Louis. *Les Masques* (Paris, 1961).

Begg, Ean. *The Cult of the Black Virgin* (London, 1985).

Benedictus, Louis. *Les Musiques bizarres à l'Exposition* (1889) comp. and transcribed by Louis Benedictus, drawings by A. Gorgnet (Paris, 1889). The exotic songs in this work were translated by Judith Gautier, but they are unsigned.

———— *Les Musiques bizarres à l'Exposition de 1900,* transcribed by Louis Benedictus (Paris, 1900). The book consists of six brochures published separately: *La Musique chinoise; Danse javanaise—danse du diable; La Musique indo-chinaise; La Musique japanaise; La Musique égyptienne;* and *Les Chants de Madagascar.*

Benjamin, Walter. "The Work of Art in the Age of Mechanical Reproduction" in *Illuminations* (New York, 1968): 217–251.

Benois, Alexandre. "Vospominaniia o balete" in *Russkie Zapiski,* 18 (1939).

———— *Reminiscences of the Russian Ballet* (New York, 1977).

Bergeron, Katherine, and Philip V. Bohlman, ed. *Disciplining Music: Musicology and Its Canons* (Chicago, 1992).

Bergstein, Barry. "Miles Davis and Karlheinz Stockhausen: A Reciprocal Relationship," *The Musical Quarterly,* 76.4 (1992): 502–525.

Berio, Luciano. *Two Interviews* (New York, 1985).

———— *Rendering* (Vienna, 1989).

Berkhofer, Robert F. *The White Man's Indian: Images of the American Indian from Columbus to the Present* (New York, 1978).

Berlin, Edward. *Ragtime: A Musical and Cultural History* (Berkeley, 1980).

Bernard, Jonathan. *The Music of Edgard Varèse* (New Haven, 1987).

Bernstein, Leonard. *The Unanswered Question* (Cambridge, Mass., 1976).

Berrett, Joshua. "Louis Armstrong and Opera," *The Musical Quarterly,* 76.2 (1992): 216–241.

Bianconi, Luigi. Preface to P. Marolo, *Secondo libro de' madrigali* (1614), *Musiche Rinascimentali Siciliane,* vol. 4 (Florence, 1973).

Bierley, Paul E. *John Philip Sousa: American Phenomenon* (New York, 1973).

Blachere, Jean-Claude. *Le Modèle nègre: Aspects littéraires du mythe primitiviste au XXe siècle chez Apollinaire, Cendrars, Tzara* (Dakar, Senegal, 1981).

Blackstone, Sarah J. *Buckskins, Bullets, and Business: A History of Buffalo Bill's Wild West* (New York, 1986).

Blanche, Jacques-Émile. *Propos de peintre: De Gauguin à la Revue nègre* (Paris, 1928).

Blok, Alexandre. *Oeuvres complètes* (Moscow, 1963).

Bloom, Harold. *The Anxiety of Influence* (New York, 1973).

Bochner, Jay. *Blaise Cendrars: Discovery and Re-creation* (Toronto, 1978).

Bohlman, Philip V. "Ethnomusicology's Challenge to the Canon; the Canon's Challenge to Ethnomusicology" in Bergeron and Bohlman 1992: 116–136.

Bois, Yve-Alain. "La leçon de Kahnweiler: Cubist Art and African Sources," *Cahiers du Musée National d'Art Moderne,* 23 (Spring 1988): 29–56.

Bordman, Gerald. *American Musical Revue* (New York, 1985).

Boschot, Adolphe. "*Le Sacre du printemps,* ballet en deux actes de MM. Roerich, Stravinsky et Nijinsky," *L'Echo de Paris,* 30 (May 30, 1913): 6.

Boulez, Pierre. "Incidences actuelles de Berg" in *Relevés d'apprenti* (Paris, 1966); first published in *Polyphonie,* 2 (1948).

———— *Notes of an Apprenticeship* (New York, 1968).

———— *Conversations with Célestin Deliège,* English trans. of interviews conducted in French in 1972–1974 (London, 1976).

———— "Existe-t-il conflit entre la pensée européenne et non-européenne?" in *Europäische Musik zwischen Nationalismus und Exotik* (Winterthur, Switz., 1984). Forum Musicologicum: Basler Beiträge zur Musikgeschichte, vol. 4.

———— *Éclats / Boulez* (Paris, 1986a).

———— *Orientations* (Cambridge, Mass., 1986b).

———— *Le pays fertile: Paul Klee* (Paris, 1989).

Bowlt, John E. *Russian Stage Design* (1982).

———— "From Studio to Stage: the Painters of the Ballets Russes" in Baer 1988.

———— "A Brazen Can-Can in the Temple of Art: The Russian Avant-Garde and Popular Culture" in Varnedoe and Gopnik 1990: 134–159.

Bozeman, Theodore Dwight. *To Live Ancient Lives: The Primitivist Dimension in Puritanism* (Chapel Hill, 1988).

Bradbury, Malcolm. "The Nonhomemade World: European and American Modernism" in Singal 1991.

———— "Isn't that Spatial?" A review of Jameson 1991 in *The New York Times Book Review* (April 12, 1992): 33.

Bradbury, Malcolm, and James McFarlane, ed. *Modernism, 1890–1930* (New York, 1978).

Brandt, Kathleen Weil-Garris. "Twenty-five Questions about Michelangelo's Sistine Ceiling," *Apollo,* 126 (December 1987): 392–400.

Braun, Edward. *The Theatre of Meyerhold: Revolution on the Modern Stage* (New York, 1979).

Brender, Richard. "Functions of Film: Léger's Cinema on Paper and on Cellulose, 1913–25," *Cinema Journal,* 24.1 (Fall 1984): 41–64.

Bridgman, Elena. "*Mir Iskusstva:* Origins of the Ballets Russes" in Baer 1988: 26–43.

Bridgman, Richard. *Gertrude Stein in Pieces* (New York, 1970).

Briscoe, James R. "Asian Music at the 1889 Paris Exposition," paper delivered at the Fourth Symposium of the International Musicological Society, Osaka, July 21–25, 1990.

Brooker, Peter, ed. *Modernism/Postmodernism* (London, 1992).

Brown, Frederick. *An Impersonation of Angels* (New York, 1968).

Brown, Howard M. "Emulation, Competition, and Homage: Imitation and Theories of Imitation in the Renaissance," *Journal of the American Musicological Society,* 35 (1982): 11.

Brown, Malcolm Hamrick. "Stravinsky and Prokofiev: Sizing Up the Competition" in Pasler 1986: 39–50.

Brown, Rae Linda. "William Grant Still, Florence Price, and William Dawson: Echoes of the Harlem Renaissance" in Floyd 1990: 71–86.

Browning, Gordon Frederick. *Tristan Tzara: The Genesis of the Dada Poem, or from Dada to Aa* (Stuttgart, 1979).

Bullard, Truman Campbell. "The First Performance of Igor Stravinsky's *Sacre du Printemps*" (Ph.D. diss., Eastman School of Music, University of Rochester, 1971), 3 vols.

Burgett, Paul. "Vindication as a Thematic Principle in the Writings of Alain Locke on the Music of Black Americans" in Floyd 1990: 29–40.

Burke, Peter. *Popular Culture in Early Modern Europe* (London, 1978).

Burkholder, J. Peter. *Charles Ives* (New Haven, 1985).

———— "Johannes Martini and the Imitation Mass of the Late Fifteenth Century," *Journal of the American Musicologcial Society,* 38 (1985a): 470–523.

————— "'Quotation' and Emulation: Charles Ives's Uses of His Models," *The Musical Quarterly*, 71.1 (1985b): 1–26.

Busoni, Ferruccio. *Tre cadenze per il concerto op. 61 per violino e orchestra di L. van Beethoven* (Milan, 1943/R1963).

Butler, Christopher. *After the Wake: An Essay on the Contemporary Avant-Garde* (Oxford, 1980).

Cage, John, and Kathleen Hoover. *Virgil Thomson* (New York, 1959).

Calvocoressi, M.-D. "Critique musicale du *Sacre du printemps*," *Comoedia illustré, supplément artistique*, 5.17 (June 5, 1913): n.p.

Camfield, William A. "Juan Gris and the Golden Section," *The Art Bulletin*, 47 (March 1965): 128–34.

Campbell, Joseph. *Renewal Myths and Rites of the Primitive Hunters and Planters* (Dallas, 1960/R1989).

————— *Transformations of Myth through Time* (New York, 1990).

Campbell, Sue Ellen. "Equal Opposites: Wyndham Lewis, Henri Bergson, and Their Philosophies of Space and Time," *Twentieth Century Literature*, 29 (Fall 1983): 351–369.

Carner, Mosco. "The Exotic Element in Puccini," *The Musical Quarterly*, 22.1 (1936): 45–67.

Cassirer, Ernst. "The Mythical Concept of Time" in *The Philosophy of Symbolic Forms*, vol. 2, *Mythical Thought*, trans. Ralph Manheim (New Haven, 1955).

Cendrars, Blaise. "The Scenario of *La Création du monde*" in Rischbieter 1970: 99.

Chambers, Iain. "Contamination, Coincidence, and Collusion: Pop Music, Urban Culture, and the Avant-Garde" in Brooker 1992: 190–196.

Chamot, Mary. *Goncharova: Stage Designs and Paintings* (London, 1979).

Chantavoine, Jean. "Au Théâtre des Champs-Élysées; *Le Sacre du printemps*," *Excelsior*, 4 (May 30, 1913): 6.

Chernoff, John Miller. *African Rhythm and African Sensibility* (Chicago, 1979).

Chilton, John. *Sidney Bechet: The Wizard of Jazz* (New York, 1987).

Chisholm, Anne. *Nancy Cunard* (London, 1979).

Clark, David R., and James B. McGuire. *W. B. Yeats: The Writing of Sophocles' King Oedipus* (Philadelphia, 1989).

Clark, Katerina, and Michael Holquist. *Mikhail Bakhtin* (Cambridge, Mass., 1984).

Clarke, Mary, and Clement Crisp. *Design for Ballet* (London, 1987).

Clerici, Naila. "Native Americans in Columbus's Home Land" in Feest 1987: 415–426.

Clifford, James. *The Predicament of Culture* (Cambridge, Mass., 1988).

————— "Notes on Theory and Travel," *Inscriptions*, 5 (1989): 177–188.

Clifton, Thomas. *Music as Heard: A Study in Applied Phenomenology* (New Haven, 1983).

Clouzot, Henri, and A. Level. *Sculptures africaines et océaniennes, colonies françaises et Congo belge* (Paris, 1925).

Cocteau, Jean. "Opinions sur l'art nègre," *Action,* 3 (April 1920).

——— *A Call to Order,* trans. Rollo H. Myers (London, 1926).

——— *Oedipe roi* (Paris, 1928).

——— *Portraits-souvenirs, 1900–1914* (Paris, 1935).

——— *"Les Mariés de la Tour Eiffel,"* in *Théâtre I* (Paris 1948).

——— *Oeuvres complètes* (Lausanne, 1950).

——— *Lettres à André Gide,* with preface and commentary by Jean-Jacques Kihm (Paris, 1970).

Coen, Ester. "Les futuristes et le moderne," *Cahiers du Musée National d'Art Moderne,* 19–20 (June 1987): 60–73.

Coeuroy, André, and André Schaeffner. *Le jazz* (Paris, 1926).

Cohen, Arthur A., ed. *The New Art of Color: The Writings of Robert and Sonia Delaunay,* trans. by David Shapiro and Arthur A. Cohen (New York, 1978).

Coleridge-Taylor, Samuel. *Negro Melodies* (London, 1904).

Collier, James Lincoln. *The Making of Jazz: A Comprehensive History* (Boston, 1978).

——— *Duke Ellington* (New York, 1987).

——— *The Reception of Jazz in America: A New View,* Institute for Studies in American Music, Monograph 27 (Brooklyn, 1988).

Comini, Alessandra. *The Changing Image of Beethoven: A Study in Mythmaking* (New York, 1987).

Cook, Susan. "*Der Zar lässt sich photographieren:* Weill and Comic Opera" in Kowalke 1986: 83–101.

——— *Opera for a New Republic: The Zeitopern of Krenek, Weill, and Hindemith* (Ann Arbor, 1988).

——— "Jazz as Deliverance: The Reception and Institution of American Jazz during the Weimar Republic," *American Music* (Spring 1989): 30–47.

Cooper, Douglas. *Picasso Theater* (New York, 1968).

Copland, Aaron. "Jazz Structure and Influence," *Modern Music,* 3 (January-February 1927): 9–13.

Courville, Xavier de. Review of *La Création du monde, Revue musicale,* 6.4 (February 1, 1925): 216.

Covach, John. "The Music and Theory of Josef Hauer" (Ph.D. diss., University of Michigan, 1990).

——— "The Sources of Schoenberg's 'Aesthetic Theology,' " *Abstracts* (American Musicological Society, Chicago) (November 6–10, 1991): 39.

Craft, Robert. *Stravinsky: Glimpses of a Life* (London, 1992).

——— ed. *Stravinsky: Selected Correspondence,* vol. 1 (New York, 1982).

——— *Stravinsky: Selected Correspondence,* vol. 2 (New York, 1984).

——— *Stravinsky: Selected Correspondence,* vol. 3 (New York, 1985).

Craig, Cairns. *Yeats, Eliot, Pound and the Politics of Poetry* (London, 1982).

Craig, Edward Gordon. "The Actor and the Über-Marionette," *The Mask* (Florence), 1.2 (April 1908): 3ff. Reprinted in Arnold Rood, ed., *Gordon Craig on Movement and Dance* (London, 1977): 50–51.

———— *Gordon Craig: The Story of His Life* (London, 1968).

Crawford, Richard. "It Ain't Necessarily Soul," *Yearbook for Inter-American Musical Research,* 8 (1972): 17–38.

———— "Gershwin's Reputation: A Note on *Porgy and Bess,*" *The Musical Quarterly,* 65 (1979): 257–264.

———— "George Gershwin," *The New Grove Dictionary of American Music,* vol. 2 (London, 1986).

———— "Porgy and Bess," *The New Grove Dictionary of Opera* (London, 1992).

———— "Duke Ellington (1899–1974) and His Orchestra" in *The American Musical Landscape* (Berkeley, 1993).

Crawford, Robert. *The Savage and the City in the Work of T. S. Eliot* (New York, 1987).

Cro, Stelio. *The Noble Savage: Allegory of Freedom* (Waterloo, Ont., 1990).

Cronk, Michael Sam. "Writing While They're Singing: A Conversation about Longhouse Social Dance Songs," *New York Folklore,* 14.3–4 (1988): 49–59.

———— "Brave Chiefs and Drowned Princesses: Images of Indianness in Popular Music, 1790 to 1925," paper presented at the Society for Ethnomusicology Annual Conference, Seattle, Wash., October 1992.

Crosland, Margaret, ed. *Cocteau's World: An Anthology of Writings by Jean Cocteau* (London, 1972).

Crowder, Henry. *As Wonderful As All That? Henry Crowder's Memoir of His Affair With Nancy Cunard, 1928–1935* (Navarro, Calif., 1987).

Cruse, Harold. *The Crisis of the Negro Intellectual* (New York, 1967).

Cunard, Nancy, ed. *Negro* (New York, 1934; rep. New York, 1969; abridged ed., New York, 1970).

Danow, David K. *The Thought of Mikhail Bakhtin: From Word to Culture* (New York, 1991).

Danto, Arthur. *Beyond the Brillo Box: The Visual Arts in Post-Historical Perspective* (New York, 1992).

Darrell, R. D. Reviews in *Phonograph Monthly Review,* 5.3 (December 1930): 102; 5.4 (January 1931): 137.

———— Review in *Disques,* 6.9 (June 1932): 153–157.

Debussy, Claude. *Lettres à deux amis* (Paris, 1942).

Denon, Vivant. *Travels in Upper and Lower Egypt,* trans. Arthur Aikin (London, 1803).

Devriès, Anik. "Les Musiques d'Extrême-Orient a l'Exposition universelle de 1889" in *Cahiers Debussy* (Saint-Germain-en-Laye, 1977): 25–36.

Diaghilev, Sergei. "The Bases of Artistic Evaluation" and "On the Exhibition of V. M. Vasnetsolv" in "Art Chronicles," *Mir Iskusstva,* 2 (1899).

Dobbins, Frank. "*Doulce mémoire:* A Study of the Parody Chanson," *Proceedings of the Royal Musical Association,* 96 (1969–70): 85.

Dodge, Roger Pryor. "Consider the Critics" in *Jazzmen,* ed. R. Ramsey, Jr., and C. E. Smith (New York, 1939): 301–342.

Doig, Allan. *Theo van Doesburg: Painting into Architecture, Theory into Practice* (New York, 1986).

Dominique, Jullien. *Proust et ses modèles* (Paris, 1989).

Donne, John. "L'art nègre dans les ateliers de l'école de Paris, 1905–1920," *Arts d'Afrique Noire,* 71 (Autumn 1989): 21–28.

Downes, Olin. "*Jonny spielt auf,* Opera of This Age," *The New York Times,* January 20, 1929.

Dubnick, Randa. *The Structure of Obscurity: Gertrude Stein, Language, and Cubism* (Urbana, 1984).

Ducharte, Pierre. *La Comédie italienne* (Paris, 1925).

Duffalo, Richard. *Trackings* (New York, 1989).

Dushkin, Samuel. "Working with Stravinsky" in Merle Armitage, *Stravinsky,* ed. Edwin Corle (New York, 1949).

Duthuit, G. "Cinématographe et fêtes," *Action,* 4 (July 1920).

Eagleton, Terry. "Nationalism: Irony and Commitment" in Terry Eagleton, Fredric Jameson, and Edward W. Said, *Nationalism, Colonialism, and Literature* (Minneapolis, 1990): 23–39.

Eaton, Katherine. *The Theater of Meyerhold and Brecht* (Westport, Conn., 1985).

Eksteins, Modris. *Rites of Spring* (Boston, 1989).

Eliot, T. S. *Selected Essays* (New York, 1950).

———— *The Elder Statesman* (London, 1959).

Ellington, Duke. "The Duke Steps Out," *Rhythm* (March 1931): 20–22.

———— *Music Is My Mistress* (Garden City, N.J., 1973).

Ellington, Mercer. *Duke Ellington In Person: An Intimate Memoir* (Boston, 1978).

Ellis, John M. "The Origins of PC," *The Chronicle of Higher Education,* 38 (January 15, 1992): B1–2.

Emerson, Ralph Waldo. *Letters and Social Aims* (Boston, 1876).

Ermath, Elizabeth Deeds. *Sequel to History: Postmodernism and the Crisis of Representational Time* (Princeton, 1992).

Eruli, Brunella. "Masques, acteurs, marionettes: Objets 'transitionnels' " in Aslan 1985: 209–217.

Eynat, Irè. "Gordon Craig, the Über-marionette, and the Dresden Theatre" in *Theatre Research International* (Oxford), 3 (1980).

———— *Beyond the Mask* (Carbondale, Ill., 1987).

Eysteinsson, Astradur. *The Concept of Modernism* (Ithaca, 1990).

Fabre, Michel. *From Harlem to Paris: Black American Writers in France, 1840–1980* (Urbana, 1991).

Falla, Manuel de. *El "cante jondo" (canto primitivo andaluz)* (Granada, 1922).

Faure, Élie. *Histoire de l'art: L'art médiéval* (Paris, 1911/R1921, 1939).

———— *Equivalences* (Paris, 1951).

Feest, Christian F. "From North America" in Rubin 1984: 85–97.

———— *Indians and Europe: An Interdisciplinary Collection of Essays* (Aachen, 1987).

Felber, Erwin. "Exotismus und Primitivismus in der neueren Musik," *Die Musik,* 21 (1925): 724–731.

Festa-McCormick, Diana. *Proustian Optics of Clothes: Mirrors, Masks, Mores* (Saratoga, Calif., 1984).

Finson, Jon. "Music and Medium: Two Versions of Manilow's 'Could it be Music,' " *The Musical Quarterly,* 65.2 (1979): 265–280.

Fiorentino, Daniele. " 'Those Red-Brick Faces': European Press Reactions to the Indians of Buffalo Bill's Wild West Show" in Feest 1987: 403–414.

Flanner, Janet. *Paris Was Yesterday: 1925–1939* (New York, 1972).

Floyd, Samuel A., Jr. "Music in the Harlem Renaissance: An Overview," in Floyd 1990: 1–28.

———— ed. *Black Music in the Harlem Renaissance* (New York, 1990).

Forte, Allen. *The Harmonic Organization of the Rite* (New Haven, 1978).

Fournier, Gabriel. "Erik Satie et son époque," *La Revue musicale,* 214 (June 1952): 129–135.

Friar, Ralph E., and Natasha A. Friar. *The Only Good Indian . . .; The Hollywood Gospel* (New York, 1972).

Funayama, Takashi. "*Three Japanese Lyrics* and japonisme." In Pasler 1986: 273.

Gable, David. "Boulez's Two Cultures: The Post-War European Synthesis and Tradition," *Journal of the American Musicological Society,* 43.3 (Fall 1990): 426–456.

Gadamer, Hans-Georg. *Truth and Method,* rev. and trans. J. Weinsheimer and D. G. Marshall (New York, 1989).

———— ed. *Truth and Historicity* (The Hague, 1972).

Gaggi, Silvio. *Modern / Postmodern: A Study in Twentieth-Century Arts and Ideas* (Philadelphia, 1989).

Gammond, Peter. *Duke Ellington: His Life and Music* (London, 1958).

Garafola, Lynn. *Diaghilev's Ballets Russes* (New York, 1989).

Garber, Marjorie. *Vested Interests: Cross-Dressing and Cultural Anxiety* (New York, 1992).

Gates, Henry Louis. *Loose Canons: Notes on the Culture Wars* (New York, 1992).

Gay, Peter. *Freud for Historians* (New York, 1985).

Geist, Sidney. *Brancusi: A Study of the Sculpture* (New York, 1983).

Gide, André. *Oedipe* (Paris, 1930). English trans. as *Oedipus* by John Russell (London, 1950).

Gillmor, Alan M. *Erik Satie* (Boston, 1988).

Gilman, Sander L. *On Blackness without Blacks: Essays on the Image of the Black in Germany* (Boston, 1982).

Gioia, Ted. "Jazz and the Primitivist Myth," *The Musical Quarterly,* 73.1 (1989): 130–143. Also appears in Gioia, *The Imperfect Art* (New York, 1988): 19–49.

Gleizes, Albert. "La Peinture et ses lois," *La Vie des lettres* (October 1922).

Gleizes, Albert, and Jean Metzinger. *Cubism* (London, 1913).

Glover, J. Garrett. *The Cubist Theatre* (Ann Arbor, 1983).

Gobineau, Joseph-Arthur de. *Essai sur l'inégalité des races humaines* (Paris, 1853).

Godet, Robert. "Claude Debussy," *La Semaine littéraire,* nos. 1267–1269 (April 13–27, 1918). Reprinted as *Claude Debussy: textes et documents inédits* (special number of *La Revue de musicologie*), ed. François Lesure (1962).

———— "En Marge de la marge," *Revue musicale,* 7.7 (May 1926): 59–61.

Goldberg, Isaac. *Tin Pan Alley* (New York, 1930).

Goldwater, Robert. "Black is Beautiful," *The New York Review of Books* (December 18, 1969).

———— *Primitivism in Modern Art* (Cambridge, Mass., 1986).

Goncharova, Natalia. "Le Loubok hindou et persan," in an extract from a preface by Goncharova for the catalogue to the Exposition Bolchaïa Dmitrovka, IIe Salon d'Art, Moscow, 1913: 11–12, translated in Loguine 1971: 36.

Goncharova, Natalia, with Michel Larionov and Pierre Vorms. *Les Ballets Russes: Serge de Diaghilew et la décoration théatrale* (Paris, 1955).

Goodwin, Andrew. *On Record: Rock, Pop, and the Written Word* (New York, 1989).

Gorak, Jan. *The Making of the Modern Canon* (London, 1991).

Gordon, Allan M. "Interactions between Art and Music during the Harlem Renaissance" in Floyd 1990: 139–149.

Gordon, Mel. "Russian Eccentric Theatre: The Rhythm of America on the Early Soviet Stage" in Baer 1992: 115–127.

Gordon, Tom. "The Cubist Metaphor: Picasso in Stravinsky Criticism," *Current Musicology,* 40 (1985): 22–33.

Grainger, Percy. "Jazz," *Anbruch,* 7 (April 1925): 210–212.

Gräner, Georg. "Jazz-Glosse," *Allgemeine Musikzeitung,* 53 (1926): 121–122.

Gray, Camilla. *The Russian Experiment in Art, 1863–1922* (London, 1962). Revised and enlarged edition by Marian Burleigh-Motley, London, 1986.

Gray, Christopher. *Cubist Aesthetic Theories* (Baltimore, 1953).

Graziano, John. "Black Musical Theater and the Harlem Renaissance Movement" in Floyd 1990: 87–110.

Green, Christopher. *Cubism and Its Enemies: Modern Movements and Reactions in French Art, 1916–1928* (New Haven, 1987).

Green, Jeffrey P. "The Negro Renaissance and England" in Floyd 1990: 151–172.

Grigoriev, Serge. "Gontcharova et Larionov, peintres-décorateurs des ballets de Diaghilev" in Loguine 1971: 105–106.

Groenendijk, Paul. *Adolf Loos: huis voor Josephine Baker* (Rotterdam, 1985).

Gropius, Walter, ed. *The Theater of the Bauhaus,* trans. Arthur S. Wensinger (Middletown, Conn., 1961).

Gross, David. "Bergson, Proust, and the Revaluation of Memory," *International Philosophical Quarterly* 25 (December 1985): 369–380.

Grove, Nancy. *Isamu Noguchi: A Study of the Sculpture* (New York, 1985).

———— *Isamu Noguchi: Portrait Sculpture* (Washington, D.C., 1989).

Gruenberg, Louis. "Der Jazz als Ausgangspunkt," *Anbruch,* 7 (April 1925): 196–199.

Grundberg, Andy. "As It Must to All, Death Comes to Post-Modernism (in Art, Photography)," *The New York Times* (September 16, 1990): H47.

Guillaume, Paul, and Thomas Munro. *Primitive Negro Sculpture* (New York, 1926).

Haar, James. "*Pace non trovo:* A Study in Literary and Musical Parody," *Musica Disciplina,* 20 (1966): 95–149.

Habermas, Jürgen. *The Philosophical Discourse of Modernity,* trans. Frederick Lawrence (Cambridge, Mass., 1987).

———— *The New Conservatism: Cultural Criticism and the Historians' Debate* (Cambridge, Mass., 1989).

Häger, Bengt. *The Swedish Ballet* (New York, 1990).

Haimo, Nathan, and Paul Johnson, ed. *Stravinsky Perspectives* (Lincoln, Neb., 1987).

Hall, Edith. *Inventing the Barbarian: Greek Self-Definition through Tragedy* (Oxford, 1989).

Hamm, Charles, Bruno Nettl, and Ronald Byrnside. *Contemporary Music and Music Cultures* (Englewood Cliffs, N.J., 1975).

Hammond, Bryan, and Patrick O'Connor. *Josephine Baker* (Boston, 1988).

Haney, Lynn. *Naked at the Feast: A Biography of Josephine Baker* (New York, 1981).

Hansen, Robert C. *Scenic and Costume Design for the Ballets Russes* (Ann Arbor, 1985).

Harbec, Jacinthe. "*Parade:* Les Influences cubistes sur la composition musicale d'Erik Satie" (Master's thesis, McGill University, 1987).

Harding, James. *The Ox on the Roof* (New York, 1972).

Harich-Schneider, Eta. *A History of Japanese Music* (London, 1971).

Hartt, Frederick. *David, By the Hand of Michelangelo: The Original Model Rediscovered* (New York, 1987).

Hauff, Andreas. "Mahagonny . . . Only a Made-Up Word?" *Kurt Weill Newsletter,* 9.1 (Spring 1991): 7–8.

Hegel, Georg Wilhelm Friedrich. *The Philosophy of History,* trans. C. J. Friedrich (New York, 1956).

Heifetz, Robin J. "European Influence upon Japanese Instrumental and Vocal Media: 1946–1977," *The Music Review,* 47 (February 1986–87): 29–43.

Hennings, Emmy. "Das Cabaret Voltaire und die Galerie Dada" in Peter Schifferli, ed., *Als Dada Begann, Bildchronik und Erinnerungen der Grunder* (Zurich, 1957).

Hess, Willy. *Sämtliche Kadenzen* [Beethoven] (Zurich, 1979).

Hewitt, Helen. "*Fors seulement* and the Cantus Firmus Technique of the Fifteenth Century" in *Essays in Musicology in Honor of Dragan Plamenac,* ed. G. Reese and R. J. Snow (Pittsburgh, 1969): 91–126.

Hirsbrunner, Theo. *Igor Strawinsky in Paris* (Laaber, 1982).

Hodeir, André. "A Masterpiece: Concerto for Cootie" in *Jazz, Its Evolution and Essence* (New York, 1956), Eng. trans. by David Noakes of *Hommes et problèmes du jazz* (Paris, 1954).

Hodson, Millicent. "Nijinsky's New Dance: Rediscovery of Ritual Design in *Le Sacre du printemps*" (Ph.D. diss., University of California, Berkeley, 1985).

———— "Nijinsky's Choreographic Method: Visual Sources from Roerich for *Le Sacre du printemps*," *Dance Research Journal,* 18.2 (Winter 1986–87): 7–15.

Hoffman, Katherine. "Collage in the Twentieth Century: An Overview" in Hoffman 1989: 1–38.

———— ed. *Collage: Critical Views* (Ann Arbor, 1989).

Honour, Hugh. *Chinoiserie: The Vision of Cathay* (New York, 1973).

———— *The European Vision of America: A Special Exhibition to Honor the Bicentennial of the United States* (Cleveland, 1975).

Hornbostel, Erich M. v. "Ethnologisches zu Jazz," *Melos,* 6 (1927): 510–512.

Howat, Roy. *Debussy in Proportion* (Cambridge, Eng., 1983).

Huelsenbeck, Richard. *Memoirs of a Dada Drummer,* trans. Joachim Neogroschel (New York, 1974).

Hughes, Richard, ed. *The American Quest for the Primitive Church* (Urbana, 1988).

Hughes, Richard, and C. Leonard Allen. *Illusions of Innocence: Protestant Primitivism in America, 1630–1875* (Chicago, 1988).

Hughes, Robert. *The Shock of the New* (New York, 1980).

Hulme, T. E. "Modern Art and Its Philosophy," a speech delivered to the Quest Society, January 1914. Published in T. E. Hulme, *Speculations: Essays on Humanism and the Philosophy of Art,* ed. Herbert Read (London, 1924).

Huxley, Aldous. *Perennial Philosophy* (New York, 1945).

Isaak, Jo Anna. *The Ruin of Representation in Modernist Art and Texts* (Ann Arbor, 1986).

Ivanov, Sergei. *Ancient Masks of Siberian Peoples,* comp. and introduced by S. Ivanov (Leningrad, 1975).

Ivernel, Philippe. "De Brecht à Brecht: métamorphose du masque, masques de la métamorphose" in Aslan 1985: 159–172. See especially "Les masques expressionnistes": 164ff.

Jablonski, Edward. *Gershwin* (New York, 1987).

Jaffe, Hans, ed. *De Stijl, 1917–1931* (Minneapolis, 1982).

James, Richard. "Avant-Garde Sound-on-Film Techniques and Their Relationship to Electro-Acoustic Music," *The Musical Quarterly,* 72.1 (1986): 74–89.

———— "Ravel's *Chansons Madécasses:* Ethnic Fantasy or Ethnic Borrowing?" *The Musical Quarterly,* 74.3 (1990): 360–384.

Jameson, Fredric. "Modernism and Imperialism" in Terry Eagleton, Fredric Jameson, and Edward Said, *Nationalism, Colonialism, and Literature* (Minneapolis, 1990): 43–66.

———— *Postmodernism, or the Cultural Logic of Late Capitalism* (Durham, 1991).

———— "Postmodernism and Consumer Society" in Brooker 1992: 139–150.

Jay, Robert. "Taller than Eiffel's Tower: The London and Chicago Tower Projects, 1889–1894," *Journal of the Society of Architectural Historians,* 46.2 (June 1987): 145–146.

Jeanneret, Albert. "Les Concerts Wiéner," *L'Esprit nouveau,* 14 (1923): 1664–1665.

Johnson, R. Stanley. *Cubism and La Section d'Or: Reflections on the Development of the Cubist Epoch, 1907–1922* (Chicago, 1991).

Jones, Louisa. *Pierrot-Watteau: A Nineteenth Century Myth* (Tubingen, 1984).

Jowitt, Deborah. *Time and the Dancing Image* (New York, 1988).

Jullien, Dominique. *Proust et ses modèles: "Les Mille et Une Nuits" et "Les Mémoires de Saint-Simon"* (Paris, 1989).

Junod, Henri Alexandre. *Les chants et les contes des Ba-Ronga* (Lausanne, 1897).

Kaes, Anton. "The Debate about Cinema," *New German Critique,* 15 (Winter 1987): 7–33.

Kahnweiler, Daniel-Henry. *Juan Gris, sa vie, son oeuvre* (Paris, 1946).

Kandinsky, Wassily. *The Art of Spiritual Harmony* (London, 1914).

Kandinsky, Wassily and Franz Marc, ed. *Der Blaue Reiter* (Munich, 1912/R1965).

Karlinsky, Simon. "Igor Stravinsky and Russian Preliterate Theater" in Pasler 1986: 3–15.

———— "A Cultural Educator of Genius" in Baer 1988.

Kartomi, Margaret J. "The Processes and Results of Musical Culture Contact: A Discussion of Terminology and Concepts," *Ethnomusicology,* 25.2 (May 1981): 227–249.

Kater, Michael H. "Forbidden Fruit? Jazz in the Third Reich," *American Historical Review,* 94 (February 1989): 11–43.

Katz, Ruth. "The Reception of Western Music in Japan as a Challenge to Contextual Theories of Culture," paper delivered at the Fourth Symposium of the International Musicological Society, Osaka, July 21–25, 1990.

Kerman, Joseph. "The State of Academic Music Criticism" in *On Criticizing Music: Five Philosophical Perspectives,* ed. Kingsley Price (Baltimore, 1981).

———— "A Few Canonic Variations" in *Canons,* ed. Robert von Hallberg (Chicago, 1983).

Kermode, Frank. *The Sense of an Ending* (London, 1968).

———— *History and Value* (Oxford, 1988).

Kershaw, Ian. *The Nazi Dictatorship: Problems and Perspectives of Interpretation* (London, 1985).

Kirk, Elise. "*Art nouveau,* Orientalism, and American Music: A Confluence of Three Cultures," paper read at the Fourth Symposium of the International Musicological Society, Osaka, July 21–25, 1990.

Klee, Paul. *Paul Klee: Puppen, Plastiken, Reliefs, Masken, Theater* (Paris, 1979).

Knowlton, Don. "The Anatomy of Jazz," *Harper's* (April 1926).

Kolakowski, Leszek. "Looking for the Barbarians" in Kolakowski's *Modernity on Endless Trial* (Chicago, 1990).

Korngold, Julius. "Jazzkultur," *Allgemeine Musikzeitung,* 53 (1926): 225–226.

Korsyn, Kevin. "Towards a New Poetics of Musical Influence," *Musical Analysis,* 10:1–2 (1991): 3–72.

Kosman, Joshua. "The Early Music Debate: Ancients, Moderns, Postmoderns," *The Journal of Musicology,* 10.1 (Winter 1992): 116–117.

Kowalke, Kim, ed. *A New Orpheus* (New Haven, 1986).

Kramer, Hilton. *The Age of the Avant-Garde* (New York: 1973).

——— "The 'Primitivism' Conundrum," *The New Criterion,* 3.4 (December 1984): 1–7.

Kramer, Jonathan D. "Discontinuity and Proportion in the Music of Stravinsky." In Pasler 1986: 174–194.

Kramer, Richard. "Cadenza Contra Text: Mozart in Beethoven's Hands," *Nineteenth Century Music,* 16.1 (Spring 1992): 116–131.

Krauss, Rosalind. *The Originality of the Avant-Garde and Other Modernist Myths* (London, 1985).

Krehbiel, Henry Edward. *Afro-American Folksong: A Study in Racial and National Music* (New York, 1914).

Krenek, Ernst. "America's Influence on Its Émigré Composers," *Perspectives of New Music,* 8.2 (Spring-Summer 1970): 112–117.

——— *Horizons Circled* (Berkeley, 1974).

Kuper, Adam. *The Invention of Primitive Society: Transformations of an Illusion* (London, 1988).

Lalo, Pierre. "Au Théâtre des Champs-Élysées," "Feuilleton du *Temps,*" *Le Temps* (June 3, 1913): 3.

Laloy, Louis. "Notes sur la musique cambodgienne," *Bericht über den Zweiten Kongress der Internationalen Musikgesellschaft* (report on the congress at Basel, September 25–27, 1906) (Leipzig, 1907): 61–64.

——— *Debussy* (Paris, 1909; rev. 1944).

——— *La Musique chinoise* (Paris, 1912), including a group of "Mélodies notées," 122–126.

——— "La Musique," *La Grande Revue* (June 25, 1913): 612–613.

——— "Stravinsky," *La Musique retrouvée* (Paris, 1928). Originally written for *Comoedia* (Autumn 1913).

Lamarque, Peter. "Expression and the Mask: The Dissolution of Personality in Noh," *The Journal of Aesthetics and Art Criticism,* 47 (Spring 1989): 157–168.

Lambert, Constant. *Music Ho! A Study of Music in Decline* (London, 1934).

Langhorne, Elizabeth. "Pollock, Picasso, and the Primitive," *Art History,* 12 (March 1989): 66–92.

Lanman, Jonathan. "The Religious Symbolism of the T in T-O Maps," *Cartographica,* 18 (1981): 18–21.

Larionov, Michel. "Icones et Loubki," extract from a preface by Larionov for the catalogue to the Exposition Bolchaïa Dmitrovka, IIᵉ Salon d'Art, Moscow, 1913: 5–10, translated in Loguine 1971: 33–35.

Laubenthal, Annegrit. *Paul Hindemiths Einakter-Triptychon* (Tutzing, 1986).

Laude, Jean. *La Peinture française (1905–1914) et "L'Art nègre"* (Paris, 1968).

Lawson, Rex. "Stravinsky and the Pianola" in Pasler 1986: 284–301.

Leach, Robert. *Vsevolod Meyerhold* (Cambridge, Eng., 1989).

Léger, Fernand. "The Invented Theater" (1924) in Rischbieter 1970: 97.

———— *The Functions of Painting,* trans. Alexandra Anderson, ed. Edward Fry (New York, 1973).

Lehmann-Haupt, Christopher. "Putting Cultural Politics into Classroom Debates," a review of Gerald Graff, *How Teaching the Conflicts Can Revitalize American Education* (New York, 1992), in *The New York Times* (December 21, 1992): B2.

Leighten, Patricia. "The White Peril and *L'Art nègre:* Picasso, Primitivism, and Anticolonialism," *The Art Bulletin,* 72.4 (December 1990): 609–630.

Lendvai, E. *Béla Bartók: An Analysis of His Music* (London, 1971).

Lerma, Dominique-René de. "Bibliography of the Music: The Concert Music of the Harlem Renaissance Composers, 1919–1935" in Floyd 1990: 175–218.

Lesure, François. *Igor Stravinsky, "Le Sacre du printemps": Dossier de presse* (Geneva, 1980a).

———— ed. *Claude Debussy: Lettres 1884–1918* (Paris, 1980b).

Létay, Miklós. " 'Redskins at the Zoo': Sioux Indians in Budapest, 1886," in Feest 1987: 375–381.

Levin, Gail. "American Art" in Rubin 1984: 453–473.

Levin, Thomas Y. "For the Record: Adorno on Music in the Age of Its Technological Reproducibility," *October,* 55 (Winter 1990): 23–47.

Levine, Lawrence. *Highbrow / Lowbrow: The Emergence of Cultural Hierarchy in America* (Cambridge, Mass., 1988).

Levinson, André. *La Danse d'aujourd'hui* (Paris, 1929).

———— *Ballet Old and New,* trans. Susan Cook Summer (New York, 1982).

———— *André Levinson on Dance: Writings from Paris in the Twenties,* ed. with an intro. by Joan Acocella and Lynn Garafola. (Hanover, N.H., 1991).

Levy, Julien. "Isamu Noguchi," *Creative Art,* 12 (January 1933): 29–35.

Lewis, David. *Constantin Brancusi* (London, 1957).

Lipsey, Roger, ed. *Coomaraswamy* (Princeton, 1977).

Lloyd, Jill. *German Expressionism: Primitivism and Modernity* (New Haven, 1991).

Lo, Kii-Ming. "In Search of a Chinese Melody: Tracing the Source of Weber's *Musik zu Turandot,* op. 37," paper read at the Fourth Symposium of the International Musicological Society, Osaka, July 21–25, 1990.

Locke, Alain, ed. *The New Negro: An Interpretation* (New York, 1925).

———— *The Negro and His Music* (Washington, D.C., 1936; rep. Port Washington, N.Y., 1968).

Lockspeiser, Edward. *Debussy* (London, 1951).

Lockwood, Lewis. "On 'Parody' as Term and Concept in Sixteenth-Century Music" in *Aspects of Medieval and Renaissance Music,* ed. Jan La Rue (New York, 1966): 560–575.

Loguine, Tatiana. *Gontcharova et Larionov: Cinquante ans à Saint-Germain-des-Prés* (Paris, 1971).

Long, Richard A. "Interactions between Writers and Music during the Harlem Renaissance" in Floyd 1990: 129–138.

Loriers, Marie Christine. "Perspective: The Pyramid Prevails," *Progressive Architecture,* 70 (June 1989): 37–38.

Lourié, Arthur. "La sonate pour piano de Strawinsky," *La Revue musicale,* 6.10 (August 1, 1925): 100–104.

———— "Leçons de Bach," *La Revue musicale,* 13.131 (1932): 60–64.

Lowinsky, Edward. "Musical Genius: Evolution and Origins of a Concept," *The Musical Quarterly,* 1 (1964): 321, 476.

Lyman, Jeffrey. "Tut Not Tah: Tracing the Development of Stravinsky's Brittle Voice," (seminar paper, University of Michigan, 1992).

Lyotard, Jean-François. *The Postmodern Condition* (Minneapolis, 1984).

Maclagan, David. *Creation Myths* (London, 1977).

Maertens, Jean-Thierry. "Le Masque primitif et la sexualité" in Aslan 1985: 33–40.

Malitz, Nancy. "Poetic Clashes Turned to Music," *The New York Times* (November 15, 1992): H27.

Malm, William. *Six Hidden Views of Japanese Music* (Berkeley, 1986).

———— "Japanese Music Performance Groups in America as Marginal Survivals," paper read at the Fourth Symposium of the International Musicological Society, Osaka, July 21–25, 1990.

Manganaro, Marc. " 'Beating a Drum in a Jungle': T. S. Eliot on the Artist as 'Primitive,' " *Modern Language Quarterly,* 47 (December 1986): 393–421.

Marcus, Greil. *Lipstick Traces* (Cambridge, Mass., 1989).

Mariani, Giorgio. " 'Was Anybody More of an Indian than Karl Marx?' The *Indiani Metropolitani* and the 1977 Movement" in Feest 1987: 585–596.

Mariz, Vasco. *Heitor Villa-Lobos* (Washington, D.C., 1970).

Martzel, Gérard. "Fêtes rituelles et danses masquées de l'ancien Japon" in Aslan 1985: 71–79.

Mason, Peter. *Deconstructing America: Representations of the Other* (London, 1990).

Matthews, David. "The Rehabilitation of the Vernacular" in Norris 1989: 240–251.

Mattis, Olivia. "Edgard Varèse's 'Progressive' Nationalism: *Amériques* meets *Américanisme,*" paper delivered at the American Musicological Society, Chicago, November 1991.

————— "New Theater and the Unrealized *Dream*," *Library Chronicle of the University of Texas at Austin,* 22 (January 1992).

Maur, Karin von. "Oskar Schlemmer und Paul Hindemith," *Hindemith-Jahrbuch,* 4 (1974–75).

————— ed. *Vom Klang der Bilder: Die Musik in der Kunst des 20. Jahrhunderts* (Munich, 1985).

Maurer, Evan. "Dada and Surrealism" in Rubin 1984: 535–593.

Mazo, Margarita. "Stravinsky's *Les Noces* and Russian Folk Wedding Ritual," *Journal of the American Musicological Society,* 43.1 (Spring 1990): 99–142.

McClary, Susan. "Terminal Prestige," *Cultural Critique,* 12 (Spring 1989): 57–81.

————— "Schubert's Sexuality and His Music," *AMS Gay/Lesbian Study Group Newsletter* (March 1992): 8–14.

McEvilley, Thomas. "Doctor, Lawyer, Indian Chief," *Artforum,* 23 (November 1984): 54–61.

McFarlane, James. "The Mind of Modernism" in Bradbury and McFarlane (1978).

McGowan, John. *Postmodernism and Its Critics* (Ithaca, 1991).

McMillan, Samuel H. "Gertrude Stein, the Cubists, and the Futurists" (Ph.D. diss., University of Texas, 1964).

McPhee, Colin. *Music in Bali* (New Haven, 1966).

McQuillan, Melissa. "Painters and the Ballet: 1917–1926" (Ph.D. diss., Institute of Fine Arts, New York University, 1979).

Mehring, Wolfram. "Le masque au théâtre de la mandragore" in Aslan 1985: 183–187. See especially "L'homme et la marionnette," 183, regarding Mehring's stagings of Büchner's *Léonce et Léna* and *Woyzeck* (illustrations 103, 106 at the end of the volume).

Messing, Scott. *Neoclassicism in Music* (Ann Arbor, 1988).

————— "Mozart and the Polemics of Modernism," *Proteus,* 8.2 (1991): 10–15.

Mestrovic, Stjepan G. *The Coming Fin de Siècle: An Application of Durkheim's Sociology to Modernity and Postmodernism* (London, 1991).

Mignolo, Walter D. "Putting the Americas on the Map: European and Amerindian Territorial Representations during the Sixteenth Century," Philip Thayer Memorial Lecture, Randolph-Macon Woman's College, Lynchburg, Va., April 3, 1991.

Milhaud, Darius. "Die Entwicklung der Jazz-Band und die Nordamerikanische Negermusik," *Anbruch,* 7 (April 1925): 200–205.

————— *Études* (Paris, 1927). Contains: "À propos de *Parade* au concert"; "L'evolution du jazz-band et de la musique des nègres d'Amerique du Nord"; "Les marionnettes"; "La musique et les clowns"; "Poulenc's *Les Biches.*"

————— *Notes sans musique* (Paris, 1949).

————— *An Autobiography: Notes without Music* (New York, 1953).

Miller, Christopher. "Theories of Africans: The Question of Literary Anthropology," *Critical Inquiry,* 13.1 (Autumn 1986): 120–139.

Misler, Nicoletta. "Siamese Dancing and the Ballets Russes" in Baer 1988.

Mitchell, W. J. T. "Spatial Form in Literature: Toward a General Theory," *Critical Inquiry,* 6.3 (1980): 541.

Morgan, Robert. "Rethinking Musical Culture: Canonic Reformulations in a Post-Tonal Age" in Bergeron and Bohlman 1992: 44–63.

Morgenstern, Sam, ed. *Composers on Modern Music* (New York, 1956).

Morrow, Edward. "Duke Ellington on Gershwin's *Porgy,*" *New Theatre* (December 1935): 5–6.

Morson, Gary, and Caryl Emerson. *Mikhail Bakhtin: Creation of a Prosaics* (Stanford, 1990).

Morton, Lawrence. "Footnotes to Stravinsky Studies: *Le Sacre du printemps,*" *Tempo,* 128 (1979): 9–16.

Mueller, Richard. "Javanese Influence on Debussy's Fantaisie and Beyond," *Nineteenth Century Music,* 10 (Fall 1986): 157–186.

Nattiez, Jean-Jacques. *Proust as Musician,* trans. Derrick Puffett (Cambridge, Eng., 1989).

Nettl, Bruno. *The Western Impact on World Music: Change, Adaptation, and Survival* (New York, 1985).

Neumann, Eckhard, ed. *Bauhaus and Bauhaus People* (New York, 1970).

Newbould, B. "Ravel's Pantoum," *Musical Times,* 116 (1975): 228–231.

Nicholls, Peter. "Anti-Oedipus? Dada and Surrealist Theatre, 1916–35," *New Theatre Quarterly,* 7 (November 1991): 331–347.

Nijinska, Bronislava. *Bronislava Nijinska: Early Memoirs,* trans. and ed. Irina Nijinska and Jean Rawlinson (New York, 1981).

Noguchi, Isamu. *A Sculptor's World* (New York, 1967).

Norden, Martin F. "The Avant-Garde Cinema of the 1920s: Connections to Futurism, Precisionism, and Suprematism," *Leonardo,* 17.2 (1984): 108–112.

Norris, Christopher. *Deconstruction: Theory and Practice* (New York, 1982).

———— *Music and the Politics of Culture* (London, 1989).

Noverre, Jean-George. *Lettres sur la danse, sur les ballets et les arts* (St. Petersburg, 1803).

Ohsaki, Shigemi. "Reception of European Music in Japan: Its Problems and the Tasks of the Musicologist," paper read at the Fourth Symposium of the International Musicological Society, Osaka, July 21–25, 1990.

Oja, Carol. *Colin McPhee: A Composer in Two Worlds* (Washington, D.C., 1990).

Oliver, Paul, ed. *Black Music in Britain: Essays on the Afro-Asian Contribution to Popular Music* (Buckingham, Eng., 1990).

Olkhovsky, Yury. *Vladimir Stasov and Russian National Culture* (Ann Arbor, 1983).

Orenstein, Arbie. *Ravel, Man and Musician* (New York, 1975).

———— ed. *A Ravel Reader* (New York, 1990).

Ortega y Gasset, José. *The Dehumanization of Art* (New York, 1948).

Ory, Pascal. *L'Expo universelle* (Brussels, 1989).

Ouellette, Fernand. *Edgard Varèse,* trans. Derek Coltman (New York, 1966).

Pakenham, Thomas. *The Scramble for Africa, 1876–1912* (New York, 1991).

Palacio, Jean de. *Pierrot fin de siècle* (Paris, 1990).

Palmer, Anthony. "To Fuse or Not to Fuse: Directions of Two Japanese Composers, Miki and Takemitsu," paper read at the Fourth Symposium of the International Musicological Society, Osaka, July 21–25, 1990.

Pasler, Jann. "Music and Spectacle in *Petrushka* and *The Rite of Spring*" in Pasler 1986: 53.

———— "New Music as Confrontation: The Musical Sources of Jean Cocteau's Identity," *The Musical Quarterly,* 75 (1991): 255–278.

———— "Stravinsky and the Apaches," *The Musical Times,* 123 (June 1982): 400.

———— ed. *Confronting Stravinsky* (Berkeley, 1986).

Pattison, Robert. *The Triumph of Vulgarity: Rock Music in the Mirror of Romanticism* (Oxford, 1987).

Pawlowski, Gustave de. "Au Théâtre des Champs-Élysées: *Le Sacre du printemps,* ballet de deux actes de M. Igor Stravinsky," *Comoedia,* 7 (May 31, 1913): 1.

Peltier, Philippe. "From Oceania" in Rubin 1984.

Penfield, Joyce. *Communicating with Quotes: The Igbo Case* (Westport, Conn., 1983).

Peppercorn, Lisa. *Villa-Lobos* (London, 1989).

Perkins, David. *A History of Modern Poetry* (Cambridge, Mass., 1976).

Perloff, Marjorie. *The Futurist Moment: Avant-Garde, Avant-Guerre, and the Language of Rupture* (Chicago, 1986).

Perloff, Nancy. *Art and the Everyday: Popular Entertainment and the Art of Erik Satie* (Oxford, 1991).

Pfrogner, Hermann. *Die Zwölfordnung der Töne* (Zurich, 1953).

Phelps, Robert. *Professional Secrets,* trans. Richard Howard (New York, 1970).

Picon-Vallin, Béatrice. "Les années 10 à Petersbourg: Meyerhold, la commedia dell'arte, et le bal masqué" in Aslan 1985: 147–158.

Pigman, G. W., III. "Versions of Imitation in the Renaissance," *Renaissance Quarterly,* 33 (1980): 1–32.

Pillaut, Léon. "Le Gamelan javanais," *Le Ménestrel,* 53.31 (3 July 1887): 244–245.

Polin, Claire. "Interviews with Soviet Composers," *Tempo,* 151 (December 1984): 10–16.

Polkow, Dennis. "Rock Meets Classical," *Musical America* (January-February 1992): 17–21.

Poole, Phoebe. "Picasso's Neo-Classicism, Second Period, 1917–25," *Apollo,* 106 (March 1967): 200–201.

Pople, Anthony. *Berg: Violin Concerto* (Cambridge, Eng., 1991).

Poulenc, Francis. *My Friends and Myself,* trans. James Harding (London, 1978).

Pousseur, Henri. "Stravinsky selon Webern selon Stravinsky," *Musique en jeu,* 4 (October 1971): 21–47 and 5 (n.d.): 107–126. English version: "Stravinsky by Way of Webern: The Consistency of a Syntax," *Perspectives of New Music,* 10.2 (1971): 13–51 and 11.1 (1972): 112–145.

Pozharskaia, Militsa Nikolaevna. *Russkie sezony v Parizhe: eskizy dekoratsii i kostimov, 1908–1929 / M. N. Pozharskaia: The Russian Seasons in Paris: Sketches of the Scenery and Costumes, 1908–1929,* in Russian and English (Moscow, 1988).

Price, Richard, and Sally Price. *Equatoria* (New York, 1992).

Price, Sally. *Primitive Art in Civilized Places* (Chicago, 1989).

Prost, Christine. "Maurice Ravel: *L'Enfant et les sortilèges,*" *Analyse musicale,* 4 (1990): 65–81.

Proust, Marcel. *À la Recherche du temps perdu: Du côté de chez Swann* (Paris, 1913).

Rambert, Marie. *Quicksilver: The Autobiography of Marie Rambert* (London, 1972).

Raksin, David, and Peggy Sherry. "David Raksin Remembers Weill, *Where Do we Go From Here?* and 'Developing' Film Music in the 1940s," *Kurt Weill Newsletter,* 10.2 (Fall 1992): 6–9.

Rattenbury, Ken. *Duke Ellington, Jazz Composer* (New Haven, 1990).

Ravel, Maurice. "Contemporary Music," *Rice Institute Pamphlet,* 15 (April 1928): 131–145.

Reich, Willi. *Schoenberg: A Critical Biography,* trans. Leo Black (London, 1971).

Restagno, Enzo, ed. *Gubaidulina* (Turin, 1991).

Richards, David. "*Woyzeck* Ricochets through a Mad World," *The New York Times* (December 13, 1992): H5.

Richardson, Joanna. *Judith Gautier: A Biography* (London, 1986).

Ries, Frank W. D. *The Dance Theatre of Jean Cocteau* (Ann Arbor, 1986).

Riis, Thomas L. *Just before Jazz* (Washington, D.C., 1989).

Rimsky-Korsakov, Nikolai. *My Musical Life,* 3rd ed., trans. Judah A. Joffe, ed. Carl Van Vechten (New York, 1942).

Ringer, Alexander. "On the Question of 'Exoticism' in Nineteenth Century Music," *Studia Musicologica,* 7 (1965): 115–123.

———— "Europäische Musik im Banne der Exotik" in *Europäische Musik zwischen Nationalismus und Exotik* (Winterthur, 1984).

Rischbieter, Hennring. *Art and the Stage in the Twentieth Century* (Greenwich, Conn., 1968).

Rivière, Jacques. "*Le Sacre du printemps,*" *La Nouvelle Revue française,* 7 (November 1913).

Robbins, Bruce. "Othering the Academy: Professionalism and Multiculturalism," *Social Research,* 58 (Summer 1991): 355–372.

Robbins, Daniel. "Albert Gleizes: Reason and Faith in Modern Painting," intro. to *Albert Gleizes, 1881–1953, A Retrospective Exhibition: The Solomon R. Guggenheim Museum, New York, 1964* (New York, 1966).

Robertson, Marta. " 'A Gift to Be Simple': The Collaboration of Aaron Copland and Martha Graham in the Genesis of *Appalachian Spring*" (Ph.D. diss., University of Michigan, 1992).

Rochberg, George. Notes to *String Quartet No. 3* (1972), Nonesuch Record H-71283.

Rockwell, John. *All American Music* (New York, 1983).

Roland-Manuel. *"Le Sacre du printemps,"* Montjoie! Organe de l'impérialisme français, 1.9–10 (June 14–29, 1913): 13.

Rood, Arnold, ed. *Gordon Craig on Movement and Dance* (London, 1977).

Roose-Evans, James. *Experimental Theatre from Stanislavsky to Today* (New York, 1970).

Rosa, Joseph G., and Robin May. *Buffalo Bill and His Wild West: A Pictorial Biography* (Lawrence, Kan., 1989).

Rosenblum, Robert. *Cubism,* 2nd ed. (New York, 1966).

——— "Picasso and the Typography of Cubism" in Hoffman 1989: 91–120.

——— "Cubism as Pop Art" in Varnedoe and Gopnik 1990: 116–133.

Rosenstock, Laura. "Léger: *The Creation of the World*" in Rubin 1984: 475–484.

Roskill, Mark. *The Interpretation of Cubism* (London, 1985).

Ross, Andrew. *The Failure of Modernism: Symptoms of American Poetry* (New York, 1986).

Roth-Mascagni, Pauline. *Musique et géométrie de trois poèmes Valéryens* (Brussels, 1979).

Rothstein, Edward. "Roll Over Beethoven: The New Musical Correctness and Its Mistakes," *The New Republic* (February 4, 1991): 29–34.

——— "Was Schubert Gay? If He Was, So What?" *The New York Times* (February 4, 1992): B3.

——— "How High Is 'Low'? It's All Relative," *The New York Times* (December 6, 1992): H23.

——— "The Rhyme and Reason of Rhythms," *The New York Times* (February 28, 1993): H25.

Rubin, William. "Picasso" in Rubin 1984: 241–343.

——— ed. *"Primitivism" in Twentieth Century Art: Affinity of the Tribal and the Modern* (New York, 1984).

Rublowsky, John. *Black Music in America* (New York, 1971).

Sachs, Curt. *The Wellsprings of Music* (New York, 1962/R1977).

Said, Edward. *Beginnings* (New York, 1975).

——— *Orientalism* (New York, 1978).

——— "Yeats and Decolonization" in Terry Eagleton, Frederic Jameson, and Edward Said, *Nationalism, Colonialism, and Literature* (Minneapolis, 1990): 69–95.

——— "The Politics of Knowledge," *Raritan,* 11 (Summer 1991): 17–31.

——— *Culture and Imperialism* (New York, 1993).

Salmon, André. "Negro Art," trans. in *Burlington Magazine* (1920): 164–172.

Sargeant, Winthrop. *Jazz, Hot and Hybrid* (New York, 1938/R1964, 1975).

Sass, Louis A. *Madness and Modernism: Insanity in the Light of Modern Art, Literature, and Thought* (New York, 1992).

Savage, Jon. "The Age of Plunder," *The Face,* 33 (January 1983): 44–49.

Schaeffner, André. "Les Chanteurs dans la 'fosse,' " *La Revue musicale,* 6.1 (November 1, 1924): 18–36.

———— "Variations Schoenberg," *Contrepoints,* 7 (1951): 110–129.

Schatt, Peter W. *Exotik in der Musik des 20. Jahrhunderts* (Munich, 1986).

Schebera, Jürgen. *Kurt Weill, 1900–1950: Eine Biographie in Texten, Bildern, and Dokumenten* (Mainz, 1990).

Schlemmer, Oskar. *The Letters and Diaries of Oskar Schlemmer,* ed. Tut Schlemmer, trans. Krishna Winston (Middletown, Conn., 1972).

———— "Abstraction dans la danse et le costume" in *Théâtre et abstraction,* trans., preface, and notes by Éric Michaud (Lausanne, 1978).

Schlesinger, Arthur M., Jr. *The Disuniting of America* (Knoxville, Tenn., 1991).

Schloezer, Boris van. "Junge Franzosen," *Die Musik,* 18 (April 1926): 502–509.

Schmalenbach, Werner. *Fernand Léger,* trans. Robert Allen with James Emmons (New York, 1985).

Schneider, Marius. "Tone and Tune in West African Music," *Ethnomusicology,* 5 (1962).

Schnittke, Alfred. *Kadenzen zu Beethoven's Violinkonzert* (1975–1977, unpublished).

———— *Kadenzen zu zwei Klavierkonzerten von W. A. Mozart,* 491 (1975), KV 467 (1980) (Hamburg, 1988).

———— *Two Cadenzas to Mozart's Concerto for Bassoon and Orchestra* (1983) (in Russian) in *Proizvedenia sovietskikh kompozitorov dlia fagota solo [Works for Solo Bassoon by Soviet Composers]* (Moscow, 1985).

Schoenberg, Arnold. "Stravinsky's *Oedipus*" in *Style and Idea,* ed. L. Stein, trans. L. Black (New York, 1975): 482–483.

Schubert, Giselher. Notes to the recording of *Mörder, Hoffnung der Frauen,* Wergo 60132-50, English trans. by John Patrick Thomas (Mainz, 1986).

———— Notes to the recording of *Das Nusch-Nuschi,* Wergo 60146-50, English trans. by John Patrick Thomas (Mainz, 1988).

Schuller, Gunther. *Early Jazz: Its Roots and Musical Development* (New York, 1968).

Schwab, Catharine. "The Mélodie française moderne" (Ph.D. diss., The University of Michigan, 1991).

Schwab, Raymond. *Oriental Renaissance* (New York, 1964).

Schwichtenberg, Cathy. *The Madonna Connection: Representational Politics, Subcultural Identities, and Cultural Theory* (Boulder, Colo., 1992).

Scott, Derek B. "Music and Sociology for the 1990s; A Changing Critical Perspective," *The Musical Quarterly,* 74 (1990): 385–410.

Seeger, Anthony. "Singing Other Peoples' Songs," *Cultural Survival Quarterly,* 15 (Summer 1991): 36–39.

Seeger, Charles. "Grassroots for American Music," *Modern Music,* 16 (1938–39): 143.

———— "The Importance to Cultural Understanding of Folk and Popular Music," a paper read at the Conference on Inter-American Relations in the Field of Music, Washington, D.C., 1939.

Sekine, Masara. *Yeats and the Noh* (Gerrards Cross, Eng., 1990).

Shanes, Eric. *Constantin Brancusi* (New York, 1989).

Shapiro, Ann Dhu, ed. *Music and Context: Essays for John M. Ward* (Cambridge, Mass., 1985).

Shattuck, Roger. *The Banquet Years* (New York, 1968).

Sherr, Laurence. "The Genesis of *Agon:* Stravinsky, Balanchine, and the New York City Ballet," (DMA diss., University of Illinois, 1988).

Sidran, Ben. *Black Talk* (New York, 1971).

Silver, Kenneth. "Jean Cocteau and the *Image d'Épinal:* An Essay on Realism and Naiveté" in Anderson and Saltus 1984.

———— *Esprit de Corps* (Princeton, 1989).

Simon, Linda. *The Biography of Alice B. Toklas* (Garden City, N.J., 1977).

Singal, Daniel Joseph. "Towards a Definition of American Modernism" in Singal 1991: 1–27.

———— ed. *Modernism and American Culture* (Belmont, Calif., 1991). Originally published in *American Quarterly,* 39.1 (Spring 1987).

Smith, Susan. *Masks in Modern Drama* (Berkeley, 1985). See particularly pp. 71–74 regarding the Cocteau-Stravinsky collaborations.

Souritz, Elizabeth. *Soviet Choreographers in the 1920s* (Durham, 1990).

Southern, Eileen. "William Grant Still," *Biographical Dictionary of Afro-American and African Musicians* (Westport, Conn., 1982).

Spector, Irwin. *Rhythm and Life: The Work of Émile Jaques-Dalcroze* (Stuyvesant, N.Y., 1990).

Sprigge, Elizabeth, and Jean-Jacques Kihm. *Jean Cocteau: The Man and The Mirror* (London, 1968).

Sproul, Barbara. *Primal Myths: Creating the World* (London, 1980).

Stearns, Marshall. *The Story of Jazz* (New York, 1975).

Steegmuller, Francis. *Cocteau: A Biography* (Boston, 1970).

Stein, Gertrude. *The Autobiography of Alice B. Toklas* (New York, 1933). Reprinted in *Selected Writings of Gertrude Stein,* ed. Carl Van Vechten (New York, 1946).

Stephen-Chauvet, Charles. *Musique nègre* (Paris, 1929).

Stiefel, Erhard. "Au retour du Japon" in Aslan 1985.

Stilwell, Robynn. "Partners in the Dance: The Collaboration of Igor Stravinsky and George Balanchine in *Agon,*" (Ph.D. diss., University of Michigan, 1994).

Stimpson, Brian. *Paul Valéry and Music: A Study of the Techniques of Composition in Valéry's Poetry* (Cambridge, Eng., 1984).

Stockhausen, Karlheinz. "Metacollage und Integration: Gefundene und erfundene Musik" in *Texte zur Musik, 1963–1970,* vol. 3 (Cologne, 1970): 224.

——— "Weltmusik" in *Texte zur Musik, 1970–1977,* vol. 4 (Cologne, 1978): 468–476.

——— *Kadenzen für Haydn's Trompetenkonzert* (1983–1985) (Kürten, Ger., 1985a).

——— *Kadenzen für Mozart's Flötenkonzerte* (1984–85) (Kürten, Ger., 1985b).

——— *Kadenzen für Mozart's Klarinettenkonzert* (1978) (Kürten, Ger., 1985c).

——— *Kadenz für Leopold Mozart's Trompetenkonzert* (1984) (Kürten, Ger., 1985d).

——— Open letter "To the International Music Council," November 21, 1984, in *Texte zur Musik, 1977–1984,* vol. 6 (Cologne, 1989a): 564–572.

——— *Stockhausen on Music,* comp. Robin Maconie (London, 1989b).

——— *Towards a Cosmic Music: Texts by Karlheinz Stockhausen,* trans. Tim Nevil (Longmead, Eng., 1989c).

Stoecker, Helmuth, ed. *German Imperialism in Africa: From the Beginnings until the Second World War,* trans. Bernd Zollner (London, 1986).

Storey, Robert. *Pierrot: A Critical History of a Mask* (Princeton, 1978).

Straus, Joseph. *Remaking the Past: Musical Modernism and the Influence of the Tonal Tradition* (Cambridge, Mass., 1990).

——— "The 'Anxiety of Influence' in Twentieth-Century Music," *The Journal of Musicology,* 9 (Fall 1991): 430–447.

Stravinsky, Igor. *An Autobiography* (New York, 1936).

——— *Poetics of Music* (Cambridge, Mass., 1939/R1954, 1977).

——— *Stravinsky: Selected Correspondence,* ed. Robert Craft, vol. 1 (New York, 1982).

Stravinsky: La carrière européenne, exhibition catalogue, Musée d'Art Moderne de la Ville de Paris (Paris, 1980).

Stravinsky. Sein Nachlass. Sein Bild, exhibition catalogue, Kunstmuseum Basel (Basel, 1984).

Stravinsky: Visages d'Igor, exhibition catalogue, Musée de Tessé (Le Mans, 1976).

Stravinsky, Igor, and Robert Craft. *Conversations* (Garden City, N.J., 1959).

——— *Memories and Commentaries* (Garden City, N.J., 1960).

——— *Expositions and Developments* (London, 1962).

Stravinsky, Vera, and Robert Craft. *Stravinsky in Pictures and Documents* (New York, 1978).

Stuckenschmidt, Hans Heinz. "Musik am Bauhaus" in Maur 1985: 408ff.

Stumpf, Karl. *Beiträge zur Akustik und Musikwissenschaft,* vol. 3 (Leipzig, 1901).

——— *Die Anfänge der Musik* (Leipzig, 1911).

Suydam, John. "*Mein Traum* and the 'Unfinished' Symphony: A Reinterpretation," paper read at the meeting of the American Musicological Society, Chicago, November 6–10, 1991.

Swain, Joseph. "Form and Function of the Classical Cadenza," *The Journal of Musicology,* 6 (Winter 1988): 27–59.

Tani, H. *Traditional Japanese Music* (Tokyo, 1970).

Taruskin, Richard. "Russian Folk Melodies in *The Rite of Spring*," *Journal of the American Musicological Society,* 33.3 (1980): 501–543.

———— "How the Acorn Took Root: A Tale of Russia," *Nineteenth Century Music,* 6.3 (1983): 189–212.

———— "From Subject to Style: Stravinsky and the Painters" in Pasler 1986: 16.

———— "Stravinsky's 'Rejoicing Discovery' and What it Meant: In Defense of His Notorious Text Setting" in Haimo and Johnson 1987: 162.

———— "The Pastness of the Present" in *Authenticity and Early Music,* ed. Nicholas Kenyon (Oxford, 1988).

Tatsumura, Ayako. "Understanding Music as 'Other': Toward an Aesthetic of Intercultural Reception of Music," paper read at the Fourth Symposium of the International Musicological Society, Osaka, July 21–25, 1990.

Taviani, Ferdinando. "Positions du masque dans la commedia dell'arte" in Aslan 1985: 119–134. See particularly "L'intérieur et l'extérieur": 124–130.

Taylor, Ronald. *Kurt Weill: Composer in a Divided World* (Boston, 1992).

Taylor, Timothy. "The Voracious Muse: Contemporary Cross-Cultural Musical Borrowings, Culture, and Postmodernism" (Ph.D. diss., University of Michigan, 1993).

Thomson, Virgil. *Virgil Thomson* (London, 1967).

———— *A Virgil Thomson Reader* (New York, 1981).

Thorp, Raymond W. *Spirit Gun of the West: The Story of Doc W. F. Carver* (Glendale, Calif., 1957).

Tick, Judith. "Ruth Crawford—A Modernist Pioneer," intro. to *Two Chamber Works of the 1920s* (Madison, 1992).

Tiersot, Julien. *Musiques pittoresques: Promenades musicales à l'Exposition de 1889* (Paris, 1889).

Toledano, Ralph de, ed. *Frontiers of Jazz* (New York, 1947).

Tomlinson, Gary. "Cultural Dialogics and Jazz: A White Historian Signifies" in Bergeron and Bohlman 1992: 64–94.

Torgovnick, Marianna. *Gone Primitive: Savage Intellect, Modern Lives* (Chicago, 1990).

Touchard, Maurice. "Ballets russes et français," *La Nouvelle Revue,* 8 (July 1, 1913): 116–125.

Tower, Beeke Sell. *Envisioning America: Prints, Drawings, and Photographs by George Grosz and His Contemporaries, 1915–1933* (Cambridge, Mass., 1990).

Treitler, Leo. "History, Criticism, and Beethoven's Ninth Symphony," *Nineteenth*

Century Music, 3 (1980): 193–210. Reprinted in *Music and the Historical Imagination* (Cambridge, Mass., 1989): 19–45.

Troy, Nancy. *The De Stijl Environment* (Cambridge, Mass., 1983).

Tucker, Mark. "Jungle Music," *The New Grove Dictionary of Jazz,* ed. Barry Kernfeld (London, 1988): 639.

———— *Ellington: The Early Years* (Urbana, 1990).

Turner, Bryan S., ed. *Theories of Modernity and Postmodernity* (London, 1990).

Van den Toorn, Pieter. *The Music of Igor Stravinsky* (New Haven, 1983).

Van Holt, J. "Eternity and Soap Bubbles," *The Mask,* 4.1 (July 1911). Reprinted in Rood 1977: 75–76.

Varèse, Edgard. "Spatial Music" in *Contemporary Composers on Contemporary Music,* ed. Barney Childs and Elliot Schwartz (New York, 1967).

Varnedoe, Kirk. Preface to Rubin 1984.

———— "On the Claims and Critics of the 'Primitivism' Show," *Art in America,* 73 (May 1985): 11–21.

Varnedoe, Kirk, and Adam Gopnik. *High and Low: Modern Art and Popular Culture* (New York, 1990a).

———— ed. *Modern Art and Popular Culture: Readings in High and Low Art* (New York, 1990b).

Vaschenko, Alexander. "Some Russian Responses to North American Indian Cultures" in Feest 1987: 307–320.

Volkov, Nikolai. *Meyerhold* (Moscow and Leningrad, 1929).

Volta, Ornella. *Erik Satie et la tradition populaire* (Paris, 1988).

Vuillemin, Louis. *"Le Sacre du printemps,"* Comoedia, 7 (May 31, 1913): 2.

Vuillermoz, Émile. "La Saison russe au Théâtre des Champs-Élysées," *S.I.M.,* 9.6 (June 15, 1913): 49–56.

———— "Le Jardin du Paradis, Ballets Suédois, La Griffes Sante-Odyle, Le Cloître," *La Revue musicale,* 5.2 (December 1923a): 166–188.

———— "Rag-Time et jazz-band" in *Musiques d'aujourd'hui* (Paris, 1923b).

Walker, John A. *Cross-Overs: Art into Pop / Pop into Art* (London, 1987).

Wallaschek, Richard. *Primitive Music: An Inquiry into the Origin and Development of Music, Songs, Instruments, Dances, and Pantomimes of Savage Races* (London, 1893/R1970).

Walsh, Richard John. *The Making of Buffalo Bill: A Study in Heroics* (Indianapolis, 1928).

Watkins, Glenn. Preface to Sigismondo D'India, *Ottavo Libro di Madrigali* (1624) (Florence, 1980).

———— "The Canon and Stravinsky's Late Style" in Pasler 1986: 217–246.

———— *Soundings: Music in the Twentieth Century* (New York, 1988).

———— "Aggiornamenti" in *Gesualdo* (Oxford, 1973; 2nd ed., 1991): 296–364.

———— Preface to Sigismondo D'India, *Terzo Libro di Madrigali* (1615) (Florence, 1994).

Watkins, Glenn, and Thomasin La May. "Imitatio and Emulatio: Changing Concepts of Originality in the Madrigals of Gesualdo and Monteverdi in the 1590s" in *Festschrift Reinhold Hammerstein,* ed. Ludwig Finscher (Munich, 1986).

Weber, Fritz. "Heroes, Meadows, and Machinery: *Fin-de-Siècle* Music" in *Fin de Siècle and Its Legacy,* ed. M. Teich and R. Porter (Cambridge, Eng., 1990): 216–234.

Wegner, Reinhard. *Der Exotismus-Streit in Deutschland: zur Auseinandersetzung mit primitiven Formen in der bildenden Kunst des 20. Jahrhunderts* (Frankfurt am Main, 1983).

Weiss, Jeffrey S. "Picasso, Collage, and the Music Hall" in Varnedoe and Gopnik 1990b: 82–115.

Wellmer, Albrecht. *The Persistence of Modernity: Essays on Aesthetics, Ethics, and Postmodernism,* trans. David Midgley (Oxford, 1991).

Werckmeister, O. K. *Citadel Culture* (Chicago, 1991).

Westphal, Kurt. "Negermusik und ihre Apostel," *Allgemeine Musikzeitung,* 54 (1927): 421–422.

White, E. W. *Stravinsky* (Berkeley, 1979).

White, Hayden. *Metahistory* (Baltimore, 1973).

————— *Tropics of Discourse: Essays in Cultural Criticism* (Baltimore, 1978).

————— *The Content of the Form* (Baltimore, 1987).

Whitesitt, Linda. *The Life and Music of George Antheil, 1900–1959* (Ann Arbor, 1983).

Whitmore, Philip. *Unpremeditated Art: The Cadenza in the Classical Keyboard Concerto* (Oxford, 1991).

Whittall, Arnold. "The Theorist's Sense of History: Concepts of Contemporaneity as Composition and Analysis," *Journal of the Royal Musical Association,* 112 (1987): 1–20.

Wichmann, Siegfried, ed. *World Cultures and Modern Art: The Encounter of the Nineteenth- and Twentieth-century European Art and Music with Asia, Africa, Oceania, Afro- and Indo-America,* catalogue for the exhibition on the occasion of the Games of the XXth Olympiad, Munich 1972 (Munich, 1972).

Wiesel, Meir. "Motivic Unity in Stravinsky's *Agon,*" *Orbis Musicae,* 7 (1979–80): 119–24.

Wilde, Oscar. *The Artist as Critic,* ed. Richard Ellmann (New York, 1969).

Wiley, Roland John. "The *Balagany* in *Petrushka*" in Shapiro 1985.

————— *A Century of Russian Ballet: Documents and Eyewitness Accounts, 1810–1910* (Oxford, 1990).

Wilson, Edmund. *Axel's Castle* (New York, 1931).

Wiseman, Carter. *I. M. Pei: A Profile in American Architecture* (New York, 1990).

Wolf, Eric R. *Europe and the People without History* (Berkeley, 1982).

Wuorinen, Charles. *Three Cadenzas for the Concerto in C for Oboe by Wolfgang Amadeus Mozart* (New York, 1990).

Wuorinen, Charles, and Jeffrey Kresky. "On the Significance of Stravinsky's Last Works." In Pasler 1986: 263.

Yeats, William Butler. *Sophocles' King Oedipus: A Version for the Modern Stage* (London, 1928).

Yost, Nellie Irene. *Buffalo Bill: His Family, Friends, Fame, Failure, and Fortune* (Chicago, 1979).

Zhang, Qian. "The History and Future of the Reception of Western Music by China in the Twentieth Century," paper read at the Fourth Symposium of the International Musicological Society, Osaka, July 21–25, 1990.

Zimmermann, Michael. "Delaunays Formes circulaires und die Philosophie Henri Bergsons: zur Methode der Interpretation abstrakter Kunst," *Wallraf-Richartz-Jahrbuch,* 48–49 (1987–88): 335–364.

Zukav, Gary. *The Dancing Wu Li Masters: An Overview of the New Physics* (New York, 1979).

Index